ALSO BY THE EDITORS AT AMERICA'S TEST KITCHEN

The Complete Slow Cooker

The Complete Make-Ahead Cookbook

The Complete Mediterranean Cookbook

The Complete Vegetarian Cookbook

The Complete Cooking for Two Cookbook

What Good Cooks Know

Cook's Science

The Science of Good Cooking

The Perfect Cookie

Bread Illustrated

Master of the Grill

Kitchen Smarts

Kitchen Hacks

100 Recipes: The Absolute Best Ways to Make
the True Essentials

The New Family Cookbook

The America's Test Kitchen Cooking
School Cookbook

The Cook's Illustrated Meat Book

The Cook's Illustrated Baking Book

The Cook's Illustrated Cookbook

The New Best Recipe

Soups, Stews, and Chilis

The America's Test Kitchen Quick Family Cookbook

The America's Test Kitchen Healthy
Family Cookbook

The America's Test Kitchen Family Baking Book

The Best of America's Test Kitchen (2007–2018 Editions)

The Complete America's Test Kitchen TV Show
Cookbook 2001–2018

Food Processor Perfection

Pressure Cooker Perfection

Vegan for Everybody

Naturally Sweet

Foolproof Preserving

Paleo Perfected

The How Can It Be Gluten-Free Cookbook: Volume 2

The How Can It Be Gluten-Free Cookbook

The Best Mexican Recipes

Slow Cooker Revolution Volume 2: The Easy-Prep Edition

Slow Cooker Revolution

The Six-Ingredient Solution

The America's Test Kitchen D.I.Y. Cookbook

Pasta Revolution

THE COOK'S ILLUSTRATED ALL-TIME BEST SERIES

All-Time Best Holiday Entertaining

All-Time Best Sunday Suppers

All-Time Best Soups

All-Time Best Appetizers

COOK'S COUNTRY TITLES

One-Pan Wonders

Cook It in Cast Iron

Cook's Country Eats Local

FOR A FULL LISTING OF ALL OUR BOOKS

CooksCountry.com

AmericasTestKitchen.com

PRAISE FOR AMERICA'S TEST KITCHEN TITLES

"Another winning cookbook from ATK. . . . The folks at America's Test Kitchen apply their rigorous experiments to determine the facts about these pans."
Booklist on *Cook It in Cast Iron*

"An exceptional resource for novice canners, though preserving veterans will find plenty here to love as well."
Library Journal (starred review) on *Foolproof Preserving*

"This book upgrades slow cooking for discriminating, 21st-century palates—that is indeed revolutionary."
The Dallas Morning News on *Slow Cooker Revolution*

"The 21st-century *Fannie Farmer Cookbook* or *The Joy of Cooking*. If you had to have one cookbook and that's all you could have, this one would do it."
CBS San Francisco on *The New Family Cookbook*

"The sum total of exhaustive experimentation . . . anyone interested in gluten-free cookery simply shouldn't be without it."
Nigella Lawson on *The How Can It Be Gluten-Free Cookbook*

"The go-to gift book for newlyweds, small families or empty nesters."
Orlando Sentinel on *The Complete Cooking for Two Cookbook*

"A one-volume kitchen seminar, addressing in one smart chapter after another the sometimes surprising whys behind a cook's best practices. . . . You get the myth, the theory, the science and the proof, all rigorously interrogated as only America's Test Kitchen can do."
NPR on *The Science of Good Cooking*

"A beautifully illustrated, 318-page culinary compendium showcasing an impressive variety and diversity of authentic Mexican cuisine."
Midwest Book Review on *The Best Mexican Recipes*

"A terrifically accessible and useful guide to grilling in all its forms that sets a new bar for its competitors on the bookshelf. . . . Packed with practical advice, simple tips, and approachable recipes to ensure that grill enthusiasts are able to get the most out of their grills and ingredients."
Publisher's Weekly (starred review) on *Master of the Grill*

"This book is a comprehensive, no-nonsense guide . . . a well-thought-out, clearly explained primer for every aspect of home baking."
The Wall Street Journal on *The Cook's Illustrated Baking Book*

"Buy this gem for the foodie in your family, and spend the extra money to get yourself a copy too."
The Missourian on *The Best of America's Test Kitchen 2015*

"Some 2,500 photos walk readers through 600 painstakingly tested recipes, leaving little room for error."
Associated Press on *The America's Test Kitchen Cooking School Cookbook*

"Cook-friendly and kitchen-oriented, illuminating the process of preparing food instead of mystifying it . . . . the perfect kitchen home companion."
The Wall Street Journal on *The Cook's Illustrated Cookbook*

"There are pasta books . . . and then there's this pasta book. Flip your carbohydrate dreams upside down and strain them through this sieve of revolutionary, creative, and also traditional recipes."
San Francisco Book Review on *Pasta Revolution*

"Further proof that practice makes perfect, if not transcendent. . . . If an intermediate cook follows the directions exactly, the results will be better than takeout or Mom's."
The New York Times on *The New Best Recipe*

10TH ANNIVERSARY EDITION

The Complete

Cook's Country

TV Show Cookbook

Every Recipe and Every Review
From All Ten Seasons

THE EDITORS AT AMERICA'S TEST KITCHEN

Photo, far right on page 279: Shutterstock

America's Test Kitchen
21 Drydock, Suite 201E
Boston, MA 02210

The Complete Cook's Country 10th Anniversary Cookbook
Every Recipe and Every Review From All Ten Seasons

ISBN 978-1-940352-93-0 (paperback edition)
ISBN 978-1-945256-34-9 (hardcover edition)
ISSN 2330-5762

Manufactured in the United States of America
10 9 8 7 6 5 4 3 2 1

Distributed by Penguin Random House Publisher Services
tel: 800-733-3000

facebook.com/americastestkitchen

twitter.com/TestKitchen

youtube.com/AmericasTestKitchen

instagram.com/TestKitchen

pinterest.com/TestKitchen

americastestkitchen.tumblr.com

google.com/+AmericasTestKitchen

Chief Creative Officer Jack Bishop
Editorial Director, Books Elizabeth Carduff
Senior Managing Editor Debra Hudak
Assistant Editor Samantha Ronan
Editorial Assistant Alyssa Langer
Design Director Carole Goodman
Deputy Art Director Jen Kanavos Hoffman
Graphic Designer Katie Barranger
Production Designer Reinaldo Cruz
Photography Director Julie Bozzo Cote
Photography Producer Mary Ball
Feature Photography Keller + Keller
Senior Staff Photographer Daniel J. van Ackere
Additional Photography Carl Tremblay
Cover Photo Carl Tremblay
Staff Photographer Steve Klise and Kevin White
Food Stylists Daniel Cellucci, Isabelle English, Catrine Kelty, Monica Mariano, Kendra McKnight, Marie Piraino, Mary Jane Sawyer, Elle Simone Scott, and Sally Staub
Photoshoot Kitchen Team
  Senior Editor Chris O'Connor
  Lead Cook Daniel Cellucci
  Assistant Test Cooks Mady Nichas and Jessica Rudolph
Production Director Guy Rochford
Senior Production Manager Jessica Lindheimer Quirk
Production Manager Christine Walsh
Imaging Manager Lauren Robbins
Production and Imaging Specialists Heather Dube, Dennis Noble, and Jessica Voas
Historical Researcher Meg Ragland
Copyeditor Cheryl Redmond
Proofreader Amanda Poulsen Dix
Indexer Elizabeth Parson

CooksCountry.com
AmericasTestKitchen.com

contents

welcome to cook's country

Where are you from?

Time was, this was an easy question to answer. The place where you lived was just down the road from where you were born. Its land and weather and people and rhythms wound themselves into you, deepening over the course of a lifetime. You ate the foods your parents, and grandparents, and great-grandparents did, and while they were similar to the foods eaten on the other side of the state, they were different, too. Everyone had a turkey on Thanksgiving, but where your family served cracker stuffing, another family had cornbread dressing or rice casserole or enchiladas. Local twists on morning biscuits or Sunday dinner helped define who you were.

But in America today, "Where are you from?" is an increasingly complicated question. Fewer and fewer of us live as adults in the same town where we were raised. We are a mobile, peripatetic people. As each generation reaches further afield, its tether to its roots frays a little. We pass on fewer traditions these days. We carry less of our history into our future. Our children know little about our own childhoods. And yet, even as we move from house to house, and city to city, we still long for something we call home.

Look at it through another lens and you'll see something hopeful: All this moving around may just be the thing that keeps a place's traditions vital and alive. Because when we travel, our traditions—especially our food traditions—travel with us.

A young woman moves from Georgia to Pittsburgh and yearns for the biscuits of her youth. She sends up a flare for a family recipe, which is by her grandmother, then uses the Internet to order the special

Southern flour she needs to get the biscuit just tender enough, in the perfect shade of gold. She brings a batch to a party and, suddenly, she's the most popular brunch guest in town. A few years on, she's teaching her son how to make them, too.

A professor relocates from Annapolis to Tacoma, and enters a seafood cooking competition at a college fundraiser. He chooses the Chesapeake crab cake recipe scrawled on a 3x5 card stuck in an old family cookbook, adapts it to a local Pacific crustacean, and wins the grand prize. By the next semester, the dining hall is serving the professor's "famous" Chesapeake crab cakes every other week.

And when each of these people returns to Georgia or to Annapolis for a visit, they seek out and re-connect with the original dishes. With their history. With home.

There are so many different kinds of "American" food, and here at Cook's Country, we celebrate them all. We look at rural foods, from low country grits to high desert tacos. We look at city foods, from New Orleans gumbo to New York cheesecake. We search high, low, and in between for recipes from every community in the country, the old ones and the new, from centuries-old switchel to modern-day monkey bread.

It's been ten years since Cook's Country presented its first recipe. Since then, our hard-working crew of test cooks, editors, and instructors have carried on the mission to find these recipes and work hard to perfect them. We look for ways to refine the ingredients and techniques to jive with contemporary cooking habits, while zealously maintaining the integrity and spirit of the originals. It can take weeks of experimentation, tinkering with seasoning amounts and cooking times until we get things just right. And we don't stop there. These recipes inspire brand-new ideas for simple, straightforward, easy meals that mix time-tested knowledge with fresh discoveries.

Our goal is to produce recipes that are easy, clear, and rewarding enough that you'll want to make them too. We work to clarify concepts, streamline processes, and shorten the distance from hunger pang to dinner time. Over the past decade, we've been proud to share thousands of recipes with you. And as we look ahead to our second decade, we've added to our cast of characters. These new faces, in our test kitchen and on our TV show and website, represent a whole new set of cooking traditions to explore.

It can take us weeks, or maybe months, to produce even a simple, two-step recipe. But it's worth it. Because by getting these dishes from our kitchens to your table, we believe we're helping to preserve, and expand, our shared American recipe book.

It's a big country, Cook's Country, and there's no better time to celebrate America's incredibly rich, incredibly broad, and incredibly deep cooking traditions. There's plenty of room in the kitchen, no matter where you're from.

Welcome home. Now, grab an apron. Let's cook.

Tucker Shaw
Executive Editor
Cook's Country magazine

This book has been tested, written, and edited by the folks at America's Test Kitchen. Located in Boston's Seaport District in the historic Innovation and Design Building, it features 15,000 square feet of kitchen space including photography and video studios. It is the home of *Cook's Illustrated* and *Cook's Country* magazines and is the Monday-through-Friday destination for more than 60 test cooks, editors, and cookware specialists. Our mission is to test recipes over and over again until we understand how and why they work and until we arrive at the "best" version.

Filmed in a rustic farmhouse kitchen, *Cook's Country from America's Test Kitchen* features the best regional home cooking in the country and relies on the same practical, no-nonsense approach to cooking that has made *Cook's Country* magazine so successful.

Bridget Lancaster and Julia Collin Davison are the hosts of the show and ask the questions you might ask. It's the job of our chefs, Ashley Moore, Bryan Roof, and Christie Morrison, to demonstrate our recipes. The chefs show Bridget and Julia what works and what doesn't, and they explain why. In the process, they discuss (and show you) the best examples from our development process as well as the worst. Jack Bishop challenges Bridget and Julia to live tastings of kitchen staples like hot dogs, apple cider vinegar, fettuccine, and sauerkraut, while Adam Ried reveals the test kitchen's top choices for equipment, including kitchen timers, Dutch ovens, cast-iron skillets, and more.

Although just seven cooks and editors appear on the television show, dozens more worked to make the show a reality. Executive producer Mary Mullaney conceived and developed each episode along with producer Kaitlin Keleher, associate producer Shan Shan Tam, and production assistant

Sara Joyner. Meg Ragland and Cara Eisenpress assisted with all the historical recipe research. Debby Paddock assisted with photography research.

Along with the on-air crew, executive chefs Erin McMurrer, Dan Zuccarello, and Morgan Bolling helped plan and organize the 13 television episodes shot in November 2016 and ran the "back kitchen," where all the food that appeared on camera originated. Lauren Savoie, Kate Shannon, Miye Bromberg, and Carolyn Grillo organized the tasting and equipment segments.

During filming, chefs Allison Berkey, Lyndsay Burginger, Steve Dunn, Matthew Fairman, Eric Haessler, Andrew Janjigian, Cecelia Jenkins, Lawman Johnson, Lan Lam, Katie Leaird, Timothy McQuinn, Anne Petito, Stephanie Pixley, and Anne Wolf cooked all the food needed on set. Kitchen assistants Ena Gudiel and Jarod Torres also worked long hours. Chefs Allison Berkey, Daniel Cellucci, Leah Colins, Afton Cyrus, Joseph Gitter, Sara Mayer, and Katherine Perry helped coordinate the kitchen with the television set by readying props, equipment, and food. Assistant test kitchen director Leah Rovner, test kitchen manager Alexxa Benson, lead senior kitchen assistant Meridith Lippard, and senior kitchen assistant Taylor Pond were charged with making sure all the ingredients and kitchen equipment we needed were on hand.

Special thanks to director and editor Herb Sevush and director of photography Stephen Hussar. We also appreciate the hard work of the video production team, including Scott Brawn, Wilson Chao, Joe Cristofori, Peter Dingle, Eric Fisher, Ken Fraser, Erik Freitas, Bob Hirsch, Jim Hirsch, Sue Willard Kiess, Joe McCleish, Gilles Morin, Tom Robertson, and Phil Teves. Thanks also to Nick Dakoulas and Conor Olmstead, our second unit camera department. We also would like to thank Judy Barlow at American Public Television, which presents the show.

Blue Apron, DCS by Fisher & Paykel, Holland America Line, and Valley Fig Growers sponsored the show, and we thank them for their support. We also thank Deborah Fagone, Christine Anagnostis, and Kate Zebrowski for serving our sponsors.

Aprons were made by Crooked Brook. Thanks to music supervisor Christopher Sabec, Aaron Redner, and the band Hot Buttered Rum.

We also thank Dona Neely from Devens Eco-Efficiency Center, Transitions at Devens, Veterans, Inc., Roche Bros, Whole Foods, Westerman Store & Restaurant Equipment Inc., Suburban Supply, T.F. Kinnealey & Co., Sid Wainer & Son, and Michael's Movers.

as good as grandma's

Why This Recipe Works To pack our mac and cheese with bright tomato flavor, we discovered that undercooking the pasta and adding petite canned diced tomatoes with their juices to the drained macaroni allowed the macaroni to soak up more of the tomato flavor. Returning the pasta to the heat afterward allowed the noodles to absorb some of the tomato juice. Finally, to avoid a curdled sauce, we added fat in the form of half-and-half (cut with some chicken broth) and a mix of sharp and mild cheddar cheeses.

MACARONI AND CHEESE WITH TOMATOES

SERVES 8 TO 10

Let the finished dish rest for 10 to 15 minutes before you serve it; otherwise, it will be soupy.

- 1 pound elbow macaroni
  Salt and pepper
- 1 (28-ounce) can petite diced tomatoes
- 6 tablespoons unsalted butter
- ½ cup all-purpose flour
- ¼ teaspoon cayenne pepper
- 4 cups half-and-half
- 1 cup chicken broth
- 1 pound mild cheddar cheese, shredded (4 cups)
- 8 ounces sharp cheddar cheese, shredded (2 cups)

1. Adjust oven rack to middle position and heat oven to 400 degrees. Bring 4 quarts water to boil in large Dutch oven. Add macaroni and 1 tablespoon salt and cook, stirring often, until just al dente, about 6 minutes. Drain pasta and return to pot. Pour diced tomatoes with their juices over pasta and stir to coat. Cook over medium-high heat, stirring occasionally, until most of liquid is absorbed, about 5 minutes. Set aside.

2. Meanwhile, melt butter in medium saucepan over medium heat. Stir in flour and cayenne and cook until golden, about 1 minute. Slowly whisk in half-and-half and broth until smooth. Bring to boil, reduce heat to medium, and simmer, stirring occasionally, until mixture is slightly thickened, about 15 minutes. Off heat, whisk in cheeses, 1 teaspoon salt, and 1 teaspoon pepper until cheeses melt. Pour sauce over macaroni and stir to combine.

3. Scrape mixture into 13 by 9-inch baking dish set in rimmed baking sheet and bake until top begins to brown, 15 to 20 minutes. Let sit for 10 to 15 minutes before serving.

To Make Ahead The macaroni and cheese can be made in advance through step 2. Scrape mixture into 13 by 9-inch baking dish, cool, lay plastic wrap directly on surface of pasta, and refrigerate for up to 2 days. When ready to bake, remove plastic, cover with aluminum foil, and bake for 30 minutes. Uncover and bake until top is golden brown, about 15 minutes. Let sit for 10 to 15 minutes before serving.

An Automat Classic

Home cooks have long put their stamp on plain-Jane macaroni and cheese, stirring in such items as hot dogs or diced ham and peas. One appealing, old-fashioned variation, however, is practically endangered: baked macaroni and cheese with tomatoes. The genius in the recipe is that the bright acid of the tomato cuts the richness of the cheese. Today, people of a certain age remember tomato mac and cheese fondly from Horn and Hardart's automats.

Automats started in Germany in 1896 as a way to quickly feed hundreds of thousands of workers during their lunch hour. The idea was very much like a vending machine. Rather than ordering their meals through a server, patrons would drop coins into a slot to open a glass door in front of a compartment holding a menu item. Frank Hardart brought back the automat idea after a visit to Germany. Hardart, along with his partner, Joseph B. Horn, hired an engineer to further simplify the German system so they could transform their traditional lunch counter into an automat in 1902.

As for one of their most popular menu items, macaroni and cheese with tomatoes, most of us have never heard of it, much less tasted it. Automats may be a thing of the past, but a good recipe for macaroni and cheese shouldn't be.

BEST POTLUCK MACARONI AND CHEESE

SERVES 8 TO 10

Block American cheese from the deli counter is best here, as prewrapped singles result in a drier macaroni and cheese.

- 4 slices hearty white sandwich bread, torn into quarters
- 4 tablespoons unsalted butter, melted, plus 4 tablespoons unsalted butter
- ¼ cup grated Parmesan cheese
- 1 pound elbow macaroni
- Salt
- 5 tablespoons all-purpose flour
- 3 (12-ounce) cans evaporated milk
- 2 teaspoons hot sauce
- 1 teaspoon dry mustard
- ⅛ teaspoon ground nutmeg
- 8 ounces extra-sharp cheddar cheese, shredded (2 cups)
- 5 ounces American cheese, shredded (1¼ cups)
- 3 ounces Monterey Jack cheese, shredded (¾ cup)

1. Adjust oven rack to middle position and heat oven to 350 degrees. Pulse bread, melted butter, and Parmesan in food processor until ground to coarse crumbs, about 8 pulses. Transfer to bowl.

2. Bring 4 quarts water to boil in large pot. Add macaroni and 1 tablespoon salt and cook, stirring often, until just al dente, about 6 minutes. Reserve ½ cup macaroni cooking water, then drain and rinse macaroni in colander under cold running water. Set aside.

3. Melt remaining 4 tablespoons butter in now-empty pot over medium-high heat. Stir in flour and cook, stirring constantly, until mixture turns light brown, about 1 minute. Slowly whisk in evaporated milk, hot sauce, mustard, nutmeg, and 2 teaspoons salt and cook until mixture begins to simmer and is slightly thickened, about 4 minutes. Off heat, whisk in cheeses and reserved cooking water until cheese melts. Stir in macaroni until completely coated.

4. Transfer mixture to 13 by 9-inch baking dish and top evenly with bread-crumb mixture. Bake until cheese is bubbling around edges and top is golden brown, 20 to 25 minutes. Let sit for 5 to 10 minutes before serving.

To Make Ahead The macaroni and cheese can be made in advance through step 3. Increase amount of reserved macaroni cooking water to 1 cup. Scrape mixture into 13 by 9-inch baking dish, cool, lay plastic wrap directly on surface of pasta, and refrigerate for up to 1 day. Bread-crumb mixture may be refrigerated for up to 2 days. When ready to bake, remove plastic, cover with aluminum foil, and bake for 30 minutes. Uncover, sprinkle bread crumbs over top, and bake until topping is golden brown, about 20 minutes longer. Let sit before serving.

Keeping It Together

Using already stabilized ingredients like American cheese and evaporated milk ensures that this cheesy sauce doesn't break in the oven.

Why This Recipe Works Unlike many macaroni and cheese recipes, our Best Potluck Macaroni and Cheese is creamy, sturdy, and rich. We prevented the sauce from separating and clumping when baked by using evaporated milk and American cheese—the stabilizers in these ingredients kept the sauce from breaking, so that it emerged from the oven satiny smooth. Homemade bread crumbs, enriched with melted butter and Parmesan cheese, created a flavorful, crisp topping.

CLASSIC TOMATO SOUP

SERVES 6 TO 8

Use unseasoned canned tomatoes.

2 (28-ounce) cans diced tomatoes
¾ cup low-sodium chicken broth
3 tablespoons unsalted butter
1 onion, chopped
1 bay leaf
1 teaspoon brown sugar
2 tablespoons tomato paste
2 tablespoons all-purpose flour
½ teaspoon baking soda
 Salt and pepper
½ cup heavy cream

1. Drain tomatoes in colander set over large bowl, pressing lightly to release juices. Transfer tomato juice and chicken broth to large measuring cup (mixture should measure about 4 cups); reserve.

2. Melt butter in Dutch oven over medium heat. Add onion and cook until softened, about 5 minutes. Add two-thirds of drained tomatoes, bay leaf, and brown sugar and cook, stirring occasionally, until tomatoes begin to brown, about 15 minutes.

3. Add tomato paste and flour to pot and cook, stirring frequently, until paste begins to darken, 1 to 2 minutes. Slowly stir in reserved tomato juice–broth mixture, remaining tomatoes, baking soda, and ½ teaspoon salt and bring to boil. Reduce heat to medium-low and simmer until slightly thickened, about 5 minutes. Remove from heat.

4. Discard bay leaf. Puree soup in batches. Return pureed soup to pot and stir in cream. Season with salt and pepper. Serve. (Soup can be refrigerated for 3 days.)

Are You Kidding Me?

You can use it to brush your teeth, scrub your counters, or make your refrigerator smell better. Still, we were shocked at the difference that a mere ½ teaspoon of baking soda made in our Classic Tomato Soup. It neutralized some of the acid in the tomatoes for a perfect sweet-tart balance. And its sodium ions weakened the pectin in the cells of the tomatoes, allowing them to puree into a silken soup.

Bay Leaves

Bay leaves are a standard addition to soups, stews, and bean dishes. We prefer dried bay leaves to fresh; they work just as well in long-cooked recipes, are cheaper, and will keep for months in the freezer. We prefer Turkish bay leaves to those from California. The California bay leaf has a medicinal and potent flavor, like something you'd put in a cough drop. The Turkish bay leaf has a mild, green, and slightly clove-like flavor.

Why This Recipe Works We were shocked that the key to a satiny, well-balanced classic tomato soup turned out to be just ½ teaspoon of baking soda, which also helped neutralize the metallic taste and acidity of the canned tomatoes. To enhance the tomatoes' complexity, we browned most of them in a Dutch oven to concentrate their flavor, and saved some to add at the end of cooking to keep the soup fresh. We were tempted to add a variety of classic seasonings, but found they made the soup taste like marinara sauce. Tasters were most satisfied with a single bay leaf, chicken broth, and the richness of heavy cream.

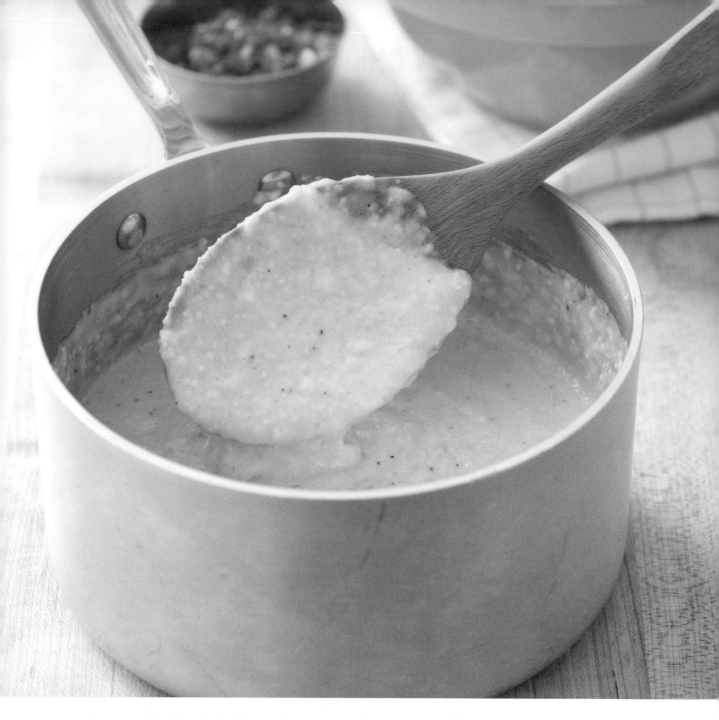

Why This Recipe Works Grits are a southern staple, but their appeal can be lost in bland, gluey incarnations. To take this down-home dish from dull to delicious, we needed to work on both texture and flavor. Replacing some of the cooking water with milk gave a creamy sweetness to the unadorned grits. As for the cheese, we found that a combination of Monterey Jack and sharp cheddar lent both smoothness and pronounced cheesy flavor. To give the dish more depth, we sautéed scallion whites and added real pureed corn for an extra boost of corn flavor.

CREAMY CHEESE GRITS

SERVES 4 TO 6

The grits are ready when they are mostly creamy but still retain a little bite. If the grits get too thick, whisk in a little water. If you are using frozen corn, thaw it first.

½ cup fresh or frozen corn kernels
3½ cups water
4 tablespoons unsalted butter
4 scallions, white parts minced,
   green parts sliced thin
1 cup milk
½ teaspoon hot sauce
   Salt and pepper
1 cup old-fashioned grits
4 ounces Monterey Jack cheese,
   shredded (1 cup)
4 ounces sharp cheddar cheese,
   shredded (1 cup)

1. Puree corn and ¼ cup water in blender until smooth, about 1 minute; set aside. Melt 2 tablespoons butter in medium saucepan over medium heat. Add scallion whites and cook until softened, about 2 minutes. Stir in remaining 3¼ cups water, milk, hot sauce, ½ teaspoon salt, and ½ teaspoon pepper and bring to boil.

2. Slowly whisk grits into saucepan until no lumps remain. Reduce heat to low and cook, stirring frequently, until thick and creamy, about 15 minutes.

3. Off heat, stir in Monterey Jack, cheddar, pureed corn, and remaining 2 tablespoons butter until incorporated. Season with salt and pepper to taste. Serve sprinkled with scallion greens.

Know Your Corn

Cornmeal Cornmeal is corn kernels that are dried and ground to a powder.

Grits Grits are cornmeal, but the name also refers to the cooked porridge popular in the South.

Hominy Grits Hominy grits are corn kernels with the hull and bran removed before grinding.

Polenta Polenta is cornmeal, but the name also refers to the cooked Italian porridge, which is traditionally enriched with butter and Parmesan.

Weighing Cheese

Our recipes specify cup amounts of cheese to reflect the habits of the typical home cook. But cheese is sold by weight, so it can be hard to determine how much to buy. Also, one person's measure may not precisely equal another's. To complicate matters, we classify cheese into three categories: hard, such as Parmesan and Pecorino Romano; semisoft, such as cheddar and Monterey Jack; and soft, such as feta, blue, and fresh goat cheeses. Each packs into cup measures differently. To develop a standard weight for each cheese category, we gathered 10 test cooks and had each weigh out 1-cup samples of each type. We averaged the weights to account for the heavy and light hands of different individuals. We found that 1 cup of grated hard cheese equals about 2 ounces, while the same measure of soft and semisoft is about 4 ounces. And remember, when measuring cheese, lightly pack measuring cups meant for dry ingredients; don't use liquid measuring cups, which will give you an inaccurate measurement for dry ingredients.

ROASTED GREEN BEANS WITH GOAT CHEESE AND HAZELNUTS

SERVES 4 TO 6

To trim green beans quickly, line up a handful so the stem ends are even and then cut off the stems with one swipe of the knife.

1½ pounds green beans, trimmed
5½ tablespoons extra-virgin olive oil
¾ teaspoon sugar
    Kosher salt and pepper
2 garlic cloves, minced
1 teaspoon grated orange zest plus 2 teaspoons juice
2 teaspoons lemon juice
1 teaspoon Dijon mustard
2 tablespoons minced fresh chives
2 ounces goat cheese, crumbled (½ cup)
¼ cup hazelnuts, toasted, skinned, and chopped

1. Adjust oven rack to lowest position and heat oven to 475 degrees. Combine green beans, 1½ tablespoons oil, sugar, ¾ teaspoon salt, and ½ teaspoon pepper in bowl. Evenly distribute green beans on rimmed baking sheet.

2. Cover sheet tightly with aluminum foil and roast for 10 minutes. Remove foil and continue to roast until green beans are spotty brown, about 10 minutes longer, stirring halfway through roasting.

3. Meanwhile, combine garlic, orange zest, and remaining ¼ cup oil in medium bowl and microwave until bubbling, about 1 minute; let steep for 1 minute. Whisk orange juice, lemon juice, mustard, ¼ teaspoon salt, and ¼ teaspoon pepper into garlic mixture.

4. Transfer green beans to bowl with dressing, add chives, and toss to combine. Transfer to serving platter and sprinkle with goat cheese and hazelnuts. Serve.

ROASTED GREEN BEANS WITH ALMONDS AND MINT

Omit orange zest and juice, substitute with 1 teaspoon grated lime zest and 4 teaspoons lime juice; ¼ cup torn fresh mint leaves for chives; and ¼ cup whole blanched almonds, toasted and chopped, for hazelnuts. Omit goat cheese.

ROASTED GREEN BEANS WITH PECORINO AND PINE NUTS

Omit orange zest and juice, substitute with 1 teaspoon grated lemon zest and 4 teaspoons lemon juice; 2 tablespoons chopped fresh basil for chives; 1½ ounces Pecorino Romano cheese, shredded, for goat cheese; and ¼ cup pine nuts, toasted, for hazelnuts.

Steam and Then Roast Uncovered

For tender green beans with a hint of flavorful browning, we found that a hybrid moist-then-dry roasting method worked best. First we roast the beans covered with foil, which traps steam and helps them cook through quickly. Then we remove the foil to allow the beans to brown in the dry heat.

Why This Recipe Works For tender green beans with a hint of flavorful browning, we developed a hybrid method—first steaming the beans under a foil cover and then removing the foil and allowing them to roast. Adding a bit of sugar to the beans promoted the browning and blistering we wanted in the oven's high heat. Tossing the beans with a light citrus dressing and goat cheese brightened their flavor, while toasted hazelnuts provided a welcome crunch.

Why This Recipe Works Too often a bright, crisp romaine salad is weighed down by an overly heavy dressing, so we set out to make a light and flavorful green goddess dressing. We achieved this by using three kinds of herbs: tarragon, parsley, and chives. To discreetly add depth, we used a single anchovy fillet, and for the creamiest texture, we used mayo and sour cream and prepared the dressing in a blender. While modern versions of green goddess dressing often contain avocado, the original version, credited to chef Philip Roemer of the Palace Hotel in San Francisco in the 1920s, does not, so we skipped it.

GREEN GODDESS DRESSING

MAKES 1¼ CUPS; ENOUGH FOR 6 WEDGES OF LETTUCE

To appreciate the full flavor of this rich dressing, drizzle it over chilled wedges of mild iceberg lettuce or romaine lettuce leaves. A blender yields a brighter, slightly more flavorful dressing, but a food processor will work, too.

  2 teaspoons dried tarragon
  1 tablespoon lemon juice
  1 tablespoon water
  ¾ cup mayonnaise
  ¼ cup sour cream
  ¼ cup coarsely chopped fresh parsley
  1 garlic clove, chopped
  1 anchovy fillet, rinsed and dried
  ¼ cup chopped chives
    Salt and pepper

  1. Combine tarragon, lemon juice, and water in small bowl and let sit for 15 minutes.
  2. Blend tarragon mixture, mayonnaise, sour cream, parsley, garlic, and anchovy in blender until smooth, scraping down sides as necessary. Transfer to medium bowl, stir in chives, and season with salt and pepper. Chill until flavors meld, about 1 hour. (Dressing can be covered and refrigerated for up to 1 day.)

Don't Fear the Fish

The single anchovy fillet we call for in this recipe may seem superfluous, but it adds savory depth to the dressing (without tasting like fish). Try adding a minced anchovy to your next batch of beef stew or tomato sauce—it will boost the flavor considerably. Anchovies are sold jarred or canned. Extra jarred anchovies can be refrigerated right in the jar according to package directions. But extra canned anchovies should be transferred to a nonreactive airtight container, covered with oil, and refrigerated for up to 2 weeks.

Juicing Lemons

We squeezed a dozen lemons—cold, rolled, and warm—and found that each yielded the same amount of juice. The only difference was that warm and room-temperature lemons were softer and therefore easier to squeeze than the cold lemons. When you use a tool like a reamer or juicer, this doesn't come into play as much, but if you're juicing by hand, we recommend room-temperature lemons. To quickly warm a cold lemon, you can heat it in the microwave until it is warm to the touch.

To quickly juice a lemon, we prefer a wooden reamer with a sharp tip that can easily pierce the flesh. Plastic reamers with rounded tips didn't work as well in our tests. Plastic and glass juicers (which sit on the counter and collect juice) are better suited to oranges and grapefruits than lemons. When purchasing lemons at the supermarket, choose large ones that give to gentle pressure; hard lemons have thicker skin and yield less juice.

CLASSIC TUNA SALAD

MAKES 2 CUPS; ENOUGH FOR 4 SANDWICHES

For slightly milder salads, use an equal amount of shallot instead of onion.

¼ cup finely chopped onion
2 tablespoons olive oil
3 (5-ounce) cans solid white tuna in water
½ cup plus 2 tablespoons mayonnaise
1 celery rib, minced
2 teaspoons lemon juice
½ teaspoon sugar
Salt and pepper

1. Combine onion and oil in small bowl and microwave until onion begins to soften, about 2 minutes. Let onion mixture cool for 5 minutes. Place tuna in fine-mesh strainer and press dry with paper towels. Transfer tuna to medium bowl and mash with fork until finely flaked.

2. Stir mayonnaise, celery, lemon juice, sugar, ½ teaspoon salt, ½ teaspoon pepper, and onion mixture into tuna until well combined. Season with salt and pepper to taste. Serve. (Salad can be refrigerated for up to 24 hours.)

TUNA SALAD WITH HARD-COOKED EGGS, RADISHES, AND CAPERS

Substitute 2 tablespoons extra-virgin olive oil for olive oil and 6 tablespoons extra-virgin olive oil for mayonnaise. Add 2 thinly sliced hard-cooked eggs; 2 trimmed, halved, and thinly sliced radishes; and ¼ cup capers, minced, to salad.

TUNA SALAD WITH APPLE, WALNUTS, AND TARRAGON

Add 1 apple, cored and cut into ½-inch pieces; ½ cup walnuts, toasted and chopped coarse; and 1 tablespoon minced fresh tarragon to salad.

TUNA SALAD WITH CORNICHONS AND WHOLE-GRAIN MUSTARD

Add ¼ cup finely chopped cornichons, 1 tablespoon minced fresh chives, and 1 tablespoon whole-grain mustard to salad.

TUNA SALAD WITH CURRY AND GRAPES

Add 1 teaspoon curry powder to bowl with onion and oil before microwaving. Add 1 cup green grapes, halved, to salad.

Draining Tuna

Place tuna in fine-mesh strainer and press dry with paper towels to remove excess moisture and prevent watery tuna salad. Once drained, transfer to medium bowl and mash with fork until finely flaked.

Why This Recipe Works A classic lunchbox staple, tuna salad too often turns out watery, chalky, and/or bland. It may sound odd, but the key to great tuna salad is to first thoroughly drain chunked tuna and dry it with paper towels. Mashing the dried tuna with a fork made for a nice, uniform consistency. To moisten the salad, we quickly infused olive oil with chopped onion in the microwave and added it to the tuna, along with a bit of sugar, lemon juice, and mayo to round out the flavor. We tasted every variety of canned tuna and the runaway winner was solid white tuna packed in water.

CHICKEN FLORENTINE

SERVES 4 TO 6

We like tender, quick-cooking bagged baby spinach here; if using curly-leaf spinach, chop it before cooking.

     2 tablespoons vegetable oil
    12 ounces (12 cups) baby spinach
     4 (6-ounce) boneless, skinless chicken
        breasts, trimmed
        Salt and pepper
     1 shallot, minced
     2 garlic cloves, minced
1¼ cups chicken broth
1¼ cups water
     1 cup heavy cream
     6 tablespoons grated Parmesan cheese
     1 teaspoon grated lemon zest
        plus 1 teaspoon juice

1. Adjust oven rack to upper-middle position and heat broiler. Heat 1 tablespoon oil in 12-inch skillet over medium-high heat until shimmering. Add spinach and cook, stirring occasionally until wilted, 1 to 2 minutes. Transfer spinach to colander set over bowl and press with spoon to release excess liquid. Discard liquid.

2. Pat chicken dry with paper towels and season with salt and pepper. Wipe out pan and heat remaining 1 tablespoon oil over medium-high heat until just smoking. Cook chicken on both sides until golden, 4 to 6 minutes. Add shallot and garlic to skillet and cook until fragrant, about 30 seconds. Stir in broth, water, and cream and bring to boil.

3. Reduce heat to medium-low and simmer until chicken is cooked through, about 10 minutes; transfer chicken to plate and tent with aluminum foil. Continue to simmer sauce until reduced to 1 cup, about 10 minutes. Off heat, stir in 4 tablespoons Parmesan and lemon zest and juice.

4. Cut chicken crosswise into ½-inch-thick slices and arrange on broiler-safe platter. Scatter spinach over chicken and pour sauce over spinach. Sprinkle with remaining Parmesan and broil until golden brown, 3 to 5 minutes. Serve.

Draining Spinach

As it cooks, spinach releases a lot of moisture, which can make dishes like our Chicken Florentine watery. To prevent that, we transferred the spinach to a colander and pressed the leaves with a spoon to force the liquid out. We drained nearly ¼ cup of liquid from the 12 ounces of spinach used in this recipe.

Enchanting Chicken—Without A Wand

The idea of chicken Florentine as a dish made from chicken, spinach, and a cheesy cream sauce appeared in print as early as 1931, when *The Lowell (Mass.) Sun* breathlessly described Chicken Mornay Florentine as served at the Manhattan restaurant, Divan Parisien: "They make magic passes over spinach, then cover it with breasts of chicken and a Mornay sauce." In the "Tables for Two" column of *The New Yorker*, April 25, 1931, the Divan Parisien was described as "a quiet and extremely civilized restaurant with an assorted clientele. . . ." What a shame then, that one of their most popular dishes morphed to a 1960s casserole (made with frozen spinach, margarine, packaged bread crumbs, and condensed soups) and then to wedding banquet fare in the 1970s and '80s (breasts stuffed with spinach, rolled, fried, and served with a cheesy sauce). We wanted to deconstruct the casserole, unroll the spirals, and return chicken Florentine to its earliest version: a bright, elegant, streamlined sauté with a pan sauce. No magic passes involved.

Why This Recipe Works To restore chicken Florentine to its elegant roots, we started with fresh spinach. To prevent the water from the spinach from washing out the other flavors in the dish, we drained excess liquid from the cooked spinach by pressing the leaves with the back of a spoon in a colander. For flavor, we seared the chicken breasts first and then poached them in the sauce before broiling. We used cream to make the sauce silky and built volume with equal amounts of chicken broth and water. We also added a squeeze of lemon juice and a hit of zest, along with Parmesan cheese for its nutty, savory punch.

Why This Recipe Works Once-trendy chicken Divan's original recipe calls for many different components and even more cooking steps. We wanted to stay true to the original flavor of the dish but streamline the cooking process. To do this, we batch-cooked the broccoli first, then the chicken. While the broccoli and chicken rested, we used the same pan to prepare our sauce. And instead of making a separate hollandaise sauce, like the traditional chicken Divan recipes demand, we whisked egg yolks and lemon juice together, then tempered the mixture with the hot pan sauce, and whisked in butter at the end.

CHICKEN DIVAN

SERVES 4

Use one small onion instead of the shallots, if desired.

 3 tablespoons vegetable oil
 1 pound broccoli florets, cut into 1-inch pieces
2½ cups chicken broth
 ¼ cup all-purpose flour
 4 (6-ounce) boneless, skinless chicken
   breasts, trimmed
   Salt and pepper
 2 shallots, minced
 1 cup heavy cream
 ½ cup dry sherry
 2 teaspoons Worcestershire sauce
 3 ounces Parmesan cheese, grated (1½ cups)
 3 large egg yolks
 1 tablespoon lemon juice
 3 tablespoons unsalted butter

1. Adjust oven rack to lower-middle position and heat broiler. Heat 1 tablespoon oil in large skillet over medium-high heat until just smoking. Add broccoli and cook until spotty brown, about 1 minute. Add ½ cup broth, cover, and steam until just tender, about 1½ minutes. Remove lid and cook until liquid has evaporated, about 1 minute. Transfer broccoli to plate lined with paper towels; rinse and wipe out skillet.

2. Heat remaining 2 tablespoons oil in now-empty skillet over medium-high heat until smoking. Meanwhile, place flour in shallow dish. Season chicken with salt and pepper and dredge in flour to coat. Cook chicken until golden brown on both sides, 4 to 6 minutes. Transfer chicken to plate.

3. Add shallots to skillet and cook until just softened, about 1 minute. Add remaining 2 cups broth and cream and scrape browned bits from bottom of pan. Return chicken to skillet and simmer over medium-high heat until cooked through, about 10 minutes. Transfer chicken to clean plate and continue to simmer sauce until reduced to 1 cup, about 10 minutes. Add sherry and Worcestershire and simmer until reduced again to 1 cup, about 3 minutes. Stir in 1 cup Parmesan.

4. Whisk egg yolks and lemon juice in small bowl, then whisk in about ¼ cup sauce. Off heat, whisk egg yolk mixture into sauce in skillet, then whisk in butter.

5. Cut chicken into ½-inch-thick slices and arrange on broiler-safe platter. Scatter broccoli over chicken and pour sauce over broccoli. Sprinkle with remaining ½ cup Parmesan and broil until golden brown, 3 to 5 minutes. Serve.

Broccoli Makes It to the Big Time

It can seem hard to believe today, but broccoli, a key ingredient in chicken Divan, an elegant chicken dish from Manhattan's Divan Parisien restaurant (see page 16), was a relative late-comer to the American diet. This headline from *The New York Times* in 1926 attests to its arrival on the scene: "New Vegetables Vary our Menus: Broccoli, Artichoke, and Avocado Naturalized, and Fennel Enters Under Foreign Name—Homely Carrot Is Still in Demand." Broccoli aside, the restaurant's recipe required a whole poached chicken and a sauce made with béchamel, hollandaise, Parmesan cheese, and whipped cream. The ingredients were combined *à la minute* (just before being plated) and broiled to perfection. Sounds good, but if we're counting right, that's at least five pots, four recipes, and more time than we'd care to spend in the kitchen. No wonder most "modern" recipes rely on canned soup. We wanted to bring Divan into the 21st century without compromising the flavors of the original dish.

Why This Recipe Works Our take on smothered chicken had two goals: big chicken flavor and weeknight ease. For perfectly tender, evenly cooked southern-style smothered chicken, we started with chicken parts rather than a whole bird. We browned the pieces and then shallow-braised them in a savory gravy built from pantry ingredients: chicken broth, flour, sautéed onions, celery, garlic, and dried sage. We found that we needed just 2 tablespoons of flour to thicken the gravy to a rich—but not stodgy—consistency. A splash of cider vinegar brightened the sauce and helped the chicken's flavor shine.

SOUTHERN-STYLE SMOTHERED CHICKEN

SERVES 4

This dish is best served with rice, but it's also good with potatoes. You may substitute ground sage for the dried sage leaves, but decrease the amount to ¼ teaspoon.

- 3 pounds bone-in chicken pieces (split breasts cut in half crosswise, drumsticks, and/or thighs), trimmed
  Salt and pepper
- ½ cup plus 2 tablespoons all-purpose flour
- ¼ cup vegetable oil
- 2 onions, chopped fine
- 2 celery ribs, chopped fine
- 3 garlic cloves, minced
- 1 teaspoon dried sage leaves
- 2 cups chicken broth
- 1 tablespoon cider vinegar
- 2 tablespoons minced fresh parsley

1. Pat chicken dry with paper towels and season with salt and pepper. Spread ½ cup flour in shallow dish. Working with 1 piece at a time, dredge chicken in flour, shaking off excess, and transfer to plate.

2. Heat oil in Dutch oven over medium-high heat. Add half of chicken to pot, skin side down, and cook until deep golden brown, 4 to 6 minutes per side; transfer to plate. Repeat with remaining chicken, adjusting heat if flour begins to burn.

3. Pour off all but 2 tablespoons fat and return pot to medium heat. Add onions, celery, 1 teaspoon salt, and ½ teaspoon pepper and cook until softened, 6 to 8 minutes. Stir in garlic, sage, and remaining 2 tablespoons flour and cook until vegetables are well coated with flour and garlic is fragrant, about 1 minute. Whisk in broth, scraping up any browned bits.

4. Nestle chicken into sauce, add any accumulated juices from plate, and bring to boil. Reduce heat to low, cover, and simmer until breasts register 160 degrees and drumsticks/thighs register 175 degrees, 30 to 40 minutes.

5. Transfer chicken to serving dish. Stir vinegar into sauce and season with salt and pepper to taste. Pour sauce over chicken, sprinkle with parsley, and serve.

How to Split and Trim Breasts

1. With whole breast skin side down on cutting board, center knife on breastbone, then apply pressure to cut through and separate breast into two halves.

2. Using kitchen shears, trim off rib section from each breast, following vertical line of fat from tapered end of breast up to socket.

3. Using chef's knife or kitchen shears, trim excess fat and skin from breasts.

GLAZED MEATLOAF

SERVES 6 TO 8

Both ground sirloin and ground chuck work well here, but avoid ground round—it is gristly and bland.

Glaze
1	cup ketchup
¼	cup packed brown sugar
2½	tablespoons cider vinegar
½	teaspoon hot sauce

Meatloaf
2	teaspoons vegetable oil
1	onion, chopped fine
2	garlic cloves, minced
17	square or 19 round saltines
⅓	cup whole milk
1	pound 90 percent lean ground beef
1	pound ground pork
2	large eggs plus 1 large yolk
⅓	cup finely chopped fresh parsley
2	teaspoons Dijon mustard
2	teaspoons Worcestershire sauce
½	teaspoon dried thyme
	Salt and pepper

1. For the Glaze Whisk all ingredients in saucepan until sugar dissolves. Reserve ¼ cup glaze mixture, then simmer remaining glaze over medium heat until slightly thickened, about 5 minutes. Cover and keep warm.

2. For the Meatloaf Line rimmed baking sheet with aluminum foil and coat lightly with vegetable oil spray. Heat oil in nonstick skillet over medium heat until shimmering. Cook onion until golden, about 8 minutes. Add garlic and cook until fragrant, about 30 seconds. Transfer to large bowl.

3. Process saltines and milk in food processor until smooth, about 30 seconds. Add beef and pork and pulse until well combined, about 10 pulses. Transfer meat mixture to bowl with cooled onion mixture. Add eggs and yolk, parsley, mustard, Worcestershire, thyme, 1 teaspoon salt, and ¾ teaspoon pepper to bowl and mix with hands until combined.

4. Adjust 1 oven rack to middle position and second rack 4 inches from broiler element; heat broiler. Transfer meat mixture to prepared baking sheet and shape into 9 by 5-inch loaf. Broil on upper rack until well browned, about 5 minutes. Brush 2 tablespoons unreduced glaze over top and sides of loaf and then return to oven and broil until glaze begins to brown, about 2 minutes.

5. Transfer meatloaf to lower rack and brush with remaining unreduced glaze. Reduce oven temperature to 350 degrees and bake until meatloaf registers 160 degrees, 40 to 45 minutes. Transfer to cutting board, tent with foil, and let rest for 20 minutes. Slice and serve, passing remaining reduced glaze at table.

Ketchup—The Truffle Oil Of The '20s?

Say "meatloaf" and most Americans think 1950s comfort food and Mom, but this humble recipe has surprisingly elegant roots in a now-forgotten dish called "cannelon." A typical cannelon recipe from the original *Boston Cooking-School Cookbook* calls for chopping and seasoning beef, shaping it into a log, and basting it with melted butter as it bakes. The wide availability of meat grinders and the advent of reliable refrigeration made ground beef a household staple in the early 20th century and meatloaf recipes gained wide circulation. As a topping, butter was usurped by tomato sauce until ketchup became popular in the 1920s. The Heinz company created a "House of Heinz" campaign to tout the gourmet appeal their products gave to everyday dishes such as meatloaf. Along with their ketchup, Heinz suggested incorporating other Heinz products, such as beefsteak sauce, chili sauce, and olives into meatloaf, or serving cubes of meatloaf with pickle slices for an easy hors d'oeuvre. For our meatloaf, we skipped the gourmet aspirations and unnecessary mix-ins for a stellar version of the 1950s favorite.

Why This Recipe Works For our old-fashioned meatloaf, we cut ground beef with an equal portion of sweet ground pork for better flavor. As for seasoning, we stuck with tradition: salt, pepper, Dijon mustard, Worcestershire sauce, thyme, parsley, sautéed onion, and garlic. To add moisture and structure, we used a panade (paste) of milk and saltines. Combining the panade in a food processor and then pulsing it with the meat gave the loaf the most cohesive, tender structure. To evaporate the surface moisture that was inhibiting the formation of a crust, we broiled the loaf prior to baking and glazing.

FROSTED MEATLOAF

SERVES 6 TO 8

If you don't have a ricer or a food mill, just mash the potatoes thoroughly.

- ¼ cup ketchup
- 1 tablespoon packed light brown sugar
- 1 tablespoon cider vinegar
- ½ teaspoon hot sauce
- 8 tablespoons unsalted butter
- 1 onion, chopped fine
- 3 garlic cloves, minced
- 17 square or 19 round saltines, crushed (⅔ cup)
- 1 cup whole milk
- 1 pound ground pork
- 2 large eggs plus 1 large yolk
- ⅓ cup minced fresh parsley
- 2 teaspoons Dijon mustard
- 2 teaspoons Worcestershire sauce
  Salt and pepper
- ½ teaspoon dried thyme
- 1 pound 90 percent lean ground beef
- 2 pounds russet potatoes, peeled and cut into 1-inch pieces

1. Adjust oven racks to upper-middle and lower-middle positions and heat broiler. Line rimmed baking sheet with aluminum foil, set wire rack in sheet, and place 14 by 6-inch piece of foil in center of rack. Whisk ketchup, sugar, vinegar, and hot sauce together in bowl; set aside glaze.

2. Melt 2 tablespoons butter in 10-inch skillet over medium heat. Add onion and cook until just softened, 3 to 5 minutes. Add garlic and cook until fragrant, about 30 seconds. Set aside off heat.

3. Combine saltines and ⅓ cup milk in large bowl and mash with fork until chunky paste forms. Add pork, eggs and yolk, parsley, mustard, Worcestershire, 1 teaspoon salt, ¾ teaspoon pepper, thyme, and onion mixture and knead with your hands until mostly combined. Add beef and knead until combined.

4. Transfer meat mixture to foil rectangle on wire rack and form into 9 by 6-inch loaf. Broil on upper-middle oven rack until well browned, 5 to 7 minutes. Brush glaze over top and sides of meatloaf, return to upper-middle rack, and broil until glaze begins to brown, 3 to 5 minutes. Move meatloaf to lower-middle oven rack, adjust oven temperature to 350 degrees, and bake until meatloaf registers 160 degrees, 40 to 45 minutes. Remove from oven.

5. Meanwhile, bring potatoes and 2 quarts water to boil in Dutch oven over high heat. Reduce heat to medium-low and simmer until potatoes are tender, 20 to 25 minutes; drain potatoes thoroughly in colander. Set ricer or food mill over now-empty pot and press or mill potatoes into pot. Stir 1 teaspoon salt, remaining 6 tablespoons butter, and remaining ⅔ cup milk into potatoes until combined.

6. Using offset spatula, spread mashed potatoes evenly over top and sides of meatloaf. Heat broiler and return meatloaf to lower-middle oven rack. Broil until potatoes are browned, about 15 minutes. Using foil as sling, transfer meatloaf to carving board and let rest for 15 minutes. Slice and serve.

Reviving Comfort Food

During World War II, meat was rationed. Americans were encouraged to extend short supplies through many means, boosting meatloaf's popularity. In the '50s, this classic was reinvented as a centerpiece for entertaining, topped with garnishes, glazes, sauces, and, of course, mashed potatoes.

Why This Recipe Works Meatloaf and potatoes are an unbeatable combination, so frosted meatloaf—meatloaf coated in a layer of mashed potatoes—was an idea we could get behind. To perfect this nearly forgotten 1950s classic, we found that we had to broil the meatloaf in stages to keep the potatoes from slipping off: First, it was broiled to create a crust and then coated with a tangy, ketchup-based glaze for flavor and broiled again. After cooking through, the meatloaf was frosted with creamy mashed potatoes and broiled for a final stint to turn the fluffy crown of potatoes beautifully brown.

Why This Recipe Works As much as we love classic meatloaf, a recipe for a rustic meatloaf with a deep brown crust and hearty mushroom gravy piqued our interest. Sliced button mushrooms plus minced porcini gave the gravy an earthy richness. To further boost the flavor of the meatloaf itself, we added the porcini soaking liquid and more button mushrooms, which we ground in a food processor and sautéed. To keep the procedure simple, we baked the meatloaf in the same skillet. Then, while the loaf was resting, we used the skillet and the meat drippings to build our gravy.

MEATLOAF WITH MUSHROOM GRAVY

SERVES 8

If you're short the 2 tablespoons of meatloaf drippings needed to make the gravy, supplement the drippings with melted butter or vegetable oil.

1 cup water
¼ ounce dried porcini mushrooms, rinsed
16 square or 18 round saltines
10 ounces white mushrooms, trimmed
1 tablespoon vegetable oil
1 onion, chopped fine
  Salt and pepper
4 garlic cloves, minced
1 pound ground pork
2 large eggs
1 tablespoon plus ¾ teaspoon Worcestershire sauce
1 pound 85 percent lean ground beef
¾ teaspoon minced fresh thyme
¼ cup all-purpose flour
2½ cups chicken broth

1. Adjust oven rack to middle position and heat oven to 375 degrees. Microwave water and porcini in covered bowl until steaming, about 1 minute. Let sit until softened, about 5 minutes. Strain porcini through fine-mesh strainer lined with coffee filter, reserving liquid. Mince and reserve porcini.

2. Process saltines in food processor until finely ground, about 30 seconds; transfer to large bowl and reserve. Pulse 5 ounces of white mushrooms in processor until finely ground, 8 to 10 pulses.

3. Heat oil in 12-inch nonstick oven-safe skillet over medium-high heat until shimmering. Add onion and cook until browned, 6 to 8 minutes. Stir in processed mushrooms and ¼ teaspoon salt and cook until liquid evaporates and mushrooms begin to brown, about 5 minutes. Add garlic and cook until fragrant, about 30 seconds. Transfer to bowl with saltines and let cool to room temperature, about 15 minutes. Wipe out skillet with paper towels.

4. Add pork, ¼ cup reserved porcini liquid, eggs, 1 tablespoon Worcestershire, 1 teaspoon salt, and ¾ teaspoon pepper to cooled mushroom-saltine mixture and knead gently until nearly combined. Add beef and knead until well combined. Transfer meat mixture to now-empty skillet and shape into 10 by 6-inch loaf. Bake until meatloaf registers 160 degrees, 45 to 55 minutes. Transfer meatloaf to carving board and tent loosely with aluminum foil.

5. Slice remaining 5 ounces white mushrooms. Discard any solids in skillet and pour off all but 2 tablespoons fat. Heat fat over medium-high heat until shimmering. Add sliced mushrooms and reserved porcini and cook, stirring occasionally, until deep golden brown, 6 to 8 minutes. Stir in thyme and ¼ teaspoon salt and cook until fragrant, about 30 seconds. Add flour and cook, stirring frequently, until golden, about 2 minutes. Slowly whisk in broth, ½ cup reserved porcini liquid, and remaining ¾ teaspoon Worcestershire, scraping up any browned bits, and bring to boil. Reduce heat to medium and simmer, whisking occasionally, until thickened, 10 to 15 minutes. Season with salt and pepper to taste. Slice meatloaf and serve with gravy.

One Skillet, Start to Finish

ON THE STOVE
We brown the onion and ground mushrooms for robust flavor.

INTO THE OVEN
We shape and bake the meatloaf in the same skillet.

BACK TO THE STOVE
While the meatloaf rests, we use its drippings to make the gravy.

BACON-WRAPPED MEATLOAF

SERVES 6 TO 8

Bull's-Eye Original is our favorite barbecue sauce. Do not use thick-cut bacon for this recipe, as the package will yield fewer strips for wrapping the meatloaf. Oscar Mayer Naturally Hardwood Smoked Bacon is our favorite thin-sliced bacon.

¼ cup barbecue sauce, plus extra for serving
1 tablespoon cider vinegar
1 tablespoon Worcestershire sauce
1 tablespoon spicy brown mustard
17 square or 19 round saltines, crushed (⅔ cup)
4 slices coarsely chopped bacon,
  plus 8 whole slices
1 onion, chopped coarse
3 garlic cloves, minced
⅓ cup whole milk
2 large eggs plus 1 large yolk
⅓ cup minced fresh parsley
¾ teaspoon salt
½ teaspoon pepper
1½ pounds 90 percent lean ground beef

1. Adjust oven rack to upper-middle position and heat oven to 375 degrees. Line rimmed baking sheet with aluminum foil and set wire rack in sheet. Whisk barbecue sauce, vinegar, Worcestershire, and mustard together in bowl; set glaze aside.

2. Process saltines in food processor until finely ground, about 30 seconds; transfer to large bowl. Pulse chopped bacon and onion in now-empty processor until coarsely ground, about 10 pulses. Transfer bacon mixture to 10-inch nonstick skillet and cook over medium heat until onion is soft and translucent, about 5 minutes. Add garlic and cook until fragrant, about 30 seconds. Set aside off heat.

3. Add milk, eggs and yolk, parsley, salt, pepper, and 2 tablespoons glaze to saltines and mash with fork until chunky paste forms. Stir in bacon mixture until combined. Add the beef and knead with your hands until combined.

4. Lightly spray 8½ by 4½-inch loaf pan with vegetable oil spray. Line pan with large sheet of plastic wrap, with extra plastic hanging over edges of pan. Push plastic into corners and up sides of pan. Line pan crosswise with remaining 8 bacon slices, overlapping them slightly and letting excess hang over edges of pan (you should have at least ½ inch of overhanging bacon). Brush bacon with 3 tablespoons glaze. Transfer meatloaf mixture to bacon-lined pan and press mixture firmly into pan. Fold bacon slices over mixture.

5. Using metal skewer or tip of paring knife, poke 15 holes in one 14 by 3-inch piece of foil. Center foil rectangle on top of meatloaf. Carefully flip meatloaf onto wire rack so foil is on bottom and bacon is on top. Gripping plastic, gently lift and remove pan from meatloaf. Discard plastic. Gently press meatloaf into 9 by 5-inch rectangle.

6. Bake until bacon is browned and meatloaf registers 150 degrees, about 1 hour. Remove from oven and heat broiler. Brush top and sides of meatloaf with remaining 2 tablespoons glaze. Broil meatloaf until glaze begins to char and meatloaf registers 160 degrees, 3 to 5 minutes. Using foil as sling, transfer meatloaf to carving board and let rest for 15 minutes. Slice and serve, passing extra barbecue sauce.

That's a Wrap

Invert the foil-topped loaf, bacon and all, onto a wire rack set in a baking sheet, remove the loaf pan and plastic, press the meatloaf into shape, and bake.

Why This Recipe Works What's even better than a bacon-wrapped meatloaf? A bacon-wrapped meatloaf that also has chopped bacon added to the ground beef inside. To make shaping easy, we lined a loaf pan with plastic wrap and then shingled slices of bacon in the pan. After pressing the meatloaf mixture into the pan, we turned it out onto a piece of foil set on a wire rack inside a rimmed baking sheet. This allowed the fat from the meat to drain away from the loaf as it cooked. A pass under the broiler ensured that the bacon was crisp and that the spicy-sweet glaze caramelized to perfection.

Why This Recipe Works The point of Swiss steak is to transform a tough, inexpensive cut of meat into a delicate meal so tender you can almost eat it with a spoon. Many recipes called for tenderizing the meat by pounding it before cooking, but we know from experience that pounding meat does nothing to tenderize it. Instead we relied on a slow braise to create the ideal texture. To flavor the Swiss steak gravy, we found a combination of sautéed onion, diced tomatoes, and sun-dried tomatoes was ideal.

SWISS STEAK WITH TOMATO GRAVY

SERVES 6 TO 8

Top blade roast may also be labeled chuck roast first cut, top chuck roast, flat iron roast, or simply blade roast.

- 1 (3½- to 4-pound) boneless top blade roast, trimmed
  Salt and pepper
- 2 tablespoons vegetable oil
- 1 onion, halved and sliced thin
- 2 tablespoons tomato paste
- 1 tablespoon all-purpose flour
- 3 garlic cloves, minced
- ½ teaspoon dried thyme
- 1 (14.5-ounce) can diced tomatoes
- 1½ cups chicken broth
- 1 tablespoon sun-dried tomatoes packed in oil, rinsed, patted dry, and minced
- 1 tablespoon minced fresh parsley

1. Adjust oven rack to middle position and heat oven to 300 degrees. Cut roast crosswise into quarters and remove center line of gristle from each quarter to yield 8 steaks.

2. Pat steaks dry with paper towels and season lightly with salt and pepper. Heat 1 tablespoon oil in Dutch oven over medium-high heat just until smoking. Brown 4 steaks on both sides, about 6 minutes. Transfer to plate and repeat with remaining oil and steaks.

3. Add onion to empty pot and cook until softened, about 5 minutes. Add tomato paste, flour, garlic, and thyme and cook until fragrant, about 1 minute. Stir in diced tomatoes and broth and bring to boil.

4. Return steaks and any accumulated juices to pan. Cover, transfer to oven and cook until steaks are fork-tender, about 2 hours. Transfer steaks to platter, tent with aluminum foil, and let rest for 5 minutes. Skim fat from sauce. Stir in sun-dried tomatoes and parsley. Season with salt and pepper to taste. Pour sauce over steaks. Serve.

Preparing Blade Roast for Swiss Steak
Top blade roast, a shoulder cut with great flavor, has a pesky line of gristle that runs horizontally through its center. Follow these simple steps to remove it and cut perfect Swiss steaks.

1. Place roast on cutting board and cut crosswise into 4 even pieces.

2. One piece at a time, turn meat on its side to expose line of gristle that runs through its center.

3. Remove by slicing through meat on either side of gristle to yield 2 "steaks."

Why This Recipe Works We wanted to rescue this American classic from the frozen foods aisle for a great weeknight option. We started by mixing a panade (a milk and bread paste) into ground beef to help bind the meat and preserve moisture, but this trick made the dish taste too much like meatloaf. On a lark, we added mashed potatoes as seen in one recipe and were impressed with the silky texture and great flavor of the patties. To make the dish easier, we swapped in instant potato flakes. We browned the patties on both sides and let them finish cooking in the extra-rich mushroom and onion sauce, which kept the beef tender.

SALISBURY STEAK

SERVES 4

When shaping the patties in step 1, be sure to wet your hands to prevent sticking. Tawny port or dry sherry can be substituted for the ruby port. Do not use potato granules, which add an off-flavor.

½ cup milk
7 tablespoons instant potato flakes
1 pound 90 percent lean ground beef
  Salt and pepper
4 tablespoons unsalted butter
1 onion, halved and sliced thin
1 pound white mushrooms, trimmed and sliced thin
1 tablespoon tomato paste
2 tablespoons all-purpose flour
1¾ cups beef broth
¼ cup ruby port

1. Whisk milk and potato flakes in large bowl. Add beef, ½ teaspoon salt, and ½ teaspoon pepper and knead until combined. Shape into four ½-inch-thick oval patties and transfer to parchment paper–lined plate. Refrigerate for at least 30 minutes or up to 4 hours.

2. Melt 1 tablespoon butter in 12-inch nonstick skillet over medium-high heat. Cook patties until well browned on each side, about 10 minutes. Transfer to plate.

3. Add onion and remaining 3 tablespoons butter to now-empty skillet and cook until onion is softened, about 5 minutes. Add mushrooms and ½ teaspoon salt and cook until liquid has evaporated, 5 to 7 minutes. Stir in tomato paste and flour and cook until browned, about 2 minutes. Slowly stir in broth and port and bring to simmer. Return patties to skillet, cover, and simmer over medium-low heat until cooked through, 12 to 15 minutes. Season sauce with salt and pepper to taste. Serve.

Take 2 Aspirin—or Have Some Salisbury Steak

It's hard to imagine that chopped steak could be considered health food, but that's just what Dr. James Henry Salisbury had in mind when he invented his eponymous dish as a "meat cure" for wounded and ill Civil War soldiers (who were instructed to eat it three times a day—with no vegetables allowed). Some 60 years later, during the period of World War I food rations, restaurateurs ground up their lean beef scraps, shaped them into patties, dressed the cooked patties with a rich mushroom cream sauce, and called it Salisbury steak. Around this time, recipes for Salisbury steak began showing up in cookbooks, but with a nod toward the original recipe, instructions indicated that invalids should skip the sauce. During World War II, Salisbury steak again enjoyed popularity because it was a great way to stretch meat: cream of wheat, oats, and soy grits were common fillers. And in 1965, Salisbury steak really hit the big time when Swanson introduced it in a special three-course TV dinner. Impressed by its storied past, we couldn't resist resurrecting this American classic.

MILK-CAN SUPPER

SERVES 6 TO 8

If your Dutch oven is slightly smaller than 8 quarts, the lid may not close all the way when you start cooking. But as the contents of the pot cook, they will decrease in volume, so you'll soon be able to clamp on the lid. Use small red potatoes, measuring 1 to 2 inches in diameter. Light-bodied American lagers, such as Budweiser, work best in this recipe.

```
 1    tablespoon vegetable oil
2½    pounds bratwurst (10 sausages)
 2    pounds small red potatoes, unpeeled
 1    head green cabbage (2 pounds),
        cored and cut into 8 wedges
 3    ears corn, husks and silk removed,
        ears cut into 3 pieces
 6    carrots, peeled and cut into 2-inch pieces
 1    onion, halved and cut through root end
        into 8 wedges
 4    garlic cloves, peeled and smashed
10    sprigs fresh thyme
 2    bay leaves
      Salt and pepper
1½    cups beer
 2    green bell peppers, stemmed, seeded,
        and cut into 1-inch-wide strips
```

1. Heat oil in 8-quart Dutch oven over medium heat until shimmering. Add bratwurst and cook until browned all over, 6 to 8 minutes. Remove pot from heat. Transfer bratwurst to cutting board and halve crosswise.

2. Place potatoes in single layer in now-empty Dutch oven. Arrange cabbage wedges in single layer on top of potatoes. Layer corn, carrots, onion, garlic, thyme, bay leaves, 1 teaspoon salt, and ½ teaspoon pepper over cabbage. Pour beer over vegetables and arrange browned bratwursts on top.

3. Bring to boil over medium-high heat (wisps of steam will be visible). Cover, reduce heat to medium, and simmer for 15 minutes. Add bell peppers and continue to simmer, covered, until potatoes are tender, about 15 minutes. (Use long skewer to test potatoes for doneness.)

4. Transfer bratwurst and vegetables to large serving platter (or roasting pan, if your platter isn't large enough); discard thyme sprigs and bay leaves. Pour 1 cup cooking liquid over platter. Season with salt and pepper to taste. Serve, passing remaining cooking liquid separately.

Trail Talk

Food often outlasts the culture that created it. Milk-can supper, for example, originated as a way of feeding cowhands after a long day of work. It is still popular in parts of the West and upper Midwest, but the food lingo of the cowboys who once ate this dish has faded away. Some names for individual dishes, such as calf slobber (for meringue), reflected the coarseness of trail language. Perhaps most revealing was the name for the 5- or 10-gallon can that served as an all-purpose cooking utensil throughout a thousand-mile cattle drive: It was called the squirrel can, the uncomplimentary moniker coming from the idea that it was never emptied during the course of the entire drive but instead became the receptacle for whatever the cook found to add to it. In her 1933 article "Ranch Diction of the Texas Panhandle," author Mary Dale Buckner declared, "It is true that when a spoon, cup, dipper or some small object was dropped into [the squirrel can], usually no one bothered to remove it." We'll stick with the milk can.

Why This Recipe Works Traditionally, cowboys layered vegetables and meat (usually sausage) into a giant milk can, then cooked it over an open fire to feed large groups of cowhands. To bring this all-in-one dish into the home kitchen, we opted to use a Dutch oven but keep the basic technique of layering ingredients according to cooking time. Browning the Bratwurst first created flavorful fond. We lined the bottom of the pot with sturdy red potatoes to protect the other vegetables from burning, and we added the quick-cooking green bell peppers halfway through cooking. Traditional lager as a cooking liquid gave our meat-and-potatoes meal toasty depth.

PAN-FRIED PORK CHOPS

SERVES 4

Chops between ¾ and 1 inch thick will work in this recipe.

- 1 teaspoon garlic powder
- ½ teaspoon paprika
- ½ teaspoon salt
- ½ teaspoon pepper
- ¼ teaspoon cayenne pepper
- 1 cup all-purpose flour
- 4 (8- to 10-ounce) bone-in pork rib or center-cut chops, about ¾ inch thick, trimmed
- 3 slices bacon, chopped
- ½ cup vegetable oil

1. Combine garlic powder, paprika, salt, pepper, and cayenne in bowl. Place flour in shallow dish. Pat chops dry with paper towels. Cut 2 slits about 2 inches apart through fat and connective tissue on edge of each chop. Season both sides of chops with spice mixture, then dredge chops lightly in flour (do not discard flour). Transfer to plate and let rest for 10 minutes.

2. Meanwhile, cook bacon in 12-inch nonstick skillet over medium heat until fat renders and bacon is crisp, 5 to 7 minutes. Using slotted spoon, transfer bacon to paper towel–lined plate and reserve for another use. Do not wipe out pan.

3. Add oil to fat in pan and heat over medium-high heat until just smoking. Return chops to flour dish and turn to coat chops again. Cook chops until well browned on each side, 6 to 8 minutes. Serve.

BBQ PAN-FRIED PORK CHOPS
Replace first 5 ingredients with 3 tablespoons light brown sugar, 1 teaspoon chili powder, 1 teaspoon paprika, ½ teaspoon salt, ½ teaspoon dry mustard, ¼ teaspoon ground cumin, and ¼ teaspoon cayenne pepper.

HERBED PAN-FRIED PORK CHOPS
Replace first 5 ingredients with ½ teaspoon dried marjoram, ½ teaspoon dried thyme, ¼ teaspoon dried basil, ¼ teaspoon dried rosemary (crumbled), ¼ teaspoon dried sage, pinch ground fennel, and ½ teaspoon salt.

Preventing Curly Chops
Pork chops—especially thin-cut chops—have a tendency to curl as they cook. When exposed to the high heat of the pan, the ring of fat and connective tissue that surrounds the exterior tightens, causing the meat to buckle and curl. To prevent it, we cut two slits about 2 inches apart through the fat and connective tissue on each chop.

BUCKLED CHOP
No slits

FLAT CHOP
Slits cut

Why This Recipe Works Not all pork chops are created alike—for pan-frying, we found that center-cut or bone-in pork chops worked best. The bone added valuable flavor to the meat and prevented it from drying out. Simply dredging the pork chops in flour, as most recipes instructed, produced a spotty, insubstantial crust that wouldn't stay put. We have had success letting floured chicken rest before re-dredging and frying, and we wondered if the same treatment would work for pork. Sure enough, our double-dipped chops emerged from the pan with a hefty, crisp, golden-brown crust.

Why This Recipe Works Bone-in chops were a must for smothered pork chops, because the bone kept the meat moist and added flavor to the sauce. Caramelizing the onions made the sauce too sweet and took almost an hour. We had better luck cooking them in butter until they were lightly browned. We swapped out chicken broth in favor of meatier beef broth, which greatly improved the flavor of our sauce. Adding dried thyme, a bay leaf, and cider vinegar bumped up the flavor even more. To thicken our broth, we made a cornstarch-and-broth slurry. The results? A silky sauce that clung to our chops.

SMOTHERED PORK CHOPS

SERVES 4

Chops thicker than ½ inch won't be fully tender in the allotted cooking time.

1	teaspoon onion powder
½	teaspoon paprika
	Salt and pepper
¼	teaspoon cayenne pepper
4	(8- to 10-ounce) bone-in blade-cut pork chops, about ½ inch thick, trimmed
1½	tablespoons vegetable oil
1	tablespoon unsalted butter
2	onions, halved and sliced ¼ inch thick
2	garlic cloves, minced
¼	teaspoon dried thyme
¾	cup plus 1 tablespoon beef broth
1	bay leaf
1	teaspoon cornstarch
1	teaspoon cider vinegar

1. Adjust oven rack to middle position and heat oven to 300 degrees. Combine onion powder, paprika, ½ teaspoon salt, ½ teaspoon pepper, and cayenne in small bowl. Pat chops dry with paper towels. Cut 2 slits about 2 inches apart through fat and connective tissue on edge of each chop. Rub chops with spice mixture.

2. Heat oil in large skillet over medium-high heat until just smoking. Brown chops on both sides, 6 to 8 minutes, and transfer to plate. Melt butter in now-empty skillet over medium heat. Cook onions until browned, 8 to 10 minutes. Add garlic and thyme and cook until fragrant, about 30 seconds. Stir in ¾ cup broth and bay leaf, scraping up any browned bits, and bring to boil. Return chops and any accumulated juices to pan, cover, and transfer to oven. Cook until chops are completely tender, about 1½ hours.

3. Transfer chops to platter and tent with aluminum foil. Discard bay leaf. Strain contents of skillet through fine-mesh strainer into large liquid measuring cup; reserve onions. Let liquid settle, then skim fat. Return 1½ cups defatted pan juices to now-empty skillet and bring to boil. Reduce heat to medium and simmer until sauce is reduced to 1 cup, about 5 minutes.

4. Whisk remaining 1 tablespoon broth and cornstarch in bowl until no lumps remain. Whisk cornstarch mixture into sauce and simmer until thickened, 1 to 2 minutes. Stir in reserved onions and vinegar. Season with salt and pepper to taste. Serve.

Pork Chop Perfection

You might think smothered pork chops were born in a diner somewhere. You'd be wrong. "Smother" is an English term that refers to a method of cooking meat, poultry, or game slowly in a covered vessel. This method, essentially a braise, goes back at least to the 16th century. Recipes for smothers first came to the United States from England during the Revolutionary War. Amelia Simmons's *American Cookery*, written in 1796, includes a recipe for smothering a chicken with oysters, though onions are the most common smothering agent. It is believed onions in smothers were used to tone down the gaminess of meat or hide off-flavors. Sailors smothered their salt beef and salt pork rations with onions and potatoes when out to sea. Regional variations soon developed throughout the country: New Englanders often made smothers with fresh pork; in the South, Creole cooking advised against smothering pork, but recommended it for beef, chicken, and veal; and while other traditions in the Deep South did smother pork, it was more typically tails, chitterlings, or other tough or gamy parts—the parts of the pig most available to African-American slaves. Eventually, pork chops did make it into the pot, and we're glad they did.

Why This Recipe Works The apple flavor in cider-braised pork chops can be fleeting. We wanted tender, juicy chops infused with deep, rich cider flavor. Tasters preferred 1-inch blade chops for their heft, silky meat, and rich taste. Patting the chops dry before adding them to the heated Dutch oven helped them develop a flavorful crust. Apple cider lent both sweetness and tartness to the braising mixture and sauce, while a bit of fresh thyme provided a heady herbal component. Jarred apple butter added further apple flavor, and its natural pectin gave the sauce a thick, glossy consistency. A splash of cider vinegar provided brightness.

CIDER-BRAISED PORK CHOPS

SERVES 6

Do not use chops thinner than 1 inch. In step 3, a fat separator makes quick work of defatting the sauce.

6 (8- to 10-ounce) bone-in blade-cut pork chops, about 1 inch thick, trimmed
  Salt and pepper
2 tablespoons vegetable oil
1 onion, chopped
¼ cup apple butter
2 tablespoons all-purpose flour
3 garlic cloves, minced
1 cup apple cider
1 sprig fresh thyme
1 teaspoon cider vinegar
1 tablespoon finely chopped fresh parsley

1. Adjust oven rack to lower-middle position and heat oven to 300 degrees. Pat chops dry with paper towels. Cut 2 slits about 2 inches apart through fat and connective tissue on edge of each chop. Season chops with salt and pepper. Heat oil in Dutch oven over medium-high heat until just smoking. Brown 3 chops on each side, about 8 minutes; transfer to plate, and then repeat with remaining 3 chops.

2. Pour off all but 1 tablespoon fat from pot and cook onion over medium heat until softened, about 5 minutes. Stir in 2 tablespoons apple butter, flour, and garlic and cook until onion is coated and mixture is fragrant, about 1 minute. Stir in cider and thyme, scraping up any browned bits with wooden spoon, and bring to boil. Add browned chops and any accumulated juices to pot, cover, and transfer to oven. Braise until chops are completely tender, about 1½ hours.

3. Transfer chops to serving platter. Strain sauce, then skim off fat. Whisk in vinegar, parsley, and remaining 2 tablespoons apple butter. Season with salt and pepper to taste. Serve, passing sauce at table. (Pork chops and sauce can be refrigerated separately for up to 2 days. To serve, reheat sauce and chops together over medium heat until chops are warmed through.)

Three Keys to Better Apple Flavor

Cider alone won't provide much apple flavor. To pack the taste of apples into our pork chops, we settled on a triple helping of apple products.

APPLE BUTTER
Apple butter provides intense apple and warm spice flavor. It also helps thicken the sauce.

CIDER VINEGAR
Finishing with a splash of cider vinegar adds brightness and complexity to the sauce.

CIDER
Sweet-tart cider provides most of the liquid for the braising mixture and sauce.

CRISPY FISH STICKS WITH TARTAR SAUCE

SERVES 4

Be sure to rinse the capers, otherwise the tartar sauce will be too salty. Halibut, haddock, or catfish can be substituted for the cod.

- 4 slices hearty white sandwich bread, torn into quarters
- 16 square or 18 round saltines
- ½ cup all-purpose flour
- 2 large eggs
- 1 cup mayonnaise
- 2 pounds skinless cod, cut into 1-inch-thick strips
  Salt and pepper
- ¼ cup finely chopped dill pickles, plus 1 tablespoon pickle juice
- 1 tablespoon capers, rinsed and minced
- 1 cup vegetable oil

1. Adjust oven rack to middle position and heat oven to 200 degrees. Pulse bread and saltines in food processor to fine crumbs, about 15 pulses; transfer to shallow dish. Place flour in second shallow dish. Beat eggs with ¼ cup mayonnaise in third shallow dish.

2. Pat fish dry with paper towels and season with salt and pepper. One at a time, coat fish strips lightly with flour, dip in egg mixture, and then dredge in crumbs, pressing on both sides to adhere. Transfer breaded fish to plate. Combine remaining ¾ cup mayonnaise, pickles, pickle juice, and capers in small bowl and set aside.

3. Heat ½ cup oil in large 12-inch nonstick skillet over medium heat until just smoking. Fry half of fish strips until deep golden and crisp on both sides, about 4 minutes. Drain on paper towel–lined plate and transfer to oven to keep warm. Discard oil, wipe out skillet, and repeat with remaining ½ cup oil and remaining fish. Serve with tartar sauce.

Fish Sticks—Pioneering the Frozen Food Landscape

Commercial freezing brought fish to the people, but it was the fish stick, introduced in 1953 by Birds Eye, that got them interested in eating fish. Why? Fish sticks have always appealed on a few levels. The breading helps prevent the fish from sticking to the pan; their mild flavor and crunchy crust appeal to children; and conveniently, fish sticks require minimal cleanup. Over the years, neither the expanded market created by freezing nor the wild popularity of fish sticks did much to boost the nation's overall fish consumption. But fish sticks did fire up the frozen foods market, both in terms of the creativity of producers and the enthusiasm of consumers for new, convenient heat-and-eat food products. Before fish sticks went commercial in the frozen foods industry, they were found at fish markets and delis along the East Coast. And of course, they were made at home. Homemade might not be as convenient as the frozen type, but we still aimed for a recipe that was easy enough for a weeknight.

Why This Recipe Works Forget the boxed varieties in the frozen foods aisle—our homemade fish sticks are fresh and crisp, and fry up in just minutes. Our recipe calls for cod, but halibut, haddock, and catfish are all worthy substitutes. Eggs beaten with mayonnaise helped our coating of crisp saltines and fresh bread crumbs adhere to the fish. We pan-fried the fish in two batches to ensure they cooked up even and crisp.

STRAWBERRY PRETZEL SALAD

SERVES 10 TO 12

For a sturdier crust, use (thinner) pretzel sticks not (fatter) rods. Thaw the strawberries in the refrigerator the night before you begin the recipe. You'll puree 2 pounds of the strawberries and slice the remaining 1 pound.

6½ ounces pretzel sticks
2¼ cups (15¾ ounces) sugar
12 tablespoons unsalted butter, melted and cooled
8 ounces cream cheese
1 cup heavy cream
3 pounds (10½ cups) frozen strawberries, thawed
¼ teaspoon salt
4½ teaspoons unflavored gelatin
½ cup cold water

1. Adjust oven rack to middle position and heat oven to 400 degrees. Spray 13 by 9-inch baking pan with vegetable oil spray. Pulse pretzels and ¼ cup sugar in food processor until coarsely ground, about 15 pulses. Add melted butter and pulse until combined, about 10 pulses. Transfer pretzel mixture to prepared pan. Using bottom of measuring cup, press crumbs into bottom of pan. Bake until crust is fragrant and beginning to brown, about 10 minutes, rotating pan halfway through baking. Set aside crust, letting it cool slightly, about 20 minutes.

2. Using stand mixer fitted with whisk, whip cream cheese and ½ cup sugar on medium speed until light and fluffy, about 2 minutes. Increase speed to medium-high and, with mixer still running, slowly add cream in steady stream. Continue to whip until soft peaks form, scraping down bowl as needed, about 1 minute longer. Spread whipped cream cheese mixture evenly over cooled crust. Refrigerate until set, about 30 minutes.

3. Meanwhile, process 2 pounds strawberries in now-empty food processor until pureed, about 30 seconds. Strain mixture through fine-mesh strainer set over medium saucepan, using underside of small ladle to push puree through strainer. Add remaining 1½ cups sugar and salt to strawberry puree in saucepan and cook over medium-high heat, whisking occasionally, until bubbles begin to appear around sides of pan and sugar is dissolved, about 5 minutes; remove from heat.

4. Sprinkle gelatin over water in large bowl and let sit until gelatin softens, about 5 minutes. Whisk strawberry puree into gelatin. Slice remaining strawberries and stir into strawberry-gelatin mixture. Refrigerate until gelatin thickens slightly and starts to cling to sides of bowl, about 30 minutes. Carefully pour gelatin mixture evenly over whipped cream cheese layer. Refrigerate salad until gelatin is fully set, at least 4 hours or up to 24 hours. Serve.

Salad Days

Baked beans, marshmallows, fruit cocktail, flavored gelatin, grated American cheese, ginger ale, sauerkraut . . . Do the words "salad fixings" spring to mind? Probably not, but then you aren't a well-bred, middle-class lady living in the first half of the 20th century. Had you been reared on the tenets of the domestic science movement that dominated American cooking at that time, such a list would indeed have suggested salad. As a "progressive housekeeper," you would have cringed at the very idea of what we call salad today. As culinary historian Laura Shapiro has detailed in *Perfection Salad: Women and Cooking at the Turn of the Century*, vegetables had to be tamed, and the very best way to render untidy raw vegetables harmless was to encase them in gelatin. After molding and chilling her salad, she could gild the lily with a few stuffed prunes, rococo swirls of thinned mayonnaise, and a carved tomato tulip. Pretzel salad is a direct descendent of such "Festive for Special Occasions Salads," as Betty Crocker's *New Picture Cook Book* grouped similar concoctions as late as 1961. Even today, despite the Cool Whip and the strawberry Jell-O, pretzel salad is not dessert—it's a salad.

Why This Recipe Works This tri-layer Midwestern specialty doesn't much resemble salad, but the sweet-salty, creamy-crunchy combination grabbed our attention. We knew we could make this slightly offbeat potluck favorite shine with some home-made elements. We replaced the "whipped topping" with real cream, which we whipped into softened cream cheese with some sugar for a tangy, not-too-sweet middle layer. The top layer, traditionally made from boxed Jell-O, got an upgrade to plain gelatin flavored with real pureed strawberry juice and sliced frozen berries. The time it took to make these elements from scratch was well worth the extra effort.

Why This Recipe Works Homemade stock tastes a lot better than even the best store-bought broths. While it's not complicated to make, it does require some babysitting on the stovetop, so instead, we turned to our slow cooker. We piled vegetables and leftover cooked chicken bones in cold water, added seasonings, and set it on high. The slow cooker prevented evaporation so the bones remained submerged, which is often a challenge with stovetop stock recipes. Refrigerating the strained stock allowed the fat to rise to the top and solidify, making it easy to discard. This rich, savory stock is remarkably easy—and thrifty too.

SLOW-COOKER CHICKEN STOCK

MAKES ABOUT 3 QUARTS

This stock is great to use in any of our recipes calling for chicken broth. You can freeze chicken carcasses one at a time until you have the 2½ pounds needed for this recipe; three to four rotisserie chicken carcasses or one 6-pound roaster carcass will weigh about 2½ pounds. This recipe was developed using bones from cooked chicken.

    3 quarts water
2½ pounds roasted chicken bones
    1 onion, chopped
    2 carrots, peeled and cut into 1-inch chunks
    2 celery ribs, chopped
    1 teaspoon black peppercorns
    1 teaspoon salt
    1 bay leaf

1. Place all ingredients in slow cooker. Cover and cook on high for 8 to 10 hours.

2. Let stock cool slightly, then strain through fine-mesh strainer set over large bowl. Use immediately or let cool completely, then refrigerate until cold. (When cold, surface fat will solidify and can be easily removed with spoon. Stock will keep, refrigerated, for up to 5 days, or frozen for up to 2 months).

Stock Storage

Frozen homemade chicken stock lasts for up to two months. Freeze small and medium amounts in ice cube trays or muffin tins; once frozen, pop out the stock blocks and keep them in zipper-lock bags for easy access when making pan sauces or gravy. Freeze larger amounts in plastic quart containers or zipper-lock bags, which are easy to stack in crowded freezers.

SMALL   **MEDIUM**   **LARGE**
AMOUNTS   **AMOUNTS**   **AMOUNTS**

Celery

Buy loose celery heads, not bagged celery heads (with clipped leaves) or bagged celery hearts. Loose celery heads tend to be fuller and fresher. Look for glossy green stalks without brown edges or yellowing leaves. Revive limp celery stalks by cutting off about 1 inch from both ends and submerging the stalks in a bowl of ice water for 30 minutes. The best way to store celery is to wrap it in foil and store it in the refrigerator. It will keep for several weeks.

Carrots

Buy fresh carrots with greens attached for the best flavor. If buying bagged carrots, check that they are evenly sized and firm (they shouldn't bend). Don't buy extra-large carrots, which are often woody and bitter. To prevent shriveling, store carrots in the crisper drawer in a partially open zipper-lock bag or in their original plastic bag. Before storing green-topped carrots, remove and discard the greens or the carrots will become limp. Both bagged and fresh carrots will keep for several weeks.

fork-in-the-road favorites

Why This Recipe Works The old-fashioned method of batter-fried chicken calls for dipping chicken parts in a batter not unlike pancake batter before frying. For juicy meat, we brined our chicken. To ensure a crisp crust, we replaced the milk in our initial batters with plain old water. With milk, the sugars in the milk solids browned too fast and produced a soft crust. Using equal parts cornstarch and flour in the batter also helped ensure a crisp crust on the chicken. And baking powder added lift and lightness without doughiness.

BATTER-FRIED CHICKEN

SERVES 4 TO 6

You will need at least a 6-quart Dutch oven for this recipe.

Brine and Chicken

¼ cup salt
¼ cup sugar
4 pounds bone-in chicken pieces (breasts halved crosswise and leg quarters separated into drumsticks and thighs), trimmed

Batter

1 cup all-purpose flour
1 cup cornstarch
5 teaspoons pepper
2 teaspoons baking powder
1 teaspoon salt
1 teaspoon paprika
½ teaspoon cayenne pepper
1¾ cups cold water
3 quarts peanut or vegetable oil

1. For the Brine and Chicken Dissolve salt and sugar in 1 quart cold water in large container. Submerge chicken in brine, cover, and refrigerate for 30 minutes or up to 1 hour.

2. For the Batter Meanwhile, combine flour, cornstarch, pepper, baking powder, salt, paprika, and cayenne in large bowl, add water, and whisk until smooth. Refrigerate batter while chicken is brining.

3. Set wire rack in rimmed baking sheet. Add oil to large Dutch oven until it measures about 2 inches deep and heat over medium-high heat to 350 degrees. Using tongs, remove chicken from brine and pat dry with paper towels. Rewhisk batter. Transfer half of chicken to batter and turn to coat. Remove chicken from batter, 1 piece at a time, allowing excess to drip back into bowl, and transfer to oil. Fry chicken, adjusting burner as necessary to maintain oil temperature between 300 and 325 degrees, until deep golden brown and breasts register 160 degrees and thighs and drumsticks register 175 degrees, 12 to 15 minutes. Drain chicken on prepared baking sheet. Return oil to 350 degrees and repeat with remaining chicken. Serve.

Keys to Best Batter-Fried Chicken

1. Whisk together flour, cornstarch, baking powder, spices, and water to make thin batter for crisp crust.

2. After dipping chicken in batter, let excess drip off (back into bowl) to avoid doughy coating.

3. To prevent chicken pieces from sticking together in oil, don't crowd pot. Fry chicken in 2 batches.

Why This Recipe Works Really good honey fried chicken is juicy and tender on the inside with a crispy, sticky, honey-flavored coating. To keep the meat moist, we brined the chicken first. For the coating, we dusted the chicken in cornstarch and dipped it in a thin cornstarch-and-water batter. The hardest part was glazing the fried chicken in honey without making the crust soggy. We found that the key was to double-fry the chicken: We partially fried the chicken, let it rest to allow moisture from the skin to evaporate, then fried it again for an incredibly crunchy crust that stayed crispy when dunked in a glaze of warm honey and hot sauce.

HONEY FRIED CHICKEN

SERVES 4

If using kosher chicken, do not brine. You will need at least a 6-quart Dutch oven for this recipe.

Brine and Chicken
½ cup salt
½ cup sugar
3 pounds bone-in chicken pieces (breasts halved crosswise and leg quarters separated into drumsticks and thighs), trimmed

Batter
1½ cups cornstarch
¾ cup cold water
2 teaspoons pepper
1 teaspoon salt
3 quarts peanut or vegetable oil

Honey Glaze
¾ cup honey
2 tablespoons hot sauce

1. For the Brine and Chicken Dissolve salt and sugar in 2 quarts cold water in large container. Submerge chicken in brine, cover, and refrigerate for 30 minutes to 1 hour.

2. For the Batter While chicken is brining, whisk 1 cup cornstarch, water, pepper, and salt together in large bowl until smooth. Refrigerate batter.

3. Set wire rack inside rimmed baking sheet. Sift remaining ½ cup cornstarch into shallow bowl. Remove chicken from brine and dry thoroughly with paper towels. Working with 1 piece at a time, coat chicken thoroughly with cornstarch, shaking to remove excess; transfer to platter.

4. Add oil to large Dutch oven until it measures about 2 inches deep and heat over medium-high heat to 350 degrees. Whisk batter to recombine. Using tongs, transfer half of chicken to batter and turn to coat. Remove chicken from batter, 1 piece at a time, allowing excess to drip back into bowl, and transfer to hot oil. Fry chicken, stirring to prevent pieces from sticking together, until slightly golden and just beginning to crisp, 5 to 7 minutes. Adjust burner, if

necessary, to maintain oil temperature between 325 and 350 degrees. (Chicken will not be cooked through at this point.) Transfer parcooked chicken to platter. Return oil to 350 degrees and repeat with remaining raw chicken and batter. Let each batch of chicken rest for 5 to 7 minutes.

5. Return oil to 350 degrees. Return first batch of chicken to oil and fry until breasts register 160 degrees and thighs/drumsticks register 175 degrees, 5 to 7 minutes. Transfer to prepared baking sheet. Return oil to 350 degrees and repeat with remaining chicken.

6. For the Honey Glaze Combine honey and hot sauce in large bowl and microwave until hot, about 1½ minutes. Add chicken pieces to honey mixture, one at a time, and turn to coat. Return to baking sheet, skin side up, to drain. Serve.

Making a Beeline West

The common honeybee (*Apis mellifera L.*) is not native to North America. British settlers bound for Virginia brought hives aboard ships, along with peacocks, pigeons, and rabbits, as the author of a letter from the Virginia Company recorded in 1621. During the next 200 years, the bee population slowly rolled westward, pollinating the prairies and the settlers' crops and providing pioneers with honey, wax, candles, and medicine. Native Americans called the honeybee the "white man's fly," and they saw the bees that swarmed ahead of the settlers as a threat. "The Indians . . . consider them the harbinger of the white man," Washington Irving wrote as he traveled through the Oklahoma Territory in 1832. "As the bee advances, the Indian and the buffalo retire." Similarly, after visiting members of the Osage tribe in the Missouri Territory in 1836, writer Alphonso Wetmore reported that "the Indians held a day of mourning because a swarm of bees had been found."

CREOLE FRIED CHICKEN

SERVES 4 TO 6

In step 1, do not soak the chicken longer than 8 hours, or it will be too salty. You will need at least a 6-quart Dutch oven for this recipe.

Seasoned Brine and Chicken
¼ cup sugar
3 tablespoons Worcestershire sauce
3 tablespoons hot sauce
2 tablespoons salt
1 tablespoon garlic powder
4 pounds bone-in chicken pieces (breasts halved crosswise and leg quarters separated into drumsticks and thighs), trimmed

Creole Seasoning
1 tablespoon pepper
1 tablespoon dried oregano
1 tablespoon garlic powder
2 teaspoons onion powder
2 teaspoons cayenne pepper
1 teaspoon white pepper
1 teaspoon celery salt
2 cups all-purpose flour
3 quarts peanut or vegetable oil

1. For the Seasoned Brine and Chicken Dissolve sugar, Worcestershire, hot sauce, salt, and garlic powder in 1 quart cold water in large container. Submerge chicken in brine, cover, and refrigerate for 1 hour or up to 8 hours.

2. For the Creole Seasoning Combine pepper, oregano, garlic powder, onion powder, cayenne, white pepper, and celery salt in large bowl; reserve ¼ cup spice mixture. Add flour to bowl with remaining spice mixture and stir to combine. Set wire rack in rimmed baking sheet.

3. Remove chicken from brine and pat dry with paper towels. Sprinkle chicken with 3 tablespoons reserved spice mixture and toss to coat. Dredge chicken pieces in flour mixture. Shake excess flour from chicken and transfer to wire rack. (Do not discard flour mixture.)

4. Adjust oven rack to middle position and heat oven to 200 degrees. Set second wire rack in second rimmed baking sheet. Add oil to large Dutch oven until it measures about 2 inches deep and heat over medium-high heat to 375 degrees. Return chicken pieces to flour mixture and turn to coat. Fry half of chicken, adjusting burner as necessary to maintain oil temperature between 300 and 325 degrees, until deep golden brown and breasts register 160 degrees and thighs and drumsticks register 175 degrees, 10 to 12 minutes. Transfer chicken to prepared baking sheet and place in oven. Return oil to 375 degrees and repeat with remaining chicken. Sprinkle crisp chicken with remaining 1 tablespoon spice mixture. Serve.

Secrets to Boldly Flavored Creole Fried Chicken

1. Soaking chicken in brine of sugar, Worcestershire, hot sauce, salt, and garlic powder seasons chicken fully.

2. After brining, homemade Creole seasoning adds flavor without dusty saltiness of packaged spice blends.

3. The homemade Creole seasoning also lends potent punch to chicken's flour coating.

4. For peppery finish, sprinkle hot chicken with more homemade Creole seasoning when it comes out of oil.

Why This Recipe Works Creole fried chicken recipes should turn out meat that is deeply seasoned with the complex, lively heat of black, white, and cayenne peppers. We built depth of flavor in our fried chicken with a three-step approach: After brining the chicken, we sprinkled it with homemade Creole seasoning for added flavor without the dusty saltiness of packaged spice blends. We also added seasoning to the chicken's flour coating to lend a potent punch. And for a peppery finish, we sprinkled the hot chicken with more seasoning when it came out of the oil.

Why This Recipe Works For fried chicken loaded with garlic flavor, we started by tossing a mix of chicken pieces in a marinade chock-full of both fresh and granulated garlic. We further reinforced our key flavor by dipping the parts in beaten egg whites and dredging them in flour boosted with more granulated garlic. After frying the chicken in peanut oil, we created a potent garlic-parsley butter that took the chicken's flavor right over the top.

GARLIC FRIED CHICKEN

SERVES 4

You will need at least a 6-quart Dutch oven for this recipe. Mince the garlic with a knife rather than with a garlic press.

Chicken

- 3 tablespoons extra-virgin olive oil
- 2 tablespoons granulated garlic
- 5 garlic cloves, minced
  Kosher salt and pepper
- 3 pounds bone-in chicken pieces (split breasts cut in half crosswise, drumsticks, thighs, and/or wings), trimmed
- 2 cups all-purpose flour
- 4 large egg whites
- 3 quarts peanut or vegetable oil

Garlic Butter

- 8 tablespoons unsalted butter, softened
- 2 tablespoons minced fresh parsley
- ¼ teaspoon kosher salt
- ¼ teaspoon pepper
- 8 garlic cloves, minced
- 1 tablespoon water

1. For the Chicken Combine olive oil, 1 tablespoon granulated garlic, minced garlic, 2 teaspoons salt, and 2 teaspoons pepper in large bowl. Add chicken and toss to thoroughly coat with garlic mixture. Cover with plastic wrap and refrigerate for at least 1 hour or up to 24 hours.

2. Set wire rack in rimmed baking sheet. Whisk flour, remaining 1 tablespoon granulated garlic, 2 teaspoons salt, and 2 teaspoons pepper together in separate bowl. Lightly beat egg whites together in shallow dish.

3. Remove chicken from marinade and brush away any solidified clumps of oil with paper towels. Working with 1 piece at a time, dip chicken into egg whites to thoroughly coat, letting excess drip back into dish; then dredge in flour mixture, pressing firmly to adhere. Transfer chicken to prepared wire rack and refrigerate, uncovered, for at least 30 minutes or up to 2 hours.

4. Set second wire rack in second rimmed baking sheet and line with triple layer of paper towels. Add peanut oil to large Dutch oven until it measures about 2 inches deep and heat over medium-high heat to 325 degrees. Add half of chicken to hot oil and fry until breasts register 160 degrees and drumsticks/thighs register 175 degrees, 13 to 16 minutes. Adjust burner, if necessary, to maintain oil temperature between 300 and 325 degrees. Transfer to paper towel–lined rack, return oil to 325 degrees, and repeat with remaining chicken.

5. For the Garlic Butter While chicken rests, combine 7 tablespoons butter, parsley, salt, and pepper in bowl; set aside. Melt remaining 1 tablespoon butter in 8-inch nonstick skillet over medium heat. Add garlic and water and cook, stirring frequently, until garlic is softened and fragrant, 1 to 2 minutes. Add hot garlic mixture to butter-parsley mixture and whisk until well combined.

6. Transfer chicken to platter and spoon garlic butter over top. Serve.

On the Road: Basque Cooking in California

Though it might seem out of place, Basque food is as comfortable in California as any other cuisine. Immigrants from the Basque lands—primarily the Pyrenees Mountains separating Spain and France—flooded California during the Gold Rush in the mid-19th century; when gold proved elusive, they turned to agriculture and shepherding in and around Bakersfield, California, which boasts one of the largest Basque populations in the United States.

During our visit to this region, we were struck by how the vibrant fare at the Pyrenees Cafe stands firmly against the city's ever-present heat. There we feasted on plates of garlic fried chicken, Basque-style green beans, cabbage and bean soup dotted with spicy salsa, thin slices of pickled veal tongue, and a few glasses of chilled house wine, before enjoying the customary Basque dessert: vanilla ice cream doused with red wine. Unusual, yes, but there are certainly worse ways to end a meal.

EXTRA-CRUNCHY FRIED CHICKEN

SERVES 4

Keeping the oil at the correct temperature is essential to producing crunchy fried chicken that is neither too brown nor too greasy. You will need at least a 6-quart Dutch oven for this recipe. If you want to produce a slightly lighter version of this recipe, you can remove the skin from the chicken before soaking it in the buttermilk. The chicken will be slightly less crunchy.

- 2 tablespoons salt
- 2 cups plus 6 tablespoons buttermilk
- 1 (3½-pound) whole chicken, cut into 8 pieces and trimmed (4 breast pieces, 2 drumsticks, 2 thighs), wings discarded
- 3 cups all-purpose flour
- 2 teaspoons baking powder
- ¾ teaspoon dried thyme
- ½ teaspoon pepper
- ¼ teaspoon garlic powder
- 1 quart peanut or vegetable oil

1. Dissolve salt in 2 cups buttermilk in large container. Submerge chicken in brine, cover, and refrigerate for 1 hour.

2. Whisk flour, baking powder, thyme, pepper, and garlic powder together in large bowl. Add remaining 6 tablespoons buttermilk; with your fingers rub flour and buttermilk together until buttermilk is evenly incorporated into flour and mixture resembles coarse, wet sand. Set wire rack inside rimmed baking sheet.

3. Dredge chicken pieces in flour mixture and turn to coat thoroughly, gently pressing flour mixture onto chicken. Shake excess flour from each piece of chicken and transfer to prepared baking sheet.

4. Line platter with triple layer of paper towels. Add oil to large Dutch oven until it measures about ¾ inch deep and heat over medium-high heat to 375 degrees. Place chicken pieces skin side down in oil, cover, and fry until deep golden brown, 8 to 10 minutes. Remove lid after 4 minutes and lift chicken pieces to check for even browning; rearrange if some pieces are browning faster than others. Adjust burner, if necessary, to maintain oil temperature between 300 and 315 degrees. Turn chicken pieces over and continue to fry, uncovered, until chicken pieces are deep golden brown on second side and breasts register 160 degrees and thighs and drumsticks register 175 degrees, 6 to 8 minutes. Using tongs, transfer chicken to prepared platter; let stand for 5 minutes. Serve.

EXTRA-SPICY, EXTRA-CRUNCHY FRIED CHICKEN

Add ¼ cup hot sauce to buttermilk-salt mixture in step 1. Replace dried thyme and garlic powder with 2 tablespoons cayenne pepper and 2 teaspoons chili powder in step 2.

Steps to an Extra-Crunchy Coating

1. Soak chicken in buttermilk-salt mixture.

2. Coat chicken with buttermilk-moistened flour.

3. Add chicken to hot oil and cover pot to capture steam.

4. Use tongs to flip chicken and finish cooking with cover off.

Why This Recipe Works For well-seasoned, extra-crunchy fried chicken we started by brining the chicken in heavily salted buttermilk. For the crunchy coating, we combined flour with a little baking powder, then added buttermilk to make a thick slurry, which clung tightly to the meat. Frying the chicken with the lid on the pot for half the cooking time contained the spatter-prone oil and kept it hot.

NASHVILLE HOT FRIED CHICKEN

SERVES 4 TO 6

Chicken quarters take longer to cook than smaller pieces. To ensure that the exterior doesn't burn before the inside cooks through, keep the oil temperature between 300 and 325 degrees while the chicken is frying. You will need at least a 6-quart Dutch oven for this recipe. Serve the chicken as they do in Nashville, on white bread with pickles.

Brine and Chicken
½ cup hot sauce
½ cup salt
½ cup sugar
1 (3½- to 4-pound) whole chicken, quartered

Coating
3 quarts peanut or vegetable oil
1 tablespoon cayenne pepper
½ teaspoon paprika
½ teaspoon sugar
¼ teaspoon garlic powder
   Salt and pepper
2 cups all-purpose flour

1. For the Brine and Chicken Dissolve hot sauce, salt, and sugar in 2 quarts cold water in large container. Submerge chicken in brine, cover, and refrigerate for 30 minutes or up to 1 hour.

2. For the Coating Heat 3 tablespoons oil in small saucepan over medium heat until shimmering. Add cayenne, paprika, sugar, garlic powder, and ½ teaspoon salt and cook until fragrant, about 30 seconds. Transfer to small bowl.

3. Set wire rack in rimmed baking sheet. Remove chicken from brine and pat with paper towels. Combine flour, ½ teaspoon salt, and ½ teaspoon pepper in large bowl. Dredge chicken pieces two at a time in flour mixture. Shake excess flour from chicken and transfer to prepared baking sheet. (Do not discard seasoned flour.)

4. Adjust oven rack to middle position and heat oven to 200 degrees. Set second wire rack in second rimmed baking sheet. Add remaining oil to large Dutch oven until it measures about 2 inches deep and heat over medium-high heat to 350 degrees. Return chicken pieces to flour mixture and turn to coat. Fry half of chicken, adjusting burner as necessary to maintain oil temperature between 300 and 325 degrees, until deep golden brown and breast meat registers 160 degrees and legs register 175 degrees, 20 to 25 minutes. Drain chicken on prepared baking sheet and place in oven. Return oil to 350 degrees and repeat with remaining chicken. Stir spicy oil mixture to recombine and brush over both sides of chicken. Serve.

NASHVILLE EXTRA-HOT FRIED CHICKEN
For spiced oil in step 2, increase oil to ¼ cup, cayenne to 3½ tablespoons, and sugar to ¾ teaspoon and add 1 teaspoon dry mustard. Continue with recipe as directed.

Quartering a Chicken

1. Slice between drumstick and breast. Use hands to bend back leg and pop out joint.

2. Cut through leg joint. Do not separate thigh from drumstick. Repeat steps 1 and 2 for other leg quarter.

3. To separate breast from backbone, cut through ribs with kitchen shears on each side of backbone.

4. Cut through breastbone to separate breast and wing section into halves.

Why This Recipe Works Mimicking the heat of this Nashville hot fried chicken was harder than we anticipated. We created a spicy exterior to the chicken by "blooming" the spices (cooking them in oil for a short period) to create a complex yet still lip-burning spicy flavor. We also added a healthy amount of hot sauce to our brine to inject spicy flavor into the chicken, making the flavor more than skin deep.

Why This Recipe Works Hot oil is the key to crunchy fried chicken, but it can be deadly to fresh herbs. To get the flavors to last throughout the frying process, the key was to fry for as little time as possible. Thin boneless chicken thighs took half the time to fry than bone-in chicken parts required, which allowed the fresh herb flavors to flourish. Also, thighs are cheaper to purchase. After a few tests, we settled on a three-part technique for the chives, dill, and cilantro; we added them to the tangy buttermilk dip, the flour coating, and the dipping sauce. This triple punch provided the classic aroma and flavor we know and love as "ranch."

RANCH FRIED CHICKEN

SERVES 4 TO 6

You will need at least a 6-quart Dutch oven for this recipe.

Chicken

8 (5- to 7-ounce) boneless, skinless chicken thighs, trimmed
Salt and pepper
2 quarts peanut or vegetable oil

Buttermilk Mixture

1 cup buttermilk
2 tablespoons minced fresh chives
2 tablespoons minced fresh cilantro
2 teaspoons minced fresh dill
2 teaspoons distilled white vinegar
1 garlic clove, minced
½ teaspoon salt
Pinch cayenne pepper

Coating

1¼ cups all-purpose flour
½ cup cornstarch
3 tablespoons minced fresh chives
3 tablespoons minced fresh cilantro
1 tablespoon minced fresh dill
1½ teaspoons garlic powder
1½ teaspoons salt
¾ teaspoon pepper

Ranch Sauce

½ cup mayonnaise
Salt and pepper

1. For the Chicken Pat chicken dry with paper towels and season with salt and pepper.

2. For the Buttermilk Mixture Whisk all ingredients together in bowl. Set aside ¼ cup buttermilk mixture for ranch sauce.

3. For the Coating Whisk all ingredients together in large bowl.

4. Set wire rack in rimmed baking sheet. Set second wire rack in second rimmed baking sheet and line half of rack with triple layer of paper towels.

5. Working with 1 piece at a time, dip chicken in remaining buttermilk mixture to coat, letting excess drip back into bowl; then dredge in coating, pressing to adhere. Transfer chicken to first wire rack (without paper towels). (At this point, coated chicken may be refrigerated, uncovered, for up to 2 hours.)

6. Heat oil in large Dutch oven over medium-high heat until it reaches 350 degrees. Add half of chicken to hot oil and fry until golden brown and registers 175 degrees, 7 to 9 minutes. Adjust burner, if necessary, to maintain oil temperature between 325 and 350 degrees.

7. Transfer chicken to paper towel–lined side of second wire rack to drain on each side for 30 seconds, then move to unlined side of rack. Return oil to 350 degrees and repeat with remaining chicken.

8. For the Ranch Sauce Whisk mayonnaise into reserved buttermilk mixture. Season with salt and pepper to taste.

9. Transfer chicken to platter and serve with ranch sauce.

Key Ingredients: Three Herbs, Three Ways

We use the defining herbs of ranch flavor—dill, chives, and cilantro—in three ways for this chicken: in the buttermilk dip, in the flour coating, and in the serving sauce.

Why This Recipe Works Some chicken nuggets recipes take the least desirable parts of the chicken and put them through a grinder. We opted for boneless, skin-less chicken breasts. Brining the chicken prevented it from drying out, and seasoning the breast meat combated its inherently bland flavor. Ground-up panko (Japanese-style bread crumbs) combined with flour and a pinch of baking soda provided a crispy brown exterior for our nuggets. Using whole eggs to adhere the coating made the nuggets too eggy. Egg whites alone didn't have enough binding power, but we found that resting the nuggets before frying solved the problem.

CHICKEN NUGGETS

SERVES 4 TO 6

Do not brine the chicken longer than 30 minutes or it will be too salty. To crush the bread crumbs, place them inside a zipper-lock bag and lightly beat it with a rolling pin. You will need at least a 6-quart Dutch oven for this recipe. This recipe doubles easily and freezes well.

- 4 (6-ounce) boneless, skinless chicken breasts, trimmed
- 2 cups water
- 2 tablespoons Worcestershire sauce
- Salt and pepper
- 1 cup all-purpose flour
- 1 cup panko bread crumbs, crushed
- 2 teaspoons onion powder
- ½ teaspoon garlic powder
- ½ teaspoon baking soda
- 3 large egg whites
- 1 quart peanut or vegetable oil
- 1 recipe dipping sauce (recipes follow)

1. Cut each chicken breast diagonally into thirds, then cut each third diagonally into ½-inch-thick pieces. Whisk water, Worcestershire, and 1 tablespoon salt in large bowl until salt dissolves. Add chicken pieces, cover, and refrigerate for 30 minutes.

2. Remove chicken from brine and pat dry with paper towels. Combine flour, panko, onion powder, 1 teaspoon salt, ¾ teaspoon pepper, garlic powder, and baking soda in shallow dish. Whisk egg whites in second shallow dish until foamy. Coat half of chicken with egg whites and dredge in flour mixture, pressing gently to adhere. Transfer to plate and repeat with remaining chicken (don't discard flour mixture). Let sit for 10 minutes.

3. Adjust oven rack to middle position and heat oven to 200 degrees. Set wire rack in rimmed baking sheet. Add oil to large Dutch oven until it measures about ¾ inch deep and heat over medium-high heat

to 350 degrees. Return chicken pieces to flour mixture and turn to coat, pressing flour mixture gently to adhere. Fry half of chicken until deep golden brown, about 3 minutes, turning halfway through cooking. Transfer chicken to prepared baking sheet and place in oven. Return oil to 350 degrees and repeat with remaining chicken. Serve with dipping sauce.

To Make Ahead Let fried nuggets cool, transfer to zipper-lock bag, and freeze for up to 1 month. To serve, adjust oven rack to middle position and heat oven to 350 degrees. Place nuggets on rimmed baking sheet and bake, flipping once, until heated through, about 15 minutes.

HONEY-MUSTARD SAUCE
MAKES ¾ CUP

- ½ cup yellow mustard
- ⅓ cup honey
- Salt and pepper

Whisk mustard and honey in medium bowl until smooth. Season with salt and pepper to taste.

SWEET AND SOUR SAUCE
MAKES ¾ CUP

- ¾ cup apple, apricot, or hot pepper jelly
- 1 tablespoon white vinegar
- ½ teaspoon soy sauce
- ⅛ teaspoon garlic powder
- Pinch ground ginger
- Pinch cayenne pepper
- Salt and pepper

Whisk jelly, vinegar, soy sauce, garlic powder, ginger, and cayenne in medium bowl until smooth. Season with salt and pepper to taste.

DELTA HOT TAMALES

SERVES 6 TO 8

Use a saucepan that holds 4 quarts or more, with at least 5-inch sides. Corn husks can be found in the international aisle of grocery stores.

24	corn husks
1½	tablespoons chili powder
1	tablespoon paprika
1	tablespoon salt
2	teaspoons ground cumin
2	teaspoons sugar
¾	teaspoon pepper
¾	teaspoon cayenne pepper
2½	cups (12½ ounces) yellow cornmeal
1	tablespoon baking powder
12	tablespoons unsalted butter, cut into 12 pieces
½	teaspoon baking soda
1	pound 85 percent lean ground beef
2	garlic cloves, minced
2	tablespoons cornstarch combined with 2 tablespoons cold water

1. Place husks in large bowl and cover with hot water; soak until pliable, about 30 minutes. Combine chili powder, paprika, salt, cumin, sugar, pepper, and cayenne in bowl.

2. Pulse cornmeal and baking powder in food processor until combined, about 3 pulses. Add butter and 1½ tablespoons spice mixture and pulse to chop butter into small pieces, about 8 pulses. Add 1¼ cups water and process until dough forms, about 30 seconds. Reserve ½ cup cornmeal mixture. Divide remaining cornmeal mixture into 24 equal portions, about 1½ tablespoons each, and place on plate.

3. Dissolve baking soda in 2 tablespoons water in large bowl. Add beef, garlic, reserved ½ cup cornmeal mixture, and 1½ tablespoons spice mixture and knead with your hands until thoroughly combined. Divide meat mixture into 24 equal portions, about 1½ tablespoons each, and place on plate.

4. Remove husks from water and pat dry with dish towel. Working with 1 husk at a time, lay husk on counter, smooth side up, with long side parallel to counter edge and wide end oriented toward right. Using small offset spatula, spread 1 portion of cornmeal mixture in 3½-inch square over lower right corner of husk, flush to bottom edge but leaving ¼-inch border on right edge.

5. Place 1 portion of meat mixture in log across center of cornmeal (end to end), parallel to long side of husk. Roll husk away from you and over meat mixture so cornmeal mixture surrounds meat and forms cylinder; continue rolling to complete tamale. Fold tapered end (left side) of tamale up leaving top open. Using scissors, trim tapered end of tamale to align with filled end (if tapered end hangs over). Set tamales aside seam side down.

6. Stack tamales on their sides in groups of 6 and tie into bundles with kitchen twine. Add remaining 2 tablespoons spice mixture to large saucepan. Stand tamales, open ends up, in pot (walls of pot should clear tops of tamales). Add about 5½ cups water to pot to come within 1 inch of tops of tamales, being careful not to pour water into tamales.

7. Bring tamales to boil. Cover, reduce heat to low to maintain gentle simmer, and cook until tamales are firm and beginning to pull away from husks, about 30 minutes. Using tongs and slotted spoon, carefully transfer tamales to serving platter and remove twine.

8. Return liquid to simmer over medium heat. Whisk in cornstarch slurry and cook until slightly thickened, about 1 minute. Serve sauce with tamales.

Cooking with Corn Husks

Cooking the tamales in corn husks—which are available in most supermarkets near the dried chiles—adds a subtle depth of flavor. Working with the husks is actually quite easy, as they become pliable when soaked in hot water.

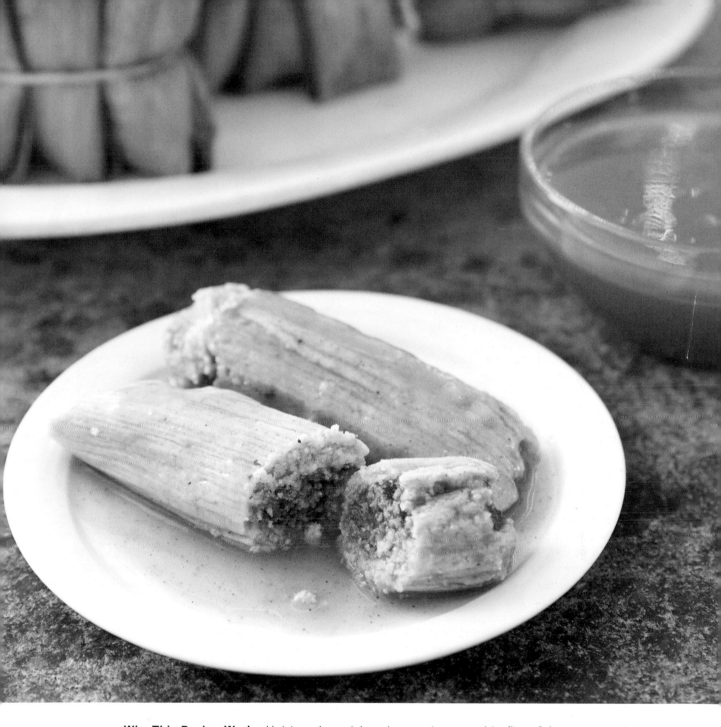

Why This Recipe Works Hot tamales—rich, spicy meat wrapped in flavorful corn dough—are a favorite in the Mississippi delta. A bit of this cornmeal mixture stirred into the uncooked ground beef kept the filling moist and baking soda was the trick for a more tender bite. We used butter instead of the traditional lard with coarsely ground cornmeal for a more balanced taste. We cooked the tamales in groups of six for more stability in the pot and made a spicy, glazy sauce with the seasoned stewing liquid and a cornstarch slurry. This was as close as we could come to being in the delta without a plane ticket.

Why This Recipe Works Our biggest challenge in making gumbo was finding an easier way to prepare the dark brown roux, the fat and flour paste that thickens the stew and adds flavor. We created a relatively hands-off roux by toasting the flour on the stovetop, adding the oil, and finishing the roux in the oven. For the soup base, we started by making our own shrimp stock, but the process was time-consuming. Instead, we switched to store-bought chicken broth fortified with fish sauce. Tasters preferred meaty chicken thighs to breasts because they had more flavor.

GUMBO

SERVES 6 TO 8

A heavy cast-iron Dutch oven yields the fastest oven roux. If a lightweight pot is all you've got, increase the oven time by 10 minutes. The chicken broth must be at room temperature to prevent lumps from forming. Fish sauce lends an essential savory quality. Since the salt content of fish sauce varies among brands, taste the finished gumbo before seasoning with salt.

- ¾ cup plus 1 tablespoon all-purpose flour
- ½ cup vegetable oil
- 1 onion, chopped fine
- 1 green bell pepper, stemmed, seeded, and chopped
- 1 celery rib, chopped fine
- 5 garlic cloves, minced
- 1 teaspoon minced fresh thyme
- ¼ teaspoon cayenne pepper
- 1 (14.5-ounce) can diced tomatoes, drained
- 3¾ cups chicken broth, room temperature
- ¼ cup fish sauce
- 2 pounds bone-in chicken thighs, skin removed, trimmed
  Salt and pepper
- 8 ounces andouille sausage, halved lengthwise and sliced thin
- 2 cups frozen okra, thawed (optional)
- 2 pounds extra-large shrimp (21 to 25 per pound), peeled and deveined

1. Adjust oven rack to lowest position and heat oven to 350 degrees. Toast ¾ cup flour in Dutch oven over medium heat, stirring constantly, until just beginning to brown, about 5 minutes. Off heat, whisk in oil until smooth. Cover, transfer pot to oven, and cook until mixture is deep brown and fragrant, about 45 minutes. (Roux can be refrigerated for 1 week. To use, heat in Dutch oven over medium-high heat, whisking constantly, until just smoking, and continue with step 2.)

2. Transfer Dutch oven to stovetop and whisk cooked roux to combine. Add onion, bell pepper, and celery and cook over medium heat, stirring frequently, until vegetables are softened, about 10 minutes. Stir in remaining 1 tablespoon flour, garlic, thyme, and cayenne and cook until fragrant, about 1 minute. Add tomatoes and cook until dry, about 1 minute. Slowly whisk in broth and fish sauce until smooth. Season chicken with pepper. Add chicken to vegetable mixture and bring to boil.

3. Reduce heat to medium-low and simmer, covered, until chicken is tender, about 30 minutes. Skim fat and transfer chicken to plate. When chicken is cool enough to handle, cut into bite-size pieces and return to pot; discard bones.

4. Stir in sausage and okra, if using, and simmer until heated through, about 5 minutes. Add shrimp and simmer until cooked through, about 5 minutes. Season with salt and pepper to taste. Serve. (Gumbo can be refrigerated for 1 day.)

To Make Ahead Gumbo can be made through step 3 and refrigerated for 3 days. To serve, bring gumbo to simmer, covered, in Dutch oven. Remove lid and proceed with recipe as directed.

Newcomer to the Bayou

Asian fish sauce? Admittedly, it's an unconventional idea. And here's the cool part: New Orleans has a well-established Vietnamese community; it began after the fall of Saigon. As far as we know, we're the first to put fish sauce in gumbo, but there's no question that these new immigrants to New Orleans are having an impact on the city's storied food traditions: They've tossed lemon grass into crawfish boils, organized a farmers' market with such exotic items as *ngo gai* (an herb), banana buds, and longan fruit, and put the *banh mi* sandwich on the city's must-eat food list, right there next to the city's signature po' boys.

NEW ORLEANS BARBECUE SHRIMP

SERVES 4

Although authentic barbecue shrimp is always made with shell-on shrimp, peeled and deveined shrimp may be used. Light- or medium-bodied beers work best here. Serve with Tabasco sauce and French bread, if desired.

2 pounds extra-large (21 to 25 per pound) shrimp
½ teaspoon salt
½ teaspoon cayenne pepper
2 tablespoons vegetable oil
6 tablespoons unsalted butter, cut into 6 pieces
2 teaspoons all-purpose flour
1 teaspoon tomato paste
1 teaspoon minced fresh rosemary
1 teaspoon minced fresh thyme
½ teaspoon dried oregano
3 garlic cloves, minced
¾ cup bottled clam juice
½ cup beer
1 tablespoon Worcestershire sauce

1. Pat shrimp dry with paper towels and sprinkle with salt and cayenne. Heat 1 tablespoon oil in large skillet over medium-high heat until just smoking. Cook half of shrimp, without moving, until spotty brown on one side, about 1 minute; transfer to large plate. Repeat with remaining oil and shrimp.

2. Melt 1 tablespoon butter in empty skillet over medium heat. Add flour, tomato paste, rosemary, thyme, oregano, and garlic and cook until fragrant, about 30 seconds. Stir in clam juice, beer, and Worcestershire, scraping up any browned bits, and bring to boil. Return shrimp and any accumulated juices to skillet. Reduce heat to medium-low and simmer, covered, until shrimp are cooked through, about 2 minutes. Off heat, stir in remaining butter until incorporated. Serve.

Not Your Average Barbecue Sauce

Barbecue sauce conjures up an image of a thick, sticky tomato-based mop, but New Orleans Barbecue Shrimp is bathed in a spicy herbed butter sauce made with these ingredients.

CLAM JUICE
The briny bite makes a simple replacement for fish stock.

BEER
The mellow, slightly hoppy bitterness balances the rich butter.

WORCESTERSHIRE
Often used to add bold, ultrasavory flavor to dishes.

BUTTER
Adding butter twice makes a rich, satiny sauce.

Why This Recipe Works Named for the "barbecue" color rather than the cooking method, this New Orleans skillet shrimp dish relies on a velvety, butter-based sauce to flavor shell-on shrimp. To achieve perfectly cooked shrimp, we started by searing them first to partially cook them and then later returned the shrimp to the finished sauce to gently cook through. By using a roux to thicken the sauce and sautéing the aromatics with tomato paste, we were able to create a silky, flavorful sauce that clung perfectly to the shrimp. We replaced time-consuming seafood stock with bottled clam juice, a technique the test kitchen has used before.

SHRIMP AND GRITS

SERVES 4

We prefer untreated shrimp—those without added sodium or preservatives like sodium tripolyphosphate. Most frozen E-Z peel shrimp have been treated (the ingredient list should tell you). If you're using treated shrimp, do not add the salt in step 4. If you use our winning grits (Anson Mills Pencil Cob) or other fresh-milled grits, you will need to increase the simmering time by 25 minutes.

Grits

3 tablespoons unsalted butter
1 cup grits
2¼ cups whole milk
2 cups water
Salt and pepper

Shrimp

3 tablespoons unsalted butter
1½ pounds extra-large shrimp (21 to 25 per pound), peeled and deveined, shells reserved
1 tablespoon tomato paste
2¼ cups water
3 slices bacon, cut into ½-inch pieces
1 garlic clove, minced
Salt and pepper
2 tablespoons all-purpose flour
1 tablespoon lemon juice
½ teaspoon Tabasco sauce, plus extra for serving
4 scallions, sliced thin

1. For the Grits Melt 1 tablespoon butter in medium saucepan over medium heat. Add grits and cook, stirring often, until fragrant, about 3 minutes. Add milk, water, and ¾ teaspoon salt. Increase heat to medium-high and bring to boil. Reduce heat to low, cover, and simmer, whisking often, until thick and creamy, about 25 minutes. Remove from heat, stir in remaining 2 tablespoons butter, and season with salt and pepper to taste. Cover and keep warm.

2. For the Shrimp Meanwhile, melt 1 tablespoon butter in 12-inch nonstick skillet over medium heat. Add shrimp shells and cook, stirring occasionally, until shells are spotty brown, about 7 minutes. Stir in tomato paste and cook for 30 seconds. Add water and bring to boil. Reduce heat to low, cover, and simmer for 5 minutes.

3. Strain shrimp stock through fine-mesh strainer set over bowl, pressing on solids to extract as much liquid as possible; discard solids. You should have about 1½ cups stock (add more water if necessary to equal 1½ cups). Wipe out skillet with paper towels.

4. Cook bacon in now-empty skillet over medium-low heat until crisp, 7 to 9 minutes. Increase heat to medium-high and stir in shrimp, garlic, ½ teaspoon salt, and ½ teaspoon pepper. Cook until edges of shrimp are just beginning to turn pink, but shrimp are not cooked through, about 2 minutes. Transfer shrimp mixture to bowl.

5. Melt 1 tablespoon butter in now-empty skillet over medium-high heat. Whisk in flour and cook for 1 minute. Slowly whisk in shrimp stock until incorporated. Bring to boil, reduce heat to medium-low, and simmer until thickened slightly, about 5 minutes.

6. Stir in shrimp mixture, cover, and cook until shrimp are cooked through, about 3 minutes. Off heat, stir in lemon juice, Tabasco, and remaining 1 tablespoon butter. Season with salt and pepper to taste. Serve over grits, sprinkled with scallions, and passing extra Tabasco.

Fresh versus Frozen

Just because shrimp are raw at the store doesn't mean they're fresh; roughly 90 percent of the shrimp sold in the United States comes from outside the country. So unless you live near a coastal area, you can bet the shrimp you're seeing were frozen and then defrosted. The problem is, once shrimp have been defrosted, their quality deteriorates quickly—and there is no way of telling how long they've been sitting in the case. We prefer to buy frozen shrimp and defrost them ourselves.

Why This Recipe Works Many modern versions of this Carolina favorite add too many frills. We set out to bring it back to basics: tender shrimp, silky sauce, and creamy grits. To avoid overcooking the shrimp, we lightly sautéed them in rendered bacon fat and set them aside while creating a flavorful sauce in the same skillet. We used the shrimp shells to make the stock that formed the base of our sauce. To finish cooking, we added the shrimp back into the sauce. Toasting the grits in butter helped coax the most corn flavor out of them before we added more-than-usual liquid. A sprinkle of chopped scallions added a fresh finish to the dish.

Why This Recipe Works Perloo (pronounced "PUHR-low"), a staple in South Carolina's Low Country, is a tomatoey rice dish simmered in broth. To start, we went the classic route and used reserved shrimp shells to create and flavor shrimp stock, which is surprisingly easy and practical to make from scratch. For the rice, we stuck to the traditional flavor base of onions, celery, and bell pepper. Sautéing the rice with the vegetables firmed up the grains' exterior and prevented mushiness. Just before removing the rice from the heat, we folded in the shrimp and let them rest, covered, for perfectly cooked shrimp and tender rice in a delicious one-pot meal.

CHARLESTON SHRIMP PERLOO

SERVES 4 TO 6

After adding the shrimp to the pot, fold it in gently; stirring the rice too vigorously will make it mushy. Any extra stock can be refrigerated for 3 days or frozen for up to 1 month. Serve with hot sauce.

5	tablespoons unsalted butter
1½	pounds extra-large shrimp (21 to 25 per pound), peeled and deveined, shells reserved
2	onions, chopped
4	celery ribs, chopped
	Salt
4	cups water
1	tablespoon peppercorns
5	sprigs fresh parsley
2	bay leaves
1	green bell pepper, stemmed, seeded, and chopped
2	cups long-grain white rice
2	garlic cloves, minced
1	teaspoon minced fresh thyme
¼	teaspoon cayenne pepper
1	(14.5-ounce) can diced tomatoes

1. Melt 1 tablespoon butter in large saucepan over medium heat. Add shrimp shells, 1 cup onion, ½ cup celery, and 1 teaspoon salt and cook, stirring occasionally, until shells are spotty brown, about 10 minutes. Add water, peppercorns, parsley, and bay leaves. Increase heat to high and bring to boil. Reduce heat to low, cover, and simmer for 30 minutes. Strain shrimp stock through fine-mesh strainer set over large bowl, pressing on solids to extract as much liquid as possible; discard solids.

2. Melt remaining 4 tablespoons butter in Dutch oven over medium heat. Add bell pepper, remaining onion and celery, and ½ teaspoon salt and cook until vegetables are beginning to soften, 5 to 7 minutes. Add rice, garlic, thyme, and cayenne and cook until fragrant and rice is translucent, about 2 minutes. Stir in tomatoes and their juice and 3 cups shrimp stock (reserve remainder for another use) and bring to boil. Reduce heat to low, cover, and cook for 20 minutes.

3. Gently fold shrimp into rice until evenly distributed, cover, and continue to cook 5 minutes longer. Remove pot from heat and let sit, covered, until shrimp are cooked through and all liquid is absorbed, about 10 minutes. Serve.

Peeling and Deveining Shrimp

1. Break shell under swimming legs, which will come off as shell is removed. Leave tail intact if desired, or tug tail to remove shell.

2. Use paring knife to make shallow cut along back of shrimp to expose vein. Use tip of knife to lift out vein. Discard vein by wiping blade against paper towel.

Why This Recipe Works This Italian sandwich is a New Orleans classic, and we wanted to do it justice. We started by inspecting Central Grocery's famous olive salad. Then we got to work on our own version and found that combining olives, capers, giardiniera, garlic, herbs, and spices gave us the salty, tangy mixture we wanted. We baked store-bought pizza dough into perfect puffy rounds, which we sprinkled with sesame seeds. Alternating layers of meats and cheese gave our sandwich stability, making it easier to eat. Lastly, we pressed the assembled sandwiches for an hour to allow the olive salad to properly soak into the bread.

NEW ORLEANS MUFFULETTAS

SERVES 8

You will need one 16-ounce jar of giardiniera to yield 2 cups drained; our favorite brand is Pastene. If you like a spicier sandwich, increase the amount of pepper flakes to ½ teaspoon.

- 2 (1-pound) balls pizza dough
- 2 cups drained jarred giardiniera
- 1 cup pimento-stuffed green olives
- ½ cup pitted kalamata olives
- 2 tablespoons capers, rinsed
- 1 tablespoon red wine vinegar
- 1 garlic clove, minced
- ½ teaspoon dried oregano
- ¼ teaspoon red pepper flakes
- ¼ teaspoon dried thyme
- ½ cup extra-virgin olive oil
- ¼ cup chopped fresh parsley
- 1 large egg, lightly beaten
- 5 teaspoons sesame seeds
- 4 ounces thinly sliced Genoa salami
- 6 ounces thinly sliced aged provolone cheese
- 6 ounces thinly sliced mortadella
- 4 ounces thinly sliced hot capicola

1. Form dough balls into 2 tight round balls on oiled baking sheet, cover loosely with greased plastic wrap, and let sit at room temperature for 1 hour.

2. Meanwhile, pulse giardiniera, green olives, kalamata olives, capers, vinegar, garlic, oregano, pepper flakes, and thyme in food processor until coarsely chopped, about 6 pulses, scraping down sides of bowl as needed. Transfer to bowl and stir in oil and parsley. Let sit at room temperature for 30 minutes. (Olive salad can be refrigerated for up to 1 week.)

3. Adjust oven rack to middle position and heat oven to 425 degrees. Keeping dough balls on sheet, flatten each into 7-inch disk. Brush tops of disks with egg and sprinkle with sesame seeds. Bake until golden brown and loaves sound hollow when tapped, 18 to 20 minutes, rotating sheet halfway through baking. Transfer loaves to wire rack and let cool completely, about 1 hour. (Loaves can be wrapped in plastic and stored at room temperature for up to 24 hours.)

4. Slice loaves in half horizontally. Spread one-fourth of olive salad on cut side of each loaf top and bottom, pressing firmly with rubber spatula to compact. Layer 2 ounces salami, 1½ ounces provolone, 3 ounces mortadella, 1½ ounces provolone, and 2 ounces capicola in order on each loaf bottom. Cap with loaf tops and individually wrap sandwiches tightly in plastic.

5. Place baking sheet on top of sandwiches and weigh down with heavy Dutch oven or two 5-pound bags of flour or sugar for 1 hour, flipping sandwiches halfway through pressing. Unwrap and slice each sandwich into quarters and serve. (Pressed, wrapped sandwiches can be refrigerated for up to 24 hours. Bring to room temperature before serving.)

A Weighty Solution

If you don't have a heavy Dutch oven, use two 5-pound bags of flour or sugar to weigh down the wrapped muffulettas.

Pressing the assembled sandwiches for an hour helps the olive salad properly soak into the bread.

CHINESE CHICKEN SALAD

SERVES 6

You can substitute 1 minced clove of garlic and ¼ teaspoon of cayenne pepper for the Asian chili-garlic sauce.

- 2 oranges
- ¼ cup rice vinegar
- ¼ cup soy sauce
- 3 tablespoons grated fresh ginger
- 3 tablespoons sugar
- 1 tablespoon Asian chili-garlic sauce
- 3 tablespoons vegetable oil
- 2 tablespoons toasted sesame oil
- 4 (6- to 8-ounce) boneless, skinless chicken breasts, trimmed
- 2 romaine lettuce hearts (12 ounces), sliced thin
- ½ small head napa cabbage, cored and sliced thin (6 cups)
- 2 red bell peppers, stemmed, seeded, and cut into 2-inch-long matchsticks
- 1 cup fresh cilantro leaves
- 1 cup salted, dry-roasted peanuts, chopped
- 6 scallions, sliced thin

1. Cut thin slice from top and bottom of each orange, exposing fruit. Slice off rind and pith, cutting from top to bottom. Working over bowl, cut orange segments from thin membrane and transfer segments to second bowl; set aside. Squeeze juice from membrane into first bowl (juice should measure ¼ cup).

2. Combine orange juice, vinegar, soy sauce, ginger, sugar, and chili-garlic sauce in bowl. Transfer ½ cup of orange juice mixture to 12-inch skillet. Slowly whisk vegetable oil and sesame oil into remaining orange juice mixture to make vinaigrette; set aside.

3. Bring orange juice mixture in skillet to boil. Add chicken, reduce heat to medium-low, cover, and simmer until meat registers 160 degrees, 10 to 15 minutes, flipping halfway through cooking. Transfer chicken to plate and let rest for 5 to 10 minutes.

4. Meanwhile, boil pan juices until reduced to ¼ cup, 1 to 3 minutes, and set aside. Using 2 forks, shred chicken into bite-size pieces. Off heat, add chicken, any accumulated juices, and 2 tablespoons vinaigrette to skillet. Toss to coat and let sit for 10 minutes.

5. Toss lettuce, cabbage, bell peppers, cilantro, peanuts, and scallions with remaining vinaigrette in large bowl. Transfer to serving platter and top with chicken and oranges. Serve.

Shopping for Aromatic Asian Ingredients

Consider keeping these three versatile ingredients on hand to add authentic Asian flavor to a variety of dishes, including our Chinese Chicken Salad.

RICE VINEGAR
This Japanese vinegar is sweet and mild.

ASIAN CHILI-GARLIC SAUCE
If you like garlic and heat, you'll reach for this bottle often.

TOASTED SESAME OIL
This aromatic, boldly flavored oil is made from roasted sesame seeds. Its flavor doesn't hold up to cooking, so add it off heat.

Why This Recipe Works We aimed to give this stale chain restaurant classic a fresh makeover. The salad-bar pile ons, from chow mein noodles to snow peas to water chestnuts, got the ax. Instead, we started with crisp romaine lettuce, napa cabbage, bell peppers, cilantro, and scallions. To keep the chicken from tasting like an after-thought, we eschewed rotisserie chicken. We poached boneless, skinless chicken breasts in a flavorful mixture of soy sauce, orange juice, rice vinegar, and ginger, set-ting aside some of the mixture to whisk with sesame and vegetable oils for a bold dressing. We finished the dish with fresh oranges and roasted peanuts.

Why This Recipe Works Like many dishes you'll find in America's Chinese restaurants, chow mein has deep roots in China, where chao mian ("fried noodles") has been around for centuries. But this takeout standard often features dry meat and a bland, pasty sauce. To help the chicken retain moisture, we soaked sliced chicken in water and baking soda followed by a quick soak in Chinese rice wine and cornstarch. For the chow mein's sauce, oyster sauce added meaty notes, and more rice wine added sweet brightness. To avoid a gloppy sauce, we used just a bit of cornstarch as thickener then added plenty of bean sprouts for fresh crunch.

CHICKEN CHOW MEIN

SERVES 4

Purchase thin, round fresh Chinese egg noodles, not flat and/or dried noodles, or substitute 6 ounces of dried chow mein, ramen, or wheat vermicelli.

- 1 (9-ounce) package fresh Chinese noodles
- 1 tablespoon toasted sesame oil
- 1 teaspoon baking soda
- 2 (6-ounce) boneless, skinless chicken breasts, trimmed and cut crosswise into 1/4-inch-thick slices
- 3 tablespoons Chinese rice wine or dry sherry
- 1 tablespoon cornstarch
- 1/2 cup chicken broth
- 3 tablespoons soy sauce
- 3 tablespoons oyster sauce
- 1/4 teaspoon white pepper
- 2 tablespoons vegetable oil
- 6 ounces shiitake mushrooms, stemmed and sliced thin
- 1 carrot, peeled and cut into 2-inch matchsticks
- 2 celery ribs, cut on bias into 1/4-inch-thick slices
- 4 scallions, white and green parts separated and sliced thin
- 3 garlic cloves, minced
- 1 tablespoon grated fresh ginger
- 4 ounces (2 cups) mung bean sprouts

1. Bring 4 quarts water to boil in large pot. Add noodles to boiling water and cook until tender, 2 to 4 minutes. Drain noodles, rinse thoroughly with cold water, then drain again. Toss noodles with sesame oil in bowl; set aside.

2. Meanwhile, dissolve baking soda in 1/2 cup cold water in bowl. Add chicken and let sit at room temperature for 15 minutes. Drain chicken, rinse under cold water, then drain again. Pat chicken dry with paper towels. Combine 1 tablespoon rice wine, 2 teaspoons cornstarch, and chicken in bowl; set aside.

3. Whisk broth, soy sauce, oyster sauce, pepper, remaining 2 tablespoons rice wine, and remaining 1 teaspoon cornstarch together in bowl; set aside.

4. Heat oil in 12-inch nonstick skillet over high heat until just smoking. Add chicken and cook, stirring frequently, until opaque, about 2 minutes. Add mushrooms and carrot and cook, stirring frequently, until tender, about 2 minutes. Add celery and cook until crisp-tender, about 1 minute. Add scallion whites, garlic, and ginger and cook until fragrant, about 30 seconds.

5. Whisk broth mixture to recombine, then add to skillet and cook until thickened and chicken is cooked through, about 2 minutes. Add bean sprouts and noodles and toss until sauce evenly coats noodles, about 1 minute. Transfer to platter and sprinkle with scallion greens. Serve.

Fresh Egg Noodles
You'll find chow mein in Chinese restaurants prepared with wheat noodles, Italian pastas, ramen noodles, or egg noodles. But our tasters preferred fresh Chinese egg noodles, available in the Asian section of most grocery stores.

SLOW-COOKER CHINESE BARBECUED PORK

SERVES 8

Pork butt roast is often labeled Boston butt in the supermarket. Look for five-spice powder and hoisin sauce in the international aisle at your supermarket.

1½ teaspoons salt
1½ teaspoons five-spice powder
 ½ teaspoon pepper
 1 (5- to 6-pound) boneless pork butt roast, trimmed and sliced crosswise into 1-inch-thick steaks
 ⅓ cup hoisin sauce
 ⅓ cup honey
 ¼ cup sugar
 ¼ cup soy sauce
 ¼ cup ketchup
 2 tablespoons dry sherry
 1 tablespoon toasted sesame oil
 1 tablespoon grated fresh ginger
 2 garlic cloves, minced

1. Combine salt, ¾ teaspoon five-spice powder, and pepper in bowl. Rub spice mixture all over pork and transfer to slow cooker. Cover and cook on low until pork is just tender, 5 to 6 hours.

2. When pork is nearly done, combine hoisin, honey, sugar, soy sauce, ketchup, sherry, oil, ginger, garlic, and remaining ¾ teaspoon five-spice powder in bowl.

Set wire rack inside aluminum foil–lined rimmed baking sheet. Pour 1 cup water into sheet. Adjust oven rack 4 inches from broiler element and heat broiler.

3. Using tongs, transfer pork from slow cooker to prepared wire rack in single layer. Brush pork with one-third of hoisin mixture and broil until lightly caramelized, 5 to 7 minutes. Flip pork, brush with half of remaining hoisin mixture, and broil until lightly caramelized on second side, 5 to 7 minutes. Brush pork with remaining hoisin mixture and broil until deep mahogany and crispy around edges, about 3 minutes. Transfer to carving board and let rest for 10 minutes. Slice crosswise into thin strips. Serve.

Pork Butt (Blade Shoulder)

This large, flavorful cut (often labeled Boston butt or pork shoulder at supermarkets) can weigh as much as 8 pounds when sold with the bone in. Many markets take out the bone and sell this cut in smaller chunks, often wrapped in netting to hold the roast together. This cut is ideal for slow roasting, barbecuing, stewing, or braising.

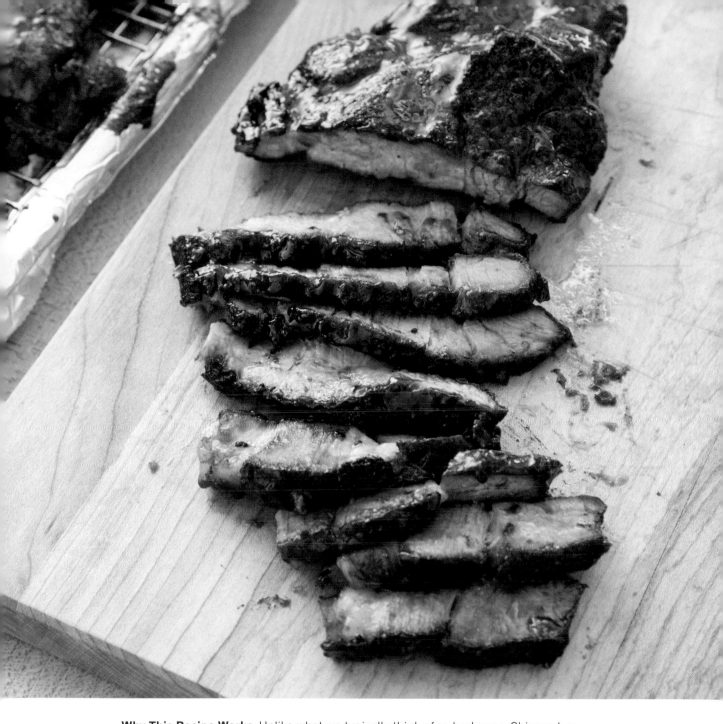

Why This Recipe Works Unlike what we typically think of as barbecue, Chinese barbecued pork is made neither on a grill nor in a smoker: It's usually cooked (and
then glazed) in an oven. But we made this dish even more convenient—by adapting
it to the slow cooker. Boneless pork butt renders lots of flavorful fat and pork juices
as it cooks. Because this fat diluted any sauce we tried, we instead used a dry rub and
then cooked the pork with a glazy sauce under the broiler. The finished "barbecued" pork was tender with a shiny, slightly charred exterior that tasted even better
than it looked, earning it the nickname "meat candy" in the test kitchen.

PATTY MELTS

SERVES 4

To make sure the melts hold together, use rye bread that's sliced about ½ inch thick.

- 10 slices hearty rye sandwich bread
- 2 tablespoons whole milk
- ¾ teaspoon onion powder
   Salt and pepper
- 1½ pounds 85 percent lean ground beef
- 3 tablespoons unsalted butter
- 2 onions, halved and sliced thin
- 8 ounces Swiss cheese, shredded (2 cups)

1. Adjust oven rack to middle position and heat oven to 200 degrees. Tear 2 pieces of bread into ½-inch pieces. Using potato masher, mash torn bread, milk, onion powder, ¾ teaspoon salt, and ½ teaspoon pepper in large bowl until smooth. Add beef and gently knead until well combined. Divide meat into 4 equal portions. Shape each portion into 6 by 4-inch oval.

2. Melt 1 tablespoon butter in 12-inch nonstick skillet over medium-high heat. Cook 2 patties until well browned on first side, about 5 minutes. Transfer to large plate, browned side up, and repeat with remaining 2 patties.

3. Pour off all but 1 teaspoon fat from pan. Add onions and ½ teaspoon salt and cook, stirring occasionally, until golden brown, 5 to 7 minutes. Arrange patties, browned side up, on top of onions, pouring any accumulated juices into pan. Reduce heat to medium and cook, shaking pan occasionally, until onions are tender and burgers are cooked through, about 5 minutes.

4. Divide 1 cup cheese among 4 slices bread. Top with patties, onions, remaining cheese, and remaining bread. Wipe out skillet with paper towels. Melt 1 tablespoon butter in now-empty skillet over medium heat. Cook 2 sandwiches until golden brown and cheese is melted, 3 to 4 minutes per side. Transfer to rimmed baking sheet and keep warm in oven. Repeat with remaining 1 tablespoon butter and remaining 2 sandwiches. Serve.

Heyday of the Sandwich

When it comes to inventive sandwiches, you can't top 1920s America. Just a decade earlier, New Yorkers were said to eat only six types of sandwich: sardine, tongue, roast beef, Swiss cheese, liverwurst, and egg, according to William Grimes's book *Appetite City: A Culinary History of New York*. But three factors—Prohibition, the newfound popularity of automobiles, and women's increasing independence—had created a tea-room craze across the country, making sandwiches so popular that one New Yorker counted nearly 1,000 different types. In these newly minted salons of sandwiches, customers chose among dubious combinations like cheese-ketchup, lemon-prune, and baked bean–celery. Cookbooks reflected the trend, offering other odd partnerships, such as peanut butter and chili sauce, not to mention shredded coconut, cucumber, and mayonnaise. Makes Elvis's prized sandwich of fried peanut butter, banana, and bacon sound almost tame.

Why This Recipe Works Because the ground beef patty for patty melts is traditionally cooked twice—browned once in butter and a second time while the sandwich is
griddled—many recipes produce something resembling dried-out hockey pucks. To
solve the problem, we incorporated a panade (a paste of bread and milk) into the
meat. To bump up the flavor of our burgers, we used rye bread and onion powder
in the panade. Covering the cooking onions with the patties trapped some of the steam
and helped the onions to soften quicker. This also allowed the flavors of the meat to
seep into the onions and vice versa.

Why This Recipe Works This Oklahoma specialty features a thin patty of ground beef topped with a crispy crust of caramelized onions cooked on a griddle. Served on a buttery grilled bun with yellow mustard, dill pickles, and a slice of American cheese, this exceptional burger is well worth a road trip. To make them at home, we sliced and salted the onions, then squeezed out their excess moisture so they'd brown quickly and stick to the burgers. We mashed the onions into the burgers, then put the burgers on a buttered skillet onion side down to brown the onions. Then we flipped the burgers and turned up the heat to finish cooking and get a nice sear.

OKLAHOMA FRIED ONION BURGERS

SERVES 4

A mandoline makes quick work of slicing the onion thinly. Squeeze the salted onion slices until they're as dry as possible, or they won't adhere to the patties. These burgers are traditionally served with yellow mustard and slices of dill pickle.

 1 large onion, halved and sliced ⅛ inch thick
    Salt and pepper
12 ounces 85 percent lean ground beef
 1 tablespoon unsalted butter
 1 teaspoon vegetable oil
 4 slices American cheese (4 ounces)
 4 hamburger buns, buttered and toasted

1. Combine onion and 1 teaspoon salt in bowl and toss to combine. Transfer to colander and let sit for 30 minutes, tossing occasionally. Using tongs, transfer onion to clean dish towel, gather edges, and squeeze onion dry. Sprinkle with ½ teaspoon pepper.

2. Divide onion mixture into 4 separate mounds on rimmed baking sheet. Form beef into 4 lightly packed balls and season with salt and pepper. Place beef balls on top of onion mounds and flatten beef firmly so onion adheres and patties measure 4 inches in diameter.

3. Melt butter with oil in 12-inch nonstick skillet over medium heat. Using spatula, transfer patties to skillet, onion side down, and cook until onion is deep golden brown and beginning to crisp around edges, 6 to 8 minutes. Flip burgers, increase heat to high, and cook until well browned on second side, about 2 minutes. Place 1 slice cheese on each bottom bun. Place burgers on buns, add desired toppings, and serve.

Keys to Fried Onion Burgers

A few tricks helped the onions adhere to the burgers and caramelize rather than burn.

1. After salting and squeezing onions dry, divide into four piles, place beef balls on top, and press.

2. Brown onion side over medium heat, then flip burgers and turn up heat to sear beef side.

Why This Recipe Works Atlanta brisket is a southern braise featuring onion soup mix, ketchup, and Atlanta's own Coca-Cola. We wanted to keep the regional charm but update the convenience-product flavor. To season the brisket, we pierced it with a fork, salted it, and let it sit overnight. For a great crust, we seared the brisket weighed down with a heavy pot. Finally, for the characteristic braising liquid, we mixed cola and ketchup and replaced the artificial-tasting soup mix with our own blend of sautéed onions, onion and garlic powders, brown sugar, and dried thyme. The mixture both flavored the meat and became a sweet, tangy sauce for serving.

ATLANTA BRISKET

SERVES 6

Parchment paper provides a nonreactive barrier between the cola-based braising liquid and the aluminum foil. A whole brisket is comprised of two smaller roasts: the flat cut and the point cut. For this recipe, we prefer the flat cut, which is rectangular in shape and leaner than the knobby, well-marbled point cut. The flat cut is topped with a thick fat cap; make sure that the fat cap isn't overtrimmed.

1 (3½-pound) beef brisket, flat cut,
  fat trimmed to ¼ inch thick
  Salt and pepper
4 teaspoons vegetable oil
1 pound onions, halved and sliced ½ inch thick
2 cups cola
1½ cups ketchup
4 teaspoons onion powder
2 teaspoons packed dark brown sugar
1 teaspoon garlic powder
1 teaspoon dried thyme

1. Using fork, poke holes all over brisket. Rub entire surface of brisket with 1 tablespoon salt. Wrap brisket in plastic wrap and refrigerate for at least 6 or up to 24 hours.

2. Adjust oven rack to lower-middle position and heat oven to 325 degrees. Pat brisket dry with paper towels and season with pepper. Heat 2 teaspoons oil in 12-inch nonstick skillet over medium-high heat until just smoking. Place brisket fat side down in skillet; weigh down brisket with heavy Dutch oven or cast-iron skillet and cook until well browned on bottom, about 4 minutes. Remove pot, flip brisket, and replace pot on top of brisket. Cook on second side until well browned, about 4 minutes longer. Transfer brisket to plate.

3. Heat remaining 2 teaspoons oil in now-empty skillet over medium heat until shimmering. Add onions and cook, stirring occasionally, until soft and golden brown, 10 to 12 minutes. Transfer onions to 13 by 9-inch baking dish and spread out in even layer.

4. Combine cola, ketchup, onion powder, sugar, garlic powder, thyme, 1 teaspoon salt, and 1 teaspoon pepper in bowl. Place brisket fat side up on top of onions and pour cola mixture over brisket. Place parchment paper over brisket and cover dish tightly with aluminum foil. Bake until tender and fork slips easily in and out of meat, 3½ to 4 hours. Let brisket rest in liquid, uncovered, for 30 minutes.

5. Transfer brisket to carving board. Skim any fat from top of sauce with large spoon. Slice brisket against grain into ¼-inch-thick slices and return to baking dish. Serve brisket with sauce.

To Make Ahead Follow recipe through step 4. Allow brisket to cool in sauce, cover, and refrigerate overnight or up to 24 hours. To serve, slice brisket, return to sauce, and cover with parchment paper. Cover baking dish with aluminum foil and cook in 350-degree oven until heated through, about 1 hour.

Getting a Great Sear

Brisket is a flat cut of meat that curls up when you try to sear it. We fixed this problem by weighing down the brisket with a heavy Dutch oven (wrapped in foil to make cleanup easier) to ensure a more even sear.

SLOW-COOKER BBQ BEEF BRISKET

SERVES 8 TO 10

Scoring the fat on the brisket at ½-inch intervals will allow the rub to penetrate the meat. Two disposable aluminum loaf pans stacked inside one another can be substituted for the metal loaf pan.

Spice Rub and Brisket
½ cup packed dark brown sugar
2 tablespoons minced canned chipotle chile in adobo sauce
1 tablespoon ground cumin
1 tablespoon paprika
2 teaspoons pepper
1 teaspoon salt
1 (4- to 5-pound) brisket roast, fat trimmed to ¼ inch thick and scored lightly

Aromatics and Sauce
3 tablespoons vegetable oil
1 onion, chopped fine
2 tablespoons tomato paste
1 tablespoon chili powder
1 tablespoon minced canned chipotle chile in adobo sauce
2 garlic cloves, minced
½ cup water, plus extra as needed
¼ cup ketchup
1 tablespoon cider vinegar
¼ teaspoon liquid smoke
   Salt and pepper

1. For the Spice Rub and Brisket Combine sugar, chipotle, cumin, paprika, pepper, and salt in bowl. Rub sugar mixture all over brisket. Cover with plastic wrap and let sit at room temperature for 1 hour or refrigerate for up to 24 hours.

2. For the Aromatics and Sauce Heat oil in 12-inch skillet over medium-high heat until shimmering. Cook onion until softened, about 5 minutes. Add tomato paste and cook until beginning to brown, about 1 minute. Stir in chili powder, chipotle, and garlic and cook until fragrant, about 30 seconds. Mound onion mixture in center of slow cooker, arrange inverted metal loaf pan over onion mixture, and place brisket fat side up on top of loaf pan. Add water

to slow cooker, cover, and cook on high until fork inserted in brisket can be removed with no resistance, 7 to 8 hours (or cook on low for 10 to 12 hours).

3. Transfer brisket to 13 by 9-inch baking dish, cover with aluminum foil, and let rest for 30 minutes. Carefully remove loaf pan from slow cooker. Pour onion mixture and accumulated juices into large bowl and skim fat. (You should have about 2 cups defatted juices; if you have less, supplement with water.)

4. Transfer brisket to carving board, slice thin against grain, and return to baking dish. Pour 1 cup reserved defatted juices over sliced brisket. Whisk ketchup, vinegar, and liquid smoke into remaining juices. Season with salt and pepper to taste. Serve, passing sauce at table.

To Make Ahead In step 3, wrap brisket tightly in foil and refrigerate for up to 3 days. (Refrigerate juices separately.) To serve, transfer foil-wrapped brisket to baking dish and heat in 350-degree oven until brisket is heated through, about 1 hour. Reheat juices in microwave or saucepan set over medium heat. Continue with recipe as directed.

Preventing Waterlogged Brisket

To minimize the moisture absorbed by the brisket, we place the meat on top of a loaf pan. The juices exuded by the meat are drawn under the pan by a vacuum effect, creating less moisture directly below the meat.

1. Pile onion mixture under inverted loaf pan and place brisket on top.

2. After cooking, release juices from loaf pan and reserve for use in barbecue sauce.

Why This Recipe Works Barbecued brisket in the slow cooker? You bet. To minimize the moisture absorbed by the brisket (which traditionally isn't cooked directly in liquid), we came up with an unorthodox solution: elevating the meat off the bottom of the slow cooker with an inverted loaf pan. The liquid exuded from the meat during cooking was drawn under the loaf pan by a vacuum effect, which meant that the slow cooker more closely mimicked the dry heat of real barbecue. To bump up the flavor of this liquid, we added sautéed onion, garlic, tomato paste, and chipotle chiles.

Why This Recipe Works We wanted a foolproof recipe for this southern specialty. We started by making a whiskey-flavored marinade, then steeped the chops in it for at least one hour prior to cooking. We cooked the chops in a hot skillet and then used the same pan to prepare the glaze—browned bits left behind by the chops in the pan added deep, meaty flavor. Allowing the cooked chops to sit in the pan in the glaze for a few minutes before serving helped ensure it clung to the meat.

TENNESSEE WHISKEY PORK CHOPS

SERVES 4

Bourbon tastes fine, but we think it's worth purchasing the real deal—Jack Daniel's Tennessee Whiskey—for this recipe. Watch the glaze closely during the last few minutes of cooking—the bubbles become very small as it approaches the right consistency.

½ cup Jack Daniel's Tennessee Whiskey
    or bourbon
½ cup apple cider
2 tablespoons packed light brown sugar
4 teaspoons cider vinegar
1 tablespoon Dijon mustard
½ teaspoon vanilla extract
⅛ teaspoon cayenne pepper
4 (8- to 10-ounce) bone-in, center-cut pork
    chops, about 1 inch thick, trimmed
2 teaspoons vegetable oil
    Salt and pepper
1 tablespoon unsalted butter

1. Whisk whiskey, cider, sugar, 2 teaspoons vinegar, mustard, vanilla, and cayenne together in bowl. Transfer ¼ cup whiskey mixture to 1-gallon zipper-lock bag, add pork chops, press air out of bag, and seal. Turn bag to coat chops with marinade and refrigerate 1 to 2 hours. Reserve remaining whiskey mixture separately.

2. Remove chops from bag, pat dry with paper towels, and discard marinade. Heat oil in 12-inch skillet over medium-high heat until just beginning to smoke. Season chops with salt and pepper and cook until well browned on both sides and a peek into thickest part of a chop using paring knife yields still-pink meat ¼ inch from surface, 6 to 8 minutes, flipping chops halfway through cooking. Transfer chops to plate and cover tightly with aluminum foil.

3. Add reserved whiskey mixture to skillet and bring to boil, scraping up any browned bits with wooden spoon. Cook until reduced to thick glaze, 3 to 5 minutes. Reduce heat to medium-low and, holding on to chops, tip plate to add any accumulated juices back to skillet. Add remaining 2 teaspoons vinegar, whisk in butter, and simmer glaze until thick and sticky, 2 to 3 minutes. Remove pan from heat.

4. Return chops to skillet and let rest in pan, turning chops occasionally to coat both sides, until sauce clings to chops and meat registers 145 degrees, about 5 minutes. Transfer chops to platter and spoon sauce over. Serve.

Break Out the Good Stuff

Bourbon was fine, but we loved the deep, caramel-flavored glaze we got when using Jack Daniel's in this recipe. Tennessee whiskey differs from Kentucky bourbon because of a distiller's trick called the Lincoln County process, in which the distilled whiskey is filtered over hard maple charcoal. Then, like bourbon, it is aged in charred oak barrels, where it picks up its distinctive caramel color and smoky flavor.

MEMPHIS-STYLE WET RIBS FOR A CROWD

SERVES 8 TO 12

Spice Rub

¼ cup paprika
2 tablespoons packed brown sugar
2 tablespoons salt
2 teaspoons pepper
2 teaspoons onion powder
2 teaspoons granulated garlic

Barbecue Sauce and Mop

1½ cups ketchup
1¼ cups apple juice
¼ cup molasses
½ cup cider vinegar
¼ cup Worcestershire sauce
3 tablespoons yellow mustard
2 teaspoons pepper

Ribs

4 (2½- to 3-pound) racks St. Louis–style spareribs, trimmed, membrane removed
2 cups wood chips, soaked in water for 15 minutes and drained
1 (13 by 9-inch) disposable aluminum roasting pan (if using charcoal) or 1 (8½ by 6-inch) disposable aluminum pan (if using gas)

1. For the Spice Rub Combine all ingredients in bowl.

2. For the Barbecue Sauce and Mop Combine ketchup, ¾ cup apple juice, molasses, ¼ cup vinegar, Worcestershire, 2 tablespoons mustard, and 2 tablespoons spice rub in medium saucepan and bring to boil over medium heat. Reduce heat to medium-low and simmer until thickened and reduced to 2 cups, about 20 minutes. Off heat, stir in pepper; set barbecue sauce aside. For the mop, whisk ½ cup apple juice, ¼ cup vinegar, 1 tablespoon mustard, and ¼ cup barbecue sauce together in bowl.

3. For the Ribs Pat ribs dry with paper towels and season with remaining spice rub. Place 1 rack of ribs, meaty side down, on cutting board. Place second rack of ribs, meaty side up, directly on top of first rack, arranging thick end over tapered end. Tie racks together at 2-inch intervals with kitchen twine. Repeat with remaining 2 racks of ribs for two bundles. Using large piece of heavy-duty aluminum foil, wrap soaked chips in foil packet and cut several vent holes in top.

4A. For a Charcoal Grill Open bottom vent halfway and place disposable roasting pan on 1 side of grill. Fill pan with 2 quarts water. Arrange 3 quarts unlit charcoal briquettes on other side of grill. Light large chimney starter half filled with charcoal briquettes (3 quarts). When top coals are partially covered with ash, pour evenly over unlit coals. Place wood chip packet on coals. Set cooking grate in place, cover, and open lid vent halfway. Heat grill until hot and wood chips are smoking, about 5 minutes.

4B. For a Gas Grill Place wood chip packet and disposable pan over primary burner and fill pan with 2 cups water. Turn primary burner to high (leave other burners off), cover, and heat grill until hot and wood chips are smoking, about 15 minutes. (Adjust primary burner as needed to maintain grill temperature of 275 to 300 degrees.)

5. Clean and oil cooking grate. Place ribs on cooler side of grill and baste with one-third of mop. Cover (positioning lid vent over ribs for charcoal) and cook for 2 hours, flipping and switching positions of ribs and basting again with half of remaining mop halfway through cooking.

6. Adjust oven racks to upper-middle and lower-middle positions and heat oven to 300 degrees. Line 2 rimmed baking sheets with foil. Cut kitchen twine from racks. Transfer 2 racks, meaty side up, to each sheet. Baste with remaining mop and bake for 2 hours, switching and rotating sheets halfway through baking.

7. Remove ribs from oven and brush evenly with ½ cup barbecue sauce. Return to oven and continue to bake until tender, basting with ½ cup barbecue sauce and switching and rotating sheets twice during baking, about 45 minutes. (Ribs do not need to be flipped and should remain meaty side up during baking.) Transfer ribs to carving board. Brush evenly with remaining ½ cup barbecue sauce, tent loosely with foil, and let rest for 20 minutes. Cut ribs in between bones to separate. Serve.

Why This Recipe Works For these saucy Memphis wet ribs, a potent spice rub performs double duty, seasoning the meat and creating the backbone for our barbecue sauce. Tying two racks together allowed us to double our yield and cook four hefty racks of ribs at once. To keep the ribs moist, we grilled them over indirect heat and basted them with a traditional "mop" of juice and vinegar. After a few hours of smoking on the grill, we brushed the ribs with our flavorful barbecue sauce and transferred them to the steady, even heat of the oven to finish tenderizing.

SLOW-COOKER MEMPHIS-STYLE WET RIBS

SERVES 4 TO 6

Try to find ribs of equal shape to ensure even cooking. These ribs should be tender but not falling off the bone.

Ribs

- 2 tablespoons paprika
- 1 tablespoon packed brown sugar
- 1 tablespoon kosher salt
- 2 teaspoons pepper
- 2 teaspoons onion powder
- 2 teaspoons granulated garlic
- 2 (2½- to 3-pound) racks St. Louis–style spareribs, trimmed and each rack cut in half

Barbecue Sauce

- ¾ cup ketchup
- 6 tablespoons apple juice
- 2 tablespoons molasses
- 2 tablespoons cider vinegar
- 2 tablespoons Worcestershire sauce
- 1 tablespoon yellow mustard
- 1 teaspoon pepper
- ¼ teaspoon liquid smoke

1. For the Ribs Combine paprika, sugar, salt, pepper, onion powder, and granulated garlic in bowl. Reserve 1 tablespoon spice rub for sauce. Pat ribs dry with paper towels and coat all over with remaining 5 tablespoons rub.

2. Arrange ribs vertically with thick ends pointing down and meaty side against interior wall of slow cooker (ribs will overlap). Cover and cook until ribs are just tender, 5 to 6 hours on high or 6 to 7 hours on low.

3. For the Barbecue Sauce Meanwhile, whisk ketchup, apple juice, molasses, vinegar, Worcestershire, mustard, pepper, liquid smoke, and reserved 1 tablespoon spice rub together in medium saucepan. Bring to boil over medium heat, then reduce heat to medium-low and simmer, stirring occasionally, until thickened and reduced to 1 cup, about 10 minutes. (Sauce can be refrigerated for up to 3 days.)

4. Line rimmed baking sheet with aluminum foil and set wire rack in sheet. Using tongs, transfer ribs, meaty side up, to prepared rack. Let ribs sit for 10 minutes to allow surface to dry out.

5. Adjust oven rack 3 inches from broiler element and heat broiler. Liberally brush ribs with ½ cup sauce and broil until sauce is bubbling and beginning to char, about 4 minutes. Remove ribs from oven, brush with remaining ½ cup sauce, tent with foil, and let rest for 20 minutes. Cut ribs in between bones to separate. Serve.

How Hot is Your Broiler?

It's good to know if your broiler runs relatively hot, average, or cold. This information allows you to adjust the cooking time for this recipe (and others) accordingly. To see how your broiler stacks up, heat it on high and place a slice of white sandwich bread directly under the heating element on the upper-middle rack. If the bread toasts to golden brown in 30 seconds or less, your broiler runs very hot, and you will need to reduce the cooking time by a minute or two. If the bread toasts perfectly in one minute, your broiler runs about average. If the bread takes two minutes or longer to toast, your broiler runs cool and you may need to increase the cooking time by a minute or two.

Why This Recipe Works To serve up saucy Memphis wet ribs without ever leaving the kitchen, we turned to our slow cooker. After applying a zesty spice rub, we arranged two racks of St. Louis–style ribs in the slow cooker. The ribs cooked low and slow in their own flavorful juices, no other liquid required. Hours later, the ribs were tender and perfectly cooked. We created a thick glazy sauce and brushed it over our deeply seasoned ribs before sliding them under the broiler to create authentic "wet" barbecue ribs indoors.

Why This Recipe Works Baltimore is known for its pit beef, replete with a well-seasoned, charred crust and a rosy pink interior. The meat is shaved paper thin, piled onto a kaiser roll, topped with a horseradish-y mayo known as tiger sauce, and finally covered with sliced onions. We started by cutting a beefy top sirloin roast in half and slow-cooked the meat on the cool side of the grill—a foil shield provided maximum protection so the meat didn't dry out. Then for maximum char, we generously seared both pieces all over.

BALTIMORE PIT BEEF

SERVES 10

When shopping for the prepared horseradish, buy the brined (not creamy) variety and, if necessary, drain it.

Tiger Sauce
½ cup mayonnaise
½ cup hot prepared horseradish
1 teaspoon lemon juice
1 garlic clove, minced
Salt and pepper

Pit Beef
4 teaspoons kosher salt
1 tablespoon paprika
1 tablespoon pepper
1 teaspoon garlic powder
1 teaspoon dried oregano
¼ teaspoon cayenne pepper
1 (4- to 5-pound) boneless top sirloin roast, trimmed and halved crosswise
10 kaiser rolls
1 onion, sliced thin

1. For the Tiger Sauce Whisk mayonnaise, horseradish, lemon juice, and garlic together in bowl. Season with salt and pepper to taste. (Sauce can be refrigerated for up to 2 days.)

2. For the Pit Beef Combine salt, paprika, pepper, garlic powder, oregano, and cayenne in bowl. Pat roasts dry with paper towels and rub with 2 tablespoons seasoning mixture. Wrap meat tightly with plastic wrap and refrigerate for 6 to 24 hours.

3A. For a Charcoal Grill Open bottom vent halfway. Light large chimney starter filled with charcoal briquettes (6 quarts). When top coals are partially covered with ash, pour evenly over half of grill. Set cooking grate in place, cover, and open lid vent halfway. Heat grill until hot, about 5 minutes.

3B. For a Gas Grill Turn all burners to high, cover, and heat grill until hot, about 15 minutes. Leave primary burner on high and turn other burner(s) off.

4. Clean and oil cooking grate. Unwrap roasts and place end to end on long side of 18 by 12-inch sheet of aluminum foil. Loosely fold opposite long side of foil around top of roasts. Place meat on cool part of grill with foil-covered side closest to heat source. Cover (positioning lid vent over meat if using charcoal) and cook until meat registers 100 degrees, 45 minutes to 1 hour.

5. Transfer roasts to plate and discard foil. Turn all burners to high if using gas. If using charcoal, carefully remove cooking grate and light large chimney starter three-quarters filled with charcoal briquettes (4½ quarts). When top coals are partially covered with ash, pour evenly over spent coals. Set cooking grate in place and cover. Heat grill until hot, about 5 minutes.

6. Pat roasts dry with paper towels and rub with remaining spice mixture. Place meat on hot part of grill. Cook (covered if using gas), turning occasionally, until charred on all sides and meat registers 120 to 125 degrees (for medium-rare), 10 to 20 minutes. Transfer meat to carving board, tent loosely with foil, and let rest for 15 minutes. Slice meat thin against grain. Transfer sliced beef to rolls, top with onion slices, and drizzle with sauce. Serve.

Preventing Pit Beef from Drying out

Even with indirect heat, the sides of the roasts closest to the fire can overcook. A simple foil shield protects them.

Why This Recipe Works Warm spices and unexpected garnishes lend Cincinnati chili recipes their unique flavors—but can sometimes muddle the dish. To recreate this Midwestern recipe in our own kitchen, we narrowed our ingredient list to four spices. Tomato paste added richness to our chili, while dark brown sugar gave it a sweet tang. Boiling the beef in water kept it tender during cooking—we cooked ours directly in our spices and liquid to infuse the meat with their intense flavor. Serving our chili over spaghetti, plus cheese, onions, red beans, and oyster crackers, gave us the true Cincinnati chili experience.

CINCINNATI CHILI

SERVES 6 TO 8

Use canned tomato sauce for this recipe—do not use jarred spaghetti sauce.

- 1 tablespoon vegetable oil
- 2 onions, chopped fine
- 2 tablespoons tomato paste
- 2 tablespoons chili powder
- 1 tablespoon dried oregano
- 1½ teaspoons ground cinnamon
- 1 garlic clove, minced
  Salt and pepper
- ¼ teaspoon ground allspice
- 2 cups chicken broth
- 2 cups canned tomato sauce
- 2 tablespoons cider vinegar
- 2 teaspoons packed dark brown sugar
- 1½ pounds 85 percent lean ground beef

1. Heat oil in Dutch oven over medium-high heat until shimmering. Cook onions until soft and browned around edges, about 8 minutes. Add tomato paste, chili powder, oregano, cinnamon, garlic, 1 teaspoon salt, ¾ teaspoon pepper, and allspice and cook until fragrant, about 1 minute. Stir in chicken broth, tomato sauce, vinegar, and sugar.

2. Add beef and stir to break up meat. Bring to boil, reduce heat to medium-low, and simmer until chili is deep brown and slightly thickened, 15 to 20 minutes. Season with salt to taste and serve. (Chili can be refrigerated for up to 3 days or frozen for up to 2 months.)

Five Ways to Cincinnati

Those in the know can order their chili without a second thought, but for the uninitiated, here's a quick guide to the five ways of Cincinnati chili. The chili is almost never served on its own (one-way). Just don't forget the oyster crackers!

TWO-WAY CHILI
Served over spaghetti.

THREE-WAY CHILI
Served over spaghetti and topped with cheese.

FOUR-WAY CHILI
Served over spaghetti and topped with onions and cheese.

FIVE-WAY CHILI
Served over spaghetti and topped with onions, red beans, and cheese.

COLORADO GREEN CHILI

SERVES 6

The chiles can be roasted and refrigerated up to 24 hours in advance.

- 3 pounds boneless pork butt roast, trimmed and cut into 1-inch pieces
  Salt
- 2 pounds (10 to 12) Anaheim chiles, stemmed, halved lengthwise, and seeded
- 3 jalapeño chiles
- 1 (14.5-ounce) can diced tomatoes
- 1 tablespoon vegetable oil
- 2 onions, chopped fine
- 8 garlic cloves, minced
- 1 tablespoon ground cumin
- ¼ cup all-purpose flour
- 4 cups chicken broth
  Cayenne pepper
  Lime wedges

1. Combine pork, ½ cup water, and ½ teaspoon salt in Dutch oven over medium heat. Cover and cook for 20 minutes, stirring occasionally. Uncover, increase heat to medium-high, and continue to cook, stirring frequently, until liquid evaporates and pork browns in its own fat, 15 to 20 minutes. Transfer pork to bowl and set aside.

2. Meanwhile, adjust 1 oven rack to lowest position and second rack 6 inches from broiler element. Heat broiler. Line rimmed baking sheet with aluminum foil and spray with vegetable oil spray. Arrange Anaheims, skin side up, and jalapeños in single layer on prepared sheet. Place sheet on upper rack and broil until chiles are mostly blackened and soft, 15 to 20 minutes, rotating sheet and flipping only jalapeños halfway through broiling. Place Anaheims in large bowl and cover with plastic wrap; let cool for 5 minutes. Set aside jalapeños. Heat oven to 325 degrees.

3. Remove skins from Anaheims. Chop half of Anaheims into ½-inch pieces and transfer to bowl. Process remaining Anaheims in food processor until smooth, about 10 seconds; transfer to bowl with chopped Anaheims. Pulse tomatoes and their juice in now-empty food processor until coarsely ground, about 4 pulses.

4. Heat oil in now-empty Dutch oven over medium heat until shimmering. Add onions and cook until lightly browned, 5 to 7 minutes. Stir in garlic and cumin and cook until fragrant, about 30 seconds. Stir in flour and cook for 1 minute. Stir in broth, Anaheims, tomatoes, and pork with any accumulated juices and bring to simmer, scraping up any browned bits. Cover pot, transfer to lower oven rack, and cook until pork is tender, 1 to 1¼ hours.

5. Without peeling, stem and seed jalapeños and reserve seeds. Finely chop jalapeños and stir into chili. Season chili with salt, cayenne, and reserved jalapeño seeds to taste. Serve with lime wedges.

Easier Roasted Chiles

Roasting chiles whole and then seeding them—the usual procedure—makes a mess: The wet seeds stick to everything. We halve and seed the raw Anaheims. It's neater and lets us skip the usual flipping step. We leave the jalapeños whole; they soften but don't deeply roast.

READY FOR ROASTING
Arrange the chiles head to foot for the best fit.

Why This Recipe Works This popular southwestern dish boasts rich bites of pork in a sauce dominated by green chiles. For our version, we used a combination of Anaheim and jalapeño peppers. To achieve the cohesive flavor and mild vegetal taste that we liked, we used canned, diced tomatoes and more than 2 pounds of chiles, along with 3 pounds of boneless pork butt—our preferred cut for its rich meatiness. To reduce the hands-on time, we started the pork with water in a covered pan to render the fat, then let the even heat of the oven cook the chili. Adding the jalapeños just before serving gave a fresh hit of heat.

Why This Recipe Works Similar to Latin American empanadas, these deep-fried hand pies from Louisiana are filled with savory ground meat and spices. For the filling, we used equal parts ground beef and pork along with the classic Creole combination of onions, green bell peppers, and a pinch of cayenne for heat. Chicken broth and flour made the filling cohesive. Using chicken broth rather than milk in the dough gave the crust a subtle savory flavor. After a few minutes in hot oil, they emerged with a crisp, flaky crust and piping-hot filling.

NATCHITOCHES MEAT PIES

MAKES 16 PIES

You can make the dough and the filling up to 24 hours ahead and refrigerate them separately. You can also shape and fill the pies, refrigerating them for up to 24 hours before frying. You will need at least a 6-quart Dutch oven for this recipe.

Filling
- 5 teaspoons vegetable oil
- ¾ pound 85 percent lean ground beef
- ¾ pound ground pork
- Salt and pepper
- 1 onion, chopped fine
- 1 green bell pepper, stemmed, seeded, and minced
- 6 scallions, white parts minced, green parts sliced thin
- 3 garlic cloves, minced
- ¼ teaspoon cayenne pepper
- 2 tablespoons all-purpose flour
- 1 cup chicken broth

Dough
- 4 cups (20 ounces) all-purpose flour
- 2 teaspoons salt
- 1 teaspoon baking powder
- 8 tablespoons vegetable shortening, cut into ½-inch pieces
- 1 cup chicken broth
- 2 large eggs, lightly beaten
- 1 quart vegetable oil for frying

1. For the Filling Heat 2 teaspoons oil in 12-inch skillet over medium-high heat until just smoking. Add beef, pork, 1 teaspoon salt, and ½ teaspoon pepper and cook, breaking up pieces with spoon, until no longer pink, 8 to 10 minutes. Transfer meat to bowl.

2. Add remaining 1 tablespoon oil to now-empty skillet and heat over medium-high heat until shimmering. Add onion, bell pepper, scallion whites, ½ teaspoon salt, and ½ teaspoon pepper and cook until vegetables are just starting to brown, 3 to 5 minutes. Stir in garlic and cayenne and cook until fragrant, about 30 seconds.

3. Return meat and any accumulated juices to skillet with vegetables. Sprinkle flour over meat and cook, stirring constantly, until evenly coated, about 1 minute. Add broth, bring to boil, and cook until slightly thickened, about 3 minutes. Transfer filling to bowl and stir in scallion greens. Refrigerate until completely cool, about 1 hour. (Filling can be refrigerated for up to 24 hours.)

4. For the Dough Process flour, salt, and baking powder in food processor until combined, about 3 seconds. Add shortening and pulse until mixture resembles coarse cornmeal, 6 to 8 pulses. Add broth and eggs and pulse until dough just comes together, about 5 pulses. Transfer dough to lightly floured counter and knead until dough forms smooth ball, about 20 seconds. Divide dough into 16 equal pieces. (Dough can be covered and refrigerated for up to 24 hours.)

5. Line rimmed baking sheet with parchment paper. Working with 1 piece of dough at a time, roll into 6-inch circle on lightly floured counter. Place ¼ cup filling in center of dough round. Brush edges of dough with water and fold dough over filling. Press to seal, trim any ragged edges, and crimp edges with tines of fork. Transfer to prepared sheet. (Filled pies can be covered and refrigerated for up to 24 hours.)

6. Adjust oven rack to middle position and heat oven to 200 degrees. Set wire rack in second rimmed baking sheet. Add oil to large Dutch oven until it measures about ¾ inch deep and heat over medium-high heat to 350 degrees. Place 4 pies in oil and fry until golden brown, 3 to 5 minutes per side, using slotted spatula or spider to flip. Adjust burner, if necessary, to maintain oil temperature between 325 and 350 degrees. Transfer pies to prepared wire rack and place in oven to keep warm. Return oil to 350 degrees and repeat with remaining pies. Serve.

ST. LOUIS–STYLE PIZZA

MAKES TWO 12-INCH PIZZAS

If you can find Provel cheese, use 10 ounces in place of the American cheese, Monterey Jack cheese, and liquid smoke.

Sauce and Cheeses

1 (8-ounce) can tomato sauce
3 tablespoons tomato paste
2 tablespoons chopped fresh basil
1 tablespoon sugar
2 teaspoons dried oregano
8 ounces white American cheese, shredded (2 cups)
2 ounces Monterey Jack cheese, shredded (½ cup)
3 drops liquid smoke

Dough

2 cups (10 ounces) all-purpose flour
2 tablespoons cornstarch
2 teaspoons sugar
1 teaspoon baking powder
1 teaspoon salt
½ cup plus 2 tablespoons water
2 tablespoons olive oil

1. For the Sauce and Cheeses Whisk together tomato sauce, tomato paste, basil, sugar, and oregano in small bowl; set aside. Toss cheeses with liquid smoke in medium bowl; set aside.

2. For the Dough Combine flour, cornstarch, sugar, baking powder, and salt in large bowl. Combine water and olive oil in liquid measuring cup. Stir water mixture into flour mixture until dough starts to come together. Turn dough onto lightly floured surface and knead 3 or 4 times, until cohesive.

3. Adjust oven rack to lower-middle position, place baking stone (or inverted baking sheet) on rack, and heat oven to 475 degrees. Divide dough into 2 equal pieces. Working with 1 piece of dough at a time, press into small circle and transfer to parchment paper dusted lightly with flour. Using rolling pin, roll and stretch dough to form 12-inch circle, rotating parchment as needed. Lift parchment and pizza off work surface onto inverted baking sheet.

4. Top each piece of dough with half of sauce and half of cheese. Carefully pull parchment paper and pizza off baking sheet onto hot baking stone. Bake until underside is golden brown and cheese is completely melted, 9 to 12 minutes. Remove pizza and parchment from oven. Transfer pizza to wire rack and let cool briefly. Assemble and bake second pizza. Cut into 2-inch squares. Serve.

To Make Ahead The dough can be made in advance. At end of step 2, tightly wrap ball of dough in plastic wrap and refrigerate for up to 2 days.

Meet Me in St. Louis

You can make terrific pizza without yeast. It may sound crazy to most of us, but folks in St. Louis have been doing it for years. With its wafer-thin crust; thick, sweet tomato sauce; gooey Provel cheese (another local secret); and signature square slices, St. Louis–style pizza is unmistakable. Imo's, a popular local chain, is credited with creating it, and it's said that founder Ed Imo, a former tile-layer, subconsciously cut the circular pizza into tile-shaped squares (the "square beyond compare," as the jingle goes). The chain and its pizza have since crossed into Illinois and Kansas.

Why This Recipe Works With its wafer-thin crust, thick, sweet tomato sauce, and gooey Provel cheese, St. Louis–style pizza is unmistakable. Adding cornstarch to the dough absorbed moisture and allowed the crust to crisp in a conventional oven. We doctored a simple pizza sauce by adding sugar, tomato paste, dried oregano, and fresh basil. The fresh herb wasn't typical, but it gave the pizza a flavorful lift. Smoky, melty Provel cheese was difficult to find outside the St. Louis area, so we crafted a respectable substitute with American cheese, Monterey Jack, and liquid smoke.

POTATO-CHEDDAR PIEROGI

MAKES ABOUT 30 PIEROGI

When rolling the dough in step 4, be sure not to dust the top surface with too much flour, as that will prevent the edges from forming a tight seal when pinched.

Filling
1 pound russet potatoes, peeled and sliced ½ inch thick
  Salt and pepper
4 ounces sharp cheddar cheese, shredded (1 cup)
2 tablespoons unsalted butter

Dough
2½ cups (13¾ ounces) bread flour
1 teaspoon baking powder
  Salt
1 cup sour cream
1 large egg plus 1 large yolk

Topping
4 tablespoons unsalted butter
1 large onion, chopped fine
½ teaspoon salt

1. For the Filling Combine potatoes and 1 tablespoon salt in large saucepan and cover with water by 1 inch. Bring to boil over medium-high heat; reduce heat to medium and cook at vigorous simmer until potatoes are very tender, about 15 minutes.

2. Drain potatoes in colander. While still hot, combine potatoes, cheddar, butter, ½ teaspoon salt, and ½ teaspoon pepper in bowl of stand mixer. Fit mixer with paddle and mix on medium speed until potatoes are smooth and all ingredients are fully combined, about 1 minute. Transfer filling to 8-inch square baking dish and refrigerate until fully chilled, about 30 minutes, or cover with plastic wrap and refrigerate for up to 24 hours.

3. For the Dough Whisk flour, baking powder, and ½ teaspoon salt together in clean bowl of stand mixer. Add sour cream and egg and yolk. Fit mixer

with dough hook and knead on medium-high speed for 8 minutes (dough will be smooth and elastic). Transfer dough to floured bowl, cover with plastic, and refrigerate until ready to assemble.

4. Line rimmed baking sheet with parchment paper and dust with flour. Roll dough on lightly floured counter into 18-inch circle, about ⅛ inch thick. Using 3-inch biscuit cutter, cut 20 to 24 circles from dough. Place 1 tablespoon chilled filling in center of each dough round. Fold dough over filling to create half-moon shape and pinch edges firmly to seal. Transfer to prepared sheet.

5. Gather dough scraps and reroll to ⅛-inch thickness. Cut 6 to 10 more circles from dough and repeat with remaining filling. (It may be necessary to reroll dough once more to yield 30 pierogi.) Cover pierogi with plastic and refrigerate until ready to cook, up to 3 hours.

6. For the Topping Melt butter in 12-inch skillet over medium-low heat. Add onion and salt and cook until onion is caramelized, 15 to 20 minutes. Remove skillet from heat and set aside.

7. Bring 4 quarts water to boil in Dutch oven. Add 1 tablespoon salt and half of pierogi to boiling water and cook until tender, about 5 minutes. Using spider or slotted spoon, remove pierogi from water and transfer to skillet with caramelized onion. Return water to boil, cook remaining pierogi, and transfer to skillet with first batch.

8. Add 2 tablespoons cooking water to pierogi in skillet. Cook over medium-low heat, stirring gently, until onion mixture is warmed through and adhered to pierogi. Transfer to platter and serve.

To Make Ahead Uncooked pierogi can be frozen for several weeks. After sealing pierogi in step 4, freeze them on baking sheet, about 3 hours. Transfer frozen pierogi to zipper-lock freezer bag. When ready to cook, extend boiling time in step 7 to about 7 minutes.

Why This Recipe Works Our take on the Polish dumplings known as *pierogi* combined potatoes and cheese tucked into a tender dough. We began by thoroughly combining boiled russet potatoes, shredded cheddar cheese, and butter in a stand mixer. The heat from the potatoes melted the butter and cheese for an even consistency. We created a pliable, rollable dough using higher-protein bread flour, sour cream, and egg. We stamped out rounds with a biscuit cutter and sealed in the filling by pinching the edges together before boiling the pierogi. A caramelized onion topping mixed with the dumplings made for an authentic sweet-savory finish.

Why This Recipe Works We wanted a recipe for fast-food-style crunchy potato wedges that we could prepare at home. Microwaving the potatoes in a tightly covered bowl helped them obtain perfectly cooked interiors and nicely crisped exteriors. For the coating, adding baking soda to buttermilk and replacing some of the flour with cornstarch resulted in crunchy, deep-golden-brown wedges. Finally, seasoning our crunchy potato wedges with a spice blend as they precooked in the microwave, then tossing the wedges in the seasonings when they came out of the oil, produced potatoes that were flavored from the inside out.

CRUNCHY POTATO WEDGES

SERVES 6

If you don't have buttermilk, substitute 1 cup milk mixed with 1 tablespoon lemon juice. Let the mixture sit 15 minutes before using. You will need at least a 6-quart Dutch oven for this recipe.

- 4 teaspoons kosher salt
- 2 teaspoons onion powder
- 1 teaspoon garlic powder
- 1 teaspoon dried oregano
- ¾ teaspoon cayenne pepper
- ½ teaspoon pepper
- 3 large russet potatoes (about 1¾ pounds), cut into ¼-inch wedges
- ¼ cup peanut or vegetable oil, plus 3 quarts for frying
- 1½ cups all-purpose flour
- ½ cup cornstarch
- 1 cup buttermilk
- ½ teaspoon baking soda

1. Combine salt, onion powder, garlic powder, oregano, cayenne, and pepper in small bowl.

2. Toss potato wedges with 4 teaspoons spice mixture and ¼ cup oil in large bowl; cover. Microwave until potatoes are tender but not falling apart, 7 to 9 minutes, shaking bowl to redistribute potatoes halfway through cooking. Uncover and drain potatoes. Arrange potatoes on rimmed baking sheet and let cool until potatoes firm up, about 10 minutes. (Potatoes can be held at room temperature for up to 2 hours.)

3. Set wire rack in rimmed baking sheet and line second baking sheet with triple layer of paper towels. Add remaining 3 quarts oil to large Dutch oven until it measures about 2 inches deep and heat over medium-high heat to 340 degrees. Meanwhile, combine flour and cornstarch in medium bowl and whisk buttermilk and baking soda together in large bowl. Working in 2 batches, dredge potato wedges in flour mixture, shaking off excess. Dip in buttermilk mixture, allowing excess to drip back into bowl, then coat again in flour mixture. Shake off excess and place on wire rack. (Potatoes can be coated up to 30 minutes in advance.)

4. When oil is ready, add half of coated wedges and fry until deep golden brown, 4 to 6 minutes. Transfer wedges to large bowl and toss with 1 teaspoon spice mixture. Drain wedges on paper towel–lined baking sheet. Return oil to 340 degrees and repeat with second batch of wedges. Serve with extra spice mixture.

To Make Ahead Our Crunchy Potato Wedges freeze very well. Follow steps 1 through 4, frying each batch of wedges until they are light golden brown, 2 to 3 minutes. Do not toss with seasoning, and drain and cool potatoes completely on baking sheet lined with paper towels. Freeze wedges on baking sheet until completely frozen, about 2 hours, then transfer potatoes to zipper-lock bag for up to 2 months. When ready to eat, heat 3 quarts oil to 340 degrees and cook in 2 batches until deep golden brown, about 3 minutes. Toss with seasonings, drain, and serve.

CREAMY BBQ SAUCE
MAKES 1¼ CUPS
Combine ¾ cup mayonnaise, ¼ cup barbecue sauce, 3 tablespoons cider vinegar, 1 minced garlic clove, ¼ teaspoon pepper, and ⅛ teaspoon salt in small bowl.

BUFFALO BLUE CHEESE SAUCE
MAKES 1½ CUPS
Combine ¾ cup mayonnaise, ¼ cup blue cheese salad dressing, 3 tablespoons hot sauce, 1 minced garlic clove, ¼ teaspoon pepper, and ⅛ teaspoon celery salt in small bowl.

CURRIED CHUTNEY SAUCE
MAKES 1¼ CUPS
Combine ¾ cup mayonnaise, ¼ cup yogurt, ¼ cup minced fresh cilantro, 3 tablespoons mango chutney, 2 teaspoons curry powder, ¼ teaspoon pepper, and ⅛ teaspoon salt in small bowl.

Why This Recipe Works Let's face it, frozen potato tots don't live up to our child-hood memories. And many recipes simply mix coarsely ground potato with flour and egg, which fry up into raw, dense nuggets. We found that parcooking the chopped potato in the microwave was a step in the right direction, but the tots were still too heavy. Reducing the flour and omitting the egg helped, but they were still not light and fluffy. To minimize the gluey texture of potato starch, we tried processing the potatoes with water. Perfection. This step rinsed off the excess starch, and a small amount of salt in the mixture kept the interior downy white.

CRISPY POTATO TOTS

MAKES 48 POTATO TOTS

If any large pieces of potato remain after processing, chop them coarsely by hand. To make handling the uncooked tots easier, use a wet knife blade and wet hands. Once the tots are added to the hot oil, they may stick together; resist the temptation to stir and break them apart until after they have browned and set. You will need at least a 6-quart Dutch oven for this recipe.

2¼ teaspoons salt
2½ pounds russet potatoes, peeled and cut into 1½-inch pieces
1½ tablespoons all-purpose flour
½ teaspoon pepper
1 quart peanut or vegetable oil

1. Whisk 1 cup water and salt together in bowl until salt dissolves. Pulse potatoes and salt water in food processor until coarsely ground, 10 to 12 pulses, stirring occasionally. Drain mixture in fine-mesh strainer, pressing potatoes with rubber spatula until dry (liquid should measure about 1½ cups); discard liquid. Transfer potatoes to bowl and microwave, uncovered, until dry and sticky, 8 to 10 minutes, stirring halfway through cooking.

2. Stir flour and pepper into potatoes. Spread potato mixture into thin layer over large sheet of aluminum foil and let cool for 10 minutes. Push potatoes to center of foil and place foil and potatoes in 8-inch square baking pan. Push foil into corners and up sides of pan, smoothing it flush to pan. Press potato mixture tightly and evenly into pan. Freeze, uncovered, until firm, about 30 minutes.

3. Meanwhile, adjust oven rack to middle position and heat oven to 200 degrees. Set wire rack in rimmed baking sheet. Add oil to large Dutch oven until it measures about ¾ inch deep and heat over high heat until 375 degrees. Using foil overhang, lift potatoes from pan and cut into 48 pieces (5 cuts in 1 direction and 7 in other). Fry half of potato tots until golden brown and crisp, 5 to 7 minutes, stirring only after they are browned and set. Transfer to prepared baking sheet and place in oven. Return oil to 375 degrees and repeat with remaining potato tots. Serve.

To Make Ahead Let fried potato tots cool, transfer to zipper-lock bag, and freeze for up to 1 month. To serve, adjust oven rack to middle position and heat oven to 400 degrees. Place potato tots on rimmed baking sheet and bake until heated through, 12 to 15 minutes.

CRISPY POTATO TOTS FOR A CROWD
Double all ingredients for Crispy Potato Tots. Process and drain potato mixture in 2 batches. Microwave entire potato mixture for 12 to 14 minutes, stirring halfway through cooking. Spread potato mixture over large sheet of foil to cool and press into 13 by 9-inch baking pan. After freezing, cut potato rectangle in half crosswise before cutting into potato tots per recipe. Fry in 4 batches.

BACON-RANCH POTATO TOTS
Stir 1 tablespoon cider vinegar into potatoes after microwaving. Add 4 slices finely chopped cooked bacon, 1 teaspoon onion powder, ½ teaspoon garlic powder, and ½ teaspoon dried dill to potatoes with flour in step 2.

PARMESAN-ROSEMARY POTATO TOTS
Stir 2 minced garlic cloves into drained potatoes before microwaving. Add 1 cup grated Parmesan cheese and 2 tablespoons minced fresh rosemary to potatoes with flour in step 2.

SOUTHWESTERN POTATO TOTS
Add ½ cup shredded smoked gouda cheese, 3 tablespoons minced fresh cilantro, and 2 tablespoons minced jarred jalapeños to potatoes with flour in step 2.

BEER-BATTERED ONION RINGS

SERVES 4 TO 6

In step 1, do not soak the onion rounds longer than 2 hours or they will turn soft and become too saturated to crisp properly. Ordinary yellow onions will produce acceptable rings here. We like full-bodied beers like Sam Adams in this recipe. Cider vinegar can be used in place of malt vinegar. You will need at least a 6-quart Dutch oven for this recipe.

- 2 sweet onions, peeled and sliced into ½-inch-thick rounds
- 3 cups ale or lager
- 2 teaspoons malt vinegar
  Salt and pepper
- 2 quarts peanut or vegetable oil
- ¾ cup all-purpose flour
- ¾ cup cornstarch
- 1 teaspoon baking powder

1. Place onion rounds, 2 cups beer, vinegar, ½ teaspoon salt, and ½ teaspoon pepper in 1-gallon zipper-lock bag; refrigerate for 30 minutes or up to 2 hours.

2. Line rimmed baking sheet with triple layer of paper towels. Add oil to large Dutch oven until it measures about 1½ inches deep and heat over medium-high heat to 350 degrees. While oil is heating, combine flour, cornstarch, baking powder, ½ teaspoon salt, and ¼ teaspoon pepper in large bowl. Slowly whisk in ¾ cup beer until just combined (some lumps will remain). Whisk in remaining beer as needed, 1 tablespoon at a time, until batter falls from whisk in steady stream and leaves faint trail across surface of batter.

3. Adjust oven rack to middle position and heat oven to 200 degrees. Remove onions from refrigerator and pour off liquid. Pat onion rounds dry with paper towels and separate into rings. Transfer one-third of rings to batter. One at a time, carefully transfer battered rings to oil. Fry until rings are golden brown and crisp, about 5 minutes, flipping halfway through frying. Drain rings on prepared baking sheet, season with salt and pepper to taste, and transfer to oven. Return oil to 350 degrees and repeat 2 more times with remaining onion rings and batter. Serve.

Troubleshooting Onion Rings

1. To prevent raw, crunchy onions, soak rings in combination of beer, vinegar, and salt, which softens and flavors raw onion.

2. If batter is too thick, rings will be doughy; too thin and it will run off. Add beer gradually until batter falls from whisk to form ribbon trail.

3. To prevent fused rings, fry battered onion rings in small batches and transfer to hot oil one at a time so they don't stick together.

Why This Recipe Works We wanted sweet, tender onions for our beer-battered onion rings. We found that sweet onions worked best, and after testing many different batters, we settled on a beer, flour, salt, pepper, baking powder, and cornstarch batter. The beer gave the coating flavor, and the carbonation also provided lift to the batter. Baking powder yielded a coating that was thick and substantial, yet light, while cornstarch added crunch to the coating. Before frying our onion rings, we soaked the onions in a mixture of beer, malt vinegar, and salt to soften them and build flavor.

steakhouse specials

Why This Recipe Works The sizzling arrival of cast-iron plates of marinated steak-house steak tips is often the most exciting part about them, because in reality, the first bite reveals chewy meat in an overly sweet marinade. For tender tips with great beefy flavor, we relied on sirloin steak tips. As for the marinade, we replaced the usual culprits—ketchup, barbecue sauce, and cola—with a mixture of soy sauce, oil, dark brown sugar, and tomato paste for enhanced meaty flavor and maximum char.

GRILLED STEAKHOUSE STEAK TIPS

SERVES 4 TO 6

Sirloin steak tips are often labeled "flap meat" and are sold as whole steaks, strips, and pieces. For even pieces, buy a whole steak of uniform size and cut it up yourself.

- ⅓ cup soy sauce
- ⅓ cup vegetable oil
- 3 tablespoons packed dark brown sugar
- 5 garlic cloves, minced
- 1 tablespoon tomato paste
- 1 tablespoon paprika
- ½ teaspoon pepper
- ¼ teaspoon cayenne pepper
- 2½ pounds sirloin steak tips, trimmed

1. Whisk soy sauce, oil, sugar, garlic, tomato paste, paprika, pepper, and cayenne together in bowl until sugar dissolves; transfer to zipper-lock bag. Pat beef dry with paper towels. Prick beef all over with fork and cut into 2½-inch pieces. Add meat to bag with soy sauce mixture and refrigerate for at least 2 or up to 24 hours, turning occasionally.

2A. For a Charcoal Grill Open bottom vent completely. Light large chimney starter filled with charcoal briquettes (6 quarts). When top coals are partially covered with ash, pour evenly over grill. Set cooking grate in place, cover, and open lid vent completely. Heat grill until hot, about 5 minutes. Leave burners on high.

2B. For a Gas Grill Turn all burners to high, cover, and heat grill until hot, about 15 minutes.

3. Clean and oil cooking grate. Grill beef (covered if using gas) until charred and registers 130 to 135 degrees (for medium), 8 to 10 minutes. Transfer meat to platter, tent loosely with aluminum foil, and let rest for 5 to 10 minutes. Serve.

Common Ingredients, Uncommon Results

We engineered our marinade to give the steak tips maximum meaty flavor and satisfying texture. These familiar ingredients make a strong team, each with its own part to play.

DARK BROWN SUGAR
Delivers depth, complexity, and a caramelized, crusty char.

VEGETABLE OIL
Distributes flavors and activates oil-soluble flavor compounds, such as those found in garlic.

TOMATO PASTE
Adds background savor and enough body to help the marinade cling.

SOY SAUCE
Its salt penetrates to deeply season the meat. Its glutamates boost meaty flavor.

Why This Recipe Works Adding sugar to steak may at first seem strange, but trust us, the sugar provides a hint of sweetness and helps create the ultimate charred crust. To keep the sugar-salt mixture from sliding off the steaks or melting away on the grill, we sprinkled the mixture onto the steaks, let them rest for at least an hour, and then seasoned the moist steaks again just before hitting the heat. Though we typically discourage fussing with meat once it's on the grill, in this case, moving the steaks around as they cooked minimized the hot spots and evened out the heavy browning caused by the sugar.

GRILLED SUGAR STEAK

SERVES 4 TO 6

These steaks need to sit for at least 1 hour after seasoning. You will have about 1 teaspoon of sugar mixture left over after the final seasoning of the steaks in step 3. If your steaks are more than 1 inch thick, pound them to 1 inch.

¼ cup sugar
3 tablespoons kosher salt
4 (9- to 11-ounce) boneless strip steaks,
   1 inch thick, trimmed
   Pepper

1. Mix sugar and salt together in bowl. Pat steaks dry with paper towels and place in 13 by 9-inch baking dish. Evenly sprinkle 1½ teaspoons sugar mixture on top of each steak. Flip steaks and sprinkle second side of each steak with 1½ teaspoons sugar mixture. Cover with plastic wrap and let sit at room temperature for 1 hour or refrigerate for up to 24 hours.

2A. For a Charcoal Grill Open bottom vent completely. Light large chimney starter mounded with charcoal briquettes (7 quarts). When top coals are partially covered with ash, pour evenly over half of grill. Set cooking grate in place, cover, and open lid vent completely. Heat grill until hot, about 5 minutes.

2B. For a Gas Grill Turn all burners to high, cover, and heat grill until hot, about 15 minutes. Turn all burners to medium-high.

3. Clean and oil cooking grate. Transfer steaks to plate. (Steaks will be wet; do not pat dry.) Sprinkle steaks with 1 teaspoon sugar mixture on each side, then season with pepper.

4. Place steaks on hotter side of grill (if using charcoal) and cook (covered if using gas) until evenly charred on first side, 3 to 5 minutes, rotating and switching positions for even cooking. Flip steaks and continue to cook until meat registers 120 to 125 degrees (for medium-rare), 3 to 5 minutes, rotating and switching positions for even cooking.

5. Transfer steaks to wire rack set in rimmed baking sheet and let rest for 5 minutes. Slice and serve.

On the Road: A Denver Gem

Shaped like a circus tent, Bastien's Restaurant is a historic family-owned restaurant in Denver, Colorado, where grilled sugar steak has been the signature dish and a customer favorite for decades. The restaurant sits prominently on Colfax Avenue, a 50-odd-mile street that bisects Denver. It's a notorious street of contrasts (one stretch abuts the state capital while the next teems with unlawful trade, and gentrification mixes with grit along its entire stretch), but as Denver's defining throughway, it was granted Heritage Corridor status in the late 1990s to help protect and preserve Bastien's and many other mid-century architectural gems.

BROILED STEAKS

SERVES 4

To minimize smoking, be sure to trim as much exterior fat and gristle as possible from the steaks before cooking. Try to purchase steaks of a similar size and shape for this recipe. Note that you will need 2 cups of salt to line the roasting pan; the salt will absorb drippings from the steak and minimize smoking.

4 tablespoons unsalted butter, softened
1 teaspoon minced fresh thyme
1 teaspoon Dijon mustard
 Salt and pepper
1 (13 by 9-inch) disposable aluminum roasting pan, 3 inches deep
4 strip, rib-eye, or tenderloin steaks, 1 to 2 inches thick, trimmed

1. Adjust oven racks to upper-middle and lower-middle positions and heat oven to 375 degrees. Beat butter, thyme, mustard, ¼ teaspoon salt, and ¼ teaspoon pepper in bowl and refrigerate.

2. Spread 2 cups salt over bottom of aluminum pan. Pat steaks dry with paper towels, season with salt and pepper, and transfer to wire rack. Set rack over aluminum pan and transfer to lower oven rack. Cook 6 to 10 minutes, then remove pan from oven. Flip steaks, pat dry with paper towels, and let rest for 10 minutes.

3. Heat broiler. Transfer pan to upper oven rack and broil steaks, flipping every 2 to 4 minutes, until meat registers 120 to 125 degrees (for medium-rare), 6 to 16 minutes, depending on thickness of steaks (see chart). Transfer steaks to platter, top with reserved butter mixture, and tent with aluminum foil. Let rest for 5 minutes. Serve.

Perfectly Broiled Steaks

The first step to perfectly broiled steaks is knowing exactly how thick your steaks are. Using a ruler, measure each steak and then follow the guidelines below.

STEAK THICKNESS	PRECOOK	BROIL
1 inch	6 minutes	Turn steaks every 2 minutes
1½ inches	8 minutes	Turn steaks every 3 minutes
2 inches	10 minutes	Turn steaks every 4 minutes

Broiler Prep

Since oven-rack positioning varies greatly from model to model, we suggest you ensure correct positioning with a dry run before turning on your oven.

Before preheating your oven and with your oven racks adjusted to the upper-middle and lower-middle positions, place a wire rack on top of a 3-inch-deep disposable aluminum pan and place it on the upper-middle rack. Place the steaks on top of the rack and use a ruler to measure the distance between the top of the steaks and the heating element of the broiler. For optimal searing, there should be ½ inch to 1 inch of space.

If there is more than 1 inch of space, here's how to close the gap: Elevate the aluminum pan by placing it on an inverted rimmed baking sheet; use a deeper-sided disposable aluminum pan; or stack multiple aluminum pans inside one another. If there's less than ½ inch of space, adjust the oven rack or use a shallower pan.

Why This Recipe Works We usually rely on a red-hot skillet or the grill for our recipes that include putting a crusty sear on steaks, but we wondered if our oven's broiler could do the job just as well. Starting the steaks at a moderate temperature took the chill off, and letting them rest before putting them under the broiler produced evenly cooked meat. Covering the bottom of the pan with salt helped absorb the grease from the meat and greatly minimized smoking. To ensure a good sear on our steaks, we placed a wire rack over a 3-inch disposable pan, to bring the meat closer to the heating element.

Why This Recipe Works In order to achieve a respectable crust on our restaurant-style grilled steak, the exterior of the meat must be dry. After trying numerous drying-out methods, including salting and aging, we considered the freezer. The freezer's intensely dry environment sufficiently dehydrated the steaks' exteriors, and since we were only freezing them for a short time, the interiors remained tender and juicy. We rubbed the steaks with a mixture of salt and cornstarch before freezing. The salt ensured they were well seasoned, and cornstarch, a champ at absorbing moisture, allowed us to cut the freezing time in half.

CHAR-GRILLED STEAKS

SERVES 4

Serve with one of the sauces that follow, if desired.

- 1 teaspoon salt
- 1 teaspoon cornstarch
- 4 strip, rib-eye, or tenderloin steaks, about 1½ inches thick, trimmed
  Pepper
- 1 recipe steak sauce (recipes follow)

1. Combine salt and cornstarch. Pat steaks dry with paper towels and rub with salt mixture. Arrange on wire rack set in rimmed baking sheet and freeze until steaks are firm and dry to touch, at least 30 minutes or up to 1 hour.

2A. For a Charcoal Grill Open bottom vent completely. Light large chimney starter filled with charcoal briquettes (6 quarts). When top coals are partially covered with ash, pour evenly over grill. Set cooking grate in place, cover, and open lid vent completely. Heat grill until hot, about 5 minutes.

2B. For a Gas Grill Turn all burners to high, cover, and heat grill until hot, about 15 minutes. Leave burners on high.

3. Clean and oil cooking grate. Season steaks with pepper. Grill (covered if using gas) until meat registers 120 to 125 degrees (for medium-rare), 8 to 16 minutes, flipping steaks halfway through cooking. Transfer to plate, tent with aluminum foil, and let rest for 5 minutes. Serve.

CLASSIC STEAK SAUCE
MAKES 1¼ CUPS
Raisins add depth and sweetness to this sauce.

- ½ cup boiling water
- ⅓ cup raisins
- ¼ cup ketchup
- 3 tablespoons Worcestershire sauce
- 2 tablespoons Dijon mustard
- 2 tablespoons distilled white vinegar
  Salt and pepper

Combine water and raisins in bowl and let sit, covered, until raisins are plump, about 5 minutes.

Puree raisin mixture, ketchup, Worcestershire, mustard, and vinegar in blender until smooth, 30 seconds to 1 minute. Season with salt and pepper to taste. (Sauce can be refrigerated for 1 week.)

SPICY RED PEPPER STEAK SAUCE
MAKES 1¼ CUPS
This peppery sauce is a simplified version of the Spanish classic, romesco.

- 1 slice hearty white sandwich bread, toasted until golden and torn into pieces
- 2 tablespoons slivered almonds, toasted
- 1 cup jarred roasted red peppers, drained
- 1 plum tomato, seeded and chopped
- 2 teaspoons red wine vinegar
- 1 garlic clove, minced
- ⅛ teaspoon cayenne pepper
- 1 tablespoon extra-virgin olive oil
  Salt

Process bread and almonds in food processor until finely ground, about 10 seconds. Add red peppers, tomato, vinegar, garlic, and cayenne and process until smooth, about 1 minute. Season with salt to taste. (Sauce can be refrigerated for 1 week.)

GARLIC-PARSLEY STEAK SAUCE
MAKES 1¼ CUPS
A little of this aromatic vinaigrette goes a long way.

- ½ cup finely chopped fresh parsley
- ¼ cup minced red onion
- ¼ cup red wine vinegar
- 2 garlic cloves, minced
- ⅛ teaspoon red pepper flakes
- ¼ cup extra virgin olive oil
  Salt and pepper

Combine parsley, onion, vinegar, garlic, and pepper flakes in bowl. Slowly whisk in oil. Season with salt and pepper to taste. (Sauce can be refrigerated for 1 week.)

GRILLED COWBOY-CUT RIB EYES

SERVES 4 TO 6

Don't start grilling until the steaks' internal temperatures have reached 55 degrees. Otherwise, the times and temperatures in this recipe will be inaccurate.

2 (1¼- to 1½-pound) double-cut bone-in rib-eye steaks, 1¾ to 2 inches thick, trimmed
4 teaspoons kosher salt
2 teaspoons vegetable oil
2 teaspoons pepper

1. Set wire rack inside rimmed baking sheet. Pat steaks dry with paper towels and sprinkle all over with salt. Place steaks on prepared rack and let stand at room temperature until meat registers 55 degrees, about 1 hour. Rub steaks with oil and sprinkle with pepper.

2A. For a Charcoal Grill Open bottom vent halfway. Arrange 4 quarts unlit charcoal briquettes in even layer over half of grill. Light large chimney starter one-third filled with charcoal briquettes (2 quarts). When top coals are partially covered with ash, pour evenly over unlit coals. Set cooking grate in place, cover, and open lid vent halfway. Heat grill until hot, about 5 minutes.

2B. For a Gas Grill Turn all burners to high, cover, and heat grill until hot, about 15 minutes. Turn primary burner to medium-low and turn off other burner(s). Adjust primary burner as needed to maintain grill temperature of 300 degrees.

3. Clean and oil cooking grate. Place steaks on cooler side of grill with bones facing fire. Cover and cook until steaks register 75 degrees, 10 to 20 minutes. Flip steaks, keeping bones facing fire. Cover and continue to cook until steaks register 95 degrees, 10 to 20 minutes.

4. If using charcoal, slide steaks to hotter part of grill. If using gas, remove steaks from grill, turn primary burner to high, and heat until hot, about 5 minutes; place steaks over primary burner. Cover and cook until well browned and steaks register 120 degrees (for medium-rare), about 4 minutes per side. Transfer steaks to clean wire rack set in rimmed baking sheet, tent loosely with foil, and let rest for 15 minutes. Transfer steaks to carving board, cut meat from bone, and slice into ½-inch-thick slices. Serve.

In Praise of Cowboy Steaks

Rib-eye steaks are deeply marbled, tender, and beefy—they're from the same part of the steer that's used for prime rib. Bone-in steaks (like these) have more flavor than boneless, and the bone protects against overcooking. Of special interest is the exterior band of fat and meat on a rib eye called the deckle; connoisseurs say it is the most flavorful part of the cow.

BIGGER IS BETTER
Cowboy-cut rib eyes are double-thick bone-in steaks. They take longer to cook than single-serving rib eyes, so they have more time to soak up smoky grill flavor.

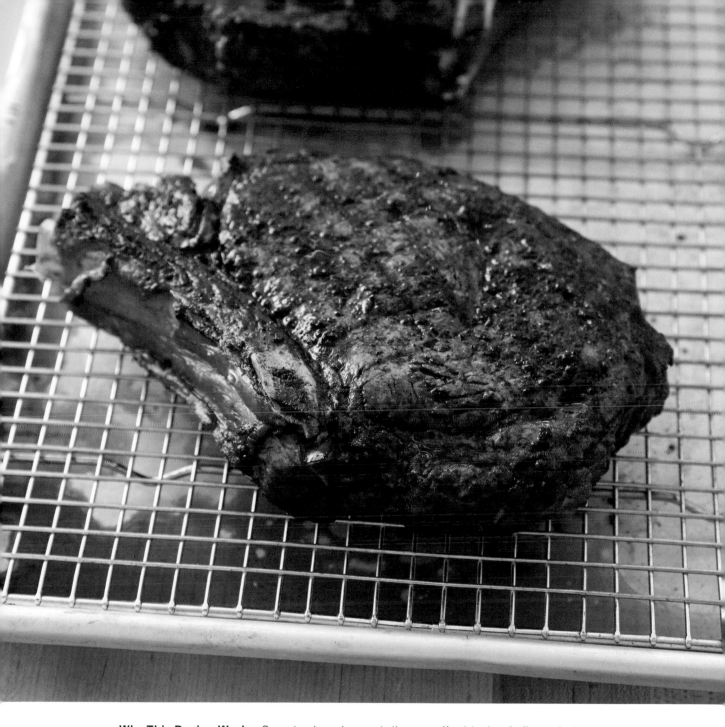

Why This Recipe Works Oversized cowboy-cut rib eyes offer big, beefy flavor, but cooking the huge steaks all the way through while achieving a flavorful seared crust is challenging. We used a bare minimum of seasonings—salt, pepper, and oil—to highlight the flavor of the steaks. To cook them, we opted for a low and slow approach to start. To keep the fire burning long enough, we layered unlit coals under lit ones. We let the steaks come to room temperature before grilling to cut down on cooking time, and then slow-roasted the steaks on the cooler side of the grill until they were almost done. A quick sear over hot coals gave them a flavorful dark crust.

GRILLED STEAK BURGERS

SERVES 4

Use kaiser rolls or other hearty buns for these substantial burgers.

Burgers

8 tablespoons unsalted butter
2 garlic cloves, minced
2 teaspoons onion powder
1 teaspoon pepper
½ teaspoon salt
2 teaspoons soy sauce
1½ pounds 90 percent lean ground sirloin
4 hamburger buns

Steak Sauce

2 tablespoons tomato paste
⅔ cup beef broth
⅓ cup raisins
2 tablespoons soy sauce
2 tablespoons Dijon mustard
2 tablespoons balsamic vinegar
1 tablespoon Worcestershire sauce

1. For the Burgers Melt butter in 8-inch skillet over medium-low heat. Add garlic, onion powder, pepper, and salt and cook until fragrant, about 1 minute. Pour all but 1 tablespoon butter mixture into bowl and let cool for about 5 minutes.

2. For the Steak Sauce Meanwhile, add tomato paste to skillet and cook over medium heat until paste begins to darken, 1 to 2 minutes. Stir in broth, raisins, soy sauce, mustard, vinegar, and Worcestershire and simmer until raisins plump, about 5 minutes. Process sauce in blender until smooth, about 30 seconds; transfer to bowl.

3. Add 5 tablespoons cooled butter mixture and soy sauce to ground beef and gently knead until well combined. Shape into four ¾-inch-thick patties and press shallow divot in center of each. Brush each patty all over with 1 tablespoon steak sauce. Combine remaining 2 tablespoons cooled butter mixture with 2 tablespoons steak sauce; set aside.

4A. For a Charcoal Grill Open bottom vent completely. Light large chimney starter filled with charcoal briquettes (6 quarts). When top coals are partially covered with ash, pour evenly over grill. Set cooking grate in place, cover, and open lid vent completely. Heat grill until hot, about 5 minutes.

4B. For a Gas Grill Turn all burners to high, cover, and heat grill until hot, about 15 minutes. Leave burners on high.

5. Clean and oil cooking grate. Grill burgers (covered if using gas) until meat registers 120 to 125 degrees (for medium-rare), 3 to 4 minutes per side, or 130 to 135 degrees (for medium), 4 to 5 minutes per side. Transfer burgers to plate, tent loosely with aluminum foil, and let rest for 5 to 10 minutes. Brush cut side of buns with butter–steak sauce mixture. Grill buns, cut side down, until golden, 2 to 3 minutes. Place burgers on buns. Serve with remaining steak sauce.

Butter Makes It Better

Why are our steakhouse burgers so good? Yep, butter. Ground sirloin has great flavor, but it's a little dry: Butter helps keep the burgers moist. Butter also gives richness and body to our homemade steak sauce. And we slather butter on the buns before toasting them on the grill.

FLAVORED BUTTER
For the meat, sauce, and buns.

Why This Recipe Works We wanted a burger with the big beefy flavor and crusty char of a grilled steak. Ground sirloin, the most flavorful ground beef, was a natural choice, but unfortunately it's also quite lean. A seasoned butter added richness to the sirloin, but something was missing. Steak sauce! In about five minutes, we simmered up our own intensely flavored sauce, perfect for serving with the burger, smearing on the bun, and even mixing into the beef before cooking.

Why This Recipe Works Despite their name, grillades are not grilled; rather, they are thinly sliced cuts of meat browned and stewed in a supersavory tomato-based gravy. For consistency and ease we opted for pork blade chops (with the bones cut off) which cooked evenly and held up to stewing. When it came time to make a roux for the base of our gravy, dry-toasting the flour in a skillet in advance helped cut down on the cooking time. Adding our own Cajun seasoning spice blend, a traditional mix of vegetables, and a dash of Tabasco provided heat and complexity to this iconic Louisiana dish.

PORK GRILLADES

SERVES 6 TO 8

We prefer pork blade chops because they hold up to stewing better than loin chops. Blade chops aren't typically available boneless; ask your butcher to bone them for you. Use our Louisiana Seasoning (recipe follows) or your favorite store-bought variety.

1 cup all-purpose flour
8 (6- to 8-ounce) bone-in pork-blade-cut chops, ½ inch thick, bones discarded, and trimmed
2 tablespoons Louisiana Seasoning
Salt and pepper
½ cup vegetable oil
1 onion, chopped
1 green bell pepper, stemmed, seeded, and chopped
1 celery rib, chopped
2 garlic cloves, minced
2 cups chicken broth
1 (14.5-ounce) can whole peeled tomatoes, crushed by hand
2 slices bacon
1 tablespoon Worcestershire sauce
1 bay leaf
1 teaspoon Tabasco sauce, plus extra for serving
4 cups cooked white rice
2 scallions, sliced thin

1. Adjust oven rack to lower-middle position and heat oven to 350 degrees. Toast ¼ cup flour in small skillet over medium heat, stirring constantly, until just beginning to brown, about 3 minutes; set aside.

2. Season chops with 1½ teaspoons Louisiana Seasoning, salt, and pepper. Whisk remaining ¾ cup flour and remaining 1½ tablespoons Louisiana Seasoning together in shallow dish. Working with 1 chop at a time, dredge in seasoned flour, shaking off excess; transfer chops to plate.

3. Heat oil in Dutch oven over medium heat until shimmering. Add 4 chops and cook until browned, 3 to 5 minutes per side; transfer to plate. Repeat with remaining 4 chops.

4. Remove all but ¼ cup oil from Dutch oven and return to medium heat. Add toasted flour to pot and cook, whisking constantly, until deep brown, about 2 minutes. Add onion, bell pepper, celery, and 1 teaspoon salt and cook, stirring often, until vegetables are just softened, about 3 minutes. Add garlic and cook until fragrant, about 30 seconds.

5. Stir in broth, tomatoes and their juice, bacon, Worcestershire, and bay leaf, scraping up any browned bits. Nestle chops into liquid and add any accumulated pork juices from plate. Bring to simmer, cover, and transfer to oven. Cook until fork slips easily in and out of pork, about 1 hour.

6. Remove grillades from oven. Discard bacon and bay leaf; stir in Tabasco. Season with salt and pepper to taste. Serve over rice, sprinkled with scallions and passing extra Tabasco.

LOUISIANA SEASONING
MAKES ABOUT ¾ CUP

5 tablespoons paprika
2 tablespoons garlic powder
1 tablespoon dried thyme
1 tablespoon cayenne pepper
1 tablespoon celery salt
1 tablespoon salt
1 tablespoon pepper

Combine all ingredients in bowl.

The Right Chop

The problem with buying pork chops is that markets call chops by different names. Since grillades are braised, it's important that you don't buy a lean chop, which would be better quickly grilled or sautéed. Flavorful blade chops may not look pretty, but their fat and connective tissue softens and melts out during braising.

BAKED STUFFED SHRIMP

SERVES 4 TO 6

In a pinch, chicken broth can be substituted for the clam juice. A sturdy rimmed baking sheet can be used in place of the broiler pan bottom. Shrimp that are labeled U12 contain 12 or less shrimp per pound.

- 4 slices hearty white sandwich bread, torn into quarters
- ½ cup mayonnaise
- ¼ cup bottled clam juice
- ¼ cup finely chopped fresh parsley
- 4 scallions, chopped fine
- 1 tablespoon Dijon mustard
- 2 garlic cloves, minced
- 2 teaspoons grated lemon zest plus 1 tablespoon juice
- ⅛ teaspoon cayenne pepper
  Salt
- 1¼ pounds colossal shrimp (U12), peeled and deveined

1. Adjust oven rack to upper-middle position and heat oven to 375 degrees. Pulse bread in food processor to coarse crumbs, about 10 pulses. Transfer crumbs to broiler pan bottom and bake until golden and dry, 8 to 10 minutes, stirring halfway through cooking time. Remove crumbs from oven and reduce temperature to 275 degrees.

2. Combine toasted bread crumbs, mayonnaise, clam juice, parsley, scallions, mustard, garlic, lemon zest and juice, cayenne, and ¼ teaspoon salt in bowl.

3. Pat shrimp dry with paper towels and season with salt. Grease empty broiler pan bottom. To butterfly shrimp, use sharp paring knife to cut along (but not through) vein line, then open up shrimp like a book. Using tip of paring knife, cut 1-inch opening through center of shrimp. Arrange shrimp cut side down on prepared pan. Divide bread-crumb mixture among shrimp, pressing to adhere. Bake until shrimp are opaque, 20 to 25 minutes.

4. Remove shrimp from oven and heat broiler. Broil shrimp until crumbs are deep golden brown and crispy, 1 to 3 minutes. Serve.

CREOLE BAKED STUFFED SHRIMP WITH SAUSAGE
The smoky, meaty flavor of kielbasa is a nice foil to the sweet shrimp in this variation.
Omit cayenne and add 1 teaspoon Creole seasoning in step 2. Fold 4 ounces kielbasa sausage, chopped fine, into filling and proceed as directed.

Easy Steps to Baked Stuffed Shrimp
Cutting a hole through the center of each butterflied shrimp helps the shrimp hold on to the stuffing.

1. Use paring knife to cut along but not through vein line, then open up shrimp like a book. Cut 1-inch opening all the way through center of shrimp.

2. After shrimp have been butterflied and openings have been cut, flip shrimp over onto broiler pan so that they will curl around stuffing.

3. Divide stuffing among shrimp, firmly pressing stuffing into opening and to edges of shrimp.

Why This Recipe Works There are often two problems with baked stuffed shrimp: mushy, bland stuffing and shrimp as chewy as rubber bands. We wanted a recipe that produced crisp, flavorful stuffing and perfectly cooked shrimp. For the stuffing, tasters preferred the sweet flavor of fresh bread crumbs, toasted to ensure crispness. Butterflying the shrimp allowed us to press the stuffing into the shrimp—as the shrimp contracted in the oven, the stuffing was sealed into place. To prevent over-cooked shrimp, yet still achieve crisp stuffing, we cooked the shrimp for a longer time at a lower temperature.

FOOLPROOF CHICKEN CORDON BLEU

SERVES 4 TO 6

To help prevent the filling from leaking, thoroughly chill the stuffed breasts before breading. We like Black Forest ham here.

25 Ritz crackers (about ¾ sleeve)
4 slices hearty white sandwich bread, torn into quarters
6 tablespoons unsalted butter, melted
8 thin slices deli ham (8 ounces)
8 ounces Swiss cheese, shredded (2 cups)
4 (8-ounce) boneless, skinless chicken breasts, trimmed
Salt and pepper
3 large eggs
2 tablespoons Dijon mustard
1 cup all-purpose flour

1. Adjust oven racks to lowest and middle positions and heat oven to 450 degrees. Pulse crackers and bread in food processor until coarsely ground, about 15 pulses. Drizzle in butter; pulse a few times to incorporate. Bake crumbs on rimmed baking sheet on middle rack, stirring occasionally, until light brown, 3 to 5 minutes. Transfer to shallow dish. Do not turn oven off.

2. Top each ham slice with ¼ cup cheese and roll tightly; set aside. Pat chicken dry with paper towels. Using paring knife, cut into thickest part of each chicken breast to create deep pocket with opening of 3 to 4 inches. Stuff each breast with 2 ham-and-cheese rolls and press closed. Season both sides of chicken with salt and pepper. Transfer chicken to plate, cover with plastic wrap, and refrigerate for at least 20 minutes.

3. Beat eggs and mustard in second shallow dish. Place flour in third shallow dish. One at a time, coat stuffed chicken lightly with flour, dip into egg mixture, and dredge in crumbs, pressing to adhere. (Breaded chicken can be refrigerated, covered, for 1 day.) Transfer chicken to clean rimmed baking sheet. Bake on lowest rack until bottom of chicken is golden brown, about 10 minutes, and then move baking sheet to middle rack and reduce oven temperature to 400 degrees. Bake until golden brown and chicken registers 160 degrees, 20 to 25 minutes. Transfer to platter, tent with aluminum foil, and let rest for 5 minutes. Serve.

Stuffing, Streamlined

1. Using paring knife, cut into thickest part of chicken breast to create deep pocket with opening of 3 to 4 inches.

2. Stuff each pocket with 2 ham-and-cheese rolls and seal. Refrigerate chicken for at least 20 minutes before breading.

Why This Recipe Works Making chicken cordon bleu can be fussy; we wanted an easier way. We found cutting a pocket into the breast to be much more efficient than the traditional method of pounding and rolling. To get the same swirl effect achieved by rolling the chicken around the ham and cheese, we simply rolled the ham slices into cylinders around shredded cheese and tucked the cylinders into each chicken breast. Adding a healthy dose of Dijon mustard to the egg wash boosted the flavor of our chicken, as did supplementing homemade bread crumbs with buttery Ritz cracker crumbs.

Why This Recipe Works It can be a hassle to stand over a pot of caramelized onions when a craving for this French classic strikes. We looked to the slow cooker for simplification. Replicating the meaty flavor of the soup was more of a challenge, as the slow, long cooking can result in washed-out flavor. We found that soy sauce, sherry, and thyme added early on helped boost flavor and the addition of beef bones to store-bought chicken and beef broths reproduced the rich meatiness of the classic. Apple butter highlighted the flavor of the onions without drawing attention to itself and also helped make for a rich, silky broth.

SLOW-COOKER FRENCH ONION SOUP

SERVES 6 TO 8

After halving the onions, slice them through the root end for hearty slices that will hold up to long cooking. Beef bones are stocked in the frozen foods aisle of most supermarkets.

Soup

 2 pounds beef bones
 4 tablespoons unsalted butter
 4 pounds yellow onions, halved and sliced through root end into ¼-inch-thick slices
    Salt and pepper
 1 tablespoon packed brown sugar
 1 teaspoon minced fresh thyme
 ¾ cup apple butter
 ¾ cup dry sherry
 5 tablespoons all-purpose flour
 ¼ cup soy sauce
 2 cups chicken broth
 2 cups beef broth

Cheese Croutons

 1 small baguette, cut into ½-inch slices
10 ounces Gruyère cheese, shredded (2½ cups)

1. For the Soup Arrange beef bones on paper towel–lined plate. Microwave until well browned, 8 to 10 minutes. Meanwhile, set slow cooker to high. Add butter, cover, and cook until melted. Add onions, 2 teaspoons salt, 1 teaspoon pepper, brown sugar, and thyme. Stir apple butter, sherry, flour, and soy sauce together in small bowl until smooth. Pour over onions and toss to coat. Tuck bones under onions around edge of slow cooker. Cover and cook on high heat until onions are softened and deep golden brown, 10 to 12 hours (start checking onions after 8 hours). (Cooked onions can be refrigerated for 1 day.)

2. Remove bones from slow cooker. Heat broths in microwave until beginning to boil. Stir into slow cooker. Season with salt and pepper to taste.

3. For the Cheese Croutons Adjust oven rack to upper-middle position (about 6 inches from broiler element) and heat oven to 400 degrees. Arrange bread slices in single layer on baking sheet and bake until bread is golden at edges, about 10 minutes. Heat broiler. Divide cheese evenly among croutons and broil until melted and bubbly, 3 to 5 minutes.

4. Ladle soup into bowls and top each with 2 croutons. Serve.

Slicing Onions for French Onion Soup

For this soup, we found that cutting onions with the grain (rather than across it) yielded slices that retained their shape through 10 to 12 hours in the slow cooker.

1. Using chef's knife, trim off both ends of onion.

2. Turn onion onto cut end to steady it and slice in half, through root end.

3. Peel each half, place flat side down, and cut onion, lengthwise, into slices.

GARLIC MASHED POTATOES

SERVES 8 TO 10

Cutting the potatoes into ½-inch pieces ensures that the maximum surface area is exposed to soak up garlicky flavor.

  4 pounds russet potatoes, peeled, quartered, and cut into ½-inch pieces
12 tablespoons unsalted butter, cut into pieces
12 garlic cloves, minced
  1 teaspoon sugar
1½ cups half-and-half
 ½ cup water
     Salt and pepper

1. Place cut potatoes in colander. Rinse under cold running water until water runs clear. Drain thoroughly.

2. Melt 4 tablespoons butter in Dutch oven over medium heat. Cook garlic and sugar, stirring often, until sticky and straw colored, 3 to 4 minutes. Add rinsed potatoes, 1¼ cups half-and-half, water, and 1 teaspoon salt to pot and stir to combine. Bring to boil, then reduce heat to low and simmer, covered and stirring occasionally, until potatoes are tender and most of liquid is absorbed, 25 to 30 minutes.

3. Off heat, add remaining 8 tablespoons butter to pot and mash with potato masher until smooth. Using rubber spatula, fold in remaining ¼ cup half-and-half until liquid is absorbed and potatoes are creamy. Season with salt and pepper to taste. Serve.

Folk Remedies for Removing Garlic Odor

Garlic odor is hard to remove from your hands, but folk remedies for doing so abound, from washing with baking soda, vinegar, lemon juice, salt, or toothpaste to rubbing your hands on stainless steel. To find out if any of these tricks worked, we rubbed minced garlic on our hands and tried each method.

Washing with all of these substances lessened the odor at least a little, with baking soda and lemon juice outperforming the others, and rubbing one's hands on stainless steel succeeding just as well. Why? Some of the aromatic compounds in garlic are weak acids that can be neutralized by alkaline baking soda. Because not all aroma compounds are acidic, baking soda can't neutralize the odor 100 percent. Stainless steel removes some of the odor when iron atoms in the stainless steel exchange some of their electrons with sulfur atoms from the volatile aroma compounds, rendering them nonvolatile (nonstinky). Lemon juice contains lemon oils that dissolve the oil-soluble aroma compounds in garlic, plus its own fragrance masks the remaining odor. The bottom line? Lemon juice, baking soda, and stainless steel all help a little, but there is no magic cure for removing garlic smell from your hands.

Secrets to Great Roasted Garlic Flavor

1. To bloom garlic flavor and temper harshness, cook minced garlic and sugar in butter until garlic is sticky and straw-colored.

2. For deeply integrated garlic flavor, toss raw potatoes with garlic-butter mixture, add half-and-half and water directly to pot, cover, and gently cook until tender.

Why This Recipe Works Making mashed potatoes isn't typically a quick endeavor—add roasted garlic to the mix and you've really got a project on your hands. We wanted a streamlined recipe. We cut the potatoes into small pieces to promote even, quicker cooking. The small pieces also meant the potatoes could better soak up garlicky flavor. To mimic the flavor of roasted garlic, we sprinkled in a little sugar while sautéing the garlic. Finally, we simmered the potatoes in half-and-half, butter, and the sautéed garlic to avoid the "washing away" of flavor that can come from boiling in just water.

Why This Recipe Works To revive this classic potato dish, we first focused on how to prep the potatoes. Boiled cubed potatoes won out over shredded because they held their texture better in the casserole. Next, we sautéed onion and garlic, added cream and chicken broth (to cut the richness of the cream), and cooked the cubed potatoes in this mixture. Lemon juice and zest brought the casserole welcome brightness. For the crusty topping, we turned to an unexpected ingredient: frozen shredded hash browns. We sautéed the thawed hash browns in butter, cream, and chicken broth to enhance their flavor before topping the casserole.

DELMONICO POTATO CASSEROLE

SERVES 8 TO 10

We prefer the buttery flavor of Yukon Gold potatoes here, but all-purpose and red potatoes also work. Do not use russets—their high starch content will make the casserole gluey. For the topping, we had good results with Ore-Ida Country Style Hash Browns, available in the frozen foods aisle of most supermarkets.

  3 tablespoons unsalted butter
  1 onion, chopped fine
  2 garlic cloves, minced
  2½ cups heavy cream
  1½ cups chicken broth
  2½ pounds Yukon Gold potatoes, peeled
     and cut into ½-inch cubes
  ⅛ teaspoon ground nutmeg
     Salt and pepper
  1 teaspoon grated lemon zest
     plus 2 teaspoons juice
  5 cups frozen shredded hash brown potatoes,
     thawed and patted dry with paper towels
  1½ ounces Parmesan cheese, grated (¾ cup)
  ¼ cup finely chopped fresh chives

1. Adjust oven rack to upper-middle position and heat oven to 450 degrees. Melt 1 tablespoon butter in Dutch oven over medium-high heat. Cook onion until softened, about 3 minutes. Stir in garlic and cook until fragrant, about 30 seconds. Stir in 2 cups cream, 1 cup broth, Yukon Golds, nutmeg, 2 teaspoons salt, and 1 teaspoon pepper. Bring to boil, then reduce heat to medium and simmer until potatoes are translucent at edges and mixture is slightly thickened, about 10 minutes. Off heat, stir in lemon zest and juice.

2. Transfer potato mixture to 13 by 9-inch baking dish and bake until bubbling around edges and surface is just golden, about 20 minutes. Meanwhile, melt remaining 2 tablespoons butter in 12-inch nonstick skillet over medium-high heat. Cook shredded potatoes until beginning to brown, about 2 minutes. Add remaining ½ cup cream, remaining ½ cup broth, and ½ teaspoon pepper to skillet and cook, stirring occasionally, until liquid has evaporated, about 3 minutes. Off heat, stir in ½ cup Parmesan and 2 tablespoons chives.

3. Remove baking dish from oven and top with shredded potato mixture. Sprinkle with remaining ¼ cup Parmesan and continue to bake until top is golden brown, about 20 minutes. Let cool for 15 minutes. Sprinkle with remaining 2 tablespoons chives. Serve.

To Make Ahead Prepare through step 1, let cool completely, transfer to baking dish, and refrigerate, covered with plastic wrap, for 1 day. To serve, proceed as directed in step 2, increasing baking time to 25 to 30 minutes.

Potatoes with Panache

In 1837, Delmonico's opened in lower Manhattan and a restaurant star was born. Owned by two Swiss men, the restaurant served French-style cuisine and became the model for many other fashionable restaurants of the era. Its lavish dining room served such luxurious fare as lobster Newburg, baked Alaska, and their signature potato side dish, Delmonico potatoes. The potatoes were boiled, finely shredded, and cooked with milk and heavy cream. When an order came in, a serving of potatoes was sprinkled with Parmesan cheese and "gratinéed" under the broiler. The result was a potato gratin with a creamy interior and a crusty, cheesy topping. But look up a modern recipe for this dish and you'll most likely find a casserole made of overboiled chunks of potatoes baked in a creamy cheddar sauce and topped with more cheese. We wanted to bring back the simplicity and elegance of the original dish, but make it more practical to feed a crowd.

Why This Recipe Works These crispy, cheesy Parmesan potatoes promised to be a habit-forming snack, but first we had to figure out how best to cook the potatoes and how to get the cheese to stick to them. Using thinly sliced, creamy Yukon Gold potatoes meant they wouldn't dry out during roasting. We tossed the potato slices with seasoned cornstarch to promote crisping. Parmesan, rosemary, and a little more cornstarch made for a savory coating that clung evenly to the slices. Baked in a very hot oven until golden brown and served with a cool chive sour cream, these were just the potatoes we craved.

CRISPY PARMESAN POTATOES

SERVES 6 TO 8

Try to find potatoes that are 2½ to 3 inches long. Spray the baking sheet with an aerosol (not pump) vegetable oil spray. Use a good-quality Parmesan cheese here. Serve with Chive Sour Cream (recipe follows), if desired.

- 2 pounds medium Yukon gold potatoes, unpeeled
- 4 teaspoons cornstarch
  Salt and pepper
- 1 tablespoon extra-virgin olive oil
- 6 ounces Parmesan cheese, cut into 1-inch chunks
- 2 teaspoons minced fresh rosemary

1. Adjust oven rack to lower-middle position and heat oven to 500 degrees. Spray rimmed baking sheet liberally with vegetable oil spray. Cut thin slice from 2 opposing long sides of each potato; discard slices. Cut potatoes crosswise into ½-inch-thick slices and transfer to large bowl.

2. Combine 2 teaspoons cornstarch, 1 teaspoon salt, and 1 teaspoon pepper in small bowl. Sprinkle cornstarch mixture over potatoes and toss until potatoes are thoroughly coated and cornstarch is no longer visible. Add oil and toss to coat.

3. Arrange potatoes in single layer on prepared sheet and bake until golden brown on top, about 20 minutes.

4. Meanwhile, process Parmesan, rosemary, ½ teaspoon pepper, and remaining 2 teaspoons cornstarch in food processor until cheese is finely ground, about 1 minute.

5. Remove potatoes from oven. Sprinkle Parmesan mixture evenly over and between potatoes (cheese should cover surface of baking sheet), pressing on potatoes with back of spoon to adhere. Using two forks, flip slices over into same spot on sheet.

6. Bake until cheese between potatoes turns light golden brown, 5 to 7 minutes. Transfer sheet to wire rack and let potatoes cool for 15 minutes. Using large metal spatula, transfer potatoes, cheese side up, and accompanying cheese to platter and serve.

CHIVE SOUR CREAM
MAKES ABOUT 1 CUP
This enhanced condiment makes an excellent topping for potatoes of all kinds.

- 1 cup sour cream
- ¼ cup minced fresh chives
- ½ teaspoon minced fresh rosemary
- ½ teaspoon salt
- ½ teaspoon pepper
- ½ teaspoon garlic powder
- ¼ teaspoon onion powder

Combine all ingredients in bowl. Cover and refrigerate at least 30 minutes to allow flavors to blend.

Flipping For Frico

Using 2 forks, turn each potato slice over and return it to the same spot on the sheet. As the Parmesan bakes, it will transform into crispy cheesey bits called frico.

ROASTED SALT-AND-VINEGAR POTATOES

SERVES 4

Use small red potatoes, measuring 1 to 2 inches in diameter. If you prefer to use kosher salt, you will need 1½ cups of Morton's or 2½ cups of Diamond Crystal. Cider vinegar is a good substitute for the malt vinegar.

- 6 tablespoons olive oil
- 2 pounds small red potatoes, scrubbed
- 1¼ cups salt
- 3 tablespoons malt vinegar
  Pepper

1. Adjust oven rack to upper-middle position and heat oven to 500 degrees. Set wire rack inside rimmed baking sheet. Brush second rimmed baking sheet evenly with oil. Bring 2 quarts water to boil in Dutch oven over medium-high heat. Stir in potatoes and salt and cook until just tender and paring knife slips easily in and out of potatoes, 20 to 30 minutes. Drain potatoes and transfer to wire rack; let dry for 10 minutes.

2. Transfer potatoes to oiled baking sheet. Flatten each potato with underside of measuring cup until ½ inch thick. Brush potatoes with half of vinegar and season with pepper. Roast until potatoes are well browned, 25 to 30 minutes. Brush with remaining vinegar. Transfer potatoes to platter, smashed side up. Serve.

Scrub the Potatoes

Because the skins will be in the finished dish, it's important to scrub the potatoes well before cooking.

Salt of the Earth (and Sea)

A variety of salts are available in supermarkets today: table, iodized, kosher, and sea salt. What's the difference? Table and iodized salt (simply table salt with iodine added) have fine grains and contain anticaking agents that help them flow freely. Kosher salt, so named because it is used in the koshering process, has larger crystals and typically contains no additives. Both table and kosher salts are considered "refined salts" because they are mined from rock salt deposits and then purified. Sea salt is harvested by evaporating seawater and therefore has a full, slightly mineral flavor. Though we use table salt in the vast majority of our recipes, the choice is a matter of preference—except when it comes to our Roasted Salt-and-Vinegar Potatoes. While table, kosher, and sea salts all performed equally well in this recipe, we advise against using iodized salt as it gives the potatoes a noticeably chemical flavor.

Malt Vinegar Substitutes

For our salt-and-vinegar potatoes, we raided the English larder for a beloved condiment: malt vinegar. Brits commonly douse fish and chips with it, so we knew it would be a perfect match for roasted potatoes. The vinegar, which is made from sprouted barley grains, gives the potatoes a pleasantly malty, tangy taste. But if you don't have it, cider or white wine vinegars are good substitutes. Avoid balsamic and rice vinegars, which tasters found too sweet, and red wine and distilled white vinegars, which were too harsh.

Why This Recipe Works Cooking red potatoes in a super-saturated salt solution gave them incredibly creamy, well-seasoned interiors. After the potatoes were parcooked, we smashed them to expose some of the potato flesh, brushed them with malt vinegar, and roasted them on a well-oiled baking sheet until the exposed surface was golden and crispy. A final brush with more vinegar when the potatoes came out of the oven reinforced the addictive salty-sour flavor of these spuds.

Why This Recipe Works Our Super-Stuffed Baked Potatoes feature fluffy potato, garlic, herbs, and creamy cheese in crispy potato-skin shells. Precooking the potatoes in the microwave shaved an hour off the cooking time. And while most stuffed baked potato recipes call for cutting the potato in half, we preferred to lop off just the top quarter of the potato. Prepared this way, the potato shells held more filling. But after hollowing out the potatoes, there wasn't enough stuffing to fill each one and mound the filling on top. To make the filling go further, we cooked an extra potato and used its flesh to top off the other stuffed baked potatoes.

SUPER-STUFFED BAKED POTATOES

SERVES 6

This recipe calls for seven potatoes but makes six servings; the remaining potato is used for its flesh.

7   large russet potatoes
3   tablespoons unsalted butter, melted,
     plus 3 tablespoons unsalted butter
     Salt and pepper
1   (5.2-ounce) package Boursin cheese, crumbled
½   cup half-and-half
2   garlic cloves, minced
¼   cup chopped fresh chives

1. Adjust oven rack to middle position and heat oven to 475 degrees. Set wire rack in rimmed baking sheet. Prick potatoes all over with fork, place on paper towel, and microwave until tender, 20 to 25 minutes, turning potatoes over after 10 minutes.

2. Slice and remove top quarter of each potato, let cool for 5 minutes, then scoop out flesh, leaving ¼-inch layer of potato on inside. Discard 1 potato shell. Brush remaining shells inside and out with 3 tablespoons melted butter and sprinkle interiors with ¼ teaspoon salt. Transfer potatoes, scooped side up, to prepared baking sheet and bake until skins begin to crisp, about 15 minutes.

3. Meanwhile, mix half of Boursin with half-and-half in bowl until blended. Cook remaining 3 tablespoons butter and garlic in saucepan over medium-low heat until garlic is straw-colored, 3 to 5 minutes. Stir in Boursin mixture until combined.

4. Set ricer or food mill over medium bowl and press or mill potatoes into bowl. Gently fold in warm Boursin mixture, 3 tablespoons chives, 1 teaspoon pepper, and ½ teaspoon salt until well incorporated. Remove potato shells from oven and fill with potato-cheese mixture. Top with remaining crumbled Boursin and bake until tops of potatoes are golden brown, about 15 minutes. Sprinkle with remaining 1 tablespoon chives. Serve.

Bigger, Better Stuffed Potatoes
During testing for our Super-Stuffed Baked Potatoes, we found that most recipes called for the baked potatoes to be cut right in half before being filled. But these skimpy spuds were far from the super-stuffed garlic potatoes we were looking for. Instead, we found the best method was to cut off only the top quarter of the potato, leaving a much more substantial spud to stuff.

1. Slice off top quarter of microwaved potato.

2. Use spoon to scoop out interior of potato, being careful to leave ¼-inch layer of potato in shell.

Why This Recipe Works For this showstopper side dish, we found that using the right kind of potato is key. The russet potato was the best choice because of its starchy flesh and fluffy texture. Taking the time to rinse the potatoes of surface starch after they were sliced prevented them from sticking together, while trimming off the end of each potato gave the remaining slices room to fan out. To prevent overcooking our spuds in the punishing oven heat, we precooked them in the microwave before baking. A topping of fresh bread crumbs, melted butter, two kinds of cheese, garlic powder, and paprika is the crowning touch.

CRISPY BAKED POTATO FANS

SERVES 4

To ensure that the potatoes fan out evenly, look for uniformly shaped potatoes.

Bread-Crumb Topping

1 slice hearty white sandwich bread, torn into quarters
4 tablespoons unsalted butter, melted
2 ounces Monterey Jack cheese, shredded (½ cup)
¼ cup grated Parmesan cheese
1 teaspoon paprika
½ teaspoon garlic powder
Salt and pepper

Potato Fans

4 russet potatoes
2 tablespoons extra-virgin olive oil
Salt and pepper

1. For the Bread-Crumb Topping Adjust oven rack to middle position and heat oven to 200 degrees. Pulse bread in food processor until coarsely ground, about 5 pulses. Bake bread crumbs on rimmed baking sheet until dry, about 20 minutes. Let cool for 5 minutes, then combine crumbs, butter, Monterey Jack, Parmesan, paprika, garlic powder, ¼ teaspoon salt, and ¼ teaspoon pepper in large bowl. (Bread-crumb topping can be refrigerated in zipper-lock bag for 2 days.)

2. For the Potato Fans Heat oven to 450 degrees. Cut ¼ inch from bottom and ends of potatoes, then slice potatoes crosswise at ¼-inch intervals, leaving ¼ inch of potato intact. Gently rinse potatoes under running water, let drain, and transfer, sliced side down, to plate. Microwave until slightly soft to touch, 6 to 12 minutes, flipping potatoes halfway through cooking.

3. Line rimmed baking sheet with aluminum foil. Arrange potatoes, sliced side up, on prepared baking sheet. Brush potatoes all over with oil and season with salt and pepper. Bake until skin is crisp and potatoes are beginning to brown, 25 to 30 minutes. Remove potatoes from oven and heat broiler.

4. Carefully top potatoes with stuffing mixture, pressing gently to adhere. Broil until bread crumbs are deep golden brown, about 3 minutes. Serve.

BLUE CHEESE AND BACON BAKED POTATO FANS

In step 1, substitute ⅓ cup crumbled blue cheese for Monterey Jack. In step 4, sprinkle 4 slices bacon, cooked until crisp and then crumbled, over potatoes just prior to serving.

Prepping Baked Potato Fans

These potatoes may look difficult to make, but we found a few simple tricks to ensure perfect potato fans every time.

1. Trim ¼-inch slices from bottom and ends of each potato to allow them to sit flat and to give slices extra room to fan out during baking.

2. Chopsticks provide a foolproof guide for slicing potato petals without cutting all the way through.

3. Gently flex open fans while rinsing under cold running water; this rids potatoes of excess starch that can impede fanning.

OLIVE OIL POTATO GRATIN

SERVES 6 TO 8

The test kitchen's favorite supermarket extra-virgin olive oil is California Olive Ranch Everyday. We prefer to use a mandoline to create thin, even slices of potato.

- 2 ounces Pecorino-Romano cheese, grated (1 cup)
- ½ cup extra-virgin olive oil
- ¼ cup panko bread crumbs
  Salt and pepper
- 2 onions, halved and sliced thin
- 2 garlic cloves, minced
- 1 teaspoon minced fresh thyme
- 1 cup low-sodium chicken broth
- 3 pounds Yukon Gold potatoes, peeled and sliced ⅛ inch thick

1. Adjust oven rack to upper-middle position and heat oven to 400 degrees. Grease 13 by 9-inch baking dish. Combine Pecorino, 3 tablespoons oil, panko, and ½ teaspoon pepper in bowl; set aside.

2. Heat 2 tablespoons oil in 12-inch skillet over medium heat until shimmering. Add onions, ½ teaspoon salt, and ¼ teaspoon pepper and cook, stirring frequently, until browned, about 15 minutes. Add garlic and ½ teaspoon thyme and cook until fragrant, about 30 seconds. Add ¼ cup broth and cook until nearly evaporated, scraping up any browned bits, about 2 minutes. Remove from heat; set aside.

3. Toss potatoes, remaining 3 tablespoons oil, 1 teaspoon salt, ½ teaspoon pepper, and remaining ½ teaspoon thyme together in bowl. Arrange half of potatoes in prepared dish, spread onion mixture in even layer over potatoes, and distribute remaining potatoes over onions. Pour remaining ¾ cup broth over potatoes. Cover dish tightly with aluminum foil and bake for 1 hour.

4. Remove foil, top gratin with reserved Pecorino mixture, and continue to bake until top is golden brown and potatoes are completely tender, 15 to 20 minutes. Let cool for 15 minutes. Serve.

Slicing Potatoes

A mandoline makes quick work of thinly slicing potatoes, but if you don't own one, cut a slice off of one side of each potato to create a flat, stable surface for thin slicing.

Why This Recipe Works Potato gratin is a notoriously heavy side dish, laden with cream and gooey cheese. We wanted to shift the focus of this classic side dish to the potatoes. We chose Yukon Gold potatoes for their rich flavor and moderate starch content, which helped them hold their shape when cooked. Tossing the potatoes with fruity, flavorful extra-virgin olive oil heightened the flavor of the potatoes but didn't overpower them. For a crisp, cheesy topping, we mixed more olive oil with panko bread crumbs and sprinkled the dish with sharp, salty Pecorino-Romano. For added depth, we added sautéed onions, fresh thyme, and garlic.

MASHED POTATO CAKES

SERVES 4 TO 6

Using two spatulas to flip the cakes helps prevent splattering. We like to change the oil after frying the first batch of cakes because any dark panko remnants left behind will freckle the second batch. You can strain the oil through a fine-mesh strainer if you prefer to reuse it, but be careful because it is very hot. Plan ahead: The cooked mashed potatoes need to chill in the refrigerator for 1 hour, which makes it easier to form the cakes.

2½ pounds russet potatoes, peeled, halved
     lengthwise, and sliced ¼ inch thick
     Salt and pepper
 1   ounce Parmesan cheese, grated (½ cup)
 ¼   cup chopped fresh chives
 1   large egg yolk plus 2 large eggs
 2   cups panko bread crumbs
 1   cup vegetable oil
     Sour cream

1. Place potatoes in medium saucepan and add water to cover by 1 inch, then stir in 1 tablespoon salt. Bring to boil over high heat. Reduce heat to medium-low and simmer until tip of paring knife inserted into potatoes meets no resistance, 8 to 10 minutes. Drain potatoes and return to saucepan; let cool for 5 minutes.

2. Add Parmesan, chives, egg yolk, ¾ teaspoon salt, and ¼ teaspoon pepper to cooled potatoes. Using potato masher, mash until smooth and well combined. Transfer potato mixture to bowl and refrigerate until completely cool, about 1 hour.

3. Beat remaining 2 eggs together in shallow dish. Place panko in second shallow dish. Divide potato mixture into 8 equal portions (about ½ cup each) and shape into 3-inch-diameter cakes, about ¾ inch thick. Working with 1 cake at a time, carefully dip cakes in egg mixture, turning to coat both sides and allowing excess to drip off; then coat with panko, pressing gently to adhere. Transfer to plate and let sit for 5 minutes.

4. Line large plate with paper towels. Heat ½ cup oil in 12-inch nonstick skillet over medium-high heat until shimmering. Place 4 cakes in skillet and cook until deep golden brown on first side, about 3 minutes. Using 2 spatulas, carefully flip cakes and continue to cook until deep golden brown on second side, about 2 minutes longer, gently pressing on cakes with spatula for even browning.

5. Transfer cakes to prepared plate. Discard oil and wipe out skillet with paper towels. Repeat with remaining ½ cup oil and remaining 4 cakes. Serve with sour cream.

BLUE CHEESE AND BACON MASHED POTATO CAKES

Substitute ¾ cup crumbled blue cheese for Parmesan. Stir 6 slices cooked chopped bacon into potato mixture after mashing in step 2.

CHEDDAR AND SCALLION MASHED POTATO CAKES

Substitute 1 cup shredded sharp cheddar cheese for Parmesan and sliced scallions for chives.

Why This Recipe Works Mashed potato cakes—soft, fluffy mashed potatoes coated in bread crumbs and fried—are equally welcome at suppertime next to a piece of meat or at breakfast under a poached egg. Using leftover mashed potatoes yielded mushy cakes, so we started from scratch, mashing russet potatoes with Parmesan, chives, and an egg yolk for extra richness. Chilling the mashed potatoes before forming the cakes made shaping them easier. For a golden-brown and crisp crust, we dipped the disks in beaten egg to help the coating adhere. Serving the potato cakes with a dollop of sour cream offered a cool, tangy finish.

Why This Recipe Works Roasting red peppers on the grill turns their juicy crunch smoky and tender. We tossed stemmed and cored peppers in garlic-infused olive oil, allowing the oil to soak into the interiors' exposed flesh. To prevent flare-ups, we grilled the peppers in a foil-covered disposable pan then drained them and placed them directly on the hot grates to char. After easily scraping the charred skins from the peppers, we tossed them in a vinaigrette made from the leftover oil and liquid released from the peppers. The finished peppers were tender, smoky, and infused with heady garlic flavor that complemented the intensified sweetness.

GRILL-ROASTED PEPPERS

SERVES 4

These peppers can be refrigerated for up to 5 days.

¼ cup extra-virgin olive oil
3 garlic cloves, peeled and smashed
  Salt and pepper
1 (13 by 9-inch) disposable aluminum pan
6 red bell peppers
1 tablespoon sherry vinegar

1. Combine oil, garlic, ½ teaspoon salt, and ¼ teaspoon pepper in disposable pan. Using paring knife, cut around stems of peppers and remove cores and seeds. Place peppers in pan and turn to coat with oil. Cover pan tightly with aluminum foil.

2A. For a Charcoal Grill Open bottom vent completely. Light large chimney starter filled with charcoal briquettes (6 quarts). When top coals are partially covered with ash, pour evenly over half of grill. Set cooking grate in place, cover, and open lid vent completely. Heat grill until hot, about 5 minutes.

2B. For a Gas Grill Turn all burners to high, cover, and heat grill until hot, about 15 minutes. Turn all burners to medium-high.

3. Clean and oil cooking grate. Place pan on grill (over hotter side for charcoal) and cook, covered, until peppers are just tender and skins begin to blister, 10 to 15 minutes, rotating and shaking pan halfway through cooking.

4. Remove pan from heat and carefully remove foil (reserve foil to use later). Using tongs, remove peppers from pan, allowing juices to drip back into pan, and place on grill (over hotter side for charcoal). Grill peppers, covered, turning every few minutes until skins are blackened, 10 to 15 minutes.

5. Transfer juices and garlic in pan to medium bowl and whisk in vinegar. Remove peppers from grill, return to now-empty pan, and cover tightly with foil. Let peppers steam for 5 minutes. Using spoon, scrape blackened skin off each pepper. Quarter peppers lengthwise, add to vinaigrette in bowl, and toss to combine. Season with salt and pepper to taste, and serve.

Steam Then Sear

We first steam the peppers in garlicky olive oil and their own juices. Then we sear the peppers and serve them with a vinaigrette made from the infused oil.

STUFFED TOMATOES

SERVES 6

Look for large tomatoes, about 3 inches in diameter.

- 6 large vine-ripened tomatoes (8 to 10 ounces each)
- 1 tablespoon sugar
  Kosher salt and pepper
- 4½ tablespoons extra-virgin olive oil
- ¼ cup panko bread crumbs
- 3 ounces Gruyère cheese, shredded (¾ cup)
- 1 onion, halved and sliced thin
- 2 garlic cloves, minced
- ⅛ teaspoon red pepper flakes
- 8 ounces (8 cups) baby spinach, chopped coarse
- 1 cup couscous
- ½ teaspoon grated lemon zest
- 1 tablespoon red wine vinegar

1. Adjust oven rack to middle position and heat oven to 375 degrees. Cut top ½ inch off stem end of tomatoes and set aside. Using melon baller, scoop out tomato pulp and transfer to fine-mesh strainer set over bowl. Press on pulp with wooden spoon to extract juice; set aside juice and discard pulp. (You should have about ⅔ cup tomato juice; if not, add water as needed to equal ⅔ cup.)

2. Combine sugar and 1 tablespoon salt in bowl. Sprinkle each tomato cavity with 1 teaspoon sugar mixture, then turn tomatoes upside down on plate to drain for 30 minutes.

3. Combine 1½ teaspoons oil and panko in 10-inch skillet and toast over medium-high heat, stirring frequently, until golden brown, about 3 minutes. Transfer to bowl and let cool for 10 minutes. Stir in ¼ cup Gruyère.

4. Heat 2 tablespoons oil in now-empty skillet over medium heat until shimmering. Add onion and ½ teaspoon salt and cook until softened, 5 to 7 minutes. Stir in garlic and pepper flakes and cook until fragrant, about 30 seconds. Add spinach, 1 handful at a time, and cook until wilted, about 3 minutes. Stir in couscous, lemon zest, and reserved tomato juice. Cover, remove from heat, and let sit until couscous has absorbed liquid, about 7 minutes.

Transfer couscous mixture to bowl and stir in remaining ½ cup Gruyère. Season with salt and pepper to taste.

5. Coat bottom of 13 by 9-inch baking dish with remaining 2 tablespoons oil. Blot tomato cavities dry with paper towels and season with salt and pepper. Pack each tomato with couscous mixture, about ½ cup per tomato, mounding excess. Top stuffed tomatoes with 1 heaping tablespoon panko mixture. Place tomatoes in prepared dish. Season reserved tops with salt and pepper and place in empty spaces in dish.

6. Bake, uncovered, until tomatoes have softened but still hold their shape, about 20 minutes. Using slotted spoon, transfer to serving platter. Whisk vinegar into oil remaining in dish, then drizzle over tomatoes. Place tops on tomatoes and serve.

STUFFED TOMATOES WITH BACON
Substitute shredded smoked cheddar for Gruyère. Stir 3 slices chopped, cooked bacon into cooked couscous mixture with cheddar in step 4.

STUFFED TOMATOES WITH CAPERS AND PINE NUTS
Substitute shredded mozzarella for Gruyère. Stir 2 tablespoons rinsed capers and 2 tablespoons toasted pine nuts into cooked couscous mixture with mozzarella in step 4.

STUFFED TOMATOES WITH CURRANTS AND PISTACHIOS
Substitute crumbled feta for Gruyère. Stir 2 tablespoons currants and 2 tablespoons chopped pistachios into cooked couscous mixture with feta in step 4.

STUFFED TOMATOES WITH OLIVES AND ORANGE
Substitute shredded Manchego for Gruyère. Substitute ¼ teaspoon grated orange zest for lemon zest. Stir ¼ cup pitted kalamata olives, chopped, into cooked couscous mixture with Manchego in step 4.

Why This Recipe Works Stuffed tomatoes always sound delicious, but too often you get tasteless tomatoes and a lackluster stuffing that falls out in a clump. To concentrate flavor and get rid of excess moisture, we seasoned hollowed-out tomato shells with salt and sugar and let them drain. Couscous proved the best base for the filling, and we rehydrated it with the reserved tomato juice, ensuring the savory tomato flavor we craved. A topping of panko bread crumbs—pretoasted for proper browning—mixed with more cheese added crunch and richness, and a drizzle of the cooking liquid mixed with red wine vinegar provided a piquant final touch.

our sunday best

OLD-FASHIONED ROAST TURKEY WITH GRAVY

SERVES 10 TO 12

You will need one 2-yard package of cheesecloth for this recipe. Because we layer the bird with salt pork, we prefer to use a natural turkey here; a self-basting turkey (such as a frozen Butterball) may become too salty. If using a self-basting turkey, omit the chicken broth in the gravy and increase the amount of water to 7 cups. Make sure to start the gravy as soon as the turkey goes into the oven.

Turkey
1   (2-yard) package cheesecloth
4   cups water
1   (12- to 14-pound) turkey, neck, giblets, and tailpiece removed and reserved for gravy
1   pound salt pork, cut into ¼-inch-thick slices

Gravy
1   tablespoon vegetable oil
1   onion, chopped
5   cups water
2   cups chicken broth
4   sprigs fresh thyme
1   bay leaf
6   tablespoons all-purpose flour
    Salt and pepper

1. For the Turkey Adjust oven rack to lowest position and heat oven to 350 degrees. Fold cheesecloth into 18-inch square, place in large bowl, and cover with water. Tuck wings behind turkey and arrange, breast side up, on V-rack set in roasting pan. Prick skin of breast and legs of turkey all over with fork, cover breast and legs with salt pork, top with soaked cheesecloth (pouring any remaining water into roasting pan), and cover cheesecloth completely with heavy-duty aluminum foil.

2. Roast turkey until breast registers 140 degrees, 2½ to 3 hours. Remove foil, cheesecloth, and salt pork and discard. Increase oven temperature to 425 degrees. Continue to roast until breast registers 160 degrees and thighs register 175 degrees, 40 minutes to 1 hour longer. Transfer turkey to carving board and let rest 30 minutes.

3. For the Gravy Meanwhile, heat oil in large saucepan over medium-high heat until shimmering. Cook turkey neck and giblets until browned, about 5 minutes. Add onion and cook until softened, about 3 minutes. Stir in water, broth, thyme, and bay leaf and bring to boil. Reduce heat to low and simmer until reduced by half, about 3 hours. Strain mixture through fine-mesh strainer into 4-cup liquid measuring cup (you should have about 3½ cups), reserving giblets if desired.

4. Carefully strain contents of roasting pan into fat separator. Let liquid settle, then skim, reserving ¼ cup fat. Pour defatted pan juices into measuring cup with giblet broth to yield 4 cups liquid.

5. Heat reserved fat in empty saucepan over medium heat until shimmering. Stir in flour and cook until golden and fragrant, about 4 minutes. Slowly whisk in giblet broth and bring to boil. Reduce heat to medium-low and simmer until slightly thickened, about 5 minutes. Chop giblets and add to gravy, if desired, and season with salt and pepper to taste. Carve turkey and serve with gravy.

Salt Pork

Covering the breast and tops of the legs of the turkey with salt pork helps to season the meat and insulate it from overcooking. Don't confuse salt pork with bacon. Although both come from the belly of the pig and are salt-cured, bacon is heavily smoked and is typically leaner and meatier. Salt pork is unsmoked and used primarily as a flavoring agent (traditionally in dishes like baked beans) and is rarely actually consumed. We recommend buying blocks of salt pork (precut slices can dry out) and portioning it as needed. Look for salt pork that has at least a few streaks of meat throughout. Salt pork can be refrigerated for up to one month.

Why This Recipe Works For a roast turkey with moist, flavorful meat, we tried a number of options until we discovered a technique used for ages: barding. Similar to larding, it is a process of wrapping strips of lard (or other animal fat) around the meat so that it slowly releases flavor and moisture throughout roasting. After piercing the skin of the turkey breast and legs with a fork, we covered it with thin slices of salt pork before layering on cheesecloth that had been soaked in water and then aluminum foil. This insulated the meat and allowed the salt pork to slowly melt in the oven, basting the turkey with rich fat.

CORNBREAD AND SAUSAGE STUFFING

SERVES 10 TO 12

We prefer spicy andouille sausage in this recipe, but chorizo or kielbasa work well, too. For the cornbread, use your favorite recipe, store-bought cornbread, or Betty Crocker Golden Corn Muffin and Bread Mix or Jiffy Corn Muffin Mix, both of which will work fine in stuffing.

12 cups prepared cornbread cut into ¾-inch cubes
1½ pounds andouille sausage, halved lengthwise and sliced into ¼-inch-thick half-moons
2 tablespoons unsalted butter
2 small onions, chopped fine
3 celery ribs, chopped fine
2 tablespoons minced fresh sage
3 garlic cloves, minced
1 teaspoon salt
1 teaspoon pepper
4 cups chicken broth

1. Adjust oven racks to upper-middle and lower-middle positions and heat oven to 400 degrees. Spread cornbread evenly over 2 rimmed baking sheets. Bake until slightly crisp, 15 to 20 minutes; let cool. Carefully remove upper-middle rack from oven.

2. Cook sausage in Dutch oven over medium-high heat until lightly browned, 5 to 7 minutes. Transfer to paper towel–lined plate and pour off fat left behind in pot. Melt butter over medium-high heat, add onions and celery, and cook until softened, about 5 minutes. Stir in sage, garlic, salt, and pepper and cook until fragrant, about 1 minute. Add broth

and sausage, scraping up browned bits with wooden spoon. Add cornbread and gently stir until liquid is absorbed. Cover and set aside for 10 minutes. (Stuffing can be refrigerated for 1 day; let sit at room temperature for 30 minutes before baking.)

3. Remove lid and bake until top of stuffing is golden brown and crisp, about 30 minutes. Serve.

CORNBREAD AND BACON STUFFING
Substitute 1 pound bacon, chopped, for sausage, 3 cups fresh or frozen corn kernels for celery, and 3 thinly sliced scallions for sage.

Drying Cornbread
Although cornbread gives stuffing great flavor, it also adds a lot of moisture, making a soggy baked mess. If you have the time, cube the cornbread, spread it out on baking sheets, and let it sit overnight on the counter. If you're in a hurry (and who isn't around the holidays?), pop the baking sheets holding the cornbread into a 400-degree oven until slightly crisp, 15 to 20 minutes.

Why This Recipe Works We wanted a stuffing rich enough to stand on its own without gravy. We found our answer in cornbread and sausage. Cornbread gives the stuffing more flavor than plain white bread. We wanted plenty of stuffing, so we chose to cook it in a Dutch oven, which is large enough to accommodate 10 to 12 portions. To compensate for the loss in richness and poultry flavor we didn't just rely on any sausage—we chose spicy andouille sausage. Adding chicken broth to the stuffing further boosted the meaty flavor of our stuffing and helped keep it from drying out.

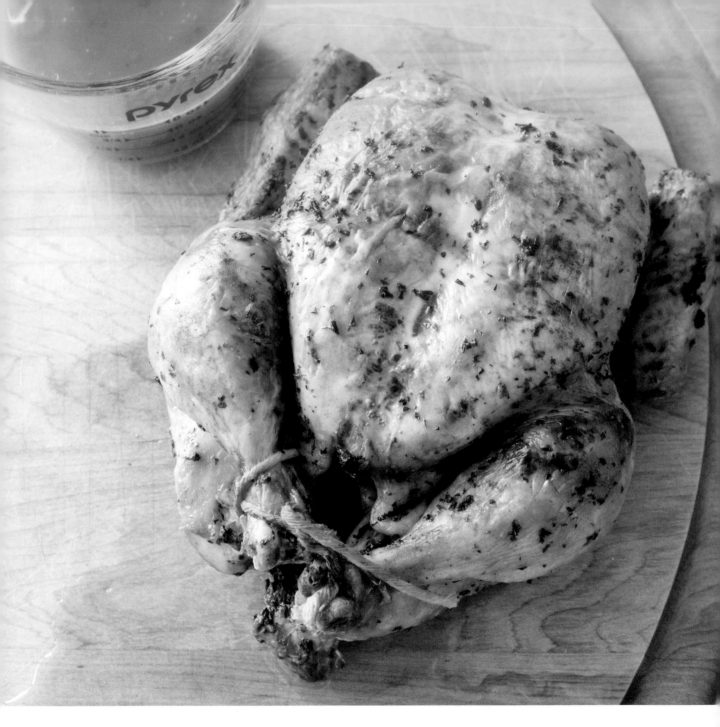

Why This Recipe Works Developing a recipe for a classic herb roast chicken proved surprisingly tricky. Stuffing the chicken with fresh herbs delivered zero flavor, herb butter melted off the chicken, and infused oil failed to really penetrate the meat. Our solution was to slather the chicken with a thick paste of fresh herbs and garlic, processed until smooth, then let it rest to develop a pronounced herbal flavor. So that there was plenty of meat to go around, we used two whole chickens instead of one. For a simple pan sauce, while the chicken rested we whisked the drippings with chicken broth, white wine, cornstarch, butter, and additional herb paste.

HERB ROAST CHICKEN

SERVES 6 TO 8

For even cooking, arrange the chickens side by side a few inches apart on the V-rack, with the legs pointing in opposite directions.

1 cup chopped fresh parsley
2 tablespoons chopped fresh thyme
1 tablespoon chopped fresh rosemary
2 garlic cloves, minced
  Salt and pepper
2 tablespoons olive oil
2 (3½- to 4-pound) whole chickens, giblets discarded
1 cup plus 2 tablespoons water
2 teaspoons cornstarch
1¼ cups chicken broth
¼ cup dry white wine
2 tablespoons unsalted butter, chilled

1. Process parsley, thyme, rosemary, garlic, 2 teaspoons salt, and 1 teaspoon pepper in food processor until paste forms, about 30 seconds. Reserve 1 teaspoon herb paste for sauce. Combine 2 tablespoons herb paste with oil in bowl. Set aside herb-oil paste and remaining herb paste.

2. Adjust oven rack to middle position and heat oven to 450 degrees. Pat chickens dry with paper towels. Using your fingers, gently loosen skin covering breast and thighs. Rub remaining herb paste under skin of each chicken, making sure to coat breast, thigh, and leg meat. Rub herb-oil paste over outside of each chicken. Tuck wings behind back and tie legs together with kitchen twine. Transfer chickens to platter. Cover and refrigerate 1 hour.

3. Arrange chickens 2 inches apart, breast side down, on V-rack set inside large roasting pan. Roast until thigh meat registers 135 to 140 degrees, 35 to 40 minutes. Remove chickens from oven and, using 2 bunches of paper towels, flip breast side up (meat that was facing in should now be facing out). Pour 1 cup water into roasting pan. Return chickens to oven and roast until breast registers 160 degrees and thighs register 175 degrees, 25 to 30 minutes. Transfer to carving board and let rest for 20 minutes.

4. Whisk cornstarch with remaining 2 tablespoons water in bowl until no lumps remain. Pour pan juices and any accumulated chicken juices into liquid measuring cup; skim fat. Transfer ½ cup defatted pan juices to medium saucepan. Add broth and wine and bring to boil. Reduce heat to medium-low and simmer until sauce is slightly thickened and reduced to 1¼ cups, 8 to 10 minutes. Whisk in cornstarch mixture and simmer until thickened, 3 to 5 minutes. Off heat, whisk in butter and reserved 1 teaspoon herb paste. Season with salt and pepper to taste. Carve chickens and serve, passing sauce at table.

Herb Flavor Times Three

To get deeply flavored roast chicken, we triple up on the herb paste.

1. Separate skin from meat and rub herb paste under skin.

2. Apply herb paste mixed with olive oil to exterior of each chicken.

3. Whisk teaspoon of herb paste into sauce for a fresh finish.

ROAST LEMON CHICKEN

SERVES 3 TO 4

Avoid using nonstick or aluminum roasting pans in this recipe. The former can cause the chicken to brown too quickly, while the latter may react with the lemon juice, producing off-flavors.

1 (3½- to 4-pound) whole chicken, giblets discarded
3 tablespoons grated lemon zest plus ⅓ cup juice (3 lemons)
1 teaspoon sugar
  Salt and pepper
2 cups chicken broth
  Water
1 teaspoon cornstarch
3 tablespoons unsalted butter
1 tablespoon finely chopped fresh parsley

1. Adjust oven rack to middle position and heat oven to 475 degrees. Pat chicken dry with paper towels. Using kitchen shears, cut along both sides of backbone to remove it. Flatten breastbone and tuck wings behind back. Using your fingers, gently loosen skin covering breast and thighs. Combine lemon zest, sugar, and 1 teaspoon salt in small bowl. Rub 2 tablespoons zest mixture under skin of chicken. Season chicken with salt and pepper and transfer to roasting pan. (Seasoned chicken can be refrigerated for 2 hours.)

2. Whisk broth, 1 cup water, lemon juice, and remaining zest mixture in 4-cup liquid measuring cup, then pour into roasting pan. (Liquid should just reach skin of thighs. If it does not, add enough water to reach skin of thighs.) Roast until skin is golden brown and breast registers 160 degrees and thighs register 175 degrees, 40 to 45 minutes. Transfer to carving board and let rest for 20 minutes.

3. Carefully pour liquid from pan, along with any accumulated chicken juices, into saucepan (you should have about 1½ cups). Skim fat, then cook over medium-high heat until reduced to 1 cup, about 5 minutes. Whisk cornstarch with 1 tablespoon water in small bowl until no lumps remain, then whisk into saucepan. Simmer until sauce is slightly thickened, about 2 minutes. Off heat, whisk in butter and parsley and season with salt and pepper. Carve chicken and serve, passing sauce at table.

More Lemon Flavor in Less Time

Butterflying the chicken may be unfamiliar, but this surprisingly simple process makes it easier to flavor the chicken with lemon—and it speeds roasting, too.

1. Use kitchen shears to cut out backbone. Flip bird over and press to flatten breastbone.

2. Carefully loosen skin, then rub zest mixture into breast, thigh, and leg meat.

3. Roast flattened chicken in lemony sauce so that its flavor can permeate meat.

Why This Recipe Works The citrus flavor in roasted lemon chicken can be harsh or, on the flip side, totally absent. To infuse the meat with bright flavor, we combined lemon zest, sugar, and salt and rubbed it into the chicken under the skin. For even more lemon flavor, we roasted the chicken in a sauce of lemon juice mixed with water, more zest, and chicken broth. Roasting the bird at a high temperature ensured that the exposed skin became crisp. Before serving, we reduced the sauce to concentrate its flavor and thickened it with butter and cornstarch for sheen, body, and richness.

APPLE CIDER CHICKEN

SERVES 3 TO 4

Plain brandy, cognac, or Calvados (a French apple brandy) can be used in place of the apple brandy.

- 3 pounds bone-in chicken pieces, (split breasts halved crosswise, legs separated into thighs and drumsticks), trimmed
  Salt and pepper
- 2 teaspoons vegetable oil
- 1 onion, chopped fine
- 2 garlic cloves, minced
- 2 teaspoons minced fresh thyme
- 2 teaspoons all-purpose flour
- 1 large Golden Delicious, Cortland, or Jonagold apple (8 ounces), peeled, cored, and cut into ¾-inch pieces
- 1 cup apple cider
- ¼ cup apple brandy
- 1 teaspoon cider vinegar

1. Adjust oven rack to middle position and heat oven to 450 degrees. Pat chicken dry with paper towels and season with salt and pepper. Heat oil in 12-inch ovenproof skillet over medium-high heat until just smoking. Cook chicken skin side down until well browned, about 10 minutes. Flip and brown on second side, about 5 minutes. Transfer to plate.

2. Pour off all but 1 tablespoon fat from skillet. Add onion and cook until softened, about 5 minutes. Stir in garlic, thyme, and flour and cook, stirring frequently, until fragrant and flour is absorbed, about 1 minute. Add apple, apple cider, and 3 tablespoons apple brandy and bring to boil.

3. Nestle chicken skin side up into sauce and roast in oven until breasts register 160 degrees and thighs/drumsticks register 175 degrees, about 10 minutes. Transfer chicken to platter. Stir vinegar and remaining 1 tablespoon brandy into sauce and season with salt and pepper to taste. Serve, passing sauce at table.

Preventing Flabby Skin

We avoid flabby skin with a hybrid technique that combines braising and pan roasting.

1. Brown chicken skin side down in skillet for 10 minutes until deep brown. Brown second side for 5 more minutes.

2. Finish chicken, skin side up and uncovered, in hot oven. Be sure liquid does not submerge chicken pieces.

Apple Cider versus Apple Juice

To make cider, apples are simply cored, chopped, mashed, and then pressed to extract their liquid. Most cider is pasteurized before sale, though unpasteurized cider is also available. To make apple juice, manufacturers follow the same steps used to make cider, but they also filter the extracted liquid to remove pulp and sediment. Apple juice is then pasteurized, and potassium sorbate (a preservative) is often mixed in to prevent fermentation. Finally, apple juice is sometimes sweetened with sugar or corn syrup. We tried using unsweetened apple juice in recipes for pork chops and glazed ham that call for cider. Tasters were turned off by excessive sweetness in the dishes made with apple juice, unanimously preferring those made with cider. This made sense: The filtration process used in making juice removes some of the complex, tart, and bitter flavors that are still present in cider. (When we tested the pH level of both liquids, the cider had a lower pH than the apple juice, confirming its higher level of acidity.) The bottom line: When it comes to cooking, don't swap apple juice for cider.

Why This Recipe Works We had a tall order with our Apple Cider Chicken: It had to taste like apples, and it had to have super-crisp skin. Cooking the chicken in a skillet, skin side down, then moving it to a hot oven kept the skin exceptionally crisp. When it came to flavor, apple cider alone didn't do the trick. We also needed fresh apples, apple brandy, and cider vinegar to flavor the chicken with apple goodness. For the sauce, Granny Smith apples were too sour, while other varieties turned to mush when cooked. In the end, we preferred Golden Delicious, Cortland, or Jonagold apples, which held their shape and offered sweet flavor.

Why This Recipe Works Cooking vegetables and chicken together in the same pan often leads to unevenly cooked chicken and greasy, soggy vegetables. To get the chicken and vegetables to cook at the same rate, we used chicken parts, which contain less overall fat than a whole chicken and don't smother the vegetables underneath, which would cause them to steam. To ensure that the delicate white meat stayed moist while the darker meat cooked through, we placed the chicken breasts in the center of the pan, with the thighs and drumsticks around the perimeter.

ONE-PAN ROAST CHICKEN WITH ROOT VEGETABLES

SERVES 4

We halve the chicken breasts crosswise for even cooking. Use Brussels sprouts no bigger than golf balls, as larger ones are often tough and woody.

12 ounces Brussels sprouts, trimmed and halved
12 ounces red potatoes, cut into 1-inch pieces
8 ounces shallots, peeled and halved
4 carrots, peeled and cut into 2-inch pieces, thick ends halved lengthwise
6 garlic cloves, peeled
4 teaspoons minced fresh thyme
1 tablespoon vegetable oil
2 teaspoons minced fresh rosemary
1 teaspoon sugar
   Salt and pepper
2 tablespoons unsalted butter, melted
3½ pounds bone-in chicken pieces (2 split breasts halved crosswise, 2 drumsticks, and 2 thighs), trimmed

1. Adjust oven rack to upper-middle position and heat oven to 475 degrees. Toss Brussels sprouts, potatoes, shallots, carrots, garlic, 2 teaspoons thyme, oil, 1 teaspoon rosemary, sugar, ¾ teaspoon salt, and ¼ teaspoon pepper together in bowl. Combine butter, remaining 2 teaspoons thyme, remaining 1 teaspoon rosemary, ¼ teaspoon salt, and ⅛ teaspoon pepper in second bowl; set aside.

2. Pat chicken dry with paper towels and season with salt and pepper. Place vegetables in single layer on rimmed baking sheet, arranging Brussels sprouts in center. Place chicken, skin side up, on top of vegetables, arranging breast pieces in center and leg and thigh pieces around perimeter of sheet.

3. Brush chicken with herb butter and roast until breasts register 160 degrees and thighs/drumsticks register 175 degrees, 35 to 40 minutes, rotating pan halfway through cooking. Transfer chicken to serving platter, tent loosely with aluminum foil, and let rest for 5 to 10 minutes. Toss vegetables in pan juices and transfer to platter with chicken. Serve.

ONE-PAN ROAST CHICKEN WITH FENNEL AND PARSNIPS

Replace Brussels sprouts and carrots with 1 fennel bulb, stalks discarded, bulb halved, cored, and sliced into ½-inch wedges, and 8 ounces (4 medium) parsnips, peeled and cut into 2-inch pieces.

Preparing Fennel

1. Cut off stalks and feathery fronds. Trim very thin slice from base and remove any tough or blemished outer layer.

2. Cut bulb in half through base. Use small sharp knife to remove pyramid-shaped cone.

3. Cut each half into ½-inch wedges.

SKILLET-ROASTED CHICKEN AND POTATOES

SERVES 4

Use uniform, medium potatoes.

3 tablespoons olive oil
2 teaspoons minced fresh thyme
1½ teaspoons smoked paprika
1½ teaspoons grated lemon zest,
 plus lemon wedges for serving
 Salt and pepper
1 (4-pound) whole chicken, giblets discarded
2 pounds Yukon Gold potatoes, peeled,
 ends squared off, and sliced into
 1-inch-thick rounds

1. Adjust oven rack to lower middle position and heat oven to 400 degrees. Combine 2 tablespoons oil, thyme, paprika, lemon zest, 1 teaspoon salt, and ½ teaspoon pepper in bowl. Pat chicken dry with paper towels and use your fingers or handle of wooden spoon to carefully separate skin from breast. Rub oil mixture all over chicken and underneath skin of breast. Tie legs together with kitchen twine and tuck wingtips behind back.

2. Toss potatoes with remaining 1 tablespoon oil, 1½ teaspoons salt, and ½ teaspoon pepper. Arrange potatoes, flat sides down, in single layer in 12-inch ovensafe nonstick skillet. Place skillet over medium heat and cook potatoes, without moving them, until brown on bottom, 7 to 9 minutes (do not flip).

3. Place chicken, breast side up, on top of potatoes and transfer skillet to oven. Roast until breast registers 160 degrees and thighs register 175 degrees, 1 to 1¼ hours. Transfer chicken to carving board, tent loosely with aluminum foil, and let rest for 20 minutes.

4. Meanwhile, cover skillet, return potatoes to oven, and roast until tender, about 20 minutes. Carve chicken and serve with potatoes and lemon wedges.

Keys to Potatoes That Are Tender and Brown

Potatoes don't cook at the same rate as a chicken. Here's how we got the dish to work.

1. On the Stove Brown one side of potatoes on stovetop, then top spuds with chicken and roast.

2. In the Oven Once chicken is done, set aside; cover pan and return to oven to finish cooking potatoes.

Prepping Fresh Thyme

For thin-stemmed thyme, chop stems along with leaves. If stems are thick, hold sprig upright and run your thumb and forefinger along stem to release leaves.

Why This Recipe Works For this convenient, one-pan meal, we were challenged to deliver tender potatoes and moist chicken at the same time. First, we quickly browned one side of the potatoes (an entire 2 pounds of potatoes fit into a 12-inch skillet when sliced into 1-inch-thick rounds). We placed the bird on top and moved everything to the oven where flavorful juices basted the potatoes. An hour later, the chicken was golden and juicy and the potatoes had a caramelized crust on the bottom. While the chicken rested, we returned the potatoes to the oven. By the time the chicken was ready to be served, the potatoes were soft and flavorful.

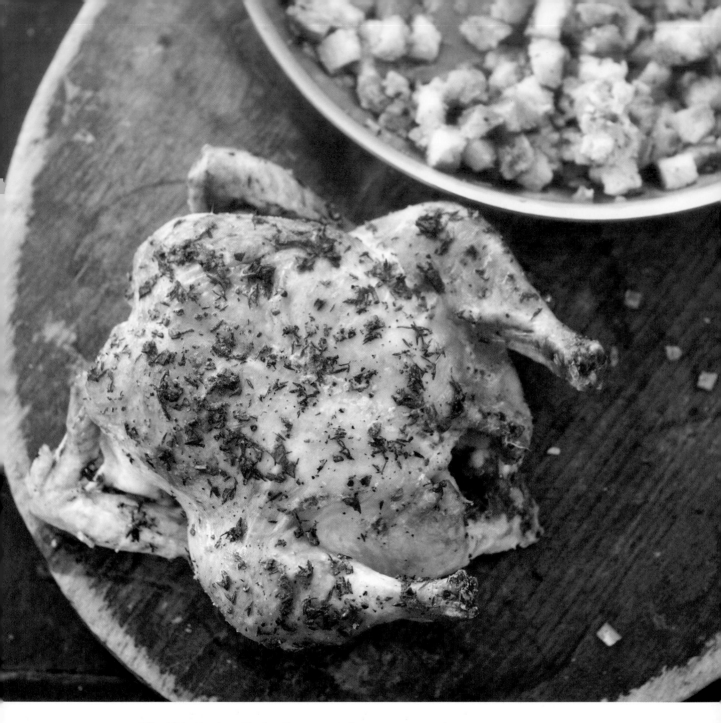

Why This Recipe Works To simplify Sunday-style stuffed chicken into a one-pan meal, we sped things up by taking the stuffing out of the chicken and making the entire dish in just one skillet. First we sautéed the aromatics for the stuffing, then we placed the chicken—brushed with a flavorful herb butter—right on top. We scattered the bread cubes around the bird and moved the skillet to the oven to simultaneously roast the chicken and toast the bread. As the chicken cooked, the bread soaked up its flavorful juices. Finally, while the chicken rested, a quick stir and a splash of broth mixed up the aromatics and moistened the stuffing.

SKILLET-ROASTED CHICKEN WITH STUFFING

SERVES 4

You can find Italian bread in the bakery section of your grocery store. Take care when stirring the contents of the skillet in steps 4 and 5, as the skillet handle will be very hot.

1 (4-pound) whole chicken, giblets discarded
6 tablespoons unsalted butter
2 tablespoons minced fresh sage
2 tablespoons minced fresh thyme
  Salt and pepper
2 onions, chopped fine
2 celery ribs, minced
7 ounces Italian bread, cut into ½-inch cubes (6 cups)
⅓ cup chicken broth

1. Adjust oven rack to lower-middle position and heat oven to 375 degrees. Pat chicken dry with paper towels. Melt 4 tablespoons butter in small bowl in microwave, about 45 seconds. Stir in 1 tablespoon sage, 1 tablespoon thyme, 1 teaspoon salt, and ½ teaspoon pepper. Brush chicken with herb butter.

2. Melt remaining 2 tablespoons butter in 12-inch ovensafe skillet over medium heat. Add onions, celery, ½ teaspoon salt, and ½ teaspoon pepper and cook until softened, about 5 minutes. Add remaining 1 tablespoon sage and remaining 1 tablespoon thyme and cook until fragrant, about 1 minute. Off heat, place chicken, breast side up, on top of vegetables. Arrange bread cubes around chicken in bottom of skillet.

3. Transfer skillet to oven and roast until breasts register 160 degrees and thighs register 175 degrees, about 1 hour, rotating skillet halfway through roasting.

4. Carefully transfer chicken to plate and tent loosely with aluminum foil. Holding skillet handle with potholder (handle will be hot), stir bread and vegetables to combine, cover, and let stand for 10 minutes.

5. Add broth and any accumulated chicken juice from plate and cavity to skillet and stir to combine. Warm stuffing, uncovered, over low heat until heated through, about 3 minutes. Remove from heat, cover, and let sit while carving chicken. Transfer chicken to carving board, carve, and serve with stuffing.

Chopping Onions Finely

1. Halve onion through root end, then peel onion and trim top. Make several horizontal cuts from one end of onion to other but don't cut through root end.

2. Make several vertical cuts. Be sure to cut up to but not through root end.

3. Rotate onion so root end is in back; slice onion thinly across previous cuts. As you slice, onion will fall apart into chopped pieces.

Why This Recipe Works A quick meal of chicken and vegetables baked in foil sounded great to us, but our first attempts were not much better than an old-style TV dinner. Seasoning the chicken with salt on both sides and refrigerating it for at least an hour proved ideal, as did using sturdy vegetables which held up during cooking. Placing the potato slices under the chicken insulated the meat from the oven's direct heat, and we found that leaving plenty of headroom above the chicken within the pouch gave the steam room to circulate, ensuring even cooking. An added bonus? No pots or pans to clean.

CHICKEN BAKED IN FOIL WITH SWEET POTATO AND RADISH

SERVES 4

To ensure even cooking, cut the vegetables as directed and buy chicken breasts of the same size. Refrigerate the pouches for at least 1 hour before cooking.

- 5 tablespoons extra-virgin olive oil
- 6 garlic cloves, sliced thin
- 1 tablespoon grated fresh ginger
- ¼ teaspoon red pepper flakes
- 12 ounces sweet potatoes, peeled and sliced ¼ inch thick
- 4 radishes, trimmed and quartered
- 2 celery ribs, quartered lengthwise and cut into 2-inch lengths
- ½ large red onion, sliced ½ inch thick, layers separated
  Kosher salt and pepper
- 4 (6-ounce) boneless, skinless chicken breasts, trimmed
- 2 tablespoons rice vinegar
- 2 tablespoons minced fresh cilantro

1. Spray centers of four 20 by 12-inch sheets of heavy-duty aluminum foil with vegetable oil spray. Microwave oil, garlic, ginger, and pepper flakes in small bowl until garlic begins to brown, 1 to 1½ minutes. Combine potato slices, radishes, celery, onion, 1 teaspoon salt, and garlic oil in large bowl.

2. Pat chicken dry with paper towels. Sprinkle ⅛ teaspoon salt evenly over each side of each chicken breast, then season with pepper. Position 1 piece of prepared foil with long side parallel to counter edge. In center of foil, arrange one-quarter of potato slices in 2 rows perpendicular to counter edge. Lay 1 chicken breast on top of potato slices. Place one-quarter of vegetables around chicken. Repeat with remaining foil, potato slices, chicken, and vegetables. Drizzle any remaining oil mixture from bowl over chicken.

3. Bring short sides of foil together and crimp to seal tightly. Crimp remaining open ends of packets, leaving as much headroom as possible inside packets. Refrigerate for at least 1 hour or up to 24 hours.

4. Adjust oven rack to lowest position and heat oven to 475 degrees. Arrange packets on rimmed baking sheet. Bake until chicken registers 160 degrees, 18 to 23 minutes. (To check temperature, poke thermometer through foil and into chicken.) Let chicken rest in packets for 3 minutes.

5. Transfer chicken packets to individual dinner plates, carefully open (steam will escape), and slide contents onto plates. Drizzle vinegar over chicken and vegetables and sprinkle with cilantro. Serve.

CHICKEN BAKED IN FOIL WITH POTATOES AND CARROTS

Substitute 12 ounces Yukon Gold potatoes (unpeeled, sliced ¼ inch thick) and 2 carrots (peeled, quartered lengthwise and cut into 2-inch lengths), for sweet potatoes, radishes, and celery; lemon juice for rice vinegar. Substitute 1 teaspoon minced fresh thyme for ginger and 2 tablespoons minced fresh chives for cilantro.

CHICKEN BAKED IN FOIL WITH FENNEL AND SUN-DRIED TOMATOES

Substitute 1 fennel bulb, stalks discarded, bulb halved, cored, and cut into ½-inch-thick wedges, layers separated, for celery; balsamic vinegar for rice vinegar; and minced fresh basil for cilantro. Add ¼ cup oil-packed sun-dried tomatoes, rinsed, patted dry, and chopped fine and ¼ cup pitted kalamata olives, chopped fine, to vegetables in step 1.

CHICKEN AND SLICKS

SERVES 4 TO 6

If you're short on chicken fat at the end of step 1, supplement it with vegetable oil.

1½ pounds bone-in chicken thighs, trimmed
2 (12-ounce) bone-in split chicken breasts, halved crosswise and trimmed
    Salt and pepper
6 tablespoons plus 2 cups all-purpose flour
3 tablespoons vegetable oil
1 onion, chopped
2 teaspoons minced fresh thyme
7½ cups chicken broth
2 bay leaves
¼ cup chopped fresh parsley

1. Pat chicken dry with paper towels and season with salt and pepper. Toast 6 tablespoons flour in Dutch oven over medium heat, stirring constantly, until just beginning to brown, about 5 minutes. Transfer flour to medium bowl and wipe out pot. Heat 1 tablespoon oil in now-empty Dutch oven over medium-high heat until just smoking. Cook chicken until browned all over, about 10 minutes; transfer to plate. When chicken is cool enough to handle, remove and discard skin. Pour fat (you should have about 2 tablespoons) into small bowl; reserve.

2. Add onion and 1 tablespoon oil to now-empty pot and cook over medium heat until softened, about 5 minutes. Stir in thyme and cook until fragrant, about 30 seconds. Add 7 cups broth, chicken, and bay leaves and bring to boil. Reduce heat to low and simmer, covered, until breasts register 160 degrees and thighs register 175 degrees, 20 to 25 minutes. Remove from heat and transfer chicken to clean plate. When chicken is cool enough to handle, shred into bite-size pieces, discarding bones.

3. Meanwhile, combine remaining ½ cup chicken broth, reserved fat, and remaining 1 tablespoon oil in liquid measuring cup. Process remaining 2 cups flour and ½ teaspoon salt in food processor until combined. With processor running, slowly pour in broth mixture and process until mixture resembles coarse meal. Turn dough onto lightly floured surface and knead until smooth. Divide in half.

4. Roll each dough half into 10-inch square about ⅛ inch thick. Cut each square into twenty 5 by 1-inch rectangles. Place handful of noodles in single layer on parchment paper–lined plate, cover with another sheet of parchment, and repeat stacking with remaining noodles and additional parchment, ending with parchment. Freeze until firm, at least 10 minutes or up to 30 minutes.

5. Return broth to simmer and add noodles. Cook until noodles are nearly tender, 12 to 15 minutes, stirring occasionally to separate. Remove 1 cup broth from pot and whisk into reserved toasted flour. Stir broth-flour mixture into pot, being careful not to break up noodles, and simmer until slightly thickened, 3 to 5 minutes. Add shredded chicken and parsley and cook until heated through, about 1 minute. Season with salt and pepper to taste. Serve.

Making Slicks

1. Roll each dough half into 10-inch square of ⅛ inch thickness. Then, using sharp knife, cut dough into twenty 5 by 1-inch rectangles.

2. Stack slicks between layers of parchment and freeze briefly before simmering.

Why This Recipe Works A distant cousin to chicken and dumplings, chicken and slicks offers tender chicken in a rich, flavorful broth but swaps the traditional biscuit-style dumpling for a thick, chewy, noodlelike version. For a flavorful base, we browned the chicken before simmering it in the broth; bone-in pieces provided the best flavor. While authentic recipes call for lard in the slicks, we replaced it with more readily available vegetable oil, plus some of the rendered fat from our chicken. Cooking the slicks in an already thickened broth caused them to break apart, so we cooked them in the broth before adding toasted flour to thicken it.

MORAVIAN CHICKEN PIE

SERVES 8

Crust

½ cup sour cream, chilled
1 large egg, lightly beaten
2½ cups (12½ ounces) all-purpose flour
1½ teaspoons salt
12 tablespoons unsalted butter,
   cut into ½-inch pieces and chilled

Filling

2 (10- to 12-ounce) bone-in split chicken
  breasts, halved crosswise and trimmed
3 (5- to 7-ounce) bone-in chicken thighs,
  trimmed
  Salt and pepper
1 tablespoon vegetable oil
3 cups chicken broth
1 bay leaf
2 tablespoons unsalted butter
¼ cup all-purpose flour
¼ cup half-and-half
1 large egg, lightly beaten

1. For the Crust Combine sour cream and egg in bowl. Process flour and salt in food processor until combined, about 3 seconds. Add butter and pulse until only pea-size pieces remain, about 10 pulses. Add half of sour cream mixture and pulse until combined, 5 pulses. Add remaining sour cream mixture and pulse until dough begins to form, about 10 pulses.

2. Transfer mixture to lightly floured counter and knead briefly until dough comes together. Divide dough in half and form each half into 4-inch disk. Wrap each disk in plastic wrap and refrigerate for at least 1 hour or up to 2 days.

3. Line rimmed baking sheet with parchment paper. Remove 1 dough disk from refrigerator and let sit for 10 minutes. Working on lightly floured counter, roll into 12-inch round and transfer to 9-inch pie plate, leaving ½-inch overhang all around. Repeat with second dough disk and transfer to prepared baking sheet. Cover both dough rounds with plastic wrap and refrigerate for 30 minutes.

4. For the Filling Pat chicken dry with paper towels and season with salt and pepper. Heat oil in large Dutch oven over medium-high heat until just smoking. Cook chicken until browned, about 10 minutes; transfer to plate. Pour fat (you should have 2 tablespoons; supplement with butter if necessary) into bowl; reserve. When chicken is cool enough to handle, remove and discard skin. Add broth, chicken, and bay leaf to now-empty pot and bring to boil. Reduce heat to low and simmer, covered, until breasts register 160 degrees and thighs register 175 degrees, 14 to 18 minutes. Transfer chicken to bowl. When chicken is cool enough to handle, shred into bite-size pieces, discarding bones. Pour broth through fine-mesh strainer into second bowl and reserve (you should have about 2¾ cups); discard bay leaf.

5. Adjust oven rack to lowest position and heat oven to 450 degrees. Heat butter and reserved fat in now-empty pot over medium heat until shimmering. Add flour and cook, whisking constantly, until golden, 1 to 2 minutes. Slowly whisk in 2 cups reserved broth and half-and-half and bring to boil. Reduce heat to medium-low and simmer gravy until thickened and reduced to 1¾ cups, 6 to 8 minutes. Season with salt and pepper to taste. Combine 1 cup gravy with shredded chicken; reserve remaining gravy for serving.

6. Transfer chicken mixture to dough-lined pie plate and spread into even layer. Top with second dough round, leaving at least ½-inch overhang all around. Fold dough under so that edge of fold is flush with rim of pie plate. Flute edges using thumb and forefinger or press with tines of fork to seal. Cut four 1-inch slits in top. Brush pie with egg and bake until top is light golden brown, 18 to 20 minutes. Reduce oven temperature to 375 degrees and continue to bake until crust is deep golden brown, 10 to 15 minutes. Let pie cool on wire rack for at least 45 minutes.

7. When ready to serve, bring remaining ¾ cup reserved gravy and remaining ¾ cup reserved broth to boil in medium saucepan. Simmer over medium-low heat until slightly thickened, 5 to 7 minutes. Season with salt and pepper to taste. Serve pie with gravy.

Why This Recipe Works Protestant immigrants from the Czech province Moravia settled in Pennsylvania and later North Carolina and brought with them such homey dishes as Moravian cake, cookies, and chicken pie, a satisfying double-crusted pie filled with shredded chicken and served with a rich gravy. Searing the chicken (a mix of breasts and thighs) helped to render its fat, which we used in a roux to thicken the gravy. For moist chicken, we poached it in chicken broth and used that broth to give our gravy flavor. As for the pie crust, we found that sour cream helped make for a rich, flaky crust that was remarkably easy to roll out.

Why This Recipe Works Guinness beef stew often captures only the bitterness and none of the deep, caramelized flavors of the beer. We found the trick to rich, malty flavor was to add some of the beer at the end of cooking so that the heat didn't dull the complex flavors. We also added a little brown sugar to balance some of the bitterness. We loved the idea of just dumping the meat into the pot without searing, but the flavor was lacking. To compensate, we first browned the onions and tomato paste, then cooked the stew uncovered so that the meat could brown in the oven.

GUINNESS BEEF STEW

SERVES 6 TO 8

Use Guinness Draught, not Guinness Extra Stout, which is too bitter.

- 1 (3½- to 4-pound) boneless beef chuck-eye roast, pulled apart at seams, trimmed, and cut into 1½-inch pieces
  Salt and pepper
- 3 tablespoons vegetable oil
- 2 onions, chopped fine
- 1 tablespoon tomato paste
- 2 garlic cloves, minced
- ¼ cup all-purpose flour
- 3 cups chicken broth
- 1¼ cups Guinness Draught
- 1½ tablespoons packed dark brown sugar
- 1 teaspoon minced fresh thyme
- 1½ pounds Yukon Gold potatoes, unpeeled, cut into 1-inch pieces
- 1 pound carrots, peeled and cut into 1-inch pieces
- 2 tablespoons minced fresh parsley

1. Adjust oven rack to lower-middle position and heat oven to 325 degrees. Season beef with salt and pepper. Heat oil in Dutch oven over medium-high heat until shimmering. Add onions and ¼ teaspoon salt and cook, stirring occasionally, until well browned, 8 to 10 minutes.

2. Add tomato paste and garlic and cook until rust-colored and fragrant, about 2 minutes. Stir in flour and cook for 1 minute. Whisk in broth, ¾ cup Guinness, sugar, and thyme, scraping up any browned bits. Bring to simmer and cook until slightly thickened, about 3 minutes. Stir in beef and return to simmer. Transfer to oven and cook, uncovered, for 90 minutes, stirring halfway through cooking.

3. Stir in potatoes and carrots and continue cooking until beef and vegetables are tender, about 1 hour, stirring halfway through cooking. Stir in remaining ½ cup Guinness and parsley. Season with salt and pepper to taste and serve.

Cook It Uncovered

Most stew recipes start by searing meat in batches on the stovetop. For an easier beef stew, we skip that step but keep the flavor by cooking the stew uncovered in the oven; the open pot allows the meat on top to take on flavorful browning. In addition, the liquid reduces, concentrating in flavor and texture, while the meat cooks.

Preparing a Chuck Roast

1. Pull apart roast at major seams (marked by lines of fat and silverskin). Use knife as necessary.

2. With sharp chef's knife or boning knife, trim off thick layers of fat and silverskin. Cut meat into 1½-inch pieces.

BRUNSWICK STEW

SERVES 4 TO 6

Our favorite kielbasa is Wellshire Farms Smoked Polska Kielbasa.

- 1 tablespoon vegetable oil
- 1 onion, chopped fine
- ¾ cup ketchup
- 4 cups water
- 2 pounds boneless, skinless chicken thighs, trimmed
- 1 pound russet potatoes, peeled and cut into ½-inch chunks
- 8 ounces kielbasa sausage, sliced ¼ inch thick
- 6–8 tablespoons cider vinegar
- 2 tablespoons Worcestershire sauce
- 1 tablespoon yellow mustard
- 1 teaspoon garlic powder
  Salt and pepper
- ¼ teaspoon red pepper flakes
- 1 cup canned crushed tomatoes
- ½ cup frozen lima beans
- ½ cup frozen corn

1. Heat oil in Dutch oven over medium-high heat until shimmering. Add onion and cook until softened, 3 to 5 minutes. Add ketchup and ¼ cup water and cook, stirring frequently, until fond begins to form on bottom of pot and mixture has thickened, about 6 minutes.

2. Add chicken, potatoes, kielbasa, 6 tablespoons vinegar, 1½ tablespoons Worcestershire, mustard, garlic powder, 1 teaspoon salt, 1 teaspoon pepper, pepper flakes, and remaining 3¾ cups water and bring to boil. Reduce heat to low, cover, and simmer until potatoes are tender, 30 to 35 minutes, stirring frequently.

3. Transfer chicken to plate and let cool for 5 minutes, then shred into bite-size pieces with 2 forks. While chicken cools, stir tomatoes, lima beans, and corn into stew and continue to simmer, uncovered, for 15 minutes. Stir in shredded chicken and remaining 1½ teaspoons Worcestershire and cook until warmed through, about 2 minutes. Season with salt, pepper, and remaining vinegar (up to 2 tablespoons) to taste. Serve.

Browning Ketchup

Ketchup offers a lot of culinary bang for the buck, with sweet, tangy, and savory flavors in a single bottle. For this recipe, we cook the ketchup until it thickens and browns, making it even more complex.

Why This Recipe Works Brunswick stew is a fixture at many Southern barbecues, but because there is no definitive recipe for the stew, many cooks use it as a kitchen sink dump-all, resulting in variations that simply aren't appealing. After testing various versions, we settled on an eastern North Carolina style made with barbecue sauce for complex flavor and potatoes for thickness. We kept the meats simple, opting for tender chicken thighs and flavorful kielbasa. Because barbecue sauce flavors vary across brands, we created our own. Browning the ketchup before adding other ingredients helped to soften its raw edge and created a rich tomato base.

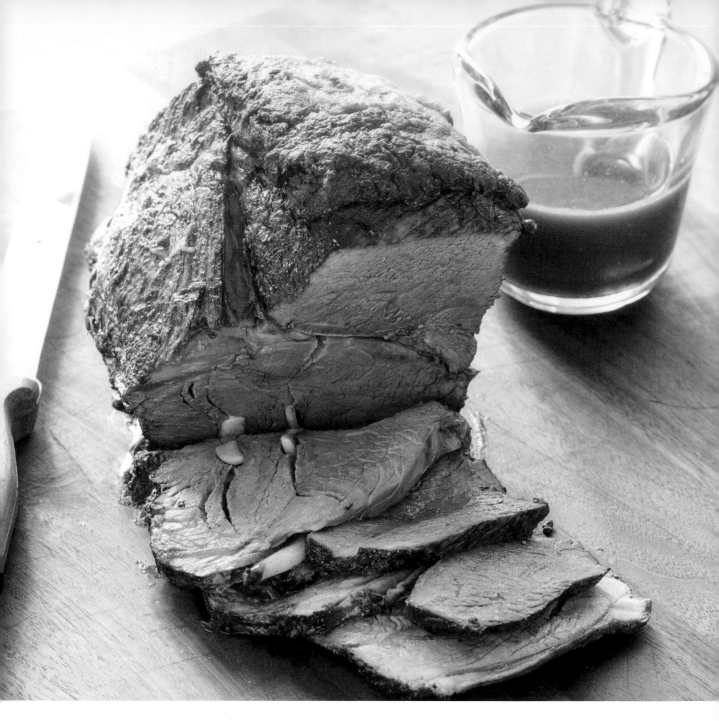

Why This Recipe Works Is there a more affordable roast beef alternative to pricey prime rib? One that is faster to cook and full of rich, beefy, tender flavor? In our testing, we found our answer with top sirloin. Skipping a stovetop sear, we browned the roast in the oven at a high temperature and then reduced the oven temperature to cook the roast through without losing too much moisture. And to give our roast an extra layer of savory flavor, we turned to garlic. A three-pronged attack yielded roast beef with great garlic flavor: We studded the roast beef with toasted garlic, rubbed it with garlic salt, and coated it while it cooked with a garlic paste.

SUNDAY-BEST GARLIC ROAST BEEF

SERVES 6 TO 8

Look for a top sirloin roast that has a thick, substantial fat cap still attached. The rendered fat will help to keep the roast moist. When making the jus, taste the reduced broth before adding any of the accumulated meat juices from the roast. The meat juices are well seasoned and may make the jus too salty. If you don't have a heavy-duty nonstick roasting pan, a broiler pan bottom works well, too.

Beef

8 large garlic cloves, unpeeled
1 (4-pound) top sirloin roast, fat trimmed to ¼ inch

Garlic-Salt Rub

3 large garlic cloves, minced
1 teaspoon dried thyme
½ teaspoon salt

Garlic Paste

½ cup olive oil
12 large garlic cloves, cut in half lengthwise
2 sprigs fresh thyme
2 bay leaves
½ teaspoon salt
 Pepper

Jus

1½ cups beef broth
1½ cups chicken broth

1. For the Beef Toast garlic in 8-inch skillet over medium-high heat, tossing frequently, until spotty brown, about 8 minutes. Set aside. When cool enough to handle, peel and cut into ¼-inch slivers. Using paring knife, make 1-inch-deep slits all over roast and insert toasted garlic into slits.

2. For the Garlic-Salt Rub Combine garlic, thyme, and salt in small bowl and rub all over roast. Place roast on large plate and refrigerate, uncovered, for at least 4 hours or preferably overnight.

3. For the Garlic Paste Heat oil, garlic, thyme, bay leaves, and salt in small saucepan over medium-high heat until bubbles start to rise to surface. Reduce heat to low and cook until garlic is soft, about 30 minutes. Let cool completely, then strain, reserving oil. Discard herbs and transfer garlic to small bowl. Mash garlic with 1 tablespoon garlic oil until paste forms. Cover and refrigerate paste until ready to use. Cover and reserve garlic oil.

4. Adjust oven rack to middle position, place nonstick roasting pan on rack, and heat oven to 450 degrees. Using paper towels, wipe garlic-salt rub off beef. Rub beef with 2 tablespoons reserved garlic oil and season with pepper. Transfer meat, fat side down, to preheated pan and roast, turning as needed until browned on all sides, 10 to 15 minutes.

5. Reduce oven temperature to 300 degrees. Remove pan from oven, turn roast fat side up, and, using spatula, coat top with garlic paste. Return meat to oven and roast until it registers 120 to 125 degrees (for medium-rare), 50 minutes to 1 hour, 10 minutes. Transfer to carving board, cover loosely with aluminum foil, and let rest for 20 minutes.

6. For the Jus Pour off fat from roasting pan and place pan over high heat. Add beef broth and chicken broth and bring to boil, scraping up browned bits with wooden spoon. Simmer, stirring occasionally, until reduced to 2 cups, about 5 minutes. Add accumulated juices from roast and cook for 1 minute, then pour through fine-mesh strainer. Slice roast crosswise into ¼-inch-thick slices. Serve with jus.

Why This Recipe Works For tender, juicy roast beef, we chose top sirloin roast with a thick fat cap, which rendered as the beef roasted and kept it moist. Searing each side before roasting helped to develop a flavorful crust. Though the right roasting temperature produced juicy meat (our roast having expelled very little liquid), it left precious few drippings in the roasting pan from which to make gravy. A good amount of beef broth, plus the rendered fat and fond left behind from searing the meat, provided volume and richness, while mushrooms, red wine, and Worcestershire sauce amped up the flavor.

CLASSIC ROAST BEEF AND GRAVY

SERVES 6 TO 8

For the best flavor and texture, refrigerate the roast overnight after salting. If you don't have a V-rack, cook the roast on a wire rack set inside a rimmed baking sheet.

1   (4-pound) top sirloin roast,
    fat trimmed to ¼ inch
    Salt and pepper
1   tablespoon vegetable oil
8   ounces white mushrooms,
    trimmed and chopped
2   onions, chopped fine
1   carrot, peeled and chopped
1   celery rib, minced
1   tablespoon tomato paste
4   garlic cloves, minced
¼   cup all-purpose flour
1   cup red wine
4   cups beef broth
1   teaspoon Worcestershire sauce

1. Pat roast dry with paper towels. Rub 2 teaspoons salt evenly over meat. Cover with plastic wrap and refrigerate for at least 1 hour or up to 24 hours.

2. Adjust oven rack to lower-middle position and heat oven to 275 degrees. Pat roast dry with paper towels and rub with 1 teaspoon pepper. Heat oil in Dutch oven over medium-high heat until just smoking. Brown roast all over, 8 to 12 minutes, then transfer to V-rack set inside roasting pan (do not wipe out Dutch oven). Transfer to oven and cook until meat registers 120 to 125 degrees (for medium-rare), 1½ to 2 hours.

3. Meanwhile, add mushrooms to fat left in Dutch oven and cook until golden, about 5 minutes. Stir in onions, carrot, and celery and cook until browned, 5 to 7 minutes. Stir in tomato paste, garlic, and flour and cook until fragrant, about 2 minutes. Stir in wine and broth, scraping up any browned bits with wooden spoon. Bring to boil, then reduce heat to medium and simmer until thickened, about 10 minutes. Strain gravy, then stir in Worcestershire and season with salt and pepper; cover and keep warm.

4. Transfer roast to carving board, tent with aluminum foil, and let rest for 20 minutes. Slice roast crosswise into ½-inch-thick slices. Serve with gravy.

Flavor Builders

A combination of sautéed mushrooms, tomato paste, beef broth, and Worcestershire sauce mimicked the roasted, beefy flavor of traditional gravy made with pan drippings.

Top Sirloin—The Right Cut

Through extensive testing of every cut of beef, the test kitchen has settled on top sirloin as our favorite inexpensive roast. Look for a roast with at least a ¼-inch fat cap on top; the fat renders in the oven, basting the roast and helping to keep it moist.

HERBED ROAST BEEF

SERVES 6 TO 8

For even deeper seasoning, refrigerate the roast overnight after filling it with the herb mixture in step 2.

⅓ cup minced fresh parsley
1 shallot, minced
2 tablespoons minced fresh thyme
2 tablespoons olive oil
1 tablespoon Dijon mustard
4 tablespoons unsalted butter, softened
1 (4-pound) top sirloin roast, fat trimmed to ¼ inch
1 tablespoon salt
1 tablespoon pepper

1. Combine parsley, shallot, and thyme in bowl. Transfer 2 tablespoons herb mixture to second bowl and stir in 1 tablespoon oil and mustard until combined; set aside. Add butter to remaining herb mixture and mash with fork until combined.

2. Butterfly roast by slicing horizontally through middle of meat, leaving about ½ inch of meat intact, and rub roast inside and out with salt and pepper. Spread herb-mustard mixture over interior of meat, fold roast back together, and tie securely with kitchen twine at 1-inch intervals. Refrigerate for at least 1 hour or up to 24 hours.

3. Adjust oven rack to middle position and heat oven to 275 degrees. Pat roast dry with paper towels.

Heat remaining 1 tablespoon oil in 12-inch skillet over medium-high heat until just smoking. Brown roast all over, 8 to 12 minutes, then arrange on V-rack set inside roasting pan. Transfer to oven and roast until meat registers 120 to 125 degrees (for medium-rare), 1½ to 2 hours.

4. Transfer roast to carving board, spread with herb-butter mixture, tent with aluminum foil, and let rest for 20 minutes. Remove twine and slice roast crosswise into ¼-inch-thick slices. Serve.

Fast Sear, Slow Roast for Beef

We brown most beef roasts on the stovetop to build a flavorful crust, then roast them gently for a uniformly rosy, juicy interior.

1. Searing roast assures a flavorful, deep brown crust.

2. Roasting at a low temperature (275 degrees) keeps the meat moist and succulent.

Herbs Galore

Fresh parsley and thyme flavor both the interior and exterior of our roast.

1. Butterfly roast by slicing horizontally through middle of the meat. Leave about ½ inch of meat intact, then open it like a book.

2. After seasoning meat, spread herb-mustard mixture over interior of meat.

3. Fold meat back to its original position, then tie securely at 1-inch intervals with kitchen twine.

4. For second hit of herb flavor after roast is cooked, spread it with herb butter.

Why This Recipe Works For a roast beef dressed to impress without much effort, we turned to a swirl of herbs and mustard. To start, we combined fresh herbs with the mustard, butterflied the roast, and spread the herbs over the interior of the meat before folding it back together and securing it with twine. A simple herb butter, spread over the resting roast, melted and mingled with the natural juices of the meat, creating a flavorful sauce without the need to dirty another pan.

HERB-CRUSTED BEEF TENDERLOIN

SERVES 12 TO 16

Make sure to begin this recipe 2 hours before you plan to put the roast in the oven. The tenderloin can be trimmed, tied, rubbed with the salt mixture, and refrigerated up to 24 hours in advance; make sure to bring the roast back to room temperature before putting it into the oven.

1 (6-pound) whole beef tenderloin, trimmed, tail end tucked, and tied at 1½-inch intervals
  Kosher salt and cracked peppercorns
2 teaspoons sugar
2 slices hearty white sandwich bread, torn into pieces
2½ ounces Parmesan cheese, grated (1¼ cups)
½ cup chopped fresh parsley
6 tablespoons olive oil
2 teaspoons plus 2 tablespoons chopped fresh thyme
4 garlic cloves, minced
1 recipe Horseradish Cream Sauce

1. Set wire rack in rimmed baking sheet. Pat tenderloin dry with paper towels. Combine 1 tablespoon salt, 1 tablespoon pepper, and sugar in small bowl and rub all over tenderloin. Transfer to prepared baking sheet and let sit at room temperature for 2 hours.

2. Meanwhile, pulse bread in food processor to fine crumbs, about 15 pulses. Transfer bread crumbs to medium bowl and toss with ½ cup Parmesan, 2 tablespoons parsley, 2 tablespoons oil, and 2 teaspoons thyme until evenly combined. Wipe out food processor with paper towels and process remaining ¾ cup Parmesan, 6 tablespoons parsley, ¼ cup oil, 2 tablespoons thyme, and garlic until smooth paste forms. Transfer herb paste to small bowl.

3. Adjust oven rack to upper-middle position and heat oven to 400 degrees. Roast tenderloin for 20 minutes and remove from oven. Using scissors, carefully cut kitchen twine and remove it. Coat tenderloin with herb paste, then bread-crumb topping. Roast until meat registers 120 to 125 degrees (for medium-rare)

and topping is golden brown, 20 to 25 minutes. (If topping browns before meat reaches preferred internal temperature, lightly cover with aluminum foil for remainder of roasting time and remove while roast rests.) Let roast rest, uncovered, for 30 minutes on wire rack. Transfer to carving board and carve. Serve with Horseradish Cream Sauce.

HORSERADISH CREAM SAUCE
MAKES ABOUT 1 CUP

½ cup sour cream
½ cup heavy cream
¼ cup prepared horseradish, drained
2 teaspoons Dijon mustard
1 garlic clove, minced
¼ teaspoon sugar
  Salt and pepper

Mix all ingredients in bowl; add salt and pepper to taste. Cover and let stand at room temperature for 1 to 1½ hours to thicken. (Sauce can be refrigerated for up to 2 days.)

Preparing Herb-Crusted Beef Tenderloin

1. To ensure even cooking, fold thin, tapered end under roast, then tie entire roast with kitchen twine every 1½ inches. Roast for 20 minutes.

2. Remove roast from oven, snip twine with scissors, and remove before adding herb paste and bread-crumb mixture. Return to oven to finish cooking.

Why This Recipe Works Though beef tenderloin offers incomparable tenderness, its flavor could often use some embellishment. To give the meat a flavor boost, we turned to a thick herbed crust. But herbs can burn easily, lose their flavor in a hot oven, or just fall off the meat. Cooking the roast in the oven at a high temperature for part of the time gave us a perfectly caramelized exterior that made applying an herb paste easy. Adding grated Parmesan cheese to the paste gave it nutty flavor and helped the paste adhere to the meat. Fresh parsley and thyme provided a flavorful coating, and for a crisp texture, we relied on bread crumbs.

Why This Recipe Works For an occasion-worthy, beefy top-loin roast, we wanted a seared crust and a perfect medium-rare throughout, but most recipes we found could only give us one or the other. Gently roasting in a low oven until the meat was almost done and then setting it under the broiler for a few minutes achieved both results without the hassle of pan-searing. Scoring the fat cap before cooking helped the fat to render and the surface to crisp. We let the meat sit overnight with a spice and herb rub (and plenty of salt) to ensure a perfectly seasoned, flavorful roast, and served it with a bright, fresh salsa verde to complement the rich meat.

HOLIDAY STRIP ROAST

SERVES 8 TO 10

Serve with Salsa Verde (recipe follows).

1 (5- to 6-pound) boneless top loin roast,
   fat trimmed to ¼ inch
2 tablespoons peppercorns
1 tablespoon coriander seeds
1 tablespoon yellow mustard seeds
3 tablespoons olive oil
2 tablespoons kosher salt
2 tablespoons chopped fresh rosemary
1 teaspoon red pepper flakes

1. Pat roast dry with paper towels. Using sharp knife, cut ½-inch crosshatch pattern through fat cap, ¼ inch deep. Tie kitchen twine around roast at 2-inch intervals. Grind peppercorns, coriander seeds, and mustard seeds to texture of coarse sand in spice grinder. Combine spice mixture, oil, salt, rosemary, and pepper flakes in bowl until thick paste forms. Rub paste all over roast and into crosshatch. Wrap roast with plastic wrap and refrigerate for 6 to 24 hours.

2. Set wire rack inside rimmed baking sheet. One hour before cooking, unwrap meat and place on prepared rack, fat side up. Adjust oven rack to middle position and heat oven to 275 degrees. Transfer roast to oven and cook until meat registers 115 degrees, about 90 minutes, rotating sheet halfway through cooking. Remove roast from oven and heat broiler.

3. Return roast to oven and broil on middle oven rack until fat cap is deep brown and interior of roast registers 125 degrees, 3 to 5 minutes. Transfer to carving board, tent loosely with aluminum foil, and let rest for 20 minutes. Remove twine and carve into thin slices. Serve.

SALSA VERDE
MAKES ABOUT 1½ CUPS
Mince the garlic before processing it, or it won't break down enough. This sauce can be prepared up to two days in advance and refrigerated. Before serving, bring it to room temperature and stir to recombine.

2 slices hearty white sandwich bread,
   torn into 1-inch pieces
1 cup extra-virgin olive oil
¼ cup lemon juice (2 lemons)
4 cups fresh parsley leaves
¼ cup capers, rinsed
4 anchovy fillets, rinsed
2 garlic cloves, minced
½ teaspoon kosher salt

Process bread, oil, and lemon juice in food processor until smooth, about 10 seconds. Add parsley, capers, anchovies, garlic, and salt and pulse until mixture is finely chopped, about 5 pulses, scraping down bowl as needed.

The Right Grind
As part of the rub for the roast, we grind peppercorns with mustard seeds and coriander seeds to the texture of coarse sand. Since these ingredients are irregularly sized and of varying densities, the texture won't be uniform, which is OK. The correct grind looks like this.

Coarse and irregular

DEVILED BEEF SHORT RIBS

SERVES 4 TO 6

English-style short ribs contain a single rib bone. For a milder sauce, use only one jalapeño and discard the seeds.

⅔ cup yellow mustard
⅓ cup orange juice
⅓ cup packed light brown sugar
1–2 jalapeño chiles, stemmed, seeds reserved, and roughly chopped
4 teaspoons dry mustard
1 tablespoon lemon juice plus 1 teaspoon grated lemon zest
Salt and pepper
½ teaspoon cayenne pepper
5 pounds bone-in English-style short ribs, bones 4 to 5 inches long, 1 to 1½ inches of meat on top of bone, trimmed
2 tablespoons unsalted butter
1½ cups panko bread crumbs
1 tablespoon chopped fresh parsley

1. Adjust oven rack to middle position and heat oven to 325 degrees. Combine yellow mustard, orange juice, sugar, jalapeños and reserved seeds, dry mustard, lemon juice, and 2 teaspoons pepper in food processor and process until smooth, about 30 seconds; set aside. (Mustard mixture can be refrigerated for up to 1 week.)

2. Combine 1 tablespoon salt, 1 tablespoon pepper, and cayenne in bowl. Sprinkle ribs all over with spice mixture. Arrange ribs, meat side down, in 13 by 9-inch baking dish. Cover dish tightly with aluminum foil and roast until meat is nearly tender, about 3 hours.

3. Meanwhile, melt butter in 12-inch skillet over medium-high heat. Add panko and cook, stirring often, until golden brown, about 3 minutes. Off heat, stir in parsley and lemon zest and transfer to shallow dish.

4. Remove baking dish from oven and increase oven temperature to 425 degrees; transfer ribs to plate. Discard rendered fat and juices from dish. Brush meat (not bone) all over with one-fourth of mustard sauce and return ribs to dish, meat side up. Roast, uncovered, until beginning to brown, about 10 minutes. Brush meat again with one-third of remaining mustard sauce and continue to roast until well browned and completely tender, 10 to 15 minutes longer. Transfer ribs to serving platter, tent loosely with foil, and let rest for 15 minutes.

5. Brush meat once more with half of remaining mustard sauce and roll in panko mixture, taking care to entirely coat meat. Serve, passing remaining mustard sauce separately.

A Roasting-Braising Hybrid Method

Most short rib recipes call for searing, then braising, and finally turning the braising liquid into a sauce. For our Deviled Beef Short Ribs, we took a different road: We put the ribs in a baking dish, meat side down, and roasted them (covered) until tender, about 3 hours. The meat cooked in its own rendered fat and juices, giving us fully rendered, supertender short ribs without much hands-on work. To finish,

 we uncovered the ribs, brushed them with a glaze, roasted them meat side up, repeated, and then rolled them in toasted crumbs.

Why This Recipe Works "Deviling" food usually involves flavoring it with mustard, black pepper, and other seasonings, but for our deviled short ribs we really wanted to feel the heat. We first roasted the seasoned ribs meat side down in a covered baking dish, allowing the meat to cook in its own rendered fat and juices. After cranking the heat and pouring off the juices, we brushed the ribs with a spicy glaze of dry and prepared mustards, citrus, brown sugar, and pureed jalapeños. A few rounds of brushing and roasting created a browned crust, and for a crunchy finish we coated the ribs with buttery, toasted panko bread crumbs.

ONE-PAN PRIME RIB AND ROASTED VEGETABLES

SERVES 8 TO 10

The roast must be salted and then refrigerated for at least 24 hours before cooking; salting and refrigerating for the full 4 days results in the most tender, flavorful meat.

1 (7-pound) first-cut beef standing rib roast (3 bones), fat trimmed to ¼ inch
  Kosher salt and pepper
  Vegetable oil
2 pounds carrots, peeled, cut into 2-inch lengths, halved or quartered lengthwise to create ½-inch-diameter pieces
1 pound parsnips, peeled and sliced ½ inch thick on bias
1 pound Brussels sprouts, trimmed and halved
1 red onion, halved and sliced through root end into ½-inch wedges
2 teaspoons minced fresh thyme

1. Using sharp knife, cut through roast's fat cap in 1-inch crosshatch pattern, being careful not to cut into meat. Rub 2 tablespoons salt over entire roast and into crosshatch. Transfer to large plate and refrigerate, uncovered, for at least 24 hours or up to 4 days.

2. Adjust oven rack to lower-middle position and heat oven to 250 degrees. Season roast with pepper and arrange, fat side up, on V-rack set in large roasting pan. Roast until meat registers 115 degrees for rare, 120 degrees for medium-rare, or 125 degrees for medium, 3 to 3½ hours. Transfer V-rack with roast to carving board, tent loosely with aluminum foil, and let rest for about 1 hour.

3. Meanwhile, increase oven temperature to 425 degrees. Pour off all but 2 tablespoons fat from pan. (If there isn't enough fat in pan, add vegetable oil to equal 2 tablespoons.) Toss carrots, parsnips, brussels sprouts, onion, thyme, 1 teaspoon salt, and ½ teaspoon pepper with fat in pan. Roast vegetables, stirring halfway through roasting, until tender and browned, 45 to 50 minutes.

4. Remove pan from oven and heat broiler. Carefully nestle V-rack with roast among vegetables in pan. Broil roast until fat cap is evenly browned, about 5 minutes, rotating pan as necessary. Transfer roast to carving board, carve meat from bones, and cut into ¾-inch-thick slices. Season vegetables with salt and pepper to taste. Serve roast with vegetables.

Buy the Right Roast

This recipe calls for a first-cut, bone-in standing rib roast, which contains ribs 9, 10, and 11 (the ribs that are closest to the tail of the steer; butchers often label this cut "loin-end"). First-cut roasts contain the largest eye of meat. While second-cut roasts are pretty good, too, they are slightly fattier and more irregular, making them more difficult to cook evenly. Since these cuts are often priced the same, it's worth your while to ask for the superior first-cut roast.

FIRST CUT
More meat, larger eye

SECOND CUT
More fat, smaller eye
(but still good)

Carving a Standing Rib Roast

To carve a bone-in rib roast, simply hold the roast in place with a carving fork and cut parallel to the rib bones to remove the meat in one big piece. Then slice and serve the meat.

Why This Recipe Works Our goal was to produce a recipe for holiday prime rib with roasted vegetables that was simple and foolproof. We scored and salted a first-cut standing rib roast and refrigerated it for 24 hours for tender beef. A low-and-slow cooking method yielded evenly red and juicy meat, and an additional stint under the broiler turned the outside crispy and golden. Instead of forcing the vegetables to work in concert with the beef, we roasted them solo in the flavorful beef fat while the prime rib was resting. It was definitely a feast fit for a holiday—with only one pan to wash.

Why This Recipe Works To ensure a juicy roast, we trimmed the excess fat, made shallow crosshatch cuts in the remaining fat cap, and rubbed the roast with salt 24 hours before cooking. We saved the trimmed fat and placed it under the roast as it cooked, creating intensely flavored drippings. To achieve a creamy interior, we precooked the potatoes in the microwave before tossing them with the rendered fat and roasting them until crisp. Searing the cooked roast in a hot skillet added some last-minute browning to the roast's exterior without overcooking it. An easy red wine–orange sauce proved a bright contrast to the savory beef.

PRIME RIB WITH POTATOES AND RED WINE–ORANGE SAUCE

SERVES 8 TO 10

The roast must be salted and refrigerated for at least 24 hours before cooking. Wait until the roast is done cooking before peeling and cutting the potatoes so they don't discolor. It is crucial to use a sturdy rimmed baking sheet for this recipe. Serve with Red Wine–Orange Sauce (recipe follows).

1 (7-pound) first-cut beef standing rib roast (3 bones), with untrimmed fat cap
  Kosher salt and pepper
4 pounds Yukon gold potatoes, peeled and cut into 1½-inch pieces
1 tablespoon minced fresh rosemary
1 tablespoon vegetable oil

1. Using sharp knife, trim roast's fat cap to even ¼-inch-thickness; reserve and refrigerate trimmings. Cut 1-inch crosshatch pattern in fat cap, being careful not to cut into meat. Rub 2 tablespoons salt over roast and into crosshatch. Transfer to large plate and refrigerate, uncovered, for at least 24 hours or up to 4 days.

2. Adjust oven rack to lower-middle position and heat oven to 250 degrees. Cut reserved trimmings into ½-inch pieces. Place 1 cup of trimmings in rimmed baking sheet, then set wire rack in sheet. Season roast with pepper and place, fat side up, on wire rack.

3. Roast until meat registers 115 degrees for rare, 120 degrees for medium-rare, or 125 degrees for medium, 3 to 3½ hours. Transfer roast to carving board, tent with aluminum foil, and let rest for 1 hour. Carefully remove wire rack and reserve beef fat in baking sheet (there should be about ½ cup; if not, add vegetable oil).

4. Increase oven temperature to 450 degrees. Microwave potatoes, covered, in large bowl until they begin to release moisture and surfaces look wet, about 7 minutes. Pat potatoes dry with paper towels. Toss potatoes with rosemary, 2 teaspoons salt, and ½ teaspoon pepper. Transfer potatoes to baking sheet and carefully toss with reserved fat (fat may be hot). Roast until tender and browned, 35 to 40 minutes,

redistributing halfway through cooking. Season potatoes with salt and pepper to taste.

5. Pat roast dry with paper towels. Heat oil in 12-inch skillet over medium-high heat until just smoking. Sear all sides until browned, 6 to 8 minutes total. Transfer roast to carving board. Carve meat from bones and cut into ¾-inch-thick slices. Serve with potatoes.

RED WINE–ORANGE SAUCE
MAKES ABOUT 1½ CUPS
Medium-bodied red wines are best for this sauce.

6 tablespoons unsalted butter, cut into 6 pieces and chilled
3 shallots, minced
1½ tablespoons tomato paste
1 tablespoon sugar
4 garlic cloves, minced
1 tablespoon all-purpose flour
3 cups beef broth
1½ cups red wine
⅓ cup orange juice
1½ tablespoons Worcestershire sauce
1 sprig fresh thyme
  Salt and pepper

1. Melt 2 tablespoons butter in medium saucepan over medium-high heat. Add shallots, tomato paste, and sugar and cook, stirring frequently, until deep brown, 4 to 5 minutes. Stir in garlic and flour and cook until garlic is fragrant and vegetables are well coated with flour, about 30 seconds.

2. Stir in broth, wine, orange juice, Worcestershire, and thyme, scraping up any browned bits. Bring to boil, reduce heat to medium, and cook at low boil until reduced to 2 cups, about 40 minutes.

3. Strain sauce through fine-mesh strainer set over bowl; discard solids. Return sauce to pot and place over low heat. Whisk in remaining 4 tablespoons butter, 1 piece at a time. Season with salt and pepper to taste.

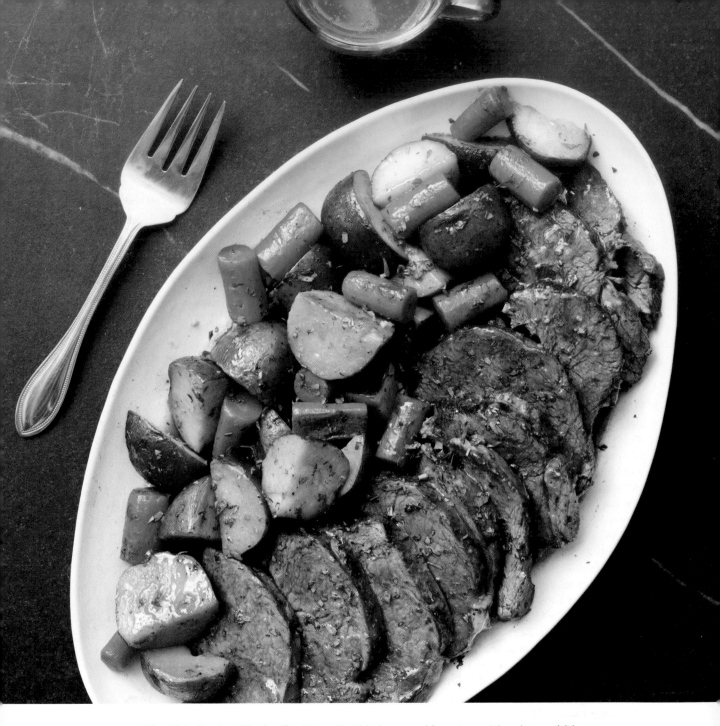

Why This Recipe Works Traditionally, this lazy cook's pot roast involves rubbing a chuck roast with onion soup mix, wrapping it in foil, and cooking it in the oven until tender. While we liked the ease of this dish, we weren't fans of its artificial, salty taste. To develop oniony flavor with ease, we started with onion powder and salt, but ditched the monosodium glutamate in favor of soy sauce, which enhanced the roast's beefy flavor. Brown sugar added sweetness and depth, while a surprise ingredient, a little espresso powder, provided toasty complexity. Dividing the roast into two halves allowed us to apply more of the flavorful spice rub to its exterior.

CHUCK ROAST IN FOIL

SERVES 4 TO 6

You will need an 18-inch-wide roll of heavy-duty aluminum foil for wrapping the roast. We prefer to use small red potatoes, measuring 1 to 2 inches in diameter, in this recipe.

Rub

3 tablespoons cornstarch
4 teaspoons onion powder
2 teaspoons packed light brown sugar
2 teaspoons salt
1 teaspoon pepper
1 teaspoon garlic powder
1 teaspoon instant espresso powder
1 teaspoon dried thyme
½ teaspoon celery seeds

Chuck Roast

1 (4-pound) boneless beef chuck-eye roast, pulled apart at seams, fat trimmed to ¼ inch, and tied at 1-inch intervals
2 onions, peeled and quartered
1 pound small red potatoes, quartered
4 carrots, peeled and cut into 1½-inch pieces
2 bay leaves
2 tablespoons soy sauce

1. For the Rub Adjust oven rack to lower-middle position and heat oven to 300 degrees. Combine all ingredients in small bowl.

2. For the Chuck Roast Pat roast dry with paper towels. Place two 30 by 18-inch sheets of heavy-duty aluminum foil perpendicular to each other inside large roasting pan. Place onions, potatoes, carrots, and bay leaves in center of foil and drizzle with soy sauce. Set roasts on top of vegetables. Rub roasts all over with rub. Fold opposite corners of foil toward each other and crimp edges tightly to seal. Transfer pan to oven and cook until meat is completely tender, about 4½ hours.

3. Remove roasts from foil pouch and place on carving board. Tent meat with foil and let rest for 20 minutes. Remove onions and bay leaves. Using slotted spoon, place carrots and potatoes on serving platter. Strain contents of roasting pan through fine-mesh strainer into fat separator. Let liquid settle, then pour defatted pan juices into serving bowl.

4. Remove kitchen twine from roasts. Slice roasts thin against grain and transfer to platter with vegetables. Pour ½ cup pan juices over meat. Serve with remaining pan juices.

Back in Fashion

Family Circle magazine once asked Peg Bracken, author of the mega-bestselling *I Hate to Cook Book,* to select her greatest-hits list for the hate-to-cook set. Her list included such gems as Stayabed Stew ("For those days when you're en negligee, en bed, with a murder story and a box of bonbons") and the Basic I-Hate-to-Cook Muffin (made by combining beer and muffin mix). But one classic super-easy dish of the day was notably absent: chuck roast with instant onion soup. "Done to death," Bracken explained, adding, "I remember years ago when every working wife in the land was sprinkling a package of dried onion soup mix onto a chunk of chuck steak...the thing was bigger than a Hula-Hoop, and it died, of course, of over-exposure." But guess what? The hula hoop is back, and in its new incarnation, chuck roast in foil is poised for a comeback, too.

CROWN ROAST OF PORK

SERVES 10 TO 12

A crown roast is two bone-in pork loin roasts tied into a crown shape, with the rib bones frenched and chine bones removed. This can be difficult to do, so ask your butcher to make this roast for you. We wrap extra kitchen twine around the widest part of the roast to provide more support when flipping. Use potatoes that measure 1 to 2 inches in diameter.

   Kosher salt and pepper
 3 tablespoons minced fresh thyme
 2 tablespoons minced fresh rosemary
 5 garlic cloves, minced
 1 (8- to 10-pound) pork crown roast
 2 pounds small red potatoes
10 ounces shallots, peeled and halved
 2 Golden Delicious apples, peeled, cored, and halved
 8 tablespoons unsalted butter, melted
 ½ cup apple cider
 1 cup chicken broth

1. Combine 3 tablespoons salt, 1 tablespoon pepper, thyme, rosemary, and garlic in bowl; reserve 2 teaspoons for vegetables. Pat pork dry with paper towels and rub with remaining herb salt. Wrap kitchen twine twice around widest part of roast and tie tightly. Refrigerate roast, covered, for 6 to 24 hours.

2. Adjust oven rack to lower-middle position and heat oven to 475 degrees. Place V-rack inside large roasting pan. Toss potatoes, shallots, apples, 4 tablespoons butter, and reserved herb salt in large bowl and transfer to pan. Arrange roast bone side down in V-rack and brush with remaining 4 tablespoons butter. Roast until meat is well browned and registers 110 degrees, about 1 hour.

3. Remove roast from oven and reduce oven temperature to 300 degrees. Using 2 bunches of paper towels, flip roast bone side up. Add apple cider to pan and return to oven, rotating direction of pan. Roast until meat registers 140 degrees, 30 to 50 minutes. Place meat on carving board, tent loosely with aluminum foil, and let rest for 15 to 20 minutes.

4. Transfer apple halves to blender and potatoes and shallots to bowl. Pour pan juices into fat separator, let liquid settle for 5 minutes, then pour into blender. Add chicken broth to blender with apples and pan juices and process until smooth, about 1 minute. Transfer sauce to medium saucepan and bring to simmer over medium heat. Season with salt and pepper to taste. Cover and keep warm. Remove twine from roast and slice meat between bones. Serve with vegetables and sauce.

Cooking Crown Roast of Pork Evenly

1. Using kitchen twine, make 2 loops around widest part of roast and tie securely to help crown hold its shape when flipped.

2. Place pork bone side down on V-rack and adjust bones to steady roast. Roast about 1 hour, until meat registers 110 degrees.

3. Using paper towels to protect your hands, flip hot roast bone side up and set it back on V-rack to finish cooking in gentle oven.

Why This Recipe Works A crown roast—two bone-in pork loin roasts tied together in a round—can feed a holiday crowd and offers a dramatic presentation, but its shape presents serious challenges to even cooking. Simply roasting it yielded meat overcooked on the outside and undercooked around the inner circle. The solution? We turned the roast upside down to allow more air to circulate and to better expose the thickest part of the roast to the heat. For a side, we opted for potatoes, shallots, and apples roasted in the pan alongside the meat. Pureeing the apples into a rich pan sauce gave us both fruity flavor and a nice, thick consistency.

Why This Recipe Works Pork shoulder's fat content and marbling mean it requires low and slow cooking to become tender—making it a natural for the slow cooker. For a full-flavored sauce, we browned the pork, then sautéed onions and garlic with tomato paste in the browned bits left behind before adding them to the slow cooker. A little instant tapioca produced just the right texture in the braising liquid. White wine added brightness and a splash of white wine vinegar, stirred in at the end of cooking, refreshed the wine flavor. Hearty root vegetables and diced tomatoes, which cooked along with the roast, balanced the flavors.

SLOW-COOKER PORK POT ROAST

SERVES 8

This roast is sometimes sold in elastic netting that must be removed before cooking. If you cannot find 2½- to 3-pound pork picnic shoulder roasts, you can substitute one 6-pound pork picnic shoulder roast; cut it into two pieces and prepare as directed.

- 2 (2½- to 3-pound) boneless pork picnic shoulder roasts, trimmed
  Salt and pepper
- 2 tablespoons vegetable oil
- 2 onions, chopped
- 6 garlic cloves, minced
- 1 tablespoon tomato paste
- ½ cup white wine
- 1 (28-ounce) can diced tomatoes, drained
- 3 tablespoons instant tapioca
- 2 teaspoons minced fresh thyme
- 1 pound carrots, peeled, halved lengthwise, and cut into 2-inch pieces
- 1 pound parsnips, peeled, halved lengthwise, and cut into 2-inch pieces
- 2 teaspoons white wine vinegar

1. Open each roast and trim any excess fat, then tie each roast with kitchen twine at 1½-inch intervals and once around length of roasts. Pat roasts dry with paper towels and season with salt and pepper. Heat 2 teaspoons oil in 12-inch skillet over medium-high heat until just smoking. Brown roasts all over, about 10 minutes. Transfer to slow cooker.

2. Add onions and 2 teaspoons oil to now-empty skillet and cook until browned, about 5 minutes. Add garlic and tomato paste and cook until fragrant, about 1 minute. Stir in wine and simmer, scraping up browned bits with wooden spoon, until thickened, about 2 minutes. Stir in tomatoes, tapioca, and thyme; transfer to slow cooker.

3. Toss carrots, parsnips, ¼ teaspoon salt, ¼ teaspoon pepper, and remaining 2 teaspoons oil in bowl until vegetables are well coated. Scatter vegetable mixture over pork. Cover and cook on low until meat is tender, 9 to 10 hours (or cook on high 4 to 5 hours).

4. Transfer roasts to carving board, tent with aluminum foil, and let rest for 10 minutes. Remove twine from roasts and cut meat into ½-inch-thick slices; transfer to serving platter. Using slotted spoon, transfer carrots and parsnips to platter with pork. Stir vinegar into sauce and season with salt and pepper to taste. Serve, passing sauce separately.

Two Roasts are Better than One

We like to use two smaller roasts for this recipe, because the meat cooks more quickly and the small roasts are easier to manage in the slow cooker—and to find in the supermarket. Most boneless pork shoulder roasts come bound in string netting, which is difficult to remove after cooking. We prefer to cut the netting off before cooking, trim the roasts, and then tie each one with kitchen twine.

1. Remove netting from pork roasts. Open each roast and trim any excess fat.

2. Tie roasts separately. To ensure even cooking, fold smaller lobes under, then tie each roast with kitchen twine every 1½ inches around circumference and once around length.

Why This Recipe Works For this Sunday dinner–worthy pork roast, we skipped lean loins and opted for a meaty and inexpensive pork butt roast, which we flavored with a spice rub of cracked peppercorns, rosemary, sage, fennel seeds, and garlic. Cooking the roast in a low oven for seven hours rendered its fat and softened its tough connective tissue. For easy slicing, we refrigerated the cooked roast overnight until firm, then reheated it in the oven while we made a simple sauce from apple cider, apple jelly, and cider vinegar.

OLD-FASHIONED ROAST PORK

SERVES 8

A heavy roasting pan with 3-inch sides is the best choice for this recipe, but a shallow broiler pan also works well. Boneless pork butt roast is often labeled Boston butt in the supermarket.

- 6 pounds boneless pork butt roast, fat trimmed to ⅛ inch, tied lengthwise and crosswise
- 3 garlic cloves, minced
- 2 teaspoons peppercorns, cracked
- 1½ teaspoons salt
- 1 tablespoon chopped fresh rosemary
- 1 tablespoon chopped fresh sage
- 1 tablespoon fennel seeds, chopped
- 2 large red onions, cut into 1-inch wedges
- 1 cup apple cider
- ¼ cup apple jelly
- 2 tablespoons cider vinegar

1. Adjust oven rack to lower-middle position and heat oven to 300 degrees. Pat pork dry with paper towels. Combine garlic, peppercorns, salt, rosemary, sage, and fennel seeds in small bowl. Rub roast with herb mixture.

2. Transfer to roasting pan and cook for 3 hours. Scatter onion wedges around roast, tossing onions in pan drippings to coat. (If roast has not produced any juices, toss onions with 1 tablespoon vegetable oil before adding to pan.) Continue roasting until meat is extremely tender and skewer inserted in center meets no resistance, 3½ to 4 hours. (Check pan juices every hour to make sure they have not evaporated. If necessary, add 2 cups water to pan and scrape up browned bits.)

3. Transfer roast to large baking dish, place onions in medium bowl, and pour pan drippings into 2-cup liquid measuring cup, adding enough water to measure 1½ cups. Let roast, onions, and drippings cool for 30 minutes, cover each with plastic wrap, and refrigerate overnight.

4. One hour before serving, adjust oven rack to middle position and heat oven to 300 degrees. Cut meat into ¼-inch slices and overlap in large baking dish. Skim off fat from pan drippings and transfer drippings and reserved onions to medium saucepan. Add cider, jelly, and vinegar and bring to boil over medium-high heat, then reduce to simmer. Spoon ½ cup sauce over pork slices and cover baking dish with aluminum foil. Place in oven and heat until very hot, 30 to 40 minutes.

5. Just before serving, reduce sauce until dark and thickened, 10 to 15 minutes. Serve pork, spooning onion mixture over meat or passing separately.

Secrets to Old-Fashioned Flavor

1. Trim any excess fat from pork, leaving behind ⅛-inch-thick layer. Tie trimmed roast tightly into uniform shape, lengthwise and then crosswise.

2. Rub mixture of rosemary, sage, fennel seeds, garlic, salt, and pepper over roast.

3. Roast pork for 3 hours, add onion wedges, and continue to roast until meat is extremely tender, 3½ to 4 hours more.

PUERTO RICAN PORK ROAST

SERVES 8 TO 10

Depending on their size, you may need two bunches of cilantro. Crimp the foil tightly over the edges of the roasting pan in step 2 to minimize evaporation. Make sure to spray the V-rack in step 3. Serve over white rice.

1½ cups chopped fresh cilantro leaves and stems
1 onion, chopped coarse
¼ cup kosher salt
¼ cup olive oil
10 garlic cloves, peeled
2 tablespoons pepper
1 tablespoon dried oregano
1 tablespoon ground cumin
1 (7-pound) bone-in pork picnic shoulder
1 tablespoon grated lime zest
   plus ⅓ cup juice (3 limes)

1. Pulse 1 cup cilantro, onion, salt, oil, garlic, pepper, oregano, and cumin in food processor until finely ground, about 15 pulses, scraping down sides of bowl as needed. Pat pork dry with paper towels and rub sofrito all over. Wrap pork in plastic wrap and refrigerate for at least 12 hours or up to 24 hours.

2. Adjust oven rack to lower-middle position and heat oven to 450 degrees. Pour 8 cups water in large roasting pan. Unwrap pork and place skin side down in pan. Cover pan tightly with aluminum foil and roast for 90 minutes. Remove foil, reduce oven temperature to 375 degrees, and continue to roast for 2½ hours.

3. Remove pan from oven. Spray V-rack with vegetable oil spray. Gently slide metal spatula under pork to release skin from pan. Using folded dish towels, grasp ends of pork and transfer to V-rack, skin side

up. Wipe skin dry with paper towels. Place V-rack with pork in roasting pan. If pan looks dry, add 1 cup water. Return to oven and roast until pork registers 195 degrees, about 1 hour. (Add water as needed to keep bottom of pan from drying out.)

4. Line rimmed baking sheet with foil. Remove pan from oven. Transfer V-rack and pork to prepared sheet and return to oven. Immediately increase oven temperature to 500 degrees. Cook until pork skin is well browned and crispy (when tapped lightly with tongs, skin will sound hollow), 15 to 30 minutes, rotating sheet halfway through cooking. Transfer pork to carving board and let rest for 30 minutes.

5. Meanwhile, pour juices from pan into fat separator. Let liquid settle for 5 minutes, then pour off 1 cup defatted juices into large bowl. (If juices measure less than 1 cup, make up difference with water.) Whisk remaining ½ cup cilantro and lime zest and juice into bowl.

6. Remove crispy skin from pork in 1 large piece. Coarsely chop skin into bite-size pieces and set aside. Trim and discard excess fat from pork. Remove pork from bone and chop coarse. Transfer pork to bowl with cilantro-lime sauce and toss to combine. Serve pork, with crispy skin on side.

Creating Crispy Skin

Elevating the roast on a V-rack to finish cooking crisps up the flavorful skin.

Why This Recipe Works Famous for its crispy skin, this Puerto Rican dish of long-cooked, heavily seasoned pork roast should result in flavorful meat along with its trademark crispy exterior. We rubbed a picnic shoulder with a salty sofrito (a paste of aromatics and herbs) the day before roasting, which kept the meat moist and packed a flavor punch. We then roasted the pork skin-side down, covered, which helped transform tough collagen into gelatin. Next, we removed the foil cover to ensure that our pork didn't taste steamed, and then turned the roast skin side up on a V-rack to dry the skin to prepare it for the last step—a quick roast at very high heat.

CIDER-BRAISED PORK ROAST

SERVES 8

Pork butt roast is often labeled Boston butt in the supermarket. Plan ahead: This roast needs to cure for 18 to 24 hours before cooking. If you can't find Braeburn apples, substitute Jonagold. If you don't have a fat separator, strain the liquid through a fine-mesh strainer into a medium bowl in step 4 and wait for it to settle.

- 1   (5- to 6-pound) bone-in pork butt roast
- ¼   cup packed brown sugar
    Kosher salt and pepper
- 3   tablespoons vegetable oil
- 1   onion, halved and sliced thin
- 6   garlic cloves, smashed and peeled
- 2   cups apple cider
- 6   sprigs fresh thyme
- 2   bay leaves
- 1   cinnamon stick
- 2   Braeburn apples, cored and cut into 8 wedges each
- ¼   cup apple butter
- 1   tablespoon cornstarch
- 1   tablespoon cider vinegar

1. Using sharp knife, trim fat cap on roast to ¼ inch. Cut 1-inch crosshatch pattern, ¹⁄₁₆ inch deep, in fat cap. Place roast on large sheet of plastic wrap. Combine sugar and ¼ cup salt in bowl and rub mixture over entire roast and into slits. Wrap roast tightly in double layer of plastic, place on plate, and refrigerate for 18 to 24 hours.

2. Adjust oven rack to middle position and heat oven to 275 degrees. Unwrap roast and pat dry with paper towels, brushing away any excess salt mixture from surface. Season roast with pepper.

3. Heat oil in Dutch oven over medium-high heat until just smoking. Sear roast until well browned on all sides, about 3 minutes per side. Turn roast fat side up. Scatter onion and garlic around roast and cook until fragrant and beginning to brown, about 2 minutes. Add 1¾ cups cider, thyme sprigs, bay leaves, and cinnamon stick and bring to simmer. Cover,

transfer to oven, and braise until fork slips easily in and out of meat and meat registers 190 degrees, 2 hours 15 minutes to 2 hours 45 minutes.

4. Transfer roast to carving board, tent with aluminum foil, and let rest for 30 minutes. Strain braising liquid through fine-mesh strainer into fat separator; discard solids and let liquid settle for at least 5 minutes.

5. About 10 minutes before roast is done resting, wipe out pot with paper towels. Spoon 1½ tablespoons of clear, separated fat from top of fat separator into now-empty pot and heat over medium-high heat until shimmering. Season apples with salt and pepper. Space apples evenly in pot, cut side down, and cook until well browned on both cut sides, about 3 minutes per side. Transfer to platter and tent with foil.

6. Wipe out pot with paper towels. Return 2 cups defatted braising liquid to now-empty pot and bring to boil over high heat. Whisk in apple butter until incorporated. Whisk cornstarch and remaining ¼ cup cider together in bowl and add to pot. Return to boil and cook until thickened, about 1 minute. Off heat, add vinegar and season with salt and pepper to taste. Cover sauce and keep warm.

7. To carve roast, cut around inverted T-shaped bone until it can be pulled free from roast (use clean dish towel to grasp bone if necessary). Slice pork and transfer to serving platter with apples. Pour 1 cup sauce over pork and apples. Serve, passing remaining sauce at table.

Removing the Bone

Holding onto tip of T-shaped bone, use long knife to cut meat away from all sides of bone until bone is loose enough to pull out of roast.

Why This Recipe Works Pork and apples are a classic combination, so we paired flavorful bone-in pork butt roast with apple cider. Rubbing the meat with a brown sugar–salt mixture and refrigerating it overnight seasoned the pork and helped keep it juicy. Onions, garlic, bay leaf, cinnamon, and thyme were welcome additions that kept the clean, sweet-tart taste of cider in focus. Apple butter and cider vinegar added more apple-y punch, and a slurry of cornstarch and reserved cider thickened the braising liquid into a beautiful sauce. Apple wedges seared in flavorful pork fat united the elements of this hearty roast.

Why This Recipe Works Ham glazed with sweet apple cider certainly sounds great, but most recipes lack serious apple flavor, not to mention they call for frequent basting. For a relatively hands-off ham that was infused with lots of apple flavor, we marinated the ham in apple cider spiked with warm spices. Baking the ham in an oven bag guarded against dried-out meat. And to give our ham a crusty, spicy-sweet exterior, we rolled back the bag once the ham was heated through, slathered on reduced apple cider, pressed a mixture of brown sugar and black pepper all over, and slid it back into the oven until it caramelized.

CIDER-BAKED HAM

SERVES 16 TO 20

We prefer a bone-in, uncut, cured ham for this recipe, because the exterior layer of fat can be scored and helps create a nice crust. A spiral-sliced ham can be used instead, but there won't be much exterior fat, so skip the trimming and scoring in step 2. This recipe requires nearly a gallon of cider and a large oven bag. In step 4, be sure to stir the reduced cider mixture frequently to prevent scorching.

 1 cinnamon stick, broken into rough pieces
 ¼ teaspoon whole cloves
3¼ quarts apple cider
 8 cups ice cubes
 1 (7- to 10-pound) cured bone-in half ham, preferably shank end
 2 tablespoons Dijon mustard
 1 cup packed dark brown sugar
 1 teaspoon pepper
    Large oven bag

1. Toast cinnamon and cloves in large saucepan over medium heat until fragrant, about 3 minutes. Add 4 cups cider and bring to boil. Pour spiced cider into large stockpot or clean bucket, add 4 cups cider and ice, and stir until melted.

2. Meanwhile, remove skin from exterior of ham and trim fat to ¼-inch thickness. Score remaining fat at 1-inch intervals in crosshatch pattern. Transfer ham to container with chilled cider mixture (liquid should nearly cover ham) and refrigerate for at least 4 hours or up to 12 hours.

3. Discard cider mixture and transfer ham to large oven bag. Add 1 cup fresh cider to bag, tie securely, and cut 4 slits in top of bag. Transfer to large roasting pan and let stand at room temperature for 1½ hours.

4. Adjust oven rack to lowest position and heat oven to 300 degrees. Bake until ham registers 100 degrees, 1½ to 2½ hours. Meanwhile, bring remaining 4 cups cider and mustard to boil in saucepan. Reduce heat to medium-low and simmer, stirring often, until mixture is very thick and reduced to ⅓ cup, about 1 hour.

5. Combine sugar and pepper in bowl. Remove ham from oven and let rest for 5 minutes. Increase oven temperature to 400 degrees. Roll back oven bag and brush ham with reduced cider mixture. Using your fingers, carefully press sugar mixture onto exterior of ham. Return to oven and bake until dark brown and caramelized, about 20 minutes. Transfer ham to carving board, tent loosely with aluminum foil, and let rest for 15 minutes. Carve and serve.

Secrets to Cider-Baked Ham

1. Soaking ham in spice-infused cider lends concentrated flavor.

2. Baking ham with cider in oven bag keeps meat moist and lends even more cider flavor.

3. Brushing ham with sticky cider reduction provides big apple flavor and base for crust.

4. Pressing mixture of brown sugar and pepper onto ham gives exterior spicy-sweet, crackly crust.

PARMESAN-CRUSTED ASPARAGUS

SERVES 4 TO 6

Avoid pencil-thin asparagus for this recipe. Work quickly when tossing the asparagus with the egg whites, as the salt on the asparagus will rapidly begin to deflate the whites.

2   pounds (½-inch-thick) asparagus, trimmed
    Salt and pepper
3   ounces Parmesan cheese, grated (1½ cups)
¾ cup panko bread crumbs
1   tablespoon unsalted butter, melted and cooled
    Pinch cayenne
2   large egg whites
1   teaspoon honey

1. Adjust oven rack to middle position and heat oven to 450 degrees. Line rimmed baking sheet with aluminum foil and spray with vegetable oil spray. Using fork, poke holes up and down stalks of asparagus. Toss asparagus with ½ teaspoon salt and let stand for 30 minutes on a paper towel–lined baking sheet.

2. Meanwhile, combine 1 cup Parmesan, panko, butter, ¼ teaspoon salt, ⅛ teaspoon pepper, and cayenne in bowl. Transfer half of panko mixture to shallow dish and reserve remaining mixture. Using stand mixer fitted with whisk, whip egg whites and honey on medium-low speed until foamy, about 1 minute. Increase speed to medium-high and whip until soft peaks form, 2 to 3 minutes. Scrape into 13 by 9-inch baking dish and toss asparagus in mixture. Working with 1 spear at a time, dredge half of asparagus in panko and transfer to aluminum foil–lined baking sheet. Refill shallow dish with reserved panko mixture and repeat with remaining half of asparagus.

3. Bake asparagus until just beginning to brown, 6 to 8 minutes. Sprinkle with remaining ½ cup Parmesan and continue to bake until cheese is melted and panko is golden brown, 6 to 8 minutes. Transfer to platter. Serve.

Making the Coating Stick

1. Perforate and salt asparagus to draw out excess moisture that could saturate crumbs.

2. Whip egg whites to help crumbs adhere. Add honey for flavor and extra sticking power.

3. Work with 1 spear at a time to keep bread crumbs from clumping.

Why This Recipe Works Simply roasting asparagus and topping it with shaved Parmesan gives you limp spears and rubbery cheese. To get perfectly crisp-tender asparagus, we first salted it to rid it of excess moisture. For a cheesy coating that would stay put on the slender spears, we whipped a combination of honey and egg whites to soft peaks, dipped the asparagus in the mixture, then coated them with a mixture of bread crumbs and Parmesan. Finally, to reinforce the Parmesan flavor, we sprinkled the spears with more cheese at the end of roasting.

BRUSSELS SPROUT SALAD

SERVES 8

Slice the sprouts as thin as possible. Shred the Pecorino Romano on the large holes of a box grater.

- 3 tablespoons lemon juice
- 2 tablespoons Dijon mustard
- 1 small shallot, minced
- 1 garlic clove, minced
  Salt and pepper
- 6 tablespoons extra-virgin olive oil
- 2 pounds Brussels sprouts, trimmed, halved, and sliced very thin
- 3 ounces Pecorino Romano cheese, shredded (1 cup)
- ½ cup pine nuts, toasted

1. Whisk lemon juice, mustard, shallot, garlic, and ½ teaspoon salt together in large bowl. Slowly whisk in oil until incorporated. Toss Brussels sprouts with vinaigrette and let sit for at least 30 minutes or up to 2 hours.

2. Fold in Pecorino and pine nuts. Season with salt and pepper to taste. Serve.

BRUSSELS SPROUT SALAD WITH CHEDDAR, HAZELNUTS, AND APPLE

Substitute 1 cup shredded sharp cheddar for Pecorino and ½ cup hazelnuts, toasted, skinned, and chopped, for pine nuts. Add 1 Granny Smith apple, cored and cut into ½-inch pieces.

BRUSSELS SPROUT SALAD WITH SMOKED GOUDA, PECANS, AND DRIED CHERRIES

Substitute 1 cup shredded smoked gouda for Pecorino and ½ cup pecans, toasted and chopped, for pine nuts. Add ½ cup chopped dried cherries.

How to Slice Brussels Sprouts

You can use the slicing disk of your food processor or slice the sprouts with a chef's knife. Follow these steps to do the latter safely and quickly.

1. Trim stem end of each sprout and then cut each sprout in half through cut end.

2. With flat surface on cutting board, thinly slice each half.

Why This Recipe Works Raw Brussels sprout salad isn't as weird as it sounds: Brussels sprouts are very much like miniature cabbages in both texture and taste. To make this slaw-like salad, we thinly sliced the sprouts and tossed them with a bright, lemony vinaigrette with a touch of Dijon. We briefly marinated the salad in the vinaigrette to soften and season the sprouts. We topped the sprouts with toasted pine nuts and salty Pecorino Romano for a salad that's so delicious it can turn Brussels sprout loathers into Brussels sprout lovers.

Why This Recipe Works Conventional wisdom holds that anything but the gentlest treatment turns mashed potatoes into wallpaper paste, but we think our mixer-whipped spuds prove otherwise. For the lightest, fluffiest potatoes, we found high-starch russets worked best. Boiling the potatoes added extra water, resulting in a flat, not fluffy, finished dish. The best technique was to rinse excess starch from the raw potatoes, steam them, and then dry them in a pot on the stovetop over low heat. This process made them fluffier and better able to absorb the warm butter-and-milk mixture during whipping.

WHIPPED POTATOES

SERVES 8 TO 10

If your steamer basket has short legs (under 1¾ inches), the potatoes will sit in water as they cook and get wet. To prevent this, use balls of aluminum foil as steamer basket stilts. A stand mixer fitted with a whisk yields the smoothest potatoes, but a hand-held mixer may be used as well.

    4   pounds russet potatoes, peeled and cut into
        1-inch pieces
1½ cups whole milk
    8   tablespoons unsalted butter, cut into 8 pieces
    2   teaspoons salt
½   teaspoon pepper

1. Place cut potatoes in colander. Rinse under cold water until water runs clear, about 1 minute. Drain potatoes. Fill Dutch oven with 1 inch water and bring to boil. Place steamer basket in Dutch oven and fill with potatoes. Reduce heat to medium and cook, covered, until potatoes are tender, 20 to 25 minutes.

2. Heat milk, butter, salt, and pepper in small saucepan over medium-low heat, whisking until smooth, about 3 minutes; cover and keep warm.

3. Pour contents of Dutch oven into colander and return potatoes to dry pot. Stir over low heat until potatoes are thoroughly dried, about 1 minute. Using stand mixer fitted with whisk, break potatoes into small pieces on low speed, about 30 seconds. Add milk mixture in steady stream until incorporated. Increase speed to high and whip until potatoes are light and fluffy and no lumps remain, about 2 minutes. Serve.

Choosing Your Mixing Method

Don't try this recipe in your food processor—its sharp blades cut open the starch granules and turn the potatoes to glue. The beating motion of the mixer makes smooth, fluffy potatoes every time.

DON'T DO IT
A food processor's blade makes gluey mashed potatoes.

WHIP SMART
Use the mixer for light, fluffy whipped potatoes.

Whip It Good

In all likelihood, whipped potatoes owe their mid 20th-century fame to the Sunbeam Mixmaster. The appliance, first manufactured in 1930 and quickly enshrined as the must-have kitchen tool for American housewives, actually had a Mix-Finder Dial setting for whipped potatoes—speed 4 or 5, depending on the model. Whipping potatoes in the Mixmaster, the manufacturer claimed, saved "one-third the time usually taken by hand." But then, this machine promised time savings on just about every kitchen task. The 17 available attachments on early models included not only a slicer/shredder and an ice cream maker, but also a butter churn, a string bean slicer, and (our personal favorite) a pea sheller. It's no wonder this kitchen tool became perhaps the most famous appliance of the 20th century.

Why This Recipe Works Duchess potatoes take mashed potatoes to the next level, enriching them with egg and piping them into decorative rosettes before baking. To cook our spuds, we tried boiling, but this made them waterlogged; baking dried them out. Parcooking them in the microwave and finishing the rosettes in a hot oven proved best. For a potato mixture that was the right texture for piping, we stirred in butter, eggs, and cream while the potatoes were still hot, then added more butter once the potatoes had cooled. Baking powder ensured our picture-perfect Duchess Potatoes had the perfect airy, light texture to match.

DUCHESS POTATOES

SERVES 8

For the smoothest, most uniform texture, use a food mill or ricer to mash the potatoes. Choose potatoes of the same size so that they cook evenly.

- 3 pounds russet potatoes
- 1 cup heavy cream
- 6 tablespoons unsalted butter, cut into ¼-inch pieces and softened
- 1 large egg plus 1 large yolk, lightly beaten
- 1¼ teaspoons salt
- ½ teaspoon pepper
- ½ teaspoon baking powder
- Pinch nutmeg
- Vegetable oil spray

1. Adjust oven rack to upper-middle position and heat oven to 475 degrees. Meanwhile, prick potatoes all over with fork, place on plate, and microwave until tender, 18 to 25 minutes, turning potatoes over after 10 minutes.

2. Cut potatoes in half. When cool enough to handle, scoop flesh into large bowl and mash until no lumps remain. Add cream, 3 tablespoons butter, egg and yolk, salt, pepper, baking powder, and nutmeg and continue to mash until potatoes are smooth. Let cool to room temperature, about 10 minutes. Gently fold in remaining butter until pieces are evenly distributed.

3. Transfer potato mixture to piping bag fitted with ½-inch star tip. Pipe eight 4-inch-wide mounds of potato onto rimmed baking sheet. Spray lightly with vegetable oil spray and bake until golden brown, 15 to 20 minutes. Serve.

To Make Ahead Once piped onto baking sheet, potatoes can be covered loosely with plastic wrap and refrigerated for 24 hours. Remove plastic and spray lightly with vegetable oil spray before baking.

Two Paths to Perfect Piping

With a pastry bag fitted with a star tip, making beautiful duchess potatoes is child's play. If you don't have a pastry bag, don't worry: There's another easy way.

With Pastry Bag
Pipe 4-inch circle of potato mixture onto baking sheet. Continue to pipe upward in circles to form 3-inch-high peak.

Without Pastry Bag
Scoop potato mixture into zipper-lock bag, snip off 1 corner, and pipe as directed. Use tines of fork to create rippled surface.

Freezer Friendly

Our Duchess Potatoes freeze beautifully, which is handy, as they're ideal for a party. Pipe the mounds onto a rimmed baking sheet and then cover lightly with plastic wrap. Freeze for 2 hours until solid and transfer the potatoes to an airtight container (or leave them on the baking sheet if you've got the space). When you are ready to bake them, arrange on a rimmed baking sheet (or simply remove the plastic), spray lightly with vegetable oil spray, and bake according to our recipe. They can go straight from freezer to oven, and they won't even need any extra time.

SYRACUSE SALT POTATOES

SERVES 6 TO 8

You will need 1¼ cups of noniodized table salt, 1½ cups of Morton kosher salt, or 2½ cups of Diamond Crystal kosher salt to equal 14 ounces. We prefer to use small potatoes, measuring 1 to 2 inches in diameter, in this recipe.

  8 cups water
14 ounces salt
  3 pounds small white or red potatoes
  8 tablespoons unsalted butter, cut into 8 pieces
  2 tablespoons minced fresh chives
  1 teaspoon pepper

1. Set wire rack in rimmed baking sheet. Bring water to boil in Dutch oven over medium-high heat. Stir in salt and potatoes and cook until potatoes are just tender, 20 to 30 minutes. Drain potatoes and transfer to prepared baking sheet. Let dry until salty crust forms, about 1 minute.

2. Meanwhile, microwave butter, chives, and pepper in medium bowl until butter is melted, about 1 minute. Transfer potatoes to serving bowl and serve, passing butter separately.

Salt Magic

Just out of the salty water, the potatoes will look like any other boiled potato.

One minute after they've been drained, the characteristic salt crust will appear on the potato skins.

The high salinity means the cooking water gets hotter than normal, resulting in extra-creamy potato flesh.

Selling Salt Potatoes

Salt potatoes have their origin in the mid-1800s when Irish salt workers in the Syracuse area would cook unpeeled new potatoes in huge evaporation vats filled with boiling salt water. In 1914, John Hinerwadel, owner of an eponymous central New York clambake company, began offering salt potatoes on his menu. They became so popular that Mr. Hinerwadel started selling salt potato kits—complete with a sack of small white potatoes and a packet of salt—so people could make the potatoes at home. The red and white bags of potatoes with the signature red and yellow sun are still sold in the Syracuse area.

Why This Recipe Works For Syracuse salt potatoes with a well-seasoned crust and ultra-creamy interior, we cut back on the usual 3 cups of salt, which resulted in overly salty potatoes. We found that white or red potatoes proved best, but they needed to be boiled in the salted water whole—if they were cut or peeled, they absorbed too much salt. Though these potatoes are usually served with plain melted butter for dipping, we found that adding chives and black pepper to the butter brought this dish to new heights.

Why This Recipe Works Most recipes for mashed potato casserole simply dump mashed potatoes in a baking dish and pop it in the oven, but these dishes always end up bland, gluey, and dense. We wanted a casserole that delivered fluffy, buttery, creamy potatoes nestled under a savory golden crust. Using half-and-half instead of the traditional heavy cream lightened the recipe, and cutting it with chicken broth kept the potatoes moist. Beating eggs into the potato mixture helped it achieve a fluffy, airy texture. For bold flavor, we added Dijon mustard and fresh chives.

MASHED POTATO CASSEROLE

SERVES 8

The casserole may also be baked in a 13 by 9-inch pan.

4 pounds russet potatoes, peeled and cut into 1-inch chunks
12 tablespoons unsalted butter, cut into 12 pieces
½ cup half-and-half
½ cup chicken broth
2 teaspoons Dijon mustard
1 garlic clove, minced
2 teaspoons salt
4 large eggs
¼ cup finely chopped fresh chives

1. Adjust oven rack to upper-middle position and heat oven to 375 degrees. Bring potatoes and water to cover by 1 inch to boil in large pot over high heat. Reduce heat to medium and simmer until potatoes are tender, about 20 minutes.

2. Heat butter, half-and-half, broth, mustard, garlic, and salt in saucepan over medium-low heat until smooth, about 5 minutes. Keep warm.

3. Drain potatoes and transfer to large bowl. Using stand mixer fitted with paddle, beat potatoes on medium-low speed, slowly adding half-and-half mixture, until smooth and creamy, about 1 minute. Scrape down bowl; beat in eggs, 1 at a time, until incorporated, about 1 minute. Fold in chives.

4. Transfer potato mixture to greased 3-quart baking dish. Smooth surface of potatoes, then use fork to make peaked design on top of casserole. Bake until potatoes rise and begin to brown, about 35 minutes. Let cool for 10 minutes. Serve.

To Make Ahead The baking dish with the potatoes can be covered with plastic and refrigerated for up to 24 hours. When ready to bake, let the casserole sit at room temperature for 1 hour. Increase baking time by 10 minutes.

Secrets to Perfect Mashed Potato Casserole

1. When poured into casserole dish, mashed potatoes will look very soupy. They will firm up and rise in oven.

2. For better browning and an impressive presentation, use fork to make peaked design on top of casserole.

Can Evaporated Milk Be Substituted for Half-and-Half?

Sorry, the answer is no. We substituted evaporated milk in a handful of recipes that call for half-and-half. The savory dishes made with evaporated milk in place of half-and-half tasted tinny, and the desserts were too sweet.

Not willing to give up, we diluted the evaporated milk with water and then used it in place of the half-and-half in our test recipes. Tasters didn't like that either, detecting a mildly cooked taste. We tried heavy cream, but its high milk-fat content muted the other flavors. Whole milk made the food less rich, but the flavors remained lively.

With heavy cream and either skim or whole milk, you can mix up a good substitute for half-and-half. If you don't mind a slightly thinner consistency and lighter flavor, whole milk will work in most recipes.

⅓ cup heavy cream + ⅔ cup skim milk =
1 cup half-and-half

¼ cup heavy cream + ¾ cup whole milk =
1 cup half-and-half

CREAMY MASHED SWEET POTATOES

SERVES 4 TO 6

This recipe can be doubled and prepared in a Dutch oven, but the cooking time will need to be doubled as well.

- 2 pounds sweet potatoes, peeled, quartered, and sliced ¼ inch thick
- 4 tablespoons unsalted butter, cut into 4 pieces
- 3 tablespoons heavy cream
- 1 teaspoon sugar
  Salt and pepper

1. Combine sweet potatoes, butter, 2 tablespoons cream, sugar, ½ teaspoon salt, and ¼ teaspoon pepper in large saucepan. Cook, covered, over low heat until potatoes are fall-apart tender, 35 to 40 minutes.

2. Off heat, add remaining 1 tablespoon cream and mash sweet potatoes with potato masher. Serve.

HERBED MASHED SWEET POTATOES WITH CARAMELIZED ONION

If you prefer, substitute ¼ teaspoon dried thyme for the thyme sprig.

Add 1 sprig fresh thyme to saucepan in step 1. While sweet potatoes are cooking, melt 1 tablespoon butter in 8-inch nonstick skillet and add 1 small onion, chopped, ¼ teaspoon sugar, and ¼ teaspoon salt. Cook over low heat until onion is caramelized, about 15 minutes. Remove thyme and mash potatoes as directed. Stir in onion and 1 tablespoon sour cream.

SMOKEHOUSE MASHED SWEET POTATOES

Add ⅛ teaspoon cayenne pepper to saucepan in step 1. Mash sweet potatoes with ½ cup shredded smoked Gouda cheese and cover with lid until cheese melts, about 1 minute. Sprinkle with 6 slices chopped cooked bacon and 1 thinly sliced scallion.

No-Boil Sweet Potatoes

Boiling sweet potatoes in lots of liquid—as you would regular potatoes—is not a good idea. Sweet potatoes will soak up too much water, and the resulting mash will be a soggy mess. Better to cook them in a small amount of liquid. Just 2 tablespoons of heavy cream (plus a little butter), along with the water released from the sweet potatoes as they cook, is enough to steam them to tenderness.

The Slice is Right

It is imperative to cut the sweet potato into thin, even slices to ensure perfect cooking.

1. Quarter each peeled sweet potato lengthwise.

2. Cut each quarter into ¼-inch slices crosswise.

Why This Recipe Works Deeply flavored, earthy, and subtly sweet, mashed sweet potatoes hardly need a layer of marshmallows to make them into a tempting side. For a silky and full-flavored mash, we found the secret was to thinly slice the potatoes and cook them covered, on the stovetop, over low heat in a small amount of butter and cream. Once the sweet potatoes were fall-apart tender, they could be mashed right in the pot—no draining, no straining, no fuss. Adding another spoonful of cream when we mashed the potatoes enriched them even more.

SWEET CORN SPOONBREAD

SERVES 6

You will need three ears of corn to yield 2 cups. Frozen corn, thawed and drained well, can be substituted for the fresh corn.

　1　cup cornmeal
2¾　cups whole milk
　4　tablespoons unsalted butter
　2　cups fresh corn
　1　teaspoon sugar
　1　teaspoon salt
　⅛　teaspoon cayenne pepper
　3　large eggs, separated
　¼　teaspoon cream of tartar

1. Adjust oven rack to middle position and heat oven to 400 degrees. Grease 1½-quart soufflé dish or 8-inch baking dish. Whisk cornmeal and ¾ cup milk in bowl until combined; set aside.

2. Melt butter in Dutch oven over medium-high heat. Cook corn until beginning to brown, about 3 minutes. Stir in remaining 2 cups milk, sugar, salt, and cayenne and bring to boil. Off heat, cover mixture and let steep for 15 minutes.

3. Transfer warm corn mixture to blender or food processor and puree until smooth. Return to pot and bring to boil. Reduce heat to low and add cornmeal mixture, whisking constantly, until thickened, 2 to 3 minutes; transfer to large bowl and let cool to room temperature, about 20 minutes. Once mixture is cool, whisk in egg yolks until combined.

4. Using stand mixer fitted with whisk, beat egg whites and cream of tartar on medium-low speed until foamy, about 1 minute. Increase speed to medium-high and whip until stiff peaks form, 3 to 4 minutes. Whisk one-third of whites into corn mixture, then gently fold in remaining whites until combined. Scrape mixture into prepared dish and transfer to oven. Reduce oven temperature to 350 degrees and bake until spoonbread is golden brown and has risen above rim of dish, about 45 minutes. Serve immediately.

INDIVIDUAL SPOONBREADS

To make individual spoonbreads, divide batter among 6 greased 7-ounce ramekins. Arrange ramekins on rimmed baking sheet and bake as directed, reducing cooking time to 30 to 35 minutes.

Egg Whites 101

Egg whites are most easily whipped in a very clean metal bowl with a pinch of cream of tartar, which promotes stabilization.

Soft Peaks
Soft peaks will droop slightly downward from tip of whisk or beater.

Stiff Peaks
Stiff peaks will stand up tall on their own.

Overwhipped
Overwhipped egg whites will look curdled and separated; if you reach this point, start over with new whites and clean bowl.

Why This Recipe Works For a fluffy, soufflé-style sweet corn spoonbread with deep corn flavor, we focused on flavor, then texture. Sautéing the corn in butter, before steeping it in milk and pureeing it, ensured that the sweet corn flavor permeated our spoonbread. To make sure the cornmeal didn't impart a gritty texture, we soaked it in the milk beforehand. And to guarantee a stable foam and an impressive rise, we beat the egg whites with a bit of cream of tartar.

tex-mex favorites

Why This Recipe Works Too often, nacho recipes produce soggy chips loaded down with bland, greasy beef, dry beans, and cold strings of cheese. Instead, we wanted hearty nachos that are crisp, flavorful, and fresh. Boldly seasoning our beef with a mixture of spices and other flavorings caused the flavor to pop. While many nacho recipes call for cheddar cheese, we found it didn't melt nearly as well as pepper Jack, which melted smoothly and added a kick, too.

ULTIMATE SPICY BEEF NACHOS

SERVES 8

In addition to our One-Minute Salsa (recipe follows), garnish the nachos with sour cream, chopped cilantro, and diced avocado.

Refried Beans
½ cup canned refried beans
3 tablespoons shredded pepper Jack cheese
1 tablespoon chopped canned jalapeños

Spicy Beef
2 teaspoons vegetable oil
1 small onion, chopped fine
3 garlic cloves, minced
1 tablespoon chili powder
1 teaspoon ground cumin
½ teaspoon dried oregano
1 teaspoon salt
1 pound 90 percent lean ground beef
2 tablespoons tomato paste
1 teaspoon packed brown sugar
1½ teaspoons minced canned chipotle chile in adobo sauce, plus 1 teaspoon adobo sauce
½ cup water
2 teaspoons lime juice

1 (9.5-ounce) bag tortilla chips
1 pound pepper Jack cheese, shredded (4 cups)
2 jalapeño chiles, sliced into thin rings
1 recipe One-Minute Salsa

1. Adjust oven rack to middle position and heat oven to 400 degrees.

2. For the Refried Beans Pulse ingredients in food processor until smooth, about 10 pulses. Transfer to bowl and cover with plastic wrap.

3. For the Spicy Beef Heat oil in large skillet over medium heat until shimmering. Cook onion until softened, about 4 minutes. Add garlic, chili powder, cumin, oregano, and salt and cook until fragrant, about 1 minute. Add beef and cook, breaking meat into small bits with wooden spoon and scraping pan bottom to prevent scorching, until no longer pink, about 5 minutes. Add tomato paste, sugar, chipotle, and adobo sauce and cook until paste begins to darken, about 1 minute. Add water, bring to simmer, and cook over medium-low until mixture is nearly dry, 5 to 7 minutes. Stir in lime juice and transfer mixture to plate lined with several layers of paper towels. Use more paper towels to blot up excess grease.

4. Spread half of chips on large ovensafe serving platter or in 13 by 9-inch baking dish. Dollop half of bean mixture over chips, then spread evenly. Scatter half of beef mixture over beans, top with 2 cups cheese and half of jalapeños. Repeat with remaining chips, beans, beef, cheese, and jalapeños. Bake until cheese is melted and just beginning to brown, 12 to 14 minutes. Serve with salsa and other suggested garnishes.

ONE-MINUTE SALSA
MAKES ABOUT 1 CUP
Make sure to drain both the tomatoes and the jalapeños before processing. The salsa will keep for two days in the refrigerator. Season to taste before serving.

½ small red onion
¼ cup fresh cilantro leaves
2 tablespoons jarred jalapeños, drained
1 tablespoon lime juice
1 garlic clove, peeled
¼ teaspoon salt
1 (14.5-ounce) can diced tomatoes, drained

Pulse onion, cilantro, jalapeños, lime juice, garlic, and salt in food processor until roughly chopped, about 5 pulses. Add tomatoes and pulse until chopped, about 2 pulses. Transfer mixture to fine-mesh strainer and drain briefly. Serve.

Why This Recipe Works With bold Southwestern flavors and an appealing ingredient list, seven-layer dip recipes sound like a hit. But most versions of this party classic assume that guests won't notice the messy layers and tired flavors. In our version, canned black beans stood in for refried beans, while garlic, chili powder, and lime juice added flavor. We found that sour cream on its own quickly watered down our dip, but combining it with cheese gave this layer more structure.

ULTIMATE SEVEN-LAYER DIP

SERVES 8 TO 10

This recipe is usually served in a clear dish so you can see the layers. For a crowd, double the recipe and serve in a 13 by 9-inch glass baking dish. If you don't have time to make fresh guacamole as called for, simply mash three avocados with 3 tablespoons lime juice and ½ teaspoon salt.

4 large tomatoes, cored, seeded, and chopped fine
2 jalapeño chiles, stemmed, seeded, and minced
3 tablespoons chopped fresh cilantro
6 scallions (2 minced, 4 with green parts sliced thin and white parts discarded)
2 tablespoons plus 2 teaspoons lime juice (2 limes)
  Salt
1 (15-ounce) can black beans, drained but not rinsed
2 garlic cloves, minced
¾ teaspoon chili powder
1½ cups sour cream
1 pound pepper Jack cheese, shredded (4 cups)
1 recipe Chunky Guacamole (page 238)
  Tortilla chips

1. Combine tomatoes, jalapeños, cilantro, minced scallions, and 2 tablespoons lime juice in medium bowl. Stir in ⅛ teaspoon salt and let stand until tomatoes begin to soften, about 30 minutes. Strain mixture into bowl and discard liquid.

2. Pulse black beans, garlic, remaining 2 teaspoons lime juice, chili powder, and ⅛ teaspoon salt in food processor until mixture resembles chunky paste, about 15 pulses. Transfer to bowl and wipe out food processor. Pulse sour cream and 2½ cups pepper Jack until smooth, about 15 pulses. Transfer to separate bowl.

3. Spread bean mixture evenly over bottom of 8-inch square baking dish or 1-quart glass bowl. Spread sour cream mixture evenly over bean layer and sprinkle evenly with remaining 1½ cups cheese. Spread guacamole over cheese and top with tomato mixture. Sprinkle with sliced scallion greens and serve with tortilla chips. (Dip can be refrigerated for up to 24 hours. Let dip stand at room temperature for 1 hour before serving.)

ULTIMATE SMOKY SEVEN-LAYER DIP
Cook 4 slices bacon in 10-inch skillet over medium-high heat until crisp, about 8 minutes. Drain on paper towel–lined plate and crumble. Pulse 1 to 3 teaspoons minced canned chipotle chile in adobo sauce with black beans in step 2. Garnish dip with crumbled bacon along with scallions.

Processing Your Pico
Although the pico de gallo topping in our Ultimate Seven-Layer Dip adds lots of fresh flavor, chopping all the ingredients by hand takes some work. We found that a food processor gets the job done, but the texture won't be as perfectly uniform as pico made by hand. To make pico de gallo in the food processor, start by pulsing jalapeños with cilantro until finely chopped. Then add quartered, cored, and seeded tomatoes and pulse in 1-second bursts until the tomatoes are evenly chopped. Add minced scallions and lime juice. Strain as instructed.

Seeding Jalapeños

Halve pepper lengthwise. Starting at end opposite stem, use melon baller to scoop down inside of each half.

CHUNKY GUACAMOLE

MAKES ABOUT 3 CUPS

Preparing the guacamole ahead of time helps the flavors marry, but it should not be prepared more than one day in advance. To prevent the dip from turning brown, press a sheet of plastic wrap directly onto the surface and refrigerate until ready to use. We prefer pebbly Hass avocados to the smoother Fuerte variety.

2   scallions, green and white parts separated and sliced thin
1   jalapeño chile, stemmed, seeded, and minced
1   small garlic clove, minced
¼   teaspoon finely grated lime zest plus 2 tablespoons juice
3   avocados, halved, pitted, and cubed
3   tablespoons chopped fresh cilantro
    Salt

1. Combine scallion whites, jalapeño, garlic, and lime juice in large bowl. Let sit for 30 minutes.

2. Add two-thirds of avocado pieces to bowl with jalapeño mixture and mash with potato masher until smooth. Gently fold remaining avocado pieces into mashed avocado mixture. Gently stir in lime zest, scallion greens, and cilantro. Season with salt to taste. Serve.

Ripening Avocados

Avocados have a small window of perfect ripeness. To see if we could broaden this time frame, we ripened avocados four ways: on the counter or refrigerator shelf, enclosed in a paper bag, and enclosed in a paper bag with pieces of green apple (fruit gives off ethylene gas, which helps many fruits and vegetables ripen more quickly). We also tried burying the avocados at room temperature in flour and in rice. In the end, the only thing that mattered was the temperature at which the avocados were stored.

At room temperature, rock-hard avocados ripened within two days, but many of them ripened unevenly, developing soft spots and air pockets on one side just as the other side was ripening. Once ripe, they lasted two days on average if kept at room temperature (stored in the fridge after ripening, they lasted five days). Avocados ripened in the refrigerator, whether in a bag or out in the open, took around four days to soften, but did so evenly. Stored in the fridge, they lasted a full five days before starting to show signs of overripening.

The bottom line: If you need avocados to ripen sooner rather than later, keep them on the counter. Otherwise, you're better off putting them in the fridge and allowing them to ripen slowly. In either case, store the ripened fruit in the fridge to extend its shelf life.

Preparing Avocado for Guacamole

1. Halve avocado. Strike pit sharply with chef's knife. Twist blade to remove pit, then use dish towel to pull pit off blade.

2. Place avocado half on dish towel to secure it and make ½-inch crosshatch slices into flesh without cutting through skin.

3. Insert spoon between skin and flesh to separate the two. Gently scoop out avocado cubes.

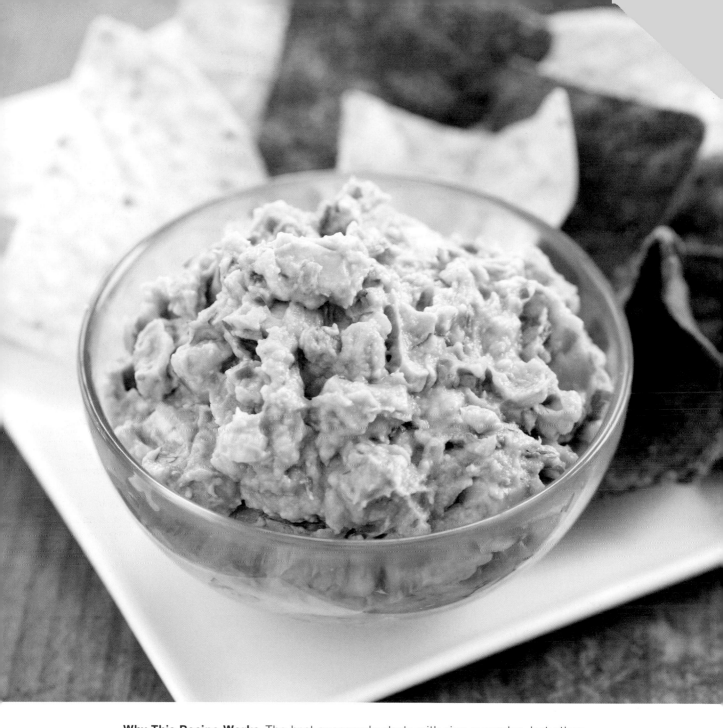

Why This Recipe Works The best guacamole starts with ripe avocados, but other ingredients often overwhelm their delicate flavor. Tasters liked the flavor of minced garlic in guacamole, but thought raw onions were just too harsh. Instead, scallions lent a mellower onion flavor. Steeping them in lime juice for a few minutes before combining them with the avocados mellowed their flavor even more. To provide some textural contrast to our guacamole, we chopped the avocados and then mashed just two-thirds of the chunks.

Why This Recipe Works Huevos rancheros has made its way northward from Mexico, becoming common on breakfast menus around the United States. To make this crowd-pleasing but involved dish of fried eggs, cheese, and tomato-chile sauce manageable for a group, we roasted the sauce components to brown the vegetables and replicate the char from a cast-iron skillet. We then transferred everything to a casserole dish and nestled the eggs into the sauce so we could cook eight eggs at once. Moving this spicy dish of eggs and charred chiles to the oven gave us a perfectly timed meal that's not just for breakfast.

HUEVOS RANCHEROS

SERVES 4

Use a heavyweight rimmed baking sheet; flimsy sheets will warp. Our winning sheet is the Nordic Ware Baker's Half Sheet. Serve with refried beans and hot sauce.

- 2 (28-ounce) cans diced tomatoes
- 1 tablespoon packed brown sugar
- 1 tablespoon lime juice
- 1 onion, chopped
- ½ cup chopped canned green chiles
- ¼ cup extra-virgin olive oil
- 3 tablespoons chili powder
- 4 garlic cloves, sliced thin
  Salt and pepper
- 4 ounces pepper Jack cheese, shredded (1 cup)
- 8 large eggs
- 1 avocado, halved, pitted, and diced
- 3 scallions, sliced thin
- ⅓ cup minced fresh cilantro
- 8 (6-inch) corn tortillas, warmed

1. Adjust oven rack to middle position and heat oven to 500 degrees. Line rimmed baking sheet with parchment paper. Drain tomatoes in fine-mesh strainer set over bowl, pressing with rubber spatula to extract as much juice as possible. Reserve 1¾ cups tomato juice and discard remainder. Whisk sugar and lime juice into reserved tomato juice and set aside.

2. In separate bowl, combine onion, chiles, oil, chili powder, garlic, ½ teaspoon salt, and drained tomatoes. Transfer tomato mixture to prepared baking sheet and spread in even layer to edges of sheet. Roast until charred in spots, 35 to 40 minutes, stirring and redistributing into even layer halfway through baking. Reduce oven temperature to 400 degrees.

3. Transfer roasted tomato mixture to 13 by 9-inch baking dish and stir in tomato juice mixture. Season with salt and pepper to taste, then spread into even layer. Sprinkle pepper Jack over tomato mixture. Using spoon, hollow out 8 holes in tomato mixture in 2 rows. Crack 1 egg into each hole. Season eggs with salt and pepper.

4. Bake until whites are just beginning to set but still have some movement when dish is shaken, 13 to 16 minutes. Transfer dish to wire rack, tent loosely with aluminum foil, and let sit for 5 minutes. Spoon avocado over top, then sprinkle with scallions and cilantro. Serve with warm tortillas.

To Make Ahead The sauce can be made 24 hours in advance. Microwave until hot, about 2 minutes (stirring halfway), before transferring to baking dish and proceeding with recipe.

Roast the Vegetables, Bake the Eggs

To evoke the charred flavors in traditional huevos rancheros, we roast vegetables in a hot oven before layering them into a dish with cheese sprinkled over. Cracking eggs into wells in the mixture allows us to bake eight servings at once—no more standing at the stove frying egg after egg for an impatient crowd.

ARROZ CON POLLO

SERVES 6

Sazón is a spice blend common in Latin American cooking. We developed this recipe with Goya Sazón with Coriander and Annatto (or con Culantro y Achiote). It can be found in the international aisle of most supermarkets; however, other brands will work. (One tablespoon of Goya Sazón equals about two packets.) If you can't find sazón, use our homemade version (recipe follows). You can substitute ¾ cup of chopped green bell pepper for the Cubanelle pepper. Allow the rice to rest for the full 15 minutes before lifting the lid to check it. Long-grain rice may be substituted for medium-grain, but the rice will be slightly less creamy.

1 cup fresh cilantro leaves and stems, chopped
1 onion, chopped (1 cup)
1 Cubanelle pepper, stemmed, seeded, and chopped (¾ cup)
5 garlic cloves, chopped coarse
1 teaspoon ground cumin
½ cup mayonnaise
3½ tablespoons lemon juice (2 lemons), plus lemon wedges for serving
   Salt and pepper
6 (5- to 7-ounce) bone-in chicken thighs, trimmed
1 tablespoon vegetable oil
2 cups medium-grain rice, rinsed
1 tablespoon Goya Sazón with Coriander and Annatto
2½ cups chicken broth
¼ cup pimento-stuffed green olives, halved
2 tablespoons capers, rinsed
2 bay leaves
½ cup frozen peas, thawed (optional)

1. Adjust oven rack to middle position and heat oven to 350 degrees. Process cilantro, ½ cup onion, Cubanelle, garlic, and cumin in food processor until finely chopped, about 20 seconds, scraping down bowl as needed. Transfer sofrito to bowl.

2. Process mayonnaise, 1½ tablespoons lemon juice, ⅛ teaspoon salt, and 2 tablespoons sofrito in now-empty processor until almost smooth, about

30 seconds. Transfer mayonnaise-herb sauce to small bowl, cover, and refrigerate until ready to serve.

3. Pat chicken dry with paper towels and sprinkle with 1 teaspoon salt and ¼ teaspoon pepper. Heat oil in Dutch oven over medium heat until shimmering. Add chicken to pot skin side down and cook without moving it until skin is crispy and golden, 7 to 9 minutes. Flip chicken and continue to cook until golden on second side, 7 to 9 minutes longer. Transfer chicken to plate; discard skin.

4. Pour off all but 2 tablespoons fat from pot and heat over medium heat until shimmering. Add remaining ½ cup onion and cook until softened, 3 to 5 minutes. Stir in rice and Sazón and cook until edges of rice begin to turn translucent, about 2 minutes.

5. Stir in broth, olives, capers, bay leaves, remaining sofrito, remaining 2 tablespoons lemon juice, 1 teaspoon salt, and ½ teaspoon pepper, scraping up any browned bits. Nestle chicken into pot along with any accumulated juices and bring to vigorous simmer. Cover, transfer to oven, and bake for 20 minutes.

6. Transfer pot to wire rack and let stand, covered, for 15 minutes. Fluff rice with fork and stir in peas, if using. Discard bay leaves. Serve with mayonnaise-herb sauce and lemon wedges.

HOMEMADE SAZÓN
MAKES 1 TABLESPOON
We add paprika in place of annatto for color. In addition to flavoring our Arroz con Pollo, this blend makes a great seasoning for eggs, beans, and fish.

1 teaspoon garlic powder
¾ teaspoon salt
½ teaspoon paprika
½ teaspoon ground coriander
¼ teaspoon ground cumin

Combine all ingredients in bowl.

Why This Recipe Works *Arroz con pollo* is a classic Latin take on chicken and rice. To serve up an all-purpose version at home, we first created the dish's flavor backbone: a *sofrito* of onions, peppers, garlic, and spices. Next, after browning meaty skin-on chicken thighs, we used the rendered fat to soften chopped onion, toast the rice, and bloom the starring spice blend, *sazón*. We removed the skin from the thighs and finished cooking them nestled into the rice, studded with halved green olives, capers, and our zesty sofrito. We served our arroz con pollo with a drizzle of herby lemon sauce for a final punch of freshness.

LATIN FRIED CHICKEN

SERVES 4

Don't let the chicken marinate any longer than 2 hours or it will toughen from the lime juice. You will need at least a 6-quart Dutch oven for this recipe.

Marinade and Chicken

2 tablespoons kosher salt
6 garlic cloves, chopped coarse
1 tablespoon pepper
1 tablespoon ground cumin
2 teaspoons smoked paprika
2 teaspoons dried oregano
2 teaspoons grated lime zest plus ¼ cup juice (2 limes)
3 pounds bone-in chicken pieces (split breasts cut in half crosswise, drumsticks, thighs, and/or wings), trimmed

Coating

1¼ cups all-purpose flour
¾ cup cornstarch
1 tablespoon pepper
1 tablespoon granulated garlic
1 teaspoon baking powder
1 teaspoon white pepper
1 teaspoon kosher salt
1 teaspoon ground cumin
¼ teaspoon cayenne pepper
3 large egg whites, lightly beaten

3 quarts peanut or vegetable oil

1. For the Marinade and Chicken Combine salt, garlic, pepper, cumin, paprika, oregano, and lime zest and juice in bowl. Add chicken and turn to coat thoroughly. Cover with plastic wrap and refrigerate for at least 1 hour or up to 2 hours.

2. For the Coating Whisk flour, cornstarch, pepper, granulated garlic, baking powder, white pepper, salt, cumin, and cayenne together in bowl. Place egg whites in shallow dish.

3. Set wire rack in rimmed baking sheet. Remove chicken from marinade and scrape off solids. Pat chicken dry with paper towels. Working with 1 piece at a time, dip chicken into egg whites to thoroughly coat, letting excess drip back into dish. Dredge chicken in flour mixture, pressing to adhere. Transfer chicken to prepared wire rack and refrigerate for at least 30 minutes or up to 2 hours.

4. Add oil to large Dutch oven until it measures about 2 inches deep and heat over medium-high heat to 325 degrees. Add half of chicken to hot oil and fry until breasts register 160 degrees and drumsticks/thighs register 175 degrees, 13 to 16 minutes. Adjust burner, if necessary, to maintain oil temperature between 300 and 325 degrees. Transfer chicken to second wire rack set in second rimmed baking sheet. Return oil to 325 degrees and repeat with remaining chicken. Serve.

White Pepper

White peppercorns are fully ripe black peppercorns—the black outer husk is removed and the berries are dried. They lose much of their heat in this process but have a sharpness and a pronounced citrus flavor. Their taste is especially welcome in our spicy Latin Fried Chicken coating. Many chefs like the way that these peppercorns blend into white sauces, while Asian cooks use them in stir-fries and hot-and-sour soup.

Why This Recipe Works While each cuisine puts its own spin on the dish, Latin-style fried chicken is set apart by its garlicky-lime marinade and an extra-crunchy coating with lots of spice. Classic Latin fried chicken has a thin and crispy crust; we used a combination of flour cut with cornstarch for a nice, light coating and a little baking powder made it extra crisp. Refrigerating the marinated dredged chicken before frying made sure the coating set up nicely and thus stayed put on the chicken. Whether your idea of "South" is Savannah or San Salvador, this is one fried chicken recipe that you're definitely going to want to make.

Why This Recipe Works We wanted our California-Style fish tacos to be light, fresh, and simple, with a perfect balance of flavors and textures. An ultrathin beer batter using a combination of flour, cornstarch, and baking powder proved to be ideal for getting a light, crispy coating on the delicate white fish. Quick-pickled onions and jalapeños added tart spiciness, and tossing shredded cabbage with the pickling liquid just before serving added flavor without overcomplicating the dish. Lime juice and sour cream added tang to the traditional creamy white sauce.

CALIFORNIA-STYLE FISH TACOS

SERVES 6

Light-bodied American lagers, such as Budweiser, work best here. Cod, haddock, or halibut are good choices for the fish. Cut the fish on a slight bias if your fillets aren't quite 4 inches wide. You should end up with about 24 pieces of fish. Serve with green salsa, if desired.

Pickled Onions

1 small red onion, halved and sliced thin
2 jalapeño chiles, stemmed and sliced into thin rings
1 cup white wine vinegar
2 tablespoons lime juice
1 tablespoon sugar
1 teaspoon salt

Cabbage

3 cups shredded green cabbage
¼ cup pickling liquid from pickled onions
½ teaspoon salt
½ teaspoon pepper

White Sauce

½ cup mayonnaise
½ cup sour cream
2 tablespoons lime juice
2 tablespoons milk

Fish

2 pounds skinless white-flesh fish fillets, cut crosswise into 4 by 1-inch strips
Salt and pepper
¾ cup all-purpose flour
¼ cup cornstarch
1 teaspoon baking powder
1 cup beer
1 quart peanut or vegetable oil

24 (6-inch) corn tortillas, warmed
1 cup fresh cilantro leaves

1. For the Pickled Onions Combine onion and jalapeños in medium bowl. Bring vinegar, lime juice, sugar, and salt to boil in small saucepan. Pour vinegar mixture over onion mixture and let sit for at least 30 minutes. (Pickled onions can be made and refrigerated up to 2 days in advance.)

2. For the Cabbage Toss all ingredients together in bowl.

3. For the White Sauce Whisk all ingredients together in bowl. (Sauce can be made and refrigerated up to 2 days in advance.)

4. For the Fish Adjust oven rack to middle position and heat oven to 200 degrees. Set wire rack inside rimmed baking sheet. Pat fish dry with paper towels and season with salt and pepper. Whisk flour, cornstarch, baking powder, and 1 teaspoon salt together in large bowl. Add beer and whisk until smooth. Transfer fish to batter and toss until evenly coated.

5. Add oil to large Dutch oven until it measures about ¾ inch deep and heat over medium-high heat to 350 degrees. Working with 5 to 6 pieces at a time, remove fish from batter, allowing excess to drip back into bowl, and add to hot oil, briefly dragging fish along surface of oil to prevent sticking. Adjust burner, if necessary, to maintain oil temperature between 325 and 350 degrees. Fry fish, stirring gently to prevent pieces from sticking together, until golden brown and crispy, about 2 minutes per side. Transfer fish to prepared wire rack and place in oven to keep warm. Return oil to 350 degrees and repeat with remaining fish.

6. Divide fish evenly among tortillas. Top with pickled onions, cabbage, white sauce, and cilantro. Serve.

EASY CHICKEN TACOS

SERVES 6

To warm the tortillas, wrap them in foil and heat them in a 350-degree oven for 15 minutes. Top the tacos with shredded lettuce, grated cheese, diced avocado, chopped tomato, and sour cream.

- 3 tablespoons unsalted butter
- 4 garlic cloves, minced
- 2 teaspoons minced canned chipotle chile in adobo sauce
- ¾ cup chopped fresh cilantro
- ½ cup orange juice
- 1 tablespoon Worcestershire sauce
- 4 (6-ounce) boneless, skinless chicken breasts, trimmed
- 1 teaspoon yellow mustard
  Salt and pepper
- 12 (6-inch) flour tortillas

1. Melt butter in large skillet over medium-high heat. Add garlic and chipotle and cook until fragrant, about 30 seconds. Stir in ½ cup cilantro, orange juice, and Worcestershire and bring to boil. Add chicken and simmer, covered, over medium-low heat until meat registers 160 degrees, 10 to 15 minutes, flipping chicken halfway through cooking. Transfer to plate and tent with aluminum foil.

2. Increase heat to medium-high and cook until liquid is reduced to ¼ cup, about 5 minutes. Off heat, whisk in mustard. Using 2 forks, shred chicken into bite-size pieces and return to skillet. Add remaining ¼ cup cilantro to skillet and toss until well combined. Season with salt and pepper to taste. Serve with tortillas.

Storing Canned Chipotle Chiles

When a recipe uses just a teaspoon or two of chipotle chiles, here's how to store the rest of the can.

Canned chipotle chiles are jalapeños that have been ripened until red, smoked, and packed in a tangy tomato-based adobo sauce. Since the size of chipotles varies, in the test kitchen we measure them by minced teaspoons. Could we store leftovers in the freezer, or would they lose their potency? To see, we pureed several cans and froze measured teaspoons on a plastic wrap–covered plate. Once our "chipotle chips" were hard, we peeled them off the plastic and transferred them to a zipper-lock freezer bag.

Weeks later we made a salsa and a casserole with the frozen chipotles and compared them with the same dishes made with chiles from a newly opened can. Most tasters couldn't tell the two apart. The chipotles will keep for up to two months in the freezer and should be thawed before you use them. The chiles will also last for two weeks in the refrigerator.

Shredding Chicken

Hold one fork in each hand, with tines facing down. Insert tines into chicken and gently pull forks away from each other, breaking meat apart and into long thin shreds.

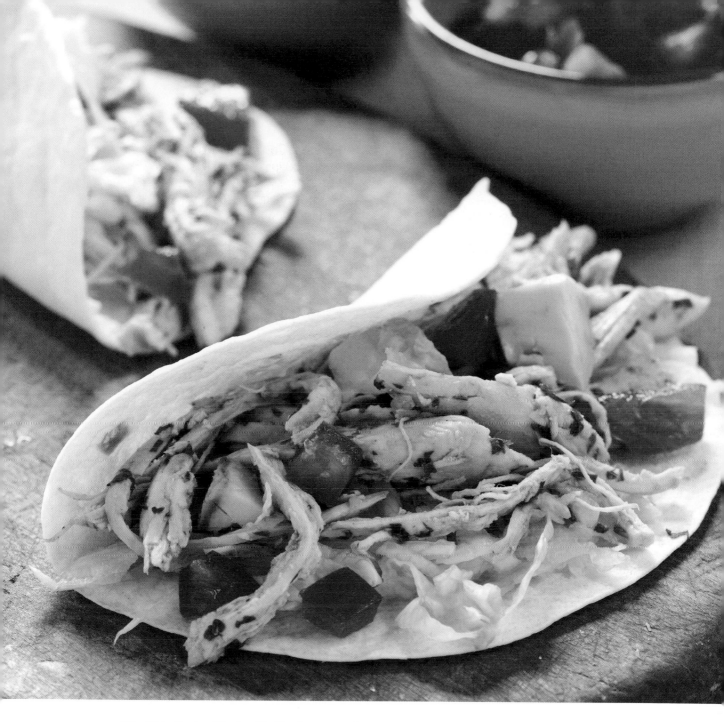

Why This Recipe Works We like the convenience of boneless, skinless chicken breasts in tacos, but they can be dry. After trying a variety of cooking methods, we found that poaching produced meat that was tender and moist. Chipotle chiles gave our poaching liquid a smoky, full-bodied flavor and orange juice offered a touch of sweetness that tempered its vivid acidity. For more robust flavor, we called on two kitchen staples: Worcestershire mimicked the complex flavor of dark meat, and mustard added sharpness that balanced the sweet orange juice and smoky chipotle.

Why This Recipe Works San Antonio's been enjoying puffy taco shells in restaurants for years, and we were determined to re-create a similar version in the test kitchen. Instead of using the traditional *masa de maíz* (finely ground hominy), we used the more widely available masa harina (dried masa flour) for our tortilla dough. Pressing the dough with a clear pie plate allowed us to gauge the diameter and to get a consistent thickness. Using a large saucepan containing just 2 quarts of oil made our taco shell prep much easier. For a flavorful filling, picadillo made with ground beef, green bell pepper, onions, garlic, and cumin fit the bill.

PUFFY TACOS

SERVES 6 TO 8

We used Maseca Instant Masa Corn Flour for our taco shells. The dough should not be sticky and should have the texture of Play-Doh. If the dough cracks or falls apart when pressing the tortillas, just reroll and press again.

Picadillo
- 12 ounces 85 percent lean ground beef
- ½ russet potato (4 ounces), peeled and cut into ¼-inch pieces
- Salt and pepper
- 1 onion, chopped fine
- 1 small green bell pepper, stemmed, seeded, and chopped fine
- 3 garlic cloves, minced
- 1½ teaspoons ground cumin
- 2 teaspoons all-purpose flour
- ¾ cup water

Taco Shells
- 2½ cups (10 ounces) masa harina
- 1 teaspoon salt
- 1⅔ cups warm water
- 2 quarts vegetable oil

- Shredded iceberg lettuce
- Chopped tomato
- Shredded sharp cheddar cheese
- Hot sauce

1. For the Picadillo Combine beef, potato, 1 teaspoon pepper, and ¾ teaspoon salt in 12-inch nonstick skillet. Cook over medium-high heat until meat and potatoes begin to brown, 6 to 8 minutes, breaking up meat with spoon. Add onion and bell pepper and cook until softened, 4 to 6 minutes. Add garlic and cumin and cook until fragrant, about 30 seconds.

2. Stir in flour and cook for 1 minute. Stir in water and bring to boil. Reduce heat to medium-low and simmer until thickened slightly, about 1 minute. Season with salt and pepper to taste. Remove from heat, cover, and keep warm.

3. For the Taco Shells Mix masa harina and salt together in medium bowl. Stir in warm water with rubber spatula. Using your hands, knead mixture in bowl until it comes together fully (dough should be soft and tacky, not sticky), about 30 seconds. Cover dough with damp dish towel and let rest for 5 minutes.

4. Divide dough into 12 equal portions, about ¼ cup each, then roll each into smooth ball between your hands. Transfer to plate and keep covered with damp dish towel. Cut sides of 1-gallon zipper-lock bag, leaving bottom seam intact.

5. Set wire rack in rimmed baking sheet and line rack with triple layer of paper towels. Add oil to large saucepan until it measures 2½ inches deep and heat over medium-high heat to 375 degrees.

6. When oil comes to temperature, enclose 1 dough ball at a time in split bag. Using clear pie plate (so you can see size of tortilla), press dough flat into 6-inch circle (about ⅛ inch thick).

7. Carefully remove tortilla from plastic and drop into hot oil. Fry tortilla until it puffs up, 15 to 20 seconds. Using 2 metal spatulas, carefully flip tortilla. Immediately press down in center of tortilla with 1 spatula to form taco shape, submerging tortilla into oil while doing so. Using second spatula, spread top of tortilla open about 1½ inches. Fry until golden brown, about 60 seconds. Adjust burner, if necessary, to maintain oil temperature between 350 and 375 degrees.

8. Transfer taco shell to prepared rack and place upside down to drain. Return oil to 375 degrees and repeat with remaining dough balls.

9. Divide picadillo evenly among taco shells, about ¼ cup each. Serve immediately, passing lettuce, tomato, cheddar, and hot sauce separately.

Why This Recipe Works Traditional *cochinita pibil* requires a suckling pig and banana leaves. To make these richly flavored tacos at home, we replaced annatto seeds with bay leaves and tomato paste and swapped in well-marbled, collagen-rich pork butt for the pig. Our savory braising liquid delivered layers of flavor. Cooking the pork butt low and slow produced luscious meat that shredded easily with a potato masher. Served on warm tortillas with punchy quick-pickled red onions and a fiery home-made habanero sauce, our supermarket-friendly tacos tasted perfectly authentic.

CITRUS-BRAISED PORK TACOS

SERVES 6

Pork butt roast is often labeled Boston butt in the super-market. For a spicier sauce, add an extra habanero or two; if you are spice-averse, substitute jalapeños for the habaneros. Pickled onions and habanero sauce can each be refrigerated for up to 1 week.

Pork

2 tablespoons vegetable oil
1 onion, chopped fine
3 garlic cloves, minced
1 teaspoon ground cumin
1 teaspoon dried oregano
½ teaspoon ground allspice
½ teaspoon ground cinnamon
⅓ cup tomato paste
1½ cups water
¼ cup frozen orange juice concentrate, thawed
3 tablespoons distilled white vinegar
1½ tablespoons Worcestershire sauce
5 bay leaves
Salt and pepper
1 (2½- to 3-pound) boneless pork butt roast, trimmed and cut into 1-inch chunks

Pickled Red Onions

1 red onion, halved and sliced thin
1 cup distilled white vinegar
⅓ cup sugar
¼ teaspoon salt

Habanero Sauce

1 cup water
1 carrot, peeled and chopped
1 vine-ripened tomato, cored and chopped
¼ cup chopped onion
½ habanero chile, stemmed
1 garlic clove, smashed and peeled
Salt and pepper
1 tablespoon distilled white vinegar
1½ teaspoons lime juice, plus lime wedges for serving

18 (6-inch) corn tortillas, warmed

1. For the Pork Adjust oven rack to lower-middle position and heat oven to 300 degrees. Heat oil in Dutch oven over medium heat until shimmering. Add onion and cook until lightly browned, 4 to 6 minutes.

2. Add garlic, cumin, oregano, allspice, and cinnamon and cook until fragrant, about 30 seconds. Stir in tomato paste and cook, stirring constantly, until paste begins to darken, about 45 seconds. Stir in water, orange juice concentrate, 2 tablespoons vinegar, Worcestershire, bay leaves, 2 teaspoons salt, and 1 teaspoon pepper, scraping up any browned bits.

3. Add pork and bring to boil. Transfer to oven, uncovered, and cook until pork is tender, about 2 hours, stirring once halfway through cooking.

4. For the Pickled Red Onions Meanwhile, place onion in medium bowl. Bring vinegar, sugar, and salt to simmer in small saucepan over medium-high heat, stirring occasionally, until sugar dissolves. Pour over onions and cover loosely. Let onions cool completely, about 30 minutes.

5. For the Habanero Sauce Combine water, carrot, tomato, onion, habanero, garlic, and ½ teaspoon salt in now-empty saucepan. Bring to boil over medium heat and cook until carrot is tender, about 10 minutes. Remove from heat and let carrot mixture cool slightly, about 5 minutes. Transfer carrot mixture to blender, add vinegar and lime juice, and process until sauce is smooth, 1 to 2 minutes. Season with salt and pepper to taste; set aside.

6. Transfer pot to stovetop; discard bay leaves. Using potato masher, mash pork until finely shredded. Bring to simmer over medium-high heat, then reduce heat to medium-low and cook until most of liquid has evaporated, 3 to 5 minutes.

7. Off heat, stir in remaining 1 tablespoon vinegar and season with salt and pepper to taste. Serve on tortillas with pickled red onions, habanero sauce, and lime wedges.

EASIER CHICKEN CHIMICHANGAS

SERVES 4

If using a cast-iron Dutch oven, increase the broth to 1¾ cups, adding 1¼ cups in step 2. Serve with Smoky Salsa Verde (page 256).

1¼ cups chicken broth
1 tablespoon minced canned chipotle chile in adobo sauce
½ cup long-grain white rice
Salt and pepper
2 (6-ounce) boneless, skinless chicken breasts, trimmed
1 tablespoon peanut or vegetable oil, plus 3 cups for frying
1 onion, chopped fine
2 garlic cloves, minced
1 teaspoon chili powder
½ teaspoon ground cumin
1 (15-ounce) can pinto beans, rinsed
4 ounces sharp cheddar cheese, shredded (1 cup)
⅓ cup chopped fresh cilantro
1 tablespoon all-purpose flour
1 tablespoon water
4 (10-inch) flour tortillas

1. Whisk broth and chipotle together in 2-cup liquid measuring cup. Combine ½ cup chipotle broth, rice, and ¼ teaspoon salt in bowl. Cover bowl and microwave until liquid is completely absorbed, about 5 minutes. Meanwhile, pat chicken dry with paper towels and season with salt and pepper.

2. Heat 1 tablespoon oil in Dutch oven over medium-high heat until just smoking. Add onion and cook until softened, about 5 minutes. Stir in garlic, chili powder, and cumin and cook until fragrant, about 30 seconds. Add remaining ¾ cup chipotle broth, parcooked rice, and beans and bring to boil.

3. Reduce heat to medium-low, add chicken, and cook, covered, until chicken registers 160 degrees and rice is tender, about 15 minutes, flipping chicken halfway through cooking. Transfer chicken to cutting board and let rest for 5 to 10 minutes. Cut chicken into ½-inch pieces and combine with rice and bean mixture, cheddar, and cilantro in large bowl. Wash now-empty pot.

4. Whisk flour and water together in small bowl. Stack tortillas on plate and microwave, covered, until pliable, about 1 minute. Working with one at a time, place one-quarter of chicken mixture in center of warm tortilla. Brush edges of tortilla with flour paste. Wrap top and bottom of tortilla tightly over filling. Brush ends of tortilla with paste and fold into center, pressing firmly to seal.

5. Set wire rack in rimmed baking sheet. Heat remaining 3 cups oil in clean pot over medium-high heat until 325 degrees. Place 2 chimichangas, seam side down, in oil. Fry, adjusting burner as necessary to maintain oil temperature between 300 and 325 degrees, until chimichangas are deep golden brown, about 4 minutes, turning them halfway through frying. Drain on prepared wire rack. Bring oil back to 325 degrees and repeat with remaining chimichangas. Serve.

Glue and Fold

The usual burrito-style wrapping method left us between the devil and the deep blue sea: Either the filling leaked out in the pot of oil or the ends of the tortilla never crisped. Our new chimichanga folding technique solves both problems.

1. Place filling in middle of tortilla. Brush tortilla's circumference with flour-and-water paste.

2. After folding opposing sides toward center and pressing to seal, brush open flaps with more paste. Fold flaps in and press firmly to seal chimichanga shut.

Why This Recipe Works Forget about tasteless fillings. We simmer the chicken and rice for our chimichangas in a chipotle broth, infusing them with a smoky bite through and through. As for construction, we noticed that the standard burrito-style wrapping method left us with doughy tortilla ends and filling that fell out. We created an easy new folding technique that kept the filling put without any floury bites.

SMOKY SALSA VERDE

MAKES 1¼ CUPS

This salsa is especially good served with our Easier Chicken Chimichangas (page 254), or try it with just about anything you'd serve salsa with, such as tortilla chips, grilled steak, or scrambled eggs.

1	pound tomatillos, husks and stems removed, rinsed well, and dried
1	small onion, quartered
1	jalapeño chile, stemmed, halved, and seeded
1	garlic clove, peeled
1	teaspoon olive oil
½	cup fresh cilantro leaves
1	tablespoon lime juice
	Salt

1. Adjust oven rack 5 inches from broiler element and heat broiler. Toss tomatillos, onion, jalapeño, and garlic with oil and place on aluminum foil–lined rimmed baking sheet. Broil, shaking pan occasionally, until vegetables are lightly charred, 10 to 12 minutes. Cool slightly, about 5 minutes.

2. Add vegetables, cilantro, lime juice, and ¼ teaspoon salt to food processor and pulse until coarsely ground, 5 to 7 pulses. Season with salt to taste. Serve. (Salsa can be refrigerated for up to 3 days.)

Tomatillos

Called *tomates verdes* (green tomatoes) in much of Mexico, small green tomatillos have a tangier, more citrusy flavor than true green tomatoes. When choosing tomatillos, look for pale-green orbs with firm flesh that fills and splits open the fruit's outer papery husk, which must be removed before cooking. Avoid tomatillos that are too yellow and soft, as these specimens are past their prime and will taste sour and muted.

Reviving Tired Herbs

We rarely use an entire bunch of herbs at once, and inevitably a few days later they are looking less-than-fresh and we have to throw them out and start all over. Is there a way to revive tired herbs? With a little research, we found that soaking herbs in water restores the pressure of the cell contents against the cell wall, causing them to become firmer as the dehydrated cells plump up. So, after purposely letting several bunches of parsley, cilantro, and mint sit in the refrigerator until they became limp, sorry-looking versions of their former selves, we tried bringing the herbs back to life by soaking them in tepid and cold water. We found that soaking herbs (stems trimmed) for 10 minutes in cold water perks them up better than tepid water. These herbs had a fresher look and an improved texture.

Why This Recipe Works Our recipe for *salsa verde* includes the typical ingredients: tomatillos, onions, garlic, jalapeño, and lots of cilantro. To temper their sharply acidic flavor, we broiled the tomatillos just until tender. We also broiled the other vegetables to provide subtle smokiness. Our recipe calls for a large amount of cilantro to ensure that its flavor stands out from the other ingredients.

Why This Recipe Works Tex-Mex cheese enchiladas are a wildly popular dish in the Lone Star State, beloved for their relative simplicity and their chile gravy, a red sauce that's a cross between beef gravy and Mexican enchilada sauce. We found that two toasted ancho chiles ground with a combination of spices gave the sauce smoky flavors that we brightened with a little white vinegar. We skipped frying the corn tortillas instead brushing them with oil and microwaving, resulting in soft, easy-to-roll tortillas without excess grease. For the cheesy filling, we combined sharp cheddar and Monterey Jack and used the oven to ensure melty, gooey cheese.

TEX-MEX CHEESE ENCHILADAS

SERVES 6

Dried chiles vary in size and weight. You'll get a more accurate measure if you seed and tear them first; you need about ½ cup of prepped chiles. You'll lose some flavor, but you can substitute 2 tablespoons ancho chile powder and 1 tablespoon ground cumin for the whole ancho chiles and cumin seeds, decreasing the toasting time to 1 minute.

Gravy

- 2 dried ancho chiles, stemmed, seeded, and torn into ½-inch pieces (½ cup)
- 1 tablespoon cumin seeds
- 1 tablespoon garlic powder
- 2 teaspoons dried oregano
- 3 tablespoons vegetable oil
- 3 tablespoons all-purpose flour
  Salt and pepper
- 2 cups chicken broth
- 2 teaspoons distilled white vinegar

Enchiladas

- 12 (6-inch) corn tortillas
- 1½ tablespoons vegetable oil
- 8 ounces Monterey Jack cheese, shredded (2 cups)
- 6 ounces sharp cheddar cheese, shredded (1½ cups)
- 1 onion, chopped fine

1. For the Gravy Toast chiles and cumin in 12-inch skillet over medium-low heat, stirring frequently, until fragrant, about 2 minutes. Transfer to spice grinder and let cool for 5 minutes. Add garlic powder and oregano and grind to fine powder.

2. Heat oil in now-empty skillet over medium-high heat until shimmering. Whisk in flour, ½ teaspoon salt, ½ teaspoon pepper, and spice mixture and cook until fragrant and slightly deepened in color, about 1 minute. Slowly whisk in broth and bring to simmer. Reduce heat to medium-low and cook, whisking frequently, until gravy has thickened and reduced to 1½ cups, about 5 minutes. Whisk in vinegar and season with salt and pepper to taste. Remove from heat, cover, and keep warm.

3. For the Enchiladas Adjust oven rack to middle position and heat oven to 450 degrees. Brush both sides of tortillas with oil. Stack tortillas, then wrap in damp dish towel. Place tortillas on plate and microwave until warm and pliable, about 1 minute.

4. Spread ½ cup gravy in bottom of 13 by 9-inch baking dish. Combine cheeses in bowl; set aside ½ cup cheese mixture for topping enchiladas. Sprinkle ¼ cup cheese mixture and 1 tablespoon onion across center of each tortilla. Tightly roll tortillas around filling and lay them seam side down in dish (2 columns of 6 tortillas will fit neatly across width of dish). Pour remaining 1 cup gravy over enchiladas, then sprinkle with reserved cheese mixture.

5. Cover dish with aluminum foil and bake until sauce is bubbling and cheese is melted, about 15 minutes. Let enchiladas cool for 10 minutes, then sprinkle with remaining onion. Serve.

To Make Ahead The sauce can be made up to 24 hours in advance. To reheat, add 2 tablespoons water and microwave until loose, 1 to 2 minutes, stirring halfway through microwaving.

Enchilada Orientation

After spreading ½ cup chile gravy in 13 by 9-inch baking dish, fit 12 enchiladas by creating two snug rows of six.

AUTHENTIC BEEF ENCHILADAS

SERVES 4 TO 6

Cut back on the jalapeños if you like your enchiladas on the mild side.

 3 tablespoons chili powder
 3 garlic cloves, minced
 2 teaspoons ground coriander
 2 teaspoons ground cumin
 1 teaspoon sugar
   Salt
1¼ pounds top blade steaks, trimmed
 1 tablespoon vegetable oil
 2 onions, chopped
 1 (15-ounce) can tomato sauce
 ½ cup water
 8 ounces Monterey Jack or mild cheddar cheese, shredded (2 cups)
 ⅓ cup chopped fresh cilantro
 ¼ cup chopped canned jalapeños
12 (6-inch) corn tortillas

1. Combine chili powder, garlic, coriander, cumin, sugar, and 1 teaspoon salt in small bowl. Pat meat dry with paper towels and sprinkle with salt. Heat oil in Dutch oven over medium-high heat until shimmering. Cook meat until browned on both sides, about 6 minutes. Transfer meat to plate. Add onions to pot and cook over medium heat until golden, about 5 minutes. Stir in garlic mixture and cook until fragrant, about 1 minute. Add tomato sauce and water and bring to boil. Return meat and juices to pot, cover, reduce heat to low, and gently simmer until meat is tender and can be broken apart with wooden spoon, about 1½ hours.

2. Adjust oven rack to middle position and heat oven to 350 degrees. Strain beef mixture over medium bowl, breaking meat into small pieces; reserve sauce. Transfer meat to bowl and mix with 1 cup cheese, cilantro, and jalapeños.

3. Spread ¾ cup sauce in bottom of 13 by 9-inch baking dish. Place 6 tortillas on plate and microwave until soft, about 1 minute. Spread ⅓ cup beef mixture down center of each tortilla, roll tortillas tightly, and set in baking dish seam side down. Repeat with remaining tortillas and beef mixture (you may have to fit 2 or more enchiladas down the sides of the baking dish). Pour remaining sauce over enchiladas and spread to coat evenly. Sprinkle remaining 1 cup cheese evenly over enchiladas, wrap with aluminum foil, and bake until heated through, 20 to 25 minutes. Remove foil and continue baking until cheese browns slightly, 5 to 10 minutes. Serve.

Trimming Blade Steaks

Halve each steak lengthwise and slice away center strip of gristle.

Why This Recipe Works Traditional beef enchilada recipes require simmering steak for hours. Convenience recipes call for hamburger and canned sauce. We wanted to find a middle ground. For a deeply flavored sauce, we relied on chili powder and tomato sauce, along with onions, garlic, and spices. Slicing beefy, inexpensive blade steaks into small pieces cut our cooking time considerably. Authentic recipes fry the corn tortillas and then dip them in sauce to soften and season them. Instead, we softened the tortillas in the microwave. Once filled, topped with sauce and cheese, and baked, our enchiladas tasted like the real deal.

CHICKEN CHILAQUILES

SERVES 6

New Mexican or Anaheim chiles can be substituted for the guajillo chiles. If queso fresco is unavailable, you can substitute farmer's cheese or a mild feta. When baking the tortillas, stir them well to promote even browning.

16 (6-inch) corn tortillas, each cut into 8 wedges
¼ cup olive oil
  Salt
5 dried guajillo chiles, stemmed and seeded
1 (28-ounce) can whole peeled tomatoes
1 cup finely chopped onion
1 poblano chile, stemmed, seeded, and chopped
1 jalapeño chile, stemmed, seeded, and chopped
8 sprigs fresh cilantro, plus 2 tablespoons chopped
3 garlic cloves, chopped
1½ cups chicken broth
1½ pounds boneless, skinless chicken breasts, trimmed
4 ounces queso fresco, crumbled (1 cup)
1 avocado, halved, pitted, and cut into ½-inch chunks
2 radishes, trimmed and sliced thin
  Sour cream
  Lime wedges

1. Adjust oven racks to upper-middle and lower-middle positions and heat oven to 425 degrees. Divide tortillas evenly between 2 rimmed baking sheets and drizzle with oil and ½ teaspoon salt. Toss until tortillas are evenly coated with oil. Bake until golden brown and crisp, 15 to 20 minutes, stirring chips and switching and rotating sheets halfway through baking.

2. Toast guajillos in Dutch oven over medium heat until fragrant and slightly darkened, about 5 minutes. Transfer to blender and process until finely ground, 60 to 90 seconds, scraping down sides of blender jar as needed.

3. Add tomatoes and their juice, ¾ cup onion, poblano, jalapeño, cilantro sprigs, garlic, and ¾ teaspoon salt to guajillos and process until very smooth, 60 to 90 seconds. Transfer sauce to now-empty Dutch oven and stir in broth. Bring sauce to boil over medium-high heat. Add chicken breasts; reduce heat to low and simmer, uncovered, until chicken registers 160 degrees, 15 to 20 minutes, flipping halfway through cooking.

4. Using tongs, transfer chicken to large plate. Increase heat to medium and continue to simmer sauce until thickened and reduced to about 4½ cups, about 5 minutes longer. While sauce simmers, shred chicken into bite-size pieces using 2 forks. Return chicken to sauce and cook until warmed through, about 2 minutes.

5. Add chips to pot and toss to coat. Remove from heat and season with salt to taste. Cover and let stand for 2 to 5 minutes, depending on how soft you like your chips.

6. Transfer chilaquiles to serving dish and top with queso fresco, avocado, radishes, remaining ¼ cup onion, and chopped cilantro. Serve with sour cream and lime wedges.

Entrée-Worthy Chilaquiles

1. Use three types of chiles.

2. Make easy homemade chips.

3. Cook chicken in sauce.

4. Finish with fresh garnishes.

Why This Recipe Works *Chilaquiles* are often made from leftover meats and are considered a side dish, but we started from scratch for the best flavor and turned the dish into a meal. We began by baking our own tortilla chips. For the tomato-based red sauce, we toasted dried guajillo chiles to intensify their flavor before pureeing them with fresh poblanos, jalapeños, and other aromatic ingredients. To make the chilaquiles a complete meal, we poached boneless, skinless chicken breasts in the red sauce before shredding and mixing the tender meat back in with the chips. Finishing the dish with sour cream and queso fresco balanced the heat.

Why This Recipe Works Many chili con carne recipes call for toasting and grinding whole chiles. We wanted to create a simpler, authentic-tasting version. For the meat, we settled on beef chuck, our favorite cut for stews because its substantial marbling provides rich flavor and tender texture after prolonged cooking. To add a smoky meatiness to our chili, we browned the beef in bacon fat instead of oil. We added a jalapeño for brightness and heat and minced chipotle for smoky, spicy depth. A few tablespoons of corn muffin mix, in place of masa harina (corn flour), helped thicken our chili and gave it a silky texture.

EASY CHILI CON CARNE

SERVES 6 TO 8

If the bacon does not render a full 3 tablespoons of fat in step 1, supplement it with vegetable oil. If desired, serve chili with chopped onion, avocado, shredded cheese, lime wedges, and/or hot sauce.

- 1 (14.5-ounce) can diced tomatoes
- 2 teaspoons minced canned chipotle chile in adobo sauce
- 4 slices bacon, chopped fine
- 1 (3½- to 4-pound) boneless beef chuck-eye roast, pulled apart at seams, trimmed, and cut into 1-inch pieces
  Salt and pepper
- 1 onion, chopped fine
- 1 jalapeño chile, stemmed, seeded, and chopped fine
- 3 tablespoons chili powder
- 4 garlic cloves, minced
- 1½ teaspoons ground cumin
- ½ teaspoon dried oregano
- 4 cups water
- 1 tablespoon packed brown sugar
- 2 tablespoons yellow corn muffin mix

1. Process tomatoes and chipotle in food processor until smooth. Cook bacon in Dutch oven over medium heat until crisp, about 8 minutes. Transfer bacon to paper towel–lined plate and reserve 3 tablespoons bacon fat.

2. Pat beef dry with paper towels and season with salt and pepper. Heat 1 tablespoon reserved bacon fat in now-empty Dutch oven over medium-high heat until just smoking. Brown half of beef, about 8 minutes. Transfer to bowl and repeat with 1 tablespoon bacon fat and remaining beef.

3. Add remaining 1 tablespoon bacon fat, onion, and jalapeño to again-empty Dutch oven and cook until softened, about 5 minutes. Stir in chili powder, garlic, cumin, and oregano and cook until fragrant, about 30 seconds. Stir in water, pureed tomato mixture, bacon, browned beef, and sugar and bring to boil. Reduce heat to low and simmer, covered, for 1 hour. Skim fat and continue to simmer uncovered until meat is tender, 30 to 45 minutes.

4. Ladle 1 cup chili liquid into medium bowl and stir in muffin mix; cover with plastic wrap. Microwave until mixture is thickened, about 1 minute. Slowly whisk mixture into chili and simmer until chili is slightly thickened, 5 to 10 minutes. Season with salt and pepper to taste. Serve. (Chili can be refrigerated for up to 3 days.)

Silky Sauce

Our chili gets silky texture and a hint of corn flavor from the addition of corn muffin mix.

Why This Recipe Works As the name implies, five-alarm chili should be spicy enough to make you break a sweat—but it has to have rich, complex chile flavor as well. We used a combination of dried anchos, smoky chipotle chiles in adobo sauce, fresh jalapeños, and chili powder to create layers of spicy flavor. Ground beef added meaty bulk, and pureeing the chiles along with canned tomatoes and corn chips added extra body and another layer of flavor. Mellowed with a bit of sugar and enriched with creamy pinto beans, our chili was well balanced and spicy without being harsh.

FIVE-ALARM CHILI

SERVES 8 TO 10

Look for ancho chiles in the international aisle at the supermarket. Light-bodied American lagers, such as Budweiser, work best here. Serve chili with lime, sour cream, diced tomato, diced avocado, scallions, and cornbread.

2 ounces (4 to 6) dried ancho chiles, stemmed, seeded, and cut into 1-inch pieces
3½ cups water
1 (28-ounce) can whole peeled tomatoes
¾ cup crushed corn tortilla chips
¼ cup canned chipotle chile in adobo sauce plus 2 teaspoons adobo sauce
2 tablespoons vegetable oil
2 pounds 85 percent lean ground beef
   Salt and pepper
2 pounds onions, chopped fine
2 jalapeño chiles, stemmed, seeds reserved, and minced
6 garlic cloves, minced
2 tablespoons ground cumin
2 tablespoons chili powder
1 tablespoon dried oregano
2 teaspoons ground coriander
2 teaspoons sugar
1 teaspoon cayenne pepper
1½ cups beer
3 (15-ounce) cans pinto beans, rinsed

1. Combine anchos and 1½ cups water in bowl and microwave until softened, about 3 minutes. Drain and discard liquid. Process anchos, tomatoes and their juice, remaining 2 cups water, tortilla chips, chipotle, and adobo sauce in blender until smooth, about 1 minute; set aside.

2. Heat 2 teaspoons oil in Dutch oven over medium-high heat until just smoking. Add beef, 1 teaspoon salt, and ½ teaspoon pepper and cook, breaking up pieces with spoon, until all liquid has evaporated and meat begins to sizzle, 10 to 15 minutes. Drain in colander and set aside.

3. Heat remaining 4 teaspoons oil in now-empty Dutch oven over medium-high heat until simmering. Add onions and jalapeños and seeds and cook until onions are lightly browned, about 5 minutes. Stir in garlic, cumin, chili powder, oregano, coriander, sugar, and cayenne and cook until fragrant, about 30 seconds. Pour in beer and bring to simmer. Stir in beans, reserved chile-tomato mixture, and reserved cooked beef and return to simmer. Cover, reduce heat to low, and cook, stirring occasionally, until thickened, 50 to 60 minutes. Season with salt to taste. Serve.

Five Hits for Five-Alarm Chili

JALAPEÑO
Brings fresh vegetable flavor

CHIPOTLE IN ADOBO
Instant shortcut to smokiness

CHILI POWDER
Wouldn't be chili without it

CAYENNE
Adds raw heat

ANCHO
Adds depth, complexity, and mild heat

SO-CAL CHURROS

MAKES ABOUT 18 CHURROS

We used a closed star #8 pastry tip, ⅝ inch in diameter, to create deeply grooved ridges in the churros. However, you can use any large, closed star tip of similar diameter, though your yield may vary slightly. It's important to mix the dough for 1 minute in step 2 before adding the eggs to keep them from scrambling.

Dough

- 2 cups water
- 2 tablespoons unsalted butter
- 2 tablespoons sugar
- 1 teaspoon vanilla extract
- ½ teaspoon salt
- 2 cups (10 ounces) all-purpose flour
- 2 large eggs
- 2 quarts vegetable oil

Chocolate Sauce

- ¾ cup heavy cream
- 4 ounces semisweet chocolate chips
- Pinch salt
- ¼ teaspoon vanilla extract

Coating

- ½ cup (3½ ounces) sugar
- ¾ teaspoon ground cinnamon

1. For the Dough Line 1 rimmed baking sheet with parchment paper and spray with vegetable oil spray. Combine water, butter, sugar, vanilla, and salt in large saucepan and bring to boil over medium-high heat. Remove from heat; add flour all at once and stir with rubber spatula until well combined, with no streaks of flour remaining.

2. Transfer dough to bowl of stand mixer. Fit mixer with paddle and mix on low speed until cooled slightly, about 1 minute. Add eggs, increase speed to medium, and beat until fully incorporated, about 1 minute.

3. Transfer warm dough to piping bag fitted with ⅝-inch closed star pastry tip. Pipe 18 (6-inch) lengths of dough onto prepared sheet, using scissors to snip dough at tip. Refrigerate, uncovered, for 15 minutes to 1 hour.

4. Adjust oven rack to middle position and heat oven to 200 degrees. Set wire rack in second rimmed baking sheet and place in oven. Line large plate with triple layer of paper towels. Add oil to Dutch oven until it measures about 1½ inches deep and heat over medium-high heat to 375 degrees.

5. Gently drop 6 churros into hot oil and fry until dark golden brown on all sides, about 6 minutes, turning frequently for even cooking. Adjust burner, if necessary, to maintain oil temperature between 350 and 375 degrees. Transfer churros to paper towel–lined plate for 30 seconds to drain off excess oil, then transfer to wire rack in oven. Return oil to 375 degrees and repeat with remaining dough in 2 more batches.

6. For the Chocolate Sauce Microwave cream, chocolate chips, and salt in bowl at 50 percent power, stirring occasionally, until melted, about 2 minutes. Stir in vanilla until smooth.

7. For the Coating Combine sugar and cinnamon in shallow dish. Roll churros in cinnamon sugar, tapping gently to remove excess. Transfer churros to platter and serve warm with chocolate sauce.

Churning Out Churros

Pipe eighteen 6-inch lengths of warm dough, snipping at tip. Refrigerate 15 minutes to 1 hour to firm up before frying.

Why This Recipe Works The fried pastries known as *churros* should be crisp on the outside and soft on the inside, but piping thick *pâte à choux* dough into hot oil is no easy feat. We began by preparing a simple dough, precooking a mixture of water, butter, sugar, vanilla, and salt before stirring in flour and beating in eggs. The dough proved easier to work with when still warm, so we transferred it to a pastry bag right away. Piping the dough onto a baking sheet and frying the churros in batches made it easier to monitor when they were done. A roll in cinnamon sugar and a dip in a simple chocolate sauce made for a sweet finish.

everybody loves italian

Why This Recipe Works To translate a classic minestrone to the slow cooker, we needed to find a combination of vegetables that would cook through in the same amount of time. Green beans took too long to become tender. We scrapped cauliflower because its flavor overwhelmed the soup. Zucchini squash and Swiss chard won out for texture and their similar cooking times. Canned beans disintegrated in the soup, so we used dried white beans. We started cooking the beans in the soup along with some softened carrots and onions, then added the squash, chard, and pasta toward the end of cooking so they would be perfectly tender.

SLOW-COOKER MINESTRONE

SERVES 6 TO 8

We recommend using great Northern or cannellini beans here. Serve the minestrone with grated Parmesan cheese.

1 cup dried medium–size white beans, rinsed and picked over
6 tablespoons extra-virgin olive oil
2 onions, chopped fine
4 carrots, peeled and cut into ½-inch pieces
8 garlic cloves, minced
1 (28-ounce) can whole peeled tomatoes, coarsely crushed by hand
8 cups chicken broth
3 cups water
2 cups fresh basil leaves, chopped
1 teaspoon dried oregano
¼ teaspoon red pepper flakes
2 medium zucchini, quartered lengthwise, seeded, and sliced ¼ inch thick
8 ounces Swiss chard, stemmed and chopped
½ cup small dried pasta, such as ditalini, orzo, or small elbows
Salt and pepper

1. Bring beans and enough water to cover by 1 inch to boil in medium saucepan over high heat. Reduce heat to low and simmer, covered, until beans are just beginning to soften, about 20 minutes. Drain beans and transfer to slow cooker.

2. Heat 3 tablespoons oil in Dutch oven over medium heat until shimmering. Add onions and carrots and cook until softened, about 5 minutes. Stir in garlic and cook until fragrant, about 30 seconds.

Add tomatoes and their juice and cook until pan is nearly dry, 8 to 12 minutes. Stir in broth, water, ½ cup basil, oregano, and pepper flakes and bring to boil; transfer to slow cooker. Cover and cook until beans are tender, 6 to 7 hours on low or 5 to 6 hours on high.

3. Stir zucchini, Swiss chard, and pasta into slow cooker and cook on high, covered, until pasta is tender, 20 to 30 minutes. Stir in remaining 1½ cups basil and remaining 3 tablespoons oil. Season with salt and pepper to taste and serve.

To Make Ahead Recipe can be made through step 2 and refrigerated for up to 2 days. To finish, bring to boil in Dutch oven. Stir in zucchini, chard, and pasta; reduce heat to low; and simmer until pasta is tender, about 10 minutes.

Timing is Everything

First the onions, carrots, and tomatoes go into the slow cooker with the broth to create a rich, long-simmered backbone of flavor. Then we add the quick-cooking zucchini, Swiss chard, and pasta toward the end so they don't overcook.

HEAD START
Sautéed vegetables and canned whole tomatoes season the broth.

LAST MINUTE
The more delicate vegetables are added with the pasta near the end of cooking.

Why This Recipe Works We love the flavor and heartiness of Sunday gravy, but not the laundry list of ingredients or hours of monitoring the stovetop. For a streamlined recipe, we turned to our slow cooker and narrowed the meat selection down to three: flank steak, for meaty flavor; country-style spareribs, for tender, fall-off-the-bone meat; and sausage, for its spicy, sweet kick. Using the flavorful drippings left behind from browning the sausage to sauté our aromatics infused the whole dish with flavor. And a combination of drained diced tomatoes, canned tomato sauce, and tomato paste ensured a rich, thick sauce.

SLOW-COOKER ITALIAN SUNDAY GRAVY

SERVES 8 TO 10

Most sausage has enough seasoning to make extra salt unnecessary. This recipe makes enough to sauce 2 pounds of pasta. We like rigatoni, ziti, or penne with this sauce.

  1 tablespoon vegetable oil
  1 pound sweet Italian sausage
  1 pound hot Italian sausage
  2 onions, chopped
12 garlic cloves, minced
  2 teaspoons dried oregano
  1 (6-ounce) can tomato paste
½ cup dry red wine
  1 (28-ounce) can diced tomatoes, drained
  1 (28-ounce) can tomato sauce
  2 pounds bone-in country-style pork spareribs, trimmed
  1 (1½-pound) flank steak, trimmed
  3 tablespoons chopped fresh basil
     Pepper

1. Heat oil in Dutch oven over medium-high heat until just smoking. Add sweet sausage and cook until well browned and fat begins to render, about 8 minutes. Using slotted spoon, transfer sausage to paper towel–lined plate to drain, then place in slow cooker. Repeat with hot sausage; transfer to slow cooker.

2. Cook onions in rendered fat over medium heat until well browned, about 6 minutes. Stir in garlic and oregano and cook until fragrant, about 1 minute. Add tomato paste and cook until it begins to brown, about 5 minutes. Stir in wine and simmer, scraping up browned bits, until wine is slightly reduced, about 3 minutes. Transfer to slow cooker. Stir in diced tomatoes and tomato sauce.

3. Submerge spareribs and steak in sauce in slow cooker. Cover and cook until meat is tender, 8 to 10 hours on low or 4 to 5 hours on high.

4. About 30 minutes before serving, remove ribs, steak, and sausages and set aside until cool enough to handle. Shred ribs and steak into small pieces, discarding excess fat and bones; slice sausages in half crosswise. Skim fat from surface of sauce, then stir sausages and shredded meat back into sauce. Stir in basil and season with pepper to taste. Serve. (Gravy can be refrigerated for up to 3 days.)

To Make Ahead Recipe can be made in advance through step 2. After stirring in diced tomatoes and tomato sauce, add browned sausages and simmer over medium-low heat until cooked through, about 12 minutes. Refrigerate sausage and sauce for up to 2 days. To cook gravy, warm sauce and sausages together over medium heat until heated through; transfer to slow cooker. Proceed with step 3.

The Meat Matters
For our easy Slow-Cooker Italian Sunday Gravy, we narrowed down the meat to the following combination, which offers the best taste and texture.

ITALIAN SAUSAGES
Browning the sausages in advance helps build deep flavor.

FLANK STEAK
This lean cut adds beefy flavor without too much grease.

COUNTRY-STYLE SPARERIBS
These meaty ribs become fall-apart tender in a slow cooker.

PORK RAGU

MAKES ABOUT 8 CUPS

This recipe makes enough sauce to coat 2 pounds of pasta. Leftover sauce may be refrigerated for up to 3 days or frozen for up to 1 month.

2   (2¼- to 2½-pound) racks baby back ribs, trimmed and each rack cut into fourths
2   teaspoons ground fennel
    Kosher salt and pepper
3   tablespoons olive oil
1   large onion, chopped fine
1   large fennel bulb, stalks discarded, bulb halved, cored, and chopped fine
2   large carrots, peeled and chopped fine
¼   cup minced fresh sage
1½ teaspoons minced fresh rosemary
1   cup plus 2 tablespoons dry red wine
1   (28-ounce) can whole peeled tomatoes, drained and chopped coarse
3   cups chicken broth
1   garlic head, outer papery skins removed and top fourth of head cut off and discarded
1   pound pappardelle or tagliatelle
    Grated Parmesan cheese

1. Adjust oven rack to middle position and heat oven to 300 degrees. Sprinkle ribs with ground fennel and generously season with salt and pepper, pressing spices to adhere. Heat oil in Dutch oven over medium-high heat until just smoking. Add half of ribs, meat side down, and cook, without moving them, until meat is well browned, 6 to 8 minutes; transfer to plate. Repeat with remaining ribs; set aside.

2. Reduce heat to medium and add onion, fennel, carrots, 2 tablespoons sage, rosemary, and ½ teaspoon salt to now-empty pot. Cook, stirring occasionally and scraping up any browned bits, until vegetables are well browned and beginning to stick to pot bottom, 12 to 15 minutes.

3. Add 1 cup wine and cook until evaporated, about 5 minutes. Stir in tomatoes and broth and bring to simmer. Submerge garlic and ribs, meat side down, in liquid; add any accumulated juices from plate. Cover and transfer to oven. Cook until ribs are fork-tender, about 2 hours.

4. Remove pot from oven and transfer ribs and garlic to rimmed baking sheet. Using large spoon, skim any fat from surface of sauce. Once cool enough to handle, shred meat from bones; discard bones and gristle. Return meat to pot. Squeeze garlic from its skin into pot. Stir in remaining 2 tablespoons sage and remaining 2 tablespoons wine. Season with salt and pepper to taste.

5. Meanwhile, bring 4 quarts water to boil in large pot. Add pasta and 2 tablespoons salt and cook, stirring often, until al dente. Reserve ½ cup cooking water, then drain pasta and return it to pot. Add half of sauce and toss to combine, adjusting consistency with reserved cooking water as needed. Serve, passing Parmesan separately.

Cutting Baby Back Ribs for Ragu

Before browning ribs, divide each rack into three-rib segments using a chef's knife.

Why This Recipe Works Earthy and intense, pork ragu takes pasta to a new level. Most recipes call for pork shoulder and a hard-to-find, bony cut like neck, shank, or feet. We tried using all baby back ribs and found the resulting ragu rich and meaty. For a classic Italian flavor profile, fennel took the place of celery in the ragu's base and ground fennel rubbed into the ribs echoed the anise flavor. Simmering the garlic head whole right in the sauce yielded sweeter softened cloves that we squeezed back into the sauce when tender. With fresh herbs and red wine, our ragu tasted balanced and far more complex than its simple preparation would suggest.

Why This Recipe Works For the long-cooked flavor of pork ragu in under 90 minutes, we looked to our food processor. Whirring fennel, onion, and fennel seeds together created a savory flavor base. Pulsing canned whole tomatoes created a silky tomato sauce, and processing sweet Italian sausage delivered bites of well-seasoned meat in every forkful. We cooked the components in stages, browning the sausage before softening the *soffritto* in the rendered fat. Minced garlic and dried oregano, bloomed in tomato paste, further defined the Italian flavors, and red wine offered brightness. A 45-minute simmer produced a rich ragu with the perfect consistency.

PASTA WITH SAUSAGE RAGU

SERVES 4 TO 6

For a spicier sauce, substitute hot Italian sausage for sweet. You will have 3 cups of extra sauce, which can be used to sauce 1 pound of pasta.

- ½ fennel bulb, stalks discarded, bulb cored and chopped coarse
- ½ onion, chopped coarse
- 1 tablespoon fennel seeds
- 1 (28-ounce) can whole peeled tomatoes
- 2 pounds sweet Italian sausage, casings removed
- 1 tablespoon extra-virgin olive oil, plus extra for drizzling
    Salt and pepper
- 2 tablespoons tomato paste
- 4 garlic cloves, minced
- 1½ teaspoons dried oregano
- ¾ cup red wine
- 1 pound pappardelle or tagliatelle
    Grated Parmesan cheese

1. Pulse fennel, onion, and fennel seeds in food processor until finely chopped, about 10 pulses, scraping down sides of bowl as needed; transfer to separate bowl. Process tomatoes in now-empty processor until smooth, about 10 seconds; transfer to second bowl. Pulse sausage in now-empty processor until finely chopped, about 10 pulses, scraping down sides of bowl as needed.

2. Heat oil in Dutch oven over medium-high heat until shimmering. Add sausage and cook, breaking up meat with spoon, until all liquid has evaporated and meat begins to sizzle, 10 to 15 minutes.

3. Add fennel mixture and ½ teaspoon salt and cook, stirring occasionally, until softened, about 5 minutes. (Fond on bottom of pot will be deeply browned.) Add tomato paste, garlic, and oregano and cook, stirring constantly, until fragrant, about 30 seconds.

4. Stir in wine, scraping up any browned bits, and cook until nearly evaporated, about 1 minute. Add 1 cup water and pureed tomatoes and bring to simmer. Reduce heat to low and simmer gently, uncovered, until thickened, about 45 minutes. (Wooden spoon should leave trail when dragged through sauce.) Season with salt and pepper to taste; cover and keep warm.

5. Bring 4 quarts water to boil in large pot. Add pasta and 1 tablespoon salt and cook, stirring often, until al dente. Reserve 1 cup cooking water, then drain pasta and return it to pot. Add 3 cups sauce and ½ cup reserved cooking water to pasta and toss to combine. Adjust consistency with remaining reserved cooking water as needed. Transfer to serving dish. Drizzle with extra oil, sprinkle with Parmesan, and serve. (Remaining 3 cups sauce can be refrigerated for up to 3 days or frozen for up to 1 month.)

Spotlight on Fennel

The vegetable that we slice and eat raw or cooked is Florence fennel, or *finocchio*; its bulb, stems, and feathery fronds boast a mildly sweet, faint anise flavor. Fennel seeds, which are a key part of the flavor profile of Italian sausage, come from a perennial herb called common fennel (also referred to as herb, sweet, or wild fennel) that has no bulb.

FLORENCE FENNEL
A vegetable grown for its edible bulb, stems, and fronds.

COMMON FENNEL
A perennial herb grown for its ornamental fronds and aromatic seeds.

PASTA WITH ROASTED GARLIC SAUCE, ARUGULA, AND WALNUTS

SERVES 4

It takes about four heads of garlic to yield 50 cloves, but you can use prepeeled.

50 garlic cloves, peeled (1 cup)
 3 tablespoons extra-virgin olive oil,
   plus extra for drizzling
 1 cup chicken broth
 2 teaspoons balsamic vinegar
   Salt and pepper
 1 pound spaghetti, linguine, or fettuccine
 8 ounces (8 cups) baby arugula
 1 cup walnuts, toasted and chopped
   Grated Pecorino Romano cheese

1. Combine garlic and oil in medium saucepan over medium-low heat. Cover and cook, stirring occasionally, until garlic is browned all over, 6 to 8 minutes. Add broth, vinegar, ¾ teaspoon salt, and ½ teaspoon pepper and bring to boil. Reduce heat to low and simmer, uncovered, until garlic is fork-tender, 5 to 7 minutes. Pour garlic mixture into food processor and process until smooth, about 1 minute.

2. Meanwhile, bring 4 quarts water to boil in large pot. Add pasta and 1 tablespoon salt and cook, stirring often, until al dente. Reserve ½ cup cooking water, then drain pasta and return it to pot. Add garlic sauce, arugula, and walnuts to pasta and toss to combine. Adjust consistency with reserved cooking water as needed. Season with salt and pepper to taste. Serve, drizzling individual servings with extra oil and passing Pecorino separately.

Speedy Stovetop "Roasting"

We love the mellow sweetness of roasted garlic, but we don't always have an hour to make it. Our stovetop method takes just 15 minutes. We sauté 50 cloves of garlic in olive oil in a covered pan for just 6 minutes or so. Later, we add balsamic vinegar, which helps mimic the complex, sweet flavor of oven-roasted garlic.

Why This Recipe Works Toasting mellows, softens, and sweetens a head of garlic. But rather than waiting the hour or more it can take to roast garlic in the oven, we set out to develop a quick pasta dish that could harness the same great flavor in short order. We browned a whopping 50 whole cloves on the stovetop, and then poached the garlic in chicken broth seasoned with sweet, tangy balsamic vinegar. After a spin in the food processor, the final result was a complex and silky sauce that we combined with walnuts and spicy arugula. The best part? The whole thing took just 15 minutes—more than enough time to cook the pasta.

PASTA WITH MUSHROOM SAUCE

SERVES 4

If you can't find shiitake mushrooms, cremini mushrooms can be substituted or white mushrooms can be used exclusively, but don't omit the dried porcini. Parmesan cheese can be substituted for the Pecorino Romano.

12 ounces shiitake mushrooms, stemmed
12 ounces white mushrooms, trimmed
4 tablespoons unsalted butter
  Salt and pepper
2 shallots, minced
2 tablespoons minced fresh sage
4 garlic cloves, minced
¼ ounce dried porcini mushrooms, rinsed and chopped fine
½ cup dry white wine
4 cups water plus ¼ cup hot water
12 ounces (3¾ cups) campanelle, penne, or fusilli
2 ounces Pecorino Romano cheese, grated (1 cup), plus extra for serving
1 tablespoon lemon juice
2 tablespoons minced fresh chives

1. Coarsely chop half of shiitake mushrooms and white mushrooms; then quarter remaining shiitake mushrooms and white mushrooms. Melt 2 tablespoons butter in Dutch oven over medium-high heat. Add all shiitake mushrooms and white mushrooms (both chopped and quartered) and ¾ teaspoon salt. Cover and cook until mushrooms release their liquid, about 5 minutes. Uncover and continue to cook, stirring occasionally, until all liquid has evaporated and mushrooms begin to brown, about 10 minutes.

2. Add shallots, sage, garlic, and porcini mushrooms and cook until fragrant, about 1 minute. Add wine and cook until evaporated, about 2 minutes. Stir in 4 cups water, pasta, and 1¼ teaspoons salt and bring to boil. Reduce heat to medium, cover, and cook, stirring occasionally, until pasta is tender, 12 to 15 minutes.

3. Off heat, stir in Pecorino, ¼ cup hot water, lemon juice, remaining 2 tablespoons butter, and ½ teaspoon pepper. Stir vigorously for 1 minute, until sauce is thickened. Season with salt and pepper to taste. Transfer to serving dish and sprinkle with chives. Serve, passing extra Pecorino separately.

Doubling Down for Big Impact

Chopping half the mushrooms creates more fond for a flavorful sauce; quartering the rest gives big, meaty mushroom texture.

Coarsely Chopped   **Quartered**

Why This Recipe Works In order to coax as much earthy, meaty flavor as possible from supermarket mushrooms, we used fresh shiitake and white mushrooms, plus dried porcini. We coarsely chopped half of them, providing better browning due to the increased surface area, and we quartered the rest for visual appeal and meaty texture. After deglazing the pan with wine, we added the pasta directly to the pot so it could absorb the flavorful liquid. One minute of vigorous stirring drew out the pasta's starch, adding structure to the sauce and helping it cling to the pasta. The end result? An elegant one-pot dish with deep mushroom flavor.

Why This Recipe Works We wanted a creamy, light polenta substantial enough to serve as an entrée. Cooking the cornmeal in water instead of dairy gave us clean, sweet corn flavor and an airy texture. Garlic oil boosted the dish's savory quality, and adding half-and-half and nutty Pecorino contributed some welcome richness. While the polenta chilled, we processed canned whole tomatoes into a smooth, thick puree and created a sweet-and-savory red sauce. We sliced and baked blocks of polenta long enough to brown and heat through before serving.

FLUFFY BAKED POLENTA WITH RED SAUCE

SERVES 6

We developed this recipe using Quaker Yellow Corn Meal for its desirable texture and relatively short cooking time. We recommend you use the same product for this recipe. The timing may be different for other types of cornmeal, so be sure to cook the polenta until it is thickened and tender. Whole milk can be substituted for the half-and-half. Plan ahead: The polenta needs to be cooled for at least 3 hours before being cut, baked, and served.

Polenta

4 tablespoons unsalted butter
2 tablespoons extra-virgin olive oil
2 garlic cloves, smashed and peeled
7 cups water
1½ teaspoons salt
½ teaspoon pepper
1½ cups cornmeal
3 ounces Pecorino Romano cheese, grated (1½ cups)
¼ cup half-and-half

Red Sauce

1 (14.5-ounce) can whole peeled tomatoes
¼ cup extra-virgin olive oil
1 onion, peeled and halved through root end
1 (15-ounce) can tomato sauce
1 ounce Pecorino Romano cheese, grated (½ cup)
1½ tablespoons sugar
¾ teaspoon salt
½ teaspoon garlic powder

1. For the Polenta Lightly grease 8-inch square baking pan. Heat butter and oil in Dutch oven over medium heat until butter is melted. Add garlic and cook until lightly golden, about 4 minutes. Discard garlic.

2. Add water, salt, and pepper to butter mixture. Increase heat to medium-high and bring to boil. Add cornmeal in slow, steady stream, whisking constantly. Reduce heat to medium-low and continue to cook, whisking frequently and scraping sides and bottom of pot, until mixture is thick and cornmeal is tender, about 20 minutes.

3. Off heat, whisk in Pecorino and half-and-half. Transfer to prepared pan and let cool completely on wire rack. Once cooled, cover with plastic wrap and refrigerate until completely chilled, at least 3 hours.

4. For the Red Sauce Process tomatoes and their juice in blender until smooth, about 30 seconds. Heat 1 tablespoon oil in large saucepan over medium heat until shimmering. Add onion, cut side down, and cook without moving until lightly browned, about 4 minutes. Add pureed tomatoes, tomato sauce, Pecorino, sugar, salt, garlic powder, and remaining 3 tablespoons oil. Bring mixture to boil, reduce heat to medium-low, and simmer until sauce is slightly thickened, about 15 minutes. Remove from heat, discard onion, cover, and keep warm.

5. Adjust oven rack to middle position and heat oven to 375 degrees. Line rimmed baking sheet with parchment paper, then grease parchment. Cut chilled polenta into 6 equal pieces (about 4 by 2⅔ inches each). Place on prepared sheet and bake until heated through and beginning to brown on bottom, about 30 minutes. Serve each portion covered with about ½ cup red sauce.

MEATBALLS AND MARINARA

SERVES 8

To keep the recipe easy and streamlined, the meatballs and sauce start with the same onion mixture. This recipe makes enough to sauce 2 pounds of pasta.

Onion Mixture
¼ cup olive oil
3 onions, chopped fine
8 garlic cloves, minced
1 tablespoon dried oregano
¾ teaspoon red pepper flakes

Marinara
1 (6-ounce) can tomato paste
1 cup dry red wine
1 cup water
4 (28-ounce) cans crushed tomatoes
1 ounce Parmesan cheese, grated (½ cup)
¼ cup chopped fresh basil
   Salt
1–2 teaspoons sugar

Meatballs
4 slices hearty white sandwich bread, torn into pieces
¾ cup milk
8 ounces sweet Italian sausage, casings removed
2 ounces Parmesan cheese, grated (1 cup)
½ cup chopped fresh parsley
2 large eggs
2 garlic cloves, minced
1½ teaspoons salt
2½ pounds 80 percent lean ground chuck

1. For the Onion Mixture Heat oil in Dutch oven over medium-high heat until shimmering. Cook onions until golden, 10 to 15 minutes. Add garlic, oregano, and pepper flakes and cook until fragrant, about 30 seconds. Transfer half of onion mixture to large bowl and set aside.

2. For the Marinara Add tomato paste to remaining onion mixture in pot and cook until fragrant, about 1 minute. Add wine and cook until slightly thickened, about 2 minutes. Stir in water and tomatoes and simmer over low heat until sauce is no longer watery, 45 minutes to 1 hour. Stir in Parmesan and basil and season with salt and sugar to taste.

3. For the Meatballs Meanwhile, adjust oven rack to upper-middle position and heat oven to 475 degrees. Add bread and milk to bowl with reserved onion mixture and mash together until smooth. Add sausage, Parmesan, parsley, eggs, garlic, and salt to bowl and mash to combine. Add beef and knead with hands until well combined. Lightly shape mixture into 2½-inch round meatballs (about 16 meatballs total), place on rimmed baking sheet, and bake until well browned, about 20 minutes.

4. Transfer meatballs to pot with sauce and simmer for 15 minutes. Serve. (Meatballs and marinara can be frozen for up to 1 month.)

Well-Seasoned Meatballs Without the Mess
We bypassed the messy frying step and baked our meatballs in a super-hot oven instead to ensure a nicely browned crust. Simmering the meatballs in the sauce briefly allows the sauce to season the meat, and vice versa.

1. Bake meatballs in very hot oven to ensure browned crust.

2. Simmer meatballs in sauce for 15 minutes before serving for flavorful sauce and meatballs

Why This Recipe Works Meatballs and marinara sauce are the epitome of comfort food, except when you're the cook. Frying the meatballs can be messy and take a good chunk of time when working in batches. For an easier method, we turned to the oven and roasted our meatballs at a high temperature, which ensured they developed a nice, browned crust. To keep our meatballs moist and tender, we added a panade (a paste of milk and bread). In addition to ground beef, using Italian sausage for the pork gave the meatballs a flavor boost, as did simmering them in the sauce after baking.

Why This Recipe Works To infuse our slow-cooker meatballs and marinara sauce with depth of flavor, we used lots of onion, garlic, and tomato paste and sautéed them before adding them to the slow cooker. Microwaving the meatballs before adding them to the slow cooker rendered just enough fat (which we discarded) to ensure the sauce wouldn't be greasy. To bind and moisten the meatballs, we traded in the usual panade (a paste of milk and bread), which caused them to break apart in the slow cooker, for cream and shredded mozzarella cheese.

SLOW-COOKER MEATBALLS AND MARINARA

SERVES 6

Microwave the meatballs on a large plate or in a casserole dish to contain the rendering fat. This recipe makes enough to sauce 1½ pounds of pasta.

Onion Mixture

2 tablespoons olive oil
2 onions, chopped fine
1 (6-ounce) can tomato paste
6 garlic cloves, minced
1 tablespoon dried oregano
½ teaspoon red pepper flakes
¼ teaspoon salt

Marinara

½ cup red wine
2 (28-ounce) cans crushed tomatoes

Meatballs

4 ounces Italian sausage, casings removed
2 ounces mozzarella cheese, shredded (½ cup)
1 ounce Parmesan cheese, grated (½ cup)
2 large eggs
2 garlic cloves, minced
¾ teaspoon salt
1¼ pounds 85 percent lean ground beef
3 tablespoons heavy cream

1 ounce Parmesan cheese, grated (½ cup)
2 tablespoons finely chopped fresh basil
Salt

1. For the Onion Mixture Heat oil in Dutch oven over medium-high heat until shimmering. Add onions, tomato paste, garlic, oregano, pepper flakes, and salt and cook until softened and lightly browned, about 8 to 10 minutes. Transfer half of onion mixture to large bowl and set aside.

2. For the Marinara Add wine to remaining onion mixture in pot and cook until slightly thickened, about 2 minutes. Stir in tomatoes, then transfer to slow cooker.

3. For the Meatballs Add sausage, mozzarella, Parmesan, eggs, garlic, and salt to bowl with reserved onion mixture. Mash with potato masher until smooth. Add beef and cream to bowl and knead with hands until well combined. Lightly shape mixture into 2-inch round meatballs (about 12 total). Microwave meatballs on large plate until fat renders and meatballs are firm, 4 to 7 minutes. Nestle meatballs into slow cooker, discarding rendered fat. Cover and cook until meatballs are tender and sauce is slightly thickened, 4 to 5 hours on low.

4. Let meatballs and sauce settle for 5 minutes, then skim fat from surface and stir in Parmesan and basil. Season with salt to taste. Serve.

To Make Ahead Recipe can be made in advance through shaping meatballs in step 3. Uncooked meatballs and sauce can be refrigerated in separate containers for up to 24 hours. When ready to cook, add sauce to slow cooker and proceed with microwaving meatballs in step 3.

Microwaving Meatballs

Microwave meatballs uncovered until fat renders and meat is firm.

Why This Recipe Works Pasta in a slow cooker? You bet. But achieving well-cooked pasta and melty cheese in the slow cooker takes some strategy. Borrowing a technique from risotto was the key to perfect pasta—we stirred the raw pasta into the browned sausage and onion mixture, coating the starch in fat and preventing the pasta from bloating in the slow cooker. To get cheese that was evenly melted, we added it after cooking and let it sit in the residual warmth of the turned-off slow-cooker.

SLOW-COOKER BAKED ZITI

SERVES 6

Our favorite crushed tomatoes are SMT Crushed Tomatoes.

- 2 tablespoons olive oil
- 1 pound hot or sweet Italian sausage, casings removed
- 1 onion, chopped
- 3 garlic cloves, minced
- ½ teaspoon dried oregano
- ½ teaspoon salt
- ½ teaspoon pepper
- 8 ounces (2½ cups) ziti
- 1 (28-ounce) can crushed tomatoes
- 1 (15-ounce) can tomato sauce
- 8 ounces (1 cup) whole-milk ricotta cheese
- 4 ounces mozzarella cheese, shredded (1 cup)
- 2 tablespoons thinly sliced fresh basil

1. Make aluminum foil collar for slow cooker by folding 2 (18-inch-long) pieces of foil to make 2 (18 by 4-inch) strips. Line perimeter of slow cooker with foil strips and spray with vegetable oil spray.

2. Heat oil in Dutch oven over medium-high heat until just smoking. Cook sausage, breaking up pieces with spoon, until well browned, 6 to 8 minutes. Add onion and cook until lightly browned, about 5 minutes. Stir in garlic, oregano, salt, and pepper and cook until fragrant, about 1 minute.

3. Reduce heat to medium-low. Add ziti and cook, stirring constantly, until edges of pasta become translucent, about 4 minutes. Off heat, stir in crushed tomatoes and tomato sauce, scraping up any browned bits. Transfer mixture to prepared slow cooker. Cover and cook on low until pasta is tender, about 3 hours.

4. Using tongs, remove foil collar from slow cooker. Dollop ricotta over ziti and sprinkle with mozzarella. Cover and let sit for 20 minutes to let cheeses melt. Garnish with basil and serve.

Key Steps to Great Slow-Cooker "Baked" Ziti

1. To prevent burning, fold aluminum foil into two strips and use them to line perimeter of slow cooker.

2. To avoid slimy, bloated pasta, sauté it with sausage and onion.

SKILLET CHICKEN PARMESAN

SERVES 4

We like the assertive flavor of sharp provolone here, but mild provolone works well, too.

2 slices hearty white sandwich bread, torn into large pieces
3 tablespoons olive oil
2½ ounces Parmesan cheese, grated (1¼ cups)
¼ cup chopped fresh basil
1 (28-ounce) can crushed tomatoes
2 garlic cloves, minced
Salt and pepper
4 (6-ounce) boneless, skinless chicken breasts, trimmed
½ cup all-purpose flour
3 tablespoons vegetable oil
3 ounces mozzarella cheese, shredded (¾ cup)
3 ounces provolone cheese, shredded (¾ cup)

1. Pulse bread in food processor to coarse crumbs, about 10 pulses. Toast bread crumbs in 12-inch nonstick skillet over medium-high heat until browned, about 5 minutes, and transfer to bowl. Toss with 1 tablespoon olive oil, ¼ cup Parmesan, and half of basil. In separate bowl, combine remaining 2 tablespoons olive oil, ¼ cup Parmesan, remaining basil, tomatoes, garlic, and salt and pepper to taste.

2. Using sharp knife, and holding chicken securely, slice each breast horizontally into 2 cutlets of even thickness. Place flour in shallow dish. Season chicken with salt and pepper and dredge in flour. Heat 2 tablespoons vegetable oil in now-empty skillet over medium-high heat until shimmering. Add 4 cutlets

and cook until golden brown on both sides, about 5 minutes. Transfer to plate and repeat with remaining cutlets and remaining 1 tablespoon vegetable oil.

3. Reduce heat to medium-low and add tomato mixture to now-empty skillet. Return cutlets to pan in even layer, pressing down to cover with sauce. Sprinkle mozzarella, provolone, and remaining ¾ cup Parmesan over chicken. Cover and cook until cheese is melted, about 5 minutes. Sprinkle with bread crumb mixture and serve.

Making Cutlets from Breasts

Use hand to hold breast in place, keeping fingers straight and parallel to breast. Starting at thickest end of breast, slice in half horizontally, producing 2 even cutlets.

Shredding Semisoft Cheese

To keep grater holes from clogging, lightly coat side of box grater with vegetable oil spray before shredding cheese.

Why This Recipe Works To streamline chicken Parmesan and still keep its flavors and textures intact, we browned boneless, skinless chicken breasts, which we had sliced into cutlets, in a nonstick pan, then made a simple tomato sauce and simmered the chicken right in the sauce so it could absorb the flavors. For the cheesy layer, we supplemented the traditional mozzarella with provolone (preferably the sharp variety) for a much richer flavor. And rather than breading the chicken, we sprinkled the bread crumbs, which we toasted and seasoned with Parmesan and basil, over the finished dish so they stayed ultra-crisp.

SKILLET LASAGNA

SERVES 4 TO 6

A 12-inch nonstick skillet with a tight-fitting lid works best for this recipe.

1 (28-ounce) can diced tomatoes
   Water
1 tablespoon olive oil
1 onion, chopped fine
   Salt and pepper
3 garlic cloves, minced
⅛ teaspoon red pepper flakes
1 pound meatloaf mix
10 curly-edged lasagna noodles,
   broken into 2-inch lengths
1 (8-ounce) can tomato sauce
1 ounce Parmesan cheese, grated (½ cup),
   plus 2 tablespoons, grated
8 ounces (1 cup) whole-milk or part-skim
   ricotta cheese
3 tablespoons chopped fresh basil

1. Place tomatoes in 4-cup liquid measuring cup. Add water until mixture measures 4 cups.

2. Heat oil in 12-inch nonstick skillet over medium heat until shimmering. Add onion and ½ teaspoon salt and cook until onion begins to brown, about 5 minutes. Stir in garlic and pepper flakes and cook until fragrant, about 30 seconds. Add meat and cook, breaking up meat into small pieces with wooden spoon, until it is no longer pink, about 4 minutes.

3. Scatter pasta over meat but do not stir. Pour tomato mixture and tomato sauce over pasta, cover, and bring to simmer. Reduce heat to medium-low and simmer, stirring occasionally, until pasta is tender, about 20 minutes.

4. Off heat, stir in ½ cup Parmesan and season with salt and pepper to taste. Dollop heaping tablespoons of ricotta over top, cover, and let sit for 5 minutes. Sprinkle with basil and remaining 2 tablespoons Parmesan. Serve.

SKILLET LASAGNA WITH SAUSAGE AND RED PEPPER

Substitute 1 pound Italian sausage, casings removed, for meatloaf mix. Add 1 chopped red bell pepper to skillet with onion.

Secrets to Skillet Lasagna

1. Sauté onion, garlic, and meat in skillet, then scatter broken lasagna noodles over meat.

2. Pour diced tomatoes and tomato sauce over noodles, cover, and cook until pasta is tender, about 20 minutes.

3. Stir in Parmesan and dollop with ricotta, then cover skillet and let cheese soften off heat.

Why This Recipe Works To get our lasagna fix without spending hours in the kitchen, we made the entire dish, from start to finish, in a 12-inch skillet. After sautéing aromatics, we browned our meat in the pan, then added the noodles and sauce. Meatloaf mix (a blend of ground beef, pork, and veal) contributed deep, meaty flavor. Canned diced tomatoes and tomato sauce, thinned with water, provided ample liquid to cook our noodles and thickened to just the right consistency after a brief simmer. For a rich, creamy topping, we dropped big dollops of ricotta cheese over the noodles and covered the pan so they'd melt.

Why This Recipe Works To make a spinach lasagna worthy of its name, we increased the amount of spinach. Frozen spinach tasted just as good as fresh and cut down on kitchen time. For the most even texture, we used the food processor to chop the spinach. For extra spinach flavor we included some of the drained spinach liquid (we combined it with the ricotta in the food processor) but not enough to make the lasagna watery. To keep the spinach flavor front and center, we nixed the traditional creamy béchamel in favor of a fresh, herb-flecked tomato sauce but still layered in plenty of mozzarella and Parmesan for richness.

SPINACH AND TOMATO LASAGNA

SERVES 8 TO 10

Our favorite brand of no-boil lasagna noodles is Barilla. You can thaw the spinach overnight in the refrigerator instead of microwaving it, but be sure to warm the spinach liquid to help smooth the ricotta.

30 ounces frozen chopped spinach
2 tablespoons olive oil
1 onion, chopped fine
5 garlic cloves, minced
⅛ teaspoon red pepper flakes
2 (28-ounce) cans crushed tomatoes
   Salt and pepper
6 tablespoons chopped fresh basil
1½ pounds (3 cups) whole-milk or part-skim ricotta cheese
3 ounces Parmesan cheese, grated (1½ cups)
2 large eggs
12 no-boil lasagna noodles
12 ounces whole-milk mozzarella cheese, shredded (3 cups)

1. Adjust oven rack to middle position and heat oven to 375 degrees. Microwave spinach in covered large bowl until completely thawed, about 15 minutes, stirring halfway through cooking. Squeeze spinach dry, reserving ⅓ cup liquid. Pulse spinach in food processor until ground, 8 to 10 pulses, scraping down bowl every few pulses. Wipe out large bowl with paper towels. Transfer spinach to now-empty bowl; set aside.

2. Heat oil in large saucepan over medium heat until shimmering. Add onion and cook until softened, about 5 minutes. Stir in garlic and pepper flakes and cook until fragrant, about 30 seconds. Add tomatoes, ½ cup processed spinach, 1 teaspoon salt, and ½ teaspoon pepper and cook until slightly thickened, about 10 minutes. Off heat, stir in 3 tablespoons basil; set aside.

3. Process ricotta and reserved spinach liquid in food processor until smooth, about 30 seconds. Add Parmesan, remaining 3 tablespoons basil, eggs, 1½ teaspoons salt, and ½ teaspoon pepper and process until combined. Stir ricotta mixture into remaining processed spinach.

4. Cover bottom of 13 by 9-inch baking dish with 1¼ cups sauce. Top with 3 noodles and spread one-third of ricotta mixture evenly over noodles. Sprinkle with ⅔ cup mozzarella and cover with 1¼ cups sauce. Repeat twice, beginning with noodles and ending with sauce. Top with remaining 3 noodles, remaining sauce, and remaining 1 cup mozzarella.

5. Cover pan tightly with aluminum foil sprayed with vegetable oil spray and bake until bubbling around edges, about 40 minutes. Discard foil and continue to bake until cheese is melted, about 10 minutes. Let cool on wire rack for 30 minutes. Serve.

Keys to Spinach Flavor

For lasagna that actually tastes like spinach, we took a three-pronged approach.

1. Increasing the amount of spinach to triple the amount called for in most recipes guaranteed it had a distinct presence.
2. Adding some of the spinach water, from squeezing the spinach dry to prevent a soggy lasagna, to the ricotta cheese ensured a creamy, spinach-flavored filling.
3. Chopping the spinach in the food processor produced a fine, even texture that distributed nicely in both the cheese filling and the sauce.

Why This Recipe Works For fuss-free but flavorful manicotti, we started by substituting no-boil lasagna noodles for the manicotti tubes. Briefly soaking them in hot water made them pliable and easy to roll up. Using the food processor to break down the ground beef allowed its flavor to permeate the sauce quickly so it needed just a short simmer. For even more meaty flavor, we added a popular pizza topping—pepperoni—which gave the sauce a spicy backbone. To liven up the filling, we included assertive provolone, plus a portion of the processed ground beef and pepperoni; a single egg helped to bind it all together.

BAKED MANICOTTI WITH MEAT SAUCE

SERVES 6 TO 8

You will need 16 no-boil lasagna noodles for this recipe. The test kitchen's preferred brand, Barilla, comes 16 noodles to a box, but other brands contain only 12. It is important to let the dish cool for 15 minutes after baking.

Meat Sauce
- 1 onion, chopped
- 6 ounces thinly sliced deli pepperoni
- 1 pound 85 percent lean ground beef
- 5 garlic cloves, minced
- 1 tablespoon tomato paste
- ¼ teaspoon red pepper flakes
- 2 (28-ounce) cans crushed tomatoes
- Salt and pepper

Manicotti
- 1½ pounds (3 cups) ricotta cheese
- 10 ounces mozzarella cheese, shredded (2½ cups)
- 6 ounces provolone cheese, shredded (1½ cups)
- 1 large egg, lightly beaten
- ¼ cup finely chopped fresh basil
- ½ teaspoon salt
- ½ teaspoon pepper
- 16 no-boil lasagna noodles

1. For the Meat Sauce Adjust oven rack to upper-middle position and heat oven to 375 degrees. Pulse onion and pepperoni in food processor until coarsely ground, about 10 pulses. Add beef and pulse until thoroughly combined, 5 to 8 pulses.

2. Transfer mixture to large saucepan and cook over medium heat, breaking up mixture with wooden spoon, until no longer pink, about 5 minutes. Using slotted spoon, transfer 1 cup meat mixture to paper towel–lined plate and reserve. Add garlic, tomato paste, and pepper flakes to pot and cook until fragrant, about 1 minute. Stir in tomatoes and simmer until sauce is slightly thickened, about 20 minutes. Season with salt and pepper to taste. (Meat sauce can be refrigerated for up to 3 days.)

3. For the Manicotti Combine ricotta, 2 cups mozzarella, 1 cup provolone, egg, basil, salt, pepper, and reserved meat mixture in large bowl. Pour 1 inch boiling water into 13 by 9-inch baking dish and slip noodles into water, one at a time. Let noodles soak until pliable, about 5 minutes, separating noodles with tip of knife to prevent sticking. Remove noodles from water and place in single layer on clean dish towels; discard water and dry off baking dish.

4. Spread half of meat sauce over bottom of baking dish. Spread ¼ cup ricotta mixture evenly over bottom of each noodle. Roll noodles up around filling and lay them seam side down in baking dish. Spread remaining sauce over top to cover pasta completely. Cover dish tightly with aluminum foil and bake until bubbling around edges, about 40 minutes. Remove foil and sprinkle with remaining ½ cup mozzarella and ½ cup provolone. Bake until cheese is melted, about 5 minutes. Let cool for 15 minutes. Serve.

Manicotti Made Easy

Manicotti shells are hard to fill without tearing. For easy-to-fill manicotti, we found a better solution in no-boil lasagna noodles.

1. After soaking no-boil lasagna noodles briefly in hot water, spread filling across bottom of each and roll into tube.

2. Arrange rolled manicotti seam side down over sauce in baking dish.

GRANDMA PIZZA

SERVES 4

If the dough snaps back when you press it to the corners of the baking sheet, cover it, let it rest for 10 minutes, and try again.

Dough

- 3 tablespoons olive oil
- ¾ cup water
- 1½ cups (8¼ ounces) bread flour
- 2¼ teaspoons instant or rapid-rise yeast
- 1 teaspoon sugar
- ¾ teaspoon salt

Topping

- 1 (28-ounce) can diced tomatoes
- 1 tablespoon olive oil
- 2 garlic cloves, minced
- 1 teaspoon dried oregano
- ¼ teaspoon salt
- 8 ounces mozzarella cheese, shredded (2 cups)
- ¼ cup grated Parmesan cheese
- 2 tablespoons chopped fresh basil

1. For the Dough Coat rimmed baking sheet with 2 tablespoons oil. Combine water and remaining 1 tablespoon oil in 1-cup liquid measuring cup. Using stand mixer fitted with dough hook, mix flour, yeast, sugar, and salt on low speed until combined. With mixer running, slowly add water mixture and mix until dough comes together, about 1 minute. Increase speed to medium-low and mix until dough is smooth and comes away from sides of bowl, about 10 minutes.

2. Transfer dough to greased baking sheet and turn to coat. Stretch dough to 10 by 6-inch rectangle. Cover loosely with plastic wrap and let rise in warm place until doubled in size, 1 to 1½ hours. Stretch dough to corners of pan, cover loosely with plastic, and let rise in warm place until slightly puffed, about 45 minutes. Meanwhile, adjust oven rack to lowest position and heat oven to 500 degrees.

3. For the Topping Place tomatoes in colander and drain well. Combine drained tomatoes, oil, garlic, oregano, and salt in bowl. Combine mozzarella and Parmesan in second bowl. Sprinkle cheese mixture over dough, leaving ½-inch border around edges. Top with tomato mixture and bake until well browned and bubbling, about 15 minutes. Slide pizza onto wire rack, sprinkle with basil, and let cool for 5 minutes. Serve.

Easy Rise

Our method lets the dough proof right on the sheet. Spread dough on oiled baking sheet, then cover with plastic wrap and set it aside to rise.

Where Was Grandma Pizza Born?

In a 2003 piece in the Long Island newspaper Newsday, writer Erica Marcus traced grandma pizza's origins to Umberto's Pizzeria in New Hyde Park. According to Marcus, in the early 1970s proprietor Umberto Corteo would ask his pizza man to create a simple pizza like the one his mother used to make in Italy. The Corteos opened a second pizzeria, King Umberto's, in nearby Elmont. It was later bought by two former Umberto's pizza makers, who built a best-selling item out of their former boss's favorite lunch, naming it grandma pizza sometime in the late 1980s. Within 10 years, other Long Island pizzerias were offering the pie, and a phenomenon was born.

Why This Recipe Works Grandma pizza is a thin-crust pan pizza topped with a modest amount of cheese and chunks of tomatoes. To re-create this Long Island specialty, bread flour and lengthy kneading gave us the chewy crust we wanted, but the dough was difficult to stretch thin. Proofing the dough on the same sheet pan that we used to bake the pizza let it stretch on its own as it proofed. For a fresh, easy tomato topping that wouldn't make our crust soggy, we tossed drained diced tomatoes with salt, olive oil, garlic, and oregano. Baking the pizza on the lowest rack then cooling it on a wire rack perfectly crisped the bottom crust.

Why This Recipe Works Getting crisp pizza crust from your oven can be a challenge, but with just a few tweaks and the right tools, you'll have homemade pizza that's miles better than offerings from the freezer case or the delivery guy. We started by rolling out pizza dough thinly and then gently pressing it into our cast-iron skillet. Heating the pizza dough in the skillet on the stove gave our crust a jump start before going into the oven. Once in the oven, the skillet functioned like a pizza stone and crisped up our crust in just minutes. Our simple, classic pizza toppings—pizza sauce, mozzarella cheese, and basil—allowed our crust to really shine.

CAST-IRON SKILLET PIZZA

SERVES 4

We like to use our Classic Pizza Dough and No-Cook Pizza Sauce (recipes follow); however, you can use ready-made pizza dough and sauce from the local pizzeria or supermarket.

- ¼ cup extra-virgin olive oil
- 1 pound pizza dough, room temperature
- 1 cup pizza sauce
- 12 ounces fresh mozzarella cheese, sliced ¼ inch thick
- 2 tablespoons chopped fresh basil

1. Adjust oven rack to upper-middle position and heat oven to 500 degrees. Grease 12-inch cast-iron skillet with 2 tablespoons oil.

2. Place dough on lightly floured counter, divide in half, and cover with greased plastic wrap. Press and roll 1 piece of dough (keeping remaining dough covered) into 11-inch round. Transfer dough to prepared skillet and gently push it to corners of pan. Spread ½ cup sauce over surface of dough, leaving ½-inch border around edge. Top with half of mozzarella.

3. Set skillet over medium-high heat and cook until outside edge of dough is set, pizza is lightly puffed, and bottom crust is spotty brown when gently lifted with spatula, 2 to 4 minutes. Transfer skillet to oven and bake until edge of pizza is golden brown and cheese is melted, 7 to 10 minutes.

4. Using potholders, remove skillet from oven and slide pizza onto wire rack using spatula; let cool slightly. Sprinkle with 1 tablespoon basil, cut into wedges, and serve. Being careful of hot skillet, repeat with remaining 2 tablespoons oil, dough, sauce, mozzarella, and 1 tablespoon basil. Cut into wedges and serve.

CLASSIC PIZZA DOUGH
MAKES 1 POUND

- 2 cups (11 ounces) plus 2 tablespoons bread flour
- 1⅛ teaspoons instant or rapid-rise yeast
- ¾ teaspoon salt
- 1 tablespoon olive oil
- ¾ cup warm water (110 degrees)

1. Pulse flour, yeast, and salt together in food processor to combine, about 5 pulses. With processor running, add oil, then water, and process until rough ball forms, 30 to 40 seconds. Let dough rest for 2 minutes, then process for 30 seconds longer. (If after 30 seconds dough is very sticky and clings to blade, add extra flour as needed.)

2. Transfer dough to lightly floured counter and knead by hand to form smooth, round ball, about 1 minute. Place dough in large, lightly greased bowl, cover tightly with greased plastic wrap, and let rise until doubled in size, 1 to 1½ hours. (Alternatively, dough can be refrigerated for at least 8 hours or up to 16 hours.)

NO-COOK PIZZA SAUCE
MAKES 2 CUPS
While it is convenient to use ready-made pizza sauce, we think it is a lot tastier to make your own.

- 1 (28-ounce) can whole peeled tomatoes, drained with juice reserved
- 1 tablespoon extra-virgin olive oil
- 1 teaspoon red wine vinegar
- 2 garlic cloves, minced
- 1 teaspoon dried oregano
  Salt and pepper

Process tomatoes with oil, vinegar, garlic, and oregano in food processor until smooth, about 30 seconds. Transfer mixture to 2-cup liquid measuring cup and add tomato juice until sauce measures 2 cups. Season with salt and pepper to taste. (Sauce can be refrigerated for up to 1 week or frozen for up to 1 month.)

ITALIAN POT ROAST

SERVES 4 TO 6

Start checking the roast for doneness after 2 hours; if there is a little resistance when prodded with a fork, it's done. Light, sweeter red wines, such as a Merlot or Beaujolais, work especially well with this recipe.

- 1 (3½- to 4-pound) boneless beef chuck-eye roast, trimmed, tied at 1-inch intervals
  Salt and pepper
- 2 tablespoons vegetable oil
- 1 onion, chopped
- 1 celery rib, minced
- 1 pound cremini or white mushrooms, trimmed and quartered
- 2 tablespoons tomato paste
- 1 (14.5-ounce) can diced tomatoes
- ½ cup canned tomato sauce
- ½ cup water
- 1 cup red wine
- 2 teaspoons sugar
- 1 large garlic head, outer papery skins removed, halved
- 1 sprig fresh thyme
- 1 sprig fresh rosemary

1. Adjust oven rack to middle position and heat oven to 300 degrees. Pat roast dry with paper towels and season with salt and pepper.

2. Heat oil in Dutch oven over medium-high heat until just smoking. Brown roast on all sides, 8 to 12 minutes. Transfer roast to large plate. Reduce heat to medium, add onion, celery, mushrooms, and tomato paste and cook until vegetables begin to soften, about 8 minutes. Add diced tomatoes, tomato sauce, water, ½ cup wine, sugar, garlic, and thyme. Add roast, with accumulated juices, to pot and bring to simmer over medium-high heat. Place piece of aluminum foil over pot, cover with lid, and transfer pot to oven.

3. Cook until roast is just fork-tender, 2½ to 3½ hours, turning roast after 1 hour. Remove lid and foil and let roast rest for 30 minutes, skimming fat from surface of liquid after 20 minutes. Transfer roast to carving board and tent with foil.

4. Remove and reserve garlic head and skim remaining fat. Add remaining ½ cup wine to pot, bring to boil over medium-high heat, and cook until sauce begins to thicken, about 12 minutes. Meanwhile, carefully squeeze garlic cloves from their skins and mash into paste. Add rosemary to pot and simmer until fragrant, about 2 minutes. Remove rosemary and thyme sprigs, stir in mashed garlic, and season with salt and pepper to taste.

5. Remove twine from roast and slice meat against grain into ½-inch-thick slices or pull apart into large pieces. Transfer meat to serving platter and pour ¾ cup sauce over meat. Serve, passing remaining sauce separately.

Fit To Be Tied

A tied roast will cook evenly and won't fall apart during the long cooking time. If your roast doesn't come tied, simply tie pieces of kitchen twine around it at 1-inch intervals.

Getting the Garlic Right

Here's how we tone down the garlic in our Italian Pot Roast so it offers mellow, not overpowering, flavor.

1. After slicing whole head of garlic in half, add it to pot to simmer with roast.

2. Once roast is done, squeeze garlic cloves from skins and mash garlic with fork to form paste. Stir garlic paste back into sauce.

Why This Recipe Works The bolder cousin of American-style pot roast, Italian Pot Roast trades the potatoes, carrots, and gravy for mushrooms, onion, and a thick sauce based on tomatoes, red wine, garlic, and herbs. For our version, we started with a chuck-eye roast for its beefy flavor and ample fat. Canned diced tomatoes, tomato sauce, and tomato paste gave us a thick, rich sauce; a double dose of red wine added depth and brightness. Simmering a whole head of garlic with our roast ensured the meat and sauce were infused with mellow garlic flavor.

PORK CHOPS WITH VINEGAR PEPPERS

SERVES 4

Our favorite chicken broth is Swanson Chicken Stock.

  3 tablespoons sugar
     Salt and pepper
  4 (8- to 10-ounce) bone-in pork rib chops,
     1 inch thick, trimmed
  ⅓ cup all-purpose flour
  2 tablespoons olive oil
  1 onion, halved and sliced thin
  8 garlic cloves, lightly crushed and peeled
  2 anchovy fillets, rinsed, patted dry, and minced
  2 cups thinly sliced sweet green vinegar peppers
  1 sprig fresh rosemary
  1 cup chicken broth
  ½ cup red wine vinegar
  1 tablespoon unsalted butter

1. Dissolve sugar and 3 tablespoons salt in 1½ quarts cold water in large container. Add chops, cover, and refrigerate for 30 minutes or up to 1 hour.

2. Place flour in shallow dish. Remove chops from brine. Pat chops dry with paper towels and season with pepper. Working with 1 chop at a time, dredge both sides in flour, shaking off excess. Heat 1 tablespoon oil in 12-inch skillet over medium-high heat until just smoking. Add chops and cook until well browned on first side, 5 to 7 minutes. Flip chops and cook on second side for 1 minute; transfer to plate, browned side up.

3. Reduce heat to medium and add remaining 1 tablespoon oil, onion, garlic, and anchovies to now-empty skillet. Cook, stirring frequently, until onion is softened and golden brown, 6 to 8 minutes. Add peppers and rosemary and cook until peppers begin to caramelize, about 5 minutes. Add broth and vinegar and bring to boil.

4. Arrange chops, browned side up, in skillet and add any accumulated juices from plate. Reduce heat to low, cover, and simmer until chops register 145 degrees, 6 to 10 minutes. Transfer chops to serving platter and tent loosely with aluminum foil.

5. Increase heat to high and boil sauce until slightly thickened, about 3 minutes. Off heat, stir in butter and season with salt and pepper to taste. Stir any accumulated juices from platter into sauce. Discard rosemary and spoon sauce over chops. Serve.

Finishing a Pan Sauce with Butter

Add butter to pan sauce off heat to prevent butter from separating and leaving an oil slick on top.

Why This Recipe Works Choosing the right pork chop and the right kind of peppers was essential to getting this dish right. We decided on thick-cut, bone-in rib chops, which we brined briefly to ensure seasoned and moist meat. Jarred sweet vinegar peppers held up to braising, and had a mild tang that we liked. To give long-cooked flavor to our quick-cooked braising sauce, we added a secret ingredient—anchovy fillets—which lent savory depth but did not impart any fishy flavor. We thickened the sauce in two ways: by flouring the chops (which also aided browning) and by reducing the sauce slightly after the pork was done.

Why This Recipe Works To make zeppoles, a cross between doughnuts and fried dough, we discovered that two leaveners were better than one. Although typically used independently, in the case of these Italian fritters, a combination of baking powder and yeast created the perfect fluffy confection. We fried the wet, sticky dough at 350 degrees, which yielded a crispy exterior that didn't overcook by the time the interior had finished cooking. These light, tender zeppoles are best served warm with a dusting of powdery confectioners' sugar.

ZEPPOLES

MAKES 15 TO 18 ZEPPOLES

This dough is very wet and sticky. If you own a 4-cup liquid measuring cup, you can combine the batter in it to make it easier to tell when it has doubled in volume in step 1. Zeppoles are best served warm.

1⅓ cups (6⅔ ounces) all-purpose flour
1 tablespoon granulated sugar
2 teaspoons instant or rapid-rise yeast
1 teaspoon baking powder
½ teaspoon salt
1 cup warm water (110 degrees)
½ teaspoon vanilla extract
2 quarts peanut or vegetable oil
    Confectioners' sugar

1. Combine flour, granulated sugar, yeast, baking powder, and salt in large bowl. Whisk water and vanilla into flour mixture until fully combined. Cover tightly with plastic wrap and let rise at room temperature until doubled in size, 15 to 25 minutes.

2. Set wire rack in rimmed baking sheet and line rack with triple layer of paper towels. Adjust oven rack to middle position and heat oven to 200 degrees. Add oil to large Dutch oven until it measures about 1½ inches deep and heat over medium-high heat to 350 degrees.

3. Using greased tablespoon measure, add 6 heaping tablespoonfuls of batter to oil. (Use dinner spoon to help scrape batter from tablespoon if necessary.) Fry until golden brown and toothpick inserted in center of zeppole comes out clean, 2 to 3 minutes, flipping once halfway through frying. Adjust burner, if necessary, to maintain oil temperature between 325 and 350 degrees.

4. Using slotted spoon, transfer zeppoles to prepared wire rack; roll briefly so paper towels absorb grease. Transfer sheet to oven to keep warm. Return oil to 350 degrees and repeat twice more with remaining batter. Dust zeppoles with confectioners' sugar and serve.

Instant Yeast

Instant, or rapid-rise, yeast is much like active dry yeast, but it has undergone a gentler drying process that has not destroyed the outer cells. Instant yeast does not require proofing and can be added directly to the dry ingredients when making bread—hence the name "instant." Our recipes call for instant yeast because it's easier to use. In breads that contain butter, sugar, and other flavorings, we find virtually no difference in flavor between instant and active dry yeasts. If you have a recipe that calls for active dry yeast, you can use instant as long as you reduce the amount of yeast by 25 percent. For example if the recipe calls for 1 packet, or 2¼ teaspoons, of active dry yeast, use 1¾ teaspoons of instant yeast.

the state of grilling

Why This Recipe Works Authentic Hawaiian huli huli chicken is typically something home cooks buy instead of make. The birds are continually basted with a sticky-sweet glaze and "huli"-ed, which means "turned" in Hawaiian. For the teriyaki-like glaze, we developed a version with soy sauce, rice vinegar, ginger, garlic, chili sauce, ketchup, brown sugar, and lots and lots of pineapple juice. We boiled the sauce down until it was thick, glossy, and sweet. To mimic a Hawaiian rotisserie, we spread the coals in a single layer. The direct heat rendered the fat and crisped the skin, but the chicken was far enough from the coals to avoid burning.

HULI HULI CHICKEN

SERVES 4 TO 6

Mesquite wood chips give this recipe authentic flavor, but you can substitute another variety.

Chicken

2 (3½- to 4-pound) whole chickens
2 quarts water
2 cups soy sauce
1 tablespoon vegetable oil
6 garlic cloves, minced
1 tablespoon grated fresh ginger

Glaze

3 (6-ounce) cans pineapple juice
¼ cup packed light brown sugar
¼ cup soy sauce
¼ cup ketchup
¼ cup rice vinegar
4 garlic cloves, minced
2 tablespoons grated fresh ginger
2 teaspoons chili-garlic sauce
2 cups wood chips, soaked in water
   for 15 minutes and drained

1. For the Chicken Using kitchen shears, cut along both sides of backbone to remove it. Trim any excess fat or skin at neck. Flip chicken over and, using chef's knife, cut through breastbone to separate chicken into halves. Repeat with other chicken. Combine water and soy sauce in large bowl. Heat oil in large saucepan over medium-high heat until shimmering. Add garlic and ginger and cook until fragrant, about 30 seconds. Stir into soy sauce mixture. Add chicken and refrigerate, covered, for at least 1 hour or up to 8 hours.

2. For the Glaze Combine pineapple juice, sugar, soy sauce, ketchup, vinegar, garlic, ginger, and chili-garlic sauce in empty saucepan and bring to boil. Reduce heat to medium and simmer until thick and syrupy (you should have about 1 cup), 20 to 25 minutes. Using large piece of heavy-duty aluminum foil, wrap soaked chips in foil packet and cut several vent holes in top.

3A. For a Charcoal Grill Open bottom vent halfway. Light large chimney starter three-quarters filled with charcoal briquettes (4½ quarts). When top coals are partially covered with ash, pour evenly over grill. Place foil packet on coals. Set cooking grate in place, cover, and open lid vent halfway. Heat grill until hot and wood chips are smoking, about 5 minutes.

3B. For a Gas Grill Place wood chip packet directly on primary burner. Turn all burners to high, cover, and heat grill until hot and wood chips are smoking, about 15 minutes. Turn all burners to medium-low. (Adjust burners as needed to maintain grill temperature of 350 degrees.)

4. Clean and oil cooking grate. Remove chicken from brine and pat dry with paper towels. Place chicken skin side up on grill (do not place chicken directly above foil packet). Cover and cook chicken until well browned on bottom and thighs register 120 degrees, 25 to 30 minutes. Flip chicken skin side down and continue to cook, covered, until skin is well browned and crisp and thighs register 175 degrees, 20 to 25 minutes longer. Transfer chicken to platter, brush with half of glaze, and let rest for 5 minutes. Serve, passing remaining glaze at table.

To Make Ahead Both brine and glaze can be made ahead and refrigerated for up to 3 days. Do not brine chicken for longer than 8 hours or it will become too salty.

Huli History Lesson

In 1955, Hawaiian chicken farmer Ernie Morgado served local farmers barbecued chickens he'd made with his mom's homemade teriyaki-style sauce. They liked it so much that he launched a catering business using specially designed barbecue troughs that held chicken halves between two grates. When the chickens were ready to turn, the workers would yell "Huli!" (turn, in Hawaiian), and all the chickens would be rotated in one go. Morgado named his sauce Huli Huli.

CORNELL BARBECUED CHICKEN

SERVES 4 TO 6

Do not brine the chicken longer than 2 hours or the vinegar will turn the meat mushy. Poultry seasoning is a mix of herbs and spices that can be found in the spice aisle of most supermarkets.

Chicken
2 (3½- to 4-pound) whole chickens
¼ cup salt
3½ cups cider vinegar

Seasoning and Sauce
1 tablespoon ground poultry seasoning
Salt and pepper
½ cup cider vinegar
3 tablespoons Dijon mustard
1 tablespoon chopped fresh sage leaves
1 tablespoon chopped fresh rosemary
½ cup olive oil

1. For the Chicken Using kitchen shears, cut along both sides of backbone to remove it. Trim any excess fat or skin at neck. Flip chicken over and, using chef's knife, cut through breastbone to separate chicken into halves. Repeat with other chicken. In large container, dissolve salt in vinegar and 2 quarts water. Submerge chickens in brine, cover, and refrigerate for 1 to 2 hours.

2. For the Seasoning and Sauce Combine poultry seasoning, 2 teaspoons salt, and 2 teaspoons pepper in small bowl; set aside. Process vinegar, mustard, sage, rosemary, ½ teaspoon salt, and ½ teaspoon pepper in blender until smooth, about 1 minute. With blender running, slowly add oil until incorporated. Transfer vinegar sauce to small bowl and reserve for basting chicken in steps 5 and 6.

3. Remove chickens from brine, pat dry with paper towels, and rub evenly with poultry seasoning mixture. Measure out ¾ cup vinegar sauce and set aside for cooking; reserve remaining sauce for serving.

4A. For a Charcoal Grill Open bottom vent completely. Light large chimney starter three-quarters filled with charcoal briquettes (4½ quarts). When top coals are partially covered with ash, pour evenly over grill. Set cooking grate in place, cover, and open lid vent halfway. Heat grill until hot, about 5 minutes.

4B. For a Gas Grill Turn all burners to high, cover, and heat grill until hot, about 15 minutes. Turn all burners to medium-low. (Adjust burners as needed to maintain grill temperature around 350 degrees.)

5. Clean and oil cooking grate. Place chicken skin side up on grill and brush with 6 tablespoons vinegar sauce for cooking. Cover and cook chicken until well browned on bottom and thighs register 120 degrees, 25 to 30 minutes, brushing with more sauce for cooking halfway through grilling.

6. Flip chicken skin side down and brush with remaining sauce for cooking. Cover and continue to cook chicken until skin is golden brown and crisp and breasts register 160 degrees and thighs register 175 degrees, 20 to 25 minutes longer.

7. Transfer chicken to carving board and let rest for 10 minutes. Carve chicken and serve with reserved sauce.

The Chicken Man of Cornell University

Robert Baker (1921–2006) developed the recipe for Cornell chicken while employed at Pennsylvania State University, but his recipe didn't take off until he had moved on to the Animal Sciences Department at Cornell University (his alma mater) and published it in a school journal. This vinegary chicken wasn't Dr. Baker's only contribution to the culinary world: He also had a hand in developing the vacuum packaging still used by much of the poultry industry and was the inventor of chicken nuggets, turkey ham, and chicken hot dogs.

Why This Recipe Works Invented in the 1940s by Robert Baker, a Cornell University professor, this tangy, crisp-skinned grilled chicken recipe has been a star attraction at the New York State Fair ever since. Grilling two split chickens over gentle direct heat worked best here. To crisp the skin without burning it, we started the chicken skin side up to render the fat slowly, then flipped the chicken skin side down to brown until crisp. The traditional poultry seasoning worked great as a rub but tasted dusty in the sauce, so we replaced it with fresh rosemary and sage. Dijon mustard contributed even more flavor to the sauce and thickened it perfectly.

ALABAMA BARBECUED CHICKEN

SERVES 4 TO 6

Hickory wood chips are traditional here; however, any type of wood chips will work fine. Two medium wood chunks, soaked in water for 1 hour, can be substituted for the wood chips on a charcoal grill.

Sauce
- ¾ cup mayonnaise
- 2 tablespoons cider vinegar
- 2 teaspoons sugar
- ½ teaspoon prepared horseradish
- ½ teaspoon salt
- ½ teaspoon black pepper
- ¼ teaspoon cayenne pepper

Chicken
- 1 teaspoon salt
- 1 teaspoon black pepper
- ½ teaspoon cayenne pepper
- 2 (3½- to 4-pound) whole chickens
- 2 cups wood chips, soaked in water for 15 minutes and drained
- 1 (13 by 9-inch) disposable aluminum roasting pan (if using charcoal)

1. For the Sauce Process ingredients in blender until smooth, about 1 minute. Refrigerate for at least 1 hour or up to 2 days.

2. For the Chicken Combine salt, pepper, and cayenne in small bowl. Using kitchen shears, cut along both sides of backbone to remove it. Trim any excess fat or skin at neck. Flip chicken over and, using chef's knife, cut through breastbone to separate chicken into halves. Repeat with other chicken. Pat chickens dry with paper towels and rub them evenly with spice mixture. Using large piece of heavy-duty aluminum foil, wrap soaked chips in foil packet and cut several vent holes in top.

3A. For a Charcoal Grill Open bottom vent halfway and place disposable pan in center of grill. Light large chimney starter filled with charcoal briquettes (6 quarts). When top coals are partially covered with ash, pour into 2 even piles on either side of pan. Place wood chip packet on 1 pile of coals. Set cooking grate in place, cover, and open lid vent halfway. Heat grill until hot and wood chips are smoking, about 5 minutes.

3B. For a Gas Grill Place wood chip packet directly on primary burner. Turn all burners to high, cover, and heat grill until hot and wood chips are smoking, about 15 minutes. Turn all burners to medium-low. (Adjust burners as needed to maintain grill temperature around 350 degrees.)

4. Clean and oil cooking grate. Place chicken skin side down on grill (in center of grill if using charcoal). Cover (positioning lid vent over chicken if using charcoal) and cook chicken until well browned on bottom and thighs register 120 degrees, 35 to 45 minutes.

5. Flip chicken skin side up. Cover and continue to cook chicken until skin is golden brown and crisp and breasts register 160 degrees and thighs register 175 degrees, 15 to 20 minutes longer.

6. Transfer chicken to carving board and brush with 2 tablespoons sauce. Tent chicken with foil and let rest for 10 minutes. Brush chicken with remaining sauce, carve, and serve.

Keeping BBQ in the Family

Big Bob Gibson's, famous for its white mayonnaise-based sauce, has been serving hickory-smoked barbecue in Decatur, Alabama, since 1925. Now run by Big Bob's grandchildren and great-grandchildren, the restaurant has expanded several times. The current pit smoker can cook 175 chickens, 110 slabs of ribs, and 60 whole turkeys at the same time. Although Big Bob used the sauce mostly on chicken, his grandson Don McLemore says nowadays people put it on everything from pork to potato chips.

Why This Recipe Works For Alabama-inspired barbecued chicken, we ditched the tomato and slathered a mayonnaise-based sauce on hickory-smoked chicken. Smoking generally takes hours, but our recipe expedites the process by cutting the chickens in half and cooking them in the middle of the grill, sandwiched between piles of smoking coals topped with hickory chips. We coated our chickens with the traditional Alabama mixture of seasoned mayonnaise and vinegar two times during cooking so the hot chicken absorbed the sauce and was flavored through and through.

Why This Recipe Works Despite its popularity, barbecued chicken recipes cause
grillers plenty of headaches. Most recipes call for searing chicken quickly over high
heat, but we found that starting the chicken over low heat slowly rendered the fat
without the danger of flare-ups. Using a method called "grill roasting" ensured that
we had almost completely cooked chicken before we were ready to add our sauce. We
created a thick, complex layer of barbecue flavor for our grilled chicken by applying
the sauce in coats and turning the chicken frequently as it cooked over moderate
heat and then finishing it over higher heat

CLASSIC BARBECUED CHICKEN

SERVES 4 TO 6

Don't try to grill more than 10 pieces of chicken at a time; you won't be able to line them up on the grill as directed in step 5.

Quick Barbecue Sauce
3 cups store-bought barbecue sauce
½ cup molasses
½ cup ketchup
¼ cup cider vinegar
3 tablespoons brown mustard
2 teaspoons onion powder
1 teaspoon garlic powder

Chicken
1 teaspoon salt
1 teaspoon pepper
¼ teaspoon cayenne pepper
3 pounds bone-in chicken pieces, breasts halved crosswise and leg quarters separated into thighs and drumsticks, trimmed
1 (13 by 9-inch) disposable aluminum roasting pan (if using charcoal)

1. For the Quick Barbecue Sauce Whisk all ingredients in medium saucepan and bring to boil over medium-high heat. Reduce heat to medium and cook until sauce is thick and reduced to 3 cups, about 20 minutes. (Sauce can be refrigerated for up to 1 week.)

2. For the Chicken Combine salt, pepper, and cayenne in small bowl. Pat chicken dry with paper towels and rub evenly with spice mixture.

3A. For a Charcoal Grill Open bottom vent completely. Place disposable pan on 1 side of grill. Light large chimney starter filled with charcoal briquettes (6 quarts). When top coals are partially covered with ash, pour evenly over half of grill, opposite pan. Set cooking grate in place, cover, and open lid vent completely. Heat grill until hot, about 5 minutes.

3B. For a Gas Grill Turn all burners to high, cover, and heat grill until hot, about 15 minutes. Leave primary burner on high and turn other burner(s) off. (Adjust primary burner as needed to maintain grill temperature around 350 degrees.)

4. Clean and oil cooking grate. Place chicken, skin side down, on cool side of grill. Cover (positioning lid vent over chicken if using charcoal) and cook until chicken begins to brown, 30 to 35 minutes. Reserve 2 cups barbecue sauce for cooking; set aside remaining 1 cup sauce for serving.

5. Slide chicken into single line between hot and cool sides of grill and continue to cook, uncovered, flipping chicken and brushing with half of sauce for cooking every 5 minutes, until sticky, about 20 minutes.

6. Slide chicken to hot side of grill and continue to cook, flipping and brushing chicken with remaining sauce for cooking, until well glazed and breasts register 160 degrees and thighs/drumsticks register 175 degrees, about 5 minutes.

7. Transfer chicken to platter, tent loosely with aluminum foil, and let rest for 10 minutes. Serve with reserved sauce.

Barbecued Chicken, Slow and Low
First grill roasting, then basting over moderate heat, and finally finishing with more basting over higher heat ensures rendered, saucy, perfectly cooked chicken.

1. Cook chicken skin side down and covered on cool side of grill for about 30 minutes.

2. Move chicken into a single line near coals; baste and turn chicken. Then move pieces directly over coals to caramelize sauce.

Why This Recipe Works The combination of bourbon and smoke flavors sounded perfect, but first we had get the savory taste we wanted while keeping the chicken from drying out. The key was a mopping sauce: a sauce that is applied during long-grilling recipes to help keep the meat moist. And since smoke is attracted to moisture, keeping the chicken skin damp enhanced the smoky flavor. For even tastier chicken, we split them in half and cut slashes into the meat to create more surface area to soak up the flavor. By basting the chicken every 15 minutes, we ended up with moist, browned chicken with smokin' good bourbon taste.

SMOKED BOURBON CHICKEN

SERVES 4

Use a bourbon you'd be happy drinking. Use all the basting liquid in step 5.

1¼ cups bourbon
1¼ cups soy sauce
½ cup packed brown sugar
1 shallot, minced
4 garlic cloves, minced
2 teaspoons pepper
2 (3½- to 4-pound) whole chickens, giblets discarded
1 cup wood chips
4 (12-inch) wooden skewers

1. Bring bourbon, soy sauce, sugar, shallot, garlic, and pepper to boil in medium saucepan over medium-high heat and cook for 1 minute. Remove from heat and let cool completely. Set aside ¾ cup bourbon mixture for basting chicken. (Bourbon mixture can be refrigerated for up to 3 days.)

2. With chickens breast side down, using kitchen shears, cut through bones on both sides of backbones; discard backbones. Flip chickens over and, using chef's knife, split chickens in half lengthwise through centers of breastbones. Cut ½-inch-deep slits across breasts, thighs, and legs, about ½ inch apart. Tuck wingtips behind backs. Divide chicken halves between two 1-gallon zipper-lock bags and divide remaining bourbon mixture between bags. Seal bags, turn to distribute marinade, and refrigerate for at least 1 hour or up to 24 hours, flipping occasionally.

3. Just before grilling, soak wood chips in water for 15 minutes, then drain. Using large piece of heavy-duty aluminum foil, wrap soaked chips in foil packet and cut several vent holes in top. Remove chicken halves from marinade and pat dry with paper towels; discard marinade. Insert 1 skewer lengthwise through thickest part of breast down through thigh of each chicken half.

4A. For a Charcoal Grill Open bottom vent halfway. Light large chimney starter filled with charcoal briquettes (6 quarts). When top coals are partially covered with ash, pour into steeply banked pile against side of grill. Place wood chip packet on coals. Set cooking grate in place, cover, and open lid vent halfway. Heat grill until hot and wood chips are smoking, about 5 minutes.

4B. For a Gas Grill Remove cooking grate and place wood chip packet directly on primary burner. Set grate in place, turn all burners to high, cover, and heat grill until hot and wood chips are smoking, about 15 minutes. Leave primary burner on high and turn off other burners. (Adjust primary burner as needed to maintain grill temperature between 350 to 375 degrees.)

5. Clean and oil cooking grate. Place chicken halves skin side up on cooler side of grill with legs pointing toward fire. Cover and cook, basting every 15 minutes with reserved bourbon mixture, until breasts register 160 degrees and thighs register 175 degrees, 75 to 90 minutes, switching placement of chicken halves after 45 minutes. (All of bourbon mixture should be used.) Transfer chicken to carving board, tent loosely with foil, and let rest for 20 minutes. Carve and serve.

How to Cut a Chicken in Half

1. Remove backbone
Using poultry shears, cut through bones on both sides of backbone; discard backbone.

2. Cut through breast
Flip chicken over and use chef's knife to halve chicken through center of breastbone.

GRILLED BUTTERFLIED LEMON CHICKEN

SERVES 8

Chicken and Rub

2 (3½- to 4-pound) whole chickens
2 teaspoons grated lemon zest
   (reserve lemon for vinaigrette)
2 teaspoons salt
1 teaspoon pepper
1 (13 by 9-inch) disposable aluminum
   roasting pan (if using charcoal)

Vinaigrette

4 lemons, halved; plus zested,
   halved lemon from rub
2 tablespoons minced fresh parsley
2 teaspoons Dijon mustard
1 garlic clove, minced
1 teaspoon sugar
½ teaspoon salt
½ teaspoon pepper
⅔ cup extra-virgin olive oil

1. For the Chicken and Rub Set wire rack in rimmed baking sheet. Using kitchen shears, cut along both sides of backbone to remove it. Flatten breastbone. Use your hands to loosen skin over breast and thighs and remove any excess fat. Repeat with other chicken. Combine lemon zest, salt, and pepper in bowl. Rub zest mixture under chicken skin and tuck wings behind back. Transfer chickens to prepared baking sheet and refrigerate, uncovered, for 30 minutes. (Chickens may be prepared up to this point 24 hours in advance; allow chickens to sit at room temperature for 30 minutes before grilling.)

2A. For a Charcoal Grill Open bottom vent completely and place disposable pan on 1 side of grill. Light large chimney starter filled with charcoal briquettes (6 quarts). When top coals are partially covered in ash, pour into steeply banked pile against side of grill (opposite disposable pan). Evenly scatter 20 unlit coals on top of hot coals. Set cooking grate in place, cover, and open lid vent completely. Heat grill until hot, about 5 minutes.

2B. For a Gas Grill Turn all burners to high, cover, and heat grill until hot, about 15 minutes. Leave primary burner on high and turn off other burner(s). (Adjust primary burner as needed to maintain grill temperature around 350 degrees.)

3. Clean and oil cooking grate. Place lemon halves, cut side down, on hot side of grill and cook until deep brown and caramelized, 5 to 8 minutes. Transfer to bowl.

4. Place chicken skin side down on cool side of grill, with legs closer to hot side. Cover (positioning lid vent over chicken if using charcoal) and cook until skin is well browned, 45 to 55 minutes.

5. Slide chicken to hot side of grill and continue to cook (covered if using gas) until deeply browned and breasts register 160 degrees and thighs register 175 degrees, about 5 minutes longer. Transfer chicken to carving board, tent loosely with aluminum foil, and let rest for 10 minutes.

6. For the Vinaigrette While chicken cooks, squeeze ⅓ cup juice from grilled lemons into bowl. Stir in parsley, mustard, garlic, sugar, salt, and pepper, then slowly whisk in oil until emulsified.

7. Carve chicken and transfer to serving platter. Pour ⅓ cup vinaigrette over chicken and serve, passing remaining vinaigrette separately.

Butterflying a Whole Chicken

1. Cut through bones on either side of backbone and trim any excess fat or skin at neck.

2. Flip chicken over and use heel of your hand to flatten breastbone.

Why This Recipe Works For perfectly grilled butterflied lemon chicken, we banked all the coals on one side of the grill, placing the chicken opposite the coals and setting the lid on the grill. This allowed the fat under the chicken's skin to render slowly and the relatively gentle heat resulted in a moister bird. Placing the chicken on the grill skin side down reduced cooking time and allowed the most fat to render—a final sear directly over the dying coals at the end of cooking crisped and browned the skin nicely. To finish the chicken with intense lemon flavor, we caramelized lemon halves over the grill and made a sauce from their juice.

Why This Recipe Works To get crisp, well-rendered chicken wings, we tossed the wings in cornstarch and pepper and grilled them over a gentle medium-low heat. We began grilling with the thicker skin side facing up so that the fat could slowly render, and then we flipped the wings at the end of cooking to crisp the skin. Also, though we normally cook white chicken meat to 160 degrees, wings are chock-full of collagen, which begins to break down upwards of 170 degrees. Cooking the wings to 180 degrees produced meltingly tender wings.

GRILLED CHICKEN WINGS

MAKES 24 WINGS

If you buy whole wings, cut them into two pieces before brining. Don't brine the wings for more than 30 minutes or they'll be too salty.

½ cup salt
2 pounds chicken wings, wingtips discarded, trimmed
1½ teaspoons cornstarch
1 teaspoon pepper

1. Dissolve salt in 2 quarts cold water in large container. Prick chicken wings all over with fork. Submerge chicken in brine, cover, and refrigerate for 30 minutes.

2. Combine cornstarch and pepper in bowl. Remove chicken from brine and pat dry with paper towels. Transfer wings to large bowl and sprinkle with cornstarch mixture, tossing until evenly coated.

3A. For a Charcoal Grill Open bottom vent completely. Light large chimney starter half filled with charcoal briquettes (3 quarts). When top coals are partially covered with ash, pour evenly over grill. Set cooking grate in place, cover, and open lid vent completely. Heat grill until hot, about 5 minutes.

3B. For a Gas Grill Turn all burners to high, cover, and heat grill until hot, about 15 minutes. Turn all burners to medium-low.

4. Clean and oil cooking grate. Grill wings (covered if using gas), thicker skin side up, until browned on bottom, 12 to 15 minutes. Flip chicken and grill until skin is crisp and lightly charred and meat registers 180 degrees, about 10 minutes. Transfer chicken to platter, tent loosely with aluminum foil, and let rest for 5 to 10 minutes. Serve.

BBQ GRILLED CHICKEN WINGS
Reduce pepper to ½ teaspoon. Add 1 teaspoon chili powder, 1 teaspoon paprika, ½ teaspoon garlic powder, ½ teaspoon dried oregano, and ½ teaspoon sugar to cornstarch mixture in step 2.

CREOLE GRILLED CHICKEN WINGS
Add ¾ teaspoon dried oregano, ½ teaspoon garlic powder, ½ teaspoon onion powder, ½ teaspoon white pepper, and ¼ teaspoon cayenne pepper to cornstarch mixture in step 2.

TANDOORI GRILLED CHICKEN WINGS
Reduce pepper to ½ teaspoon. Add 1 teaspoon garam masala, ½ teaspoon ground cumin, ¼ teaspoon garlic powder, ¼ teaspoon ground ginger, and ⅛ teaspoon cayenne pepper to cornstarch mixture in step 2.

Prepping Grilled Chicken Wings

1. Puncturing each wing with fork lets brine easily penetrate meat and helps fat render away.

2. Quick saltwater brine seasons wings and keeps them juicy.

3. Dusting wings with cornstarch and black pepper prevents sticking and encourages crisping.

GRILLED CHICKEN LEG QUARTERS

SERVES 4

A garlic press makes quick work of mincing the 6 cloves called for here. You can use 1 teaspoon of dried oregano in place of the fresh called for in the dressing. Do not (ever) use dried cilantro.

- 6 garlic cloves, minced
- 4 teaspoons kosher salt
- 1 tablespoon sugar
- 2 teaspoons grated lime zest plus 2 tablespoons juice
- 2 teaspoons plus ¼ cup extra-virgin olive oil
- 1½ teaspoons ground cumin
- 1 teaspoon pepper
- ½ teaspoon cayenne pepper
- 4 (10-ounce) chicken leg quarters, trimmed
- 2 tablespoons chopped fresh cilantro
- 2 teaspoons chopped fresh oregano

1. Combine garlic, salt, sugar, lime zest, 2 teaspoons oil, cumin, pepper, and cayenne in bowl and mix to form paste. Reserve 2 teaspoons garlic paste for dressing.

2. Position chicken skin side up on cutting board and pat dry with paper towels. Leaving drumsticks and thighs attached, make 4 parallel diagonal slashes in chicken: 1 across drumsticks, 1 across leg joints; and 2 across thighs (each slash should reach bone). Flip chicken over and make 1 more diagonal slash across back of drumsticks. Rub remaining garlic paste all over chicken and into slashes. Refrigerate chicken for at least 1 hour or up to 24 hours.

3A. For a Charcoal Grill Open bottom vent completely. Light large chimney starter filled with charcoal briquettes (6 quarts). When top coals are partially covered with ash, pour two-thirds evenly over half of grill, then pour remaining coals over other half of grill. Set cooking grate in place, cover, and open lid vent completely. Heat grill until hot, about 5 minutes.

3B. For a Gas Grill Turn all burners to high, cover, and heat grill until hot, about 15 minutes. Turn primary burner to medium and turn other burner(s) to low. (Adjust primary burner as needed to maintain grill temperature of 400 to 425 degrees.)

4. Clean and oil cooking grate. Place chicken on cooler side of grill, skin side up. Cover and cook until underside of chicken is lightly browned, 9 to 12 minutes. Flip chicken, cover, and cook until leg joint registers 165 degrees, 7 to 10 minutes.

5. Transfer chicken to hotter side of grill, skin side down, and cook (covered if using gas) until skin is well browned, 3 to 5 minutes. Flip chicken and continue to cook until leg joint registers 175 degrees, about 3 minutes longer. Transfer to platter, tent loosely with aluminum foil, and let rest for 5 to 10 minutes.

6. Meanwhile, whisk lime juice, remaining ¼ cup oil, cilantro, oregano, and reserved garlic paste together in bowl. Spoon half of dressing over chicken and serve, passing remaining dressing separately.

Making Flavorful, Well-Cooked Chicken Leg Quarters

1. Slash Make bone-deep slashes in each quarter so the seasonings can penetrate and the meat cooks more readily.

2. Rub Massage the garlicky seasoning paste into the slashes and all over the chicken and refrigerate for up to 24 hours.

Why This Recipe Works Chicken leg quarters seem like a perfect candidate for the grill—the rich leg and thigh meat has plenty of skin to crisp up. But the thick joint takes longer to cook than the rest of the leg, so grilling often results in overcooking. To remedy this, we took a two-pronged approach. To prepare the chicken, we made slashes down to the bone, a technique often used for large cuts of meat. This helped the chicken cook evenly, and also ensured deep seasoning. We then used our two-level grilling technique, starting the chicken over a low flame, then searing it over a hot fire. A citrus-y dressing provided a welcome hit of brightness.

BBQ CHICKEN THIGHS

SERVES 4 TO 6

The seasoned chicken thighs need to sit for 1 hour before grilling. We prefer Frank's RedHot Original Cayenne Pepper Sauce for this recipe. If you use Tabasco, reduce the amount to 2 teaspoons in the broth mixture and 1 teaspoon in the glaze.

  2 tablespoons packed brown sugar
  1 tablespoon kosher salt
  1 tablespoon paprika
  1 teaspoon pepper
  1 teaspoon white pepper
  ¾ teaspoon granulated garlic
  4 pounds bone-in chicken thighs, trimmed
  1 (13 by 9-inch) disposable aluminum
     roasting pan
  ½ cup plus 2 tablespoons bottled
     barbecue sauce
  ½ cup chicken broth
  7 garlic cloves (6 sliced thin, 1 minced)
  3 tablespoons Worcestershire sauce
  3 tablespoons hot sauce
  2 tablespoons apple jelly
1½ cups wood chips

1. Combine 1 tablespoon sugar, salt, paprika, pepper, white pepper, and granulated garlic in bowl. Set aside 4 teaspoons spice mixture. Place chicken in disposable pan and season all over with remaining spice mixture. Flip chicken skin side down and let sit at room temperature for 1 hour.

2. Meanwhile, whisk ½ cup barbecue sauce, broth, sliced garlic, Worcestershire sauce, and 2 tablespoons hot sauce together in bowl; set aside. In separate bowl, microwave jelly until melted, about 30 seconds. Stir minced garlic, remaining 2 tablespoons barbecue sauce, remaining 1 tablespoon sugar, and remaining 1 tablespoon hot sauce into jelly; set glaze aside.

3. Just before grilling, soak wood chips in water for 15 minutes, then drain. Using large piece of heavy-duty aluminum foil, wrap soaked chips in foil packet and cut several vent holes in top.

4A. For a Charcoal Grill Open bottom vent completely. Light large chimney starter mounded with charcoal briquettes (7 quarts). When top coals are partially covered with ash, pour into steeply banked pile against side of grill. Place wood chip packet on coals. Set cooking grate in place, cover, and open lid vent completely. Heat grill until hot and wood chips are smoking, about 5 minutes.

4B. For a Gas Grill Remove cooking grate and place wood chip packet directly on primary burner. Set grate in place, turn all burners to high, cover, and heat grill until hot and wood chips are smoking, about 15 minutes. Leave primary burner on high and turn off other burners. (Adjust primary burner as needed to maintain grill temperature of 350 to 375 degrees.)

5. Pour broth mixture over chicken in pan. Place pan on cooler side of grill, cover (positioning lid vent over chicken for charcoal), and cook for 30 minutes (chicken will be about 140 degrees).

6. Remove pan from grill. Using tongs, transfer chicken skin side up to cooler side of grill. (Discard cooking liquid.) Brush chicken skin with half of glaze, then sprinkle with reserved spice rub. Cover and cook for 15 minutes.

7. Brush chicken skin with remaining glaze. Cover and cook until glaze has set and chicken registers 175 degrees, 25 to 30 minutes longer. Transfer chicken to platter, tent loosely with foil, and let rest for 15 minutes. Serve.

Why This Recipe Works For juicy grilled chicken thighs slick with a shiny barbecue glaze, we started by applying a sweet-meets-spicy rub. We braised spice-rubbed chicken thighs in a pan of flavorful bottled barbecue sauce and chicken broth. After 30 minutes, we poured off the cooking liquid, applied a sticky glaze and more spice rub, and arranged the thighs directly on the grill to render the skin. With a final layer of glaze and a brief rest, we had the ultimate finger-licking chicken.

Why This Recipe Works To make a chicken diavolo that was fiery and smoky, we took it to the grill. A mixture of herbs, spices, lemon, oil, sugar, and both black and red pepper performed double duty as a marinade and as a sauce. We built a two-level fire, starting the chicken on the cooler side of the grill to cook through and then searing it over the hotter side to char the outside and crisp the skin. For extra smoky flavor, we added a foil-wrapped packet of soaked wood chips. We cooked the reserved marinade mixture to mellow the garlic bite, added a shot of lemon juice, and spooned our supercharged vinaigrette over the grilled chicken.

GRILLED CHICKEN DIAVOLO

SERVES 4

If you are buying a whole chicken and cutting it into pieces yourself, reserve the backbone and wings to make stock. To use wood chunks on a charcoal grill, substitute one medium wood chunk, soaked in water for 1 hour, for the wood chip packet.

3 pounds bone-in chicken pieces (split breasts cut in half, drumsticks, and/or thighs), trimmed
½ cup extra-virgin olive oil
4 garlic cloves, minced
1 tablespoon chopped fresh rosemary
2 teaspoons grated lemon zest plus 4 teaspoons juice
2 teaspoons red pepper flakes
1 teaspoon sugar
Salt and pepper
½ teaspoon paprika
1 cup wood chips

1. Pat chicken dry with paper towels. Whisk oil, garlic, rosemary, lemon zest, pepper flakes, sugar, 1 teaspoon pepper, and paprika together in bowl until combined. Reserve ¼ cup oil mixture for sauce. (Oil mixture can be covered and refrigerated for up to 24 hours.) Whisk 2¼ teaspoons salt into oil mixture remaining in bowl and transfer to 1-gallon zipper-lock bag. Add chicken, turn to coat, and refrigerate for at least 1 hour or up to 24 hours. Just before grilling, soak wood chips in water for 15 minutes, then drain. Using large piece of heavy-duty aluminum foil, wrap soaked chips in foil packet and cut several vent holes in top.

2A. For a Charcoal Grill Open bottom vent halfway. Light large chimney starter filled with charcoal briquettes (6 quarts). When top coals are partially covered with ash, pour two-thirds evenly over half of grill, then pour remaining coals over other half of grill. Place wood chip packet on larger pile of coals. Set cooking grate in place, cover, and open lid vent halfway. Heat grill until hot and wood chips are smoking, about 5 minutes.

2B. For a Gas Grill Place wood chip packet over primary burner. Turn all burners to high, cover, and heat grill until hot and wood chips are smoking, about 15 minutes. Turn primary burner to medium and turn other burner(s) to low. (Adjust primary burner as needed to maintain grill temperature of 400 to 425 degrees.)

3. Remove chicken from marinade and pat dry with paper towels. Discard used marinade. Clean and oil cooking grate. Place chicken on cooler side of grill, skin side up. Cover and cook until underside of chicken is lightly browned, 8 to 12 minutes. Flip chicken, cover, and cook until white meat registers 155 degrees and dark meat registers 170 degrees, 7 to 10 minutes.

4. Transfer chicken to hotter side of grill, skin side down, and cook (covered if using gas) until skin is well browned, about 3 minutes. Flip and continue to cook (covered if using gas) until white meat registers 160 degrees and dark meat registers 175 degrees, 1 to 3 minutes. Transfer chicken to platter, tent loosely with foil, and let rest for 5 to 10 minutes.

5. Meanwhile, heat reserved oil mixture in small saucepan over low heat until fragrant and garlic begins to brown, 3 to 5 minutes. Off heat, whisk in lemon juice and ¼ teaspoon salt. Spoon sauce over chicken. Serve.

The Right Fire

A two-level fire lets us gently cook the chicken on the cooler side and then sear it on the hotter side for flavorful char. To get good smoky flavor, we place an aluminum foil–wrapped packet of soaked wood chips on the larger pile of charcoal.

Why This Recipe Works Barbecuing is the perfect method for cooking fatty cuts of pork or beef, but relatively lean chicken is another story. For barbecued pulled chicken with a smoky flavor and moist, tender meat, we'd have to come up with some tricks. Brining the birds kept the white meat moist and juicy, and arranging the chickens on the grill with the breast meat farther from the heat source than the dark meat evened out the cooking times. We tweaked our favorite barbecue sauce to better complement the chicken, increasing the vinegar to balance the sweetness and swapping the root beer for coffee to boost the smoky flavor.

BARBECUED PULLED CHICKEN

MAKES ENOUGH FOR 8 SANDWICHES

We prefer to halve the chickens ourselves, but you may be able to buy halved chickens from your butcher.

Chicken
1   cup salt
2   (4-pound) whole chickens, giblets discarded
    Pepper
2   cups wood chips, soaked in water
    for 15 minutes and drained

Sauce
2   teaspoons vegetable oil
1   onion, chopped fine
4   cups chicken broth
1¼   cups cider vinegar
1   cup brewed coffee
¾   cup molasses
½   cup tomato paste
½   cup ketchup
2   tablespoons brown mustard
1   tablespoon hot sauce
½   teaspoon garlic powder
¼   teaspoon liquid smoke

1. For the Chicken Dissolve salt in 4 quarts cold water in large container. Remove backbones from chickens and split chickens in half lengthwise through center of breastbone. Using metal skewer, poke 20 holes all over each chicken half. Submerge chicken halves in brine, cover, and refrigerate for 1 hour. Remove chicken halves from brine, pat dry with paper towels, and season with pepper. Using large piece of heavy-duty aluminum foil, wrap soaked wood chips in foil packet and cut several vent holes in top.

2. For the Sauce Meanwhile, heat oil in Dutch oven over medium-high heat until shimmering. Add onion and cook until softened, about 5 minutes. Whisk in broth, vinegar, coffee, molasses, tomato paste, ketchup, mustard, hot sauce, and garlic powder and bring to boil. Reduce heat to medium-low and simmer until mixture is thick and reduced to 4 cups, about 65 to 75 minutes. Stir in liquid smoke; reserve 1 cup sauce for serving. (Sauce can be refrigerated for up to 2 days.)

3A. For a Charcoal Grill Open bottom vent halfway. Light large chimney starter filled with charcoal briquettes (6 quarts). When top coals are partially covered with ash, pour into steeply banked pile against side of grill. Place wood chip packet on coals. Set cooking grate in place, cover, and open lid vent halfway. Heat grill until hot and wood chips are smoking, about 5 minutes.

3B. For a Gas Grill Place wood chip packet over primary burner. Turn all burners to high, cover, and heat grill until hot and wood chips are smoking, about 15 minutes. Leave primary burner on high and turn off other burner(s).

4. Clean and oil cooking grate. Place chicken halves skin side up on cool side of grill with legs closest to heat source. Cover and cook until breasts register 160 degrees and thighs register 175 degrees, 75 to 85 minutes. Transfer chicken to carving board, tent loosely with foil, and let rest until cool enough to handle, about 15 minutes. Remove and discard skin. Pull meat off bones, separating dark and light meat. Roughly chop dark meat into ½-inch pieces. Shred white meat into thin strands.

5. Add chicken to pot with sauce and cook over medium-low heat until chicken is warmed through, about 5 minutes. Serve on hamburger rolls, passing reserved sauce separately.

BARBECUED BURNT ENDS

SERVES 8 TO 10

Look for a brisket with a significant fat cap. This recipe takes about 8 hours to prepare. The meat can be brined ahead of time, transferred to a zipper-lock bag, and refrigerated for up to a day. If you don't have ½ cup of juices from the rested brisket, supplement with beef broth.

Brisket and Rub
- 2 cups plus 1 tablespoon kosher salt
- ½ cup granulated sugar
- 1 (5- to 6-pound) beef brisket, flat cut, untrimmed
- ¼ cup packed brown sugar
- 2 tablespoons pepper
- 4 cups wood chips
- 1 (13 by 9-inch) disposable aluminum roasting pan (if using charcoal) or 2 (8½ by 6-inch) disposable aluminum pans (if using gas)

Barbecue Sauce
- ¾ cup ketchup
- ¼ cup packed brown sugar
- 2 tablespoons cider vinegar
- 2 tablespoons Worcestershire sauce
- 2 teaspoons granulated garlic
- ¼ teaspoon cayenne pepper

1. For the Brisket and Rub Dissolve 2 cups salt and granulated sugar in 4 quarts cold water in large container. Slice brisket with grain into 1½-inch-thick strips. Add brisket strips to brine, cover, and refrigerate for 2 hours. Remove brisket from brine and pat dry with paper towels.

2. Combine brown sugar, pepper, and remaining 1 tablespoon salt in bowl. Season brisket all over with rub. Just before grilling, soak wood chips in water for 15 minutes, then drain. Using 2 large pieces of heavy-duty aluminum foil, wrap soaked chips in 2 foil packets and cut several vent holes in tops.

3A. For a Charcoal Grill Open bottom vent halfway and place disposable pan filled with 2 quarts water on one side of grill, with long side of pan facing center of grill. Arrange 3 quarts unlit charcoal briquettes on opposite side of grill and place 1 wood chip packet on coals. Light large chimney starter filled halfway with charcoal briquettes (3 quarts). When top coals are partially covered with ash, pour evenly over unlit coals and wood chip packet. Place remaining wood chip packet on lit coals. Set cooking grate in place, cover, and open lid vent halfway. Heat grill until hot and wood chips are smoking, about 5 minutes.

3B. For a Gas Grill Add ½ cup ice cubes to 1 wood chip packet. Remove cooking grate and place both wood chip packets directly on primary burner; place disposable pans each filled with 2 cups water directly on secondary burner(s). Set grate in place, turn all burners to high, cover, and heat grill until hot and wood chips are smoking, about 15 minutes. Leave primary burner on high and turn off other burner(s). (Adjust primary burner as needed to maintain grill temperature of 275 to 300 degrees.)

4. Clean and oil cooking grate. Arrange brisket on cooler side of grill as far from heat source as possible. Cover (positioning lid vent over brisket for charcoal) and cook without opening for 3 hours.

5. Adjust oven rack to middle position and heat oven to 275 degrees. Remove brisket from grill and transfer to rimmed baking sheet. Cover sheet tightly with foil. Roast until fork slips easily in and out of meat and meat registers 210 degrees, about 2 hours. Remove from oven, leave covered, and let rest for 1 hour. Remove foil, transfer brisket to carving board, and pour accumulated juices into fat separator.

6. For the Barbecue Sauce Combine ketchup, sugar, vinegar, Worcestershire, granulated garlic, cayenne, and ½ cup defatted brisket juices in medium saucepan. Bring to simmer over medium heat and cook until slightly thickened, about 5 minutes.

7. Cut brisket strips crosswise into 1- to 2-inch chunks. Combine brisket chunks and barbecue sauce in large bowl and toss to combine. Serve.

Why This Recipe Works Real burnt ends are all about moist meat and plenty of flavorful, charred bark, but most pit masters use fatty point-cut brisket. To make the leaner (and more widely available) flat-cut brisket work, we cut it into strips and brine it for maximum moisture and flavor. Three hours of smoke on the grill—with a water pan for more moisture—followed by a few more hours in a low oven ensures fully tender brisket with plenty of char. We cut the meat into cubes before tossing it with a flavorful, homemade sauce. Home pit masters, take note.

GRILLED BOURBON STEAKS

SERVES 6 TO 8

Use a bourbon you'd be happy drinking. Plan ahead: These steaks need to marinate for at least 4 hours before grilling.

- 1 cup bourbon
- 1 cup Worcestershire sauce
- 1 shallot, minced
- 2 garlic cloves, minced
  Kosher salt and pepper
- 4 (1-pound) boneless rib-eye steaks, 1 to 1½ inches thick, trimmed
- 2 tablespoons vegetable oil

1. Whisk bourbon, Worcestershire, shallot, garlic, 2 teaspoons salt, and 2 teaspoons pepper together in bowl. Place 2 steaks in each of two 1-gallon zipper-lock bags and divide bourbon mixture between bags, about 1 cup each. Seal bags, turn to distribute marinade, and refrigerate for at least 4 hours or up to 24 hours, flipping occasionally.

2. Remove steaks from marinade and pat dry with paper towels; discard marinade. Brush steaks all over with oil and season liberally with salt and pepper.

3A. For a Charcoal Grill Open bottom vent completely. Light large chimney starter filled with charcoal briquettes (6 quarts). When top coals are partially covered with ash, pour evenly over grill. Set cooking grate in place, cover, and open lid vent completely. Heat grill until hot, about 5 minutes.

3B. For a Gas Grill Turn all burners to high, cover, and heat grill until hot, about 15 minutes. Turn all burners to medium-high. (Adjust burners as needed to maintain grill temperature between 350 and 400 degrees.)

4. Clean and oil cooking grate. Place steaks on grill and cook (covered if using gas) until well charred and meat registers 125 degrees (for medium-rare), 6 to 8 minutes per side.

5. Transfer steaks to wire rack set in rimmed baking sheet, tent with aluminum foil, and let rest for 10 minutes. Serve.

The World of Whiskey

The word whiskey comes from the Celtic *uisqebaugh* (whis-kee-BAW), meaning "water of life." It is traditionally made from barley, corn, rye, wheat, or oats, but artisanal makers now incorporate everything from buckwheat to farro to spelt.

A whiskey's distinct flavor is determined by a number of factors including the type of grain used, the aging time, the type of wood in which it is stored, and the distillation method. There are many types of whiskey, but American, Irish, Canadian, and Scotch are the most widely consumed. (Scotch and Canadian whiskys drop the e.)

AMERICAN

- Bourbon is the most popular form of American whiskey.
- It must contain at least 51 percent corn.
- It must be aged in charred new oak barrels for two years.
- Bourbon can't go into the barrel for aging at higher than a 62.5-percent alcohol level.

IRISH

- Irish whiskey is made from a blend of malted barley (grain that's been germinated or sprouted, which converts its starch to sugar) and unmalted barley.
- It's aged in wood for a minimum of three years.
- Often, it is triple-distilled, so it's extra-smooth.

CANADIAN

- Canadian whisky is typically made from a base whisky (usually a mix of grains but predominantly corn) and a flavoring whisky (often rye).
- Fifty-one percent of each batch must be aged in wood for three years.

SCOTCH

- Single-malt scotches are made from malted barley.
- Blends are made from a mix of single malt(s) and grain whisky made from various unmalted grains.
- Scotch whisky is usually distilled twice and is aged in oak for three years.

Why This Recipe Works Why marinate rib eyes in bourbon? The bourbon not only enhances the beef's meatiness, it also increases the char. To maximize the steaks' flavor, we soaked four hefty rib eyes in a mixture of bourbon, Worcestershire, shallot, and garlic. After marinating the meat for four hours, we fired up the grill, brushed the steaks with oil and a liberal dose of salt and pepper, and cooked them to a juicy medium-rare. The boozy marinade really delivered, giving us sweet-savory flavors and perfect char.

Why This Recipe Works Unlike other barbecue recipes, California barbecued tri-tip recipes call for cooking the meat (bottom sirloin roast) over high heat and seasoning it only with salt, pepper, garlic, and the sweet smoke of the grill. This consistently produces a charred exterior and very rare center—but we wanted the outside cooked less and the inside cooked more. To achieve this, we pushed all the coals in our grill to one side, which created a hot zone for cooking and a cooler one for finishing the meat slowly. To prevent the meat from tasting too smoky, we held off on the wood chips until after we'd seared the meat.

CALIFORNIA BARBECUED TRI-TIP

SERVES 4 TO 6

If you can't find tri-tip, bottom round steak will also work. Two medium wood chunks, soaked in water for 1 hour, can be substituted for the wood chips on a charcoal grill. Serve with Santa Maria Salsa (recipe follows) and California Barbecued Beans (page 392). We prefer this roast cooked medium-rare.

- 6 garlic cloves, minced
- 2 tablespoons olive oil
- ¾ teaspoon salt
- 1 (2-pound) tri-tip roast, trimmed
- 1 teaspoon pepper
- ¾ teaspoon garlic salt
- 2 cups wood chips, soaked in water for 15 minutes and drained

1. Combine garlic, oil, and salt in bowl. Pat meat dry with paper towels, poke it about 20 times on each side with fork, and rub it evenly with garlic mixture. Wrap meat in plastic wrap and let sit at room temperature for at least 1 hour or refrigerate for up to 24 hours. (If refrigerated, let sit at room temperature for 1 hour before grilling.) Before cooking, unwrap meat, wipe off garlic paste using paper towels, and rub it evenly with pepper and garlic salt. Using large piece of heavy-duty aluminum foil, wrap soaked chips in foil packet and cut several vent holes in top.

2A. For a Charcoal Grill Open bottom vent completely. Light large chimney starter filled with charcoal briquettes (6 quarts). When top coals are partially covered with ash, pour evenly over half of grill. Set cooking grate in place, cover, and open lid vent completely. Heat grill until hot, about 5 minutes.

2B. For a Gas Grill Turn all burners to high, cover, and heat grill until hot, about 15 minutes.

3. Clean and oil cooking grate. Grill meat on hot side of grill until well browned on both sides, about 10 minutes. Transfer meat to plate.

4. Place wood chip packet directly on coals or primary burner. If using gas, leave primary burner on high and turn other burner(s) off.

5. Place meat on cool side of grill. Cover (positioning lid vent over meat if using charcoal) and cook until meat registers 120 to 125 degrees (for medium-rare), about 20 minutes.

6. Transfer meat to carving board, tent loosely with aluminum foil, and let rest for 20 minutes. Slice meat thin against grain and serve.

SANTA MARIA SALSA
MAKES ABOUT 4 CUPS
The distinct texture of each ingredient is part of this salsa's identity and appeal, so we don't recommend using a food processor.

- 2 pounds tomatoes, cored and chopped
- 2 teaspoons salt
- 2 jalapeño chiles, stemmed, seeded, and chopped fine
- 1 small red onion, chopped fine
- 1 celery rib, chopped fine
- ¼ cup lime juice (2 limes)
- ¼ cup chopped fresh cilantro
- 1 garlic clove, minced
- ⅛ teaspoon dried oregano
- ⅛ teaspoon Worcestershire sauce

1. Place tomatoes in strainer set over bowl and sprinkle with salt; drain for 30 minutes. Discard liquid. Meanwhile, combine jalapeños, onion, celery, lime juice, cilantro, garlic, oregano, and Worcestershire in large bowl.

2. Add drained tomatoes to jalapeño mixture and toss to combine. Cover with plastic wrap and let stand at room temperature for 1 hour before serving. (Salsa can be refrigerated for up to 2 days.)

Why This Recipe Works For our Shredded Barbecued Beef, we cut a chuck roast into quarters. The smaller pieces of beef absorbed more smoke flavor and cooked much faster. After cooking the meat in a disposable roasting pan on the cooler side of the grill for a few hours, we flipped all 4 pieces, wrapped the pan in foil, and placed the roast in the oven to finish cooking. For a barbecue sauce with richer flavor, we sautéed the onions in beef fat from the pan. Chili powder and pepper added bite, while ketchup, vinegar, coffee, Worcestershire sauce, brown sugar, and the beef juices rounded out the flavors.

SHREDDED BARBECUED BEEF

SERVES 8 TO 10

If you prefer a smooth barbecue sauce, strain the sauce before tossing it with the beef in step 5. We like to serve this beef on white bread with plenty of pickle chips. Three medium wood chunks, soaked in water for 1 hour, can be substituted for the wood chips on a charcoal grill.

1 tablespoon salt
1 tablespoon pepper
1 teaspoon cayenne pepper
1 (5- to 6-pound) boneless beef chuck-eye roast, trimmed and quartered
1 (13 by 9-inch) disposable aluminum roasting pan
3 cups wood chips, soaked in water for 15 minutes and drained
1 onion, chopped fine
4 garlic cloves, minced
½ teaspoon chili powder
1¼ cups ketchup
¾ cup brewed coffee
½ cup cider vinegar
½ cup packed brown sugar
3 tablespoons Worcestershire sauce
½ teaspoon pepper

1. Combine salt, pepper, and cayenne in small bowl. Pat meat dry with paper towels and rub evenly with spice mixture. Wrap meat in plastic wrap and let sit at room temperature for at least 1 hour or refrigerate up to 24 hours. (If refrigerated, let sit at room temperature for 1 hour before grilling.) Before cooking, unwrap meat and transfer to disposable pan. Using 2 large pieces of heavy-duty aluminum foil, wrap soaked chips in 2 foil packets and cut several vent holes in tops.

2A. For a Charcoal Grill Open bottom vent completely. Light large chimney starter half filled with charcoal briquettes (3 quarts). When top coals are partially covered with ash, pour into steeply banked pile against 1 side of grill. Place wood chip packets on coals. Set cooking grate in place, cover, and open lid vent halfway. Heat grill until hot and wood chips are smoking, about 5 minutes.

2B. For a Gas Grill Place wood chip packets directly on primary burner. Turn all burners to high, cover, and heat grill until hot and wood chips are smoking, about 15 minutes. Leave primary burner on high and turn other burner(s) off. (Adjust primary burner as needed to maintain grill temperature between 250 and 300 degrees.)

3. Place pan of meat on cool side of the grill. Cover (positioning lid vent over meat if using charcoal) and cook until meat is deep red, about 2 hours. During final 20 minutes of grilling, adjust oven rack to lower-middle position and heat oven to 300 degrees.

4. Flip meat over in pan, cover pan tightly with foil, and roast beef in oven until fork slips easily in and out of beef, 2 to 3 hours.

5. Transfer meat to large bowl, tent loosely with foil, and let rest for 30 minutes. While meat rests, skim fat from accumulated juices in pan; reserve 2 tablespoons fat. Strain defatted juices; reserve ½ cup juice. Combine onion and reserved fat in medium saucepan and cook over medium heat until onion has softened, about 10 minutes. Add garlic and chili powder and cook until fragrant, about 30 seconds. Stir in ketchup, coffee, vinegar, sugar, Worcestershire, pepper, and any accumulated meat juices and simmer until thickened, about 15 minutes. Using 2 forks, pull meat into shreds, discarding any excess fat or gristle. Toss meat with ½ cup barbecue sauce. Serve, passing remaining sauce separately.

JUCY LUCY BURGERS

SERVES 4

Buy the American cheese from the deli counter, and ask them to slice it into a ½-inch slab from which you can cut four big cubes to fill the center of the burgers. One or two percent low-fat milk can be substituted for the whole milk. The cheesy center of these burgers is molten hot when first removed from the grill, so be sure to let the burgers rest for at least 5 minutes before serving.

- 2 slices hearty white sandwich bread, torn into 1-inch pieces
- ¼ cup whole milk
- 1 teaspoon garlic powder
- ¾ teaspoon salt
- ½ teaspoon pepper
- 1½ pounds 85 percent lean ground beef
- 1 slice deli American cheese (½-inch-thick), quartered

1. In large bowl using potato masher, mash bread, milk, garlic powder, salt, and pepper into smooth paste. Add beef and lightly knead mixture until well combined.

2. Divide meat into 4 equal portions. Using half of each portion of meat, encase cheese to form mini burger patty. Mold remaining half-portion of meat around mini patty and seal edges to form ball. Flatten ball with palm of your hand, forming ¾-inch-thick patty. Cover and refrigerate patties for at least 30 minutes or up to 24 hours.

3A. For a Charcoal Grill Open bottom vent completely. Light large chimney starter half filled with charcoal briquettes (3 quarts). When top coals are partially covered with ash, pour evenly over grill. Set cooking grate in place, cover, and heat grill until hot, about 5 minutes.

3B. For a Gas Grill Turn all burners to high, cover, and heat grill until hot, about 15 minutes. Turn all burners to medium.

4. Clean and oil cooking grate. Lay burgers on grill and cook, without pressing on them, until well browned on both sides and cooked through, 12 to 16 minutes, flipping burgers halfway through grilling. Transfer burgers to platter, tent loosely with aluminum foil, and let rest for 5 minutes before serving.

How to Form a Jucy Lucy
To avoid a burger blowout, it's essential to completely seal in the cheese.

1. Using half of each portion of meat, encase cheese to form mini burger patty.

2. Mold remaining half-portion of meat around mini patty and seal edges to form a ball and flatten to form ¾-inch patty.

The Great Lucy Debate
A debate still rages as to where the Jucy Lucy was created. Two Minnesota taverns, Matt's Bar and the 5–8 Club, claim to have created the burger in the 1950s. As the story goes, a customer requested a burger with the cheese sealed in the middle. When he bit in, the hot cheese spurted out and he exclaimed, "That's one juicy Lucy!" As for the unusual spelling, that's still a mystery.

Why This Recipe Works Minneapolis taverns are famous for the Jucy Lucy, a moist beef burger stuffed with American cheese. Replicating the Jucy Lucy seemed easy enough—but our burgers, cooked to well-done to melt the cheese inside, were dry and tough or the cheese melted through the meat, leaving an empty cavern where the cheese had been. To keep the cheese in place, we created a double-sealed pocket by wrapping the cheese inside a small beef patty and then molding a second patty around it. Adding a mixture of bread and milk, mashed into a paste, to the ground beef kept the burgers moist and juicy.

Why This Recipe Works For our version of New Mexico's green chile cheeseburgers—ground beef patties grilled to a crusty brown and topped with chopped fire-roasted chiles and a slice of cheese—we preferred the flavor and fat of 85 percent lean ground beef. For the topping, we used mild Anaheim chiles and spicy jalapeños for a complex chile flavor. We grilled the chiles with onions, then quickly chopped them with fresh garlic in the food processor. For even more chile flavor, we pureed some of the chile topping into a smooth paste and mixed it into the raw ground beef. This gave us burgers with satisfying heat through and through.

GREEN CHILE CHEESEBURGERS

SERVES 4

In step 3, you may need to add a teaspoon or two of water to the food processor to help process the chile mixture. Pressing a shallow divot in the center of each burger patty keeps the burgers flat during grilling.

3 Anaheim chiles, stemmed, halved, and seeded
3 jalapeño chiles, stemmed, halved, and seeded
1 onion, sliced into ½-inch-thick rounds
1 garlic clove, minced
   Salt and pepper
1½ pounds 85 percent lean ground beef
4 slices deli American cheese

1A. For a Charcoal Grill Open bottom vent completely. Light large chimney starter filled with charcoal briquettes (6 quarts). When top coals are partially covered with ash, pour evenly over grill. Set cooking grate in place, cover, and open lid vent completely. Heat grill until hot, about 5 minutes.

1B. For a Gas Grill Turn all burners to high, cover, and heat grill until hot, about 15 minutes.

2. Clean and oil cooking grate. Place Anaheims, jalapeños, and onion on grill, cover, and cook until vegetables are lightly charred and tender, 4 to 6 minutes, flipping halfway through cooking. Transfer vegetables to bowl, cover, and let cool 5 minutes. Remove skins from chiles and discard; separate onion rounds into rings.

3. Transfer chiles and onion to food processor, add garlic, and pulse until coarsely chopped, about 5 pulses. Transfer all but ¼ cup chopped chile mixture to empty bowl and season with salt and pepper; set aside. Process remaining mixture until finely chopped, about 45 seconds, scraping down bowl as needed.

4. Combine beef, finely chopped chile mixture, ½ teaspoon salt, and ¼ teaspoon pepper in large bowl and lightly knead until well combined. Shape into four ¾-inch-thick patties and press shallow depression in center of each.

5. Place burgers on grill, cover, and cook until well browned on first side, 3 to 5 minutes. Flip burgers, top with reserved coarsely chopped chile mixture and cheese, and continue to cook, covered, until cheese is melted and burgers are cooked to desired doneness, 3 to 5 minutes. Serve.

Chile Pinch Hitter

For complex green chile flavor outside of New Mexico, we found that a combination of mild Anaheims and spicy jalapeños has a nice peppery balance.

MILD HEAT
Anaheim chiles
add a mildly sweet,
grassy flavor.

SPICE IS NICE
Jalapeño chiles have
just enough heat
to stand up to the
beefiness of the burger.

CHICAGO-STYLE BARBECUED RIBS

SERVES 4 TO 6

The dry spices are used to flavor both the rub and the barbecue sauce. One medium wood chunk, soaked in water for 1 hour, can be substituted for the wood chips on a charcoal grill. When removing the ribs from the oven, be careful to not spill the hot water in the bottom of the baking sheet.

Spice Rub and Ribs

- 1 tablespoon dry mustard
- 1 tablespoon paprika
- 1 tablespoon packed dark brown sugar
- 1½ teaspoons garlic powder
- 1½ teaspoons onion powder
- 1½ teaspoons celery salt
- 1 teaspoon cayenne pepper
- ½ teaspoon ground allspice
- 2 racks baby back ribs (about 1½ pounds each), trimmed
- 1 cup wood chips, soaked in water for 15 minutes and drained
- 1 (13 by 9-inch) disposable aluminum roasting pan

Sauce

- 1¼ cups ketchup
- ¼ cup molasses
- ¼ cup cider vinegar
- ¼ cup water
- ⅛ teaspoon liquid smoke

1. For the Spice Rub and Ribs Combine dry mustard, paprika, sugar, garlic powder, onion powder, celery salt, cayenne, and allspice in bowl. Measure out and reserve 2 tablespoons spice mixture for sauce. To remove chewy membrane from ribs, loosen it with tip of paring knife and, with aid of paper towel, pull it off slowly in 1 big piece. Pat ribs dry with paper towels and rub evenly with spice mixture. Wrap meat in plastic wrap and let sit at room temperature for at least 1 hour or refrigerate for up to 24 hours. (If refrigerated, let sit at room temperature for 1 hour before grilling.)

2. For the Sauce Whisk all ingredients with reserved 2 tablespoons spice rub in bowl. Using large piece of heavy-duty aluminum foil, wrap soaked chips in foil packet and cut several vent holes in top.

3A. For a Charcoal Grill Open bottom vent completely. Light large chimney starter filled with charcoal briquettes (6 quarts). Add 2 cups water to disposable pan and place it on 1 side of grill. When top coals are partially covered with ash, pour into steeply banked pile against other side of grill, opposite pan of water. Place wood chip packet on coals. Set cooking grate in place, cover, and open lid vent completely. Heat grill until hot and wood chips are smoking, about 5 minutes.

3B. For a Gas Grill Place wood chip packet directly on primary burner. Add 2 cups water to disposable pan and place it on secondary burner. Turn all burners to high, cover, and heat grill until hot and wood chips are smoking, about 15 minutes. Turn primary burner to medium and turn other burner(s) off. (Adjust primary burner as needed to maintain grill temperature around 325 degrees.)

4. Clean and oil cooking grate. Place ribs meat side down on grill over water-filled pan; ribs may overlap slightly. Cover (positioning lid vent over meat if using charcoal) and cook until ribs are deep red and smoky, about 1½ hours, flipping and rotating racks halfway through grilling. During final 20 minutes of grilling, adjust oven rack to middle position and heat oven to 250 degrees.

5. Set wire rack in rimmed baking sheet and add just enough water to cover pan bottom. Transfer ribs to rack and cover tightly with foil. Continue to cook ribs in oven until fork slips easily in and out of meat, 1½ to 2 hours.

6. Remove ribs from oven, tent with foil, and let rest for 30 minutes. Brush ribs evenly with half of sauce. Slice ribs between bones and serve with remaining sauce.

Why This Recipe Works Chicago-style barbecued ribs recipes typically call for smoking the ribs at about 200 degrees for at least 8 hours. This slow-and-low cooking method delivers the moist, tender meat that defines Chicago ribs. We wanted to replicate the same method at home. To shorten cooking time, we started our recipe on the grill—where the ribs picked up good color and smoke flavor—and finished them in the oven. Placing pans of water on the grill and in the oven steamed the ribs, making them extra moist and tender. For Chicago-style barbecue sauce, we used celery salt, allspice, and plenty of cayenne pepper.

TEXAS BARBECUED BEEF RIBS

SERVES 4

Beef ribs are sold in slabs with up to seven bones, but slabs with three to four bones are easier to manage on the grill. If you cannot find ribs with a substantial amount of meat on the bones, don't bother making this recipe. One medium wood chunk, soaked in water for 1 hour, can be substituted for the wood chips on a charcoal grill.

Texas Barbecue Sauce

- 2 tablespoons unsalted butter
- ½ small onion, chopped fine
- 2 garlic cloves, minced
- 1½ teaspoons chili powder
- 1½ teaspoons pepper
- ½ teaspoon dry mustard
- 2 cups tomato juice
- 6 tablespoons distilled white vinegar
- 2 tablespoons Worcestershire sauce
- 2 tablespoons packed brown sugar
- 2 tablespoons molasses
- Salt

Ribs

- 3 tablespoons packed brown sugar
- 4 teaspoons chili powder
- 1 tablespoon salt
- 2 teaspoons pepper
- ½ teaspoon cayenne pepper
- 3–4 beef rib slabs (3 to 4 ribs per slab, about 5 pounds total), trimmed
- 1 cup wood chips, soaked in water for 15 minutes and drained

1. For the Texas Barbecue Sauce Melt butter in medium saucepan over medium heat. Add onion and cook until softened, about 5 minutes. Stir in garlic, chili powder, pepper, and dry mustard and cook until fragrant, about 30 seconds. Stir in tomato juice, vinegar, Worcestershire, sugar, and molasses and simmer until sauce is reduced to 2 cups, about 20 minutes. Season with salt to taste. (Sauce can be refrigerated for 1 week.)

2. For the Ribs Combine sugar, chili powder, salt, pepper, and cayenne in bowl. Pat ribs dry with paper towels and rub them evenly with spice mixture. Cover ribs with plastic wrap and let sit at room temperature for 1 hour.

3. Adjust oven rack to middle position and heat oven to 300 degrees. Set wire rack in rimmed baking sheet and add just enough water to cover pan bottom. Arrange ribs on rack and cover tightly with aluminum foil. Bake until fat has rendered and meat begins to pull away from bones, about 2 hours. Using large piece of heavy-duty foil, wrap soaked chips in foil packet and cut several vent holes in top.

4A. For a Charcoal Grill Open bottom vent halfway. Light large chimney starter filled with charcoal briquettes (6 quarts). When top coals are partially covered with ash, pour into steeply banked pile against 1 side of grill. Place wood chip packet on coals. Set cooking grate in place, cover, and open lid vent halfway. Heat grill until hot and wood chips are smoking, about 5 minutes.

4B. For a Gas Grill Place wood chip packet directly on primary burner. Turn all burners to high, cover, and heat grill until hot and wood chips are smoking, about 15 minutes. Leave primary burner on high and turn other burner(s) off. (Adjust primary burner as needed to maintain grill temperature between 250 and 300 degrees.)

5. Clean and oil cooking grate. Place ribs meat side down on cool side of grill; ribs may overlap slightly. Cover (positioning lid vent over meat if using charcoal) and cook until ribs are lightly charred and smoky, about 1½ hours, flipping and rotating racks halfway through grilling. Transfer to cutting board, tent with foil, and let rest for 10 minutes. Serve with barbecue sauce.

Why This Recipe Works Traditional Texas barbecued beef ribs are placed in pits for up to 10 hours. The smoke slowly permeates the meat, melting away fat, building flavor, and creating an unforgettable crust. We wanted a streamlined recipe. To speed things up, we first turned to steaming the ribs in the oven on a tray of water covered with aluminum foil, which tenderized the ribs. We then moved the ribs to the grill, where we smoked them over indirect heat (banking all the coals to one side of the grill and placing the ribs on the empty side) using wood chips. The surface of the meat dried and formed a spicy, crusty bark.

Why This Recipe Works For a new take on pulled pork, we started with a shank-end fresh ham. We rubbed it with only salt to keep the flavor pure and let it rest overnight for deeply seasoned, juicy meat. To speed up the usually long cooking time, we smoked the ham on the grill to infuse it with flavor before covering it with foil and transferring it to the oven. For crisp and crackling skin, we removed the skin when the meat hit 200 degrees and roasted it separately. From there, we chopped the ham, stirring in the crisp bits of skin and the flavorful rendered juices, and served it on soft buns with a smear of tangy mustard sauce.

SOUTH CAROLINA SMOKED FRESH HAM

SERVES 8 TO 10

Plan ahead: The ham must be salted at least 18 hours before cooking. You'll have about 2½ cups of mustard sauce.

Ham

1 (6- to 8-pound) bone-in, skin-on shank-end fresh ham
  Kosher salt
2 cups wood chips

Mustard Sauce

1½ cups yellow mustard
½ cup cider vinegar
6 tablespoons packed brown sugar
2 tablespoons ketchup
2 teaspoons hot sauce
2 teaspoons Worcestershire sauce
1 teaspoon pepper

Hamburger buns

1. For the Ham Pat ham dry with paper towels. Place ham on large sheet of plastic wrap and rub all over with 2 tablespoons salt. Wrap tightly in plastic and refrigerate for 18 to 24 hours.

2. Just before grilling, soak wood chips in water for 15 minutes, then drain. Using large piece of heavy-duty aluminum foil, wrap soaked chips in 8 by 4½-inch foil packet. (Make sure chips do not poke holes in sides or bottom of packet.) Cut 2 evenly spaced 2-inch slits in top of packet.

3A. For a Charcoal Grill Open bottom vent completely. Light large chimney starter three-quarters filled with charcoal briquettes (4½ quarts). When top coals are partially covered with ash, pour evenly over half of grill. Place wood chip packet on coals. Set cooking grate in place, cover, and open lid vent completely. Heat grill until hot and wood chips are smoking, about 5 minutes.

3B. For a Gas Grill Remove cooking grate and place wood chip packet directly on primary burner. Set cooking grate in place, turn all burners to high, cover, and heat grill until hot and wood chips are smoking, about 15 minutes. Turn primary burner to medium-high and turn off other burner(s). (Adjust primary burner as needed to maintain grill temperature of 300 degrees.)

4. Clean and oil cooking grate. Unwrap ham and place flat side down on cooler side of grill. Cover grill (position lid vent directly over ham if using charcoal) and cook for 2 hours. Thirty minutes before ham comes off grill, adjust oven rack to middle position and heat oven to 300 degrees.

5. For the Mustard Sauce Meanwhile, whisk all ingredients together in bowl. (Sauce can be refrigerated for up to 1 week.)

6. Transfer ham to 13 by 9-inch baking pan, flat side down. Cover pan tightly with foil. Transfer to oven and roast until fork inserted in ham meets little resistance and meat registers 200 degrees, about 2½ hours.

7. Remove ham from oven and increase oven temperature to 400 degrees. Line rimmed baking sheet with foil. Using tongs, remove ham skin in 1 large piece. Place skin fatty side down on prepared sheet. Transfer to oven and roast until skin is dark and crispy and sounds hollow when tapped with fork, about 25 minutes, rotating sheet halfway through roasting. Tent ham with foil and let rest while skin roasts.

8. Transfer ham to carving board. Strain accumulated juices from pan through fine-mesh strainer set over bowl; discard solids. Trim and discard excess fat from ham. Remove bone and chop meat into bite-size pieces; transfer to large bowl.

9. When cool enough to handle, chop skin fine. Rewarm reserved ham juices in microwave for 1 minute. Add juices and chopped skin to ham and toss to combine. Season with salt to taste. Serve on buns, topped with mustard sauce.

Why This Recipe Works Traditional vinegar-based Lexington-style pulled pork recipes take hours to prepare. We wanted to simplify this recipe without sacrificing flavor. To do so, we used a combination of grilling and oven roasting to reduce the cooking time from all day to just a few hours. To infuse our Lexington-style pulled pork with ample smoke flavor despite the abbreviated cooking time, we doubled the amount of wood chips we used.

LEXINGTON-STYLE PULLED PORK

SERVES 8

Boneless pork butt (also labeled Boston butt) is often wrapped in elastic netting; be sure to remove the netting before rubbing the meat with the spices in step 1. Four medium wood chunks, soaked in water for 1 hour, can be substituted for the wood chips on a charcoal grill.

Spice Rub and Pork

2 tablespoons paprika
2 tablespoons pepper
2 tablespoons packed brown sugar
1 tablespoon salt
1 (4- to 5-pound) boneless pork butt roast, trimmed
4 cups wood chips, soaked in water for 15 minutes and drained

Lexington Barbecue Sauce

1 cup water
1 cup cider vinegar
½ cup ketchup
1 tablespoon granulated sugar
¾ teaspoon salt
½ teaspoon pepper
½ teaspoon red pepper flakes

1. For the Spice Rub and Pork Combine paprika, pepper, sugar, and salt in bowl. Pat meat dry with paper towels and rub it evenly with spice mixture. Wrap meat in plastic wrap and let sit at room temperature for at least 1 hour or refrigerate for up to 24 hours. (If refrigerated, let sit at room temperature for 1 hour before grilling.) Using 2 large pieces of heavy-duty aluminum foil, wrap soaked chips in 2 foil packets and cut several vent holes in tops.

2A. For a Charcoal Grill Open bottom vent halfway. Light large chimney starter half filled with charcoal briquettes (3 quarts). When top coals are partially covered with ash, pour into steeply banked pile against 1 side of grill. Place wood chip packets on coals. Set cooking grate in place, cover, and open lid vent halfway. Heat grill until hot and wood chips are smoking, about 5 minutes.

2B. For a Gas Grill Place wood chip packets directly on primary burner. Turn all burners to high, cover, and heat grill until hot and wood chips are smoking, about 15 minutes. Turn primary burner to medium and turn other burner(s) off. (Adjust primary burner as needed to maintain grill temperature around 275 degrees.)

3. Clean and oil cooking grate. Place meat on cool side of grill. Cover (positioning lid vent over meat if using charcoal) and cook until pork has dark, rosy crust, about 2 hours. During final 20 minutes of grilling, adjust oven rack to lower-middle position and heat oven to 325 degrees.

4. Transfer pork to large roasting pan, cover pan tightly with foil, and roast pork in oven until fork slips easily into and out of meat, 2 to 3 hours. Remove pork from the oven and let rest, still covered with foil, for 30 minutes.

5. For the Lexington Barbecue Sauce Whisk together all ingredients until sugar and salt are dissolved. When cool enough to handle, unwrap pork and pull meat into thin shreds, discarding excess fat and gristle. Toss pork with ½ cup barbecue sauce, serving remaining sauce at table.

North Carolina Barbecue Battle

In the eastern part of North Carolina, it's just not barbecue unless it's a whole hog. Known as a pig pickin', this type of barbecue starts with a split hog and ends with succulent meat and crackling-crisp skin. The meat is then literally picked from the bones and lightly seasoned with a thin vinegar and pepper sauce. Western Carolinians eschew the whole hog and go straight for the pork shoulder—the most marbled and meatiest chunk of the animal. The pork shoulder is cooked just like the whole hog, but the sauce is enriched with just enough ketchup and sugar to take the edge off the acidity.

SOUTH CAROLINA PULLED PORK

SERVES 8

Boneless pork butt (also labeled Boston butt) is often wrapped in elastic netting; be sure to remove the netting before rubbing the meat with the spices in step 1. The cooked meat can be shredded or chopped. Four medium wood chunks, soaked in water for 1 hour, can be substituted for the wood chip packet on a charcoal grill.

Spice Rub and Pork

- 3 tablespoons dry mustard
- 2 tablespoons salt
- 1½ tablespoons packed light brown sugar
- 2 teaspoons pepper
- 2 teaspoons paprika
- ¼ teaspoon cayenne pepper
- 1 (4- to 5-pound) boneless pork butt roast, trimmed
- 4 cups wood chips, soaked in water for 15 minutes and drained

Mustard Barbecue Sauce

- ½ cup yellow mustard
- ½ cup packed light brown sugar
- ¼ cup distilled white vinegar
- 2 tablespoons Worcestershire sauce
- 1 tablespoon hot sauce
- 1 teaspoon salt
- 1 teaspoon pepper

1. For the Spice Rub and Pork Combine dry mustard, salt, sugar, pepper, paprika, and cayenne in bowl. Pat meat dry with paper towels and rub it evenly with spice mixture. Wrap meat in plastic wrap and let sit at room temperature for at least 1 hour or refrigerate up to 24 hours. (If refrigerated, let sit at room temperature for 1 hour before grilling.) Using 2 large pieces of heavy-duty aluminum foil, wrap soaked chips in 2 foil packets and cut several vent holes in tops.

2A. For a Charcoal Grill Open bottom vent completely. Light large chimney starter half filled with charcoal briquettes (3 quarts). When top coals are partially covered with ash, pour into steeply banked pile against 1 side of grill. Place wood chip packets on coals. Set cooking grate in place, cover, and open lid vent halfway. Heat grill until hot and wood chips are smoking, about 5 minutes.

2B. For a Gas Grill Place wood chip packets directly on primary burner. Turn all burners to high, cover, and heat grill until hot and wood chips are smoking, about 15 minutes. Turn primary burner to medium-high and turn other burner(s) off. (Adjust primary burner as needed to maintain grill temperature around 325 degrees.)

3. Clean and oil cooking grate. Place meat on cool side of grill. Cover (positioning lid vent over meat if using charcoal) and cook until pork has dark, rosy crust, about 2 hours. During final 20 minutes of grilling, adjust oven rack to lower-middle position and heat oven to 325 degrees.

4. For the Mustard Barbecue Sauce Whisk yellow mustard, sugar, vinegar, Worcestershire, hot sauce, salt, and pepper in bowl until smooth. Measure out ½ cup sauce and set aside for cooking, reserving remaining sauce for serving.

5. Transfer pork to roasting pan and brush evenly with sauce for cooking. Cover pan tightly with foil and roast pork in oven until fork slips easily in and out of meat, 2 to 3 hours.

6. Remove pork from oven and let rest, still covered with foil, for 30 minutes. When cool enough to handle, unwrap pork and pull meat into thin shreds, discarding excess fat and gristle. Toss pork with reserved sauce and serve.

Why This Recipe Works This regional recipe, nicknamed Carolina Gold, demands more than just a last-minute dose of bold flavors. A combination of grilling and oven roasting reduces the cooking time from all day to just four or five hours. We used a spice rub, which included dry mustard to jump-start the mustard flavor of the sauce. Most South Carolina barbecue sauce recipes use yellow mustard, which our tasters praised for its bright tang. Brushing the pork with the sauce before it went into the oven produced a second hit of mustard flavor; tossing the shredded pork with the remaining sauce gave the meat a final layer of mustard flavor.

TENNESSEE PULLED PORK SANDWICHES

SERVES 8 WITH LEFTOVERS

In step 8, shred the pork while it's still hot. Leftover pork can be refrigerated for up to three days.

Pork

1 (5- to 6-pound) bone-in pork butt roast, trimmed
  Kosher salt
2 cups wood chips
1 (13 by 9-inch) disposable aluminum roasting pan

Barbecue Sauce

1 cup ketchup
¼ cup cider vinegar
¼ cup water
2 tablespoons yellow mustard
1 tablespoon Worcestershire sauce
1 teaspoon granulated garlic
1 teaspoon pepper

1 recipe Hoecakes (page 359)
  Dill pickle chips
  Coleslaw

1. For the Pork Using sharp knife, cut 1-inch crosshatch pattern about ¼ inch deep in fat cap of roast, being careful not to cut into meat. Pat roast dry with paper towels. Place roast on large sheet of plastic wrap and rub 2 tablespoons salt over entire roast and into slits. Wrap tightly with plastic and refrigerate for 18 to 24 hours.

2. Just before grilling, soak wood chips in water for 15 minutes, then drain. Using large piece of heavy-duty aluminum foil, wrap soaked chips in foil packet and cut several vent holes in top.

3A. For a Charcoal Grill Open bottom vent completely. Light large chimney starter three-quarters filled with charcoal briquettes (4½ quarts). When top coals are partially covered with ash, pour evenly over half of grill. Place wood chip packet on coals. Set cooking grate in place, cover, and open lid vent completely. Heat grill until hot and wood chips are smoking, about 5 minutes.

3B. For a Gas Grill Remove cooking grate and place wood chip packet directly on primary burner. Set cooking grate in place, turn all burners to high, cover, and heat grill until hot and wood chips are smoking, about 15 minutes. Turn primary burner to medium-high and turn off other burner(s). (Adjust primary burner as needed to maintain grill temperature of 300 degrees.)

4. Unwrap pork and place fat side down in disposable pan. Place disposable pan on cooler side of grill. Cover grill (with lid vent directly over pork for charcoal) and cook until pork registers 120 degrees, about 2 hours. Thirty minutes before pork comes off grill, adjust oven rack to middle position and heat oven to 300 degrees.

5. Transfer disposable pan from grill to rimmed baking sheet. Cover pan tightly with foil and transfer to oven (still on sheet). Cook until fork inserted in pork meets little resistance and meat registers 210 degrees, about 3 hours.

6. For the Barbecue Sauce Meanwhile, combine all ingredients in medium saucepan and bring to boil over medium-high heat. Reduce heat to medium-low and simmer, whisking constantly, until slightly thickened, about 3 minutes. Transfer sauce to bowl and let cool completely.

7. Carefully remove foil from disposable pan (steam will escape). Remove blade bone from roast using tongs. Immediately transfer hot pork to bowl of stand mixer fitted with paddle attachment. Strain accumulated juices from pan through fine-mesh strainer set over separate bowl; discard solids.

8. Mix pork on low speed until meat is finely shredded, about 1½ minutes. Whisk pork juices to recombine, if separated, and add 1½ cups juices to shredded pork. Continue to mix pork on low speed until juices are incorporated, about 15 seconds longer. Season with salt to taste, adding more pork juices if desired. Serve pork on hoecakes with barbecue sauce, pickles, and coleslaw.

Why This Recipe Works Inspired by a central Tennessee sandwich of pulled pork on cornmeal griddle cakes called hoecakes, we wanted pork shredded so finely that it resembled pâté. A combination of grill smoking and oven roasting brought our meat to a higher temperature for a softer pork butt roast. Instead of hand-shredding the meat, we used a stand mixer fitted with a paddle attachment to handily get a superfine shred. To keep the meat moist, we returned some of the pork juices to the shredded meat and served our sandwich with barbecue sauce just like they do at Papa KayJoe's (see "A 30-Year Journey to Pulled Pork Perfection," page 359).

Why This Recipe Works To fully recreate our Papa KayJoe's experience in Centerville, Tennessee, we felt obligated to serve our Tennessee pulled pork on hoecakes. These cornmeal griddle cakes can be served on their own (with butter and syrup) or, in this case, as the perfect vehicle for a delicious barbecue sandwich. A loose batter with plenty of tangy buttermilk flavor gives the hoecakes a light texture, and the cornmeal makes them sturdy enough to hold up to a sandwich filling. Frying them in bacon fat adds a nice hit of smoky pork richness. Although our pulled pork is great on hamburger buns, we prefer to serve it on hoecakes.

HOECAKES

MAKES 16 HOECAKES

Papa KayJoe's makes their hoecakes with bacon fat.

 3 cups (15 ounces) white cornmeal
 2 tablespoons sugar
 2 teaspoons baking powder
1½ teaspoons salt
 2 cups buttermilk
 2 large eggs
 2 tablespoons bacon fat or vegetable oil

1. Adjust oven rack to middle position and heat oven to 200 degrees. Set wire rack in rimmed baking sheet and place in oven. Whisk cornmeal, sugar, baking powder, and salt together in large bowl. Beat buttermilk and eggs together in separate bowl. Whisk buttermilk mixture into cornmeal mixture until combined.

2A. For a Skillet Heat 1 teaspoon fat in 12-inch nonstick skillet over medium heat until shimmering. Using level ¼-cup dry measuring cup, drop 3 evenly spaced scoops of batter into skillet, smoothing tops slightly if necessary.

2B. For a Griddle Heat 1 tablespoon fat on 400-degree nonstick griddle until shimmering. Using level ¼-cup dry measuring cup, drop 8 evenly spaced scoops of batter onto griddle, smoothing tops slightly if necessary.

3. Cook until small bubbles begin to appear on surface of cakes and edges are set, about 2 minutes. Flip and cook until second side is golden brown, about 2 minutes longer. Transfer hoecakes to prepared sheet in oven. Repeat with remaining fat and batter: 5 additional batches for skillet or 1 additional batch for griddle. Serve.

A 30-Year Journey to Pulled Pork Perfection

Papa KayJoe's in Centerville, Tennessee, is a gray wooden building with a red tin roof at the end of a steep driveway. In the dining room, patrons tuck into Papa KayJoe's for their signature sandwiches—pulled pork on cornmeal griddle cakes—and share local news. Each morning owner Devin Pickard feeds armloads of hickory sticks into an outdoor furnace, where they slowly burn down to coals. Pickard then carries the hot embers to a nearby dirt-floored barbecue shack where a pair of cinder block pits sit waiting. At 11 a.m., Pickard lines up 24 heavily salted pork butts on the thick, black metal grate that sits over the pit and covers them with sheets of corrugated steel to trap the heat. The pork spends 6 to 8 hours on the grill, picking up the woodsy aroma of the smoldering hickory. After a day on the grill, the pork butts are packed into large aluminum roasting pans and transferred to a low oven where they'll spend the night. The next morning, Pickard slips on a pair of thick fireproof rubber gloves, picks out a pork butt, removes the blade bone and attacks the meat. In a clapping motion, he brings his fingertips together, pinching the pork; in less than a minute, the pork is in tiny shreds. He works in cupfuls of the juices that have accumulated in the roasting pan, moistening the pork with its own essence. Inside, Pickard's mother (Debbie) and daughter (Ruby) help pile the pork onto hot cornmeal griddle cakes (hoecakes) made to order with buttermilk and bacon fat. They'll produce dozens of these sandwiches today, and every day—including one for Pickard. "I would eat a barbecue sandwich every day of my life, that's how much I love it."

Why This Recipe Works Big chops demand big flavor. Soaking thick pork chops in a salt and sugar brine promised juicy, seasoned meat that would brown beautifully on the grill. For authentic Hill Country flavor, we applied a rub of kosher salt, pepper, onion powder, and granulated garlic and smoked the chops over mesquite chips. Before firing up the grill, we readied a kicked-up barbecue sauce, rendering strips of bacon and stirring in grated onion and cider vinegar for a pop of acidity; liquid smoke added extra flavor and hot sauce introduced some heat. Brushing the chops with some sauce before serving doubled down on the pork's smoky goodness.

TEXAS THICK-CUT SMOKED PORK CHOPS

SERVES 8

Each chop can easily serve two people. Grate the onion for the sauce on the large holes of a box grater. Our preferred hot sauce is Frank's RedHot Original Cayenne Pepper Sauce. If you'd like to use wood chunks instead of wood chips when using a charcoal grill, substitute two medium chunks, soaked in water for 1 hour, for the wood chip packet.

Pork
Kosher salt and pepper
3 tablespoons sugar
4 (18- to 20-ounce) bone-in pork rib chops, 2 inches thick
2 teaspoons onion powder
2 teaspoons granulated garlic
2 cups mesquite wood chips

Barbecue Sauce
2 slices bacon
¼ cup grated onion
Kosher salt and pepper
¾ cup cider vinegar
1¼ cups chicken broth
1 cup ketchup
2 tablespoons hot sauce
½ teaspoon liquid smoke

1. For the Pork Dissolve 6 tablespoons salt and sugar in 1½ quarts cold water in large container. Submerge chops in brine, cover, and refrigerate for 1 hour. Combine onion powder, granulated garlic, 1½ tablespoons salt, and 2 tablespoons pepper in bowl; set aside.

2. For the Barbecue Sauce Cook bacon in medium saucepan over medium heat until fat begins to render and bacon begins to brown, 4 to 6 minutes. Add onion and ¼ teaspoon salt and cook until softened, 2 to 4 minutes. Stir in vinegar, scraping up any browned bits, and cook until slightly thickened, about 2 minutes.

3. Stir in broth, ketchup, hot sauce, liquid smoke, and ¼ teaspoon pepper. Bring to simmer and cook until slightly thickened, about 15 minutes, stirring occasionally. Discard bacon and season with salt and pepper to taste. Remove from heat, cover, and keep warm.

4. Just before grilling, soak wood chips in water for 15 minutes, then drain. Using large piece of heavy-duty aluminum foil, wrap soaked chips in 8 by 4½-inch foil packet. (Make sure chips do not poke holes in sides or bottom of packet.) Cut 2 evenly spaced 2-inch slits in top of packet. Remove chops from brine and pat dry with paper towels. Season chops all over with reserved spice mixture.

5A. For a Charcoal Grill Open bottom vent completely. Light large chimney starter three-quarters filled with charcoal briquettes (4½ quarts). When top coals are partially covered with ash, pour evenly over half of grill. Place wood chip packet on coals. Set cooking grate in place, cover, and open lid vent completely. Heat grill until hot and wood chips are smoking, about 5 minutes.

5B. For a Gas Grill Remove cooking grate and place wood chip packet directly on primary burner. Set grate in place, turn all burners to high, cover, and heat grill until hot and wood chips are smoking, about 15 minutes. Leave primary burner on medium-high and turn off other burner(s). (Adjust primary burner as needed to maintain grill temperature around 325 degrees.)

6. Clean and oil cooking grate. Arrange chops on cooler side of grill with bone ends toward fire. Cook, covered (positioning lid vent over chops if using charcoal), until chops register 140 degrees, 45 to 50 minutes, flipping halfway through cooking.

7. Transfer chops to platter, tent with foil, and let rest for 10 minutes. Brush chops generously with warm sauce and serve, passing remaining sauce separately.

SMOKED DOUBLE-THICK PORK CHOPS

SERVES 6 TO 8

We prefer blade chops, which have more fat to prevent drying out on the grill, but leaner loin chops will also work. Two medium wood chunks, soaked in water for 1 hour, can be substituted for the wood chips on a charcoal grill. These chops are huge. You may want to slice the meat off the bone before serving.

¼ cup packed dark brown sugar
1 tablespoon ground fennel
1 tablespoon ground cumin
1 tablespoon ground coriander
1 tablespoon paprika
1 teaspoon salt
1 teaspoon pepper
4 (1¼- to 1½-pound) bone-in blade-cut pork chops, about 2 inches thick, trimmed
2 cups wood chips, soaked in water for 15 minutes and drained

1. Combine sugar, fennel, cumin, coriander, paprika, salt, and pepper in bowl. Pat pork chops dry with paper towels and rub them evenly with spice mixture. Wrap chops in plastic wrap and refrigerate for at least 1 hour or up to 24 hours. Using large piece of heavy-duty aluminum foil, wrap soaked chips in foil packet and cut several vent holes in top.

2A. For a Charcoal Grill Open bottom vent halfway. Light large chimney starter filled with charcoal briquettes (6 quarts). When top coals are partially covered with ash, pour into pile on 1 side of grill. Place wood chip packet on coals. Set cooking grate in place, cover, and open lid vent halfway. Heat grill until hot and wood chips are smoking, about 5 minutes.

2B. For a Gas Grill Place wood chip packet directly on primary burner. Turn all burners to high, cover, and heat grill until hot and wood chips are smoking, about 15 minutes. Turn primary burner to medium and turn other burner(s) off. (Adjust primary burner as needed to maintain grill temperature around 275 degrees.)

3. Clean and oil cooking grate. Place pork chops on cool side of grill with bone sides facing hot side of grill. Cover (positioning lid vent over pork if using charcoal) and cook until meat registers 145 degrees, 50 minutes to 1 hour. Slide chops directly over fire (hot side on gas grill) and cook, uncovered, until well browned, about 4 minutes, flipping chops halfway through grilling. Transfer to platter and let rest for 20 minutes. Serve.

Cutting Your Own Double-Thick Pork Chops

We like juicy blade-end chops that are at least 2 inches thick for our Smoked Double-Thick Pork Chops recipe. If you can't find them prepackaged at your grocery store, just buy a 4½- to 5-pound bone-in blade roast and cut it into 2-inch portions yourself. If cutting your own chops, ask your butcher or meat department manager if the chine bone (a part of the backbone) has been removed from the base of the roast—this thick bone can make carving difficult. If the chine bone has not been removed, ask the butcher to cut the chops for you.

Why This Recipe Works Most grilled double-thick pork chop recipes result in a charred exterior and raw meat, or gray meat that tastes steamed. We wanted our pork chops to have great taste and tenderness. Cooking our pork chops over indirect heat made for juicy and tender meat. We used wood chips on the grill to infuse the pork with a nice level of smoke flavor. Coating the double-thick pork chops with a rub of brown sugar and potent herbs and spices helped produce a flavorful crust, and quick grilling over hot coals at the end of cooking gave the crust a crisp texture and rich mahogany color.

Why This Recipe Works Usually, by the time thin-cut pork chops pick up char on the grill, the insides have dried out. To ensure that our pork chops would brown quickly, we partially froze them to eliminate excess moisture from the exterior. Salting them first prevented them from drying out and allowed us to skip brining. A combination of softened butter and brown sugar spread over the chops resulted in a flavorful golden-brown crust when they came off the grill. And a chive-mustard butter added even more flavor to the finished chops.

GRILLED THIN-CUT PORK CHOPS

SERVES 4 TO 6

To prevent the chops from curling, cut two slits about 2 inches apart through the fat around the outside of each raw chop.

- 6 bone-in rib or center-cut pork chops, about ½ inch thick, trimmed
- ¾ teaspoon salt
- 4 tablespoons unsalted butter, softened
- 1 teaspoon packed brown sugar
- ½ teaspoon pepper
- 1 teaspoon minced fresh chives
- ½ teaspoon Dijon mustard
- ½ teaspoon grated lemon zest

1. Set wire rack in rimmed baking sheet. Pat chops dry with paper towels. Cut 2 slits, about 2 inches apart, through outer layer of fat and silverskin on each chop. Rub chops with salt. Arrange on prepared rack and freeze until chops are firm, at least 30 minutes but no more than 1 hour. Combine 2 tablespoons butter, sugar, and pepper in small bowl; set aside. Mix remaining 2 tablespoons butter, chives, mustard, and zest in second small bowl and refrigerate until firm, about 15 minutes. (Butter-chive mixture can be refrigerated, covered, for 1 day.)

2A. For a Charcoal Grill Open bottom vent completely. Light large chimney starter filled with charcoal briquettes (6 quarts). When top coals are partially covered with ash, pour evenly over grill. Set cooking grate in place, cover, and open lid vent completely. Heat grill until hot, about 5 minutes.

2B. For a Gas Grill Turn all burners to high, cover, and heat grill until hot, about 15 minutes.

3. Pat chops dry with paper towels. Spread softened butter-sugar mixture evenly over both sides of each chop. Grill, covered, over hot fire until well browned and meat registers 145 degrees, 6 to 8 minutes, flipping chops halfway through grilling. Transfer chops to platter and top with chilled butter-chive mixture. Tent with aluminum foil and let rest for 5 minutes. Serve.

SPICY THAI GRILLED THIN-CUT PORK CHOPS

Substitute 1½ teaspoons Asian chili-garlic sauce, 1 teaspoon minced fresh cilantro, and ½ teaspoon grated lime zest for chives, mustard, and lemon zest.

CARIBBEAN GRILLED THIN-CUT PORK CHOPS

Substitute 1 teaspoon grated fresh ginger, ½ teaspoon minced fresh thyme, and ½ teaspoon grated orange zest for chives, mustard, and lemon zest.

MEDITERRANEAN GRILLED THIN-CUT PORK CHOPS

Substitute 1½ teaspoons black olive tapenade and ½ teaspoon minced fresh oregano for chives and mustard.

Thin Is the New Thick

For juicy, nicely charred chops, try our method: salting, freezing, and brushing with softened butter before grilling. Salting ensures juicy chops; freezing promotes crust formation by drying the exterior and adding valuable minutes to the cooking time; and butter accelerates browning and adds richness to the lean meat.

WOULD YOU EAT THIS?
Grilled straight from the package, this chop is dry, pale, and bland.

NOW WE'RE TALKING
Salted, frozen, buttered, then grilled, this chop is juicy, browned, and flavorful.

ST. LOUIS BBQ PORK STEAKS

SERVES 4

Boneless pork butt is also labeled Boston butt. If pork steaks are available, use them and increase the cooking time in the sauce to 1 to 1½ hours. We use Budweiser in this recipe, since it's made in St. Louis, but any mild-tasting beer will do.

Spice Rub and Pork Steaks
1 tablespoon packed brown sugar
1 tablespoon paprika
2 teaspoons dry mustard
2 teaspoons pepper
1 teaspoon onion powder
1 teaspoon garlic powder
1 teaspoon ground cumin
1 teaspoon salt
¼ teaspoon cayenne pepper
1 (5- to 6-pound) boneless pork butt roast, sliced crosswise, trimmed, and each half cut into three or four 1-inch-thick steaks

Barbecue Sauce
2 cups beer
1½ cups ketchup
¼ cup Heinz 57 Steak Sauce
¼ cup packed dark brown sugar
2 tablespoons cider vinegar
2 tablespoons Worcestershire sauce
1 teaspoon garlic powder
1 teaspoon hot sauce
1 teaspoon liquid smoke
1 (13 by 9-inch) disposable aluminum roasting pan

1. For the Spice Rub and Pork Steaks Combine sugar, paprika, dry mustard, pepper, onion powder, garlic powder, cumin, salt, and cayenne in bowl. Pat pork steaks dry with paper towels and rub them evenly with spice mixture. Wrap pork in plastic wrap and refrigerate for at least 1 hour or up to 24 hours.

2. For the Barbecue Sauce Whisk all ingredients together in bowl and transfer to disposable pan.

3A. For a Charcoal Grill Open bottom vent half-way. Light large chimney starter filled with charcoal briquettes (6 quarts). When top coals are partially covered with ash, pour evenly over grill. Set cooking grate in place, cover, and open lid vent halfway. Heat grill until hot, about 5 minutes.

3B. For a Gas Grill Turn all burners to high, cover, and heat grill until hot, about 15 minutes. Leave primary burner on high and turn other burner(s) off. (Adjust primary burner as needed to maintain grill temperature around 350 degrees.)

4. Clean and oil cooking grate. Place pork steaks on hot side of grill. Cook (covered if using gas) until well browned on both sides, about 10 minutes, flipping steaks halfway through grilling.

5. Transfer pork steaks to sauce in pan and coat thoroughly. Cover pan with aluminum foil and place on grill. Cover (positioning lid vent over pan if using charcoal) and cook steaks until fork-tender and they register 190 degrees, 45 minutes to 1 hour. Remove steaks from pan and grill until lightly charred around edges, 4 to 8 minutes, flipping steaks half-way through grilling.

6. Transfer steaks to serving platter, tent loosely with foil, and let rest for 10 minutes. Skim excess fat from sauce and serve with steaks.

Making Pork Steaks

1. Slice pork crosswise in half and remove any large pieces of fat.

2. Rotate and stand each half of pork butt on its cut end and cut each half into three or four 1-inch-thick steaks.

Why This Recipe Works St. Louis BBQ pork steaks are little-known in other parts of America, but in St. Louis, they are so popular that pork steaks are on permanent sale in family packs at the supermarket. We found there was no substitute for pork steak, so the only option was to cut our own. We ordered a boneless Boston butt and cut it in half crosswise, then turned each piece on end to slice 1-inch-thick steaks. Inspired by a test kitchen recipe for brats and beer, we used a method of sear, simmer, sear again. This untraditional process gives the steaks a nice char, candy-like edges, and succulent, slightly chewy interiors.

CHINESE-STYLE GLAZED PORK TENDERLOIN

SERVES 4 TO 6

Leftover pork makes an excellent addition to fried rice or noodle soup.

- 2 (12- to 16-ounce) pork tenderloins, trimmed
- ½ cup soy sauce
- ½ cup apricot preserves
- ¼ cup hoisin sauce
- ¼ cup dry sherry
- 2 tablespoons grated fresh ginger
- 1 tablespoon toasted sesame oil
- 2 garlic cloves, minced
- 1 teaspoon five-spice powder
- 1 teaspoon pepper
- ¼ cup ketchup
- 1 tablespoon molasses
- 2 teaspoons vegetable oil

1. Lay tenderloins on cutting board with long side running parallel to counter edge. Cut horizontally down length of each tenderloin, stopping ½ inch from edge so tenderloin remains intact. Working with one at a time, open up tenderloins, place between 2 sheets of plastic wrap, and pound to ¾-inch thickness.

2. Combine soy sauce, preserves, hoisin, sherry, ginger, sesame oil, garlic, five-spice powder, and pepper in bowl. Reserve ¾ cup marinade. Place pork in large zipper-lock bag and pour remaining marinade into bag with pork. Seal bag, turn to coat, and refrigerate for at least 30 minutes or up to 4 hours.

3. Combine reserved marinade, ketchup, and molasses in small saucepan. Cook over medium heat until syrupy and reduced to ¾ cup, 3 to 5 minutes. Reserve ¼ cup glaze for glazing cooked pork.

4A. For a Charcoal Grill Open bottom vent completely. Light large chimney starter filled with charcoal briquettes (6 quarts). When top coals are partially covered with ash, pour evenly over grill. Set cooking grate in place, cover, and open lid vent completely. Heat grill until hot, about 5 minutes.

4B. For a Gas Grill Turn all burners to high, cover, and heat grill until hot, about 15 minutes. Turn all burners to medium-high.

5. Clean and oil cooking grate. Pat pork dry with paper towels, then rub with vegetable oil. Grill pork (covered if using gas) until lightly charred on first side, about 2 minutes. Flip and brush grilled side of pork evenly with 2 tablespoons glaze. Continue grilling until lightly charred on second side, about 2 minutes. Flip and brush evenly with 2 more tablespoons glaze. Repeat flipping and glazing twice more, until pork registers 140 degrees and is thickly glazed, about 4 minutes longer. Transfer pork to cutting board and brush with reserved glaze. Tent loosely with aluminum foil and let rest for 5 minutes. Slice and serve.

Preparing the Tenderloins

1. Place tenderloins on cutting board and slice each down side, leaving ½ inch of meat uncut. Open each tenderloin like a book.

2. Place each butterflied tenderloin between two sheets of plastic wrap. Using meat pounder, pound each to ¾-inch thickness.

Why This Recipe Works For an easy take on Chinese-style glazed and charred pork, we turned to the grill and opted for pork tenderloin, which cooks quickly over a hot fire. Butterflying and pounding the meat gave us maximum surface area for our glaze. A combination of thick, sweet apricot preserves and ketchup flavored with hoisin, fresh ginger, sesame oil, sherry, garlic, and five-spice powder gave us a salty-sweet sauce that acted as both marinade and glaze. Continuously flipping and glazing the pork creates a charred, caramelized—but not burnt—exterior.

Why This Recipe Works We began our Chinese-Style Barbecue Spareribs by removing the tough membrane on the underside of the ribs. Instead of cooking the ribs on the grill the entire time, we found that cooking them in the sauce in the oven and then finishing them on the grill allowed for deeply seasoned Chinese-style ribs and eliminated the need to marinate them. Since the smoke from wood chips was overpowering, we replaced the wood chips with orange spice or Earl Grey tea bags soaked in water, wrapped in foil, and placed on the hot coals for a mellow, smoky flavor that complemented the Asian seasonings.

CHINESE-STYLE BARBECUED SPARERIBS

SERVES 6

Full-size spareribs are fatty, plus they're too large to fit on the grill. If you can't find St. Louis–style spareribs (which have been trimmed of the brisket bone and surrounding meat), substitute baby back ribs and begin to check for doneness after 1 hour on the grill. Cover the edges of the ribs loosely with foil if they begin to burn while grilling.

- 2 (2½- to 3-pound) racks St. Louis–style spareribs, trimmed
- 8 black tea bags, preferably orange spice or Earl Grey
- 1½ cups ketchup
- 1 cup soy sauce
- 1 cup hoisin sauce
- 1 cup sugar
- ½ cup dry sherry
- 6 garlic cloves, minced
- 2 tablespoons grated fresh ginger
- 2 teaspoons toasted sesame oil
- 1½ teaspoons cayenne pepper
- 1 (13 by 9-inch) disposable aluminum roasting pan
- 1 cup red currant jelly

1. To remove chewy membrane from ribs, loosen it with tip of paring knife and, with aid of paper towel, pull it off slowly in 1 big piece. Cut rib racks in half. Cover tea bags with water in small bowl and soak for 5 minutes. Squeeze water from tea bags. Using large piece of heavy-duty aluminum foil, wrap tea bags in foil packet and cut several vent holes in top.

2. Adjust oven rack to middle position and heat oven to 300 degrees. Whisk 1 cup ketchup, soy sauce, hoisin sauce, sugar, sherry, garlic, ginger, sesame oil, and cayenne in large bowl; reserve ½ cup for glaze. Arrange ribs, meaty side down, in disposable pan and pour remaining ketchup mixture over ribs. Cover pan tightly with foil and cook until fat has rendered and meat begins to pull away from bones, 2 to 2½ hours. Transfer ribs to large plate. Pour pan juices into fat separator. Let liquid settle and reserve 1 cup defatted pan juices.

3. Simmer reserved pan juices in medium saucepan over medium-high heat until reduced to ½ cup, about 5 minutes. Stir in jelly, reserved ketchup mixture, and remaining ½ cup ketchup and simmer until reduced to 2 cups, 10 to 12 minutes. Reserve one-third of glaze for serving.

4A. For a Charcoal Grill Open bottom vent completely. Light large chimney starter filled with charcoal briquettes (6 quarts). When top coals are partially covered with ash, pour evenly over half of grill. Place tea packet on coals. Set cooking grate in place, cover, and open lid vent completely. Heat grill until hot and tea is smoking, about 5 minutes.

4B. For a Gas Grill Place tea packet directly on primary burner. Turn all burners to high, cover, and heat grill until hot and tea is smoking, about 15 minutes. Leave primary burner on high and turn other burner(s) off.

5. Clean and oil cooking grate. Arrange ribs, meaty side down, on cool side of grill and cook, covered, until ribs are smoky and edges begin to char, about 30 minutes.

6. Brush ribs with glaze, flip, rotate, and brush again. Cover and cook, brushing with glaze every 30 minutes, until ribs are fully tender and glaze is browned and sticky, 1 to 1½ hours. Transfer ribs to cutting board, tent with foil, and let rest for 10 minutes. Serve with reserved glaze.

To Make Ahead Ribs and glaze can be prepared through step 3 up to 2 days in advance. Once ribs are cool, wrap tightly in foil and refrigerate. Transfer glaze to microwave-safe bowl, cover with plastic wrap, and refrigerate. Before proceeding with step 4, allow ribs to stand at room temperature for 1 hour. Before proceeding with step 6, microwave glaze until warm, about 1 minute.

Why This Recipe Works Boneless country-style ribs present several cooking challenges. Each piece not only varies wildly from the next, but is also a mishmash of lean white meat and rich dark meat. Unfortunately, if the ribs are cooked to optimize the white meat, then the dark meat stays tough, and if they are cooked to optimize the dark meat, the white meat turns dry. To even out the cooking, we brined the ribs so that the white meat would stay juicy and pounded the ribs to an even ¾-inch thickness to "break down" the fattier dark meat. As for flavor, a double layer of barbecue spice and sauce and a quick smoke on the grill worked wonders.

BARBECUED COUNTRY-STYLE RIBS

SERVES 4 TO 6

For easier pounding, cut any ribs that are longer than 5 inches in half crosswise.

- 1 tablespoon salt
- 2 pounds boneless country-style pork ribs, trimmed
- ¾ cup packed dark brown sugar
- 2 tablespoons chili powder
- 2 tablespoons paprika
- 1 tablespoon dry mustard
- 1 tablespoon onion powder
- ¾ teaspoon pepper
- ¼ teaspoon cayenne pepper
- 6 tablespoons ketchup
- 1 tablespoon cider vinegar
- ¼ cup wood chips, soaked in water for 15 minutes and drained

1. Dissolve salt in 2 cups cold water in large container. Place ribs, cut side down, between 2 sheets of plastic wrap and pound to ¾ inch thickness. Submerge pork in brine, cover, and refrigerate for 30 minutes to 1 hour.

2. Combine sugar, chili powder, paprika, dry mustard, onion powder, pepper, and cayenne in shallow dish. Transfer half of mixture to bowl and stir in ketchup and vinegar; set aside.

3. Remove pork from brine and pat dry with paper towels. Dredge pork in remaining spice mixture and transfer to plate. Using large piece of heavy-duty aluminum foil, wrap soaked chips in foil packet and cut several vent holes in top.

4A. For a Charcoal Grill Open bottom vent halfway. Light large chimney starter filled with charcoal briquettes (6 quarts). When top coals are partially covered with ash, pour evenly over half of grill. Place wood chip packet on coals. Set cooking grate in place, cover, and open lid vent halfway. Heat grill until hot and wood chips are smoking, about 5 minutes.

4B. For a Gas Grill Place wood chip packet directly on primary burner. Turn all burners to high, cover, and heat grill until hot and wood chips are smoking, about 15 minutes. Leave primary burner on high and turn other burner(s) off.

5. Clean and oil cooking grate. Place pork on cool side of grill, cover (positioning lid vent over meat if using charcoal), and cook until meat registers 125 degrees, 3 to 5 minutes. Brush pork with ketchup mixture and grill, brushed side down, over hot side of grill until lightly charred, 2 to 3 minutes. Brush second side of pork, flip, and grill until lightly charred and meat registers 145 degrees, 2 to 3 minutes. Transfer pork to platter, tent loosely with foil, and let rest for 5 to 10 minutes. Serve.

Country-Style Ribs

Country-style ribs aren't ribs at all. They're well-marbled pork chops cut from the blade end of the loin. We bought dozens of these chops while testing this recipe and found that they were inconsistently shaped and sized. What's more, these "ribs" had widely varying proportions of light and dark meat. To help level the culinary playing field and ensure even cooking, we pounded each piece into an even ¾ inch thickness.

MISMATCHED MEAT
Each "rib" contains both light and dark meat.

Ensuring Even Cooking

The white and dark meat in country-style ribs cook at different rates—the white meat cooks quickly, while the dark meat is slower to tenderize. To equalize them, we brined and pounded. Brining kept the white meat from drying out, while pounding the ribs thin let them cook faster, helpful since long cooking times accentuate differences in cooking. Think of a fast car and a slow car starting from a stoplight at the same time: 30 seconds after the light turns green, the two cars won't be far apart, but after 10 minutes, they will be.

SOUTH DAKOTA CORNCOB-SMOKED RIBS

SERVES 4 TO 6

A gas grill can't do these corncob ribs justice, so please use charcoal. The test kitchen's favorite ketchup is Heinz Organic. To use up some of the leftover corn, try our recipe for Sweet Corn Spoonbread (page 230).

Sauce

1 cup ketchup
¼ cup water
1 tablespoon pepper
1 tablespoon onion powder
1 tablespoon Worcestershire sauce
1 tablespoon light corn syrup
1 tablespoon granulated garlic
2 teaspoons celery seeds
½ teaspoon liquid smoke

Ribs

5 tablespoons packed light brown sugar
1 teaspoon salt
½ teaspoon pepper
2 (2½- to 3-pound) racks baby back pork ribs, trimmed and membrane removed
1 cup cornmeal
6 corncobs, kernels removed and reserved for another use
1 (13 by 9-inch) disposable aluminum roasting pan

1. For the Sauce Whisk all ingredients together in medium bowl; set aside.

2. For the Ribs Combine sugar, salt, and pepper in bowl. Pat ribs dry with paper towels and rub with sugar mixture; set aside. Using large piece of heavy-duty aluminum foil, wrap cornmeal in foil packet and cut several vent holes in top.

3. Open bottom vents of charcoal grill halfway. Place disposable pan on 1 side of grill and fill pan with 2 quarts water. Arrange 3 quarts unlit charcoal briquettes on opposite side of grill. Place cobs on top of unlit briquettes. Light large chimney starter filled halfway with charcoal briquettes (3 quarts). When top coals are partially covered with ash, pour over cobs and unlit briquettes. Place cornmeal packet on coals. Set cooking grate in place, cover, and open lid vent halfway. Heat grill until hot and cornmeal is smoking, about 5 minutes.

4. Clean and oil cooking grate. Place ribs, meat side up, on cool part of grill opposite coals. Cover, positioning lid vent over ribs, and cook until ribs are deep red and tender, 3½ to 4 hours, rotating and switching ribs every hour. (Do not flip ribs.) During last 30 minutes of cooking, baste ribs every 10 minutes, rotating and switching ribs each time. Transfer ribs to carving board, tent loosely with foil, and let rest for 15 to 20 minutes. Cut ribs in between bones. Serve, passing remaining sauce separately.

Failed Corncob Tests

In South Dakota, bushels of dried, stripped corncobs impart a special flavor to ribs. To replicate it, we left no kernel unturned. It was A for effort, but these attempts were a bust.

SOOTY
Unhusked ears of corn.

SOOTY
Husked ears with the corn intact.

TOO MUCH WORK
Husked, stripped, and oven-dried.

BURNT TASTE
Popped popcorn.

Why This Recipe Works Corncob-smoking, a South Dakota specialty, may seem odd, but it gives meat a subtle smokiness hardwoods can't match. For barbecued ribs with mild, nutty sweetness, but without the complicated barbecuing rig, we layered charcoal on our grill with fresh corncobs (with the kernels removed) and a foil packet of cornmeal. The cornmeal gave the ribs an initial blast of smoky flavor, and the fresh cobs offered long-lasting smoke and a nutty aroma. We basted the ribs with a simple ketchup-based barbecue sauce with plenty of garlic and some celery seeds for sticky, sweet ribs that we couldn't get enough of.

Why This Recipe Works Two surefire ways to dress up a pork roast are to give it a flavorful, deeply caramelized crust on the grill and serve it with a savory-sweet mustard glaze. Our mustard-glazed pork loin has the best of both worlds. Leaving our roast untrimmed added moisture and flavor—and scoring the fat kept it from tasting too fatty. For the mustard glaze, apple jelly was a perfect complement to the spicy crunch of grainy mustard, and both married well with the other glaze ingredients—brown sugar, garlic, and fresh thyme. To fully infuse our pork loin with mustard flavor, we applied the glaze before, during, and after grilling.

GRILLED MUSTARD-GLAZED PORK LOIN

SERVES 6 TO 8

Dijon and yellow mustards also work well in the glaze, but make certain to use apple jelly, not apple butter. Look for a pork roast with about ¼ inch of fat on top and tie the roast at 1-inch intervals to ensure an even shape.

½ cup whole-grain mustard
6 tablespoons apple jelly
2 tablespoons packed dark brown sugar
2 tablespoons extra-virgin olive oil
1 large garlic clove, minced
2 teaspoons minced fresh thyme
¾ teaspoon pepper
½ teaspoon salt
1 boneless pork loin roast (2½ to 3 pounds), fat scored lightly, tied at 1-inch intervals

1. Whisk mustard, jelly, sugar, oil, garlic, thyme, pepper, and salt together in bowl. Measure out ⅔ cup sauce and set aside for cooking; reserve remaining sauce for serving. Before grilling, pat pork loin dry with paper towels and coat it evenly with ⅓ cup sauce for cooking.

2A. For a Charcoal Grill Open bottom vent halfway. Light large chimney starter filled with charcoal briquettes (6 quarts). When top coals are partially covered with ash, pour evenly over half of grill. Set cooking grate in place, cover, and open lid vent halfway. Heat grill until hot, about 5 minutes.

2B. For a Gas Grill Turn all the burners to high, cover, and heat grill until hot, about 15 minutes. Leave primary burner on high and turn other burner(s) off. (Adjust primary burner as needed to maintain grill temperature around 350 degrees.)

3. Clean and oil cooking grate. Place pork loin on hot side of grill. Cook (covered if using gas) until well browned on all sides, 12 to 15 minutes, turning as needed.

4. Flip pork loin fat side up and slide to cool side of grill. Brush pork with 2 tablespoons sauce for cooking. Cover (positioning lid vent over pork if using charcoal) and continue to cook until meat registers 140 degrees, 25 to 40 minutes longer, brushing every 10 minutes with remaining sauce for cooking.

5. Transfer pork loin to carving board, tent loosely with aluminum foil, and let rest for 15 minutes. Remove twine, cut meat into ¼-inch-thick slices, and transfer to serving platter. Whisk any accumulated juices into reserved sauce, spoon over meat, and serve.

The Benefits of Scoring

Gently scoring the fat helps it render (basting the meat and keeping it moist as it cooks) and creates an uneven surface that holds the glaze.

WOOD-GRILLED SALMON

SERVES 4

Any variety of wood chips will work here, but aromatic woods such as cedar and alder give the most authentic flavor.

1½ teaspoons sugar
½ teaspoon salt
¼ teaspoon pepper
4 (6- to 8-ounce) skin-on salmon fillets, about 1¼ inches thick
1 tablespoon olive oil
2 cups wood chips, soaked in water for 15 minutes and drained

1. Combine sugar, salt, and pepper in bowl. Pat salmon fillets dry with paper towels, then brush flesh sides with oil and rub evenly with sugar mixture. Using 4 large sheets of heavy-duty aluminum foil, crimp edges of each sheet to make 4 trays, each measuring 7 by 5 inches. Perforate bottom of each tray with tip of paring knife. Divide wood chips among trays and lay 1 fillet skin side down on top of wood chips in each tray.

2A. For a Charcoal Grill Open bottom vent completely. Light large chimney starter filled with charcoal briquettes (6 quarts). When top coals are partially covered with ash, pour evenly over grill. Set cooking grate in place, cover, and open lid vent completely. Heat grill until hot, about 5 minutes.

2B. For a Gas Grill Turn all burners to high, cover, and heat grill until hot, about 15 minutes.

3. Clean and oil cooking grate. Place trays on grill. Cook (covered if using gas) until center is still translucent when checked with tip of paring knife and registers 125 degrees (for medium-rare), about 10 minutes.

4. Transfer trays to wire rack, tent loosely with foil, and let rest for 5 minutes. Slide metal spatula between skin and flesh of fish, transfer fish to platter, and serve.

BARBECUED WOOD-GRILLED SALMON

Add ¾ teaspoon chili powder and ¼ teaspoon cayenne pepper to sugar mixture and substitute 1 tablespoon Dijon mustard mixed with 1 tablespoon maple syrup for oil in step 1.

LEMON-THYME WOOD-GRILLED SALMON

Add 2 teaspoons minced fresh thyme and 1½ teaspoons grated fresh lemon zest to sugar mixture and substitute 2 tablespoons Dijon mustard for oil in step 1.

An Easier Way to Planked Salmon

Cooking salmon on a cedar plank infuses it with gentle wood flavor rather than overwhelming smokiness. Here's how to get the same great taste, minus the mail-order plank.

1. Crimp 4 sheets of foil to make trays. Using paring knife, poke small slits in bottom of trays.

2. Place soaked wood chips in foil trays and arrange salmon skin side down directly on top of wood chips.

3. Once salmon is cooked, slide metal spatula between flesh and skin; fish should release easily.

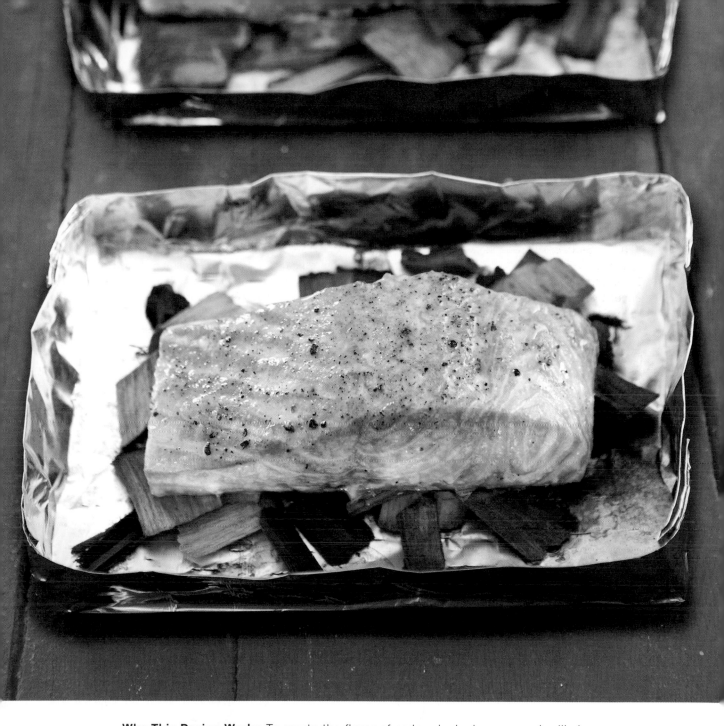

Why This Recipe Works To create the flavor of cedar planks in our wood-grilled salmon (without having to mail-order them), we settled on wood chips and made individual aluminum foil trays to hold the chips and salmon. To prevent the salmon from sticking to the wood chips, we left the skin on, which easily separated from the cooked fish. Poking a few slits in the bottom of the foil allowed more heat to reach the wood chips, which caused them to release more of their woodsy—but not overly smoky—flavor. Coating each fillet with a thin layer of olive oil and a light sprinkling of granulated sugar produced a golden, mildly sweet exterior.

CEDAR-PLANKED SALMON WITH CUCUMBER-YOGURT SAUCE

SERVES 4

Be sure to buy an untreated cedar plank specifically intended for cooking. To ensure uniform pieces of fish, we prefer to purchase a whole center-cut salmon fillet and cut it into four equal pieces. Note that the seasoned fillets must be refrigerated for at least 1 hour before grilling. When preheating the cedar plank, you will know it's ready when it is just giving off wisps of smoke. It should not ignite. Serve with lemon wedges and our Cucumber-Yogurt Sauce (recipe follows).

- 1 (2-pound) center-cut, skinless salmon fillet, about 1½ inches thick
- 2 tablespoons packed brown sugar
- 1½ tablespoons kosher salt
- 1 tablespoon chopped fresh dill
- 1 teaspoon pepper
- 1 (16 by 7-inch) cedar plank
- 1 teaspoon vegetable oil
  Lemon wedges

1. Cut salmon crosswise into 4 equal fillets and pat dry with paper towels. Combine sugar, salt, dill, and pepper in bowl. Sprinkle salmon all over with sugar mixture, place on plate, and refrigerate, uncovered, for at least 1 hour or up to 24 hours. One hour before grilling, soak cedar plank in water for 1 hour (or according to manufacturer's directions).

2A. For a Charcoal Grill Open bottom vent completely. Light large chimney starter filled with charcoal briquettes (6 quarts). When top coals are partially covered with ash, pour evenly over grill. Set cooking grate in place. Place cedar plank in center of grill. Cover and open lid vent completely. Heat grill until plank is lightly smoking and crackling (it should not ignite), about 5 minutes.

2B. For a Gas Grill Place cedar plank in center of grill. Turn all burners to medium-low, cover, and heat grill until plank is smoking and crackling (it should not ignite), about 15 minutes. Leave all burners on medium-low. Adjust burners as needed to maintain grill temperature between 300 and 325 degrees.

3. Brush 1 side of salmon fillets with oil, then place oiled side down on plank. Cover grill and cook until center of salmon is translucent when checked with tip of paring knife and registers 125 degrees (for medium-rare), 12 to 15 minutes. Using tongs, transfer plank with salmon to baking sheet, tent with aluminum foil, and let rest for 5 minutes. Serve with lemon wedges.

CUCUMBER-YOGURT SAUCE
MAKES ABOUT ¾ CUP

A spoon makes easy work of removing the cucumber seeds. Using Greek yogurt here is key; don't substitute regular plain yogurt, or the sauce will be very watery.

- ½ cucumber, peeled, halved lengthwise, and seeded
- ½ cup plain whole-milk Greek yogurt
- 1 tablespoon extra-virgin olive oil
- 1 tablespoon chopped fresh mint
- 1 tablespoon chopped fresh dill
- 1 small garlic clove, minced
- ¼ teaspoon pepper
- ⅛ teaspoon salt

Shred cucumber on large holes of box grater. Combine yogurt, oil, mint, dill, garlic, pepper, salt, and shredded cucumber in bowl. Cover and refrigerate until chilled, about 20 minutes. Serve.

Why This Recipe Works Our smoky, succulent salmon is surprisingly easy to make. Grilling the delicate fish on a cedar plank prevented it from sticking to the grill and provided subtle smoky flavor while keeping the grill grates pristine. While the plank soaked in water, we seasoned the salmon with a simple "cure" of brown sugar, kosher salt, fresh dill, and pepper. We preheated the plank on the grill before adding the salmon to get just the right woodsy flavor that wouldn't overwhelm the fish. Opting for skinless fillets allowed just enough cedar flavor to permeate the salmon. A Greek yogurt–cucumber tzatziki sauce balanced the salmon's smoky richness.

Why This Recipe Works Salmon steaks are a common choice for grilling: Their bone and thickness make them a far sturdier cut than a fillet. But the steak's thickness can also work against it, making it difficult for the interior and exterior to finish cooking at the same time. We began by tucking the belly flaps in toward the center of the steak and tying them to create medallions that would cook evenly and be easily maneuvered. To make sure our steaks were packed with flavor, we finished cooking them in a pan of zesty sauce on the cooler part of the grill. When they were done, our salmon steaks were flavorful, juicy, and moist.

GRILLED SALMON STEAKS WITH LEMON-CAPER SAUCE

SERVES 4

Before eating, lift out the small circular bone from the center of each steak.

- 4 (10-ounce) salmon steaks, 1 to 1½ inches thick
  Salt and pepper
- 2 tablespoons olive oil
- 1 teaspoon grated lemon zest and 6 tablespoons juice (2 lemons)
- 1 shallot, minced
- 3 tablespoons unsalted butter, cut into 3 pieces
- 1 tablespoon capers, rinsed
- 2 tablespoons minced fresh parsley
- 1 (13 by 9-inch) disposable aluminum pan

1. Pat salmon steaks dry with paper towels. Working with 1 steak at a time, carefully trim 1½ inches of skin from 1 tail. Tightly wrap other tail around skinned portion and tie steaks with kitchen twine. Repeat with remaining salmon steaks. Season salmon steaks with salt and pepper and brush both sides with oil. Combine lemon zest, lemon juice, shallot, butter, capers, and ⅛ teaspoon salt in disposable pan.

2A. For a Charcoal Grill Open bottom vent completely. Light large chimney starter filled with charcoal briquettes (6 quarts). When top coals are partially covered with ash, pour evenly over half of grill. Set cooking grate in place, cover, and open lid vent completely. Heat grill until hot, about 5 minutes.

2B. For a Gas Grill Turn all burners to high, cover, and heat grill until hot, about 15 minutes. Leave primary burner on high and turn off other burner(s).

3. Clean and oil cooking grate. Place salmon medallions on hot part of grill. Cook until browned, 2 to 3 minutes per side. Meanwhile, set pan on cool part of grill and cook until butter has melted, about 2 minutes. Transfer medallions to pan and gently turn to coat. Cook (covered if using gas) until center is still translucent when checked with tip of paring knife and registers 125 degrees (for medium-rare), 6 to 14 minutes, flipping salmon and rotating pan halfway through grilling. Remove twine and transfer salmon to platter. Off heat, whisk parsley into sauce and drizzle sauce over salmon. Serve.

Prepping Salmon Medallions

1. For salmon steaks sturdy enough to grill easily, remove 1½ inches of skin from one tail of each steak.

2. Tuck skinned portion into center of steak, wrap other tail around it, and tie with kitchen twine.

Why This Recipe Works We wanted tender, juicy, shrimp with a smoky, charred crust and chile flavor that was more than just superficial. To achieve this, we sprinkled one side of the shrimp with sugar to promote browning and cooked the shrimp sugar side down over the hot side of the grill for a few minutes. We then flipped the skewers to gently finish cooking on the cool side of the grill. Creating a flavorful marinade that doubled as a sauce gave our shrimp skewers a spicy, assertive kick. And butterflying the shrimp before marinating and grilling them opened up more shrimp flesh for the marinade and finishing sauce to flavor.

GRILLED JALAPEÑO AND LIME SHRIMP SKEWERS

SERVES 4

We prefer flat metal skewers that are at least 14 inches long for this recipe.

Marinade

1–2 jalapeño chiles, stemmed, seeded, and chopped
  3 tablespoons olive oil
  6 garlic cloves, minced
  1 teaspoon grated lime zest plus 5 tablespoons juice (3 limes)
½ teaspoon ground cumin
¼ teaspoon cayenne pepper
½ teaspoon salt

Shrimp

1½ pounds extra-large shrimp (21 to 25 per pound), peeled and deveined
½ teaspoon sugar
  1 tablespoon minced fresh cilantro

1. For the Marinade Process all ingredients in food processor until smooth, about 15 seconds. Reserve 2 tablespoons marinade; transfer remaining marinade to medium bowl.

2. For the Shrimp Pat shrimp dry with paper towels. To butterfly shrimp, use paring knife to make shallow cut down outside curve of shrimp. Add shrimp to bowl with marinade and toss to coat. Cover and refrigerate for 30 minutes to 1 hour.

3A. For a Charcoal Grill Open bottom vent completely. Light large chimney starter filled with charcoal briquettes (6 quarts). When top coals are partially covered with ash, pour evenly over half of grill. Set cooking grate in place, cover, and open lid vent completely. Heat grill until hot, about 5 minutes.

3B. For a Gas Grill Turn all burners to high, cover, and heat grill until hot, about 15 minutes.

4. Clean and oil cooking grate. Thread marinated shrimp on skewers. (Alternate direction of each shrimp as you pack them tightly on skewer to allow about a dozen shrimp to fit snugly on each skewer.) Sprinkle 1 side of skewered shrimp with sugar. Grill shrimp, sugared side down, over hot side of grill (covered if

using gas), until lightly charred, 3 to 4 minutes. Flip skewers and move to cool side of grill (if using charcoal) or turn all burners off (if using gas), and cook, covered, until other side of shrimp is no longer translucent, 1 to 2 minutes. Using tongs, slide shrimp into clean medium bowl and toss with reserved marinade. Sprinkle with cilantro and serve.

GRILLED RED CHILE AND GINGER SHRIMP SKEWERS

Replace marinade with 1 to 3 seeded and chopped small red chiles (or jalapeños), 1 minced scallion, 3 tablespoons rice vinegar, 2 tablespoons soy sauce, 1 tablespoon toasted sesame oil, 1 tablespoon grated fresh ginger, 2 teaspoons sugar, and 1 minced garlic clove. Prepare and grill shrimp as directed. Replace cilantro with 1 thinly sliced scallion and serve with lime wedges.

GRILLED CARIBBEAN SHRIMP SKEWERS

Replace marinade with 1 to 2 seeded and chopped habanero or serrano chiles, ¼ cup pineapple juice, 2 tablespoons olive oil, 1 tablespoon white wine vinegar, 3 minced garlic cloves, 1 teaspoon grated fresh ginger, 1 teaspoon packed brown sugar, 1 teaspoon dried thyme, ½ teaspoon salt, and ¼ teaspoon ground allspice. Prepare and grill shrimp as directed. Replace cilantro with 1 tablespoon minced fresh parsley.

How to Skewer Shrimp

1. Make shallow cut down outside curve of shrimp to open up flesh.

2. Alternate direction of each shrimp as you pack them tightly on skewer.

HUSK-GRILLED CORN

SERVES 6

The flavored butter can be made ahead and refrigerated for up to three days; bring it to room temperature before using. Set up a cutting board and knife next to your grill to avoid traveling back and forth between the kitchen and grill.

6 ears corn (unshucked)
6 tablespoons unsalted butter, softened
½ teaspoon salt
½ teaspoon pepper

1. Cut and remove silk protruding from top of each ear of corn. Combine butter, salt, and pepper in bowl. Fold one 14 by 12-inch piece heavy-duty aluminum foil in half to create 7 by 12-inch rectangle; then crimp into boat shape long and wide enough to accommodate 1 ear of corn. Transfer butter mixture to prepared foil boat.

2A. For a Charcoal Grill Open bottom vent completely. Light large chimney starter mounded with charcoal briquettes (7 quarts). When top coals are partially covered with ash, pour evenly over half of grill. Set cooking grate in place, cover, and open lid vent completely. Heat grill until hot, about 5 minutes.

2B. For a Gas Grill Turn all burners to high, cover, and heat grill until hot, about 15 minutes.

3. Clean and oil grate. Place corn on grill (over coals, with stem ends facing cooler side of grill, for charcoal). Cover and cook, turning corn every 3 minutes, until husks have blackened all over, 12 to 15 minutes. (To check for doneness, carefully peel down small portion of husk. If corn is steaming and bright yellow, it is ready.) Transfer corn to cutting board. Using chef's knife, cut base from corn. Using dish towel to hold corn, peel away and discard husk and silk with tongs.

4. Roll each ear of corn in butter mixture to coat lightly and return to grill (over coals for charcoal). Cook, turning as needed to char corn lightly on each side, about 5 minutes total. Remove corn from grill and roll each ear again in butter mixture. Transfer corn to platter. Serve, passing any remaining butter mixture.

HUSK-GRILLED CORN WITH MUSTARD-PAPRIKA BUTTER

Stir 2 tablespoons spicy brown mustard and 1 teaspoon smoked paprika into butter mixture in step 1.

HUSK-GRILLED CORN WITH CILANTRO-LIME BUTTER

Stir ¼ cup minced fresh cilantro, 2 teaspoons grated lime zest plus 1 tablespoon juice, and 1 minced small garlic clove into butter mixture in step 1.

HUSK-GRILLED CORN WITH ROSEMARY-PEPPER BUTTER

Increase pepper to 1 teaspoon. Stir 1 tablespoon minced fresh rosemary and 1 minced small garlic clove into butter mixture in step 1.

HUSK-GRILLED CORN WITH BROWN SUGAR-CAYENNE BUTTER

Stir 2 tablespoons packed brown sugar and ¼ teaspoon cayenne pepper into butter mixture in step 1.

Why This Recipe Works Corn is the perfect vegetable to grill because its sweet flavor loves a smoky accent and it's large enough not to fall through the grate. But grilled corn seldom tastes as good as it sounds. Our goal was to prevent the corn from drying out while achieving a classic char. To keep the kernels moist, we found that initially cooking the ears of corn within their husks worked best. We then shucked the hot corn, rolled the ears in seasoned butter, and returned them to the grill to caramelize. This way, the kernels achieved a good char but weren't on the grill long enough to dry out. One last roll in the butter and our corn was ready.

Why This Recipe Works Grilling corn sounds like a simple proposition—but our research found dozens of variations on the cooking method for this classic summer vegetable. For a recipe that produced corn with a distinctly grilled taste and lightly charred kernels, we grilled the corn unhusked. The grill imparted great flavor to our grilled corn, but also made the kernels tough and dry. To avoid this, we soaked the husked corn in salted water before grilling, which kept the kernels moist and seasoned them as well.

GRILLED CORN ON THE COB

SERVES 4 TO 6

If your corn isn't as sweet as you'd like, stir ½ cup of sugar into the water along with the salt. Avoid soaking the corn for more than 8 hours, or it will become overly salty.

Salt and pepper
8 ears corn, husks and silks removed
8 tablespoons unsalted butter, softened, or 1 recipe flavored butter (recipes follow)

1. In large pot, stir ½ cup salt into 4 quarts cold water until dissolved. Add corn and let soak for at least 30 minutes or up to 8 hours.

2A. For a Charcoal Grill Open bottom vent completely. Light large chimney starter filled with charcoal briquettes (6 quarts). When top coals are partially covered with ash, pour evenly over grill. Set cooking grate in place, cover, and open lid vent completely. Heat grill until hot, about 5 minutes.

2B. For a Gas Grill Turn all burners to high, cover, and heat grill until hot, about 15 minutes.

3. Clean and oil cooking grate. Grill corn, turning every 2 to 3 minutes, until kernels are lightly charred all over, 10 to 14 minutes. Remove corn from grill, brush with softened butter, and season with salt and pepper. Serve.

CHESAPEAKE BAY BUTTER
MAKES ABOUT ½ CUP

Using fork, beat 8 tablespoons softened, unsalted butter with 1 tablespoon hot sauce, 1 teaspoon Old Bay seasoning, and 1 minced garlic clove.

LATIN-SPICED BUTTER
MAKES ABOUT ½ CUP

Using fork, beat 8 tablespoons softened, unsalted butter with 1 teaspoon chili powder, ½ teaspoon ground cumin, ½ teaspoon grated lime zest, and 1 minced garlic clove. (Sprinkle cobs with ½ cup grated Parmesan, if desired.)

BASIL PESTO BUTTER
MAKES ABOUT ½ CUP

Using fork, beat 8 tablespoons softened, unsalted butter with 1 tablespoon basil pesto and 1 teaspoon lemon juice.

BARBECUE-SCALLION BUTTER
MAKES ABOUT ½ CUP

Using fork, beat 8 tablespoons softened, unsalted butter with 2 tablespoons barbecue sauce and 1 minced scallion.

A Good Soak
The grill imparts great flavor but can make corn tough and dry. Soaking the husked corn in salted water keeps the kernels moist and seasons them, too.

Why This Recipe Works For a standout backyard barbecue side, we turned canned beans into a savory showstopper. Baked beans gave us an easy starting point, and mixing in pinto and cannellini beans built a multifaceted bean base. We boosted the beans' flavor with an easy pantry sauce made with cider vinegar, granulated garlic, cayenne, and liquid smoke for that off-the-grill flavor. Browned bratwurst gave the sauce some meaty heft. We stirred the beans into this rich mixture, arranged bite-size pieces of bacon over the surface, and baked, allowing the bacon to render, crisp, and infuse the dish with its smoky flavor.

BACKYARD BARBECUE BEANS

SERVES 12 TO 16

Be sure to use a 13 by 9-inch metal baking pan; the volume of the beans is too great for a 13 by 9-inch ceramic baking dish, and it will overflow. We found that Bush's Original Recipe Baked Beans are the most consistent product for this recipe. Our favorite supermarket barbecue sauce is Bull's-Eye Original Barbecue Sauce.

½   cup barbecue sauce
½   cup ketchup
½   cup water
2   tablespoons spicy brown mustard
2   tablespoons cider vinegar
1   teaspoon liquid smoke
1   teaspoon granulated garlic
¼   teaspoon cayenne pepper
1¼ pounds bratwurst, casings removed
2   onions, chopped
2   (28-ounce) cans baked beans
2   (15-ounce) cans pinto beans, drained
2   (15-ounce) cans cannellini beans, drained
1   (10-ounce) can Ro-Tel Original Diced Tomatoes
    and Green Chilies, drained
6   slices thick-cut bacon, cut into 1-inch pieces

1. Adjust oven rack to middle position and heat oven to 350 degrees. Whisk barbecue sauce, ketchup, water, mustard, vinegar, liquid smoke, granulated garlic, and cayenne together in large bowl; set aside.

2. Cook bratwurst in 12-inch nonstick skillet over medium-high heat, breaking up into small pieces with spoon, until fat begins to render, about 5 minutes. Stir in onions and cook until sausage and onions are well browned, about 15 minutes.

3. Transfer bratwurst mixture to bowl with sauce. Stir in baked beans, pinto beans, cannellini beans, and tomatoes. Transfer bean mixture to 13 by 9-inch baking pan and place pan on rimmed baking sheet. Arrange bacon pieces in single layer over top of beans.

4. Bake until beans are bubbling and bacon is rendered, about 1½ hours. Let cool for 15 minutes. Serve.

To Make Ahead At end of step 3, beans can be wrapped in plastic and refrigerated for up to 24 hours. Proceed with recipe from step 4, increasing baking time to 1¾ hours.

Best for Baking

We tried several varieties of baked beans and found that firm, creamy **Bush's Original Recipe Baked Beans** held their shape best in this recipe. Plus, their meaty flavor is ideal for doctoring.

CALIFORNIA BARBECUED BEANS

SERVES 4 TO 6

If you can find them, pinquito beans (a variety grown in the Santa Maria Valley) are traditional in this dish. Bottled taco sauce is available in the Mexican aisle of most grocery stores. Don't add the tomato puree, taco sauce, brown sugar, and salt before the beans have simmered for an hour; they will hinder the proper softening of the beans.

4 slices bacon, chopped fine
½ pound deli ham, chopped fine
1 onion, chopped fine
4 garlic cloves, minced
1 pound pink kidney beans, soaked in 6 cups water overnight and drained
6 cups water
1 cup canned tomato puree
½ cup bottled taco sauce
5 tablespoons packed light brown sugar
1 tablespoon dry mustard
   Salt
¼ cup chopped fresh cilantro
2 tablespoons cider vinegar

1. Cook bacon and ham in Dutch oven over medium heat until fat renders and bacon and ham are lightly browned, 5 to 7 minutes. Add onion and cook until softened, about 5 minutes. Stir in garlic and cook until fragrant, about 30 seconds. Add beans and water and bring to simmer. Reduce heat to medium-low, cover, and cook until beans are just soft, about 1 hour.

2. Stir in tomato puree, taco sauce, sugar, dry mustard, and 2 teaspoons salt. Continue to simmer, uncovered, until beans are completely tender and sauce is thickened, about 1 hour. (If mixture becomes too thick, add water.) Stir in cilantro and vinegar and season with salt. Serve. (Beans can be refrigerated for up to 4 days.)

Sorting Dried Beans

It is important to rinse and pick over dried beans to remove any stones or debris before cooking. To make the task easier, sort dried beans on a large white plate or on a white, rimmed cutting board. The neutral background makes any unwanted matter a cinch to spot and discard.

Quick-Soaking Beans

If you don't want to soak the beans overnight, there is a faster way. Simply cover the beans with water in a Dutch oven, bring them to a boil over high heat, and let them boil for 5 minutes. Remove the beans from the heat and allow them to sit, covered, in the hot water for 1 hour. Drain the beans and proceed with the recipe as directed. The quick-soaked beans taste just as good as beans that are soaked overnight.

Why This Recipe Works California barbecued beans recipes use a bean variety and chili sauce rarely found outside of California. We wanted to re-create this recipe with nationally available supermarket ingredients. Pink kidney beans proved to be a good stand-in for the hard-to-find pinquito beans. Some recipes suggest using jarred taco sauce alone if the original recipe's requisite red chili sauce can't be found, but we found its taste and texture too thin. Instead, augmenting the sauce with a combination of fried bacon, ham, onion, and garlic with tomato puree, brown sugar, and dry mustard perfectly captured the chili sauce's bite.

GRILLED POTATO HOBO PACKS

SERVES 4

To keep the packs from tearing, use heavy-duty aluminum foil or two layers of regular foil. Also, scrape the cooking grate clean before grilling.

- 2 pounds Yukon Gold potatoes (about 3 large), scrubbed
- 1 tablespoon olive oil
- 2 garlic cloves, peeled and chopped
- 1 teaspoon minced fresh thyme
- 1 teaspoon salt
- ½ teaspoon pepper

1. Cut each potato in half crosswise, then cut each half into 8 wedges. Place potatoes in large bowl and wrap tightly with plastic wrap. Microwave until edges of potatoes are translucent, 4 to 7 minutes, shaking bowl (without removing plastic) to redistribute potatoes halfway through cooking. Carefully remove plastic and drain well. Gently toss potatoes with oil, garlic, thyme, salt, and pepper.

2. Cut four 14 by 10-inch sheets of heavy-duty aluminum foil. Working with 1 at a time, spread one-quarter of potato mixture over half of foil, fold foil over potatoes, and crimp edges tightly to seal.

3A. For a Charcoal Grill Open bottom vent completely. Light large chimney starter filled with charcoal briquettes (6 quarts). When top coals are partially covered with ash, pour evenly over grill. Set cooking grate in place, cover, and open lid vent completely. Heat grill until hot, about 5 minutes.

3B. For a Gas Grill Turn all burners to medium-high, cover, and heat grill until hot, about 15 minutes.

4. Grill hobo packs over hot fire, covered, until potatoes are completely tender, about 10 minutes, flipping packs halfway through cooking. Cut open foil and serve.

SPANISH-STYLE GRILLED POTATO HOBO PACKS
Prepare Grilled Potato Hobo Packs, adding 6 ounces thinly sliced cured chorizo sausage, 1 seeded and chopped red bell pepper, and 1 teaspoon paprika to cooked potatoes as they are tossed in step 1.

VINEGAR AND ONION GRILLED POTATO HOBO PACKS
Prepare Grilled Potato Hobo Packs, microwaving 1 halved and thinly sliced small onion with potatoes in step 1. Add 2 tablespoons white wine or red wine vinegar to cooked potatoes as they are tossed in step 1.

SPICY HOME FRY GRILLED POTATO HOBO PACKS
Prepare Grilled Potato Hobo Packs, omitting chopped garlic. Add 1 teaspoon paprika, ½ teaspoon garlic powder, ½ teaspoon onion powder, and ¼ teaspoon cayenne pepper to cooked potatoes as they are tossed in step 1.

Making Potato Hobo Packs

1. Microwave potatoes first to help them cook quickly on grill.

2. Arrange microwaved potatoes on foil, fold over, and crimp.

3. Flip packs halfway through grilling for evenly charred potatoes.

Why This Recipe Works We wanted to rescue this campfire classic, which too often results in unevenly cooked spuds. After multiple tests, we found that Yukon Golds were preferred to starchy, mealy russets and "slippery" red potatoes. To ensure evenly grilled potatoes, we cut them into evenly sized wedges and microwaved them for a few minutes before grilling them. Tossing the potatoes with a little oil prevented them from sticking to the foil.

Why This Recipe Works Steaming or sautéing broccoli is fine, but if you want vivid green florets with flavorful char, there's no beating the grill. To avoid toughness, we peeled the stalks with a vegetable peeler and cut the head into spears small enough to cook quickly but large enough to grill easily. Since grilling alone would yield dry broccoli, we tossed the spears in olive oil and water and steamed them in sealed foil packets on the grill. As soon as the stems and florets were evenly cooked, we placed them directly on the grill to give them plenty of char. A squeeze of grilled lemon and a sprinkling of Parmesan sealed the deal.

GRILLED BROCCOLI WITH LEMON AND PARMESAN

SERVES 4

To keep the packs from tearing, use heavy-duty aluminum foil. Use the large holes of a box grater to shred the Parmesan.

- ¼ cup extra-virgin olive oil, plus extra for drizzling
- 1 tablespoon water
  Salt and pepper
- 2 pounds broccoli
- 1 lemon, halved
- ¼ cup shredded Parmesan cheese

1. Cut two 26 by 12-inch sheets of heavy-duty aluminum foil. Whisk oil, water, ¾ teaspoon salt, and ½ teaspoon pepper together in large bowl.

2. Trim stalk ends so each entire head of broccoli measures 6 to 7 inches long. Using vegetable peeler, peel away tough outer layer of broccoli stalks (about ⅛ inch). Cut stalks in half lengthwise into spears (stems should be ½ to ¾ inch thick and florets 3 to 4 inches wide). Add broccoli spears to oil mixture and toss well to coat.

3. Divide broccoli between sheets of foil, cut side down and alternating direction of florets and stems. Bring short sides of foil together and crimp tightly. Crimp long ends to seal packs tightly.

4A. For a Charcoal Grill Open bottom vent completely. Light large chimney starter filled with charcoal briquettes (6 quarts). When top coals are partially covered with ash, pour evenly over half of grill. Set cooking grate in place, cover, and open lid vent completely. Heat grill until hot, about 5 minutes.

4B. For a Gas Grill Turn all burners to high, cover, and heat grill until hot, about 15 minutes. Turn all burners to medium-high. (Adjust burners as needed to maintain grill temperature around 400 degrees.)

5. Clean and oil cooking grate. Arrange packs evenly on grill (over coals if using charcoal), cover, and cook for 8 minutes, flipping packs halfway through cooking.

6. Transfer packs to rimmed baking sheet and, using scissors, carefully cut open, allowing steam to escape away from you. (Broccoli should be bright green and fork inserted into stems should meet some resistance.)

7. Discard foil and place broccoli and lemon halves cut side down on grill (over coals if using charcoal). Grill (covered if using gas), turning broccoli about every 2 minutes, until stems are fork-tender and well charred on all sides, 6 to 8 minutes total. Transfer broccoli to now-empty sheet as it finishes cooking. Grill lemon halves until well charred on cut side, 6 to 8 minutes.

8. Transfer broccoli to cutting board and cut into 2-inch pieces; transfer to platter. Season with salt and pepper to taste. Squeeze lemon over broccoli to taste, sprinkle with Parmesan, and drizzle with extra oil. Serve.

GRILLED BROCCOLI WITH ANCHOVY-GARLIC BUTTER

Omit lemon and Parmesan cheese. In step 1, whisk together 4 tablespoons melted unsalted butter, 3 rinsed and minced anchovy fillets, 1 minced garlic clove, 1 teaspoon lemon juice, ¼ teaspoon red pepper flakes, ½ teaspoon salt, and ⅛ teaspoon pepper. Set aside, then rewarm in step 8 and drizzle over broccoli before serving.

GRILLED BROCCOLI WITH SWEET CHILI SAUCE

Omit lemon and Parmesan cheese. In step 1, whisk together 4 teaspoons toasted sesame oil, 1 teaspoon distilled white vinegar, 2½ teaspoons sugar, 2 teaspoons Asian chili-garlic sauce, and ¼ teaspoon salt. Set aside, then drizzle over broccoli before serving.

GRILLED CAESAR SALAD

SERVES 6

Our favorite Parmesan cheese is Boar's Head Parmigiano-Reggiano.

Dressing
1 tablespoon lemon juice
1 garlic clove, minced
½ cup mayonnaise
½ ounce Parmesan cheese, grated (¼ cup)
1 tablespoon white wine vinegar
1 tablespoon Worcestershire sauce
1 tablespoon Dijon mustard
2 anchovy fillets, rinsed
½ teaspoon salt
½ teaspoon pepper
¼ cup extra-virgin olive oil

Salad
1 (12-inch) baguette, cut on bias into 5-inch-long, ½-inch-thick slices
3 tablespoons extra-virgin olive oil
1 garlic clove, peeled
3 romaine lettuce hearts (18 ounces), halved lengthwise through cores
½ ounce Parmesan cheese, grated (¼ cup)

1. For the Dressing Combine lemon juice and garlic in bowl and let stand for 10 minutes. Process mayonnaise, Parmesan, lemon-garlic mixture, vinegar, Worcestershire, mustard, anchovies, salt, and pepper in blender for about 30 seconds. With blender running, slowly add oil. Reserve 6 tablespoons dressing for brushing romaine.

2A. For a Charcoal Grill Open bottom vent completely. Light large chimney starter filled with charcoal briquettes (6 quarts). When top coals are partially covered with ash, pour evenly over half of grill. Set cooking grate in place, cover, and open lid vent completely. Heat grill until hot, about 5 minutes.

2B. For a Gas Grill Turn all burners to high, cover, and heat grill until hot, about 15 minutes. Leave all burners on high.

3. For the Salad Clean and oil cooking grate. Brush bread with oil and grill (over coals if using charcoal), uncovered, until browned, about 1 minute per side. Transfer to platter and rub with garlic clove. Brush cut sides of romaine with reserved dressing; place half of romaine, cut side down, on grill (over coals if using charcoal). Grill, uncovered, until lightly charred, 1 to 2 minutes. Move to platter with bread. Repeat. Drizzle romaine with remaining dressing. Sprinkle with Parmesan. Serve.

Salad Prep for Grilled Caesar
We get twice the flavor by using the dressing before and after grilling.

1. Brush homemade Caesar dressing onto halved romaine hearts before grilling.

2. Grill dressed romaine halves on just one side to keep lettuce from wilting.

3. Once charred lettuce comes off grill, finish with more Caesar dressing.

Why This Recipe Works Grilled salad may seem like an oxymoron, but we were intrigued by the idea of the flavors of a classic Caesar salad enriched with the smoky char of the grill. We found that compact romaine hearts held their shape better than whole heads. We halved them lengthwise to increase their surface area, making sure to keep the core intact so the leaves didn't fall apart on the grill. To prevent sticking, we brushed the leaves with dressing. Just 1 to 2 minutes over a hot grill gave us a smoky and charred (not wilted) exterior. To keep things simple, we replaced the croutons with slices of crusty bread grilled alongside the lettuce.

Why This Recipe Works We wanted to discover the secrets to tender cabbage, crunchy apples, and the sweet and spicy dressing that brings them together in this Southern barbecue side dish. Because cabbage is relatively watery, we salted the cut cabbage to draw out excess moisture before dressing it, which prevented moisture from diluting the dressing later and leaving us with a watery slaw. Granny Smith apples work best in this slaw recipe—tasters loved their sturdy crunch and tart bite. Cider vinegar gave the dressing a fruity flavor, while red pepper flakes, chopped scallions, and mustard added some punch.

TANGY APPLE CABBAGE SLAW

SERVES 6 TO 8

In step 1, the salted, rinsed, and dried cabbage can be refrigerated in a zipper-lock bag for up to 24 hours. To prep the apples, cut the cored apples into ¼-inch-thick planks, then stack the planks and cut them into thin matchsticks.

- 1 medium head green cabbage (2 pounds), cored and chopped fine (12 cups)
- 2 teaspoons salt
- 2 Granny Smith apples, cored and cut into thin matchsticks
- 2 scallions, sliced thin
- 6 tablespoons vegetable oil
- ½ cup cider vinegar
- ½ cup sugar
- 1 tablespoon Dijon mustard
- ¼ teaspoon red pepper flakes

1. Toss cabbage and salt in colander set over medium bowl. Let stand until wilted, about 1 hour. Rinse cabbage under cold water, drain, dry well with paper towels, and transfer to large bowl. Add apples and scallions and toss to combine.

2. Bring oil, vinegar, sugar, mustard, and pepper flakes to boil in saucepan over medium heat. Pour over cabbage mixture and toss to coat. Cover with plastic wrap and refrigerate at least 1 hour or up to 1 day. Serve.

Cutting Apples for Slaw

1. Cut each side of apple squarely away from core and cut each piece into ¼-inch-thick slices.

2. Stack planks and cut them into thin matchsticks.

Vinegar Primer

Although cider vinegar and white vinegar are made by the same process, the similarities end there. Vinegar is made by turning fermented liquid into acetic acid by adding certain bacteria to the liquid. Cider and distilled vinegars are made by the same process but start with different liquids: Cider vinegar begins with apple cider and distilled vinegar with ethyl alcohol (also known as grain alcohol). Although both vinegars are commonly used in pickle recipes (and are often substituted for each other), they do have distinctly different flavors. We like to use sweeter cider vinegar in sweet pickles, reserving white vinegar for applications such as sour pickles, where we want acidity without added flavor. While cider vinegar is fine in a sweet salad dressing, we don't think distilled vinegar adds much to any dressing. In general, we find that vinegars that start with wine are the best choice for salad dressings.

CIDER VINEGAR
Sweet cider vinegar begins with apple cider.

DISTILLED VINEGAR
Acidic distilled vinegar begins with ethyl alcohol.

Why This Recipe Works The high water content of cabbage is typically to blame for watery slaws. We salted our cabbage to draw out the excess moisture. Memphis Chopped Coleslaw is usually studded with celery seeds and crunchy green peppers and tossed with an unapologetically sugary mustard dressing that's balanced by a bracing hit of vinegar. To ensure our slaw boasted brash, balanced flavor, we quickly cooked the spicy dressing to meld the flavors and tossed the hot dressing with the cabbage. The salted cabbage absorbed the dressing and became seasoned inside and out.

MEMPHIS CHOPPED COLESLAW

SERVES 8 TO 10

In step 1, the salted, rinsed, and dried cabbage mixture can be refrigerated in a zipper-lock bag for up to 24 hours.

1 head green cabbage (2 pounds), cored and chopped fine (12 cups)
1 jalapeño chile, stemmed, seeded, and minced
1 carrot, peeled and shredded on box grater
1 small onion, peeled and shredded on box grater
2 teaspoons salt
¼ cup yellow mustard
¼ cup chili sauce
¼ cup mayonnaise
¼ cup sour cream
¼ cup cider vinegar
1 teaspoon celery seeds
⅔ cup packed light brown sugar

1. Toss cabbage, jalapeño, carrot, onion, and salt in colander set over medium bowl. Let stand until wilted, about 1 hour. Rinse cabbage mixture under cold water, drain, dry well with paper towels, and transfer to large bowl.

2. Bring mustard, chili sauce, mayonnaise, sour cream, vinegar, celery seeds, and sugar to boil in saucepan over medium heat. Pour over cabbage and toss to coat. Cover with plastic wrap and refrigerate 1 hour or up to 1 day. Serve.

How to Chop Cabbage

1. Cut cabbage into quarters, then trim and discard hard core.

2. Separate cabbage into small stacks of leaves that flatten when pressed.

3. Cut each stack of cabbage leaves into ¼-inch strips.

4. Cut strips into ¼-inch pieces.

ALL-AMERICAN POTATO SALAD

SERVES 4 TO 6

Make sure not to overcook the potatoes or the salad will be quite sloppy. Keep the water at a gentle simmer and use the tip of a paring knife to judge the doneness of the potatoes. If the knife inserts easily into the potato pieces, they are done.

2 large eggs
   Salt
2 pounds Yukon Gold potatoes, peeled and cut into ¾-inch cubes
3 tablespoons dill pickle juice, plus ¼ cup finely chopped dill pickles
1 tablespoon yellow mustard
¼ teaspoon pepper
½ teaspoon celery seeds
½ cup mayonnaise
¼ cup sour cream
½ small red onion, chopped fine
1 celery rib, chopped fine

1. Bring eggs, 1½ teaspoons salt, and 1 quart water to boil in small saucepan. Remove pan from heat, cover and let sit for 10 minutes. Transfer eggs to bowl filled with ice water and let cool for 5 minutes, then peel and chop coarse.

2. Place potatoes in large saucepan with cold water to cover by 1 inch. Bring to boil over high heat, add 1 teaspoon salt, reduce heat to medium-low, and simmer until potatoes are tender, 10 to 15 minutes.

3. Drain potatoes thoroughly, then spread out on rimmed baking sheet. Mix 2 tablespoons pickle juice and mustard together in small bowl, drizzle pickle juice mixture over hot potatoes, and toss until evenly coated. Refrigerate until cooled, about 30 minutes.

4. Mix remaining tablespoon pickle juice, chopped pickles, ½ teaspoon salt, pepper, celery seeds, mayonnaise, sour cream, red onion, and celery in large bowl. Toss in cooled potatoes, cover, and refrigerate until well chilled, about 30 minutes. (Salad can be refrigerated for up to 2 days.) Gently stir in eggs, just before serving.

Don't Throw Out the Juice

Pickle juice tossed with just-cooked potatoes gives them a tangy flavor that's not as harsh as straight vinegar and has a gentle sweetness, too.

Why This Recipe Works For flavorful all-American potato salad, we decided to use firm-textured Yukon Gold potatoes because they hold their shape after cooking and won't turn mushy in the salad. Our recipe benefited from the sweetness of an unexpected ingredient: pickle juice. We drizzled the still-warm potatoes with a mixture of pickle juice and mustard. The hot potatoes easily absorbed the acidic liquid and tasted seasoned through to the middle. A combination of mayonnaise and sour cream formed the base of our creamy dressing, seasoned with classic additions like celery seeds, celery, and chopped hard-cooked eggs.

SMOKY POTATO SALAD

SERVES 8

Use small red potatoes 1½ to 2 inches in diameter. If you don't have 2 tablespoons of fat in the skillet after frying the bacon, add olive oil to make up the difference.

- 6 slices bacon
- 3 tablespoons red wine vinegar
- 2 tablespoons mayonnaise
- 2 teaspoons minced canned chipotle chile in adobo sauce
  Salt and pepper
- 3 tablespoons olive oil, plus extra for brushing
- 3 pounds small red potatoes, unpeeled, halved
- 1 large onion, sliced into ½-inch-thick rounds
- 4 scallions, sliced thin

1. Cook bacon in 12-inch skillet over medium heat until crisp, 7 to 9 minutes; transfer to paper towel–lined plate. Set aside 2 tablespoons bacon fat. When cool enough to handle, crumble bacon and set aside. Whisk vinegar, mayonnaise, chile, ½ teaspoon salt, and ½ teaspoon pepper together in large bowl. Slowly whisk in 3 tablespoons oil until combined; set aside.

2A. For a Charcoal Grill Open bottom vent completely. Light large chimney starter three-quarters filled with charcoal briquettes (4½ quarts). When top coals are partially covered with ash, pour evenly over grill. Set cooking grate in place, cover, and open lid vent completely. Heat grill until hot, about 5 minutes.

2B. For a Gas Grill Turn all burners to high, cover, and heat grill until hot, about 15 minutes. Turn all burners to medium.

3. Clean and oil cooking grate. Toss potatoes with reserved bacon fat and ½ teaspoon salt. Push a toothpick horizontally through each onion round to keep rings intact while grilling. Brush onion rounds lightly with extra oil and season with salt and pepper. Place potatoes, cut side down, and onion rounds on grill and cook, covered, until charred on first side, 10 to 14 minutes.

4. Flip potatoes and onion rounds and continue to cook, covered, until well browned all over and potatoes are easily pierced with tip of paring knife, 10 to 16 minutes longer. Transfer potatoes and onion rounds to rimmed baking sheet and let cool slightly.

5. When cool enough to handle, halve potatoes; remove toothpicks and coarsely chop onion rounds. Add potatoes, onion, scallions, and bacon to dressing and toss to combine. Season with salt and pepper to taste. Serve warm or at room temperature.

Why This Recipe Works For a summery potato salad cooked on the grill from start to finish featuring smoky, tender potatoes with crispy outsides, we began with halved, unpeeled red potatoes: The skin helped them to stay intact, and their firm, waxy texture stood up to the heat of the grill. Prior to grilling, we coated the potatoes with flavorful bacon fat. For even more smokiness, we grilled rounds of onions along with the potatoes. A spicy, smoky vinaigrette with a touch of mayo, chipotle, and crumbled bacon was the perfect match for this backyard-ready potato salad.

Why This Recipe Works Amish potato salad is distinct for its creamy cooked dressing and sweet-and-sour flavor. We modernized this recipe by ditching the labor-intensive dressing, which is traditionally enriched with eggs and gently cooked over a double-boiler. To keep the rich taste with less work, we processed a hard-cooked egg yolk into the dressing base of vinegar and sugar. Sprinkling a few tablespoons of the tangy dressing over the hot potatoes infused them with flavor. Then we tossed the cooled potatoes with the rest of the dressing, enriched with sour cream, for a cool, creamy potato salad with great old-fashioned flavor.

AMISH POTATO SALAD

SERVES 8

You can substitute an equal amount of celery salt for the celery seed, but if you do, eliminate the table salt from the dressing. Make sure to use sturdy Yukon Golds here; fluffy russets will fall apart in the salad.

3 pounds Yukon Gold potatoes, peeled and cut into ¾-inch chunks
Salt and pepper
⅓ cup cider vinegar
¼ cup sugar
2 tablespoons yellow mustard
4 large hard-cooked eggs, peeled (recipe follows)
½ teaspoon celery seeds
¾ cup sour cream
1 celery rib, chopped fine

1. Bring potatoes, 1 tablespoon salt, and enough water to cover by 1 inch to boil in large pot over high heat. Reduce heat to medium and simmer until potatoes are just tender, about 10 minutes.

2. Meanwhile, microwave vinegar and sugar in small bowl until sugar dissolves, about 30 seconds. Process vinegar mixture, mustard, 1 hard-cooked egg yolk (reserve white), celery seeds, and ½ teaspoon salt in food processor until smooth, about 30 seconds. Transfer to medium bowl.

3. Drain potatoes thoroughly and transfer to large bowl. Drizzle 2 tablespoons dressing over hot potatoes and, using rubber spatula, gently toss until evenly coated. Refrigerate until cooled, at least 30 minutes, stirring gently once to redistribute dressing.

4. Whisk sour cream into remaining dressing. Add reserved egg white and 3 hard-cooked eggs to dressing and, using potato masher, mash until only small pieces remain. Add dressing and celery to cooled potatoes, tossing gently to combine. Cover and refrigerate until chilled, about 30 minutes. Season with salt and pepper to taste. Serve. (Salad can be refrigerated for up to 2 days.)

FOOLPROOF HARD-COOKED EGGS
MAKES 4 EGGS
You can double or triple this recipe as long as you use a pot large enough to hold the eggs in a single later, covered by an inch of water.

4 large eggs

Bring eggs and enough water to cover by 1 inch to boil in medium saucepan over high heat. Remove pan from heat, cover, and let sit 10 minutes. Meanwhile, fill medium bowl with 4 cups water and 1 tray of ice cubes. Transfer eggs to ice water bath with slotted spoon; let sit for 5 minutes. Peel eggs.

Sweet on Sweet-and-Sour

Like most other resourceful Colonial Americans, the Amish turned to pickling as a way to preserve fruits and vegetables for long (prerefrigeration) winters. It wasn't just practicality that drove them to pickling, however. The Amish people's penchant for these sweet-and-sour flavors is also rooted in the group's native Germany, where rich dishes are often finished with a splash of vinegar or served with vinegar-spiked sides, such as sauerkraut. The Amish table, it's said, is incomplete without "seven sweets and seven sours." A cornucopia of delicious foods reflects this Amish predilection, from watermelon rind and cantaloupe pickles to chow chow, pickled beets and eggs, and Amish potato salad, which is seasoned with plenty of vinegar and sugar.

RANCH POTATO SALAD

SERVES 6 TO 8

We prefer white wine vinegar here, but white and cider vinegars are acceptable substitutes.

- 3 pounds red potatoes, peeled and cut into ¾-inch chunks
  Salt
- ¾ cup mayonnaise
- ½ cup buttermilk
- ¼ cup white wine vinegar
- ¼ cup drained jarred roasted red peppers, chopped fine
- 3 tablespoons finely chopped fresh cilantro
- 3 scallions, chopped fine
- 1 garlic clove, minced
- ⅛ teaspoon dried dill
- 2 teaspoons pepper
- 2 tablespoons Dijon mustard

1. Bring potatoes, 1 tablespoon salt, and enough water to cover potatoes by 1 inch to boil in large pot over high heat. Reduce heat to medium and simmer until potatoes are just tender, about 10 minutes. While potatoes simmer, whisk mayonnaise, buttermilk, 2 tablespoons vinegar, red peppers, cilantro, scallions, garlic, dill, 1 teaspoon salt, and pepper in large bowl.

2. Drain potatoes thoroughly, then spread out on rimmed baking sheet. Whisk mustard and remaining vinegar in small bowl. Drizzle mustard mixture over hot potatoes and toss until evenly coated. Refrigerate until cooled, about 30 minutes.

3. Transfer cooled potatoes to bowl with mayonnaise mixture and toss to combine. Cover and refrigerate until well chilled, about 30 minutes. Serve. (Salad can be refrigerated for up to 2 days.)

Better Potato Texture, and Faster, Too

We discovered some interesting information about boiling potatoes while developing our recipe for Ranch Potato Salad. Most recipes for boiled potatoes call for starting the spuds in cold water so that they will come up to temperature slowly and cook evenly throughout. In an attempt to shorten the cooking time, we tried letting the water boil before adding the potatoes. In a side-by-side test, we weren't surprised that tasters preferred the potatoes started in cold water for their uniformly creamy texture. We were surprised, however, to find that the total cooking time for potatoes started in cold water was less than for those started in boiling water.

Hidden Valley Ranch Dressing

The original ranch dressing first became popular at the Hidden Valley Guest Ranch near Santa Barbara, Calif., in the late 1950s. It began as a dried herb mixture that Steve Henson, the ranch's owner, combined with mayonnaise and buttermilk to make a creamy, tangy dressing for the ranch's house salad. It was so well received that guests clamored for bottles of the dressing to take home with them. Recognizing the potential of his concoction, Henson began marketing the mix in small packets, and the rest is culinary history. The little packets are still around, but the dressing really took off in 1983 when manufacturers figured out how to bottle this creamy dressing in a shelf-stable format.

Why This Recipe Works Bottled ranch dressing sounds like a quick way to dress up potato salad, but many recipes are surprisingly dull and bland. We found that peeling the potatoes (we liked red spuds) allowed them to absorb more dressing. For the dressing, we doubled the amount of cilantro used in most recipes and added fresh garlic and scallions for a welcome bite. Dijon mustard and vinegar provided acidity and bite, while chopped roasted red peppers made a sweet counterpoint. To better season the potatoes, we tossed the hot spuds first with just the Dijon mustard and vinegar. And just a dash of dried dill lent more herb flavor.

Why This Recipe Works We wanted potato salad with vibrant dill flavor through and through. To do so, we seasoned our potato salad with three rounds of dill: first as an herb sachet while the potatoes simmered, next as a piquant dill vinegar, and finally as a fresh sprinkle. A dressing based on a combination of creamy mayonnaise and tangy sour cream, accented with Dijon mustard, provided the perfect backdrop for our dill flavor to shine.

DILL POTATO SALAD

SERVES 8

Use both dill stems and chopped leaves (sometimes called fronds) in the herb sachet. Trois Petits Cochons is our favorite brand of Dijon mustard.

¼ cup white wine vinegar
3 tablespoons minced fresh dill, plus ½ cup leaves and stems, chopped coarse
3 pounds Yukon Gold potatoes, peeled and cut into ¾-inch pieces
Salt and pepper
½ cup mayonnaise
¼ cup sour cream
1 tablespoon Dijon mustard
3 scallions, green parts only, sliced thin

1. Combine vinegar and 1 tablespoon minced dill in bowl and microwave until steaming, 30 to 60 seconds. Set at room temperature until cool, 15 to 20 minutes.

2. Meanwhile, place chopped dill inside disposable coffee filter and tie closed with kitchen twine. Bring potatoes, dill sachet, 1 tablespoon salt, and enough water to cover potatoes by 1 inch to boil in large pot over high heat. Reduce heat to medium and simmer until potatoes are just tender, about 10 minutes.

3. Drain potatoes thoroughly, then transfer to large bowl; discard sachet. Drizzle 2 tablespoons dill vinegar over hot potatoes and gently toss until evenly coated. Refrigerate until cooled, about 30 minutes, stirring once.

4. Whisk mayonnaise, sour cream, remaining dill vinegar, mustard, ½ teaspoon salt, and ¼ teaspoon pepper together until smooth. Add dressing to cooled potatoes. Stir in scallions and remaining 2 tablespoons minced dill. Cover and refrigerate to let flavors meld, about 30 minutes. Season with salt and pepper to taste. Serve. (Salad can be refrigerated for up to 2 days.)

Dill Three Ways

Three rounds of fresh dill season our Dill Potato Salad.

Infuse
We add a packet of chopped dill to the water in which the potatoes simmer.

Marinate
We steep vinegar with minced dill and use it to dress the hot potatoes.

Mince
We sprinkle extra minced dill over the dressed potato salad.

Why This Recipe Works Texans take their potato salad up a notch with plenty of mustard and spicy chopped jalapeños. For our version, we started with classic potato salad, using firm Yukon Gold potatoes, which have a rich earthy flavor and hold their shape after cooking, and a mayonnaise-based dressing seasoned with onion, celery seeds, and dill pickles. To this we added plenty of bold yellow mustard and spicy jalapeños. We tempered the jalapeños' raw bite by quick-pickling them in a mixture of vinegar, sugar, and mustard seeds. We used the leftover pickling solution to flavor the hot potatoes. A pinch of cayenne added extra kick.

TEXAS POTATO SALAD

SERVES 8

Annie's Naturals Organic Yellow Mustard is our favorite brand of yellow mustard.

½ cup red wine vinegar
1½ tablespoons sugar
   Salt and pepper
1 teaspoon yellow mustard seeds
½ small red onion, sliced thin
2 jalapeño chiles (1 sliced into thin rings; 1 stemmed, seeded, and minced)
3 pounds Yukon Gold potatoes, peeled and cut into ¾-inch pieces
6 tablespoons mayonnaise
6 tablespoons yellow mustard
¼ teaspoon cayenne pepper
2 large hard-cooked eggs, cut into ¼-inch pieces
1 celery rib, minced

1. Combine vinegar, sugar, 1½ teaspoons salt, and mustard seeds in bowl and microwave until steaming, about 2 minutes. Whisk until sugar and salt are dissolved. Add onion and jalapeños and set aside until cool, 15 to 20 minutes. Strain onion and jalapeños through fine-mesh strainer set over bowl. Reserve pickled vegetables and vinegar mixture separately.

2. Meanwhile, combine potatoes, 8 cups water, and 1 tablespoon salt in Dutch oven and bring to boil over high heat. Reduce heat to medium and simmer until potatoes are just tender, 10 to 15 minutes.

3. Drain potatoes thoroughly, then transfer to large bowl. Drizzle 2 tablespoons reserved vinegar mixture over hot potatoes and toss gently until evenly coated. (Reserve remaining vinegar mixture for another use.) Refrigerate until cool, about 30 minutes, stirring once halfway through chilling.

4. Whisk mayonnaise, mustard, ½ teaspoon pepper, and cayenne together in bowl until combined. Add mayonnaise mixture, reserved pickled vegetables, eggs, and celery to potatoes and stir gently to combine. Season with salt and pepper to taste. Cover and refrigerate to let flavors blend, about 30 minutes. Serve. (Salad can be refrigerated for up to 2 days.)

Keeping Potato Salad Safe

Though mayonnaise is often blamed for spoiled potato salads, it is rarely the problem. In fact, it's the potatoes that are more likely to go bad. The bacteria usually responsible for spoiled potato salad is found in soil and dust, and it thrives on starchy foods like potatoes. No matter what kind of dressing you use, don't leave any potato salad out for more than 2 hours (1 hour if the temperature is above 90 degrees), and promptly refrigerate any leftovers in a covered container.

SMASHED POTATO SALAD

SERVES 8 TO 10

Use the tip of a paring knife to judge the doneness of the potatoes. If the tip inserts easily into the potato pieces, they are done. Hellmann's Real Mayonnaise is our favorite nationally available mayonnaise. Note that the salad needs to be refrigerated for about 2 hours before serving.

3 pounds Yukon Gold potatoes, unpeeled, cut into 1-inch chunks
  Salt and pepper
2 tablespoons distilled white vinegar
1 cup mayonnaise
3 tablespoons yellow mustard
¼ teaspoon cayenne pepper
3 hard-cooked large eggs, chopped
3 scallions, sliced thin
½ cup chopped sweet pickles
½ cup finely chopped celery
¼ cup finely chopped onion

1. Combine potatoes, 8 cups water, and 1 tablespoon salt in Dutch oven and bring to boil over high heat. Reduce heat to medium and cook at vigorous simmer until potatoes are tender, 14 to 17 minutes.

2. Drain potatoes in colander. Transfer 3 cups potatoes to large bowl, add 1 tablespoon vinegar, and coarsely mash with potato masher. Transfer remaining potatoes to rimmed baking sheet, drizzle with remaining 1 tablespoon vinegar, and toss gently to combine. Let cool completely, about 15 minutes.

3. Whisk mayonnaise, ½ cup water, mustard, cayenne, 1 teaspoon salt, and 1 teaspoon pepper together in bowl. Stir mayonnaise mixture into mashed potatoes. Fold in eggs, scallions, pickles, celery, onion, and remaining potatoes until combined. (Mixture will be lumpy.)

4. Cover and refrigerate until fully chilled, about 2 hours. Season with salt and pepper to taste. Serve.

Mayo Showdown

Commercial mayonnaise is one of the most hotly debated ingredients out there, with impassioned salad- and sandwich-makers insisting that only their favorite will do. Here are three of the most well-loved mayos.

HELLMANN'S
(Sold as Best Foods west of the Rockies) The most popular brand in the U.S., Hellmann's accounts for about half of all mayonnaise sales.

DUKE'S
This spread is made with cider vinegar, which gives it a sharp flavor. It has ardent fans in many Southern states.

BLUE PLATE
The test kitchen's favorite mayo is made with egg yolks, not whole eggs. It must be mail-ordered in most of the country.

Why This Recipe Works For our take on this Southern picnic staple, wanted both the creamy texture of mashed potatoes and the tender chunks of traditional potato salad. Yukon Gold potatoes worked best—their soft skins cooked up tender and saved us from peeling. For a mix of textures, we smashed a third of the boiled spuds with some vinegar before tossing the mashed portion with the cubes. Yellow mustard contributed some extra bite, which we balanced with chopped sweet pickles, and a touch of cayenne gave. Hard-cooked eggs, scallions, celery, and onion added even more textural variety to finish off our smooth-yet-chunky potato salad.

LEMON AND HERB RED POTATO SALAD

SERVES 8

To rinse the onion, place it in a fine-mesh strainer and run it under cold water. This removes some of the onion's harshness. Drain, but do not rinse, the capers here.

- 3 pounds red potatoes, unpeeled, cut into 1-inch chunks
- 2 tablespoons distilled white vinegar
  Salt and pepper
- 2 teaspoons grated lemon zest plus 3 tablespoons juice
- ⅓ cup extra-virgin olive oil
- ½ cup finely chopped onion, rinsed
- 3 tablespoons minced fresh tarragon
- 3 tablespoons minced fresh parsley
- 3 tablespoons minced fresh chives
- 2 tablespoons capers, minced

1. Combine potatoes, 8 cups water, vinegar, and 2 tablespoons salt in Dutch oven and bring to boil over high heat. Reduce heat to medium and cook at strong simmer until potatoes are just tender, 10 to 15 minutes.

2. Meanwhile, whisk lemon zest and juice, 1 teaspoon salt, and ½ teaspoon pepper together in large bowl. Slowly whisk in oil until emulsified; set aside.

3. Drain potatoes thoroughly, then transfer to rimmed baking sheet. Drizzle 2 tablespoons dressing over hot potatoes and toss gently until evenly coated. Let potatoes cool, about 30 minutes, stirring once halfway through cooling.

4. Whisk dressing to recombine and stir in onion, tarragon, parsley, chives, and capers. Add cooled potatoes to dressing and stir gently to combine. Season with salt and pepper to taste. Serve warm or at room temperature.

Capers 101

Capers are actually pickles made from the unopened flower buds of the *Capparis spinosa* shrub, which grows in the Mediterranean. In France, Italy, and Spain, the shrubs are cultivated for capers, and Roquevaire, in Provence, is known as the "caper capital." Capers are never used fresh, and are preserved one of two ways: in a salt and water brine, sometimes with added vinegar, or in salt. More often, the flower buds are soaked in saltwater, then packed in brine or a mixture of brine and vinegar. This is how capers are sold in most supermarkets. The other option is to cure them with salt. This kind of caper costs more and is available only in specialty markets. Capers also vary in size, from the tiny non-pareilles to surfines, capucines, fines, and capotes—increasing in size and decreasing in value.

Why This Recipe Works Too often potato salad is weighed down by a heavy mayonnaise-based dressing; we sought a lighter alternative. We used waxy red potatoes, as they are lower in starch than russets and more colorful than Yukon Golds. To prevent them from breaking down too much, we added vinegar to the cooking water, giving us tender but firm potatoes that held their shape. A mixture of capers, olive oil, and lemon juice and zest complemented the potatoes' earthiness, while tarragon, parsley, and chives provided freshness. Adding some of the herbed vinaigrette while the potatoes were still hot ensured they best absorbed all of its flavor.

rise-and-shine breakfast and breads

Why This Recipe Works For a tall, fluffy diner-worthy omelet, we ditched the whisk for an electric mixer, which helped us incorporate air into the eggs. Cream added richness, but when we added it to the whipped eggs, the omelet lost its fluffiness. Combining the cream and eggs before whipping didn't work either—the fat in the cream made it impossible to whip air into the eggs. Instead, we whipped the dairy first, then folded it into the whipped eggs. After letting the bottom of the omelet set on the stovetop, we popped the skillet into a preheated oven, and just six minutes later had a puffy, fluffy omelet, cooked to perfection.

FLUFFY DINER-STYLE CHEESE OMELET

SERVES 2

Although this recipe will work with a stand mixer, a hand-held mixer makes quick work of whipping such a small amount of cream. To make two omelets, double this recipe and cook the omelets simultaneously in two skillets. If you have only one skillet, prepare a double batch of ingredients and set half aside for the second omelet. Be sure to wipe out the skillet in between omelets.

- 3 tablespoons heavy cream, chilled
- 5 large eggs, room temperature
- ¼ teaspoon salt
- 2 tablespoons unsalted butter
- 2 ounces sharp cheddar cheese, shredded (½ cup)
- 1 recipe omelet filling (optional) (recipes follow)

1. Adjust oven rack to middle position and heat oven to 400 degrees. Using stand mixer fitted with whisk, whip cream on medium-low speed until foamy, about 1 minute. Increase speed to high and whip until soft peaks form, 1 to 3 minutes. Set whipped cream aside. Using dry, clean bowl and whisk attachment, whip eggs and salt on high speed until frothy and eggs have tripled in size, about 2 minutes. Gently fold whipped cream into eggs.

2. Melt butter in ovensafe 10-inch nonstick skillet over medium-low heat, swirling pan to coat bottom and sides. Add egg mixture and cook until edges are nearly set, 2 to 3 minutes. Sprinkle with ¼ cup cheddar and half of omelet filling, if using, and transfer to oven. Bake until eggs are set and edges are beginning to brown, 6 to 8 minutes.

3. Carefully remove pan from oven (handle will be very hot), sprinkle eggs with remaining ¼ cup cheddar and remaining omelet filling, if using, and let sit, covered, until cheese begins to melt, about 1 minute. Tilt pan and, using rubber spatula, push half of omelet onto cutting board, then fold omelet over itself to form half-moon shape. Cut omelet in half and serve.

SAUSAGE AND PEPPER FILLING
MAKES ABOUT 1 CUP

- 4 ounces hot or sweet Italian sausage, casings removed
- 1 tablespoon unsalted butter
- 1 small onion, chopped
- ½ red bell pepper, chopped
  Salt and pepper

Cook sausage in 10-inch nonstick skillet over medium heat, breaking up clumps with wooden spoon, until browned, about 6 minutes. Transfer to paper towel–lined plate. Add butter, onion, and bell pepper to now-empty skillet and cook until softened, about 10 minutes. Stir in sausage and season with salt and pepper to taste.

LOADED BAKED POTATO FILLING
MAKES ABOUT 1 CUP

- 1 large Yukon Gold potato, peeled and cut into ½-inch pieces
- 4 slices bacon, chopped
- 2 scallions, sliced thin
  Salt and pepper

Microwave potato, covered, in large bowl until just tender, 2 to 5 minutes. Cook bacon in 10-inch nonstick skillet over medium heat until crisp, about 8 minutes. Transfer bacon to paper towel–lined plate; pour off all but 1 tablespoon bacon fat. Add potato to skillet and cook until golden brown, about 6 minutes. Transfer potato to bowl, add cooked bacon, and stir in scallions. Season with salt and pepper to taste.

Why This Recipe Works "Impossible" pie is a 1970s phenomenon that promises a pie "crust" without rolling out finicky dough. Traditionally, a simple Bisquick batter was whisked with eggs and poured over vegetables, meat, and cheese and baked. To give our "crust" a crispy, browned exterior, we buttered the pie dish and coated it with Parmesan cheese. We replaced the Bisquick with a simple batter of flour, baking powder, eggs, and creamy half-and-half. Doubling the number of eggs made for a richer, custardy pie. For the filling, we chose ingredients that required a minimum of prep work: scallions, diced deli ham, and Gruyère cheese.

"IMPOSSIBLE" HAM-AND-CHEESE PIE

SERVES 8

Use a rasp-style grater or the smallest holes on a box grater for the Parmesan.

- 1 tablespoon unsalted butter, softened, plus 2 tablespoons melted
- 3 tablespoons finely grated Parmesan cheese
- 8 ounces Gruyère cheese, shredded (2 cups)
- 4 ounces thickly sliced deli ham, chopped
- 4 scallions, minced
- ½ cup (2½ ounces) all-purpose flour
- ¾ teaspoon baking powder
- ½ teaspoon pepper
- ¼ teaspoon salt
- 1 cup half-and-half
- 4 large eggs, lightly beaten
- 2 teaspoons Dijon mustard
- ⅛ teaspoon ground nutmeg

1. Adjust oven rack to lowest position and heat oven to 350 degrees. Grease 9-inch pie plate with softened butter, then coat plate evenly with Parmesan.

2. Combine Gruyère, ham, and scallions in bowl. Sprinkle cheese-and-ham mixture evenly in bottom of prepared pie dish. Combine flour, baking powder, pepper, and salt in now-empty bowl. Whisk in half-and-half, eggs, melted butter, mustard, and nutmeg until smooth. Slowly pour batter over cheese-and-ham mixture in pie dish.

3. Bake until pie is light golden brown and filling is set, 30 to 35 minutes. Let cool on wire rack for 15 minutes. Slice into wedges. Serve warm.

Finger Food

To serve our "Impossible" Ham-and-Cheese Pie as an hors d'oeuvre at your next party, forgo the pie plate and instead bake it in an 8-inch square baking dish. Slice it into 1-inch squares and serve warm or at room temperature.

Grating Hard Cheese

Using a rasp-style grater to grate hard cheeses like Parmesan produces lighter, fluffier shreds that melt seamlessly into all kinds of dishes.

BREAKFAST PIZZA

SERVES 6

Small-curd cottage cheese is sometimes labeled "country-style." Room-temperature dough is much easier to shape than cold, so pull the dough from the fridge about 1 hour before you start cooking.

- 3 tablespoons extra-virgin olive oil, plus extra for drizzling
- 6 slices bacon
- 8 ounces mozzarella cheese, shredded (2 cups)
- 1 ounce Parmesan cheese, grated (½ cup)
- 4 ounces (½ cup) small-curd cottage cheese
- ¼ teaspoon dried oregano
  Salt and pepper
  Pinch cayenne pepper
- 1 pound store-bought pizza dough, room temperature
- 6 large eggs
- 2 scallions, sliced thin
- 2 tablespoons minced fresh chives

1. Adjust oven rack to lowest position and heat oven to 500 degrees. Grease rimmed baking sheet with 1 tablespoon oil.

2. Cook bacon in 12-inch skillet over medium heat until crisp, 7 to 9 minutes. Transfer to paper towel–lined plate; when cool enough to handle, crumble bacon. Combine mozzarella and Parmesan in bowl; set aside. Combine cottage cheese, oregano, ¼ teaspoon pepper, cayenne, and 1 tablespoon oil in separate bowl; set aside.

3. Press and roll dough into 15 by 11-inch rectangle on lightly floured counter, pulling on corners to help make distinct rectangle. Transfer dough to prepared sheet and press to edges of sheet. Brush edges of dough with remaining 1 tablespoon oil. Bake dough until top appears dry and bottom is just beginning to brown, about 5 minutes.

4. Remove crust from oven and, using spatula, press down on any air bubbles. Spread cottage cheese mixture evenly over top, leaving 1-inch border around edges. Sprinkle bacon evenly over cottage cheese mixture.

5. Sprinkle mozzarella mixture evenly over pizza, leaving ½-inch border. Create 2 rows of 3 evenly spaced small wells in cheese, each about 3 inches in diameter (6 wells total). Crack 1 egg into each well, then season each with salt and pepper.

6. Return pizza to oven and bake until crust is light golden around edges and eggs are just set, 9 to 10 minutes for slightly runny yolks or 11 to 12 minutes for soft-cooked yolks, rotating sheet halfway through baking.

7. Transfer pizza to wire rack and let cool for 5 minutes. Transfer pizza to cutting board. Sprinkle with scallions and chives and drizzle with extra oil. Slice and serve.

SMOKED SALMON BREAKFAST PIZZA

In step 7, after cooling, omit scallions and top pizza with ¼ cup sliced red onion, 3 ounces sliced smoked salmon (cut into thin strips), and ¼ cup sour cream. Sprinkle with chives and 1 tablespoon chopped fresh dill and drizzle with extra oil.

SAUSAGE AND RED BELL PEPPER BREAKFAST PIZZA

Substitute 6 ounces bulk breakfast sausage for bacon and extra-sharp cheddar for mozzarella. Combine sausage; 1 stemmed, seeded, and chopped red bell pepper; 1 chopped onion; and ¼ teaspoon salt in 12-inch skillet. Cook over medium heat, breaking up sausage with spoon, until sausage begins to brown and bell pepper and onion are translucent, about 6 minutes. Transfer to paper towel–lined plate. Let mixture cool completely before proceeding.

CHORIZO AND MANCHEGO BREAKFAST PIZZA

Substitute 6 ounces chorizo sausage, halved lengthwise and cut into ½-inch slices, for bacon and 1 cup shredded Manchego cheese for Parmesan. Cook chorizo in 12-inch skillet over medium heat until lightly browned, 7 to 9 minutes. Let cool completely before proceeding.

Why This Recipe Works Eggs and bacon on a cheese pizza? Sounded like an excellent breakfast to us. Our challenge was to achieve a crisp, golden-brown crust without overcooking the eggs. We gave the crust a head start by parbaking it for 5 minutes. The remaining oven time cooked the eggs and other toppings to perfection. To keep the eggs in place while they cooked, we created wells in the cheese. Though we initially used ricotta, it became dry and grainy in the oven. Then we tried cottage cheese and were pleasantly surprised to find the curds melted in the oven, leaving a creamy, silky cheese layer that tied everything together.

Why This Recipe Works Commercially made breakfast sausage always disappoints when it comes to flavor, tasting either too sweet or salty, or too bland or highly seasoned, so we decided to make our own. We started with ground pork with some fat in it (lean meat was neither fatty nor flavorful enough) and amped up its mild flavor with classic breakfast sausage flavors: garlic, sage, thyme, and cayenne pepper. A spoonful of maple syrup sweetened the patties nicely. To combine the meat mixture, we kneaded it gently with our hands, but were careful not to overmix it, which would toughen the meat.

HOMEMADE BREAKFAST SAUSAGE

MAKES 16 PATTIES

Avoid lean or extra-lean ground pork; it makes the sausage dry, crumbly, and less flavorful.

- 2 pounds ground pork
- 1 tablespoon maple syrup
- 1 garlic clove, minced
- 2 teaspoons dried sage
- 1½ teaspoons pepper
- 1 teaspoon salt
- ½ teaspoon dried thyme
- ⅛ teaspoon cayenne pepper
- 2 tablespoons unsalted butter

1. Combine pork, maple syrup, garlic, sage, pepper, salt, thyme, and cayenne in large bowl. Gently mix with hands until well combined. Using greased ¼-cup measure, divide mixture into 16 patties and place on rimmed baking sheet. Cover patties with plastic wrap, then gently flatten each one to ½-inch thickness.

2. Melt 1 tablespoon butter in 12-inch nonstick skillet over medium heat. Cook half of patties until well browned and cooked through, 6 to 10 minutes. Transfer to paper towel–lined plate and tent with aluminum foil. Wipe out skillet. Repeat with remaining butter and patties. Serve.

To Make Ahead Follow recipe through step 1. Refrigerate uncooked patties for up to 1 day or freeze for up to 1 month. To serve, proceed as directed in step 2, increasing cooking time to 14 to 18 minutes.

Dried Herbs

We use plenty of dried herbs in the test kitchen, but we don't use every dried herb. Delicate leafy herbs, such as basil, parsley, chives, mint, and cilantro become stale-tasting when dried. Heartier herbs, such as oregano, sage, and thyme, dry well and are good substitutes for fresh in most recipes—especially those in which the herbs will cook in liquid. We've found that tarragon and dill fall into a middle category: They do add flavor in their dried form, but that flavor is more muted than that provided by other dried herbs.

A few general rules: Use only half as much dried herbs as fresh, and add them at the same time as you would add fresh. Dried herbs lose potency 6 to 12 months after opening; you can test dried herbs for freshness by rubbing them between your fingers—if they don't smell bright, throw them away.

OREGANO
Great in tomato sauces, chili, Mexican and Latin dishes, and sprinkled on pizza. Dried does not have the same sharp bite as fresh, but it does have a distinct and recognizable floral element.

SAGE
We prefer rubbed (or finely crumbled) sage to the ground or chopped kinds. Use with poultry, stuffings, pork, full-flavored vegetables (like squash), and in butter sauces.

ROSEMARY
Works well in long-cooked dishes like soups, stews, and braises. Too much dried rosemary can turn a dish bitter, so use sparingly.

THYME
Good for long-cooked soups and stews and roasted meats and poultry; pairs well with mustard and lemon flavors.

SHORT-ORDER HOME FRIES

SERVES 4

Although we prefer the sweetness of Yukon Gold potatoes, other medium-starch potatoes, such as red potatoes, can be substituted. If you want to spice things up, add a pinch of cayenne pepper.

1½ pounds Yukon Gold potatoes, cut into ¾-inch pieces
4 tablespoons unsalted butter
1 onion, chopped fine
½ teaspoon garlic salt
½ teaspoon salt
Pepper

1. Place potatoes and 1 tablespoon butter in large bowl and microwave, covered, until edges of potatoes begin to soften, 5 to 7 minutes, stirring halfway through cooking.

2. Meanwhile, melt 1 tablespoon butter in 12-inch nonstick skillet over medium heat. Add onion and cook until softened and golden brown, 8 to 10 minutes. Transfer to small bowl.

3. Melt remaining 2 tablespoons butter in now-empty skillet over medium heat. Add potatoes and pack down with spatula. Cook, without moving, until bottoms of potatoes are brown, 5 to 7 minutes. Turn potatoes, pack down again, and continue to cook until well browned and crisp, 5 to 7 minutes. Reduce heat to medium-low and continue to cook until potatoes are crusty, 9 to 12 minutes, stirring occasionally. Stir in onion, garlic salt, and salt and season with pepper to taste. Serve.

GREEK DINER-STYLE HOME FRIES
Omit garlic salt and add 1 tablespoon lemon juice, 2 minced garlic cloves, and ½ teaspoon dried oregano to potatoes along with onion in step 3.

HOME FRIES WITH FRESH HERBS
Add 1 teaspoon each chopped fresh basil, parsley, thyme, and tarragon to potatoes along with onion in step 3.

The Right Spuds for Home Fries
High-starch, low-moisture potatoes, such as russets, may be great for baking and mashing, but when it comes to home fries, they are not the best choice. The fluffy flesh of these potatoes breaks down in the skillet, leaving nothing but a greasy pool of stodgy spuds. For tender tubers that retain their texture, we prefer medium-starch varieties, such as Yukon Gold and red potatoes. They hold their shape in the skillet, develop a great crust, and fry up to a beautiful golden brown.

RUSSET POTATOES
A falling-apart mess

YUKON GOLD POTATOES
Intact, crisp, and browned

Why This Recipe Works Though a commercial-grade griddle helps our local diner serve up home fries with a perfectly crispy exterior, the real secret is precooking the potatoes. Roasting or boiling our spuds took too much time for a quick breakfast side, so we turned to the microwave to jump-start their cooking before frying them in a large skillet. We found that packing the potatoes down with a spatula and cooking them a few minutes before turning them and then repeating these steps ensured they were evenly browned and extra-crunchy. Finally, we stirred in some sautéed onion and garlic salt to give our home fries a deep, savory flavor.

BETTER-THAN-THE-BOX PANCAKE MIX

MAKES ABOUT 6 CUPS; ENOUGH FOR 24 PANCAKES

Malted milk powder might seem odd here, but it gives the pancakes a deeper, more complex flavor.

- 2 cups (10 ounces) all-purpose flour
- 2 cups (8 ounces) cake flour
- 1 cup (3 ounces) nonfat dry milk powder
- ¾ cup (3⅓ ounces) malted milk powder
- ⅓ cup (2⅓ ounces) sugar
- 2 tablespoons baking powder
- 1 teaspoon baking soda
- 1 tablespoon salt
- 12 tablespoons unsalted butter, cut into ½-inch pieces

Process all ingredients in food processor until no lumps remain and mixture resembles wet sand, about 2 minutes. (Pancake mix can be frozen for up to 2 months.)

BETTER-THAN-THE-BOX PANCAKES

To make 8 pancakes, whisk 2 cups Better-Than-the-Box Pancake Mix, 2 lightly beaten large eggs, and ½ cup buttermilk in large bowl until smooth. Using ¼-cup measure, portion batter into lightly oiled 12-inch nonstick skillet or griddle in 4 places and cook over medium-low heat until golden brown, about 2 minutes per side. Repeat with remaining batter. Serve. (If you don't have buttermilk, whisk 1½ teaspoons lemon juice or white vinegar into ½ cup whole or low-fat milk and let sit until slightly thickened, about 10 minutes.)

Not Just for Milkshakes

To give our pancakes complexity and depth, we added malted milk powder to the mix. This product is made from malted barley that has been evaporated and pulverized, and sometimes includes flour or evaporated milk powder. Though it is more commonly used to make milkshakes, we found it added a sweet, nutty flavor to the pancakes made from our Better-Than-the-Box Pancake Mix.

Is the Pan Ready for Pancakes?

A properly heated pan or griddle is essential to making perfect, golden-brown, fluffy pancakes. A skillet that has not been properly heated and is too cool will produce pale, gummy pancakes. Here's a test to make sure your pan is hot enough: Drop a tablespoon of batter in its center. If, after one minute, the pancake is golden brown on the bottom, the pan is ready. If it remains blond—or is close to burning—adjust the heat accordingly.

PALE, GUMMY PANCAKE

PERFECT, FLUFFY PANCAKE

Why This Recipe Works For our take on pancake mix that delivers both store-bought ease and from-scratch taste, we combined all-purpose flour with cake flour; this duo yielded sturdy yet tender cakes. To give pancakes made from our mix complexity and depth, we added an unusual ingredient, malted milk powder, which imparted a sweet, nutty flavor. Though most mixes call for shortening, we opted for butter, which gave us moister, more flavorful pancakes. Using buttermilk instead of milk when mixing the batter gave us high-rising pancakes—the acid of the buttermilk reacts with the baking soda, causing the batter to bubble and rise.

Why This Recipe Works Getting the height and lightness of traditional pancakes with the robust flavor and texture of cornmeal pancakes is tougher than it seems. Coarsely ground cornmeal can be sandy, and it lacks the gluten necessary to support a fluffy internal structure. We found that we could use more cornmeal by heating it with some of the buttermilk to soften it first. Soaking the cornmeal also thickened the batter, helping it ride higher in the pan instead of spreading out. Letting the batter sit for a few minutes before griddling the cakes allowed the buttermilk to react with the baking soda, which resulted in fluffier, airier pancakes.

FLUFFY CORNMEAL PANCAKES

MAKES ABOUT 15 (4-INCH) PANCAKES

Our favorite cornmeal is Arrowhead Mills Organic Yellow Cornmeal.

1¾ cups buttermilk
1¼ cups (6¼ ounces) cornmeal
2 tablespoons unsalted butter,
    cut into ¼-inch pieces
¾ cup (3¾ ounces) all-purpose flour
2 tablespoons sugar
1¾ teaspoons baking powder
½ teaspoon baking soda
½ teaspoon salt
2 large eggs
2½ teaspoons vegetable oil

1. Adjust oven rack to middle position and heat oven to 200 degrees. Set wire rack inside rimmed baking sheet and place in oven. Whisk 1¼ cups buttermilk and cornmeal together in medium bowl. Stir in butter, cover, and microwave until slightly thickened around edges, about 90 seconds, stirring once halfway through cooking. Let sit, covered, for 5 minutes.

2. Whisk flour, sugar, baking powder, baking soda, and salt in large bowl. Beat eggs and remaining ½ cup buttermilk together in 1-cup liquid measuring cup. Whisk egg mixture into cornmeal mixture. Whisk cornmeal mixture into flour mixture. Let sit for 10 minutes.

3. Heat ½ teaspoon oil in 12-inch nonstick skillet over medium-low heat until shimmering. Using paper towels, carefully wipe out oil, leaving thin film on bottom of pan. Using level ¼-cup measure for each pancake, drop batter for 3 pancakes into pan.

Cook until edges are set and bubbles begin to form on tops of pancakes, about 90 seconds. Flip, then cook until second side is golden brown, about 2 minutes longer. Transfer to prepared baking sheet in oven, cover loosely with aluminum foil, and repeat with remaining oil and batter. Serve.

The Virtues of Pancake Patience

For the fluffiest pancakes, let the finished batter sit for 10 minutes before griddling the cakes. The rest gives the baking soda extra time to react and form large air bubbles, lightening the batter, ergo the pancakes. With a hearty whole grain like cornmeal, you want all the lift you can get. This trick works with any pancake batter made with whole grains.

Choosing the Right Cornmeal

Cornmeal, or ground processed corn kernels, is available in all manner of sizes for use in different applications. In most cases, we recommend choosing stone-ground over commercially produced cornmeal on two counts: First of all, stone-ground cornmeal has a more rustic texture because of the stone's rough grinding surface (companies like Quaker use smooth steel rollers that produce very fine, uniform cornmeal). And secondly, stone-ground cornmeal has a fuller flavor because it contains both the hull and oil-rich germ of the corn kernel, which commercial producers extract for better shelf life.

Why This Recipe Works A big, puffy pancake, a Dutch baby puffs and rises as it bakes, then falls in the center a few minutes out of the oven, resulting in a bowl-shaped breakfast treat with crisp sides and a thin, custardy bottom. For our version we started with a 12-inch skillet; its gently sloping walls promoted an even rise. Brushing the pan with oil and preheating it in the oven helped ensure the sides had the texture we wanted and jump-started the pancake's rise. Since fats tend to make baked goods tender rather than crisp, we used skim milk in our batter. For even more crispness, we replaced some of the flour with cornstarch.

DUTCH BABY

SERVES 4

You can use whole or low-fat milk instead of skim, but the texture won't be as crisp. Serve with an assortment of berries and lightly sweetened whipped cream, if desired.

- 2 tablespoons vegetable oil
- 1 cup (5 ounces) all-purpose flour
- ¼ cup cornstarch
- 2 teaspoons grated lemon zest plus 2 tablespoons juice
- 1 teaspoon salt
- 3 large eggs
- 1¼ cups skim milk
- 1 tablespoon unsalted butter, melted and cooled
- 1 teaspoon vanilla extract
- 3 tablespoons confectioners' sugar

1. Adjust oven rack to middle position and heat oven to 450 degrees. Brush bottom and sides of 12-inch skillet with oil. Heat skillet in oven until oil is shimmering, about 10 minutes.

2. Meanwhile, combine flour, cornstarch, lemon zest, and salt in large bowl. Whisk eggs in second bowl until frothy and light, about 1 minute. Whisk milk, butter, and vanilla into eggs until incorporated. Whisk one-third of milk mixture into flour mixture until no lumps remain, then slowly whisk in remaining milk mixture until smooth.

3. Carefully pour batter into skillet and bake until edges are deep golden brown and crisp, about 20 minutes. Transfer skillet to wire rack, sprinkle pancake with lemon juice and confectioners' sugar, and cut into wedges. Serve.

Easy Steps to Making a Dutch Baby

1. Brush bottom and sides of pan with vegetable oil to guarantee crisp exterior.

2. Heat greased pan before carefully pouring in batter to initiate rise.

3. Bake in 450-degree oven to ensure high rise.

4. Sprinkle deflated pancake with lemon juice and confectioners' sugar before serving.

BEIGNETS

MAKES 24 BEIGNETS

This dough is very wet and sticky, so flour the counter and baking sheet generously. You'll need at least a 6-quart Dutch oven for this recipe.

- 1 cup water, heated to 110 degrees
- 3 tablespoons granulated sugar
- 1 tablespoon instant or rapid-rise yeast
- 3 cups (15 ounces) all-purpose flour
- ¾ teaspoon salt
- 2 large eggs
- 2 tablespoons plus 2 quarts vegetable oil
  Confectioners' sugar

1. Combine water, 1 tablespoon granulated sugar, and yeast in large bowl and let sit until foamy, about 5 minutes. Combine flour, remaining 2 tablespoons granulated sugar, and salt in second bowl. Whisk eggs and 2 tablespoons oil into yeast mixture. Add flour mixture and stir vigorously with rubber spatula until dough comes together. Cover bowl with plastic wrap and refrigerate until nearly doubled in size, about 1 hour.

2. Set wire rack inside rimmed baking sheet. Line second sheet with parchment paper and dust generously with flour. Place half of dough on well-floured counter and pat into rough rectangle with floured hands, flipping to coat with flour. Roll dough into ¼-inch-thick rectangle (roughly 12 by 9 inches). Using pizza wheel, cut dough into twelve 3-inch squares and transfer to floured baking sheet. Repeat with remaining dough.

3. Add remaining oil to large Dutch oven until it measures about 1½ inches deep and heat over medium-high heat to 350 degrees. Fry 6 beignets, adjusting burner as necessary to maintain oil temperature between 325 and 350 degrees, until golden brown, about 3 minutes, flipping halfway through frying. Using slotted spoon or tongs, transfer beignets to prepared baking sheet. Return oil to 350 degrees and repeat with remaining beignets. Dust beignets with confectioners' sugar and serve immediately.

Forming Beignets

This dough is very wet, which allows a network of delicate holes to develop in the beignets. However, wet dough can be tricky to work with. Here's how to easily shape and cut the beignets:

1. Dust counter and rolling pin generously with flour before you roll out chilled beignet dough.

2. Cut 3-inch squares with pizza wheel.

A Faster Way to Flavor

Starting with a full tablespoon of yeast and proofing it in warm water jump-starts the fermentation process, giving our beignets complex flavor after just a 1-hour rise.

Why This Recipe Works To replicate the crisp, airy texture and tangy flavor of these classic New Orleans doughnuts, we began by using plenty of yeast, kick-starting it with warm water and sugar to develop its flavor. We added extra water for a super-hydrated dough, so that as soon as the wet dough hits the hot oil, it created lots of steam, giving our beignets an open, honeycombed structure. Since wet dough is tricky to roll out, we let it rise in the refrigerator to firm it up. A few minutes of frying and a shower of powdered sugar, and our beignets were ready to be enjoyed, Big Easy style.

Why This Recipe Works A good cornmeal biscuit combines the tender, fluffy crumb of a traditional biscuit with the distinct cornmeal flavor of cornbread. To make the dough, we used a food processor to cut chilled butter quickly into our dry ingredients. So our biscuits would taste like cornmeal, but wouldn't have its dry, gritty texture, we soaked the cornmeal in buttermilk; just 10 minutes was enough to soften it. A bit of honey provided a subtle sweetness that drew out the corn flavor even more. Kneading the dough briefly prior to cutting out rounds ensured evenly textured biscuits that rose to an impressive height.

CORNMEAL BISCUITS

MAKES 12 BISCUITS

If you don't have buttermilk, you can substitute clabbered milk; whisk 1 tablespoon lemon juice into 1¼ cups of milk and let the mixture sit until slightly thickened, about 10 minutes. Avoid coarsely ground cornmeal, which makes gritty biscuits.

- 1 cup (5 ounces) cornmeal
- 1¼ cups buttermilk
- 1 tablespoon honey
- 2 cups (10 ounces) all-purpose flour
- 1 tablespoon baking powder
- ½ teaspoon baking soda
- 1 teaspoon salt
- 12 tablespoons unsalted butter, cut into ½-inch pieces and chilled

1. Adjust oven rack to middle position and heat oven to 450 degrees. Line rimmed baking sheet with parchment paper. Whisk cornmeal, buttermilk, and honey together in large bowl; let sit for 10 minutes.

2. Pulse flour, baking powder, baking soda, and salt in food processor until combined, about 3 pulses. Scatter butter evenly over top and continue to pulse until mixture resembles coarse meal, about 15 pulses. Add flour mixture to buttermilk mixture and stir until dough forms.

3. Turn dough out onto lightly floured counter and knead until smooth, 8 to 10 times. Pat dough into 9-inch circle, about ¾ inch thick. Using 2½-inch biscuit cutter dipped in flour, cut out rounds and transfer to prepared baking sheet, dipping cutter in flour after each cut. Pat remaining dough into ¾-inch-thick circle, cut rounds from dough, and transfer to baking sheet.

4. Bake until biscuits begin to rise, about 5 minutes, then reduce oven temperature to 400 degrees and bake until golden brown, 8 to 12 minutes longer, rotating baking sheet halfway through baking. Let biscuits cool on baking sheet for 5 minutes, then transfer to wire rack. Serve warm or let cool to room temperature. (Biscuits can be stored at room temperature for up to 2 days.)

Steps to Tender, Fluffy Cornmeal Biscuits

Our Cornmeal Biscuits have the moist, flavor-packed crumb of cornbread and the fluffy stature of a stamped biscuit.

1. Soak cornmeal in buttermilk for soft crumb without too much cornmeal grit before mixing with dough.

2. Transfer dough to lightly floured counter and knead briefly before patting into 9-inch circle.

3. Use biscuit cutter to cut dough into rounds, dipping cutter into flour between cuts.

CAT HEAD BISCUITS

MAKES 6 BISCUITS

If you don't have buttermilk, you can substitute clab-bered milk; whisk 1 tablespoon lemon juice into 1¼ cups milk and let the mixture sit until slightly thickened, about 10 minutes. The recipe will also work with 3 cups White Lily flour in place of both the all-purpose and cake flours.

1½ cups (7½ ounces) all-purpose flour
1½ cups (6 ounces) cake flour
  1 tablespoon baking powder
  ½ teaspoon baking soda
  1 teaspoon salt
  8 tablespoons unsalted butter, cut into ½-inch pieces and softened
  4 tablespoons vegetable shortening, cut into ½-inch pieces
1¼ cups buttermilk

1. Adjust oven rack to upper-middle position and heat oven to 425 degrees. Grease 9-inch round cake pan. Combine all-purpose flour, cake flour, baking powder, baking soda, and salt in large bowl. Using fingertips, rub butter and shortening into flour mixture until mixture resembles coarse meal. Stir in buttermilk until combined.

2. Using greased ½-cup measure or large spring-loaded ice cream scoop, transfer 6 heaping portions of dough into prepared pan, placing five around edge and one in center.

3. Bake until puffed and golden brown, 20 to 25 minutes, rotating pan halfway through baking. Let biscuits cool in pan for 10 minutes, then transfer to wire rack. Serve. (Biscuits can be stored at room temperature for up to 2 days.)

Forming Cat Head Biscuits

Instead of kneading, rolling, and stamping, Cat Head Biscuits are scooped.

Scoop dough and nestle biscuits in cake pan using spring-loaded ice cream scoop.

Flour Mixology

Southern bakers swear by White Lily all-purpose flour, which they say makes biscuits soft and downy, exactly the texture we sought for our Cat Head Biscuits. We found we could replicate it by combining equal amounts of all-purpose flour and cake flour.

ALL-PURPOSE FLOUR
Contributes structure

CAKE FLOUR
Contributes softness

WHITE LILY
The soft and fluffy standard-bearer

Why This Recipe Works As big as a cat's head, these tender, moist biscuits that originated in the Appalachian region boast a golden-brown, craggy top and downy, soft sides. Many Southern bakers rely on White Lily flour to ensure a tender texture, but since this flour isn't readily available everywhere, we substituted an equal mix of cake flour and all-purpose flour. For biscuits with a fluffy texture, we relied on softened butter and shortening, worked in with warm hands. Scooping the dough into a round cake pan, so the mounds were touching, gave us baked biscuits with tender, soft sides.

MIXED BERRY SCONES

MAKES 8 SCONES

Work the dough as little as possible, just until it comes together. Work quickly to keep the butter and berries as cold as possible for the best results. Note that the butter is divided in this recipe. An equal amount of frozen blueberries, raspberries, blackberries, or strawberries (halved) can be used in place of the mixed berries.

Scones

1¾ cups (8¾ ounces) frozen mixed berries
3 tablespoons confectioners' sugar
3 cups (15 ounces) all-purpose flour
12 tablespoons unsalted butter, cut into ½-inch pieces, chilled
⅓ cup (2⅓ ounces) granulated sugar
1 tablespoon baking powder
1¼ teaspoons salt
¾ cup plus 2 tablespoons whole milk
1 large egg plus 1 large yolk

Glaze

2 tablespoons unsalted butter, melted
1 tablespoon honey

1. For the Scones Adjust oven rack to upper-middle position and heat oven to 425 degrees. Line rimmed baking sheet with parchment paper. (If your berry mix contains strawberries, cut them in half.) Toss berries with confectioners' sugar in bowl; freeze until needed.

2. Combine flour, 6 tablespoons butter, granulated sugar, baking powder, and salt in food processor and process until butter is fully incorporated, about 15 seconds. Add remaining 6 tablespoons butter and pulse until butter is reduced to pea-size pieces, 10 to 12 pulses. Transfer mixture to large bowl. Stir in berries.

3. Beat milk and egg and yolk together in separate bowl. Make well in center of flour mixture and pour in milk mixture. Using rubber spatula, gently stir mixture, scraping from edges of bowl and folding inward until very shaggy dough forms and some bits of flour remain. Do not overmix.

4. Turn out dough onto well-floured counter and, if necessary, knead briefly until dough just comes together, about 3 turns. Using your floured hands and bench scraper, shape dough into 12 by 4-inch rectangle, about 1½ inches tall. Using knife or bench scraper, cut dough crosswise into 4 equal rectangles. Cut each rectangle diagonally into 2 triangles (you should have 8 scones total). Transfer scones to prepared sheet. Bake until scones are lightly golden on top, 16 to 18 minutes, rotating pan halfway through baking.

5. For the Glaze While scones bake, combine melted butter and honey in small bowl.

6. Remove scones from oven and brush tops evenly with glaze mixture. Return scones to oven and continue to bake until golden brown on top, 5 to 8 minutes longer. Transfer scones to wire rack and let cool for at least 10 minutes before serving.

To Make Ahead Unbaked scones can be frozen for several weeks. After cutting scones into triangles in step 4, freeze them on baking sheet. Transfer frozen scones to zipper-lock freezer bag. When ready to bake, heat oven to 375 degrees and extend cooking time in step 4 to 23 to 26 minutes. Glaze time in step 6 will remain at 5 to 8 minutes.

Why This Recipe Works A random stop at a rural Massachusetts antique store—which had a coffee shop attached—provided the inspiration for these berry-filled scones. To recreate them, we discovered that treating the butter in two different ways was key: We processed half the cold butter to fully incorporate it into the dough, then we pulsed in the remaining butter, processing it to pea-size pieces that created pockets of steam as the scones baked. Adding confectioners' sugar to the frozen berries counteracted their tartness and helped control them from "bleeding" into the dough. A simple glaze added a nice sheen and sweet finish.

Why This Recipe Works Savory skillet-baked Southern-style cornbread should boast hearty corn flavor, a sturdy, moist crumb, and a dark brown crust. For the right texture, we used finely ground cornmeal. Toasting it in the oven for a few minutes intensified the corn flavor. Buttermilk added a sharp tang that worked well with the corn, and soaking the cornmeal in the buttermilk helped to soften it so our cornbread was moist and tender. When it came to the fat, a combination of butter (for flavor) and vegetable oil (which can withstand high heat without burning) worked best, and greasing the pan with both delivered the crisp crust we were after.

SOUTHERN-STYLE SKILLET CORNBREAD

SERVES 12

If you don't have buttermilk, you can substitute clabbered milk; whisk 2 tablespoons lemon juice into 2 cups of milk and let the mixture sit until slightly thickened, about 10 minutes. We prefer a cast-iron skillet here, but any ovensafe 10-inch skillet will work fine. Avoid coarsely ground cornmeal, as it will make the cornbread gritty.

2¼ cups (11¼ ounces) cornmeal
2 cups buttermilk
¼ cup vegetable oil
4 tablespoons unsalted butter, cut into 4 pieces
2 large eggs
1 teaspoon baking powder
1 teaspoon baking soda
¾ teaspoon salt

1. Adjust oven racks to lower-middle and middle positions and heat oven to 450 degrees. Heat 10-inch cast-iron skillet on middle rack for 10 minutes. Spread cornmeal over rimmed baking sheet and bake on lower-middle rack until fragrant and color begins to deepen, about 5 minutes. Transfer hot cornmeal to large bowl and whisk in buttermilk; set aside.

2. Carefully add oil to hot skillet and continue to bake until oil is just smoking, about 5 minutes. Remove skillet from oven and add butter, carefully swirling pan until butter is melted. Pour all but 1 tablespoon oil mixture into cornmeal mixture, leaving remaining oil mixture in pan. Whisk eggs, baking powder, baking soda, and salt into cornmeal mixture.

3. Pour cornmeal mixture into hot skillet and bake until top begins to crack and sides are golden brown, 12 to 16 minutes, rotating pan halfway through baking. Let cornbread cool in pan for 5 minutes, then turn out onto wire rack. Serve.

Secrets to Savory Southern-Style Skillet Cornbread

1. Toast cornmeal to give bread richer corn flavor.

2. Soak cornmeal in buttermilk to soften cornmeal and ensure tender yet sturdy crumb.

3. Grease and thoroughly heat skillet to create crisp crust.

Why This Recipe Works Stella's Bakery in Madison, Wisconsin, is known for its spicy cheese bread. One challenge we had while trying to recreate this addictive bread was finding a way to incorporate the cheese without stunting the dough's rise. We found the key was to make sure the cheese cubes came to room temperature before adding them to the dough. To help keep its shape, we baked the bread in a cake pan. An egg wash and a generous sprinkle of red pepper flakes finished off the loaf. A final brush of melted butter helped the crust stay supple and gave it a nice shine.

SPICY CHEESE BREAD

MAKES 1 LOAF

Take the cheese out of the refrigerator when you start the recipe to ensure that it comes to room temperature by the time you need it. Cold cheese will retard rising. The dough needs to rise for several hours before baking.

Bread

- 3¼ cups (16¼ ounces) all-purpose flour
- ¼ cup (1¾ ounces) sugar
- 1 tablespoon instant or rapid-rise yeast
- 1½ teaspoons red pepper flakes
- 1¼ teaspoons salt
- ½ cup warm water (110 degrees)
- 2 large eggs plus 1 large yolk
- 4 tablespoons unsalted butter, melted
- 6 ounces Monterey Jack cheese, cut into ½-inch cubes (1½ cups), room temperature
- 6 ounces provolone cheese, cut into ½-inch cubes (1½ cups), room temperature

Topping

- 1 large egg, lightly beaten
- 1 teaspoon red pepper flakes
- 1 tablespoon unsalted butter, melted

1. For the Bread Whisk flour, sugar, yeast, pepper flakes, and salt together in bowl of stand mixer. Whisk warm water, eggs and yolk, and melted butter together in liquid measuring cup. Add egg mixture to flour mixture. Fit stand mixer with dough hook and knead on medium speed until dough clears bottom and sides of bowl, about 8 minutes.

2. Transfer dough to unfloured counter, shape into ball, and transfer to greased bowl. Cover with plastic wrap and let rise in warm place until doubled in size, 1½ to 2 hours.

3. Grease 9-inch round cake pan. Transfer dough to unfloured counter and press to deflate. Roll dough into 18 by 12-inch rectangle with long side parallel to counter's edge. Distribute Monterey Jack and provolone evenly over dough, leaving 1-inch border around edges. Starting with edge closest to you, roll dough into log. Pinch seam and ends to seal, then roll log so seam side is down. Roll log back and forth on counter, applying gentle, even pressure, until log reaches 30 inches in length. If any tears occur, pinch to seal.

4. Starting at one end, wind log into coil; tuck end underneath coil. Place loaf in prepared cake pan and cover loosely with clean dish towel. Let rise in warm place until doubled in size, 1 to 1½ hours. Adjust oven rack to lower-middle position and heat oven to 350 degrees.

5. For the Topping Brush top of loaf with egg, then sprinkle with pepper flakes. Place cake pan on rimmed baking sheet. Bake until loaf is golden brown, about 25 minutes. Rotate loaf, tent with aluminum foil, and continue to bake until loaf registers 190 degrees, 25 to 30 minutes longer.

6. Transfer pan to wire rack and brush bread with butter. Let cool for 10 minutes. Run knife around edge of pan to loosen bread. Slide bread onto wire rack, using spatula as needed for support. Let cool for 30 minutes before slicing. Serve warm.

PERFECT POPOVERS

MAKES 6 POPOVERS

Greasing the pan with shortening ensures the best release, but vegetable oil spray may be substituted; do not use butter. Bread flour makes for the highest and sturdiest popovers, but 2 cups (10 ounces) of all-purpose flour may be substituted.

- 3 large eggs
- 2 cups 1 percent or 2 percent low-fat milk, heated to 110 degrees
- 3 tablespoons unsalted butter, melted and cooled
- 2 cups (11 ounces) bread flour
- 1 teaspoon salt
- 1 teaspoon sugar

1. Adjust oven rack to lower-middle position and heat oven to 450 degrees. Grease 6-cup popover pan with shortening, then flour pan lightly. Whisk eggs until light and foamy in medium bowl. Slowly whisk in milk and butter until incorporated.

2. Combine flour, salt, and sugar in large bowl. Whisk three-quarters of milk mixture into flour mixture until no lumps remain, then whisk in remaining milk mixture. Transfer batter to 4-cup liquid measuring cup, cover with plastic wrap, and let sit at room temperature for 1 hour. (Alternatively, batter can be refrigerated for up to 1 day. Bring to room temperature before proceeding.)

3. Whisk batter to recombine, then pour into prepared pan (batter will not reach top of cups). Bake until just beginning to brown, about 20 minutes. Without opening oven door, decrease oven temperature to 300 degrees and continue to bake until popovers are golden brown, 35 to 40 minutes longer. Poke small hole in top of each popover with skewer and continue to bake until deep golden brown, about 10 minutes longer. Transfer pan to wire rack, poke popovers again with skewer, and let cool for 2 minutes. Remove from pan and serve.

To Make Ahead Cooled popovers can be stored at room temperature for up to 2 days. To serve, adjust oven rack to middle position and heat oven to 400 degrees. Heat popovers on rimmed baking sheet until crisp and heated through, 5 to 8 minutes.

MUFFIN TIN POPOVERS

If you don't have a popover pan, you can bake the popovers in a 12-cup muffin tin—with a sacrifice in stature. To ensure even cooking, use only the outer 10 cups of the tin.

Grease and flour outer 10 cups of muffin tin, then fill ¼ inch from the top (you may have some batter left over). Reduce initial baking time in step 3 to 15 minutes, and reduce secondary baking time to 20 to 25 minutes after oven temperature has been lowered. Poke popovers as directed and continue to bake for another 10 minutes.

Popovers Gone Wrong

POP NEVER
Short, squat popovers occur when the recipe calls for cake flour, which doesn't provide enough structure to the batter. Using too little batter can also make for squat popovers, as can an oven that's not hot enough.

POP UNDER
Deflated popovers occur when they aren't baked long enough to set up properly or aren't poked during baking to allow the steam to escape.

POP UGLY
Misshapen popovers are caused by using a preheated, oiled pan. The batter that first hits the pan immediately rises up through the wet batter, resulting in an ugly shape.

Why This Recipe Works For golden-brown popovers that really popped, we used bread flour instead of all-purpose flour in the batter—the bread flour's higher protein content ensured the highest rise and crispiest crust. Resting the batter before baking prevented the popovers from setting up too quickly. We first baked our popovers at a high temperature to jump-start the initial rise, then turned the oven down so they would cook through evenly. To let steam escape (which can cause popovers to collapse), we poked a hole in the top of each one when they were almost done baking, and then again as they cooled.

WHOLE-WHEAT BLUEBERRY MUFFINS

MAKES 12 MUFFINS

Do not overmix the batter. You can substitute frozen (unthawed) blueberries for fresh in this recipe.

Streusel
- 3 tablespoons granulated sugar
- 3 tablespoons packed brown sugar
- 3 tablespoons whole-wheat flour
- Pinch salt
- 2 tablespoons unsalted butter, melted

Muffins
- 3 cups (16½ ounces) whole-wheat flour
- 2½ teaspoons baking powder
- ½ teaspoon baking soda
- 1 teaspoon salt
- 1 cup (7 ounces) granulated sugar
- 2 large eggs
- 4 tablespoons unsalted butter, melted
- ¼ cup vegetable oil
- 1¼ cups buttermilk
- 1½ teaspoons vanilla extract
- 7½ ounces (1½ cups) blueberries

1. For the Streusel Combine granulated sugar, brown sugar, flour, and salt in bowl. Add melted butter and toss with fork until evenly moistened and mixture forms large chunks with some pea-size pieces throughout; set aside.

2. For the Muffins Adjust oven rack to middle position and heat oven to 400 degrees. Spray 12-cup muffin tin, including top, generously with vegetable oil spray. Whisk flour, baking powder, baking soda, and salt together in large bowl. Whisk sugar, eggs, melted butter, and oil together in separate bowl until combined, about 30 seconds. Whisk buttermilk and vanilla into sugar mixture until combined.

3. Stir sugar mixture into flour mixture until just combined. Gently stir in blueberries until incorporated. Using a heaping ¼-cup dry measuring cup, divide batter evenly among prepared muffin cups (cups will be filled to rim); sprinkle evenly with streusel.

4. Bake until golden brown and toothpick inserted in center comes out with few crumbs attached, 18 to 20 minutes, rotating muffin tin halfway through baking. Let muffins cool in muffin tin on wire rack for 5 minutes. Remove muffins from muffin tin and let cool 5 minutes longer. Serve.

Don't Make this Mistake: Heavy and Dense Muffins

You can't simply swap whole-wheat flour into any muffin recipe and expect it to work. But if you know the science behind baking and account for the variables, you can make great blueberry muffins using 100 percent whole-wheat flour.

Why This Recipe Works When it comes to baking with whole wheat, the benefits—added fiber, bran, and nutty sweetness—are often trumped by the drawbacks: dense texture and squat appearance. To use one hundred percent whole wheat, we had to revise our standard blueberry muffin recipe. The resulting whole-wheat muffins were light and tender thanks to two leaveners and several high-moisture ingredients (buttermilk, eggs, blueberries, melted butter, and oil). As a final step we added a crumbly streusel topping to round out our now light and delicate muffins with hearty whole-wheat flavor.

Why This Recipe Works Morning glory muffins are chock-full of nuts, fruit, carrots, and spices. But all these tempting add-ins can make for heavy, dense muffins, so our first move was to strain the fruit and press out the extra juice to prevent our muffins from being soggy. To keep the bright, fruity flavor intact, we simply saved the released fruit juice, reduced it on the stovetop, and added the concentrated syrup back to the batter. To keep the nuts and coconut from becoming mealy or soggy in the finished muffins, we toasted and processed them. At last, our muffins were truly glorious.

MORNING GLORY MUFFINS

MAKES 12 MUFFINS

Though we prefer golden raisins here, ordinary raisins will work, too.

- ¾ cup (2¼ ounces) sweetened shredded coconut, toasted
- ½ cup walnuts, toasted
- 2¼ cups (11¼ ounces) all-purpose flour
- ¾ cup (5¼ ounces) sugar
- 1½ teaspoons baking soda
- ½ teaspoon baking powder
- 1 teaspoon ground cinnamon
- ¾ teaspoon salt
- 1 (8-ounce) can crushed pineapple
- 1 Granny Smith apple, peeled, cored, and shredded
- 8 tablespoons unsalted butter, melted
- 3 large eggs
- 1 teaspoon vanilla extract
- 1½ cups shredded carrots (2 to 3 carrots)
- 1 cup golden raisins

1. Adjust oven rack to middle position and heat oven to 350 degrees. Spray 12-cup muffin tin with vegetable oil spray. Process coconut and walnuts in food processor until finely ground, 20 to 30 seconds. Add flour, sugar, baking soda, baking powder, cinnamon, and salt and pulse until combined. Transfer mixture to large bowl.

2. Place pineapple and shredded apple in fine-mesh strainer set over liquid measuring cup. Press fruit dry (you should have about 1 cup juice). Bring juice to boil in 12-inch skillet over medium-high heat and cook until reduced to ¼ cup, about 5 minutes. Let cool slightly. Whisk melted butter, cooled juice, eggs, and vanilla together until smooth. Stir wet mixture into dry mixture until combined. Stir in pineapple-apple mixture, carrots, and raisins.

3. Divide batter evenly among muffin cups. Bake until toothpick inserted in center comes out clean, 24 to 28 minutes, rotating pan halfway through baking. Let muffins cool in muffin tin on wire rack for 10 minutes. Remove muffins from tin and let cool for at least 10 minutes before serving. (Muffins can be stored at room temperature for up to 3 days.)

Secrets to Glorious Morning Glory Muffins

1. Toasting the coconut and walnuts heightens their flavor, and processing them in a food processor until finely ground prevents soggy, stringy coconut and mealy nuts.

2. Pressing the juice out of the shredded apple and pineapple before stirring them into the batter keeps the muffins from being gummy and wet.

3. Reducing the released fruit juice on the stovetop (down from 1 cup to ¼ cup) and adding the syrup to the batter provides a bright, fruity flavor without adding too much moisture.

MUFFIN TIN DOUGHNUTS

MAKES 12 DOUGHNUTS

In step 3, brush the doughnuts generously, using up all the melted butter. Use your hand to press the cinnamon sugar onto the doughnuts to coat them completely.

Doughnuts

2¾ cups (13¾ ounces) all-purpose flour
1 cup (7 ounces) sugar
¼ cup cornstarch
1 tablespoon baking powder
1 teaspoon salt
½ teaspoon ground nutmeg
1 cup buttermilk
8 tablespoons unsalted butter, melted
2 large eggs plus 1 large yolk

Coating

1 cup sugar
2 teaspoons ground cinnamon
8 tablespoons unsalted butter, melted

1. For the Doughnuts Adjust oven rack to middle position and heat oven to 400 degrees. Spray 12-cup muffin tin with vegetable oil spray. Whisk flour, sugar, cornstarch, baking powder, salt, and nutmeg together in bowl. Whisk buttermilk, melted butter, and eggs and yolk together in separate bowl. Add wet ingredients to dry ingredients and stir with rubber spatula until just combined.

2. Scoop batter into prepared tin. Bake until doughnuts are lightly browned and toothpick inserted in center comes out clean, 19 to 22 minutes. Let doughnuts cool in tin for 5 minutes.

3. For the Coating Whisk sugar and cinnamon together in bowl. Remove doughnuts from tin. Working with 1 doughnut at a time, brush all over with melted butter, then roll in cinnamon sugar, pressing lightly to adhere. Transfer to wire rack and let cool for 15 minutes. Serve.

Brush with Butter

We brush the warm muffins liberally with melted butter before rolling them in the cinnamon sugar. The butter helps the coating stick and makes the muffins taste more fried.

Why This Recipe Works To capture the best of breakfast baking, we set out to create a muffin that tasted like a cake doughnut in disguise with a tender crumb, a crisp exterior, and a buttery spiced coating. Adding an extra yolk and cutting all-purpose flour with cornstarch gave the muffins a tender crumb that wouldn't break apart. To replicate a fried exterior, we turned up the oven temperature, which crisped the crust nicely. Lastly we brushed the muffins with butter and rolled them in cinnamon sugar. From coating to crumb, these doughnut muffins combined the essence of a doughnut and the ease of a muffin (without a deep fryer in sight).

ULTIMATE CINNAMON BUNS

MAKES 8 BUNS

For smaller cinnamon buns, cut the dough into 12 pieces in step 3.

Dough

¾ cup whole milk, heated to 110 degrees
2¼ teaspoons instant or rapid-rise yeast
3 large eggs, room temperature
4¼ cups (21¼ ounces) all-purpose flour
½ cup cornstarch
½ cup (3½ ounces) granulated sugar
1½ teaspoons salt
12 tablespoons unsalted butter,
cut into 12 pieces and softened

Filling

1½ cups packed (10½ ounces) light brown sugar
1½ tablespoons ground cinnamon
¼ teaspoon salt
4 tablespoons unsalted butter, softened

Glaze

1½ cups confectioners' sugar
4 ounces cream cheese, softened
1 tablespoon whole milk
1 teaspoon vanilla extract

1. For the Dough Make foil sling for 13 by 9-inch baking pan by folding 2 long sheets of aluminum foil; first sheet should be 13 inches wide and second sheet should be 9 inches wide. Lay sheets of foil in pan perpendicular to each other, with extra foil hanging over edges of pan. Push foil into corners and up sides of pan, smoothing foil flush to pan. Grease foil. Whisk milk and yeast together in liquid measuring cup until yeast dissolves, then whisk in eggs.

2. Adjust oven rack to middle position and place loaf or cake pan on bottom of oven. Using stand mixer fitted with dough hook, mix flour, cornstarch, sugar, and salt on low speed until combined. Add warm milk mixture in steady stream and mix until dough comes together, about 1 minute. Increase speed to medium and add butter, 1 piece at a time, until incorporated. Continue to mix until dough is smooth and comes away from sides of bowl, about 10 minutes (if dough is still wet and sticky, add up to ¼ cup flour, 1 tablespoon at a time, until it releases from bowl). Turn dough out onto counter and knead to form smooth, round ball. Transfer dough to medium greased bowl, cover with plastic wrap, and transfer to middle rack of oven. Pour 3 cups boiling water into loaf pan in oven, close oven door, and let dough rise until doubled in size, about 2 hours.

3. For the Filling Combine sugar, cinnamon, and salt in small bowl. Remove dough from oven and turn out onto lightly floured counter. Roll dough into 18-inch square and, leaving ½-inch border around edges, spread with butter, then sprinkle evenly with sugar mixture and lightly press sugar mixture into dough. Starting with edge closest to you, roll dough into tight cylinder, pinch lightly to seal seam, and cut into 8 pieces. Transfer pieces, cut side up, to prepared pan. Cover with plastic and let rise in oven until doubled in size, about 1 hour.

4. For the Glaze Remove buns and water pan from oven and heat oven to 350 degrees. Whisk all glaze ingredients together in medium bowl until smooth. Remove plastic and bake buns until deep golden brown and filling is melted, 35 to 40 minutes, rotating pan halfway through baking. Transfer to wire rack, top buns with ½ cup glaze, and let cool for 30 minutes. Using foil overhang, lift buns from pan and top with remaining glaze. Serve.

To Make Ahead Follow recipe through step 3, skipping step of letting buns rise. Place buns in pan, cover with plastic wrap, and refrigerate for up to 1 day. To bake, let sit at room temperature for 1 hour. Remove plastic and proceed with step 4.

Why This Recipe Works Gooey softball-size cinnamon buns are the ultimate break-fast treat. For the base of ours, we turned to a buttery, tender brioche dough. Adding cornstarch to the all-purpose flour in the dough made the buns especially tender. For a filling with great flavor, we combined a good amount of cinnamon—no other spices necessary—with brown sugar. Softened butter helped keep the filling from spilling out as we rolled up the dough. Baked together, the butter and cinnamon sugar turned into a rich, gooey filling. A thick, tangy glaze of cream cheese, confectioners' sugar, and milk ensured our buns really looked the part.

Why This Recipe Works Rich, gooey, homemade cinnamon buns can take upwards of 3 hours to prepare. We wanted the same tender, yeasty results in half the time. For a quicker rise, we supplemented the yeast (which we proofed in warm milk for extra speed) with baking powder. A mere 2 minutes of hand-kneading and a single 30-minute rise were enough to give us the flavor and texture we were looking for. We used a cooler-than-normal oven to give the yeast time to rise and develop flavor before the tops of the buns set. Brown sugar and butter in the filling and a touch of vanilla in our tangy cream cheese glaze made these buns ultra-rich and indulgent.

QUICKER CINNAMON BUNS

MAKES 8 BUNS

Since the filling, dough, and glaze all require melted butter, it's easier to melt all 10 tablespoons in a liquid measuring cup and divvy it up as needed. Stir the melted butter before each use to redistribute the milk solids. We developed this recipe using a dark cake pan, which produces deeply caramelized buns. If your cake pan is light-colored, adjust the oven rack to the lowest position, heat the oven to 375 degrees, and increase the baking time to 29 to 32 minutes.

Filling
¾ cup packed (5¼ ounces) light brown sugar
¼ cup (1¾ ounces) granulated sugar
1 tablespoon ground cinnamon
⅛ teaspoon salt
2 tablespoons unsalted butter, melted
1 teaspoon vanilla extract

Dough
1¼ cups whole milk, room temperature
4 teaspoons instant or rapid-rise yeast
2 tablespoons granulated sugar
2¾ cups (13¾ ounces) all-purpose flour
2½ teaspoons baking powder
¾ teaspoon salt
6 tablespoons unsalted butter, melted

Glaze
3 ounces cream cheese, softened
2 tablespoons unsalted butter, melted
2 tablespoons whole milk
½ teaspoon vanilla extract
⅛ teaspoon salt
1 cup (4 ounces) confectioners' sugar, sifted

1. For the Filling Combine brown sugar, granulated sugar, cinnamon, and salt in bowl. Stir in melted butter and vanilla until mixture resembles wet sand; set aside.

2. For the Dough Grease dark 9-inch round cake pan, line with parchment paper, and grease parchment. Pour ¼ cup milk in small bowl and microwave until 110 degrees, 15 to 20 seconds. Stir in yeast and 1 teaspoon sugar and let sit until mixture is bubbly, about 5 minutes.

3. Whisk flour, baking powder, salt, and remaining 5 teaspoons sugar together in large bowl. Stir in 2 tablespoons butter, yeast mixture, and remaining 1 cup milk until dough forms (dough will be sticky). Transfer dough to well-floured counter and knead until smooth ball forms, about 2 minutes.

4. Roll dough into 12 by 9-inch rectangle, with long side parallel to counter edge. Brush dough all over with 2 tablespoons butter, leaving ½-inch border on far edge. Sprinkle dough evenly with filling, then press filling firmly into dough. Using bench scraper or metal spatula, loosen dough from counter. Roll dough away from you into tight log and pinch seam to seal.

5. Roll log seam side down and cut into 8 equal pieces. Stand buns on end and gently re-form ends that were pinched during cutting. Place 1 bun in center of prepared pan and others around perimeter of pan, seam sides facing in. Brush tops of buns with remaining 2 tablespoons butter. Cover buns loosely with plastic wrap and let rise for 30 minutes. Adjust oven rack to middle position and heat oven to 350 degrees.

6. Discard plastic and bake buns until edges are well browned, 23 to 25 minutes. Loosen buns from sides of pan with paring knife and let cool for 5 minutes. Invert large plate over cake pan. Using potholders, flip plate and pan upside down; remove pan and parchment. Reinvert buns onto wire rack, set wire rack inside parchment-lined rimmed baking sheet, and let cool for 5 minutes.

7. For the Glaze Place cream cheese in large bowl and whisk in butter, milk, vanilla, and salt until smooth. Whisk in sugar until smooth. Pour glaze evenly over tops of buns, spreading with spatula to cover. Serve.

Why This Recipe Works Morning buns rely on a complicated croissant-like dough that requires both substantial effort and time. For an easier path, we switched to a quick dough closer to puff pastry. Instead of rolling the butter into the dry ingredients on the counter, we moved it all to a zipper-lock bag and rolled everything right in the bag. To produce multiple layers in this rich pastry, we rolled the dough into a rectangle, then into a cylinder, and gently patted it flat. A blend of brown and white sugar added a subtle molasses flavor to the filling, while orange zest instilled it with bright citrus notes.

MORNING BUNS

MAKES 12 BUNS

If the dough becomes too soft to work with at any point, refrigerate it until it's firm enough to easily handle.

Dough

- 3 cups (15 ounces) all-purpose flour
- 1 tablespoon sugar
- 2¼ teaspoons instant or rapid-rise yeast
- ¾ teaspoon salt
- 24 tablespoons (3 sticks) unsalted butter, cut into ¼-inch-thick slices and chilled
- 1 cup sour cream, chilled
- ¼ cup orange juice, chilled
- 3 tablespoons ice water
- 1 large egg yolk

Filling

- ½ cup (3½ ounces) granulated sugar
- ½ cup packed (3½ ounces) light brown sugar
- 1 tablespoon grated orange zest
- 2 teaspoons ground cinnamon
- 1 teaspoon vanilla extract

1. For the Dough Combine flour, sugar, yeast, and salt in large zipper-lock bag. Add butter to bag, seal, and shake to coat. Press air out of bag and reseal. Roll over bag several times with rolling pin, shaking bag after each roll, until butter is pressed into large flakes. Transfer mixture to large bowl and stir in sour cream, orange juice, water, and egg yolk until combined.

2. Turn dough onto floured counter and knead briefly to form smooth, cohesive ball. Roll dough into 20 by 12-inch rectangle. Starting with short edge, roll dough into tight cylinder. Pat cylinder flat to 12 by 4-inch rectangle and transfer to parchment paper–lined rimmed baking sheet. Cover with plastic wrap and freeze for 15 minutes.

3. For the Filling Line 12-cup muffin tin with paper or foil liners and spray with vegetable oil spray. Combine granulated sugar, brown sugar, orange zest, cinnamon, and vanilla in medium bowl. Remove dough from freezer and place on lightly floured counter. Roll dough into 20 by 12-inch rectangle and sprinkle evenly with filling, leaving ½-inch border

around edges. Starting at long edge, roll dough into tight cylinder and pinch lightly to seal seam. Trim ½ inch dough from each end and discard. Cut dough into 12 pieces and transfer, cut side up, to prepared tin. Cover loosely with plastic and refrigerate for at least 4 hours or up to 1 day.

4. Adjust oven rack to middle position and place loaf or cake pan on bottom of oven. Remove plastic from buns and place in oven. Pour 3 cups boiling water into loaf pan in oven, close oven door, and let buns rise until puffed and doubled in size, 20 to 30 minutes. Remove buns and water pan from oven and heat oven to 425 degrees. Bake until buns begin to rise, about 5 minutes, then reduce oven temperature to 325 degrees. Bake until deep golden brown, 40 to 50 minutes, rotating pan halfway through baking. Let buns cool in muffin tin on wire rack for 5 minutes, then transfer to wire rack and discard liners. Serve warm.

To Make Ahead Follow recipe through step 3, skipping step of refrigerating buns. Freeze buns, in muffin tin, until firm, about 30 minutes. Transfer buns, with liners, to zipper-lock bag and freeze for up to 1 month. To bake, return buns to muffin tin, cover with plastic, and refrigerate for at least 8 hours or up to 1 day. Proceed with step 4.

Key Steps to Flaky Pastry

1. Flatten flour-coated butter into long flakes by pressing air out of bag, sealing it, and rolling over it a few times with rolling pin.

2. Add butter-flour mixture to bowl and stir in sour cream, orange juice, water, and egg yolk. Then mix and knead briefly before rolling dough.

KOLACHES

MAKES 16 KOLACHES

Do not use nonfat ricotta cheese in this recipe. In step 1, if the dough hasn't cleared the sides of the bowl after 12 minutes, add more flour, 1 tablespoon at a time, up to 2 tablespoons. In step 6, to prevent sticking, reflour the bottom of the measuring cup (or drinking glass) after making each indentation.

Dough

- 1 cup whole milk
- 10 tablespoons unsalted butter, melted
- 1 large egg plus 2 large yolks
- 3½ cups (17½ ounces) all-purpose flour
- ⅓ cup (2⅓ ounces) sugar
- 2¼ teaspoons instant or rapid-rise yeast
- 1½ teaspoons salt

Cheese Filling

- 6 ounces cream cheese, softened
- 3 tablespoons sugar
- 1 tablespoon all-purpose flour
- ½ teaspoon grated lemon zest
- 6 ounces (¾ cup) whole-milk or part-skim ricotta cheese

Streusel

- 2 tablespoons plus 2 teaspoons all-purpose flour
- 2 tablespoons plus 2 teaspoons sugar
- 1 tablespoon unsalted butter, cut into 8 pieces and chilled

- 1 large egg beaten with 1 tablespoon milk

1. For the Dough Grease large bowl. Whisk milk, melted butter, and egg and yolks together in 2-cup liquid measuring cup (butter will form clumps). Whisk flour, sugar, yeast, and salt together in bowl of stand mixer. Fit stand mixer with dough hook, add milk mixture to flour mixture, and knead on low speed until no dry flour remains, about 2 minutes. Increase speed to medium and knead until dough clears sides of bowl but still sticks to bottom, 8 to 12 minutes.

2. Transfer dough to greased bowl and cover with plastic wrap. Adjust oven racks to upper-middle and lower-middle positions. Place dough on lower-middle rack and place loaf pan on bottom of oven. Pour 3 cups boiling water into loaf pan, close oven door, and let dough rise until doubled, about 1 hour.

3. For the Cheese Filling Using stand mixer fitted with paddle, beat cream cheese, sugar, flour, and lemon zest on low speed until smooth, about 1 minute. Add ricotta and beat until just combined, about 30 seconds. Transfer to bowl, cover with plastic, and refrigerate until ready to use.

4. For the Streusel Combine flour, sugar, and butter in bowl and rub between fingers until mixture resembles wet sand. Cover with plastic and refrigerate until ready to use.

5. Line 2 rimmed baking sheets with parchment paper. Punch down dough and place on lightly floured counter. Divide into quarters and cut each quarter into 4 equal pieces. Form each piece into rough ball by pulling dough edges underneath so top is smooth. On unfloured counter, cup each ball in your palm and roll into smooth, tight ball. Arrange 8 balls on each prepared sheet and cover loosely with plastic. Place sheets on oven racks. Replace water in loaf pan with 3 cups boiling water, close oven door, and let dough rise until doubled, about 90 minutes.

6. Remove sheets and loaf pan from oven. Heat oven to 350 degrees. Grease and flour bottom of ⅓-cup measuring cup (or 2¼-inch-diameter drinking glass). Make deep indentation in center of each dough ball by slowly pressing until cup touches sheet. (Perimeter of balls may deflate slightly.)

7. Gently brush kolaches all over with egg-milk mixture. Divide filling evenly among kolaches (about 1½ tablespoons per kolache) and smooth with back of spoon. Sprinkle streusel over kolaches, avoiding filling. Bake until golden brown, about 25 minutes, switching and rotating sheets halfway through baking. Let kolaches cool on pans for 20 minutes. Serve warm.

Why This Recipe Works Brought to Texas by Czech immigrants, kolaches are palm-size rounds of sweetened bread with dollops of sweet cheese or fruit filling in the center and a streusel topping. We discovered that long mixing with a dough hook developed plenty of stretchy gluten, making the finished pastries light and pleasantly chewy. For a Texas-style filling, a combination of tangy cream cheese and milkier, slightly salty ricotta created a perfect base, while a little sugar and lemon zest balanced the flavor. At the end of the day, our kolaches were subtly sweet, tender, buttery, and . . . gone.

MONKEY BREAD

SERVES 6 TO 8

Make sure to use light brown sugar in the coating mix; dark brown sugar has a stronger molasses flavor that can be overwhelming. After baking, don't let the bread cool in the pan for more than 5 minutes or it will stick to the pan and come out in pieces. Monkey bread is best served warm.

Dough

- 2 tablespoons unsalted butter, softened, plus 2 tablespoons melted
- 1 cup milk, heated to 110 degrees
- ⅓ cup water, heated to 110 degrees
- ¼ cup (1¾ ounces) granulated sugar
- 2¼ teaspoons instant or rapid-rise yeast
- 3¼ cups (16¼ ounces) all-purpose flour
- 2 teaspoons salt

Brown Sugar Coating

- 1 cup packed (7 ounces) light brown sugar
- 2 teaspoons ground cinnamon
- 8 tablespoons unsalted butter, melted

Glaze

- 1 cup (4 ounces) confectioners' sugar
- 2 tablespoons milk

1. For the Dough Grease 12-cup nonstick Bundt pan with softened butter; set aside. Combine milk, water, melted butter, sugar, and yeast in 2-cup liquid measuring cup.

2. Adjust oven rack to middle position and place loaf or cake pan on bottom of oven. Using stand mixer fitted with dough hook, mix flour and salt on low speed. Slowly add milk mixture and mix until dough comes together (if dough is too wet and doesn't come together, add up to 2 tablespoons more flour). Increase speed to medium and knead until dough is shiny and smooth, 6 to 7 minutes. Turn dough onto lightly floured counter and knead briefly to form smooth, round ball. Place dough in large greased bowl, coat surface with vegetable oil spray, and transfer to oven. Pour 3 cups boiling water into loaf pan in oven, close oven door, and let dough rise until doubled in size, 50 minutes to 1 hour.

3. For the Brown Sugar Coating While dough rises, combine sugar and cinnamon in small bowl. Place melted butter in second bowl. Set aside.

4. Gently remove dough from bowl and pat into rough 8-inch square. Using bench scraper or knife, cut square into quarters, then cut each quarter into 16 pieces. Roll each piece of dough into a ball. Working with one at a time, dip each ball in melted butter, allowing excess butter to drip off, then roll in sugar mixture. Layer dough balls in prepared pan, staggering seams where dough balls meet. Cover pan tightly with plastic wrap, transfer to oven, and let rest until dough balls are puffy and have risen 1 to 2 inches from top of pan, 50 minutes to 1 hour, 10 minutes.

5. Remove Bundt pan and water pan from oven; adjust oven rack to medium-low position and heat oven to 350 degrees. Remove plastic and bake until top of dough is deeply browned and caramel begins to bubble around edges, 30 to 35 minutes, rotating pan halfway through baking. Let monkey bread cool in pan for 5 minutes, then turn out on platter and let cool slightly, about 10 minutes.

6. For the Glaze Meanwhile, whisk sugar and milk together in small bowl until smooth. Using whisk, drizzle glaze over warm monkey bread, letting it run over top and sides of bread. Serve warm.

Forming Monkey Bread

After forming dough balls, dip each one in melted butter and sugar and then place in greased Bundt pan, staggering seams where dough balls meet.

Why This Recipe Works It might have a funny name, but monkey bread is a soft, sweet, sticky, ultra-cinnamony treat (its moniker probably refers to how it's pulled apart and stuffed into eager mouths). To expedite the rising and proofing of the dough, and ensure our bread had plenty of yeasty flavor, we used a good amount of instant yeast. Butter and milk helped keep the dough rich and moist, and a little sugar made the bread sweet enough to eat on its own. A dip in butter and cinnamon sugar gave the monkey bread a thick, caramel-like coating after its stint in the oven. And a drizzle of a simple glaze finished it off.

Why This Recipe Works With their chewy interiors, crunchy crusts, and craggy texture, English muffins are a treat—but they're also a lot of work. For a no-fuss recipe without the kneading, rolling, cutting, or griddling, we made a simple loaf bread with the flavor and texture of English muffins. Protein-rich bread flour gave the loaf a chewy yet light consistency, and baking soda created the all-important honeycombed texture. Heating the milk before mixing the dough activated the yeast and shortened the rising time. We simply mixed the dough, let it rise, then baked it in loaf pans until the crust was well browned and the interior was perfectly craggy.

ENGLISH MUFFIN BREAD

MAKES 2 LOAVES

Serve this bread with butter and jam.

Cornmeal
5 cups (27½ ounces) bread flour
4½ teaspoons instant or rapid-rise yeast
1 tablespoon sugar
2 teaspoons salt
1 teaspoon baking soda
3 cups whole milk, heated to 120 degrees

1. Grease two 8½ by 4½-inch loaf pans and dust with cornmeal. Combine flour, yeast, sugar, salt, and baking soda in large bowl. Stir in hot milk until combined, about 1 minute. Cover dough with greased plastic wrap and let rise in warm place for 30 minutes, or until dough is bubbly and has doubled.

2. Stir dough and divide between prepared loaf pans, pushing into corners with greased rubber spatula. (Pans should be about two-thirds full.) Cover pans with greased plastic and let dough rise in warm place until it reaches edges of pans, about 30 minutes. Adjust oven rack to middle position and heat oven to 375 degrees.

3. Discard plastic and transfer pans to oven. Bake until loaves are well browned and register 200 degrees, about 30 minutes, rotating and switching pans halfway through baking. Turn loaves out onto wire rack and let cool completely, about 1 hour. Slice, toast, and serve.

Tricks to the Right Texture

To give our English Muffin Bread the proper chew and porous texture, we needed a few tricks. High-protein bread flour allows more gluten to develop in the batter for a satisfyingly chewy loaf. Stirring baking soda in with the other dry ingredients gives the bread extra rise for an appropriately coarse, honeycombed texture.

A Well-Dressed Table

By the end of the 19th century, the English were losing their taste for English-style muffins, but in the U.S. they had become such a popular breakfast bread that the properly set breakfast table required special dishes for serving them. Victorians, of course, were ardent believers that the correct home environment shaped correct behavior; proper dining and tableware, especially, equated with proper civilization. So wealthy families had specific dishware for everything, from glass or silver vases for celery to custom dishes to hold bananas to specialized vessels and utensils for serving sardines. And don't forget asparagus forks.

Why This Recipe Works For a brown soda bread with good wheaty flavor but without a gummy, dense texture, we started by finding the right ratio of whole-wheat to all-purpose flour. Toasted wheat germ played up the sweet, nutty flavor of the whole wheat. To keep the texture light, we needed plenty of leavening; baking soda alone gave the bread a soapy taste, so we used a combination of baking soda and baking powder. Just a touch of sugar and a few tablespoons of butter kept our bread wholesome but not "health foody," and brushing a portion of the melted butter on the loaf after baking gave it a rich crust.

BROWN SODA BREAD

MAKES 1 LOAF

Toasted wheat germ is sold in jars at well-stocked supermarkets.

2 cups (10 ounces) all-purpose flour
1½ cups (8¼ ounces) whole-wheat flour
½ cup toasted wheat germ
3 tablespoons sugar
1½ teaspoons salt
1 teaspoon baking powder
1 teaspoon baking soda
1¾ cups buttermilk
3 tablespoons unsalted butter, melted

1. Adjust oven rack to lower-middle position and heat oven to 400 degrees. Line rimmed baking sheet with parchment paper. Whisk all-purpose flour, whole-wheat flour, wheat germ, sugar, salt, baking powder, and baking soda together in large bowl. Combine buttermilk and 2 tablespoons melted butter in 2-cup liquid measuring cup.

2. Add wet ingredients to dry ingredients and stir with rubber spatula until dough just comes together. Turn out dough onto lightly floured counter and knead until cohesive mass forms, about 8 turns. Pat dough into 7-inch round and transfer to prepared baking sheet. Using sharp serrated knife, make ¼-inch-deep cross about 5 inches long on top of loaf. Bake until skewer inserted in center comes out clean and loaf registers 195 degrees, 45 to 50 minutes, rotating baking sheet halfway through baking.

3. Remove bread from oven. Brush with remaining 1 tablespoon melted butter. Transfer loaf to wire rack and let cool for at least 1 hour. Serve.

BROWN SODA BREAD WITH CURRANTS AND CARAWAY

Add 1 cup dried currants and 1 tablespoon caraway seeds to dry ingredients in step 1.

Fastest Bread Ever
No yeast, no rise time, and almost no kneading or shaping.

Measure and whisk dry ingredients	5 minutes
Measure and combine wet ingredients	2 minutes
Stir wet into dry	1 minute
Knead briefly	1 minute
Shape simply	1 minute
Total work time	10 minutes

Mimicking Whole-Meal Flour
Brown Irish soda bread boasts a delicious wheaty sweetness. Traditionally, this bread adds whole-meal flour to the all-purpose flour used in the more familiar Irish soda bread to get that uniquely wheaty flavor. Many recipes simply substitute ordinary whole-wheat flour, while others skip the white flour entirely, combining the whole-wheat flour with practically the entire contents of a natural foods store. The former produced bland loaves while the latter offered great taste but crumbly textures.

For our recipe, we tried various ratios of all-purpose and whole-wheat flours until we landed on 2 cups of white flour combined with 1½ cups of whole-wheat. To play up the toasty, nutty flavor, we tried adding by turns wheat germ, wheat bran, and oatmeal. All of them gave our loaf complex wheatiness, but the bran required a trip to a specialty store and the oats required toasting and processing. Toasted wheat germ comes in convenient jars at the supermarket, so that's what we used.

A combination of whole-wheat flour, toasted wheatgerm, and all-purpose flour gives our loaf both robust flavor and tender, moist texture.

DAKOTA BREAD

MAKES ONE 10-INCH LOAF

In step 2, if the dough is still sticking to the sides of the mixing bowl after 2 minutes, add more flour 1 tablespoon at a time, up to 3 tablespoons. Be sure to use hot cereal mix, not boxed cold breakfast cereals, which may also be labeled "seven-grain."

2	cups warm water (110 degrees)
1½	cups (7½ ounces) seven-grain hot cereal mix
2	tablespoons honey
2	tablespoons vegetable oil
3½	cups (19¼ ounces) bread flour
1¾	teaspoons salt
1	teaspoon instant or rapid-rise yeast
3	tablespoons raw, unsalted pepitas
3	tablespoons raw, unsalted sunflower seeds
1	teaspoon sesame seeds
1	teaspoon poppy seeds
1	large egg, lightly beaten

1. Grease large bowl. Line rimmed baking sheet with parchment paper. In bowl of stand mixer, combine water, cereal, honey, and oil and let sit for 10 minutes.

2. Add flour, salt, and yeast to cereal mixture. Fit stand mixer with dough hook and knead on low speed until dough is smooth and elastic, 4 to 6 minutes. Add 2 tablespoons pepitas and 2 tablespoons sunflower seeds to dough and knead for 1 minute longer. Turn out dough onto lightly floured counter and knead until seeds are evenly distributed, about 2 minutes.

3. Transfer dough to greased bowl and cover with plastic wrap. Let dough rise at room temperature until almost doubled in size and fingertip depression in dough springs back slowly, 60 to 90 minutes.

4. Gently press down on center of dough to deflate. Transfer dough to lightly floured counter and shape into tight round ball. Place dough on prepared sheet. Cover dough loosely with plastic and let rise at room temperature until almost doubled in size, 60 to 90 minutes.

5. Adjust oven racks to upper-middle and lowest positions and heat oven to 425 degrees. Combine remaining 1 tablespoon pepitas, remaining 1 tablespoon sunflower seeds, sesame seeds, and poppy seeds in small bowl. Using sharp knife, make ¼-inch-deep cross, 5 inches long, on top of loaf. Brush loaf with egg and sprinkle seed mixture evenly over top.

6. Place 8½ by 4½-inch loaf pan on lowest oven rack and fill with 1 cup boiling water. Place baking sheet with dough on upper-middle rack and reduce oven to 375 degrees. Bake until crust is dark brown and bread registers 200 degrees, 40 to 50 minutes. Transfer loaf to wire rack and let cool completely, about 2 hours. Serve.

The Right Mix

Our Dakota Bread recipe calls for bread flour (for an appropriately chewy texture) supplemented with seven-grain hot cereal mix, which provides the bread with nutty depth. Don't confuse seven-grain hot cereal with seven-grain cold cereal; the latter will harm the texture of the loaf.

HOT TO TROT
Seven-grain hot cereal

Why This Recipe Works This hearty loaf from the breadbasket of America usually contains a daunting variety of flours and seeds. We shortened the ingredient list by using seven-grain cereal mix. This easy addition gave our loaf hearty texture and complex flavor. To round it out, we stirred some seeds into the batter and sprinkled more on top of the loaf. Starting the bread in a hot oven created an initial "spring," giving the loaf a lighter crumb, then lowering the temperature prevented the seeds from burning. High-protein bread flour allowed our loaf to rise high, and a pan of water in the oven prevented the crust from setting before the bread had fully risen.

great american cakes and cookies

RED VELVET CAKE

SERVES 12

This recipe must be prepared with natural cocoa powder. Dutch-processed cocoa will not yield the proper color or rise.

Cake

2¼ cups (11¼ ounces) all-purpose flour
1½ teaspoons baking soda
    Pinch salt
  1 cup buttermilk
  2 large eggs
  1 tablespoon distilled white vinegar
  1 teaspoon vanilla extract
  2 tablespoons cocoa powder
  2 tablespoons (1 ounce) red food coloring
12 tablespoons unsalted butter, softened
1½ cups (10½ ounces) granulated sugar

Frosting

16 tablespoons unsalted butter, softened
  4 cups (16 ounces) confectioners' sugar
16 ounces cream cheese, cut into 8 pieces, softened
1½ teaspoons vanilla extract
    Pinch salt

1. For the Cake Adjust oven rack to middle position and heat oven to 350 degrees. Grease two 9-inch round cake pans, line with parchment paper, grease parchment, then flour pans. Whisk flour, baking soda, and salt in medium bowl. Whisk buttermilk, eggs, vinegar, and vanilla in 4-cup liquid measuring cup. Mix cocoa with food coloring in small bowl until smooth paste forms.

2. Using stand mixer fitted with paddle, beat butter and sugar together on medium-high speed until pale and fluffy, about 3 minutes. Reduce speed to medium-low and add flour mixture in 3 additions, alternating with buttermilk mixture in 2 additions, scraping down bowl as needed. Add cocoa mixture and beat on medium speed until completely incorporated, about 30 seconds. Give batter final stir by hand. Scrape batter into prepared pans and bake until toothpick inserted in center comes out clean, about 25 minutes. Let cakes cool in pans on wire rack for 10 minutes. Remove cakes from pans, discarding parchment, and let cool completely on rack, about 2 hours. (Cooled cakes can be wrapped tightly in plastic wrap and kept at room temperature for up to 1 day.)

3. For the Frosting Using stand mixer fitted with paddle, beat butter and sugar on medium-high speed until pale and fluffy, about 2 minutes. Add cream cheese, 1 piece at a time, and beat until incorporated, about 30 seconds. Beat in vanilla and salt. Refrigerate until ready to use.

4. When cakes are cooled, cover edges of cake platter with strips of parchment. Place 1 cake layer on platter. Spread 2 cups frosting evenly over top, right to edge of cake. Top with second cake layer, press lightly to adhere, then spread remaining frosting evenly over top and sides of cake. Carefully remove parchment strips before serving. (Cake can be refrigerated for up to 3 days.)

Lost and Found

Red velvet cake fell out of fashion in the 1970s amidst health scares relating to red dye #2 (a similar fate befell red M&Ms, even though the candies never contained the dye in question). Once consumers were convinced that other red dyes were safe, red candies made it back into the M&Ms assortment (in 1987) and red velvet cakes started a comeback in bakeries.

Why This Recipe Works Although the exact origins of this cake are muddled, the appeal of a tender, shockingly bright red cake swathed in fluffy cream cheese frosting is undeniable. For a cake with an extra-tender crumb, we used two unexpected ingredients: buttermilk and vinegar. They reacted with our recipe's baking soda to create a fine, tender crumb. We also zeroed in on the perfect amount of cocoa that would add a dark hue to our cake as well as lending it a pleasant cocoa flavor.

CHOCOLATE BLACKOUT CAKE

SERVES 10 TO 12

Be sure to give the pudding and the cake enough time to cool or you'll end up with runny pudding and gummy cake.

Pudding

1¼ cups (8¾ ounces) granulated sugar
¼ cup cornstarch
½ teaspoon salt
2 cups half-and-half
1 cup whole milk
6 ounces unsweetened chocolate, chopped
2 teaspoons vanilla extract

Cake

1½ cups (7½ ounces) all-purpose flour
2 teaspoons baking powder
½ teaspoon baking soda
½ teaspoon salt
8 tablespoons unsalted butter
¾ cup (2¼ ounces) Dutch-processed cocoa powder
1 cup brewed coffee
1 cup buttermilk
1 cup packed (7 ounces) light brown sugar
1 cup (7 ounces) granulated sugar
2 large eggs
1 teaspoon vanilla extract

1. For the Pudding Whisk sugar, cornstarch, salt, half-and-half, and milk in large saucepan. Set pan over medium heat. Add chocolate and whisk constantly until chocolate melts and mixture begins to bubble, 2 to 4 minutes. Stir in vanilla and transfer pudding to large bowl. Place plastic wrap directly on surface of pudding and refrigerate until cold, at least 4 hours or up to 1 day.

2. For the Cake Adjust oven rack to middle position and heat oven to 325 degrees. Grease two 8-inch round cake pans, line with parchment paper, grease parchment, then flour pans. Whisk flour, baking powder, baking soda, and salt in bowl.

3. Melt butter in large saucepan over medium heat. Stir in cocoa and cook until fragrant, about 1 minute.

Off heat, whisk in coffee, buttermilk, brown sugar, and granulated sugar until dissolved. Whisk in eggs and vanilla, then slowly whisk in flour mixture.

4. Divide batter evenly between prepared pans and bake until toothpick inserted in center comes out clean, 30 to 35 minutes. Let cakes cool in pans on wire rack for 15 minutes. Remove cakes from pans, discarding parchment, and let cool completely on wire rack, about 2 hours.

5. Working with 1 cake layer at a time, cut cakes horizontally into 2 layers using long, serrated knife. Crumble 1 cake layer into medium crumbs and set aside. Cover edges of cake platter with strips of parchment. Place 1 cake layer on platter. Spread 1 cup pudding over top, right to edge of cake. Top with second layer; press lightly to adhere. Repeat with 1 cup pudding and last cake layer. Spread remaining pudding evenly over top and sides of cake. Sprinkle cake crumbs evenly over top and sides of cake, pressing lightly to adhere crumbs. Carefully remove parchment strips before serving. (Cake can be refrigerated for up to 2 days.)

Lost Icon

Ebinger's Baking Company opened in 1898 on Flatbush Avenue in Brooklyn and grew into a chain of more than 60 stores before going bankrupt in 1972. Started by Arthur Ebinger, a baker who emigrated from Germany with a vast collection of recipes, the business grew to include his wife and their three sons. During its heyday, Ebinger's was a point of bragging rights for Brooklynites, as celebrities and the well-to-do from Manhattan never went to Brooklyn without taking home a cake or one of Ebinger's other specialties, which included challah, rye bread, pumpkin pie, Othellos (filled mini sponge cakes covered in chocolate), and crumb buns.

Why This Recipe Works Chocolate blackout cake, a tender chocolate layer cake sandwiched together with a puddinglike filling and covered with cake crumbs, was created by the now-shuttered Ebinger's bakery in Brooklyn. We set out to create our own version. We started by adding cocoa powder to the butter we were already melting for the cake. Heating the cocoa in the butter produced a cake that was dark and rich. And to complement the chocolate flavor of the cake, we made a chocolaty, dairy-rich pudding with a combination of milk and half-and-half, which gave it a velvety, lush quality.

Why This Recipe Works We wanted to resurrect the classic childhood favorite tunnel of fudge cake without the benefit of a prepackaged cake mix. Dutch-processed cocoa gave our cake deep chocolate flavor. Adding melted chocolate to the batter made our cake moister and contributed more chocolate punch. Slightly underbaking the cake was the first step toward achieving the ideal consistency for the tunnel. Replacing some of the granulated sugar with brown sugar and cutting back on the flour and butter provided the perfect environment for the fudgy interior to form.

TUNNEL OF FUDGE CAKE

SERVES 12 TO 14

For an accurate measurement of boiling water, bring a full kettle of water to a boil, then measure out the desired amount. Do not use a cake tester, toothpick, or skewer to test the cake—the fudgy interior won't give an accurate reading. Instead, remove the cake from the oven when the sides just begin to pull away from the pan and the surface of the cake springs back when pressed gently with your finger.

Cake

- ¾ cup (2¼ ounces) Dutch-processed cocoa powder, plus extra for dusting pan
- ½ cup boiling water
- 2 ounces bittersweet chocolate, chopped
- 2 cups (10 ounces) all-purpose flour
- 2 cups pecans or walnuts, chopped fine
- 2 cups (8 ounces) confectioners' sugar
- 1 teaspoon salt
- 5 large eggs, room temperature
- 1 tablespoon vanilla extract
- 20 tablespoons (2½ sticks) unsalted butter, softened
- 1 cup (7 ounces) granulated sugar
- ¾ cup packed (5¼ ounces) light brown sugar

Chocolate Glaze

- ¾ cup heavy cream
- ¼ cup light corn syrup
- 8 ounces bittersweet chocolate, chopped
- ½ teaspoon vanilla extract

1. For the Cake Adjust oven rack to lower-middle position and heat oven to 350 degrees. Grease 12-cup Bundt pan and dust with cocoa powder. Pour boiling water over chocolate in medium bowl and whisk until smooth. Let cool to room temperature. Whisk cocoa, flour, pecans, confectioners' sugar, and salt in large bowl. Whisk eggs and vanilla in 4-cup liquid measuring cup.

2. Using stand mixer fitted with paddle, beat butter, granulated sugar, and brown sugar on medium-high speed until light and fluffy, about 2 minutes. On low speed, add egg mixture until combined, about 30 seconds. Add chocolate mixture and beat until incorporated, about 30 seconds. Beat in flour mixture until just combined, about 30 seconds.

3. Scrape batter into prepared pan, smooth batter, and bake until edges are beginning to pull away from pan, about 45 minutes. Let cool in pan on wire rack for 1½ hours, then invert onto serving plate and let cool completely, at least 2 hours.

4. For the Chocolate Glaze Heat cream, corn syrup, and chocolate in small saucepan over medium heat, stirring constantly, until smooth. Stir in vanilla and set aside until slightly thickened, about 30 minutes. Drizzle glaze over cake and let set for at least 10 minutes. Serve. (Cake can be stored at room temperature for up to 2 days.)

Birth of the Bundt Pan

Metallurgical engineer H. David Dalquist invented the Bundt pan in 1950 at the request of bakers in Minneapolis who were using old-fashioned ceramic pans of the same design. Dalquist turned to cast aluminum to produce a pan that was much lighter and easier to use. Sales of his Bundt pan (a name he trademarked) were underwhelming until Ella Helfrich's Tunnel of Fudge Cake made its debut in 1966. The Pillsbury Company quickly received over 200,000 requests for the pan, and to meet demand Dalquist's company, Nordic Ware, went into 24-hour production. Over 50 million Bundt pans have been sold worldwide.

Why This Recipe Works Lane cake is a tall, fluffy, snow white cake filled with a rich, sweet mixture of egg whites, butter, raisins, and "a wineglass full of good whiskey." Our simplified recipe capped the number of layers at two, and using a food processor streamlined much of the tedious prep work. Replacing sugar with boiled corn syrup in our frosting quickly brought the whipped egg whites to a safe temperature without resorting to a candy thermometer or complicated (and unreliable) guesswork.

LANE CAKE

SERVES 10 TO 12

Cake

1 cup whole milk, room temperature
6 large egg whites, room temperature
2 teaspoons vanilla extract
2¼ cups (9 ounces) cake flour
1¾ cups (12¼ ounces) sugar
4 teaspoons baking powder
1 teaspoon salt
12 tablespoons unsalted butter,
    cut into 12 pieces and softened

Filling

5 tablespoons bourbon
1 tablespoon heavy cream
1 teaspoon cornstarch
    Pinch salt
⅓ cup sweetened shredded coconut
¾ cup pecans
¾ cup golden raisins
4 tablespoons unsalted butter
¾ cup sweetened condensed milk
½ teaspoon vanilla extract

Frosting

2 large egg whites, room temperature
¼ teaspoon cream of tartar
¼ cup (1¾ ounces) sugar
⅔ cup light corn syrup
1 teaspoon vanilla extract

1. For the Cake Adjust oven rack to middle position and heat oven to 350 degrees. Grease two 9-inch round cake pans, line with parchment paper, grease parchment, then flour pans. Whisk milk, egg whites, and vanilla in 4-cup liquid measuring cup. Using stand mixer fitted with paddle, mix flour, sugar, baking powder, and salt on low speed until combined. Add butter, 1 piece at a time, and beat until only pea-size pieces remain. Add half of milk mixture, increase speed to medium-high, and beat until light and fluffy, about 1 minute. Reduce speed to medium-low, add remaining milk mixture, and beat until incorporated, about 30 seconds. Give batter final stir by hand.

2. Scrape batter into prepared pans and bake until toothpick inserted in center comes out clean, 20 to 25 minutes. Let cakes cool in pans on wire rack for 10 minutes. Remove cakes from pans, discarding parchment, and let cool completely on racks, about 2 hours. (Cooled cakes can be tightly wrapped in plastic wrap and stored at room temperature for up to 2 days.)

3. For the Filling Whisk bourbon, cream, cornstarch, and salt in bowl until smooth. Process coconut in food processor until finely ground, about 15 seconds. Add pecans and raisins and pulse until coarsely ground, about 10 pulses. Melt butter in large skillet over medium-low heat. Add processed coconut mixture and cook, stirring occasionally, until golden brown and fragrant, about 5 minutes. Stir in bourbon mixture and bring to boil. Remove from heat and add condensed milk and vanilla. Transfer to medium bowl and let cool to room temperature, about 30 minutes. (Filling can be refrigerated for 2 days. Bring filling to room temperature before using.)

4. For the Frosting Using stand mixer fitted with whisk, whip egg whites and cream of tartar on medium-high speed until frothy, about 30 seconds. With mixer running, slowly add sugar and whip until soft peaks form, about 2 minutes; set aside. Bring corn syrup to boil in small saucepan over medium-high heat and cook until large bubbles appear around perimeter of pan, about 1 minute. With mixer running, slowly pour hot syrup into whites (avoid pouring syrup onto beaters or it will splash). Add vanilla and beat until mixture has cooled and is very thick and glossy, 3 to 5 minutes.

5. Cover edges of cake platter with strips of parchment. Place 1 cake layer on platter. Spread filling over cake, then top with second cake layer, pressing lightly to adhere. Spread remaining frosting evenly over top and sides of cake. Carefully remove parchment strips before serving. (Cake can be refrigerated for up to 2 days.)

STRAWBERRY DREAM CAKE

SERVES 8 TO 10

Be sure to allow the cream cheese to soften so that it blends into a smooth frosting.

Cake

10 ounces frozen whole strawberries (2 cups)
¾ cup whole milk, room temperature
6 large egg whites, room temperature
2 teaspoons vanilla extract
2¼ cups (9 ounces) cake flour
1¾ cups (12¼ ounces) granulated sugar
4 teaspoons baking powder
1 teaspoon salt
12 tablespoons unsalted butter, cut into 12 pieces and softened

Frosting

10 tablespoons unsalted butter, softened
2¼ cups (9 ounces) confectioners' sugar
12 ounces cream cheese, cut into 12 pieces and softened
   Pinch salt
8 ounces fresh strawberries, hulled and sliced thin (about 1½ cups)

1. For the Cake Adjust oven rack to middle position and heat oven to 350 degrees. Grease two 9-inch round cake pans, line with parchment paper, grease parchment, then flour pans.

2. Transfer strawberries to bowl, cover, and microwave until strawberries are soft and have released their juices, about 5 minutes. Place in fine-mesh strainer set over small saucepan. Firmly press fruit dry (juice should measure at least ¾ cup); reserve strawberry solids. Bring juice to boil over medium-high heat and cook, stirring occasionally, until syrupy and reduced to ¼ cup, 6 to 8 minutes. Whisk milk into juice until combined.

3. Whisk strawberry-milk mixture, egg whites, and vanilla in bowl. Using stand mixer fitted with paddle, mix flour, sugar, baking powder, and salt on low speed until combined. Add butter, 1 piece at a time, and mix until only pea-size pieces remain, about 1 minute. Add half of milk mixture, increase speed to medium-high, and beat until light and fluffy, about 1 minute. Reduce speed to medium-low, add remaining milk mixture, and beat until incorporated, about 30 seconds. Give batter final stir by hand.

4. Scrape batter into prepared pans and bake until toothpick inserted in center comes out clean, 20 to 25 minutes, rotating pans halfway through baking. Let cakes cool in pans on wire rack for 10 minutes. Remove cakes from pans, discarding parchment, and let cool completely on rack, about 2 hours. (Cooled cakes can be tightly wrapped with plastic wrap and stored at room temperature for up to 2 days.)

5. For the Frosting Using stand mixer fitted with paddle, mix butter and sugar on low speed until combined, about 30 seconds. Increase speed to medium-high and beat until pale and fluffy, about 2 minutes. Add cream cheese, 1 piece at a time, and beat until incorporated, about 1 minute. Add reserved strawberry solids and salt and mix until combined, about 30 seconds. Refrigerate until ready to use, up to 2 days.

6. Pat strawberries dry with paper towels. Cover edges of cake platter with strips of parchment. Place 1 cake layer on platter. Spread ¾ cup frosting evenly over top, right to edge of cake. Press 1 cup strawberries in even layer over frosting and cover with additional ¾ cup frosting. Top with second cake layer, press lightly to adhere, then spread remaining frosting evenly over top and sides of cake. Garnish with remaining strawberries. Carefully remove parchment strips before serving. (Cake can be refrigerated for up to 2 days.)

Why This Recipe Works Strange as it may seem, the vast majority of existing strawberry cake recipes turn to strawberry Jell-O for flavor. Hoping to avoid this artificial solution, we performed test after test to figure out the best way to flavor our cake with actual strawberries. Any strawberry solids wreaked havoc on the tender cake, but strained and reduced strawberry juices kept our cake light and packed a strawberry punch. Not to be left behind, the reserved strawberry solids enriched the frosting with more berry flavor.

Why This Recipe Works Strawberry poke cake was invented in 1969 as a way to increase Jell-O sales. It quickly became popular thanks to its festive look and easy assembly. But we encountered two problems: dull strawberry flavor and soggy box mix cake. For a sturdier cake that would hold up to hot gelatin, we opted to make our own white cake from scratch. And to improve the strawberry flavor of the Jell-O, we combined it with the juice from cooked strawberries. Making a homemade "jam" from the berry solids and spreading the mixture on top of the cake gave our cake an extra layer of flavor.

STRAWBERRY POKE CAKE

SERVES 12

The top of the cake will look slightly overbaked—this keeps the crumb from becoming too soggy after the gelatin is poured on top.

Cake
2¼ cups (11¼ ounces) all-purpose flour
4 teaspoons baking powder
1 teaspoon salt
1 cup whole milk
2 teaspoons vanilla extract
6 large egg whites
12 tablespoons unsalted butter, softened
1¾ cups (12¼ ounces) sugar

Syrup and Topping
4 cups frozen strawberries
½ cup water
6 tablespoons (2⅔ ounces) sugar
2 tablespoons orange juice
2 tablespoons strawberry-flavored gelatin
2 cups heavy cream, chilled

1. For the Cake Adjust oven rack to middle position and heat oven to 350 degrees. Grease 13 by 9-inch baking pan, line with parchment paper, grease parchment, then flour pan. Whisk flour, baking powder, and salt in bowl. Whisk milk, vanilla, and egg whites in 4-cup liquid measuring cup.

2. Using stand mixer fitted with paddle, beat butter and sugar on medium-high speed until pale and fluffy, about 2 minutes, scraping down bowl as needed. Reduce speed to low and add flour mixture in 3 additions, alternating with milk mixture in 2 additions, beating after each addition until combined, about 30 seconds each time, scraping down bowl as needed. Give batter final stir by hand. Scrape into prepared pan and bake until toothpick inserted in center comes out clean, about 35 minutes. Let cake cool completely in pan, at least 1 hour. (Once cool, cake can be wrapped in plastic wrap and kept at room temperature for up to 2 days.)

3. For the Syrup and Topping Heat 3 cups strawberries, water, 2 tablespoons sugar, and orange juice in medium saucepan over medium-low heat. Cover and cook until strawberries are softened, about 10 minutes. Strain liquid into bowl, reserving solids, then whisk gelatin into liquid. Let cool to room temperature, at least 20 minutes.

4. Meanwhile, poke 50 deep holes all over top of cake with skewer, taking care not to poke through to dish bottom and twisting skewer to enlarge holes. Pour cooled liquid over top of cake. Wrap with plastic wrap and refrigerate until gelatin is set, at least 3 hours or up to 2 days.

5. Pulse reserved strained strawberries, 2 tablespoons sugar, and remaining 1 cup strawberries in food processor until mixture resembles strawberry jam, about 15 pulses. Spread mixture evenly over cake. Using stand mixer fitted with whisk, whip cream with remaining 2 tablespoons sugar on medium-low speed until foamy, about 1 minute. Increase speed to high and whip until soft peaks form, 1 to 3 minutes. Spread cream over strawberries. Serve. (Cake can be refrigerated for up to 2 days.)

Perfecting the Poke
Finding the right poking device wasn't as simple as you might think. Toothpicks were too small, while straws, handles of wooden spoons, pencils, and fingers were too big. A wooden skewer finally did the trick. But just poking didn't create a large enough hole for the liquid to seep into. In order to create deep lines of red color against the white crumb, we had to poke and then twist the skewer to really separate the crumb.

1. Using skewer, poke about 50 deep holes over cake, being careful not to poke through to bottom. Twist skewer to enlarge holes.

2. Slowly pour cooled gelatin mixture evenly over surface of cake and it will slowly soak into cake.

TEXAS SHEET CAKE

SERVES 24

Toast the pecans in a dry skillet over medium heat, shaking the pan occasionally, until golden and fragrant, about 5 minutes.

Cake

- 2 cups (10 ounces) all-purpose flour
- 2 cups (14 ounces) granulated sugar
- ½ teaspoon baking soda
- ½ teaspoon salt
- 2 large eggs plus 2 large yolks
- ¼ cup sour cream
- 2 teaspoons vanilla extract
- 8 ounces semisweet chocolate, chopped
- ¾ cup vegetable oil
- ¾ cup water
- ½ cup (1½ ounces) Dutch-processed cocoa powder
- 4 tablespoons unsalted butter

Chocolate Icing

- 8 tablespoons unsalted butter
- ½ cup heavy cream
- ½ cup (1½ ounces) Dutch-processed cocoa powder
- 1 tablespoon light corn syrup
- 3 cups (12 ounces) confectioners' sugar
- 1 tablespoon vanilla extract
- 1 cup pecans, toasted and chopped

1. For the Cake Adjust oven rack to middle position and heat oven to 350 degrees. Grease 18 by 13-inch rimmed baking sheet. Combine flour, sugar, baking soda, and salt in large bowl. Whisk eggs and yolks, sour cream, and vanilla in another bowl until smooth.

2. Heat chocolate, oil, water, cocoa, and butter in large saucepan over medium heat, stirring occasionally, until smooth, 3 to 5 minutes. Whisk chocolate mixture into flour mixture until incorporated. Whisk egg mixture into batter, then pour into prepared baking pan. Bake until toothpick inserted into center comes out clean, 18 to 20 minutes. Transfer to wire rack.

3. For the Chocolate Icing About 5 minutes before cake is done, heat butter, cream, cocoa, and corn syrup in large saucepan over medium heat, stirring occasionally, until smooth. Off heat, whisk in sugar and vanilla. Spread warm icing evenly over hot cake and sprinkle with pecans. Let cake cool to room temperature on wire rack, about 1 hour, then refrigerate until icing is set, about 1 hour longer. Cut into 3-inch squares. Serve. (Cake can be refrigerated for up to 2 days.)

Timing Is Everything

The key to perfectly moist Texas sheet cake is to let the warm icing soak into the hot cake. As soon as the cake comes out of the oven, pour the warm icing over the cake and use a spatula to spread the icing to the edges of the cake. This creates the fudgy layer between the icing and the cake.

Why This Recipe Works Texas sheet cake is a huge, pecan-topped chocolate-glazed cake. For the cake, we relied on a combination of butter and vegetable oil, which produced a dense, brownielike texture. To increase the fudgy chocolate flavor, we used both cocoa powder and melted semisweet chocolate. Replacing milk with heavy cream gave the icing more body, while adding corn syrup produced a lustrous finish. The key to creating the signature fudgy layer between cake and icing was to let the warm icing soak into the hot cake. We poured the icing over the sheet cake straight out of the oven and smoothed it with a spatula.

CHOCOLATE ÉCLAIR CAKE

SERVES 15

Six ounces of finely chopped semisweet chocolate can be used in place of the chips.

1¼ cups (8¾ ounces) sugar
6 tablespoons cornstarch
1 teaspoon salt
5 cups whole milk
4 tablespoons unsalted butter, cut into 4 pieces
5 teaspoons vanilla extract
1¼ teaspoons unflavored gelatin
2 tablespoons water
2¾ cups heavy cream, chilled
14 ounces graham crackers
1 cup semisweet chocolate chips
5 tablespoons light corn syrup

1. Combine sugar, cornstarch, and salt in large saucepan. Whisk milk into sugar mixture until smooth and bring to boil, scraping bottom of pan with heatproof rubber spatula, over medium-high heat. Immediately reduce heat to medium-low and cook, continuing to scrape bottom, until thickened and large bubbles appear on surface, 4 to 6 minutes. Off heat, whisk in butter and vanilla. Transfer pudding to large bowl and place plastic wrap directly on surface of pudding. Refrigerate until cool, about 2 hours.

2. Sprinkle gelatin over water in bowl and let sit until gelatin softens, about 5 minutes. Microwave until mixture is bubbling around edges and gelatin dissolves, 15 to 30 seconds. Using stand mixer fitted with whisk, whip 2 cups cream on medium-low speed until foamy, about 1 minute. Increase speed to high and whip until soft peaks form, 1 to 3 minutes. Add gelatin mixture and whip until stiff peaks form, about 1 minute.

3. Whisk one-third of whipped cream into chilled pudding, then gently fold in remaining whipped cream, 1 scoop at a time, until combined. Cover bottom of 13 by 9-inch baking dish with layer of graham crackers, breaking crackers as necessary to line bottom of pan. Top with half of pudding–whipped cream mixture (about 5½ cups) and another layer of graham crackers. Repeat with remaining pudding–whipped cream mixture and remaining graham crackers.

4. Microwave chocolate chips, remaining ¾ cup cream, and corn syrup in bowl, on 50 percent power, stirring occasionally, until smooth, 1 to 2 minutes. Let glaze cool to room temperature, about 10 minutes. Cover graham crackers with glaze and refrigerate cake for 6 to 24 hours. Serve. (Cake can be refrigerated for up to 2 days.)

The Worst College Food Ever

The Reverend Sylvester Graham, the inventor of the graham cracker, wasn't quite as much fun as that crisp treat might have you believe. In fact, he was a food zealot, convinced that a diet of nothing but water and graham crackers—originally a "health food" made from whole-wheat flour and honey—would turn you into a better person. Some 170 years ago, the administrators at Oberlin College, a small liberal arts school in Ohio, grew enamored of Graham's ideas and decided to feed students according to his principles. (And you think your college food was bad?) Oberlin students were encouraged to abstain from consuming meat, tea, and coffee—except for "crust coffee" made from toast and boiled water. They were discouraged from eating butter and pastries and even from seasoning their food. (As legend has it, a professor actually lost his job for bringing a pepper shaker to the dining hall.) Oberlin students complained so vociferously that the college was forced to abandon its dining plan, and the Graham diet (if not his eponymous cracker) faded into culinary history.

Why This Recipe Works This no-bake dessert is typically made by layering a mixture of instant vanilla pudding and Cool Whip between graham crackers and topping it with chocolate frosting. We loved the convenience of these store-bought items, but our enthusiasm waned when confronted by their flavor. With a couple of easy techniques (a quick stovetop pudding, whipped cream, and a microwave-and-stir glaze) and very little active time, we produced a from-scratch version that easily trumped its inspiration.

Why This Recipe Works This unique dessert combines a layer of fudgy chocolate cake and a layer of rich, caramel-coated flan that "magically" switch places as they bake. We started with an easy dump-and-stir cake recipe. The cake's flavor was great, but it was soggy due to the moisture from the flan. Cutting some of the buttermilk and sugar from the cake batter did the trick. To help our flan firm up, we swapped some of the egg yolks for whole eggs and added cream cheese. The cream cheese also lent the flan a tanginess that offset its sweetness. Convenient store-bought caramel sauce topped it all off.

MAGIC CHOCOLATE FLAN CAKE

SERVES 16

It's worth using good-quality caramel sauce, such as Fat Toad Farm Goat's Milk Caramel. If your blender doesn't hold 2 quarts, process the flan in two batches. The cake needs to chill for at least 8 hours before you can unmold it.

Cake

½ cup caramel sauce or topping
½ cup plus 2 tablespoons (3⅛ ounces) all-purpose flour
⅓ cup (1 ounce) cocoa powder
½ teaspoon baking soda
⅛ teaspoon salt
4 ounces bittersweet chocolate, chopped
6 tablespoons unsalted butter
½ cup buttermilk
½ cup (3½ ounces) sugar
2 large eggs
1 teaspoon vanilla extract

Flan

2 (14-ounce) cans sweetened condensed milk
2½ cups whole milk
6 ounces cream cheese
6 large eggs plus 4 large yolks
1 teaspoon vanilla extract

1. For the Cake Adjust oven rack to middle position and heat oven to 350 degrees. Grease 12-cup nonstick Bundt pan. Microwave caramel until easily pourable, about 30 seconds. Pour into pan to coat bottom. Combine flour, cocoa, baking soda, and salt in bowl; set aside. Combine chocolate and butter in large bowl and microwave at 50 percent power, stirring occasionally, until melted, 2 to 4 minutes.

Whisk buttermilk, sugar, eggs, and vanilla into chocolate mixture until incorporated. Stir in flour mixture until just combined. Pour batter over caramel in pan.

2. For the Flan Process all ingredients in blender until smooth, about 1 minute. Gently pour flan over cake batter and place Bundt pan in large roasting pan. Place roasting pan on oven rack and pour warm water into roasting pan until it reaches halfway up side of Bundt pan. Bake until toothpick inserted in cake comes out clean and flan registers 180 degrees, 75 to 90 minutes. Transfer Bundt pan to wire rack. Let cool to room temperature, about 2 hours, then refrigerate until set, at least 8 hours. (Remove roasting pan from oven once water has cooled.)

3. Place bottom third of Bundt pan in bowl of hot tap water for 1 minute. Invert completely flat cake platter, place platter over top of pan, and gently turn platter and pan upside down. Slowly remove pan, allowing caramel to drizzle over top of cake. Serve.

Modulate the Heat

A water bath, or bain-marie, makes for a more even, temperate baking environment. Simply place your baking vessel in a larger vessel (we use a roasting pan) and partially fill the latter with water.

Why This Recipe Works A great tres leches cake—a sponge cake soaked with a mixture of "three milks" (heavy cream, evaporated milk, and sweetened condensed milk)—should be moist but not mushy and sweet but not sickeningly so. For an ideal version, we needed to make our cake sturdy enough to handle the milk mixture, so we used whipped whole eggs instead of the usual egg whites. Although some tres leches recipes use equal amounts of evaporated milk, sweetened condensed milk, and cream, we found that cutting back on the cream produced a thicker mixture that didn't oversaturate the cake.

TRES LECHES CAKE

SERVES 12

The cake is best frosted right before serving.

Milk Mixture
1 (14-ounce) can sweetened condensed milk
1 (12-ounce) can evaporated milk
1 cup heavy cream
1 teaspoon vanilla extract

Cake
2 cups (10 ounces) all-purpose flour
2 teaspoons baking powder
1 teaspoon salt
½ teaspoon ground cinnamon
8 tablespoons unsalted butter
1 cup whole milk
4 large eggs, room temperature
2 cups (14 ounces) sugar
2 teaspoons vanilla extract

Topping
1 cup heavy cream
3 tablespoons corn syrup
1 teaspoon vanilla extract

1. For the Milk Mixture Pour condensed milk into large bowl. Microwave covered at 50 percent power, stirring every 3 to 5 minutes, until slightly darkened and thickened, 9 to 15 minutes. Remove from microwave and slowly whisk in evaporated milk, cream, and vanilla. Let cool to room temperature.

2. For the Cake Adjust oven rack to middle position and heat oven to 325 degrees. Grease and flour 13 by 9-inch baking dish. Whisk flour, baking powder, salt, and cinnamon in bowl. Heat butter and milk in small saucepan over low heat until butter is melted; remove from heat and set aside.

3. Using stand mixer fitted with whisk, whip eggs on medium speed until foamy, about 30 seconds. Slowly add sugar and continue to whip until fully incorporated, 5 to 10 seconds. Increase speed to medium-high and whip until mixture is thick and glossy, 5 to 7 minutes. Reduce speed to low, add milk-butter mixture and vanilla, and mix until combined, about 15 seconds. Add flour mixture in 3 additions, mixing on medium speed after each addition and scraping down bowl as needed, until flour is fully incorporated, about 30 seconds. Using rubber spatula, scrape batter into prepared dish. Bake until toothpick inserted in center comes out clean, 30 to 35 minutes. Transfer cake to wire rack and let cool for 10 minutes.

4. Using skewer, poke holes at ½-inch intervals in top of cake. Slowly pour milk mixture over cake until completely absorbed. Let sit at room temperature for 15 minutes, then refrigerate, uncovered, for 3 hours or up to 24 hours.

5. For the Topping Remove cake from refrigerator 30 minutes before serving. Using stand mixer fitted with whisk, whip cream, corn syrup, and vanilla on medium-low speed until foamy, about 1 minute. Increase speed to high and whip until soft peaks form, 1 to 3 minutes. Spread over cake and cut into 3-inch squares. Serve.

SWISS HAZELNUT CAKE

SERVES 12 TO 16

We toast and grind the hazelnuts with their skins for better color and flavor. When working with the marshmallow crème, grease the inside of your measuring cup and spatula with vegetable oil spray to prevent sticking. You may use a vegetable peeler or the large holes of a box grater to shave the chocolate.

Cake

½	cup (2 ounces) skin-on hazelnuts, toasted and cooled
1¼	cups (5 ounces) cake flour
1	cup (7 ounces) granulated sugar
1½	teaspoons baking powder
½	teaspoon salt
½	cup vegetable oil
¼	cup water
3	large egg yolks, plus 5 large whites
2½	teaspoons vanilla extract
¼	teaspoon cream of tartar

Frosting

24	tablespoons (3 sticks) unsalted butter, softened
¼	teaspoon salt
1¾	cups (7 ounces) confectioners' sugar
12	ounces (2⅔ cups) Fluff brand marshmallow crème
2	tablespoons hazelnut liqueur
6	ounces bittersweet chocolate

1. For the Cake Adjust oven rack to middle position and heat oven to 350 degrees. Line the bottoms of 2 light-colored 9-inch round cake pans with parchment paper; grease parchment but not pan sides.

2. Process hazelnuts in food processor until finely ground, about 30 seconds. Whisk flour, sugar, baking powder, salt, and ground hazelnuts together in large bowl. Whisk oil, water, egg yolks, and vanilla together in separate bowl. Whisk egg yolk mixture into flour mixture until smooth batter forms.

3. Using stand mixer fitted with whisk, whip egg whites and cream of tartar on medium-low speed until foamy, about 1 minute. Increase speed to medium-high and whip until soft peaks form, 2 to 3 minutes. Gently whisk one-third of whipped egg

whites into batter. Using rubber spatula, gently fold remaining egg whites into batter until incorporated.

4. Divide batter evenly between prepared pans and gently tap pans on counter to release air bubbles. Bake until tops are light golden brown and cakes spring back when pressed lightly in center, 25 to 28 minutes, rotating pans halfway through baking.

5. Let cakes cool in pans for 15 minutes. Run knife around edges of pans; invert cakes onto wire rack. Discard parchment and let cakes cool completely, at least 1 hour. (To prepare to make chocolate shavings, place food processor shredding disk and chocolate in freezer.)

6. For the Frosting Using clean stand mixer fitted with whisk, whip butter and salt on medium speed until smooth, about 1 minute. Reduce speed to low and slowly add sugar. Increase speed to medium and whip until smooth, about 2 minutes, scraping down sides of bowl as needed. Add marshmallow crème, increase speed to medium-high, and whip until light and fluffy, 3 to 5 minutes. Reduce speed to low, add hazelnut liqueur, return speed to medium-high, and whip to incorporate, about 30 seconds.

7. Line rimmed baking sheet with parchment paper. Fit food processor with chilled shredding disk. Turn on processor and feed chocolate through hopper. Transfer shaved chocolate to prepared baking sheet and spread into even layer. Place in freezer to harden, about 10 minutes.

8. Place 1 cake layer on cake stand. Spread 2 cups frosting evenly over top, right to edge of cake. Top with second cake layer, pressing lightly to adhere. Spread remaining 2 cups frosting evenly over top and sides of cake.

9. Fold 16 by 12-inch sheet of parchment paper into 6 by 4-inch rectangle. Using parchment rectangle, scoop up half of chocolate shavings and sprinkle over top of cake. Once top of cake is coated, scoop up remaining chocolate shavings and press gently against sides of cake to adhere, scooping and reapplying as needed. Serve.

Why This Recipe Works This sweet, nutty cake is famous in Philadelphia, but when the Swiss Haus pastry chef wouldn't disclose the recipe, we played detective. We settled on a chiffon base, knowing that the beaten egg whites would give the cake a fluffy texture. For full hazelnut flavor, we ground the nuts in a food processor, then substituted this hazelnut "flour" for a portion of the cake flour. Since meringue buttercream frosting is a project, we found an excellent shortcut using marshmallow crème. To prevent the chocolate from melting, we froze it before and after shaving and used parchment paper to gently press the curls into the frosting.

Why This Recipe Works The beauty of blitz torte is that you get five impressive layers—cake, meringue, fruit-and-cream filling, more cake, and more meringue—for about the same amount of work as a two-layer cake. That's because the recipe is incredibly clever: Each meringue layer is baked directly atop the yellow cake batter. The recipe is also pleasingly symmetrical: The egg yolks go into the cake, while the whites go into the meringue. For our filling, we mimicked the rich egginess of custard by folding store-bought lemon curd into whipped cream, stabilizing it with gelatin, and layering it with raspberries. Bliss torte is more like it!

BLITZ TORTE

SERVES 8 TO 10

If your pans are dark, reduce the baking time in step 6 to 30 to 35 minutes.

Filling

- 1 teaspoon unflavored gelatin
- 2 tablespoons water
- 1 cup heavy cream, chilled
- 1 teaspoon vanilla extract
- ½ cup lemon curd
- 10 ounces (2 cups) raspberries
- 2 tablespoons orange liqueur
- 1 tablespoon sugar

Cake

- ½ cup whole milk
- 4 large egg yolks
- 1½ teaspoons vanilla extract
- 1¼ cups (5 ounces) cake flour
- 1 cup (7 ounces) sugar
- 1½ teaspoons baking powder
- ½ teaspoon salt
- 12 tablespoons unsalted butter, cut into 12 pieces and softened

Meringue

- 4 large egg whites
- ¼ teaspoon cream of tartar
- ¾ cup (5¼ ounces) sugar
- ½ teaspoon vanilla extract
- ½ cup sliced almonds

1. For the Filling Sprinkle gelatin over water in small bowl and let sit until gelatin softens, about 5 minutes. Microwave until mixture is bubbling around edges and gelatin dissolves, 15 to 30 seconds. Using stand mixer fitted with whisk, whip cream and vanilla on medium-low speed until foamy, about 1 minute. Increase speed to medium-high and whip until soft peaks form, about 2 minutes. Add gelatin mixture and whip until firm, stiff peaks form, about 1 minute.

2. Whisk lemon curd in large metal bowl to loosen. Fold whipped cream mixture into curd. Refrigerate cream filling for 1½ to 3 hours.

3. For the Cake Meanwhile, adjust oven rack to middle position and heat oven to 325 degrees. Grease 2 light-colored 9-inch round cake pans, line with parchment paper, grease parchment, and flour pans.

4. Beat milk, yolks, and vanilla together with fork. Using stand mixer fitted with paddle, mix flour, sugar, baking powder, and salt on low speed until combined, about 5 seconds. Add butter, 1 piece at a time, and mix until only pea-size pieces remain, about 1 minute. Add half of milk mixture, increase speed to medium-high, and beat until light and fluffy, about 1 minute. Reduce speed to medium-low, add remaining milk mixture, and beat until incorporated, about 30 seconds. Give batter final stir by hand. Divide batter evenly between prepared pans and spread into even layer using small offset spatula.

5. For the Meringue Using clean, dry stand mixer fitted with a whisk, whip egg whites and cream of tartar on medium-low speed until foamy, about 1 minute. Increase speed to medium-high and whip whites to soft, billowy mounds, 1 to 3 minutes. Gradually add sugar and whip until glossy, stiff peaks form, 3 to 5 minutes. Add vanilla and whip until incorporated.

6. Divide meringue evenly between cake pans and spread evenly over cake batter to edges of pan. Use back of spoon to create peaks in meringue. Sprinkle meringue with almonds. Bake cakes until meringue is golden and has pulled away from sides of pan, 50 to 55 minutes, switching and rotating pans halfway through baking. Let cakes cool completely in pans on wire rack. (Cakes can be baked up to 24 hours in advance and stored, uncovered, in pans at room temperature.)

7. To finish filling, 10 minutes before assembling cake, combine raspberries, liqueur, and sugar in bowl.

8. Gently remove cakes from pans, discarding parchment. Place 1 cake layer on platter, meringue side up. Spread half of cream filling evenly over top. Using slotted spoon, spoon raspberries evenly over filling. Gently spread remaining cream filling over raspberries, covering raspberries completely. Top with second cake layer, meringue side up. Serve cake within 2 hours of assembly.

Why This Recipe Works The key to angel food cake is voluminous, stable egg whites. A mere speck of yolk precludes them from whipping to peaks. We had equal success with both cold and room-temperature egg whites. Cold whites achieved the same volume as room-temperature whites; they just took a few minutes longer. Cream of tartar offered some insurance against deflated whites because its acidity helped stabilize the egg whites. Cake flour was also important—all-purpose flour produced a chewy, gummy cake.

ANGEL FOOD CAKE

SERVES 10 TO 12

Do not use all-purpose flour in this recipe as it will give the cake a breadlike texture. You will need a 12-cup tube pan with a removable bottom for this recipe. If your pan has "feet" that rise above the top edge of the pan, let the cake cool upside down; otherwise, invert the tube pan over a large metal kitchen funnel or the neck of a sturdy bottle. Cake can be served plain or dusted with confectioners' sugar.

1 cup plus 2 tablespoons (4½ ounces) cake flour
¼ teaspoon salt
1¾ cups (12¼ ounces) sugar
12 large egg whites
1½ teaspoons cream of tartar
1 teaspoon vanilla extract

1. Adjust oven rack to lower-middle position and preheat oven to 325 degrees. Whisk flour and salt in bowl. Process sugar in food processor until fine, about 1 minute. Reserve half of sugar in small bowl. Add flour mixture to food processor with remaining sugar and process until aerated, about 1 minute.

2. Using stand mixer fitted with whisk, whip egg whites and cream of tartar on medium-low speed until foamy, about 1 minute. Increase speed to medium-high. Slowly add reserved sugar and whip until soft peaks form, about 6 minutes. Add vanilla and mix until incorporated.

3. Sift flour-sugar mixture over egg whites in 3 additions, folding gently with rubber spatula after each addition until incorporated. Scrape mixture into 12-cup ungreased tube pan.

4. Bake until skewer inserted into center comes out clean and cracks in cake appear dry, 40 to 45 minutes. Let cool, inverted, to room temperature, about 3 hours. To unmold, run knife along interior of pan. Turn out onto platter. Serve.

CHOCOLATE-ALMOND ANGEL FOOD CAKE

Replace ½ teaspoon vanilla extract with ½ teaspoon almond extract in step 2. Fold 2 ounces finely grated bittersweet chocolate into batter following flour in step 3.

CAFÉ AU LAIT ANGEL FOOD CAKE

Add 1 tablespoon instant coffee or espresso powder to food processor along with flour in step 1. Replace ½ teaspoon vanilla with 1 tablespoon coffee liqueur in step 2.

Key Steps to Angel Food Cake

1. Grind Sugar Process granulated sugar in food processor until powdery. It'll be fine, light, and won't deflate egg whites.

2. Stabilize Egg Whites Add cream of tartar to egg whites at start of whipping. Once whites become foamy, add half of sugar—gradually.

3. Sift Flour in Batches Gently sift flour-sugar mixture over beaten egg whites in batches to avoid deflating whites.

4. Cool Upside Down Invert cake until it is completely cool, about 3 hours. If you don't have pan with feet, invert it over neck of sturdy bottle.

CHIFFON CAKE

SERVES 10 TO 12

Separate the eggs when they're cold; it's easier. You will need a 16-cup tube pan with a removable bottom for this recipe. If your pan has "feet" that rise above the top edge of the pan, let the cake cool upside down; otherwise, invert the tube pan over a large metal kitchen funnel or the neck of a sturdy bottle.

  5 large eggs, separated
  1 teaspoon cream of tartar
1½ cups (10½ ounces) sugar
1⅓ cups (5⅓ ounces) cake flour
  2 teaspoons baking powder
  ½ teaspoon salt
  ¾ cup water
  ½ cup vegetable oil
  1 tablespoon vanilla extract

1. Adjust oven rack to lower-middle position and heat oven to 325 degrees. Using stand mixer fitted with whisk, whip egg whites and cream of tartar on medium-high speed until soft peaks form, about 2 minutes. With mixer running, slowly add 2 tablespoons sugar and whip until just stiff and glossy, about 1 minute; set aside.

2. Combine flour, remaining sugar, baking powder, and salt in large bowl. Whisk water, oil, egg yolks, and vanilla in medium bowl until smooth. Whisk wet mixture into flour mixture until smooth. Whisk one-third whipped egg whites into batter, then gently fold in remaining whites, 1 scoop at a time, until well combined. Scrape mixture into 16-cup ungreased tube pan.

3. Bake until skewer inserted into center comes out clean and cracks in cake appear dry, 55 minutes to 1 hour, 5 minutes. Let cool, inverted, to room temperature, about 3 hours. To unmold, turn pan right side up and run flexible knife around tube and outer edge. Use tube to pull cake out of pan and set it on inverted baking pan. Cut bottom free. Invert cake onto serving plate and gently twist tube to remove. Serve.

ORANGE CHIFFON CAKE
Reduce total sugar to 1¼ cups. Replace water with ¾ cup orange juice and add 1 tablespoon grated orange zest along with vanilla in step 2. For glaze, whisk 3 tablespoons orange juice, 2 tablespoons softened cream cheese, and ½ teaspoon grated orange zest in medium bowl until smooth. Add 1½ cups confectioners' sugar and whisk until smooth. Pour glaze over cooled cake. Let glaze set for 15 minutes. Serve.

Let Me Outta Here!
Like angel food cake, chiffon cake is baked in an ungreased pan. Why? The stiffly beaten egg whites need to cling to the pan to rise. If the pan were greased, they couldn't. Here's how to remove it from the pan.

1. When cake is cool, turn pan right side up and run flexible knife around tube and outer edge.

2. Use tube to pull cake out of pan and set it on inverted baking pan. Cut bottom free.

3. Invert cake onto serving plate and gently twist tube to remove.

Why This Recipe Works Chiffon cake should have the airy height of angel food cake with the richness of pound cake. For our chiffon cake recipe, we eliminated the unnecessary step of sifting the dry ingredients. We also perfected the method for beating our egg whites—slowly adding sugar once the eggs had been beaten to soft peaks and then continuing to beat them until just stiff and glossy—to avoid little pockets of cooked egg whites.

ITALIAN CREAM CAKE

SERVES 8 TO 10

Toast the coconut and nuts in a 350-degree oven until golden brown, 10 to 12 minutes. Watch carefully and stir occasionally to prevent burning.

Cake

- 1½ cups sweetened shredded coconut, toasted
- 1 cup buttermilk, room temperature
- 2 teaspoons vanilla extract
- 2½ cups (10 ounces) cake flour
- 2 teaspoons baking powder
- ¾ teaspoon salt
- ½ teaspoon baking soda
- 12 tablespoons unsalted butter, cut into 12 pieces and softened
- 4 tablespoons shortening, cut into 4 pieces
- 1¾ cups (12¼ ounces) sugar
- 5 large eggs, room temperature
- 2 cups (8 ounces) pecans, toasted and chopped

Frosting

- 12 tablespoons unsalted butter, softened
- 2¼ cups (9 ounces) confectioners' sugar
- ½ cup cream of coconut
- ½ teaspoon vanilla extract
   Pinch salt
- 16 ounces cream cheese, cut into 8 pieces and softened

1. For the Cake Adjust oven rack to middle position and heat oven to 350 degrees. Grease two 9-inch round cake pans, line with parchment paper, grease parchment, then flour pans. Process coconut in food processor until finely ground, about 1 minute. Combine coconut, buttermilk, and vanilla in 2-cup liquid measuring cup and let sit until coconut is slightly softened, about 10 minutes; reserve.

2. Combine flour, baking powder, salt, and baking soda in bowl. Using stand mixer fitted with paddle, beat butter, shortening, and sugar on medium-high speed until pale and fluffy, about 3 minutes. Add eggs, one at a time, and beat until combined. Reduce speed to low and add flour mixture in 3 additions, alternating with 2 additions of reserved coconut-buttermilk mixture, scraping down bowl as needed. Add ¾ cup pecans and give batter final stir by hand.

3. Scrape equal amounts of batter into prepared pans and bake until toothpick inserted in center comes out clean, 28 to 32 minutes. Cool cakes in pans on wire rack for 10 minutes. Remove cakes from pans, discarding parchment, and cool completely, about 2 hours. (Cooled cakes can be wrapped with plastic wrap and stored at room temperature for up to 2 days.)

4. For the Frosting Using stand mixer fitted with paddle, mix butter and sugar on low speed until combined, about 30 seconds. Increase speed to medium-high and beat until pale and fluffy, about 2 minutes. Add cream of coconut, vanilla, and salt and beat until smooth, about 30 seconds. Add cream cheese, one piece at a time, and beat until incorporated, about 1 minute. Refrigerate until ready to use.

5. When cakes are cooled, spread 1½ cups frosting over 1 cake round. Top with second cake round and spread remaining frosting evenly over top and sides of cake. Press remaining pecans onto sides of cake. Serve. (Cake can be refrigerated for up to 2 days. Bring to room temperature before serving.)

Coconut: Toast, Grind, Soak

To bring out the flavor of the shredded coconut, we toast it in a 350-degree oven until it is golden brown (about 10 minutes). To help the coconut flavor permeate the cake, we grind it to meal in the food processor. But toasted, ground coconut is hard and dry, a real problem in such a deliciously soft, moist cake. To moisten and soften the coconut meal, we soak it in buttermilk before adding it to the cake batter.

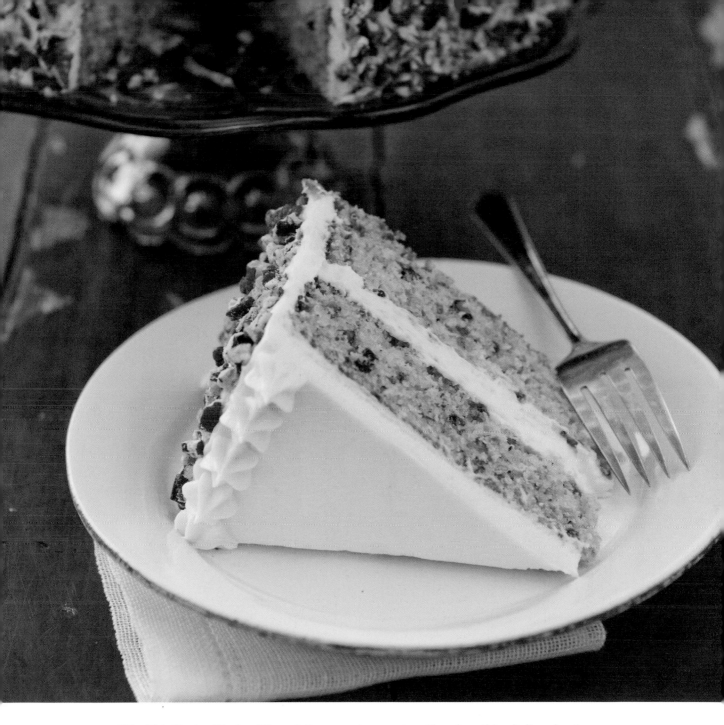

Why This Recipe Works Although the name is a mystery (there's nothing Italian about this cake), the appeal of this Southern specialty is obvious: tender yellow cake with coconut and pecans, doused in tangy cream cheese frosting. But the recipes we found produced gummy cakes with weak coconut flavor. Cake flour made a more tender crumb, and heat-activated baking powder ensured the cake would rise evenly in the oven. To boost coconut flavor, we added it twice—pulverized, toasted coconut added flavor to the cake without drying it out, and cream of coconut amped up the frosting. Finally, we coated the sides in a blanket of toasted pecans.

Why This Recipe Works In this delicious variation on classic pound cake, we added cream cheese for richness, tangy flavor, and an especially velvety texture. We let the pure flavors of eggs, butter, and the cream cheese take center stage, adding only a few teaspoons of vanilla and a moderate amount of sugar. To achieve a tight, fine crumb and a velvety texture, we left the leavener out altogether and used lower-protein cake flour. Extra egg yolks kept the cake moist and tender. Finally, a low oven took a little longer, but it produced a perfect golden-brown crust and a moist, tender interior.

CREAM CHEESE POUND CAKE

SERVES 12 TO 14

If you do not have cake flour on hand, you can substitute ⅞ cup all-purpose flour and 2 tablespoons cornstarch for each cup of flour. Serve with Strawberry-Rhubarb Compote (recipe follows).

- 3 cups (12 ounces) cake flour
- 1 teaspoon salt
- 4 large eggs plus 2 large yolks, room temperature
- ¼ cup milk
- 2 teaspoons vanilla extract
- 3 cups (21 ounces) sugar
- 24 tablespoons (3 sticks) unsalted butter, softened
- 6 ounces cream cheese, softened

1. Adjust oven rack to middle position and heat oven to 300 degrees. Grease and flour 12-cup nonstick Bundt pan. Combine flour and salt in bowl. Whisk eggs and yolks, milk, and vanilla together in 2-cup liquid measuring cup.

2. Using stand mixer fitted with paddle, beat sugar, butter, and cream cheese on medium-high speed until pale and fluffy, about 3 minutes. Reduce speed to low and very slowly add egg mixture, mixing until incorporated (batter may look slightly curdled). Add flour mixture in 3 additions, scraping down bowl as needed. Give batter final stir by hand.

3. Scrape batter into prepared pan and gently tap pan on counter to release air bubbles. Bake until toothpick inserted in center comes out clean, 80 to 90 minutes, rotating pan halfway through baking. Cool cake in pan on wire rack for 15 minutes. Remove cake from pan and cool completely, about 2 hours. Serve. (Cake can be stored, wrapped in plastic wrap, at room temperature for 3 days.)

STRAWBERRY-RHUBARB COMPOTE
MAKES 4 CUPS
The compote can be refrigerated for up to one week. It's delicious drizzled on Cream Cheese Pound Cake or ice cream or stirred into yogurt or oatmeal.

- 1 pound strawberries, hulled and chopped (3 cups)
- 1 cup (7 ounces) sugar
- 1 tablespoon lemon juice
- 1 pound rhubarb, sliced ¼-inch thick
  Pinch salt

1. Toss strawberries with ½ cup sugar and lemon juice in medium bowl. Transfer strawberry mixture to fine-mesh strainer set over medium saucepan and let stand, stirring occasionally, for 30 minutes. Do not wash bowl.

2. Return strawberries to bowl. Add rhubarb, remaining ½ cup sugar, and salt to strawberry juices in pan and bring to boil over medium-high heat. Reduce heat to medium-low and cook, stirring occasionally, until rhubarb is soft and liquid has thickened, 6 to 8 minutes.

3. Stir strawberries into pan and remove from heat. Transfer compote to bowl and let cool to room temperature, about 45 minutes. Serve.

Preparing a Bundt Pan

To ensure a clean release, apply paste of 1 tablespoon melted butter and 1 tablespoon flour to pan using pastry brush.

COLD-OVEN POUND CAKE

SERVES 12

You'll need a 16-cup tube pan for this recipe; if not using a nonstick pan, make sure to thoroughly grease a traditional pan. In step 2, don't worry if the batter looks slightly separated.

- 3 cups (12 ounces) cake flour
- ½ teaspoon baking powder
- 1 teaspoon salt
- 1 cup whole milk
- 2 teaspoons vanilla extract
- 20 tablespoons (2½ sticks) unsalted butter, softened
- 2½ cups (17½ ounces) sugar
- 6 large eggs

1. Adjust oven rack to lower-middle position. Grease and flour 16-cup tube pan. Combine flour, baking powder, and salt in bowl. Whisk milk and vanilla in measuring cup.

2. Using stand mixer fitted with paddle, beat butter and sugar on medium-high speed until light and fluffy, about 2 minutes. Beat in eggs, one at a time, until combined. Reduce speed to low and add flour mixture in 3 additions, alternating with milk mixture in 2 additions, scraping down bowl as needed. Mix on low until smooth, about 30 seconds. Give batter final stir by hand.

3. Pour batter into prepared pan and smooth top. Place cake in cold oven. Adjust oven temperature to 325 degrees and bake, without opening oven door, until cake is golden brown and skewer inserted in center comes out clean, 1 hour, 5 minutes to 1 hour, 20 minutes.

4. Let cake cool in pan on wire rack for 15 minutes. Remove cake from pan and let cool completely on rack about 2 hours. Serve. (Cake can be stored at room temperature for up to 2 days.)

A Cold Oven Really Makes a Difference

Curiosity led us to try baking our Cold-Oven Pound Cake in a preheated oven. The cake baked more quickly (no surprise), but it was squat and lacked the thick crust we'd come to expect. Evidently, the hot oven stopped the small amount of leavener in our recipe before its work was done. And it turns out the crust on our Cold-Oven Pound Cake is formed by moisture in the oven reacting with starch in the batter. A hot oven is drier than a cold oven (heat evaporates moisture), so there wasn't enough moisture in the preheated oven to form a nice, thick crust.

SQUAT CAKE
A preheated oven produces a squat, crustless cake with this recipe.

PERFECT CAKE
In contrast, a cold oven produces a high rise and a thick crust.

Why Pay for Preheating?

Gas ovens became widely available in the United States during the first decades of the 20th century. Because these ovens were more expensive than their wood- and coal-fired counterparts, gas companies had to get creative in marketing them. One popular tactic was to develop and promote recipes started in a cold oven, with the hook that consumers could save money in their gas ovens by not paying for "needless" preheating. Hence: cold-oven pound cake.

Why This Recipe Works This thrifty pound cake, which was designed to save on gas by not requiring a preheated oven, is an especially tall cake and boasts a crisp crust. To create a light crumb, we used leaner whole milk instead of the heavy cream called for in most recipes. Swapping out all-purpose flour for cake flour yielded an even finer, more delicate crumb for our pound cake. We also used baking powder, which produced carbon dioxide bubbles that gave our cake its rise. Putting the pound cake into a cold oven, as is tradition, gave the carbon dioxide more time to produce greater rise.

Why This Recipe Works Packaged chocolate cream cupcakes are a childhood treat. But try one today and you're met with wan chocolate cake encasing salty whipped vegetable shortening. We knew we could do better. Blooming cocoa powder in boiling water and adding chocolate chips and espresso powder gave our cupcakes plenty of chocolate depth. Combining marshmallow crème and the right amount of gelatin gave us the perfect creamy filling. To fill our cupcakes without a pastry bag, we used a paring knife to cut inverted cones from the tops of the cupcakes, added the frosting, and plugged the holes.

CHOCOLATE CREAM CUPCAKES

MAKES 12 CUPCAKES

To ensure an appropriately thick filling, be sure to use marshmallow crème (such as Fluff), not marshmallow sauce. For an accurate measurement of boiling water, bring a full kettle of water to a boil, then measure out the desired amount.

Cupcakes

- 1 cup (5 ounces) all-purpose flour
- ½ teaspoon baking soda
- ¼ teaspoon salt
- ½ cup boiling water
- ⅓ cup (1 ounce) cocoa powder
- ⅓ cup (2 ounces) semisweet chocolate chips
- 1 tablespoon instant espresso powder
- ¾ cup (5¼ ounces) sugar
- ½ cup sour cream
- ½ cup vegetable oil
- 2 large eggs
- 1 teaspoon vanilla extract

Filling

- ¾ teaspoon unflavored gelatin
- 3 tablespoons water
- 4 tablespoons (½ stick) unsalted butter, softened
- 1 teaspoon vanilla extract
  Pinch salt
- 1¼ cups marshmallow crème

Glaze

- ½ cup semisweet chocolate chips
- 3 tablespoons unsalted butter

1. For the Cupcakes Adjust oven rack to middle position and heat oven to 325 degrees. Spray 12-cup muffin tin with vegetable oil spray and flour. Combine flour, baking soda, and salt in bowl. Whisk water, cocoa, chocolate chips, and espresso powder in large bowl until smooth. Add sugar, sour cream, oil, eggs, and vanilla and mix until combined. Whisk in flour mixture until incorporated. Divide batter evenly among muffin cups. Bake until toothpick inserted in center comes out with few dry crumbs attached, 18 to 22 minutes. Let cupcakes cool in tin on wire rack for 10 minutes, then turn out onto wire rack and let cool completely.

2. For the Filling Sprinkle gelatin over water in large bowl and let sit until gelatin softens, about 5 minutes. Microwave until mixture is bubbling around edges and gelatin dissolves, about 30 seconds. Stir in butter, vanilla, and salt until combined. Let mixture cool until just warm to touch, about 5 minutes, then whisk in marshmallow crème until smooth; refrigerate until set, about 30 minutes. Transfer ⅓ cup marshmallow mixture to pastry bag fitted with small plain tip; reserve remaining mixture for filling cupcakes.

3. For the Glaze Microwave chocolate and butter in small bowl, stirring occasionally, until smooth, about 30 seconds. Let glaze cool to room temperature, about 10 minutes.

4. Insert tip of paring knife at 45-degree angle and about ¼ inch from edge of cupcake, cut cone from top of each cupcake, and cut off all but top ¼ inch of cone, leaving circular disk of cake. Fill cupcakes with 1 tablespoon filling each. Replace tops, frost with 2 teaspoons cooled glaze, and let sit 10 minutes. Using pastry bag, pipe curlicues across glazed cupcakes. Serve. (Cupcakes can be stored at room temperature for up to 2 days.)

Filling the Cupcakes

1. Insert tip of paring knife at 45-degree angle about ¼ inch from edge of cupcake. Cut out and remove cake cone. Cut off all but top ¼ inch of cone, leaving circular disk of cake.

2. Using spoon, fill each cupcake with marshmallow mixture and then top with reserved cake "plug." The glaze and the curlicues will hide your handiwork.

Why This Recipe Works Most hot fudge pudding cakes end up looking rich and fudgy but have very little chocolate flavor. For chocolate pudding cake that tasted as good as it looked, we folded semisweet chocolate chips into the batter, which added another layer of chocolate flavor and ensured plenty of gooey pockets in the baked cake. Vegetable oil, which most recipes call for, was flavorless, and we found substituting melted butter improved our pudding cake's flavor. Using Dutch-processed cocoa, which is less acidic than natural cocoa powder, produced a richer chocolate taste.

HOT FUDGE PUDDING CAKE

SERVES 6 TO 8

For an accurate measurement of boiling water, bring a full kettle of water to a boil, then measure out the desired amount. Do not overbake this cake or the pudding sauce will burn in the pan and the cake will be dry, not fudgy. Store leftovers, covered with plastic wrap, in the refrigerator. Reheat individual servings in a microwave on high power until hot (about 1 minute).

- 1 cup (7 ounces) sugar
- ½ cup (1½ ounces) Dutch-processed cocoa powder
- 1 cup (5 ounces) all-purpose flour
- 2 teaspoons baking powder
- ¼ teaspoon salt
- ½ cup milk
- 4 tablespoons unsalted butter, melted
- 1 large egg yolk
- 2 teaspoons vanilla extract
- ½ cup semisweet chocolate chips
- 1 cup boiling water
  Vanilla ice cream or whipped cream

1. Adjust oven rack to middle position and heat oven to 350 degrees. Spray 8-inch square baking pan with vegetable oil spray. Whisk ½ cup sugar with ¼ cup cocoa in small bowl.

2. Whisk flour, remaining ½ cup sugar, remaining ¼ cup cocoa, baking powder, and salt in large bowl. Whisk milk, butter, egg yolk, and vanilla in medium bowl until smooth. Stir milk mixture into flour mixture until just combined. Fold in chocolate chips (batter will be stiff).

3. Using rubber spatula, scrape batter into prepared pan and spread into corners. Sprinkle reserved cocoa mixture evenly over top. Gently pour boiling water over cocoa. Do not stir.

4. Bake until top of cake looks cracked, sauce is bubbling, and toothpick inserted into cakey area comes out with moist crumbs attached, about 25 minutes. Let cool in pan on wire rack for at least 10 minutes. To serve, scoop warm cake into individual serving bowls and top with vanilla ice cream or whipped cream.

BABY PUDDING CAKES

Put a fancy spin on this homey recipe by baking up individual pudding cakes.

Spray eight 6-ounce ovenproof ramekins or coffee cups with vegetable oil spray. Fill each with 2 tablespoons batter. Top each with 1½ tablespoons cocoa mixture, followed by 2 tablespoons boiling water. Arrange cups on rimmed baking sheet and bake until tops are just cracked, 20 to 25 minutes.

Is It Done Yet?

This highly unconventional cake breaks most of the usual rules, including how to judge when it's ready to come out of the oven.

1. Start testing for doneness when top is crackled like a brownie and sauce is bubbling up from bottom. Insert toothpick close to the edge, where the cake is firmest. (Don't insert the toothpick in center, where cake should be gooey.)

2. Toothpick should have large, moist crumbs—but no gooey batter—attached. Check at least two spots to be certain that what's sticking to toothpick isn't just melted chocolate.

LEMON PUDDING CAKE

SERVES 8

This dessert is best served warm or at room temperature the same day it is made.

- ¼ cup (1¼ ounces) all-purpose flour
- 2 teaspoons cornstarch
- 1¼ cups (8¾ ounces) sugar
- 5 tablespoons unsalted butter, softened
- 2 tablespoons grated zest and ½ cup juice from 4 lemons
- 5 large eggs, separated
- 1¼ cups whole milk, room temperature
- 2 quarts boiling water

1. Adjust oven rack to lowest position and heat oven to 325 degrees. Grease 8-inch square baking dish. Whisk flour and cornstarch in bowl. Using stand mixer fitted with paddle, beat ½ cup sugar, butter, and lemon zest on medium-high speed until light and fluffy, about 2 minutes. Beat in egg yolks, 1 at a time, until incorporated. Reduce speed to medium-low. Add flour mixture and mix until incorporated. Slowly add milk and lemon juice, mixing until just combined.

2. Using clean bowl and whisk attachment, beat egg whites on medium-high speed until soft peaks form, about 2 minutes. With mixer running, slowly add remaining ¾ cup sugar until whites are firm and glossy, about 1 minute. Whisk one-third of whites into batter, then gently fold in remaining whites, 1 scoop at a time, until well combined.

3. Place clean dish towel in bottom of roasting pan and arrange prepared baking dish on towel. Spoon batter into prepared dish. Carefully place pan on oven rack and pour boiling water into pan until water comes halfway up sides of baking dish. Bake until surface is golden brown and edges are set (center should jiggle slightly when gently shaken), about 1 hour. Transfer dish to wire rack and let cool for at least 1 hour. To serve, scoop warm cake into individual serving bowls.

Using a Water Bath
The water lowers the temperature surrounding the baking dish for gentle, even cooking.

1. To prevent baking dish from sliding, line bottom of roasting pan with clean dish towel and place baking dish on top.

2. Set roasting pan on oven rack and carefully pour boiling water into pan, halfway up sides of baking dish.

3. After baking, promptly remove baking dish from water. Let water cool before moving water bath.

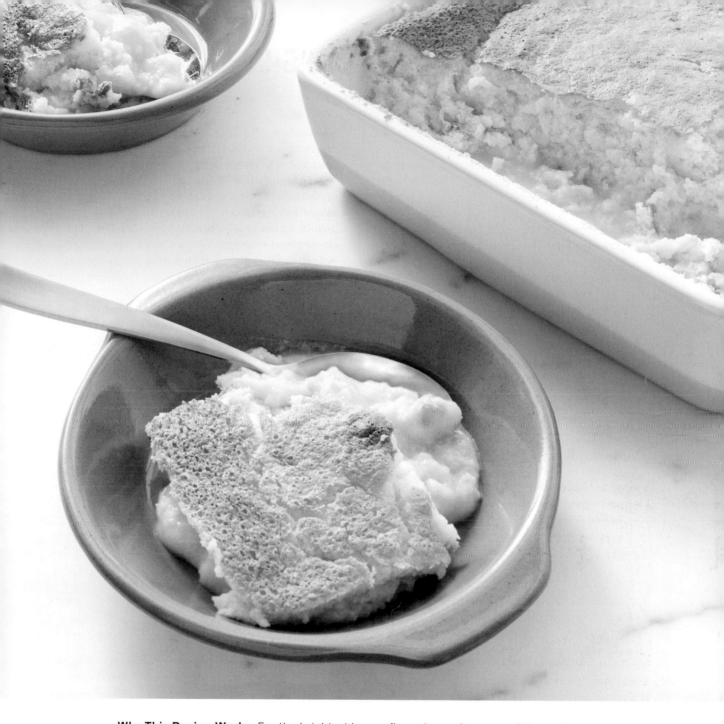

Why This Recipe Works For the brightest lemon flavor in our lemon pudding cake, we used a half cup of lemon juice. To coax even more flavor from the lemons, we creamed a bit of grated zest with the butter and sugar. A bit of cornstarch gently firmed the pudding layer without muddying the lemon flavor. To prevent the top layer of the cake from deflating, we beat sugar into the egg whites. This stabilized the whites and resulted in a high, golden, and fluffy cake. For the creamiest texture, it was important to bake the cake in a water bath. The hot water protected the pudding from cooking too quickly.

LEMON ICEBOX CHEESECAKE

SERVES 12 TO 16

Let the dissolved gelatin mixture cool down for a few minutes, or the gelatin will seize before combining with the filling. We tested our cheesecake with several store brands of lemon sandwich cookies; all worked well.

Crust
10 lemon sandwich cookies, broken into pieces (about 1¼ cups)
2 tablespoons unsalted butter, melted
1 teaspoon grated lemon zest

Curd
¼ cup (1¾ ounces) sugar
1 large egg plus 1 large yolk
    Pinch salt
2 tablespoons lemon juice
1 tablespoon unsalted butter
1 tablespoon heavy cream

Filling
2¾ teaspoons unflavored gelatin
¼ cup lemon juice (2 lemons)
1½ pounds cream cheese, cut into 1-inch pieces and softened
¾ cup (5¼ ounces) sugar
    Pinch salt
1¼ cups heavy cream, room temperature

1. For the Crust Adjust oven rack to middle position and heat oven to 350 degrees. Process cookies in food processor until finely ground, about 30 seconds. Add butter and zest and pulse until combined, about 10 pulses. Press mixture into bottom of 9-inch springform pan. Bake until lightly browned and set, about 10 minutes. Let cool completely on wire rack, at least 30 minutes.

2. For the Curd While crust is cooling, whisk sugar, egg and yolk, and salt together in small saucepan. Add lemon juice and cook over medium-low heat, stirring constantly, until thick and puddinglike, about

3 minutes. Remove from heat and stir in butter and cream. Press through fine-mesh strainer into small bowl and refrigerate lemon curd until needed.

3. For the Filling Sprinkle gelatin over lemon juice in small bowl and let stand until gelatin softens, about 5 minutes. Microwave until mixture is bubbling around edges and gelatin dissolves, about 30 seconds. Set aside.

4. Using stand mixer fitted with paddle beat cream cheese, sugar, and salt on medium speed until smooth and creamy, scraping down sides of bowl as needed, about 2 minutes. Slowly add cream and beat until light and fluffy, about 2 minutes. Add gelatin mixture and ¼ cup curd, increase speed to medium-high, and beat until smooth and airy, about 3 minutes.

5. Pour filling into cooled crust and smooth top. Pour thin lines of remaining curd on top of cake and lightly drag paring knife or skewer perpendicularly through lines to create marbled appearance. Refrigerate until set, at least 6 hours. Remove sides of pan. Serve. (Cheesecake can be refrigerated for up to 3 days.)

Swirl Showstopper
Making a swirl with the lemon curd on top of the cheesecake is absurdly easy and awfully impressive.

1. Use measuring cup to pour curd in 4 thin lines on top of cheesecake.

2. Drag paring knife or skewer perpendicularly through lines to create marbled design.

Why This Recipe Works In a baked cheesecake, tart lemon juice is mellowed by the heat of the oven. For our icebox version of lemon cheesecake, we needed to dial back the lemon juice to compensate for the lack of baking. Lemon curd, a rich, tangy spread made from eggs, butter, cream, sugar, and lemon juice, added crisp lemon flavor without the undesirable chewiness of zest or the processed flavor of lemon extract. Using lemon cookies instead of graham crackers for the crust created an additional layer of lemon flavor.

Why This Recipe Works Too often, chocolate's bitter side can clash with the tangy flavor of cream cheese, but we were determined to create a fluffy chocolate cheesecake without the bitterness. After making dozens of versions, we figured out that switching from dark to mild-mannered milk chocolate was the secret to a sweet, creamy cheesecake. Adding cocoa powder added depth and rounded out the chocolate flavor. Unlike traditional cheesecake that is baked in a water bath, we simplified our recipe by baking it in a low 250-degree oven. For an easy and crunchy, chocolaty crust, we used Oreo cookies processed with butter and a bit of sugar.

MILK CHOCOLATE CHEESECAKE

SERVES 12

Our favorite milk chocolate is Dove Silky Smooth Milk Chocolate. For the crust, use the entire Oreo cookie, filling and all. The cheesecake needs to be refrigerated for at least 8 hours before serving.

16 Oreo sandwich cookies, broken into rough pieces
1 tablespoon sugar plus ½ cup (3½ ounces)
2 tablespoons unsalted butter, melted
8 ounces milk chocolate, chopped
⅓ cup heavy cream
2 tablespoons unsweetened cocoa powder
¼ teaspoon salt
1½ pounds cream cheese, softened
4 large eggs, room temperature
2 teaspoons vanilla extract

1. Adjust oven rack to middle position and heat oven to 350 degrees. Grease bottom and sides of 9-inch nonstick springform pan.

2. Process cookies and 1 tablespoon sugar in food processor until finely ground, about 30 seconds. Add melted butter and pulse until combined, about 6 pulses. Transfer crumb mixture to prepared pan and press firmly with bottom of dry measuring cup into even layer in bottom of pan. Bake until fragrant and set, about 10 minutes. Let cool completely on wire rack.

3. Reduce oven temperature to 250 degrees. Combine 6 ounces chocolate and cream in medium bowl and microwave at 50 percent power, stirring occasionally, until melted and smooth, 60 to 90 seconds. Let cool for 10 minutes. In small bowl, whisk cocoa, salt, and remaining ½ cup sugar until no lumps remain.

4. Using stand mixer fitted with paddle, beat cream cheese and cocoa mixture on medium speed until creamy and smooth, about 3 minutes, scraping down bowl as needed. Reduce speed to medium-low, add chocolate mixture, and beat until combined.

Gradually add eggs, one at a time, until incorporated, scraping down bowl as needed. Add vanilla and give batter final stir by hand until no streaks of chocolate remain.

5. Pour cheesecake mixture into cooled crust and smooth top with spatula. Tap cheesecake gently on counter to release air bubbles. Cover pan tightly with aluminum foil (taking care not to touch surface of cheesecake with foil) and place on rimmed baking sheet. Bake for 1 hour, then remove foil. Continue to bake until edges are set and center registers 150 degrees and jiggles slightly when shaken, 30 to 45 minutes. Let cool completely on wire rack, then cover with plastic wrap and refrigerate in pan until cold, about 8 hours. (Cake can be refrigerated for up to 4 days.)

6. To unmold cheesecake, remove sides of pan, slide thin metal spatula between crust and pan bottom to loosen, and slide cake onto serving platter. Microwave remaining 2 ounces chocolate in small bowl at 50 percent power, stirring occasionally, until melted, 60 to 90 seconds. Let cool for 5 minutes. Transfer to small zipper-lock bag, cut small hole in corner, and pipe chocolate in thin zigzag pattern across top of cheesecake. Let cheesecake stand at room temperature for 30 minutes. Using warm, dry knife, cut into wedges and serve.

Melt Milk Chocolate Carefully

Because milk chocolate contains milk solids, its protein content is generally higher than that of dark chocolate. The extra protein means that milk chocolate melts at a slightly lower temperature than dark; what's more, when you add heat to protein and sugar, new molecules may form, introducing unwelcome scorched or burned flavors. Microwaves are generally gentle, but notoriously inconsistent, so choose 50 percent power, keep a close eye on the chocolate, and give it a stir every 15 seconds.

CHOCOLATE CHIP SKILLET COOKIE

SERVES 8

Top with ice cream for an extra-decadent treat.

- 12 tablespoons unsalted butter
- ¾ cup packed (5¼ ounces) dark brown sugar
- ½ cup (3½ ounces) granulated sugar
- 2 teaspoons vanilla extract
- 1 teaspoon salt
- 1 large egg plus 1 large yolk
- 1¾ cups (8¾ ounces) all-purpose flour
- ½ teaspoon baking soda
- 1 cup (6 ounces) semisweet chocolate chips

1. Adjust oven rack to upper-middle position and heat oven to 375 degrees. Melt 9 tablespoons butter in 12-inch cast-iron skillet over medium heat. Continue to cook, stirring constantly, until butter is dark golden brown, has nutty aroma, and bubbling subsides, about 5 minutes; transfer to large bowl. Stir remaining 3 tablespoons butter into hot butter until completely melted.

2. Whisk brown sugar, granulated sugar, vanilla, and salt into melted butter until smooth. Whisk in egg and yolk until smooth, about 30 seconds. Let mixture sit for 3 minutes, then whisk for 30 seconds. Repeat process of resting and whisking 2 more times until mixture is thick, smooth, and shiny.

3. Whisk flour and baking soda together in separate bowl, then stir flour mixture into butter mixture until just combined, about 1 minute. Stir in chocolate chips, making sure no flour pockets remain.

4. Wipe skillet clean with paper towels. Transfer dough to now-empty skillet and press into even layer with spatula. Transfer skillet to oven and bake until cookie is golden brown and edges are set, about 20 minutes, rotating skillet halfway through baking. Using potholders, transfer skillet to wire rack and let cookie cool for 30 minutes. Slice cookie into wedges and serve.

Making a Skillet Cookie

To ensure a uniformly baked cookie, transfer dough to skillet and press into even layer with spatula.

Seasoning Your Skillet

1. While the skillet is still warm, wipe it clean with paper towels to remove excess food bits and oil.

2. Rinse the skillet under hot running water, scrubbing with a brush or nonabrasive scrub pad to remove traces of food. Use a small amount of soap if you like, but make sure to rinse it all off.

3. Dry the skillet thoroughly (do not let it drip-dry) and put it back on the burner over medium-low heat until all traces of moisture disappear (this keeps rusting at bay). Never put a wet cast-iron skillet away or stack anything on top of a skillet that hasn't been properly dried.

4. Add ½ teaspoon of vegetable oil to the warm, dry skillet and wipe the interior with a wad of paper towels until it is lightly covered with oil.

5. Continue to rub oil into the skillet, replacing the paper towels as needed, until the skillet looks dark and shiny and does not have any remaining oil residue.

6. Turn off the heat and allow the skillet to cool completely before putting it away.

A well-seasoned skillet should have a smooth, dark black, semiglossy finish.

Why This Recipe Works A cookie in a skillet? Unlike baking a traditional batch of cookies, a skillet cookie can go straight from the oven to the table for a fun, hands-on dessert. This scaled-up cookie benefits from the hot bottom and tall sides of a well-seasoned cast-iron pan to create a great crisp crust. Reeling in the butter and chocolate chips from our usual cookie dough recipe allowed our oversized cookie to bake through in the middle while staying perfectly chewy. We increased the baking time to accommodate the giant size, but otherwise this recipe was simpler and faster than baking regular cookies.

Why This Recipe Works These delicate butter cookies literally melt in your mouth, thanks to the generous amount of cornstarch in the dough. Unfortunately, the cornstarch leaves behind a chalky residue with each bite. After settling on the maximum amount of cornstarch we could use without detection, we scoured supermarket shelves in search of other low-protein dry ingredients to replace the remainder. We replaced all-purpose flour with cake flour and chose confectioners' sugar over granulated, but we still needed more bulk. The solution? Rice Krispies! The ground cereal added the volume we were looking for without toughening the crumb.

MELTING MOMENTS

MAKES ABOUT 70 COOKIES

If the dough gets too soft to slice, return it to the refrigerator to firm up.

- ½ cup Rice Krispies cereal
- 16 tablespoons unsalted butter, cut into 16 pieces and softened
- 3 tablespoons heavy cream
- 1 teaspoon vanilla extract
- 1¼ cups (5 ounces) cake flour
- ¼ cup (1¼ ounces) cornstarch
- ⅛ teaspoon salt
- ⅔ cup (2⅔ ounces) confectioners' sugar

1. Process Rice Krispies in blender until finely ground, about 30 seconds. Combine 4 tablespoons butter and cream in large bowl and microwave until butter is melted, about 30 seconds. Whisk in processed Rice Krispies and vanilla until combined. Let cool slightly, 5 to 7 minutes.

2. Combine flour, cornstarch, and salt in medium bowl; reserve. Whisk sugar into cooled butter mixture until incorporated. Add remaining 12 tablespoons butter, whisking until smooth. Stir in flour mixture until combined.

3. Working with half of dough at a time, dollop dough into 8-inch strip down center of 14 by 12-inch sheet of parchment paper. Fold 1 long side of parchment over dough. Using ruler, press dough into tight 1-inch-wide log. Repeat with remaining dough and another sheet of parchment. Refrigerate dough until firm, about 1 hour. (Dough can be wrapped in plastic wrap and aluminum foil and frozen for up to 1 month.)

4. Adjust oven racks to upper-middle and lower-middle positions and heat oven to 300 degrees. Line 2 baking sheets with parchment. Cut dough into ¼-inch slices and place 1 inch apart on prepared baking sheets. Bake until set but not brown, 18 to 22 minutes, switching and rotating baking sheets halfway through baking. Let cool completely on sheets, about 15 minutes. Repeat with remaining dough. Serve. (Cookies can be stored at room temperature for up to 2 days.)

CRESCENT COOKIES
After step 2, transfer dough to pastry bag fitted with ½-inch star tip. Pipe 1½-inch-long crescents onto prepared baking sheets. Refrigerate dough until firm, about 30 minutes. Bake as directed.

JAM THUMBPRINT COOKIES
After step 2, transfer dough to pastry bag fitted with ½-inch plain tip. Pipe 1-inch-wide and ½-inch-high dough rounds onto prepared baking sheets. Using back of ¼-teaspoon measuring spoon dipped in water, make indentation in center of each round. Refrigerate dough until firm, about 30 minutes. Bake until set, 18 to 20 minutes, switching and rotating sheets halfway through baking. Fill each dimple with ½ teaspoon jam and bake for 5 minutes.

ROUND SPRITZ COOKIES
After step 2, transfer dough to pastry bag fitted with ½-inch star tip. Pipe 1-inch-wide and ½-inch-high dough rounds onto prepared baking sheets. Refrigerate dough until firm, about 30 minutes. Bake as directed.

Handling Soft Dough
The high proportion of butter to flour makes the dough for these cookies very soft and challenging to handle. With this technique, you can easily roll it into a log.

1. Dollop half of dough in strip down center of sheet of parchment.

2. Pulling parchment taut, use ruler to press dough into tight log

Why This Recipe Works We set out to create a slice-and-bake cookie recipe that would combine both crispness and rich butter and vanilla flavors—in effect, shortbread shaped into a convenient slice-and-bake log. Using both granulated sugar and light brown sugar gave the cookies a richness and complexity that tasters liked. We used the food processor to combine our recipe ingredients quickly without whipping in too much air—our cookies had the fine, shortbreadlike texture we were after.

SLICE-AND-BAKE COOKIES

MAKES ABOUT 40 COOKIES

Be sure that the cookie dough is well chilled and firm so that it can be uniformly sliced.

- ⅓ cup (2⅓ ounces) granulated sugar
- 2 tablespoons packed light brown sugar
- ½ teaspoon salt
- 12 tablespoons unsalted butter, cut into pieces and softened
- 2 teaspoons vanilla extract
- 1 large egg yolk
- 1½ cups (7½ ounces) all-purpose flour

1. Process granulated sugar, brown sugar, and salt in food processor until no lumps of brown sugar remain, about 30 seconds. Add butter, vanilla, and yolk and process until smooth and creamy, about 20 seconds. Scrape down sides of bowl, add flour, and pulse until dough forms, about 15 seconds.

2. Turn out dough onto lightly floured counter and roll into 10-inch log. Wrap tightly with plastic wrap and refrigerate until firm, at least 2 hours or up to 3 days. (Dough can be wrapped in foil and frozen for up to 1 month.)

3. Adjust oven racks to upper-middle and lower-middle positions and heat oven to 350 degrees. Line 2 baking sheets with parchment paper. Slice chilled dough into ¼ inch rounds and place 1 inch apart on prepared baking sheets. Bake until edges are just golden, about 15 minutes, switching and rotating baking sheets halfway through baking. Let cool 10 minutes on sheets, then transfer to wire rack and let cool completely. Repeat with remaining dough. (Cookies can be stored at room temperature for up to 1 week.)

COCONUT-LIME COOKIES

In step 1, add 2 cups sweetened shredded coconut and 2 teaspoons grated lime zest to food processor along with sugars and salt.

WALNUT–BROWN SUGAR COOKIES

In step 1, add 2 more tablespoons brown sugar and 1 cup chopped walnuts to food processor along with sugars and salt.

ORANGE–POPPY SEED COOKIES

In step 1, add ¼ cup poppy seeds and 1 tablespoon grated orange zest to food processor along with sugars and salt.

Glaze Me

We love the simplicity of our Slice-and-Bake Cookies, but a confectioners' sugar glaze is an easy way to dress them up. If the glaze is too thick to spread, thin it with 1 tablespoon water. Each glaze makes enough for 1 recipe Slice-and-Bake Cookies.

Ginger-Lime Glaze Whisk 1 tablespoon softened cream cheese, 1 teaspoon ground ginger, and 2 tablespoons lime juice in medium bowl until combined. Whisk in 1½ cups confectioners' sugar until smooth.

Malted Milk Glaze Whisk 1 tablespoon softened cream cheese, 1 tablespoon malted milk powder, 1 teaspoon vanilla extract, and 2 tablespoons milk in medium bowl until combined. Whisk in 1½ cups confectioners' sugar until smooth.

Cappuccino Glaze Whisk 1 tablespoon softened cream cheese, 1 tablespoon instant espresso powder, and 2 tablespoons milk in medium bowl until combined. Whisk in 1½ cups confectioners' sugar until smooth.

Peanut Butter and Jelly Glaze Whisk 1 tablespoon creamy peanut butter, 2 tablespoons strawberry jelly, and 1 tablespoon water in medium bowl until combined. Whisk in 1½ cups confectioners' sugar until smooth.

FAIRY GINGERBREAD

MAKES 60 COOKIES

Use cookie or baking sheets that measure at least 15 by 12 inches. Don't be disconcerted by the scant amount of batter: You really are going to spread it very thin. Use the edges of the parchment paper as your guide, covering the entire surface thinly and evenly. For easier grating, freeze a 2-inch piece of peeled ginger for 30 minutes, then use a rasp-style grater.

1½ teaspoons ground ginger
¾ cup plus 2 tablespoons (4⅜ ounces) all-purpose flour
½ teaspoon baking soda
¼ teaspoon salt
5 tablespoons unsalted butter, softened
9 tablespoons (4 ounces) packed light brown sugar
4 teaspoons grated fresh ginger
¾ teaspoon vanilla extract
¼ cup whole milk, room temperature

1. Adjust oven racks to upper-middle and lower-middle positions and heat oven to 325 degrees. Spray 2 rimless baking sheets (or inverted rimmed baking sheets) with vegetable oil spray and cover each with 15 by 12-inch sheet parchment paper. Heat ground ginger in small skillet over medium heat until fragrant, about 1 minute. Combine flour, toasted ginger, baking soda, and salt in medium bowl.

2. Using stand mixer fitted with paddle, beat butter and sugar on medium-high speed until light and fluffy, about 2 minutes. Add fresh ginger and vanilla and mix until incorporated. Reduce speed to low and add flour mixture in 3 additions, alternating with milk in 2 additions; scrape down bowl as needed.

3. Evenly spread ¾ cup batter to cover parchment on each prepared sheet (batter will be very thin). Bake until deep golden brown, 16 to 20 minutes, switching and rotating baking sheets halfway through baking. Immediately score cookies into 3 by 2-inch rectangles. Let cool completely, about 20 minutes. Using tip of paring knife, separate cookies along score marks. (Cookies can be stored at room temperature for 3 days.)

Making Fairy Gingerbread

While making several dozen batches of Fairy Gingerbread, we had time to perfect our technique. The cookies are made with an unusual method we'd never encountered before. Here's how:

1. To form cookies of requisite thinness, use small offset spatula to spread batter to edges of 15 by 12-inch sheet of parchment paper.

2. Immediately after removing cookies from oven, use chef's knife or pizza wheel to score 3 by 2-inch rectangles. Work quickly to prevent breaking.

3. Once cookies are cool, trace over scored lines with paring knife and gently break cookies apart along lines.

Why This Recipe Works Original recipes for fairy gingerbread, a cookie popular in the 19th century, melted in our mouths but were also severely lacking in flavor. A bit of vanilla extract and salt helped boost the flavor. Doubling the ginger added a much-needed kick, but without any competing flavors it was overwhelming. We cut back a little and toasted the ground ginger to bring out its natural flavor. Grating fresh ginger straight into the batter added even more intense ginger flavor. Switching from bread flour to all-purpose flour made the batter slightly easier to spread. A little baking soda helped retain the cookies' airy crispness.

JOE FROGGERS

MAKES 24 COOKIES

Place only six cookies on each baking sheet—they will spread. If you don't own a 3½-inch cookie cutter, use a drinking glass. Use mild (not robust or blackstrap) molasses. Make sure to chill the dough for a full 8 hours or it will be too hard to roll out.

⅓ cup dark rum (such as Myers's)
1 tablespoon water
1½ teaspoons salt
3 cups (15 ounces) all-purpose flour
¾ teaspoon ground ginger
½ teaspoon ground allspice
¼ teaspoon ground nutmeg
⅛ teaspoon ground cloves
1 cup molasses
1 teaspoon baking soda
8 tablespoons unsalted butter, softened but still cool
1 cup (7 ounces) sugar

1. Stir rum, water, and salt in small bowl until salt dissolves. Whisk flour, ginger, allspice, nutmeg, and cloves in medium bowl. Stir molasses and baking soda in liquid measuring cup (mixture will begin to bubble) and let sit until doubled in volume, about 15 minutes.

2. Using stand mixer fitted with paddle, beat butter and sugar on medium-high speed until fluffy, about 2 minutes. Reduce speed to medium-low and gradually beat in rum mixture. Add flour mixture in 3 additions, beating on medium-low until just incorporated, alternating with molasses mixture in 2 additions, scraping down sides of bowl as needed. Give dough final stir by hand (dough will be extremely sticky). Cover bowl with plastic wrap and refrigerate until stiff, at least 8 hours or up to 3 days.

3. Adjust oven racks to upper-middle and lower-middle positions and heat oven to 375 degrees. Line 2 baking sheets with parchment paper. Working with half of dough at a time on heavily floured counter, roll out to ¼-inch thickness. Using 3½-inch cookie cutter, cut out 12 cookies. Transfer 6 cookies to each baking sheet, spacing cookies about 1½ inches apart. Bake until cookies are set and just beginning to crack, about 8 minutes, switching and rotating baking sheets halfway through baking time. Let cookies cool on sheets on wire rack 10 minutes, then transfer cookies to rack to cool completely. Repeat with remaining dough. (Cookies may be stored for up to 1 week.)

Salty History

Joe froggers date back more than 200 years to Black Joe's Tavern, located in Marblehead, Massachusetts, a seaside town north of Boston. A freed slave and Revolutionary War veteran, Joseph Brown (known as Old Black Joe), and his wife, Lucretia (affectionately known as Auntie Cresse), opened the tavern in a part of Marblehead called Gingerbread Hill. Besides serving drinks (mostly rum), Joe and Auntie Cresse baked cookies: large, moist molasses and rum cookies made salty by the addition of Marblehead seawater. These cookies were popular sustenance on long fishing voyages, as they had no dairy to spoil and the combination of rum, molasses, and seawater kept them chewy for weeks.

According to Samuel Roads Jr.'s *History and Traditions of Marblehead*, published in 1879, the funny name for these cookies referred to the lily pads (similar in size and shape to the cookies) and large croaking frogs that would fill the pond behind Joe's tavern. Thus the cookies became known as Joe froggers.

Why This Recipe Works Joe froggers, from a recipe that dates back more than 200 years, are incredibly moist, spicy, slightly salty cookies, found in bakeries along the North Shore of Massachusetts. We wanted to develop our own recipe. Dissolving salt into our recipe's rum and water gave the cookie its distinctive salty flavor. Ginger, allspice, nutmeg, and cloves contributed warm spice flavor. Many recipes we found in our research called for lard, but we found that using butter made for a more flavorful cookie.

Why This Recipe Works These cakey cookies are a deli favorite in New York, but rarely do they live up to the hype. We wanted to improve upon the classic chocolate-vanilla combination. To get the "cookie" just right, we made several small but high-impact adjustments. We dialed back the amount of baking soda and baking powder to get rid of unwanted air bubbles, added more vanilla extract to heighten the flavor, and used just enough sour cream to make the cookies tender but not sticky. Corn syrup made the glaze thick and shiny, while milk made it creamy and spreadable. Cocoa powder kept the chocolate glaze flavorful and simple.

BLACK AND WHITE COOKIES

MAKES 12 COOKIES

Twelve cookies doesn't sound like much, but these cookies are huge. You'll get neater cookies if you spread on the vanilla glaze first. This recipe provides a little extra glaze, just in case.

Cookies

- 1¾ cups (8¾ ounces) all-purpose flour
- ½ teaspoon baking powder
- ¼ teaspoon baking soda
- ⅛ teaspoon salt
- 10 tablespoons unsalted butter, softened
- 1 cup (7 ounces) granulated sugar
- 1 large egg
- 2 teaspoons vanilla extract
- ⅓ cup sour cream

Glaze

- 5 cups (20 ounces) confectioners' sugar, sifted
- 7 tablespoons whole milk
- 2 tablespoons corn syrup
- 1 teaspoon vanilla extract
- ½ teaspoon salt
- 3 tablespoons Dutch-processed cocoa powder, sifted

1. For the Cookies Adjust oven racks to upper-middle and lower-middle positions and heat oven to 350 degrees. Line 2 baking sheets with parchment paper. Combine flour, baking powder, baking soda, and salt in bowl.

2. Using stand mixer fitted with paddle, beat butter and sugar on medium-high speed until pale and fluffy, about 2 minutes. Add egg and vanilla and beat until combined. Reduce speed to low and add flour mixture in 3 additions, alternating with 2 additions of sour cream, scraping down bowl as needed. Give dough final stir by hand.

3. Using greased ¼-cup measure, drop cookie dough 3 inches apart onto prepared baking sheets. Bake until edges are lightly browned, 15 to 18 minutes, switching and rotating sheets halfway through baking. Let cookies cool on sheets for 5 minutes, then transfer to wire rack to cool completely, about 1 hour.

4. For the Glaze Whisk sugar, 6 tablespoons milk, corn syrup, vanilla, and salt together in bowl until smooth. Transfer 1 cup glaze to small bowl; reserve. Whisk cocoa and remaining 1 tablespoon milk into remaining glaze until combined.

5. Working with 1 cookie at a time, spread 1 tablespoon vanilla glaze over half of underside of cookie. Refrigerate until glaze is set, about 15 minutes. Cover other half of cookies with 1 tablespoon chocolate glaze and let cookies sit at room temperature until glaze is firm, at least 1 hour. Serve. (Cookies can be stored at room temperature for up to 2 days.)

Glazing Black and White Cookies

1. Using butter knife or offset mini spatula, glaze half of underside of each cookie with vanilla glaze. Chill cookies in refrigerator for 15 minutes so glaze can start to harden.

2. Glaze other half of each cookie with chocolate glaze, and let cookies sit until glaze sets, about 1 hour.

WHOOPIE PIES

MAKES 6 PIES

Don't be tempted to bake all the cakes on one baking sheet; the batter needs room to spread in the oven.

Cakes

 2 cups (10 ounces) all-purpose flour
½ cup (1½ ounces) Dutch-processed cocoa powder
 1 teaspoon baking soda
½ teaspoon salt
 8 tablespoons unsalted butter, softened but still cool
 1 cup packed (7 ounces) light brown sugar
 1 large egg, room temperature
 1 teaspoon vanilla extract
 1 cup buttermilk

Filling

12 tablespoons unsalted butter, softened but still cool
1¼ cups (5 ounces) confectioners' sugar
1½ teaspoons vanilla extract
⅛ teaspoon salt
2½ cups marshmallow crème

1. For the Cakes Adjust oven racks to upper-middle and lower-middle positions and heat oven to 350 degrees. Line 2 baking sheets with parchment paper. Whisk flour, cocoa, baking soda, and salt in medium bowl.

2. Using stand mixer fitted with paddle, beat butter and sugar on medium-high speed until fluffy, about 4 minutes. Beat in egg until incorporated, scraping down sides of bowl as necessary, then beat in vanilla. Reduce speed to low and beat in flour mixture in 3 additions, alternating with buttermilk in 2 additions. Give batter final stir by hand.

3. Using ⅓-cup measure, scoop 6 mounds of batter onto each baking sheet, spacing mounds about 3 inches apart. Bake until cakes spring back when pressed, 15 to 18 minutes, switching and rotating baking sheets halfway through baking. Let cool completely on baking sheets, at least 1 hour.

4. For the Filling Using stand mixer fitted with paddle, beat butter and sugar on medium speed until fluffy, about 2 minutes. Beat in vanilla and salt.

Beat in marshmallow crème until incorporated, about 2 minutes. Refrigerate filling until slightly firm, about 30 minutes. (Bowl can be wrapped and refrigerated for up to 2 days.)

5. Dollop ⅓ cup filling on center of flat side of 6 cakes. Top with flat side of remaining 6 cakes and gently press until filling spreads to edges of cakes. Serve. (Whoopie pies can be refrigerated for up to 3 days.)

What's Up, Whoopie Pie?

Where did whoopie pies originate? Both Maine and Pennsylvania—the Pennsylvania Dutch of Lancaster County, to be specific—claim whoopie pies as their own. Maine's earliest claim dates back to 1925, when Labadie's Bakery in Lewiston first sold whoopie pies to the public. Some research showed that the Berwick Cake Company began manufacturing Whoopie! Pies (the exclamation point was part of the name) in 1927. These sources claim that whoopie pies were named after the musical *Whoopie*; *Whoopie* had its debut in Boston in 1927. In addition, Marshmallow Fluff, a key ingredient in many whoopie pie recipes, had been invented in nearby Lynn seven years earlier.

What about Pennsylvania's claim on whoopie pies? We found an article in a copy of the *Gettysburg Times* from 1982 that spoke of a chocolate cake sandwich with a fluffy cream center. These sandwiches were called gobs and were sold by the Dutch Maid Bakery of Geistown. While the name was different, the description (and a huge picture) showed that these were no doubt whoopie pies. The Dutch Maid Bakery purchased the rights to the gob in 1980 from the Harris and Boyer Baking Company, also of Pennsylvania, which had started manufacturing gobs in 1927. Maine might have a few years on Pennsylvania when it comes to whoopie pies, but who's to know for sure?

Why This Recipe Works We wanted a light, airy cake for our whoopie pies, so we used the creaming mixing method—blending the butter and sugar with a mixer until fluffy and nearly white in color. We also used lots of Dutch-processed cocoa powder and vanilla in our recipe for full flavor and a deep, dark-colored crumb. And for a cleaner, fuller flavor, we replaced the shortening (or lard) found in most recipes with butter.

Why This Recipe Works Chocolate truffles are often reserved for special occasions because they can be laborious to make. We wanted a streamlined, foolproof recipe, making the process as simple as possible. We utilized the microwave to melt the chocolate and cream ganache base, stirred the mixture with a rubber spatula (a whisk incorporates too much air), and chilled it. Rolling truffles can get messy, so we wore disposable gloves for easy clean up. A dusting of cocoa powder and confectioners' sugar keeps the truffles from sticking together during chilling and storing.

BASIC CHOCOLATE TRUFFLES

MAKES 24 TRUFFLES

Wear latex gloves when forming the truffles to keep your hands clean.

- ¼ cup (¾ ounce) unsweetened cocoa powder
- 1 tablespoon confectioners' sugar
- 8 ounces bittersweet chocolate, chopped fine
- ½ cup heavy cream
- Pinch salt

1. Sift cocoa and sugar through fine-mesh strainer into pie plate. Microwave chocolate, cream, and salt in bowl at 50 percent power, stirring occasionally with rubber spatula, until melted, about 1 minute. Stir truffle mixture until fully combined; transfer to 8-inch square baking dish and refrigerate until set, about 45 minutes.

2. Using heaping teaspoon measure, scoop truffle mixture into 24 portions, transfer to large plate, and refrigerate until firm, about 30 minutes. Roll each truffle between your hands to form uniform balls (balls needn't be perfect).

3. Transfer truffles to cocoa mixture and roll to evenly coat. (Coated truffles can be refrigerated along with excess cocoa mixture for up to 1 week.) Lightly shake truffles in your hand over pie plate to remove excess coating; transfer to platter. Refrigerate for 30 minutes. Let sit at room temperature for 10 minutes before serving.

CHOCOLATE-ALMOND TRUFFLES

Substitute 1 cup sliced almonds, toasted and chopped fine, for cocoa mixture coating. Add ½ teaspoon almond extract to chocolate mixture before microwaving in step 2.

CHOCOLATE-CINNAMON TRUFFLES

Sift ¼ teaspoon ground cinnamon with cocoa powder and sugar for coating. Add 1 teaspoon ground cinnamon and ⅛ teaspoon cayenne pepper to chocolate mixture before microwaving.

CHOCOLATE-GINGER TRUFFLES

Add 2 teaspoons ground ginger to chocolate mixture before microwaving.

CHOCOLATE-LEMON TRUFFLES

Add 1 teaspoon grated lemon zest to chocolate mixture before microwaving.

No-Stick Solution

The best way to store chocolate truffles is in the cocoa mixture you dredged them in. This keeps the chocolates from sticking and avoids the need to use more cocoa to touch them up.

old-fashioned fruit desserts and puddings

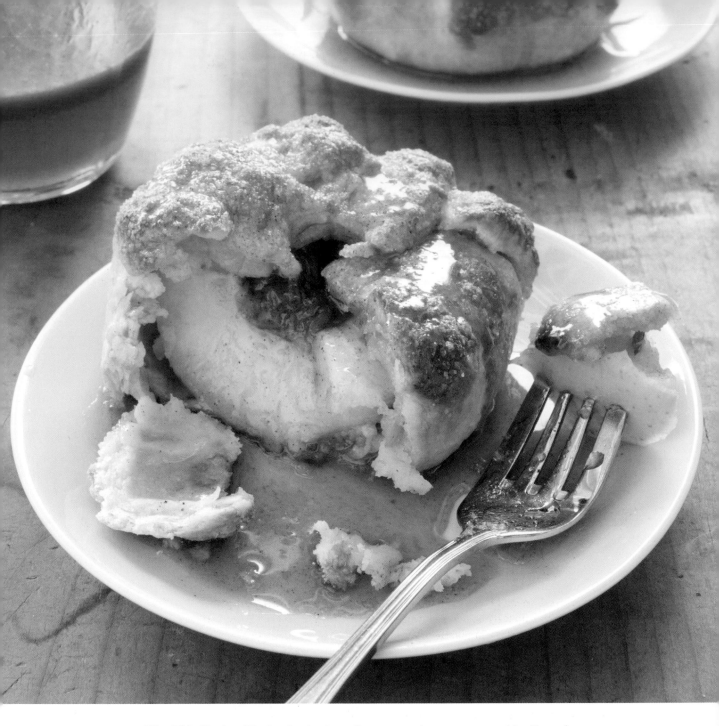

Why This Recipe Works Apple dumplings are a homespun combination of warm pastry, concentrated apple flavor, raisins, butter, and cinnamon, but too often the apples turn too soft or are unevenly baked. The pastry can also turn gummy from the apples' juices. We found that biscuit dough was easier to work with than pie dough and did a great job of absorbing the liquid from the apples without getting mushy. Rather than baking the dumplings in syrup as some recipes instruct, we served our sauce on the side, which preserved the dumplings' texture.

BAKED APPLE DUMPLINGS

MAKES 8 DUMPLINGS

Use a melon baller or a metal teaspoon measure to core the apples. Serve warm, with Cider Sauce (recipe follows).

Dough

2½ cups (12½ ounces) all-purpose flour
3 tablespoons sugar
2 teaspoons baking powder
¾ teaspoon salt
10 tablespoons unsalted butter,
   cut into ½-inch pieces and chilled
5 tablespoons vegetable shortening,
   cut into ½-inch pieces and chilled
¾ cup cold buttermilk

Apple Dumplings

6 tablespoons (2⅔ ounces) sugar
1 teaspoon ground cinnamon
3 tablespoons unsalted butter, softened
3 tablespoons golden raisins, chopped
4 Golden Delicious apples
2 egg whites, lightly beaten

1. For the Dough Process flour, sugar, baking powder, and salt in food processor until combined, about 15 seconds. Scatter butter and shortening over flour mixture and pulse until mixture resembles wet sand, about 10 pulses; transfer to bowl. Stir in buttermilk until dough forms. Turn out onto lightly floured work surface and knead briefly until dough is cohesive. Press dough into 8 by 4-inch rectangle. Cut in half, wrap each half tightly in plastic wrap, and refrigerate until firm, about 1 hour.

2. For the Apple Dumplings Adjust oven rack to middle position and heat oven to 425 degrees. Combine sugar and cinnamon in small bowl. In second bowl, combine butter, raisins, and 3 table-spoons cinnamon sugar mixture. Peel apples and halve through equator. Remove core and pack butter mixture into each apple half.

3. On lightly floured counter, roll each dough half into 12-inch square. Cut each 12-inch square into four 6-inch squares. Working with one at a time, lightly brush edges of dough square with egg white and place apple, cut side up, in center of each square. Gather dough 1 corner at a time on top of apple, crimping edges to seal. Using paring knife, cut vent hole in top of each dumpling.

4. Line rimmed baking sheet with parchment paper. Arrange dumplings on prepared baking sheet, brush tops with egg white, and sprinkle with remaining cinnamon sugar. Bake until dough is golden brown and juices are bubbling, 20 to 25 minutes. Let cool on baking sheet for 10 minutes. Serve.

CIDER SAUCE
MAKES ABOUT 1½ CUPS

1 cup apple cider
1 cup water
1 cup (7 ounces) sugar
½ teaspoon ground cinnamon
2 tablespoons unsalted butter
1 tablespoon lemon juice

Bring cider, water, sugar, and cinnamon to simmer in small saucepan and cook over medium-high heat until thickened and reduced to 1½ cups, about 15 minutes. Off heat, whisk in butter and lemon juice. Drizzle over dumplings to serve.

Wrapping Dumplings

1. Fold corners of dough up to enclose apple halves, overlapping and crimping to seal.

2. Arrange dumplings on baking sheet, brush with egg white, and sprinkle with cinnamon sugar.

Why This Recipe Works Apple fritters should be crisp on the outside, moist within, and sing out apple flavor. Too often, recipes for fritters produce leaden, soggy pastries with undercooked interiors. We found that the best solution was to dry the apples with paper towels and mix them with the dry ingredients. The dry ingredients absorbed the moisture that would otherwise have leached out during frying. As for the batter, we found that replacing the milk with apple cider reinforced the sweet apple flavor. And a quick glaze, spiked with more cider and warm spices and spooned over the warm fritters, added another layer of apple flavor.

APPLE FRITTERS

MAKES 10 FRITTERS

We like Granny Smith apples in these fritters because they are tart and crisp. Apple juice doesn't have enough flavor—you really do need the cider.

Fritters

- 2 Granny Smith apples, peeled, cored, and cut into ¼-inch pieces
- 2 cups (10 ounces) all-purpose flour
- ⅓ cup (2⅓ ounces) granulated sugar
- 1 tablespoon baking powder
- 1 teaspoon salt
- 1 teaspoon ground cinnamon
- ¼ teaspoon ground nutmeg
- ¾ cup apple cider
- 2 large eggs, lightly beaten
- 2 tablespoons unsalted butter, melted
- 3 cups peanut or vegetable oil

Glaze

- 2 cups (8 ounces) confectioners' sugar
- ¼ cup apple cider
- ½ teaspoon ground cinnamon
- ¼ teaspoon ground nutmeg

1. For the Fritters Spread prepared apples in single layer on paper towel–lined baking sheet and pat thoroughly dry with paper towels. Combine flour, sugar, baking powder, salt, cinnamon, and nutmeg in large bowl. Whisk cider, eggs, and melted butter in medium bowl until combined. Stir apples into flour mixture. Stir in cider mixture until incorporated.

2. Set wire rack in rimmed baking sheet. Heat oil in Dutch oven over medium-high heat to 350 degrees. Use ⅓-cup measure to transfer 5 heaping portions of batter to oil. Press batter lightly with back of spoon to flatten. Fry, adjusting burner as necessary to maintain oil temperature between 325 and 350 degrees, until deep golden brown, 2 to 3 minutes per side. Transfer fritters to prepared wire rack. Bring oil back to 350 degrees and repeat with remaining batter. Let fritters cool for 5 minutes.

3. For the Glaze While fritters cool, whisk sugar, cider, cinnamon, and nutmeg in medium bowl until smooth. Top each fritter with 1 heaping tablespoon glaze. Let glaze set for 10 minutes. Serve.

Forming Fritters

1. Use ⅓-cup measure and spoon to carefully and gently portion batter into hot oil.

2. Use spoon to gently press on each fritter. Flattened shape helps interior cook through.

APPLE PANDOWDY

SERVES 6

Disturbing the crust, or "dowdying," allows juices from the filling to rise over the crust and caramelize as the dessert continues to bake. Removing the skillet from the oven allows you to properly press down on the crust. Do not use store-bought pie crust in this recipe; it yields gummy results.

Pie Dough

- 3 tablespoons ice water
- 1 tablespoon sour cream
- ⅔ cup (3⅓ ounces) all-purpose flour
- 1 teaspoon granulated sugar
- ½ teaspoon salt
- 6 tablespoons unsalted butter, cut into ¼-inch pieces and frozen for 15 minutes

Filling

- 2½ pounds Golden Delicious apples, peeled, cored, halved, and cut into ½-inch-thick wedges
- ¼ cup packed (1¾ ounces) light brown sugar
- ½ teaspoon ground cinnamon
- ¼ teaspoon salt
- 3 tablespoons unsalted butter
- ¾ cup apple cider
- 1 tablespoon cornstarch
- 2 teaspoons lemon juice

Topping

- 1 tablespoon granulated sugar
- ¼ teaspoon ground cinnamon
- 1 large egg, lightly beaten

   Vanilla ice cream

1. For the Pie Dough Combine ice water and sour cream in bowl. Process flour, sugar, and salt in food processor until combined, about 3 seconds. Add butter and pulse until size of large peas, 6 to 8 pulses. Add sour cream mixture and pulse until dough forms large clumps and no dry flour remains, 3 to 6 pulses, scraping down sides of bowl as needed.

2. Form dough into 4-inch disk, wrap tightly in plastic wrap, and refrigerate for 1 hour. (Wrapped dough can be refrigerated for up to 2 days or frozen for up to 1 month. If frozen, let dough thaw completely on counter before rolling.)

3. Adjust oven rack to middle position and heat oven to 400 degrees. Let chilled dough sit on counter to soften slightly, about 5 minutes, before rolling. Roll dough into 10-inch circle on lightly floured counter. Using pizza cutter, cut dough into four 2½-inch-wide strips, then make four 2½-inch-wide perpendicular cuts to form squares. (Pieces around edges of dough will be smaller.) Transfer dough pieces to parchment paper–lined baking sheet, cover with plastic, and refrigerate until firm, at least 30 minutes.

4. For the Filling Toss apples, sugar, cinnamon, and salt together in large bowl. Melt butter in 10-inch skillet over medium heat. Add apple mixture, cover, and cook until apples become slightly pliable and release their juices, about 10 minutes, stirring occasionally.

5. Whisk cider, cornstarch, and lemon juice in bowl until no lumps remain; add to skillet. Bring to simmer and cook, uncovered, stirring occasionally, until sauce is thickened, about 2 minutes. Off heat, press lightly on apples to form even layer.

6. For the Topping Combine sugar and cinnamon in small bowl. Working quickly, shingle dough pieces over filling until mostly covered, overlapping as needed. Brush dough pieces with egg and sprinkle with cinnamon sugar.

7. Bake until crust is slightly puffed and beginning to brown, about 15 minutes. Remove skillet from oven. Using back of large spoon, press down in center of crust until juices come up over top of crust. Repeat four more times around skillet. Make sure all apples are submerged and return skillet to oven. Continue to bake until crust is golden brown, about 15 minutes longer.

8. Transfer skillet to wire rack and let cool for at least 20 minutes. Serve with ice cream, drizzling extra sauce over top.

Why This Recipe Works Unlike traditional skillet pie, apple pandowdy's crust is gently pressed into the filling (or "dowdied") during baking so the juices flood the top and caramelize in the oven. We tossed wedges of buttery Golden Delicious apples in cinnamon and brown sugar for sweet-spiced flavor and partially cooked them before simmering in an apple cider–lemon juice slurry to thicken the filling. Topping the apples with squares of dough allowed steam to escape during baking, preventing the apples from overcooking. Dowdying the crust partway through created the dessert's sweet finish.

CRANBERRY-APPLE CRISP

SERVES 8 TO 10

If you can't find Braeburn apples, Golden Delicious will work. Serve with vanilla ice cream or whipped cream.

Topping
¾ cup (3¾ ounces) all-purpose flour
½ cup packed (3½ ounces) light brown sugar
½ cup (3½ ounces) granulated sugar
1 teaspoon ground cinnamon
12 tablespoons unsalted butter, cut into ½-inch pieces and chilled
¾ cup (2¼ ounces) old-fashioned rolled oats

Filling
1 pound (4 cups) fresh or frozen cranberries
1¼ cups (8¾ ounces) granulated sugar
¼ cup water
2½ pounds Granny Smith apples, peeled, cored, halved, and cut into ½-inch pieces
2½ pounds Braeburn apples, peeled, cored, halved, and cut into ½-inch pieces
1 cup dried sweetened cranberries
3 tablespoons instant tapioca

1. For the Topping Adjust oven rack to middle position and heat oven to 400 degrees. Pulse flour, brown sugar, granulated sugar, cinnamon, and butter in food processor until mixture has texture of coarse crumbs (some pea-size pieces of butter will remain), about 12 pulses. Transfer to medium bowl, stir in oats, and use fingers to pinch topping into peanut-size clumps. Refrigerate while preparing filling.

2. For the Filling Bring fresh cranberries, ¾ cup sugar, and water to simmer in Dutch oven over medium-high heat and cook until cranberries are completely softened and mixture is jamlike, about 10 minutes. Scrape mixture into bowl. Add apples, remaining ½ cup sugar, and dried cranberries to now-empty Dutch oven and cook over medium-high heat until apples begin to release their juices, about 5 minutes.

3. Off heat, stir cranberry mixture and tapioca into apple mixture. Pour into 13 by 9-inch baking dish set in rimmed baking sheet and smooth surface evenly with spatula.

4. Mound topping over filling in center of dish, then use your fingers to rake topping out toward edges of dish and bake until juices are bubbling and topping is deep golden brown, about 30 minutes. (If topping is browning too quickly, loosely cover with piece of aluminum foil.) Let cool on wire rack for 10 minutes. Serve.

To Make Ahead After pinching topping into small clumps in step 1, transfer mixture to zipper-lock bag and refrigerate for up to 5 days or freeze for up to 1 month. The cooked filling can be refrigerated for up to 2 days. To bake, sprinkle chilled topping evenly over chilled filling, loosely cover with foil, and bake for 20 minutes. Uncover and bake until juices are bubbling and topping is deep golden brown, 15 to 20 minutes longer.

Crisp Essentials

1. Cook cranberries, sugar, and water until mixture is thick and jammy.

2. Mound topping in center of dish, then use your fingers to rake topping out toward edges of dish.

Why This Recipe Works Although it's hard to imagine that apple crisp needs much improving upon, we liked the tartness and texture that cranberries added to one of our favorite standard dessert recipes. Raw cranberries proved too bitter, but we found dried cranberries and cooked fresh berries made cranberry-apple crisp with the best taste and texture. And we used tapioca to thicken the fruit juices instead of cornstarch or flour.

Why This Recipe Works This 19th-century fruit dessert boasts sweetened stewed berries covered with drop biscuit dough that is covered to steam and cook through. We found the idea of a simple stovetop fruit dessert appealing, but standard recipes produced washed-out fruit and a soggy topping. To improve the recipe, we cooked down half of the berries until jammy, and then stirred in the remaining berries. A bit of cornstarch further thickened the filling. For a fluffy biscuit topping, we placed a dish towel under the lid during cooking to absorb condensation. A sprinkle of cinnamon sugar over the finished dessert provided sweet crunch.

MAINE BLUEBERRY GRUNT

SERVES 12

Do not use frozen blueberries here, as they will make the filling watery. You will need a clean dish towel for this recipe.

Filling
2½ pounds (8 cups) blueberries
½ cup (3½ ounces) sugar
½ teaspoon ground cinnamon
2 tablespoons water
1 teaspoon grated lemon zest plus 1 tablespoon juice
1 teaspoon cornstarch

Topping
¾ cup buttermilk
6 tablespoons unsalted butter, melted and cooled slightly
1 teaspoon vanilla extract
2¼ cups (11¼ ounces) all-purpose flour
1½ teaspoons baking powder
½ teaspoon baking soda
½ teaspoon salt
½ cup (3½ ounces) sugar
½ teaspoon ground cinnamon

1. For the Filling Cook 4 cups blueberries, sugar, cinnamon, water, and lemon zest in Dutch oven over medium-high heat, stirring occasionally, until mixture is thick and jamlike, 10 to 12 minutes. Whisk lemon juice and cornstarch in small bowl, then stir into blueberry mixture. Add remaining 4 cups blueberries and cook until heated through, about 1 minute; remove pot from heat, cover, and keep warm.

2. For the Topping Combine buttermilk, butter, and vanilla in 2-cup liquid measuring cup. Whisk flour, baking powder, baking soda, salt, and 6 tablespoons sugar in large bowl. Slowly stir buttermilk mixture into flour mixture until dough forms.

3. Using small ice cream scoop or 2 large spoons, spoon golf ball–size dough pieces on top of warm berry mixture (you should have 14 pieces). Wrap lid of Dutch oven with clean dish towel (keeping towel away from heat source) and cover pot. Simmer gently until biscuits have doubled in size and toothpick inserted in center comes out clean, 16 to 22 minutes.

4. Combine remaining 2 tablespoons sugar and cinnamon in small bowl. Remove lid and sprinkle biscuit topping with cinnamon sugar. Serve immediately.

Secrets to Great Grunt

1. Use small ice cream scoop to drop evenly sized balls of biscuit dough over warm filling.

2. A clean dish towel beneath lid absorbs condensation during cooking, keeping biscuit topping light and fluffy.

3. A sprinkling of cinnamon sugar adds crunchy contrast to steamed biscuits.

SKILLET PEACH COBBLER

SERVES 6 TO 8

You can substitute 4 pounds of frozen sliced peaches for fresh; there is no need to defrost them. Start step 2 when the peaches are almost done.

Filling

- 4 tablespoons unsalted butter
- 5 pounds peaches, peeled, halved, pitted, and cut into ½-inch wedges
- 6 tablespoons (2⅔ ounces) sugar
- ⅛ teaspoon salt
- 1 tablespoon lemon juice
- 1½ teaspoons cornstarch

Topping

- 1½ cups (7½ ounces) all-purpose flour
- 6 tablespoons (2⅔ ounces) sugar
- 1½ teaspoons baking powder
- ¼ teaspoon baking soda
- ¼ teaspoon salt
- ¾ cup buttermilk
- 4 tablespoons unsalted butter, melted and cooled
- 1 teaspoon ground cinnamon

1. For the Filling Adjust oven rack to middle position and heat oven to 425 degrees. Melt butter in 12-inch ovensafe nonstick skillet over medium-high heat. Add two-thirds of peaches, sugar, and salt and cook, covered, until peaches release their juices, about 5 minutes. Remove lid and simmer until all liquid has evaporated and peaches begin to caramelize, 15 to 20 minutes. Add remaining peaches and cook until heated through, about 5 minutes. Whisk lemon juice and cornstarch in small bowl, then stir into peach mixture. Cover skillet and set aside off heat.

2. For the Topping Meanwhile, whisk flour, 5 tablespoons sugar, baking powder, baking soda, and salt in medium bowl. Stir in buttermilk and butter until dough forms. Turn dough out onto lightly floured work surface and knead briefly until smooth, about 30 seconds.

3. Combine remaining 1 tablespoon sugar and cinnamon. Break dough into rough 1-inch pieces and space them about ½ inch apart on top of hot peach mixture. Sprinkle with cinnamon sugar and bake until topping is golden brown and filling is thickened, 18 to 22 minutes. Let cool on wire rack for 10 minutes. Serve.

Peeling Peaches

1. With paring knife, score small X at base of each peach.

2. Lower peaches into boiling water and simmer until skins loosen, 30 to 60 seconds.

3. Transfer peaches immediately to ice water and let cool for about 1 minute.

4. Use paring knife to remove strips of loosened peel, starting at X on base of each peach.

Why This Recipe Works We wanted a peach cobbler that avoided a watery filling and soggy topping. To do this, we turned to a skillet and concentrated the peach flavor by first sautéing the peaches in butter and sugar to release their juices, then cooking them down until all the liquid had evaporated. To keep the filling from being too mushy, we withheld some of the peaches from sautéing, adding them just before baking. We also made the biscuits sturdy enough to stand up to the fruit by mixing melted butter rather than cold butter into the dry ingredients.

DAKOTA PEACH KUCHEN

MAKES TWO 9-INCH KUCHENS

The dough will need 2 hours to rise plus 1 hour to chill in the refrigerator. We developed this recipe using dark cake pans; if your pans are light, increase the baking time in step 7 to 55 to 60 minutes.

Crust

½ cup whole milk
2 large eggs
2½ cups (12½ ounces) all-purpose flour
1 tablespoon sugar
2 teaspoons instant or rapid-rise yeast
½ teaspoon salt
8 tablespoons unsalted butter, cut into 8 pieces and softened

Fruit and Custard

1 pound fresh peaches, peeled, halved, pitted, and cut into ½-inch wedges or 12 ounces frozen sliced peaches, thawed
2 tablespoons plus ¾ cup (5¼ ounces) sugar
1 large egg plus 1 large yolk
¼ teaspoon salt
1¼ cups heavy cream
4 tablespoons unsalted butter, cut into 4 pieces
½ teaspoon vanilla extract
¼ teaspoon ground cinnamon

1. For the Crust Grease large bowl. Whisk milk and eggs in 2-cup liquid measuring cup until combined. Using stand mixer fitted with dough hook, mix flour, sugar, yeast, and salt on medium-low speed until combined, about 5 seconds. With mixer running, slowly add milk mixture and knead until dough forms, about 1 minute.

2. With mixer still running, add butter 1 piece at a time until incorporated. Continue kneading until dough clears sides of bowl but still sticks to bottom, 8 to 12 minutes (dough should be soft and sticky).

3. Transfer dough to greased bowl, cover with plastic wrap, and let rise on counter until doubled in size, about 1 hour. Punch down dough and divide into 2 equal balls. Wrap each ball in plastic, transfer to refrigerator, and let rest for at least 1 hour or up to 24 hours.

4. Grease 2 dark-colored 9-inch round cake pans. Roll each chilled dough balls into a 9-inch disk on lightly floured counter. Transfer to prepared pans, pushing dough to edges of pans. Cover pans loosely with plastic and let rise on counter until puffy, about 1 hour. Adjust oven rack to middle position and heat oven to 350 degrees.

5. For the Fruit and Custard Meanwhile, toss peaches with 2 tablespoons sugar in bowl, then transfer to colander set in sink; let sit for 25 minutes. Whisk remaining ¾ cup sugar, egg and yolk, and salt in medium bowl until combined. Heat cream in medium saucepan over medium heat until just beginning to simmer.

6. Slowly whisk hot cream into egg mixture. Transfer cream mixture back to saucepan and cook over medium-low heat, stirring constantly, until mixture thickens and coats back of spoon, 3 to 5 minutes. Strain custard through fine-mesh strainer set over medium bowl. Whisk in butter and vanilla and transfer to refrigerator to cool until dough is ready. (Custard can be made up to 24 hours in advance but does not need to be fully chilled before going into crust.)

7. Leaving 1-inch border all around, press down centers of doughs with bottom of dry measuring cup to deflate and create wells for peaches and custard. Arrange peaches, evenly spaced, in circular pattern in depressed dough, avoiding border. Pour custard evenly over peaches in each pan, about 1 cup per pan (you may have a few tablespoons extra). Sprinkle with cinnamon. Bake until crusts are golden brown and centers jiggle slightly when shaken, 35 to 40 minutes, switching and rotating pans halfway through baking. Let cool completely. Remove kuchens from pans using flexible spatula. Slice and serve.

Why This Recipe Works Kuchen, the official state dessert of South Dakota, features a tender yeasted dough, peaches full of flavor, and a layer of smooth, delicately sweet custard. We created a buttery crust by slowly adding softened butter to the dough, letting the dough rise and then rest in the fridge. An extra egg yolk made our custard thick and rich, without the eggy flavor found in egg whites. Finally, to ready the peaches, we sprinkled them with sugar and let them sit in a colander to pull out their excess juice and prevent the kuchen from becoming soggy. This dessert might come from South Dakota, but it felt right at home in our kitchen.

Why This Recipe Works We wanted our banana pudding to be rich and creamy, so we opted for half-and-half instead of milk in the pudding component. Roasting the bananas intensified their flavor and helped break them down so we could incorporate them more easily into the pudding. Adding a squeeze of lemon juice to the roasted bananas prevented them from browning in the refrigerator. Even whole cookies became sodden and pasty when layered with hot pudding. We solved the problem by simply waiting for the pudding to cool a little before assembling the dessert.

BANANA PUDDING

SERVES 12

If your food processor bowl holds less than 11 cups, puree half the pudding with the roasted bananas and lemon juice in step 3, transfer it to a large bowl, and whisk in the rest of the pudding.

Pudding
7 slightly underripe large bananas (2½ pounds), unpeeled
1½ cups (10½ ounces) sugar
8 large egg yolks
6 tablespoons cornstarch
6 cups half-and-half
½ teaspoon salt
3 tablespoons unsalted butter
1 tablespoon vanilla extract
3 tablespoons lemon juice
1 (12-ounce) box vanilla wafers

Whipped Topping
1 cup heavy cream, chilled
1 tablespoon sugar
½ teaspoon vanilla extract

1. For the Pudding Adjust oven rack to upper-middle position and heat oven to 325 degrees. Place 3 unpeeled bananas on baking sheet and bake until skins are completely black, about 20 minutes. Let cool for 5 minutes.

2. Meanwhile, whisk ½ cup sugar, egg yolks, and cornstarch in medium bowl until smooth. Bring half-and-half, remaining 1 cup sugar, and salt to simmer over medium heat in large saucepan. Whisk ½ cup simmering half-and-half mixture into egg yolk mixture to temper. Slowly whisk tempered yolk mixture into saucepan. Cook, whisking constantly, until mixture is thick and large bubbles appear at surface, about 2 minutes. Remove from heat and stir in butter and vanilla.

3. Transfer pudding to food processor. Add warm peeled roasted bananas and 2 tablespoons lemon juice and process until smooth. Scrape into large bowl and place plastic wrap directly on surface of pudding. Refrigerate until slightly cool, about 45 minutes.

4. Peel and cut remaining bananas into ¼-inch slices and toss in bowl with remaining 1 tablespoon lemon juice. Spoon one-quarter of pudding into 3-quart trifle dish and top with layer of cookies, layer of sliced bananas, and another layer of cookies. Repeat twice, ending with pudding. Place plastic wrap directly on surface of pudding and refrigerate until wafers have softened, at least 8 hours or up to 2 days.

5. For the Whipped Topping Using stand mixer fitted with whisk, whip cream, sugar, and vanilla on medium-low speed until foamy, about 1 minute. Increase speed to high and whip until stiff peaks form, 1 to 3 minutes. (Whipped cream can be refrigerated for 4 hours.) Top banana pudding with whipped cream. Serve.

TOASTED COCONUT BANANA PUDDING

Replace 2 cups half-and-half with one 16-ounce can unsweetened coconut milk in step 2. Sprinkle ¼ cup toasted sweetened shredded coconut over whipped cream–topped pudding before serving.

PEANUT-Y BANANA PUDDING

In step 4, sandwich 2 vanilla wafers around 1 banana slice and ½ teaspoon creamy peanut butter (you'll need ½ cup total). Assemble by alternating layers of pudding and cookie-banana sandwiches, ending with pudding. Sprinkle ¼ cup chopped salted dry-roasted peanuts over whipped cream–topped pudding before serving.

Why This Recipe Works The best bourbon bread pudding is a rich, "scoopable" custard that envelops the bread with a balance of sweet spiciness and robust bourbon flavor. Tearing a crusty baguette into ragged pieces, then toasting them, gave the pudding a rustic look and kept the bread from turning soggy in the custard. We used a mixture of 3 parts cream to 1 part milk and replaced the whole eggs with yolks for a rich, creamy custard that didn't curdle. Once the custard set up in the oven, we sprinkled cinnamon, sugar, and butter on top and let it bake until the topping was caramelized.

NEW ORLEANS BOURBON BREAD PUDDING

SERVES 8 TO 10

This bread pudding is great on its own, but for a little more punch, drizzle Bourbon Sauce over individual servings (recipe follows). A bakery-quality French baguette makes this dish even better.

1 (18- to 20-inch) baguette,
   torn into 1-inch pieces (10 cups)
1 cup golden raisins
¾ cup bourbon
6 tablespoons unsalted butter, cut into 6 pieces
   and chilled, plus extra for baking dish
8 large egg yolks
1½ cups packed (10½ ounces) light brown sugar
3 cups heavy cream
1 cup whole milk
1 tablespoon vanilla extract
1½ teaspoons ground cinnamon
¼ teaspoon nutmeg
¼ teaspoon salt
3 tablespoons granulated sugar

1. Adjust oven rack to middle position and heat oven to 450 degrees. Arrange bread in single layer on baking sheet and bake until crisp and browned, about 12 minutes, turning pieces over and switching baking sheets halfway through baking. Let bread cool. Reduce oven temperature to 300 degrees.

2. Meanwhile, heat raisins with ½ cup bourbon in small saucepan over medium-high heat until bourbon begins to simmer, 2 to 3 minutes. Strain mixture, reserving bourbon and raisins separately.

3. Butter 13 by 9-inch broiler-safe baking dish. Whisk egg yolks, brown sugar, cream, milk, vanilla, 1 teaspoon cinnamon, nutmeg, and salt together in large bowl. Whisk in reserved bourbon plus remaining ¼ cup bourbon. Add toasted bread and toss until evenly coated. Let mixture sit until bread begins to absorb custard, about 30 minutes, tossing occasionally. If majority of bread is still hard, continue to soak for 15 to 20 minutes.

4. Pour half of bread mixture into prepared baking dish and sprinkle with half of raisins. Pour remaining bread mixture into dish and sprinkle with remaining raisins. Cover with aluminum foil and bake for 45 minutes.

5. Meanwhile, mix granulated sugar and remaining ½ teaspoon cinnamon in small bowl. Using your fingers, cut 6 tablespoons butter into sugar mixture until size of small peas. Remove foil from pudding, sprinkle with butter mixture, and bake, uncovered, until custard is just set, 20 to 25 minutes. Remove pudding from oven and heat broiler.

6. Once broiler is heated, broil pudding until top forms golden crust, about 2 minutes. Transfer to wire rack and cool at least 30 minutes or up to 2 hours. Serve.

BOURBON SAUCE
MAKES ABOUT 1 CUP

1½ teaspoons cornstarch
¼ cup bourbon
¾ cup heavy cream
2 tablespoons sugar
   Pinch salt
2 teaspoons unsalted butter, cut into 8 pieces

Whisk cornstarch and 2 tablespoons bourbon in small bowl until well combined. Heat cream and sugar in small saucepan over medium heat until sugar dissolves. Whisk in cornstarch mixture and bring to boil. Reduce heat to low and cook until sauce thickens, 3 to 5 minutes. Off heat, stir in salt, butter, and remaining 2 tablespoons bourbon. Drizzle warm sauce over individual servings. (Sauce can be refrigerated for up to 5 days.)

SUMMER BERRY PUDDING

SERVES 6

Fill in any gaps in pudding crusts with toast trimmings.

8 (¼-inch-thick) slices challah, crusts removed
12 ounces strawberries, hulled and chopped (2 cups)
8 ounces blackberries, halved (1½ cups)
8 ounces (1½ cups) blueberries
5 ounces (1 cup) raspberries
½ cup (3½ ounces) granulated sugar
1 teaspoon unflavored gelatin
2 tablespoons cold water
½ cup (5½ ounces) apricot preserves
1 cup heavy cream, chilled
1 tablespoon confectioners' sugar

1. Adjust oven rack to middle position and heat oven to 350 degrees. Line 8½ by 4½-inch loaf pan with plastic wrap, pushing plastic into corners and up sides of pan and allowing excess to overhang long sides. Make cardboard cutout just large enough to fit inside pan.

2. Place challah on wire rack set in rimmed baking sheet. Bake until dry, about 10 minutes, flipping challah and rotating sheet halfway through baking. Let challah cool completely.

3. Combine strawberries, blackberries, blueberries, and raspberries in bowl. Transfer half of mixture to medium saucepan, add granulated sugar, and bring to simmer over medium-low heat, stirring occasionally. Reduce heat to low and continue to cook until berries release their juices and raspberries begin to break down, about 5 minutes. Off heat, stir in remaining berries. After 2 minutes, strain berries through fine-mesh strainer set over medium bowl for 10 minutes, stirring berries once halfway through straining (do not press on berries). Reserve berry juice. (You should have ¾ to 1 cup.)

4. Sprinkle gelatin over water in bowl and let sit until gelatin softens, about 5 minutes. Microwave until mixture is bubbling around edges and gelatin dissolves, about 30 seconds. Whisk preserves and gelatin mixture together in large bowl. Fold in strained berries.

5. Trim 4 slices of challah to fit snugly side by side in bottom of loaf pan (you may have extra challah). Dip slices in reserved berry juice until saturated, about 30 seconds per side, then place in bottom of pan. Spoon berry mixture over challah. Trim remaining 4 slices of challah to fit snugly side by side on top of berries (you may have extra challah). Dip slices in reserved berry juice until saturated, about 30 seconds per side, then place on top of berries. Cover pan loosely with plastic and place in 13 by 9-inch baking dish. Place cardboard cutout on top of pudding. Top with 3 soup cans to weigh down pudding. Refrigerate pudding for at least 8 hours or up to 24 hours.

6. Using stand mixer fitted with whisk, whip cream and confectioners' sugar on medium-low speed until foamy, about 1 minute. Increase speed to high and whip until soft peaks form, 1 to 3 minutes. Transfer to serving bowl. Remove cans, cardboard, and plastic from top of pudding. Loosen pudding by pulling up on edges of plastic. Place inverted platter over top of loaf pan and flip platter and pan upside down to unmold pudding. Discard plastic. Slice pudding with serrated knife and serve with whipped cream.

Constructing Summer Berry Pudding

1. Saturate dried, trimmed challah with reserved berry juices and place in bottom of plastic wrap–lined pan.

2. Spoon sweetened four-berry mixture over challah, and top with four more slices of saturated challah.

Why This Recipe Works Although our initial tests of this traditional British "pudding" were fairly disastrous, we knew that good bread and fresh summer berries could make a delicious dessert. The rectangular shape of a loaf pan proved a more stable mold than traditional round bowls. We staled challah bread (our top choice for its flavor and texture) in the oven for added support. Since the moisture content of fresh berries can vary, we strained the juice from the filling and dipped the bread in it ourselves. Cooking only half of the berries and mixing the rest in later brightened the filling, and apricot preserves and gelatin helped the pudding keep its shape.

Why This Recipe Works There's nothing like a cone of creamy frozen custard on a hot summer day—or really any day. While stores use industrial condensers to produce the consistency we know and love, we set out to find a way to achieve super smooth custard at home without a machine. After combining our heated cream and egg yolk mixtures, we strained the custard to remove any pieces of cooked egg. To achieve the smoothest possible custard, we cooled the mixture on ice, let it chill in the refrigerator, then whipped it in a stand mixer to add air. This prevented ice crystals from building up and made the final texture silky and creamy.

OLD-FASHIONED VANILLA FROZEN CUSTARD

MAKES ABOUT 1 QUART

One teaspoon of vanilla extract can be substituted for the vanilla bean; stir the extract into the strained custard in step 3. Use an instant-read thermometer for the best results.

6 large egg yolks
¼ cup (1¾ ounces) sugar
2 tablespoons nonfat dry milk powder
1 cup heavy cream
½ cup whole milk
⅓ cup light corn syrup
⅛ teaspoon salt
1 vanilla bean

1. Whisk egg yolks, sugar, and milk powder in bowl until smooth, about 30 seconds; set aside. Combine cream, milk, corn syrup, and salt in medium saucepan. Cut vanilla bean in half lengthwise. Using tip of paring knife, scrape out vanilla seeds and add to cream mixture, along with vanilla bean. Heat cream mixture over medium-high heat, stirring occasionally, until it steams steadily and registers 175 degrees, about 5 minutes. Remove saucepan from heat.

2. Slowly whisk heated cream mixture into yolk mixture to temper. Return cream-yolk mixture to saucepan and cook over medium-low heat, stirring constantly, until mixture thickens and registers 180 degrees, 4 to 6 minutes.

3. Immediately pour custard through fine-mesh strainer set over large bowl; discard vanilla bean. Fill slightly larger bowl with ice and set custard bowl in bowl of ice. Transfer to refrigerator and let chill until custard registers 40 degrees, 1 to 2 hours, stirring occasionally.

4. Transfer chilled custard to stand mixer fitted with whisk and whip on medium-high speed for 3 minutes, or until mixture increases in volume to about 3¾ cups. Pour custard into airtight 1-quart container. Cover and freeze until firm, at least 6 hours, before serving. (Frozen custard is best eaten within 10 days.)

OLD-FASHIONED CHOCOLATE FROZEN CUSTARD

Omit vanilla bean. Add ½ ounce finely chopped 60 percent cacao bittersweet chocolate and 1 tablespoon Dutch-processed cocoa powder to cream mixture in step 1 before cooking. Add ½ teaspoon vanilla extract to strained custard in step 3.

Steps to Smooth Frozen Custard

1. TEMPER Heating cream mixture before slowly adding it to cold yolk mixture prevents eggs from curdling.

2. STRAIN Pouring warm custard through strainer removes any pieces of cooked egg.

3. CHILL Cooling custard on ice primes it for adding air.

4. WHIP Whipping cooled custard adds air to make final texture especially creamy.

save room for pie

DOUBLE-CRUST PIE DOUGH

MAKES ENOUGH FOR ONE 9-INCH PIE

2½ cups (12½ ounces) all-purpose flour
  2 tablespoons sugar
  1 teaspoon salt
  8 tablespoons vegetable shortening,
    cut into ¼-inch pieces and chilled
 12 tablespoons unsalted butter,
    cut into ¼-inch pieces and chilled
6–8 tablespoons ice water

1. Process flour, sugar, and salt in food processor until combined, about 5 seconds. Scatter shortening over top and process until mixture resembles coarse cornmeal, about 10 seconds. Scatter butter over top and pulse until mixture resembles coarse crumbs, about 10 pulses. Transfer to bowl.

2. Sprinkle 6 tablespoons water over flour mixture. Using rubber spatula, stir and press dough until it sticks together. If dough does not come together, stir in remaining water, 1 tablespoon at a time, until it does.

3. Divide dough into 2 even pieces and flatten each into 4-inch disk. Wrap disks tightly in plastic wrap and refrigerate for 1 hour. Let chilled dough soften slightly on counter before rolling.

CLASSIC SINGLE-CRUST PIE DOUGH

MAKES ENOUGH FOR ONE 9-INCH PIE

1¼ cups (6¼ ounces) all-purpose flour
  1 tablespoon sugar
  ½ teaspoon salt
  4 tablespoons vegetable shortening,
    cut into ¼-inch pieces and chilled
  6 tablespoons unsalted butter,
    cut into ¼-inch pieces and chilled
3–4 tablespoons ice water

1. Process flour, sugar, and salt in food processor until combined, about 5 seconds. Scatter shortening over top and process until mixture resembles coarse cornmeal, about 10 seconds. Scatter butter over top and pulse until mixture resembles coarse crumbs, about 10 pulses. Transfer to bowl.

2. Sprinkle 3 tablespoons water over flour mixture. Using rubber spatula, stir and press dough until it sticks together. If dough does not come together, add remaining 1 tablespoon water. Flatten dough into 4-inch disk, wrap tightly in plastic wrap, and refrigerate for 1 hour.

3. Let chilled dough soften slightly. Lightly flour counter, then roll dough into 12-inch circle and fit it into 9-inch pie plate. Trim, fold, and crimp edges of dough. Wrap dough-lined pie plate in plastic and place in freezer until dough is fully chilled and firm, about 30 minutes, before using.

Rolling and Fitting Pie Dough

1. Roll dough outward from its center into 12-inch circle. Between every few rolls, give dough quarter turn.

2. Toss additional flour underneath dough as needed to keep dough from sticking to counter.

3. Loosely roll dough around rolling pin, then gently unroll it over pie plate.

4. Lift dough and gently press it into pie plate, letting excess hang over plate.

NO-FEAR SINGLE-CRUST PIE DOUGH

MAKES ENOUGH FOR ONE 9-INCH PIE

Anyone can make this pat-in-the-pan pie dough—no rolling or transferring of dough to the dish required. Cream cheese helps make this dough easy to handle and helps ensure a tender crust. Make sure you press the dough evenly into a glass pie plate; if you hold the dough-lined plate up to the light, you will be able to clearly see any thick or thin spots.

1¼ cups (6¼ ounces) all-purpose flour
 2 tablespoons sugar
 ¼ teaspoon salt
 8 tablespoons unsalted butter, softened but still cool
 2 ounces cream cheese, softened but still cool

1. Lightly coat 9-inch Pyrex pie plate with vegetable oil spray. Whisk flour, sugar, and salt together in bowl.

2. Using stand mixer fitted with paddle, beat butter and cream cheese on medium-high speed until completely homogeneous, about 2 minutes, stopping once or twice to scrape down beater and sides of bowl. Add flour mixture and mix on medium-low speed until mixture resembles coarse cornmeal, about 20 seconds. Scrape down sides of bowl. Increase mixer speed to medium-high and beat until dough begins to form large clumps, about 30 seconds. Reserve 3 tablespoons of dough. Turn remaining dough onto lightly floured counter, gather into ball, and flatten into 6-inch disk. Transfer disk to greased pie plate.

3. Press dough evenly over bottom of pie plate toward sides, using heel of your hand. Hold plate up to light to ensure that dough is evenly distributed. With your fingertips, continue to work dough over bottom of plate and up sides until evenly distributed.

4. On floured counter, roll reserved dough into 12-inch rope. Divide into 3 pieces and roll each piece into 8-inch rope. Arrange ropes, evenly spaced, around top of pie plate, pressing and squeezing to join them with dough in plate and form uniform edge. Use your fingers to flute edge of dough. Wrap dough-lined pie plate in plastic wrap and place in freezer until dough is fully chilled and firm, about 30 minutes, before using.

No-Fear Pie Dough

1. Hold pie plate up to light to check thickness of dough; it should be translucent, not opaque. Pay attention to curved edges.

2. Roll reserved dough into three 8-inch ropes. Arrange ropes around perimeter of pie plate, leaving small (about 1-inch) gaps between them.

3. Squeeze ropes together.

4. Create a fluted edge, dipping your fingers in flour if dough is sticky.

Why This Recipe Works Most Shaker lemon pie recipes mix lemon slices—peel and all—with sugar and eggs to form a custardy filling. But unless we macerated the lemon slices for 24 hours, the pie turned out bitter. We wanted to speed up this recipe for modern times. First, we squeezed the seeded lemon slices and reserved the juice for the filling. Then, we simmered the slices and then added them to the filling with the uncooked juice for bright lemon flavor without any macerating time.

SHAKER LEMON PIE

SERVES 8

Have an extra lemon on hand in case the three sliced lemons do not yield enough juice. See page 562 for more information on rolling and fitting pie dough.

1   recipe Double-Crust Pie Dough (page 562)
3   large lemons, sliced thin and seeded
1¾ cups (12¼ ounces) sugar
⅛   teaspoon salt
1   tablespoon cornstarch
4   large eggs
1   tablespoon heavy cream

1. Roll 1 disk of dough into 12-inch circle on lightly floured counter, then fit it into 9-inch pie plate, letting excess dough hang over edge; cover with plastic wrap and refrigerate for 30 minutes. Roll other disk of dough into 12-inch circle on lightly floured counter, then transfer to parchment paper–lined baking sheet; cover with plastic and refrigerate for 30 minutes.

2. Adjust oven rack to lowest position and heat oven to 425 degrees. Squeeze lemon slices in fine-mesh strainer set over bowl; reserve juice (you should have 6 tablespoons). Bring drained slices and 2 cups water to boil in saucepan, then reduce heat to medium-low and simmer until slices are softened, about 5 minutes. Drain well and discard liquid. Combine softened lemon slices, sugar, salt, and ¼ cup reserved lemon juice in bowl; stir until sugar dissolves.

3. Whisk cornstarch and remaining 2 tablespoons lemon juice in large bowl. Whisk eggs into cornstarch mixture, then slowly stir in lemon slice mixture until combined. Pour into chilled pie shell. Brush edges of dough with 1 teaspoon cream. Loosely roll second piece of dough around rolling pin then gently unroll it over pie. Trim, fold, and crimp edges, and cut 4 vent holes in top. Brush top with remaining 2 teaspoons cream.

4. Bake until light golden, about 20 minutes, then decrease oven temperature to 375 degrees and continue to bake until golden brown, 20 to 25 minutes. Let pie cool on wire rack for at least 1 hour. Serve. (Pie can be refrigerated for 2 days.)

Building Bold, Not Bitter, Lemon Flavor

Using sliced whole lemons, pith and all, can produce an overwhelmingly bitter filling. We found a few tricks to create bright lemon flavor while tempering the bitterness of the pith.

1. Squeeze seeded lemon slices and reserve juice for filling.

2. Simmer slices to mellow bitterness of pith and then add them to filling with uncooked juice.

Shaker Cooking

The Shakers' food was never ornate and was always healthy and hearty enough to support their industrious, hard-working lifestyle. Shakers scrubbed—rather than peeled—their vegetables (and, in the case of Shaker Lemon Pie, their citrus fruit) to minimize waste. They were also pioneers in using exact measurements in cooking at a time when many recipes called for a "dash," "glob," or "handful" of something.

The Slice is Right

While developing our recipe for Shaker Lemon Pie, we found that cutting the lemons into paper-thin slices was a difficult and time-consuming task. We had better results with a mandoline (or V-slicer), which produced perfectly thin slices in no time at all. If you don't have a mandoline, another piece of kitchen equipment will make the process easier: the freezer. Freezing the lemons for about 30 minutes firms them up for better hand slicing, which is best accomplished with a serrated knife.

Why This Recipe Works Think of sour orange pie as Northern Florida's answer to Key lime: Its custard-like filling is made with the juice of wild sour oranges. Since fresh sour oranges are hard to source, we re-created their ultrasour taste with frozen orange juice concentrate, lemon juice, and orange and lemon zests. We mixed the juice with sweetened condensed milk for sweetness and egg yolks for structure. Slightly sweet animal crackers made a crunchy crust to contrast the tart filling. Chilled and topped with orange-flavored whipped cream, this sunny pie was bright and refreshing.

SOUR ORANGE PIE

MAKES ONE 9-INCH PIE

If sour oranges are available, use ¾ cup strained sour orange juice in place of the lemon juice and orange juice concentrate in the filling.

Crust
5 ounces animal crackers
3 tablespoons sugar
Pinch salt
4 tablespoons unsalted butter, melted

Filling
1 (14-ounce) can sweetened condensed milk
6 tablespoons thawed orange juice concentrate
4 large egg yolks
2 teaspoons grated lemon zest plus 6 tablespoons juice (2 lemons)
1 teaspoon grated orange zest
Pinch salt

Whipped Cream
¾ cup heavy cream, chilled
2 tablespoons sugar
½ teaspoon grated orange zest

1. For the Crust Adjust oven rack to middle position and heat oven to 325 degrees. Process crackers, sugar, and salt in food processor until finely ground, about 30 seconds. Add melted butter and pulse until combined, about 8 pulses. Transfer crumbs to 9-inch pie plate.

2. Using bottom of dry measuring cup, press crumbs firmly into bottom and up sides of pie plate. Bake until fragrant and beginning to brown, 12 to 14 minutes. Cool to room temperature, about 30 minutes.

3. For the Filling When crust is cool, whisk condensed milk, orange juice concentrate, egg yolks, lemon zest and juice, orange zest, and salt together in bowl until fully combined. Pour filling into cooled crust.

4. Bake until center of pie jiggles slightly when shaken, 15 to 17 minutes. Cool to room temperature, then refrigerate until fully chilled, at least 3 hours; or cover with greased plastic wrap and refrigerate for up to 24 hours.

5. For the Whipped Cream Whisk cream, sugar, and orange zest together in medium bowl until stiff peaks form, 2 to 4 minutes.

6. Slice chilled pie and serve with whipped cream.

No Sour Oranges? No Problem.

Since fresh sour oranges can be hard to find, we recreated their ultrasour, slightly bitter taste by combining thawed frozen orange juice concentrate with fresh lemon juice and bolstering the mixture with lots of orange and lemon zest.

 + =

FRESH LEMON JUICE
Provides plenty of sourness

ORANGE JUICE CONCENTRATE
Adds potent orange flavor

SOUR ORANGE
Intense tartness

PEACHES AND CREAM PIE

SERVES 8

Keep an eye on the peaches at the end of their baking time to ensure that they don't scorch. You can use Classic Single-Crust Pie Dough (page 562) or No-Fear Single-Crust Pie Dough (page 563) for this pie.

- 1 recipe single-crust pie dough, fitted into 9-inch pie plate and chilled
- 2 pounds ripe but firm peaches, peeled, halved, and pitted
- 2 tablespoons plus ½ cup (4⅓ ounces) sugar
- 3 tablespoons all-purpose flour
- ¼ teaspoon salt
- ⅓ cup heavy cream
- 2 large egg yolks
- ½ teaspoon vanilla extract

1. Adjust oven racks to upper-middle and lower-middle positions and heat oven to 375 degrees. Line chilled crust with double layer of aluminum foil and fill with pie weights.

2. Place peach halves cut side up on foil-lined rimmed baking sheet and sprinkle with 2 tablespoons sugar. Bake peaches on upper-middle rack until softened and juice is released, about 30 minutes, flipping halfway through baking.

3. After 30 minutes, place crust on lower-middle rack and, while peaches continue to roast, bake until edges are lightly browned, about 15 minutes. Remove crust from oven and carefully remove foil and weights. Continue to bake until bottom of crust is light golden brown and peaches are caramelized, about 5 minutes longer. Cool crust and peaches for 15 minutes.

4. Reduce oven temperature to 325 degrees. Cut peach halves lengthwise into quarters. Arrange peaches in single layer over crust. Combine remaining ½ cup sugar, flour, and salt in bowl. Whisk in cream, egg yolks, and vanilla until smooth. Pour cream mixture over peaches. Bake until filling is light golden brown and firm in center, 45 to 55 minutes. Cool pie on wire rack for at least 3 hours. Serve.

Twice-Baked Peaches

Eat a peach out of hand, and its juiciness is no small part of what makes it so good. But cook the fruit, and that same high water content can ruin peach pie, especially when coupled with cream. To evaporate the peach juices and concentrate the peach flavor, we roasted the fruit before filling the pie. A sprinkle of sugar helps the peach halves caramelize. Plus, to save time, while you're roasting the fruit on one rack of the oven, you can prebake the crust on another.

Blind Baking a Pie Crust

The crusts for many pies and tarts are baked before filling (this is called blind baking) so that they stay golden brown, crisp, and flaky once filled.

1. Line chilled pie crust with double layer of aluminum foil, fill crust with pie weights or pennies, and bake until lightly browned, about 15 minutes.

2. Remove pie weights and foil and continue to bake until light golden brown, about 5 minutes longer.

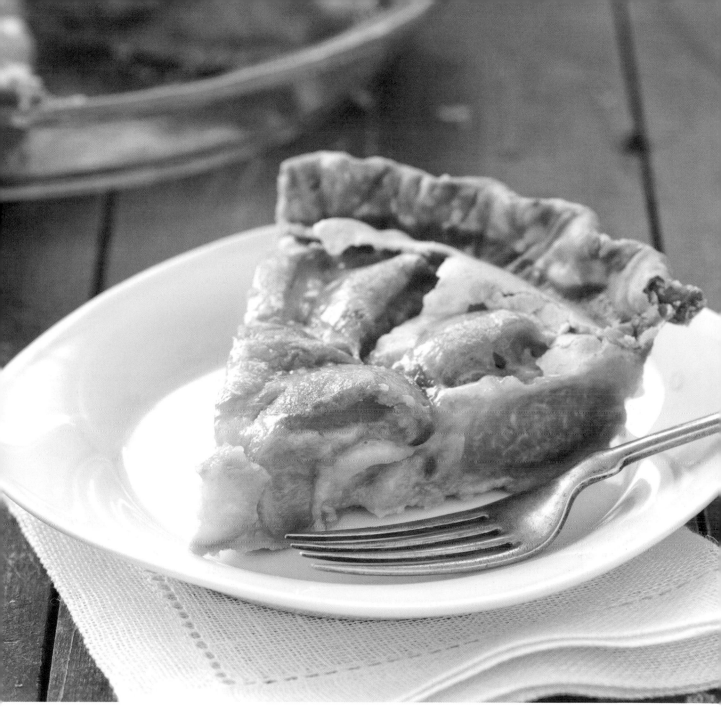

Why This Recipe Works Old-fashioned recipes for this pie call for simply arranging peaches in a pie crust, dousing them with fresh cream, and baking. But today's commercial cream gave us a milky, lumpy, and bland puddle rather than a rich filling. To thicken the cream, we whisked in a little flour and two egg yolks. But the juicy peaches wreaked watery havoc on our custardy pie filling. Roasting them in the oven evaporated their excess liquid, and a dusting of sugar encouraged caramelizing for even more flavor. Prebaking the crust ensured it would stay crisp and flaky after the roasted fruit and filling were added.

FRIED PEACH HAND PIES

MAKES 8 HAND PIES

If using frozen peaches, purchase a no-sugar-added product; we prefer Earthbound Farm or Cascadian Farm frozen peaches. There is no need to thaw the frozen peaches, but they will take longer to cook; times for both fresh and frozen are given in step 1. Use a Dutch oven that holds 6 quarts or more for frying. The assembled pies can be refrigerated for up to 24 hours before frying.

- 4 ripe peaches, peeled, halved, pitted, and cut into ½-inch wedges, or 20 ounces frozen peaches
- ½ cup (3½ ounces) sugar
  Salt
- 2 teaspoons lemon juice
- 2 cups (10 ounces) all-purpose flour
- 2 teaspoons baking powder
- 6 tablespoons unsalted butter, melted and cooled
- ½ cup whole milk
- 2 quarts peanut or vegetable oil

1. Combine peaches, sugar, and ⅛ teaspoon salt in medium saucepan. Cover and cook over medium heat, stirring occasionally and breaking up peaches with spoon, until tender, about 5 minutes for fresh peaches and 16 to 19 minutes for frozen peaches.

2. Uncover and continue to cook, stirring and mashing frequently with potato masher to coarse puree, until mixture is thickened and measures about 1⅔ cups, 7 to 13 minutes. Remove from heat, stir in lemon juice, and let cool completely. (Filling can be refrigerated for up to 3 days.)

3. Line rimmed baking sheet with parchment paper. Pulse flour, baking powder, and ¾ teaspoon salt in food processor until combined, about 3 pulses. Add melted butter and pulse until mixture resembles wet sand, about 8 pulses, scraping down sides of bowl as needed. Add milk and process until no floury bits remain and dough looks pebbly, about 8 seconds.

4. Turn dough onto lightly floured counter, gather into disk, and divide into 8 equal pieces. Roll each piece between your hands into ball, then press to flatten into round. Place rounds on prepared sheet, cover with plastic wrap, and refrigerate for 20 minutes.

5. Working with 1 piece of dough at a time, roll into 6- to 7-inch circle about ⅛ inch thick on lightly floured counter. Place 3 tablespoons filling in center of circle. Brush edges of dough with water and fold dough over filling to create half-moon shape, lightly pressing out air at seam. Trim any ragged edges and crimp edges with tines of fork to seal. Return pies to prepared sheet, cover with plastic, and refrigerate until ready to fry, up to 24 hours.

6. Line platter with triple layer of paper towels. Add oil to large Dutch oven until it measures about 1½ inches deep and heat over medium-high heat to 375 degrees. Gently place 4 pies in hot oil and fry until golden brown, about 1½ minutes per side, using slotted spatula or spider to flip. Adjust burner, if necessary, to maintain oil temperature between 350 and 375 degrees. Transfer to prepared platter. Return oil to 375 degrees and repeat with remaining 4 pies. Let cool for 10 minutes before serving.

On the Road: Peach Park

The massive, peach-shaped water tower looming over Clanton, Alabama, heralds Peach Park, a roadside retail attraction and restaurant that serves as the spiritual center of Alabama's peach-producing region. Out front, an open-air market sells fresh produce (peaches, mostly) and peach-based pantry products; inside, a long cafeteria case houses meat-and-three fare (preludes, perhaps, to peach ice cream and peach cobbler). Portraits of the reigning Miss Peach and her younger counterparts Junior Miss Peach, Young Miss Peach, and Little Miss Peach honor their regal stone-fruit court.

But the best reason to visit Peach Park is the fried peach hand pies. Rumor has it these sweet, warm pies were created as a way to use up overripe peaches, too soft and ugly to sell as is but still full of peach flavor. At Peach Park, we left no leftovers.

Why This Recipe Works These hand pies have it all: A crust that is delicate and tender but crumbly and a filling that's pure peach flavor. Starting with the filling, we cooked peeled, sliced peaches with sugar and a pinch of salt on the stovetop before gently mashing the fruit and letting it thicken. A bit of lemon juice added vibrancy. For the crust, we created a soft dough using melted butter and flour. Adding baking powder and milk created the dainty crumble we wanted. We divided, rolled out, and filled the dough, sealing in the filling before frying the pies in a Dutch oven, achieving peachy little pie perfection in minutes.

Why This Recipe Works Apple pie and cheddar cheese share a history, and we wanted to incorporate this sweet-savory pairing into a single recipe. For a flaky crust infused with cheesy flavor, extra-sharp cheddar and a teaspoon of dry mustard amped up the crust's savory qualities. Traditional apple filling got a kick from some cayenne, and precooking the filling allowed us to cram in twice as many apples. Starting with a hotter oven browned the bottom crust, and then reducing the heat kept the top from burning. The result: a moist, sweet-tart filling that perfectly complemented our flaky, cheesy crust.

APPLE PIE WITH CHEDDAR CRUST

SERVES 8

For the best flavor, be sure to use extra-sharp cheddar here. Freezing the butter for 15 minutes promotes flakiness in the crust—do not skip this step.

Crust

2½ cups (12½ ounces) all-purpose flour
1 tablespoon granulated sugar
1 teaspoon salt
1 teaspoon dry mustard
⅛ teaspoon cayenne pepper
8 ounces extra-sharp cheddar cheese, shredded (2 cups)
8 tablespoons unsalted butter, cut into ¼-inch pieces and frozen for 15 minutes
⅓ cup ice water, plus extra as needed

Filling

2 pounds Granny Smith, Empire, or Cortland apples, peeled, cored, halved, and sliced ¼-inch thick
2 pounds Golden Delicious, Jonagold, or Braeburn apples, peeled, cored, halved, and sliced ¼-inch thick
6 tablespoons (2⅔ ounces) granulated sugar
¼ cup packed (1¾ ounces) light brown sugar
½ teaspoon grated lemon zest plus 1 tablespoon juice
¼ teaspoon salt
⅛ teaspoon ground cinnamon

1. For the Crust Process flour, sugar, salt, mustard, and cayenne in food processor until combined, about 5 seconds. Scatter cheddar and butter over top and pulse until butter is size of large peas, about 10 pulses.

2. Pour half of ice water over flour mixture and pulse until incorporated, about 3 pulses. Repeat with remaining ice water. Pinch dough with your fingers; if dough feels dry and does not hold together, sprinkle 1 to 2 tablespoons extra ice water over mixture and pulse until dough forms large clumps and no dry flour remains, 3 to 5 pulses.

3. Divide dough in half and form each half into 4-inch disk. Wrap disks tightly in plastic wrap and refrigerate for 1 hour. Let chilled dough sit on counter to soften slightly, about 10 minutes, before rolling. (Wrapped dough can be refrigerated for up to 2 days or frozen for up to 1 month. If frozen, let dough thaw completely on counter before rolling.)

4. For the Filling Stir apples, granulated sugar, brown sugar, lemon zest, salt, and cinnamon together in Dutch oven. Cover and cook over medium heat, stirring frequently, until apples are just tender but still hold their shape, 10 to 15 minutes. Off heat, stir in lemon juice. Spread apple mixture on rimmed baking sheet and let cool completely, about 30 minutes. (Filling can be refrigerated for up to 24 hours.)

5. Roll 1 disk of dough into 12-inch circle between 2 sheets of parchment paper or plastic. Loosely roll dough around rolling pin and gently unroll it onto 9-inch pie plate, letting excess dough hang over edge. Ease dough into plate by gently lifting edge of dough with your hand while pressing into plate bottom with your other hand. Trim overhang to ½ inch beyond lip of pie plate. Wrap dough-lined pie plate loosely in plastic and refrigerate until dough is firm, about 15 minutes.

6. Adjust oven rack to lowest position and heat oven to 425 degrees. Fill pie shell with apple mixture. Roll other disk of dough into 12-inch circle between 2 sheets of parchment or plastic. Loosely roll dough around rolling pin and gently unroll it onto filling.

7. Trim overhang to ½ inch beyond lip of pie plate. Pinch edges of top and bottom crusts firmly together. Tuck overhang under itself; folded edge should be flush with edge of pie plate. Crimp dough around edge of pie plate using your fingers. Cut four 2-inch slits in top of dough.

8. Set pie on foil or parchment-lined baking sheet and bake for 20 minutes. Reduce oven temperature to 375 degrees and continue to bake until crust is deep golden brown and filling is bubbling, 35 to 45 minutes. Transfer pie to wire rack and let cool for at least 1½ hours. Serve.

APPLE SLAB PIE

SERVES 18 TO 20

We prefer an 18 by 13-inch nonstick rimmed baking sheet for this pie. If using a conventional baking sheet, coat it lightly with vegetable oil spray.

Pie

3½ pounds Granny Smith apples, peeled, cored, halved, and sliced thin
3½ pounds Golden Delicious apples, peeled, cored, halved, and sliced thin
1½ cups (10½ ounces) granulated sugar
½ teaspoon salt
1½ cups (4 ounces) animal crackers
2 (16-ounce) boxes refrigerated pie dough
4 tablespoons unsalted butter, melted and cooled
6 tablespoons instant tapioca
2 teaspoons ground cinnamon
3 tablespoons lemon juice

Glaze

¾ cup reserved apple juice (from filling)
2 tablespoons lemon juice
1 tablespoon unsalted butter, softened
1¼ cups (5 ounces) confectioners' sugar

1. For the Pie Combine apples, 1 cup sugar, and salt in colander set over large bowl. Let sit, tossing occasionally, until apples release their juices, about 30 minutes. Press gently on apples to extract liquid and reserve ¾ cup juice. Adjust oven rack to lower-middle position and heat oven to 350 degrees.

2. Pulse crackers and remaining ½ cup sugar in food processor until finely ground, about 20 pulses. Dust counter with cracker mixture, brush half of 1 pie round with water, overlap with second pie round, and dust top with cracker mixture. Roll out dough to 19 by 14 inches and transfer to rimmed baking sheet. Brush dough with butter, cover loosely with plastic wrap and refrigerate.

3. Roll remaining 2 dough rounds together with remaining cracker mixture to a 19 by 14-inch rectangle.

4. Toss drained apples with tapioca, cinnamon, and lemon juice and arrange evenly over bottom crust, pressing lightly to flatten. Brush edges of bottom crust with water and arrange top crust on pie. Press crusts together. Use paring knife to trim any excess dough. Use fork to crimp and seal outside edge of pie and then pierce top of pie at 2-inch intervals. Bake until pie is golden brown and juices are bubbling, about 1 hour. Let pie cool on wire rack for 1 hour.

5. For the Glaze While pie is cooling, simmer reserved apple juice in saucepan over medium heat until syrupy and reduced to ¼ cup, about 6 minutes. Stir in lemon juice and butter and let cool to room temperature. Whisk in sugar and brush glaze evenly over warm pie. Let pie cool completely, at least 1 hour longer. Serve. (Pie can be refrigerated for up to 1 day.)

How to Make Apple Slab Pie

1. Use water to "glue" together 2 store-bought pie crusts.

2. Add flavor to the bottom crust by rolling it out in mixture of crushed cookie crumbs and sugar.

3. After transferring bottom crust to baking dish, brush with melted butter for extra richness.

4. Top filled pie with second "double" crust and use fork to tightly seal edges of crust.

Why This Recipe Works Unlike a traditional apple pie, a slab pie is prepared in a baking sheet and can feed up to 20 people. Its filling is thickened to ensure neat slicing, and its crust is topped with a sugary glaze. But rolling out the dough for this mammoth pie proved problematic, as did making the filling thick enough to hold up to slicing. Gluing two sturdy store-bought crusts together with water and then rolling the dough into a large rectangle allowed us to get the crust into the large pan without a tear. To give the crust a sweet, buttery flavor, we rolled it in crushed animal crackers. Tapioca thickened the filling well without making it starchy.

OLD-FASHIONED PECAN PIE

SERVES 8 TO 10

Serve with Bourbon Whipped Cream (recipe follows), if desired. You can use Classic Single-Crust Pie Dough (page 562) or No-Fear Single-Crust Pie Dough (page 563) for this pie.

1 cup maple syrup
1 cup packed (7 ounces) light brown sugar
½ cup heavy cream
1 tablespoon molasses
4 tablespoons unsalted butter, cut into ½-inch pieces
½ teaspoon salt
6 large egg yolks, lightly beaten
1½ cups (6 ounces) pecans, toasted and chopped
1 recipe single-crust pie dough, fitted into 9-inch pie plate and chilled

1. Adjust oven rack to lowest position and heat oven to 450 degrees. Heat syrup, sugar, cream, and molasses in saucepan over medium heat, stirring occasionally, until sugar dissolves, about 3 minutes. Remove from heat and let cool for 5 minutes. Whisk butter and salt into syrup mixture until combined. Whisk in egg yolks until incorporated.

2. Scatter pecans in pie shell. Carefully pour filling over. Place pie in oven and immediately reduce oven temperature to 325 degrees. Bake until filling is set and center jiggles slightly when pie is gently shaken, 45 minutes to 1 hour. Let pie cool on rack for 1 hour, then refrigerate until set, about 3 hours or up to 1 day. Bring to room temperature before serving.

BOURBON WHIPPED CREAM
MAKES ABOUT 2 CUPS
Although any style of whiskey will work here, we like the smokiness of bourbon.

1 cup heavy cream
2 tablespoons bourbon
1½ tablespoons packed light brown sugar
½ teaspoon vanilla extract

Using stand mixer fitted with whisk, whip cream, bourbon, sugar, and vanilla on medium-low speed until foamy, about 1 minute. Increase speed to high and whip until stiff peaks form, about 2 minutes. (Whipped cream can be refrigerated for 4 hours.)

Move Over, Karo

Before cloying Karo syrup monopolized the market, pies were made with many other, less processed types of syrup, including sorghum (made from a cereal grass) and cane (made from the boiled-down juice of the sugarcane plant). These syrups still exist, and you can mail-order them, or travel to places like Louisiana or Kentucky to find them. We tasted a range of such syrups, including Steen's 100% Pure Cane Syrup and Townsend's Sweet Sorghum, then tried to duplicate their complex flavors from products we could buy at the supermarket. In the end, a combination of three ordinary sweeteners created an old-fashioned flavor that easily bested Karo.

Molasses brings a robust, slightly bitter quality.

Light brown sugar adds warmth and caramel tones.

Maple syrup adds delicate complexity.

Why This Recipe Works The pecan pies of today bear little resemblance to their 19th-century inspiration. Could we re-create old-fashioned pecan pie without using modern-day processed corn syrup? Many traditional syrups (cane, sorghum) produced a great pie, but we had to mail away for those ingredients. In the end, combining maple syrup with brown sugar and molasses replicated the old-fashioned versions perfectly. We started the pie at a high oven temperature to ensure the bottom crust was crisp and golden brown and then dropped the temperature to finish baking.

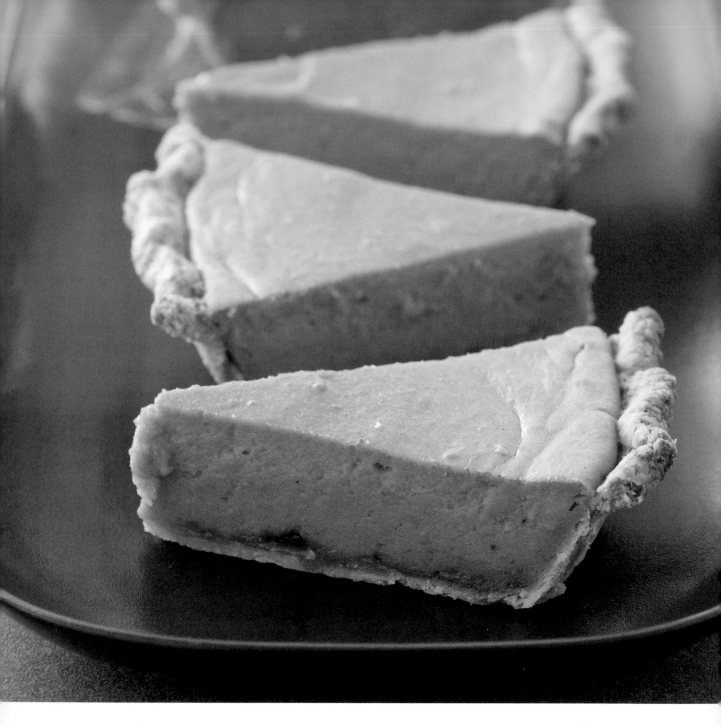

Why This Recipe Works Hoping to streamline this holiday dessert, we started by "baking" whole sweet potatoes in the microwave. A food processor made quick work of pureeing the flesh and lent a super-smooth texture. Sour cream added subtle tang while smoothing out the custard even more, and supplementing whole eggs with extra yolks added richness and helped with sliceability. We heated the spices in butter to intensify (or bloom) their flavor before adding them, along with some bourbon and vanilla, to the filling. First we sprinkled brown sugar onto the crust, which melted into a gooey faux caramel and took this pie to the next level.

SWEET POTATO PIE

SERVES 8

The best pies use homemade crust. You can use Classic Single-Crust Pie Dough (page 562) or No-Fear Single-Crust Pie Dough (page 563) for this pie. If you're pressed for time, try our favorite store-bought crust, Wholly Wholesome 9" Certified Organic Traditional Bake at Home Rolled Pie Dough. Choose sweet potatoes that are about the same size so that they'll cook evenly. Serve with Bourbon Whipped Cream (page 576), if desired.

1 (9-inch) single-crust pie dough
1¼ cups packed (8¾ ounces) light brown sugar
1¾ pounds sweet potatoes, unpeeled
½ teaspoon salt
4 tablespoons unsalted butter
½ teaspoon ground cinnamon
¼ teaspoon ground nutmeg
1 cup sour cream
3 large eggs plus 2 large yolks
2 tablespoons bourbon (optional)
1 teaspoon vanilla extract

1. Adjust oven rack to middle position and heat oven to 375 degrees. Roll dough into 12-inch circle on lightly floured counter. Loosely roll dough around rolling pin and gently unroll it onto 9-inch pie plate, letting excess dough hang over edge. Ease dough into plate by gently lifting edge of dough with your hand while pressing into plate bottom with your other hand. Trim overhang to ½ inch beyond lip of pie plate. Tuck overhang under itself; folded edge should be flush with edge of pie plate. Crimp dough evenly around edge of pie using your fingers. Wrap dough-lined pie plate loosely in plastic and freeze until dough is firm, about 15 minutes.

2. Line chilled pie shell with two 12-inch squares of parchment paper, letting parchment lie over edges of dough, and fill with pie weights. Bake until lightly golden around edges, 18 to 25 minutes. Carefully remove parchment and weights, rotate crust, and continue to bake until center begins to look opaque and slightly drier, 3 to 6 minutes. Remove from oven. Let crust cool completely. Sprinkle ¼ cup sugar over bottom of crust; set aside. Reduce oven temperature to 350 degrees.

3. Meanwhile, prick potatoes all over with fork. Microwave on large plate until potatoes are very soft and surface is slightly wet, 15 to 20 minutes, flipping every 5 minutes. Immediately slice potatoes in half to release steam. When cool enough to handle, scoop flesh into bowl of food processor. Add salt and remaining 1 cup sugar and process until smooth, about 60 seconds, scraping down sides of bowl as needed. Melt butter with cinnamon and nutmeg in microwave, 15 to 30 seconds; stir to combine. Add spiced butter, sour cream, eggs and yolks, bourbon, if using, and vanilla to potatoes and process until incorporated, about 10 seconds, scraping down sides of bowl as needed.

4. Pour potato mixture into prepared pie shell. Bake until filling is set around edges but center registers 165 degrees and jiggles slightly when pie is shaken, 35 to 40 minutes. Let pie cool completely on wire rack, about 2 hours. Serve.

Why This Recipe Works French coconut pie, a southern favorite, is a coconut-custard pie that is often too eggy, too sweet, or lacking in coconut flavor. We set out to tackle all of these issues. First, we found that two whole eggs plus one extra yolk provided just the right amount of richness. To better control the sweetness, we tried unsweetened shredded coconut which also intensified the coconut flavor. Since the dried coconut was not fully softening as the pie baked, we soaked it in buttermilk and vanilla before adding it to the filling. The finished pie was golden brown—from the pie crust to the lovely sugar crust that formed on top of the custard.

FRENCH COCONUT PIE

SERVES 8 TO 10

Look for shredded unsweetened coconut, about ¼ inch in length, in the natural foods section of the supermarket. It sometimes goes by the name "coconut flakes." Do not use large flaked coconut in this recipe. Our favorite shredded unsweetened coconut is NOW Real Food Organic Unsweetened Coconut, Shredded.

1 (9-inch) store-bought pie dough round
1¼ cups (3¾ ounces) unsweetened shredded coconut
½ cup buttermilk
1 teaspoon vanilla extract
1 cup (7 ounces) sugar
8 tablespoons unsalted butter, melted and cooled
2 large eggs plus 1 large yolk
2 tablespoons all-purpose flour
¼ teaspoon salt

1. Adjust oven rack to lower-middle position and heat oven to 325 degrees. Roll dough into 12-inch circle on lightly floured counter. Loosely roll dough around rolling pin and gently unroll it onto 9-inch pie plate, letting excess dough hang over edge. Ease dough into plate by gently lifting edge of dough with your hand while pressing into plate bottom with your other hand.

2. Trim overhang to ½ inch beyond lip of plate. Tuck overhang under itself; folded edge should be flush with edge of plate. Crimp dough evenly around edge of plate using your fingers. Wrap dough-lined plate loosely in plastic wrap and freeze until dough is firm, about 15 minutes.

3. Discard plastic wrap and line chilled pie shell with two 12-inch squares of parchment paper, letting parchment lie over edges of dough, and fill with pie weights. Bake until lightly golden around edges, 18 to 25 minutes. Transfer to wire rack and carefully remove parchment and weights. (Pie shell needn't cool completely before proceeding.)

4. Meanwhile, combine coconut, buttermilk, and vanilla in bowl. Cover with plastic and let sit for 15 minutes.

5. Whisk sugar, butter, eggs and yolk, flour, and salt together in large bowl. Stir in coconut mixture until fully incorporated. Pour filling into warm pie shell. Bake until custard is set and golden-brown crust forms on top of pie, 40 to 55 minutes.

6. Transfer pie to wire rack and let cool completely, about 4 hours. Serve at room temperature. (Cooled pie can be covered with plastic and refrigerated for up to 2 days. Let come to room temperature before serving.)

Crimping a Single Crust Pie Shell
Our easy crimping technique makes a decorative, sturdy edge.

1. Use scissors to trim overhanging dough to uniform ½ inch.

2. Tuck dough under to form thick, even edge on lip of pie plate.

3. Use both hands to pinch dough into ridges, working around perimeter.

ICEBOX KEY LIME PIE

SERVES 8 TO 10

Use instant pudding, which requires no stovetop cooking, for this recipe. Do not be tempted to use bottled lime juice, which lacks depth of flavor.

Crust

8 whole graham crackers, broken into small pieces
2 tablespoons sugar
5 tablespoons unsalted butter, melted

Filling

¼ cup (1¾ ounces) sugar
1 tablespoon grated lime zest plus 1 cup juice (8 limes)
8 ounces cream cheese, softened
1 (14-ounce) can sweetened condensed milk
⅓ cup instant vanilla pudding mix
1¼ teaspoons unflavored gelatin
1 teaspoon vanilla extract

1. For the Crust Adjust oven rack to middle position and heat oven to 350 degrees. Process crackers and sugar in food processor until finely ground, about 30 seconds. Add melted butter in steady stream while pulsing until crumbs resemble damp sand. Sprinkle mixture into 9-inch pie plate and use bottom of dry measuring cup to press crumbs firmly into bottom and sides. Bake until fragrant and browned around edges, 12 to 14 minutes. Let cool completely.

2. For the Filling Process sugar and zest in clean food processor until sugar turns bright green, about 30 seconds. Add cream cheese and process until combined, about 30 seconds. Add condensed milk and pudding mix and process until smooth, about 30 seconds. Scrape down sides of bowl. Sprinkle gelatin over 2 tablespoons lime juice in small bowl and let sit until gelatin softens, about 5 minutes. Heat in microwave for 15 seconds; stir until dissolved. With processor running, pour in gelatin mixture, remaining lime juice, and vanilla and mix until thoroughly combined, about 30 seconds.

3. Pour filling into cooled crust, cover with plastic wrap, and refrigerate for at least 3 hours or up to 2 days. To serve, let pie sit at room temperature for 10 minutes before slicing.

Bigger Limes = Less Work

When developing our recipe for Icebox Key Lime Pie, we found the flavor of Key limes and regular supermarket limes (called Persian limes) to be almost identical in our pie recipe. But there was a big difference in squeezing time.

KEY LIMES
We had to squeeze 40 Key limes to yield 1 cup of juice.

PERSIAN LIMES
Just six to eight Persian limes gave us all the juice we needed.

A Mystery of Pie History

Before Gail Borden invented sweetened condensed milk in 1856, drinking milk was a health risk, as there was no pasteurization or refrigeration for fresh milk. The shelf-stability and safety of sweetened condensed milk made it especially popular in areas like the Florida Keys, where the hot climate promoted rapid spoilage of anything perishable. Like many of our iconic foods, no one knows for sure when or by whom the first Key lime pie was made, but with canned milk in every pantry by the 1870s and an abundance of tiny Key limes throughout the area, it was only a matter of time. Most food historians trace the history of this pie back to the 1890s, but there are those—especially in the Keys—who claim the recipe is decades older.

Why This Recipe Works Authentic Key lime pie recipes used to be simple and uncooked—but they contained raw eggs, a no-no in modern times. We wanted to develop an eggless Key lime pie recipe as bright and custardy as the original. In lieu of using egg yolks, we found the right ratio of instant vanilla pudding, gelatin, and cream cheese to thicken our Icebox Key Lime Pie's filling into a perfect, smooth consistency. A full cup of fresh lime juice produced a pie with bracing lime flavor. Lime zest added another layer of flavor, and processing the zest with a little sugar offset its sourness and eliminated the annoying chewy bits.

Why This Recipe Works We wanted a lemon meringue pie with an impressively tall and fluffy topping, so we made the meringue with a hot sugar syrup and added a bit of cream of tartar to the egg whites as we beat them. This ensured that the meringue was cooked through and stable enough to be piled high on top of the filling. For our pie's bright citrus flavor, we flavored the filling with lemon zest and lemon juice and then, to ensure the filling was silky smooth, we strained out the zest.

MILE-HIGH LEMON MERINGUE PIE

SERVES 8 TO 10

You can use Classic Single-Crust Pie Dough (page 562) or No-Fear Single-Crust Pie Dough (page 563) for this pie. This pie is best served on the day it's made.

1 recipe single-crust pie dough,
   fitted into 9-inch pie plate and chilled

Lemon Filling

1¼ cups (8¾ ounces) sugar
1 cup lemon juice plus 2 tablespoons
   grated zest (5 lemons)
½ cup water
3 tablespoons cornstarch
¼ teaspoon salt
8 large egg yolks
4 tablespoons unsalted butter,
   cut into 4 pieces and softened

Meringue

1 cup (7 ounces) sugar
½ cup water
4 large egg whites
   Pinch salt
½ teaspoon cream of tartar
½ teaspoon vanilla extract

1. Adjust oven rack to middle position and heat oven to 375 degrees. Line chilled crust with double layer of aluminum foil and fill with pie weights. Bake until pie dough looks dry and is light in color, 25 to 30 minutes. Remove weights and foil and continue to bake crust until deep golden brown, 10 to 12 minutes longer. Let crust cool on wire rack to room temperature.

2. For the Lemon Filling Whisk sugar, lemon juice, water, cornstarch, and salt together in large saucepan until cornstarch is dissolved. Bring to simmer over medium heat, whisking occasionally until mixture becomes translucent and begins to thicken, about 5 minutes. Whisk in egg yolks until combined. Stir in lemon zest and butter. Bring to simmer and stir constantly until mixture is thick enough to coat back of spoon, about 2 minutes. Strain through fine-mesh strainer into cooled pie shell and scrape filling off underside of strainer. Place plastic wrap directly on surface of filling and refrigerate until set and well chilled, at least 2 hours or up to 1 day.

3. For the Meringue Adjust oven rack to middle position and heat oven to 400 degrees. Combine sugar and water in small saucepan. Bring to vigorous boil over medium-high heat. Once syrup comes to rolling boil, cook 4 minutes (mixture will become slightly thickened and syrupy). Remove from heat and set aside while beating whites.

4. Using stand mixer fitted with whisk, whip egg whites in large bowl at medium-low speed until frothy, about 1 minute. Add salt and cream of tartar and whip, gradually increasing speed to medium-high, until whites hold soft peaks, about 2 minutes. With mixer running, slowly pour hot syrup into whites (avoid pouring syrup onto whisk or it will splash). Add vanilla and whip until meringue has cooled and becomes very thick and shiny, 5 to 9 minutes.

5. Using rubber spatula, mound meringue over filling, making sure meringue touches edges of crust. Use spatula to create peaks all over meringue. Bake until peaks turn golden brown, about 6 minutes. Let pie cool on wire rack to room temperature. Serve.

Making a Meringue Mountain

1. Use rubber spatula to press meringue onto edge of pie crust. This will keep meringue from shrinking.

2. Use spatula to make dramatic peaks and swirls all over meringue.

RASPBERRY CHIFFON PIE

SERVES 8 TO 10

You can use Classic Single-Crust Pie Dough (page 562) or No-Fear Single-Crust Pie Dough (page 563) for this pie. The raspberry-flavored gelatin is important for the color and flavor of the chiffon layer; do not substitute unflavored gelatin. For an accurate measurement of boiling water, bring a full kettle of water to a boil, then measure out the desired amount.

1 recipe single-crust pie dough, fitted into 9-inch pie plate and chilled

Fruit
12 ounces (2½ cups) frozen raspberries
3 tablespoons pectin (Sure-Jell)
1½ cups (10½ ounces) sugar
   Pinch salt
5 ounces (1 cup) fresh raspberries

Chiffon
3 tablespoons raspberry-flavored gelatin
3 tablespoons boiling water
3 ounces cream cheese, softened
1 cup heavy cream, chilled

Topping
1¼ cups heavy cream, chilled
2 tablespoons sugar

1. Adjust oven rack to middle position and heat oven to 375 degrees. Line chilled crust with double layer of aluminum foil and fill with pie weights. Bake until pie dough looks dry and is light in color, 25 to 30 minutes. Remove weights and foil and continue to bake crust until deep golden brown, 10 to 12 minutes longer. Let crust cool on wire rack to room temperature.

2. For the Fruit Cook frozen berries in medium saucepan over medium-high heat, stirring occasionally, until berries begin to give up their juices, about 3 minutes. Stir in pectin and bring to full boil, stirring constantly. Stir in sugar and salt and return to full boil. Cook, stirring constantly, until slightly thickened, about 2 minutes. Pour through fine-mesh strainer into medium bowl, pressing on solids to extract as much puree as possible. Scrape puree off underside of strainer into bowl.

3. Transfer ⅓ cup raspberry puree to small bowl and let cool to room temperature. Gently fold fresh raspberries into remaining puree. Spread fruit mixture evenly over bottom of cooled pie shell and set aside.

4. For the Chiffon Dissolve gelatin in boiling water in bowl of stand mixer. Fit stand mixer with paddle, add cream cheese and reserved ⅓ cup raspberry puree, and beat on high speed, scraping down bowl once or twice, until smooth, about 2 minutes. Add cream and beat on medium-low speed until incorporated, about 30 seconds. Scrape down bowl. Increase speed to high and beat until cream holds stiff peaks, 1 to 2 minutes. Spread evenly over fruit in pie shell. Cover pie with plastic wrap. Refrigerate until set, at least 3 hours or up to 2 days.

5. For the Topping When ready to serve, fit stand mixer with whisk and whip cream and sugar on medium-low speed until foamy, about 1 minute. Increase speed to high and whip until stiff peaks form, 1 to 3 minutes. Spread or pipe over chilled filling. Serve.

Two Layers, Two Thickeners

For the Fruit Layer
For the bottom layer, we used Sure-Jell (pectin) to achieve a concentrated raspberry flavor and texture. There are two formulations of Sure-Jell. We found that the original formula made the smoothest, thickest bottom layer of fruit.

For the Chiffon Layer
A few tablespoons of raspberry gelatin made for great stability and color in the creamy chiffon layer and reinforced the berry flavor.

Why This Recipe Works Raspberry chiffon pie can often be weak on berry flavor. We wanted to produce an intensely flavored pie, so we included a layer of sweetened, thickened fruit on the crust and beneath the chiffon. We also stiffened our recipe's chiffon filling by using extra gelatin and a little cream cheese, which enabled it to hold additional raspberry puree for even more flavor.

ICEBOX STRAWBERRY PIE

SERVES 8

You can use Classic Single-Crust Pie Dough (page 562) or No-Fear Single-Crust Pie Dough (page 563) for this pie. In step 2, it is imperative that the cooked strawberry mixture measure 2 cups; any more and the filling will be loose. If your fresh berries aren't fully ripe, you may want to add extra sugar to taste in step 3.

1   recipe single-crust pie dough,
    fitted into 9-inch pie plate and chilled

Filling
2   pounds (7 cups) frozen strawberries
1   tablespoon unflavored gelatin
2   tablespoons lemon juice
2   tablespoons water
1   cup (7 ounces) sugar
    Pinch salt
1   pound fresh strawberries,
    hulled and sliced thin

Topping
4   ounces cream cheese, softened
3   tablespoons sugar
½   teaspoon vanilla extract
1   cup heavy cream

1. Adjust oven rack to middle position and heat oven to 375 degrees. Line chilled crust with double layer of aluminum foil and fill with pie weights. Bake until pie dough looks dry and is light in color, 25 to 30 minutes. Remove weights and foil and continue to bake crust until deep golden brown, 10 to 12 minutes longer. Let crust cool to room temperature on wire rack.

2. For the Filling Cook frozen berries in large saucepan over medium-low heat until berries begin to release juice, about 3 minutes. Increase heat to medium-high and cook, stirring frequently, until thick and jamlike, about 25 minutes (mixture should measure 2 cups).

3. Sprinkle gelatin over lemon juice and water in small bowl. Let stand until gelatin is softened and mixture has thickened, about 5 minutes. Stir gelatin mixture, sugar, and salt into cooked berry mixture and return to simmer, about 2 minutes. Transfer to bowl and cool to room temperature, about 30 minutes.

4. Fold fresh berries into filling. Spread evenly in pie shell and refrigerate until set, about 4 hours. (Filled pie can be refrigerated for 24 hours.)

5. For the Topping Using stand mixer fitted with whisk, beat cream cheese, sugar, and vanilla on medium speed until smooth, about 30 seconds. With mixer running, add cream and whip until stiff peaks form, about 2 minutes. Dollop individual slices of pie with topping and serve.

Don't Make This Mistake
In step 2, be sure to accurately measure the reduced strawberry mixture: You'll need exactly 2 cups. Scrape the strawberry mixture into a large liquid measuring cup. If it measures more than 2 cups, return it to the pan to cook down. It may seem fussy to stop to measure, but the pie will not set or slice properly if you have more than 2 cups of the strawberry mixture.

Why This Recipe Works Frozen strawberries, which are great for cooking, form the base of our strawberry pie. We cooked them down in a dry saucepan until they released their juice and the mixture was thick, concentrated, and flavorful. Because strawberries are low in pectin, the natural thickener found in citrus fruits and many other plants, we added some lemon juice, which perked up the flavor and tightened the texture of the filling a little. To thicken the filling further, we added a bit of unflavored gelatin. Then we mixed in fresh strawberries for a fresh finish with big berry flavor.

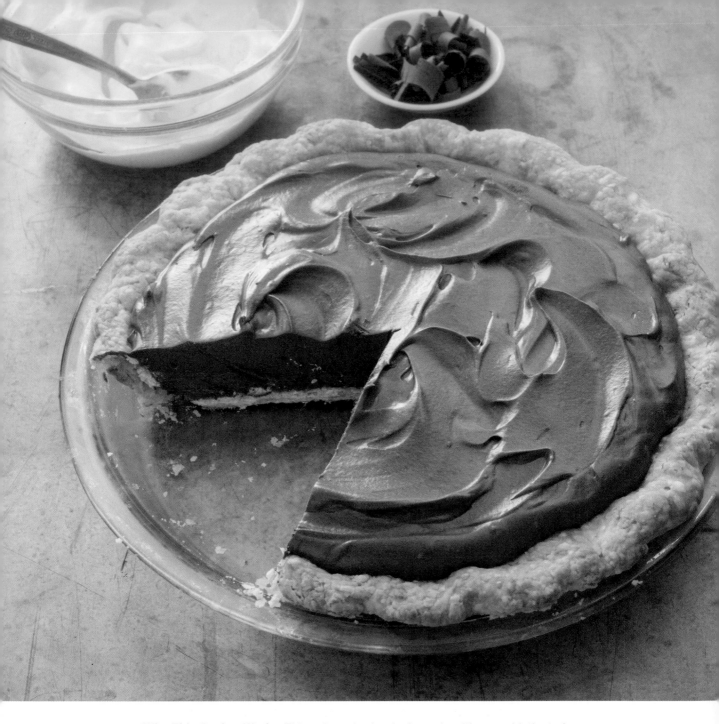

Why This Recipe Works This prize-winning icebox pie with a sophisticated name originally called for raw eggs. Testing showed that we could cook the eggs with sugar on the stovetop, almost like making a custard. Once the egg and sugar mixture was light and thick, we removed it from the heat and continued whipping it until it was fully cooled. Bittersweet chocolate folded into the cooled egg and sugar mixture made for a pie with more intense chocolate flavor. And to lighten the filling's texture, we incorporated whipped cream.

FRENCH SILK CHOCOLATE PIE

SERVES 8 TO 10

You can use Classic Single-Crust Pie Dough (page 562) or No-Fear Single-Crust Pie Dough (page 563) for this pie. Serve with lightly sweetened whipped cream.

1   recipe single-crust pie dough,
     fitted into 9-inch pie plate and chilled
1   cup heavy cream, chilled
3   large eggs
¾   cup (5¼ ounces) sugar
2   tablespoons water
8   ounces bittersweet chocolate,
     melted and cooled
1   tablespoon vanilla extract
8   tablespoons unsalted butter,
     cut into ½-inch pieces and softened

1. Adjust oven rack to middle position and heat oven to 375 degrees. Line chilled crust with double layer of aluminum foil and fill with pie weights. Bake until pie dough looks dry and is light in color, 25 to 30 minutes. Remove weights and foil and continue to bake crust until deep golden brown, 10 to 12 minutes longer. Let crust cool on wire rack to room temperature.

2. Using stand mixer fitted with whisk, whip cream on medium-low speed until foamy, about 1 minute. Increase speed to high and whip until stiff peaks form, 1 to 3 minutes. Transfer whipped cream to small bowl and refrigerate.

3. Combine eggs, sugar, and water in large heat-proof bowl set over medium saucepan filled with ½ inch barely simmering water (don't let bowl touch water). Using hand-held mixer set at medium speed, beat egg mixture until thickened and registers 160 degrees, 7 to 10 minutes. Remove bowl from heat and continue to beat egg mixture until fluffy and cooled to room temperature, about 8 minutes.

4. Add chocolate and vanilla to cooled egg mixture and beat until incorporated. Beat in butter, few pieces at a time, until well combined. Using spatula, fold in whipped cream until no streaks of white remain. Scrape filling into pie shell and refrigerate until set, at least 3 hours or up to 24 hours. Serve.

Whisking Chocolate into Silk

1. Beat eggs and sugar together in double boiler to incorporate air for filling with light, ethereal texture. Remove from heat when egg mixture reaches 160 degrees; it will be very thick.

2. Continue beating egg mixture until fluffy and cool. Add melted chocolate and beat in softened butter for rich flavor and silky-smooth texture.

The Pillsbury Bake-Off

In 1949, General Mills launched the "Grand National Recipe and Baking Contest" (later known as the Pillsbury Bake-Off). It was held at the posh Waldorf-Astoria Hotel in New York. The grand-prize winner (for No-Knead Water Rising Twists) brought home $50,000; Eleanor Roosevelt was one of the luminaries on hand to present the awards. Since then, many prize-winning Pillsbury recipes have become part of our culinary heritage, among them French Silk Chocolate Pie (the exotic name reflects the international curiosity of postwar America), Open Sesame Pie (which caused a run on sesame seeds nationwide), and Peanut Blossom Cookies (with a Hershey's Kiss in the middle).

CHOCOLATE ANGEL PIE

SERVES 8 TO 10

Serve the assembled pie within 3 hours of chilling.

Filling
9 ounces milk chocolate, chopped fine
5 ounces bittersweet chocolate, chopped fine
3 large egg yolks
1½ tablespoons granulated sugar
½ teaspoon salt
½ cup half-and-half
1¼ cups heavy cream, chilled

Meringue Crust
1 tablespoon cornstarch, plus extra for pie plate
½ cup (3½ ounces) granulated sugar
3 large egg whites
   Pinch cream of tartar
½ teaspoon vanilla extract

Topping
1⅓ cups heavy cream, chilled
2 tablespoons confectioners' sugar
   Unsweetened cocoa powder

1. For the Filling Microwave milk chocolate and bittersweet chocolate in large bowl at 50 percent power, stirring occasionally, until melted, 2 to 4 minutes. Whisk egg yolks, sugar, and salt together in medium bowl until combined, about 1 minute. Bring half-and-half to simmer in small saucepan over medium heat. Whisking constantly, slowly add hot half-and-half to egg yolk mixture in 2 additions until incorporated. Return half-and-half mixture to now-empty saucepan and cook over low heat, whisking constantly, until thickened slightly, 30 seconds to 1 minute. Stir half-and-half mixture into melted chocolate until combined. Let cool slightly, about 8 minutes.

2. Using stand mixer fitted with whisk, whip cream on medium-low speed until foamy, about 1 minute. Increase speed to high and whip until soft peaks form, 1 to 3 minutes. Gently whisk one-third of whipped cream into cooled chocolate mixture. Fold in remaining whipped cream until no white streaks

remain. Cover and refrigerate for at least 3 hours, or until ready to assemble pie. (Filling can be made up to 24 hours in advance.)

3. For the Meringue Crust Adjust oven rack to lower-middle position and heat oven to 275 degrees. Grease 9-inch pie plate and dust well with extra cornstarch, using pastry brush to distribute evenly. Combine sugar and 1 tablespoon cornstarch in bowl. Using stand mixer fitted with whisk, whip egg whites and cream of tartar on medium-low speed until foamy, about 1 minute. Increase speed to medium-high and whip whites to soft, billowy mounds, 1 to 3 minutes. Gradually add sugar mixture and whip until glossy, stiff peaks form, 3 to 5 minutes. Add vanilla to meringue and whip until incorporated.

4. Spread meringue into prepared pie plate, following contours of plate to cover bottom, sides, and edges. Bake for 1½ hours. Rotate pie plate, reduce oven temperature to 200 degrees, and bake until completely dried out, about 1 hour longer. (Shell will rise above rim of pie plate; some cracking is OK.) Let cool completely, about 30 minutes.

5. For the Topping Spoon cooled chocolate filling into cavity of pie shell, distributing evenly. Using stand mixer fitted with whisk, whip cream and sugar on medium-low speed until foamy, about 1 minute. Increase speed to high and whip until stiff peaks form, 1 to 3 minutes. Spread whipped cream evenly over chocolate. Refrigerate until filling is set, about 1 hour. Dust with cocoa. Slice with sharp knife and serve.

Busted Crust

The egg white crust is part of what distinguishes angel pie. To avoid a sticky, broken meringue shell, we added cornstarch to the whites, and we greased the pie plate and dusted it with more cornstarch.

MERINGUE MESS
Don't let this happen to you.

Why This Recipe Works Chocolate angel pie is a lavish version of chocolate cream pie with creamy chocolate mousse, fluffy whipped cream, and an airy meringue crust. For a light, crisp crust, 2½ hours in a low oven was necessary. To prevent the crust from sticking to the pan, we relied on cornstarch, both in the egg whites and dusted over the pie plate. We loaded nearly a pound of chocolate into the filling by making a cooked custard. Using two kinds of chocolate lent depth and complexity. To finish, we topped the pie with lightly sweetened whipped cream and a sprinkling of cocoa powder for a decadent, supremely chocolaty dessert.

MISSISSIPPI MUD PIE

SERVES 8 TO 12

This recipe takes at least 5 hours from start to finish. We used Nabisco Famous Chocolate Wafers in this recipe. Be sure to use milk chocolate in the mousse, as bittersweet chocolate will make the mousse too firm. Do not begin making the mousse until the brownie layer is fully chilled.

Crust
25 chocolate wafer cookies (5½ ounces), broken into coarse pieces
4 tablespoons unsalted butter, melted

Brownie Layer
4 ounces bittersweet chocolate, chopped fine
3 tablespoons unsalted butter
3 tablespoons vegetable oil
1½ tablespoons Dutch-processed cocoa powder
⅔ cup packed (4⅔ ounces) dark brown sugar
2 large eggs
2 teaspoons vanilla extract
¼ teaspoon salt
3 tablespoons all-purpose flour

Topping
10 chocolate wafer cookies (2 ounces)
2 tablespoons confectioners' sugar
1 tablespoon Dutch-processed cocoa powder
⅛ teaspoon salt
2 tablespoons unsalted butter, melted

Mousse
6 ounces milk chocolate, chopped fine
1 cup heavy cream, chilled
2 tablespoons Dutch-processed cocoa powder
2 tablespoons confectioners' sugar
⅛ teaspoon salt

1. For the Crust Adjust oven rack to middle position and heat oven to 325 degrees. Process cookie pieces in food processor until finely ground, about 30 seconds. Add melted butter and pulse until combined, about 6 pulses. Using bottom of dry measuring cup, press crumbs firmly into bottom and up sides of 9-inch pie plate. Bake until fragrant and set, about 15 minutes. Transfer to wire rack.

2. For the Brownie Layer Combine chocolate, butter, oil, and cocoa in bowl and microwave at 50 percent power, stirring often, until melted, about 1½ minutes. In separate bowl, whisk sugar, eggs, vanilla, and salt until smooth. Whisk in chocolate mixture until incorporated. Whisk in flour until just combined.

3. Pour brownie batter into crust (crust needn't be cool at this point). Bake pie until edges begin to set and toothpick inserted in center comes out with thin coating of batter attached, about 15 minutes. Transfer to wire rack and let cool for 1 hour, then refrigerate until fully chilled, about 1 hour longer.

4. For the Topping Meanwhile, line rimmed baking sheet with parchment paper. Place cookies in zipper-lock bag, press out air, and seal bag. Using rolling pin, crush cookies into ½- to ¾-inch pieces. Combine sugar, cocoa, salt, and crushed cookies in bowl. Stir in melted butter until mixture is moistened and clumps begin to form. Spread crumbs in even layer on prepared sheet and bake until fragrant, about 10 minutes, shaking sheet to break up crumbs halfway through baking. Transfer sheet to wire rack and let cool completely.

5. For the Mousse Once brownie layer has fully chilled, microwave chocolate in large bowl at 50 percent power, stirring often, until melted, 1½ to 2 minutes. Let cool until just barely warm and registers between 90 and 100 degrees, about 10 minutes.

6. Microwave 3 tablespoons cream in small bowl until it registers 105 to 110 degrees, about 15 seconds. Whisk in cocoa until homogeneous. Combine cocoa-cream mixture, sugar, salt, and remaining cream in bowl of stand mixer. Fit mixer with whisk and whip cream mixture on medium speed until beginning to thicken, about 30 seconds, scraping down bowl as needed. Increase speed to high and whip until soft peaks form, 30 to 60 seconds.

7. Using whisk, fold one-third of whipped cream mixture into melted chocolate to lighten. Using rubber spatula, fold in remaining whipped cream mixture until no dark streaks remain. Spoon mousse into chilled pie and spread evenly from edge to edge. Sprinkle with cooled topping and refrigerate for at least 3 hours or overnight. Serve.

Why This Recipe Works This pie is so named because its chocolate layers are reminiscent of the Mississippi River's silty bottom, but there's nothing muddy about its flavor. To simplify each layer of the pie, we started with a press-in chocolate wafer cookie crust. For a perfectly soft, chewy middle layer, we created a brownie-like batter and underbaked it slightly. Once this layer was fully chilled, we spread on a simple milk chocolate mousse and sprinkled on a crunchy chocolate cookie topping to finish off our striated chocolate showstopper.

SHOPPING FOR EQUIPMENT

With a well-stocked kitchen, you'll be able to take on any recipe. But there's so much equipment out there on the market, how do you figure out what's what? Price often correlates with design, not performance. Over the years, our test kitchen has evaluated thousands of products. We've gone through copious rounds of testing and have identified the most important attributes in every piece of equipment, so when you go shopping you'll know what to look for. And because our test kitchen accepts no support from product manufacturers, you can trust our ratings. Prices in this chart are based on shopping at online retailers and will vary. See AmericasTestKitchen.com for updates to these testings.

KNIVES AND MORE	ITEM	WHAT TO LOOK FOR	TEST KITCHEN FAVORITES
	CHEF'S KNIFE	• High-carbon stainless steel knife • Thin, curved 8-inch blade • Lightweight • Comfortable grip and nonslip handle	**Victorinox Swiss Army Fibrox Pro 8-Inch Chef's Knife** $39.95
	PARING KNIFE	• 3- to 3½-inch blade • Thin, flexible blade with pointed tip • Comfortable grip	**Victorinox Swiss Army Fibrox Pro 3¼-Inch Spear Point Paring Knife** $9.47
	SERRATED KNIFE	• 10-inch blade • Fewer broader, deeper, pointed serrations • Thinner blade angle • Comfortable, grippy handle • Medium weight	**Mercer Culinary Millenia 10" Wide Bread Knife** $22.10
	SLICING KNIFE	• Tapered 12-inch blade for slicing large cuts of meat • Oval scallops (called a granton edge) carved into blade • Fairly rigid blade with rounded tip	**Victorinox Swiss Army Fibrox Pro 12-Inch Granton Edge Slicing/Carving Knife** $54.65
	STEAK KNIVES	• Super-sharp, straight-edged blade • Sturdy, not wobbly, blade	**Victorinox Swiss Army 6-Piece Rosewood Steak Set, Spear Point, Straight Edge** $170.74 for a set of six Best Buy: **Chicago Cutlery Walnut Tradition 4-Piece Steak Knife Set** $17.95 for a set of four

MUST-HAVE ITEMS

KNIVES AND MORE	ITEM	WHAT TO LOOK FOR	TEST KITCHEN FAVORITES
	SANTOKU KNIFE	• 6½-inch blade • Narrow, curved, and short blade • Comfortable grip	**MAC Superior Santoku Knife** $74.95
	BONING KNIFE	• 6-inch blade • Narrow, highly maneuverable and razor-sharp blade • Comfortable grip and nonslip handle	**Victorinox 6-Inch Fibrox Pro Flexible Boning Knife** $27.20
	MEAT CLEAVER	• Razor-sharp blade • Balanced weight between handle and blade • Comfortable grip	**Global 6-Inch Meat Cleaver** $144.95 Best Buy: **LamsonSharp 7-Inch Meat Cleaver** $48
	HYBRID CHEF'S KNIFE	• High-carbon stainless steel knife • Lightweight • Thin blade that tapers from spine to cutting edge and from handle to tip	**Masamoto VG-10 Gyutou, 8.2 Inches** $136.50
	MANDOLINE	• Razor-sharp blade(s) • Hand guard to shield fingers • Gripper prongs to grasp food • Measurement-marked dial for precision cuts • Storage for extra blades	**Swissmar Börner Original V-Slicer Plus Mandoline** $29.99
	CARVING BOARD	• Trenches can contain ½ cup of liquid • Large and stable enough to hold large roasts • Midweight for easy carrying, carving, and cleaning	**J.K. Adams Maple Reversible Carving Board** $69.95
MUST-HAVE ITEM	CUTTING BOARD	• Roomy work surface at least 20 by 15 inches • Teak board for minimal maintenance • Durable edge-grain construction (wood grain runs parallel to surface of board)	**Proteak Edge Grain Teak Cutting Board** $84.99 Best Buy: **OXO Good Grips Carving and Cutting Board** $21.99

KNIVES AND MORE	ITEM	WHAT TO LOOK FOR	TEST KITCHEN FAVORITES
MUST-HAVE ITEM	KNIFE SHARPENER	• Diamond abrasives and a spring-loaded chamber to precisely guide blade • Quickly removes nicks in blades • Can convert a 20-degree edge to a sharper 15 degrees	Electric: **Chef'sChoice Trizor XV Knife Sharpener, Model #15** $149.99 Electric, Best Buy: **Chef'sChoice Diamond Sharpener for Asian Knives, Model #316** $79.99 Manual: **Chef'sChoice Pronto Manual Diamond Hone Asian Knife Sharpener** $49.99

POTS AND PANS	ITEM	WHAT TO LOOK FOR	TEST KITCHEN FAVORITES
MUST-HAVE ITEM	TRADITIONAL SKILLET	• Stainless steel interior and fully clad for even heat distribution • 12-inch diameter and flared sides • Comfortable, ovensafe handle • Tight-fitting lid included	**All-Clad 12-inch Stainless Steel Fry Pan with Lid** $96.85
	INEXPENSIVE SKILLET	• Could fit 8 pieces of chicken • Helper handle eased moving the hefty pan in and out of the oven	**Cuisinart 12-Inch Multiclad Pro Skillet** $69.95
MUST-HAVE ITEM	NONSTICK SKILLET	• Dark, nonstick surface • 12- or 12½-inch diameter, thick bottom • Comfortable, ovensafe handle • Cooking surface of at least 9 inches	**OXO Good Grips Non-Stick 12-Inch Open Frypan** $39.99
	CAST-IRON SKILLET	• Thick bottom and straight sides • Roomy interior (cooking surface of 9¼ inches or more) • Preseasoned	**Lodge Classic 12-Inch Cast Iron Skillet** $33.31

POTS AND PANS	ITEM	WHAT TO LOOK FOR	TEST KITCHEN FAVORITES
MUST-HAVE ITEMS	CAST-IRON SKILLET, ENAMELED	• Boasts flaring sides, an oversize helper handle, wide pour spouts, satiny interior, and balanced weight	**Le Creuset Signature 11¾" Iron Handle Skillet** $179.95 Best Buy: **Mario Batali by Dansk 12" Open Sauté Pan** $59.95
	DUTCH OVEN	• Enameled cast iron or stainless steel • Capacity of at least 6 quarts • Diameter of at least 9 inches • Tight-fitting lid • Wide, sturdy handles	Heavier: **Le Creuset 7¼-Quart Round French Oven** $349.95 Lighter: **All-Clad Stainless 8-Quart Stockpot** $279.95 Best Buy: **Cuisinart 7 Qt. Round Covered Casserole** $121.94
	SAUCEPAN	• Large saucepan with 3- to 4-quart capacity and small nonstick saucepan with 2- to 2½-quart capacity • Tight-fitting lids • Pans with rounded corners that a whisk can reach into • Long, comfortable handles that are angled for even weight distribution	Large: **All-Clad Stainless 4-Quart Saucepan with Lid and Loop** $224.95 Best Buy: **Cuisinart MultiClad Unlimited 4-Quart Saucepan** $69.99 Small: **Calphalon Contemporary Nonstick 2½-Quart Shallow Saucepan** $39.95
	RIMMED BAKING SHEET	• Light-colored surface (heats and browns evenly) • Thick, sturdy pan • Dimensions of 18 by 13 inches • Good to have at least two	**Nordic Ware Baker's Half Sheet** $14.97
	SAUTÉ PAN	• Aluminum core surrounded by layers of stainless steel • Hefty but well-balanced pan • 9½- to 10-inch diameter • Helper handle and tight-fitting lid	**All-Clad Stainless Steel 3-Quart Tri-Ply Sauté Pan** $224.95 Best Buy: **Cuisinart MultiClad Pro Stainless 3½-Quart Sauté Pan with Helper and Cover** $78.13

POTS AND PANS	ITEM	WHAT TO LOOK FOR	TEST KITCHEN FAVORITES
	OMELET PAN	• Gently sloped sides for easy turning and rolling of omelets • Nonstick finish • Heavy construction for durability and even heat distribution • 8-inch size for French omelets	**Original French Chef Omelette Pan** $139.95
	STOCKPOT	• 12-quart capacity • Thick bottom to prevent scorching • Wide body for easy cleaning and storage • Flat or round handles that extend at least 1¾ inches	**All-Clad Stainless 12-Quart Stock Pot** $389.95 Best Buy: **Cuisinart Chef's Classic Stainless 12-Quart Stock Pot** $69.99
MUST-HAVE ITEM	ROASTING PAN	• At least 15 by 11 inches • Stainless steel interior with aluminum core for even heat distribution • Upright handles for easy gripping • Light interior for better food monitoring	**Calphalon Contemporary Stainless Roasting Pan with Rack** $99.99 Best Buy: **Calphalon Commercial Hard-Anodized Roasting Pan with Nonstick Rack** $59.99
	ROASTING RACK	• Fixed, not adjustable, to provide sturdiness • Tall, vertical handles positioned on long side of rack	**All-Clad Nonstick Large Rack** $24.95
	COOKWARE SET	• Fully clad stainless steel with aluminum core for even heat distribution • Moderately heavy, durable construction • Lids included • Ideal mix of pans includes 12-inch skillet, 10-inch skillet, 2-quart saucepan, 4-quart saucepan, 8-quart stockpot	**All-Clad Stainless Steel Cookware Set, 10-Piece** $799.95 Best Buy: **Tramontina 18/10 Stainless Steel TriPly-Clad Cookware Set, 8-piece** $144.97

HANDY TOOLS	ITEM	WHAT TO LOOK FOR	TEST KITCHEN FAVORITES
	KITCHEN SHEARS	• Take-apart scissors (for easy cleaning) • Super-sharp blades • Sturdy construction • Work for both right- and left-handed users	**Kershaw 1120M Taskmaster Shears/Shun Multipurpose** $49.95 Best Buy: **J.A. Henckels International Kitchen Shears—Take Apart** $14.95
	TONGS	• Scalloped edges • Slightly concave pincers • Length of 12 inches (to keep your hand far from the heat) • Open and close easily	**OXO Good Grips 12-Inch Locking Tongs** $12.09
	WOODEN SPOON	• Slim yet broad bowl • Stain-resistant bamboo • Comfortable handle	**SCI Bamboo Wood Cooking Spoon** $2.40
	SLOTTED SPOON	• Wide, shallow, thin bowl • Long, hollow, comfortable handle • Steep, ladle-like angle between handle and bowl	**Cuisinart Stainless Steel Slotted Spoon** $9.12
	BASTING SPOON	• Thin, shallow bowl • Handle at least 9 inches in length • Slight dip from handle to bowl	**Rösle Basting Spoon with Hook Handle** $28.95
	ALL-AROUND SPATULA	• Head about 3 inches wide and 5½ inches long • 11 inches in length (tip to handle) • Long, vertical slots • Good to have a metal spatula to use with traditional cookware and plastic for nonstick cookware	Metal: **Wüsthof Gourmet Turner/Fish Spatula** $44.95 Plastic: **Matfer Bourgeat Pelton Spatula** $8.23
	SILICONE SPATULA	• Firm, wide blade ideal for efficient scraping and scooping • All-silicone design made for easy cleanup	**Di Oro Seamless Silicone Spatula—Large** $10.97

The first column is labeled **MUST-HAVE ITEMS** (kitchen shears through basting spoon), and the all-around spatula and silicone spatula rows are also labeled **MUST-HAVE ITEMS**.

HANDY TOOLS	ITEM	WHAT TO LOOK FOR	TEST KITCHEN FAVORITES
	OFFSET SPATULA	• Flexible blade offset to a roughly 30-degree angle • Enough usable surface area to frost the radius of a 9-inch cake • Comfortable handle	Large: **OXO Good Grips Bent Icing Knife** $9.99 Small: **Wilton 9-inch Angled Spatula** $4.79
	COOKIE SPATULA	• Small, silicone blade with thin, flexible edge • Angled handle	**OXO Good Grips Cookie Spatula** $6.99
MUST-HAVE ITEMS	ALL-PURPOSE WHISK	• At least 10 wires • Wires of moderate thickness • Comfortable rubber handle • Balanced, lightweight feel	**OXO Good Grips 11-Inch Balloon Whisk** $9.99
	PEPPER MILL	• Easy-to-adjust, clearly marked grind settings • Efficient, comfortable grinding mechanism • Generous capacity	**Cole and Mason Derwent Gourmet Precision Pepper Mill** $40
	ONE-HANDED PEPPER MILL	• Grinds quickly and easily • Accurately grinds in five textures from fine to coarse • Long-lasting rechargeable battery	**Peppermills Supreme Electric Pepper Mill** $39.95
	SUGAR SHAKER	• Mesh head that produces a fine, even dusting • Narrow cylinder that fits comfortably in your hand	**Ateco Stainless Steel Fine Mesh Shaker** $3.88
MUST-HAVE ITEM	LADLE	• Stainless steel • Hook handle • Pouring rim to prevent dripping • Handle 9 to 10 inches in length	**Rösle Ladle with Pouring Rim** $34 Best Buy: **OXO Good Grips Brushed Stainless Steel Ladle** $9.99

HANDY TOOLS	ITEM	WHAT TO LOOK FOR	TEST KITCHEN FAVORITES
MUST-HAVE ITEM	CAN OPENER	• Intuitive and easy to attach • Smooth turning motions • Dishwasher safe	**Fissler Magic Smooth-Edge Can Opener** $29
	JAR OPENER	• Strong, sturdy clamp grip • Adjusts quickly to any size jar	**Amco Swing-A-Way Comfort Grip Jar Opener** $5.99
MUST-HAVE ITEM	GARLIC PRESS	• Conical holes that press garlic through efficiently • Solid, stainless steel construction • Comfortable handle • Easy to clean	**Kuhn Rikon Stainless Steel Epicurean Garlic Press** $39.95
	GARLIC PEELER	• Thick, comfortable silicone sleeve • Removes skins without bruising • Easy to wash	**Zak! Designs E-Z Rol Garlic Peeler** $8.79
	SERRATED FRUIT PEELER	• Comfortable grip and nonslip handle • Sharp blade	**Messermeister Serrated Swivel Peeler** $5.50
MUST-HAVE ITEM	VEGETABLE PEELER	• Sharp, carbon steel blade • 1-inch space between blade and peeler to prevent jamming • Lightweight and comfortable	**Kuhn Rikon Original Swiss Peeler** $3.50
	RASP GRATER	• Sharp teeth (require little effort or pressure when grating) • Maneuverable over round shapes • Comfortable handle	**Microplane Classic Zester Grater** $12.35
MUST-HAVE ITEM	GRATER	• Paddle-style grater • Sharp, extra-large holes and generous grating plane • Rubber-lined feet for stability • Comfortable handle	**Rösle Coarse Grater** $35.95
	ROTARY GRATER	• Barrel at least 2 inches in diameter • Classic turn-crank design • Comfortable handle • Simple to disassemble for easy cleanup	**Zyliss All Cheese Grater** $19.95

HANDY TOOLS	ITEM	WHAT TO LOOK FOR	TEST KITCHEN FAVORITES
	MANUAL JUICER	• Directs juice in a steady stream with no splattering or overflowing • Large, rounded handles that are easy to squeeze	**Chef'n FreshForce Citrus Juicer** $23.04
	ICE CREAM SCOOP	• Forms perfectly round orbs that release easily • Wide, comfortable handle contains heat-conductive fluid that warms up instantly when a hand grips the exterior and also warms the bowl, making scooping easy	**Zeroll Original Ice Cream Scoop** $18.44
	MEAT POUNDER	• At least 1½ pounds in weight • Vertical handle for better leverage and control	**Norpro Grip-EZ Meat Pounder** $17.50
	BENCH SCRAPER	• Sturdy blade • Beveled edge for easy cutting and scraping • Comfortable handle with plastic, rubber, or nylon grip	**Dexter-Russell 6" Dough Cutter/Scraper–Sani-Safe Series** $7.01
	BOWL SCRAPER	• Curved shape with comfortable grip • Rigid enough to move dough but flexible enough to scrape up batter • Thin, straight edge doubles as dough cutter or bench scraper	**iSi Basics Silicone Scraper Spatula** $5.99
	ROLLING PIN	• Moderate weight (1 to 1½ pounds) • 19-inch straight barrel • Slightly textured wooden surface to grip dough for easy rolling	**J.K. Adams Plain Maple Rolling Dowel** $13.95
	MIXING BOWLS	• Good to have both stainless steel and glass (for mixing, microwaving, and holding prepped ingredients) • Sets of 6 to 9 nesting bowls ranging in capacity from about 1¼ ounces to 4 quarts (for glass) and 2 cups to 8 quarts (for stainless steel)	Stainless Steel: **Vollrath Economy Stainless Steel Mixing Bowls** $2.90–$6.90 Glass: **Pyrex Smart Essentials with Colored Lids** $27.98 for 4-bowl set

MUST-HAVE ITEMS

HANDY TOOLS	ITEM	WHAT TO LOOK FOR	TEST KITCHEN FAVORITES
	MINI PREP BOWLS	• Wide, shallow bowls • Easy to hold, fill, empty, and clean • Microwave-safe and oven-safe	**Anchor Hocking 6-Piece Nesting Prep Bowl Set** $11
MUST-HAVE ITEM — OVEN MITT	OVEN MITT	• Form-fitting and not overly bulky for easy maneuvering • Machine washable • Flexible, heat-resistant material	**Kool-Tek 15-Inch Oven Mitt by KatchAll** $44.95 each
	INNOVATIVE POT HOLDER	• Combines cotton for flexibility with grippy silicone for high-heat protection • Superior maneuverability	**OXO Good Grips Silicone Pot Holder with Magnet** $9.99
	COOKIE CUTTERS	• Metal cutters • Thin, sharp cutting edge and round or rubber-grip top • Depth of at least 1 inch	**Little difference among various brands**
	PASTRY BRUSH	• Silicone bristles (heat-resistant, durable, and easy to clean) • Perforated flaps (to trap liquid) • Angled head to reach tight spots • Comfortable handle	**OXO Good Grips Silicone Pastry Brush** $6.99
	BOUILLON STRAINER/ CHINOIS	• Conical shape • Depth of 7 to 8 inches • At least one hook on rim for stability	**Winco Reinforced Extra Fine Mesh Bouillon Strainer** $33.78
MUST-HAVE ITEMS	COLANDER	• 4- to 7-quart capacity • Metal ring attached to bottom for stability • Many holes for quick draining • Small holes so pasta doesn't slip through	**RSVP International Endurance Precision Pierced 5-Qt. Colander** $25.99
	FINE-MESH STRAINER	• Stiff, tightly woven mesh • Capacity of at least 5 cups with large, durable hooks for support over bowls and pots	**Rösle Fine-Mesh Strainer, Round Handle, 7.9 inches, 20 cm** $45

HANDY TOOLS	ITEM	WHAT TO LOOK FOR	TEST KITCHEN FAVORITES
	FOOD MILL	• Sturdy but lightweight plastic construction • Easy to turn	**RSVP Classic Rotary Food Mill** $24.95
	FAT SEPARATOR	• Bottom-draining model • Detachable bowl for easy cleaning • Strainer for catching solids	**Cuisipro Fat Separator** $33.95
	SPLATTER SCREEN	• At least 13-inches wide with a small handle • Fits over a range of pans • Minimized mess	**HIC Stainless Steel Splatter Screen** $9.99
MUST-HAVE ITEMS	POTATO MASHER	• Solid mashing disk with many small holes • Comfortable grip • Long handle	**Zyliss Stainless Steel Potato Masher** $12.99
	SALAD SPINNER	• Ergonomic and easy-to-operate hand pump • Wide base for stability • Flat lid for easy cleaning and storage	**OXO Good Grips Salad Spinner** $29.99
	STEAMER BASKET	• Collapsible stainless steel basket with feet • Adjustable and removable center rod for easy removal from pot and easy storage	**OXO Good Grips Pop-Up Steamer** $16.99
	MORTAR AND PESTLE	• Heavy, stable base with tall, narrow walls • Rough interior to help grip and grind ingredients • Comfortable, heavy pestle	**Frieling "Goliath" Mortar and Pestle Set** $49.95

MEASURING EQUIPMENT	ITEM	WHAT TO LOOK FOR	TEST KITCHEN FAVORITES
MUST-HAVE ITEMS	DRY MEASURING CUPS	• Accurate measurements • Easy-to-read measurement markings • Durable measurement markings • Stable when empty and filled • Strong and durable design • Handles perfectly flush with cups • Stacks and stores neatly	**OXO Good Grips Stainless Steel Measuring Cups** $19.99
	LIQUID MEASURING CUP	• Crisp, unambiguous markings that include ¼ and ⅓ cup measurements • Heatproof, sturdy cup with handle • Good to have in a variety of sizes (1, 2, and 4 cups)	**Pyrex 2-Cup Measuring Cup** $5.99
	ADJUSTABLE MEASURING CUP	• Plungerlike bottom (with a tight seal between plunger and tube) that you can set to correct measurement, then push up to cleanly extract sticky ingredients (such as shortening or peanut butter) • 1- or 2-cup capacity • Dishwasher-safe	**KitchenArt Pro Adjust-A-Cup Professional Series** $12.95
MUST-HAVE ITEMS	MEASURING SPOONS	• Long, comfortable handles • Rim of bowl flush with handle (makes it easy to "dip" into a dry ingredient and "sweep" across the top for accurate measuring) • Slim design	**Cuisipro Stainless Steel Measuring Spoons Set** $11.95
	KITCHEN RULER	• Stainless steel and easy to clean • 18 inches in length • Large, easy-to-read markings	**Empire 18-Inch Stainless Steel Ruler** $8.49
	DIGITAL SCALE	• Easy-to-read display not blocked by weighing platform • At least 7-pound capacity • Accessible buttons • Gram-to-ounce conversion feature • Roomy platform	**OXO Good Grips 11 lb. Food Scale with Pull Out Display** $49.99 Best Buy: **Ozeri Pronto Digital Multifunction Kitchen and Food Scale** $11.79

THERMOMETERS AND TIMERS	ITEM	WHAT TO LOOK FOR	TEST KITCHEN FAVORITES
MUST-HAVE ITEMS	INSTANT-READ THERMOMETER	• Display auto-rotates • Lights up in low light • Wakes up when unit is picked up • Takes a single AAA alkaline battery • Water resistant	**ThermoWorks Thermapen Mk4** $99 Best Buy: **ThermoWorks ThermoPop** $29
	OVEN THERMOMETER	• Wide, sturdy base • Clear temperature markings • Fairly easy to read	**CDN Pro Accurate Oven Thermometer** $8.70
	MEAT PROBE/ CANDY/ DEEP-FRY THERMOMETER	• Digital model • Easy-to-read console • Mounting clip (to attach probe to the pan)	**ThermoWorks ChefAlarm** $59 Best Buy: **Polder Classic Digital Thermometer/Timer** $24.99
	BARBECUE THERMOMETER	• Simultaneously checks food and grill temperature • Easy to read • Heatproof finger-grip • Dishwasher-safe	**Polder Dual Sensor Meat and Oven Thermometer** $10
	REFRIGERATOR/ FREEZER THERMOMETER	• Large, easy-to-read display • Accurate, and carefully monitors fluctuations in temperature	**ThermoWorks Fridge/ Freezer Alarm** $22
	REMOTE THERMOMETER	• Bluetooth device connects quickly to smart phones and delivers accurate temperature readouts • Easy to use	**iDevices Kitchen Thermometer** $78

THERMOMETERS AND TIMERS	ITEM	WHAT TO LOOK FOR	TEST KITCHEN FAVORITES
	KITCHEN TIMER	• Lengthy time range (1 second to at least 10 hours) • Able to count up after alarm goes off • Easy to use and read • Able to track multiple events	**OXO Good Grips Triple Timer** $19.99
	WEARABLE KITCHEN TIMER	• Combines a clock, timer, and stopwatch • Vertical orientation fits comfortably in hand and pockets • 38-inch lanyard is comfortable and long enough to slip overhead	**ThermoWorks TimeStick** $25

BAKEWARE	ITEM	WHAT TO LOOK FOR	TEST KITCHEN FAVORITES
MUST-HAVE ITEM	GLASS BAKING DISH	• Dimensions of 13 by 9 inches • Lightweight with large handles for easy grip and maneuvering	**Pyrex Easy Grab 3-Quart Oblong Baking Dish** $7.29
	BROILER-SAFE BAKING DISH	• Large, easy-to-grip handles • Straight sides for easy serving • Lightweight porcelain	**HIC Porcelain Lasagna Baking Dish** $29.95
MUST-HAVE ITEMS	METAL BAKING PAN	• Dimensions of 13 by 9 inches • Straight sides • Nonstick coating for even browning and easy release of cakes and bar cookies	**Williams-Sonoma Goldtouch Nonstick Rectangular Cake Pan, 9" x 13"** $32.95
	SQUARE BAKING PAN	• Straight sides • Light gold or dark nonstick surface for even browning and easy release of cakes • Good to have both 9-inch and 8-inch square pans	**Williams-Sonoma Goldtouch Nonstick Square Cake Pan, 8"** $21

BAKEWARE	ITEM	WHAT TO LOOK FOR	TEST KITCHEN FAVORITES
MUST-HAVE ITEMS	ROUND CAKE PAN	• Best for cake • Straight sides • Light finish for tall, even baking • Nonstick surface for easy release	Best All-Around: **Nordic Ware Naturals Nonstick 9-inch Round Cake Pan** $14.32
		• Dark finish is ideal for pizza and cinnamon buns • Nonstick	Best for Browning: **Chicago Metallic Non-Stick 9" Round Cake Pan** $10.97
	PIE PLATE	• Glass promotes even browning and allows progress to be monitored • ½-inch rim (makes it easy to shape decorative crusts) • Shallow angled sides prevent crusts from slumping • Good to have two	**Pyrex Bakeware 9 Inch Pie Plate** $8.16
	LOAF PAN	• Light gold or dark nonstick surface for even browning and easy release • Good to have both 8½ by 4½-inch and 9 by 5-inch pans	**Williams-Sonoma Nonstick Goldtouch Loaf Pan** $21 Best Buy: **Baker's Secret 9 x 5-Inch Nonstick Loaf Pan** $5
	SPRINGFORM PAN	• Tall sides make for an easy grip • Gold-toned pan produces evenly-baked crusts • Wide, raised base provides support	**Williams-Sonoma Goldtouch Springform Pan, 9"** $49.95 Best Buy: **Nordic Ware 9" Leakproof Springform Pan** $16.22
	COOKIE SHEET	• Thick aluminum heats and browns evenly • Won't warp with repeated use • Raised edges for easy maneuvering • Nonstick, spacious surface	**Vollrath Wear-Ever Cookie Sheet (Natural Finish)** $15.99

BAKEWARE	ITEM	WHAT TO LOOK FOR	TEST KITCHEN FAVORITES
MUST-HAVE ITEMS	MUFFIN TIN	• Gold nonstick surface for perfect browning and easy release • Wide, extended rims and raised lip for easy handling	**OXO Good Grips Non-Stick 12-Cup Muffin Pan** $24.99
	COOLING RACK	• Grid-style rack with tightly woven, heavy-gauge bars • Should fit inside a standard 18 by 13-inch rimmed baking sheet • Dishwasher-safe	**CIA Bakeware 12-Inch x 17-Inch Cooling Rack** $15.95
	BAKER'S COOLING RACK	• Sturdy rack • Four collapsible shelves • Unit folds down for easy storage	**Linden Sweden Baker's Cooling Rack** $17.99
	BISCUIT CUTTERS	• Sharp edges • A set with a variety of sizes	**Ateco 5357 11-Piece Plain Round Cutter Set** $14.95
	BUNDT PAN	• Heavyweight cast aluminum • Thick, easy-to-grip handles • Clearly defined ridges for elegant cakes • 15-cup capacity	**Nordic Ware Anniversary Bundt Pan** $30.99
	TART PAN	• Nonstick mold released tarts more readily than traditional finish • Deep grooves for impressive edges • Dark surface for deeply, evenly browned edges	**Matfer Steel Non-Stick Fluted Tart Mold** $27
	TUBE PAN	• Heavy pan (at least 1 pound) • Heavy bottom for leak-free seal • Dark nonstick surface for even browning and easy release • 16-cup capacity • Feet on rim	**Chicago Metallic Professional Nonstick Angel Food Cake Pan with Feet** $19.95

BAKEWARE	ITEM	WHAT TO LOOK FOR	TEST KITCHEN FAVORITES
	PULLMAN LOAF PAN	• Squared-off pan (4 by 4 inches) • Nonstick aluminized steel for easy cleanup • Light surface for even browning	**USA Pan 13 by 4-inch Pullman Loaf Pan & Cover** $33.95
	BAKER'S EDGE PAN	• Attached cutting grid • Dark nonstick surface for easy release	**Baker's Edge Brownie Pan** $34.95
	RAMEKINS	• Sturdy, high-fired porcelain (chip-resistant and safe for use in oven, broiler, microwave, and dishwasher) • For one all-purpose set, capacity of 6 ounces and diameter of 3 inches	**Apilco 6-Ounce Ramekins** $29 for a set of four
	BAKING STONE	• Substantial but not too heavy to handle • Dimensions of 16 by 14 inches • Clay, not cement, for evenly browned crusts	**Old Stone Oven Pizza Baking Stone** $59.95

SMALL APPLIANCES	ITEM	WHAT TO LOOK FOR	TEST KITCHEN FAVORITES
MUST-HAVE ITEM	FOOD PROCESSOR	• 14-cup capacity • Sharp and sturdy blades • Wide feed tube • Should come with basic blades and discs: steel blade, dough blade, shredding/slicing disc	**Cuisinart Custom 14-Cup Food Processor** $199.99 Mini Food Processor: **Cuisinart Elite Collection 4-Cup Chopper/Grinder** $59.95
	STAND MIXER	• Planetary action (stationary bowl and single mixing arm) • Powerful motor • Bowl size of at least 4½ quarts • Slightly squat bowl to keep ingredients in beater's range • Should come with basic attachments: paddle, dough hook, metal whisk	**Kitchen-Aid Pro Line Series 7-Qt Bowl Lift Stand Mixer** $549.95 Best Buy: **KitchenAid Classic Plus Series 4.5-Quart Tilt-Head Stand Mixer** $199.99

SMALL APPLIANCES	ITEM	WHAT TO LOOK FOR	TEST KITCHEN FAVORITES
MUST-HAVE ITEMS	HAND-HELD MIXER	• Lightweight model • Slim wire beaters without central post • Variety of speeds	**KitchenAid 5-Speed Ultra Power Hand Mixer** $69.99 Best Buy: **Cuisinart PowerSelect 3-Speed Hand Mixer** $26.77
	BLENDER	• Mix of straight and serrated blades at different angles • Jar with curved base • At least 44-ounce capacity • Heavy base for stability	**Vitamix 5200** $449 Best Buy: **Breville The Hemisphere Control** $199.99
	IMMERSION BLENDER	• Easy to maneuver and lightweight with a slim, grippy body • Well-designed blade and cage • Detachable handle for easy cleanup	**Braun Multiquick 5** $59.99
	ELECTRIC GRIDDLE	• Large cooking area (about 21 by 12 inches) • Attached pull-out grease trap (won't tip over) • Nonstick surface for easy cleanup	**BroilKing Professional Griddle** $99.99
	ELECTRIC JUICER	• Ideal for making a large amount of fruit or vegetable juice • Centrifugal, not masticating, model for fresher-tasting juice • 3-inch-wide feed tube • Easy to assemble and clean	**Breville Juice Fountain Plus** $149.99

SMALL APPLIANCES	ITEM	WHAT TO LOOK FOR	TEST KITCHEN FAVORITES
	ELECTRIC KETTLE	• Heats water rapidly • Secure base and wide comfortable handle • Removable filter in spout	**OXO On Clarity Cordless Glass Electric Kettle** $89.95 Best Buy: **Capresso Silver H2O Electric Kettle** $55.69
	COFFEE MAKER	• Thermal carafe that keeps coffee hot and fresh with capacity of at least 10 cups • Short brewing time (6 minutes is ideal) • Copper, not aluminum, heating element • Easy-to-fill water tank • Clear, intuitive controls	**Technivorm Moccamaster 10-Cup Coffee Maker with Thermal Carafe** $299 Best Buy: **Bonavita 8-Cup Coffee Maker with Thermal Carafe** $189.99
	MEAT GRINDER	• Grinds pounds of meat easily, even on older KitchenAid stand mixers • Mostly dishwasher safe	**KitchenAid Food Grinder Attachment** $48.74
	PORTABLE INDUCTION BURNER	• Large cooking surface for even heating of pans • Basic push buttons and dial controls for ease of use	**Max Burton Induction Cooktop** $124.25
	ICE CREAM MAKER	• Simple to use and very compact • Modestly priced • Made ice cream that rivaled the smooth texture of our favorite store-bought ice creams	**Cuisinart Automatic Frozen-Yogurt, Ice Cream & Sorbet Maker** $49.95

SMALL APPLIANCES	ITEM	WHAT TO LOOK FOR	TEST KITCHEN FAVORITES
	STOVETOP PRESSURE COOKER	• Stainless steel rather than aluminum for more durable construction that doesn't react to acidic foods • Stovetop model with low sides and wide base for easy access and better browning and heat retention • Pressure indicator that is easy to see and interpret at a glance	**Fissler Vitaquick 8 ½-Quart Pressure Cooker** $279.95 Best Buy: **Fagor Duo 8-Quart Stainless Steel Pressure Cooker** $109.95
	SLOW COOKER	• At least 6-quart capacity (4-quart capacity for small slow cookers) • Insert handles • Clear lid to see progress of food • Dishwasher-safe insert • Intuitive controls with programmable timer and warming mode	**KitchenAid 6-Quart Slow Cooker with Solid Glass Lid** $99.99
	TWO-SLOT TOASTER	• Quartz heating element for even heating • Clear window to monitor browning • Ample room for large or thick bread slices or bagels	**Magimix by Robot-Coupe Vision Toaster** $249.95
	TOASTER OVEN	• Quartz heating elements for steady, controlled heat • Roomy but compact interior • Simple to use	**The Smart Oven by Breville** $249.95 Best Buy: **Hamilton Beach Set & Forget Toaster Oven with Convection Cooking** $99.99
	TABLETOP GRILL	• Large grilling area • Easy to clean	**Delonghi Alfredo Healthy Indoor Grill** $53.99
	WAFFLE IRON	• Indicator lights and audible alert • Makes two waffles at a time • Six-point dial for customizing waffle doneness	**Cuisinart Double Belgian Waffle Maker** $99.95

GRILLING EQUIPMENT	ITEM	WHAT TO LOOK FOR	TEST KITCHEN FAVORITES
	GAS GRILL	• Large main grate • Built-in thermometer • Two burners for varying heat levels (three is even better) • Made of thick, heat-retaining materials such as cast aluminum and enameled steel	**Weber Spirit E-310 Gas Grill** $499
	CHARCOAL GRILL	• Sturdy construction to efficiently maintain heat • Well-designed cooking grate, handles, lids, and wheels • Generous cooking surface • Large charcoal capacity • Well-positioned air vents • Gas ignition to instantly and easily light coals • Ash catcher for easy cleanup	**Weber Performer Deluxe Charcoal Grill** $349 Best Buy: **Weber Original Kettle Premium Charcoal Grill, 22-Inch** $149
	PORTABLE CHARCOAL GRILL	• Ample cooking surface with raised lip • Cover that can be secured for travel • Lightweight but durable	**Weber Smokey Joe Gold Portable Charcoal Grill** $34.70
	SMOKER	• Large cooking area • Water pan • Multiple vents for precise temperature control	**Weber Smokey Mountain Cooker Smoker, 18"** $298.95
	CHIMNEY STARTER	• 6-quart capacity • Holes in canister so air can circulate around coals • Sturdy construction • Heat-resistant handle • Dual handle for easy control	**Weber Rapidfire Chimney Starter** $14.99

GRILLING EQUIPMENT	ITEM	WHAT TO LOOK FOR	TEST KITCHEN FAVORITES
	GRILL TONGS	• 16 inches in length • Scalloped, not sharp and serrated, edges • Open and close easily • Lightweight • Moderate amount of springy tension	**OXO Good Grips 16-Inch Locking Tongs** $14.99
	GRILL BRUSH	• Long handle • Replaceable, long-lasting steel pads for scrubbing	**Grill Wizard 18-inch China Grill Brush** $31.50
	GRILL SPATULA	• Handle at least 12 inches in length • Sharp cutting edge	**Weber Original Stainless Steel Spatula** $14.99
	BARBECUE BASTING BRUSH	• Silicone bristles • Angled brush head • Handle between 8 and 13 inches • Heat-resistant	**Elizabeth Karmel's Super Silicone Angled Barbecue Brush** $9.16
	GRILL GLOVES	• Excellent heat protection • Gloves, rather than mitts, for dexterity • Long sleeves to protect forearms	**Steven Raichlen Ultimate Suede Grilling Gloves** $29.99 per pair
	SKEWERS	• Flat and metal • $3/16$ inch thick	**Norpro 12-Inch Stainless Steel Skewers** $6.85 for a set of 6
	RIB RACK	• Sturdily supports six racks of ribs • Doubles as roasting rack (when flipped upside down) • Nonstick coating for easy cleanup	**Charcoal Companion Reversible Rib Rack** $14.95
	GRILL LIGHTER	• Flexible neck • Refillable chamber with large, easy-to-read fuel window • Comfortable grip	**Zippo Flexible Neck Utility Lighter** $18.35

GRILLING EQUIPMENT	ITEM	WHAT TO LOOK FOR	TEST KITCHEN FAVORITES
	ELECTRIC CHARCOAL STARTER	• Long, offset heating element • Quick-to-heat	**Grill Dome Rapid-Lite Electric Charcoal Starters** $34.95
	OUTDOOR GRILL PAN	• Narrow slits and raised sides so food can't fall through or off • Sturdy construction with handles	**Weber Professional-Grade Grill Pan** $19.99
	SMOKER BOX	• Cast iron for slow heating and steady smoke • Easy to fill, empty, and clean	**GrillPro Cast Iron Smoker Box by Onward Manufacturing Company** $12.79
	WOOD, FOR SMOKING	• Hickory wood for bold, smoky flavor • Long-lasting chunks for charcoal grills • Wood chips for gas grills	**Little difference among various brands**
	VERTICAL ROASTER	• Helps poultry cook evenly • 8-inch shaft keeps chicken above fat and drippings in pan • Attached basin catches drippings for pan sauce • Sturdy construction	**Vertical Roaster with Infuser by Norpro** $22.11 Best Buy: **Elizabeth Karmel's Grill Friends Porcelain Chicken Sitter** $11.99
	PROPANE INDICATOR	• Easy-to-read dial • Accurately measures propane by weight	**Grill Gauge Propane Tank Scale** $13.99
	GRILL LIGHT	• Bright, even, wide spread of warm light • Stood freely on side tables and clipped to handles	**Ivation Multipurpose Gooseneck 7-LED Dimmable Clip Light** $24.99

SPECIALTY PIECES	ITEM	WHAT TO LOOK FOR	TEST KITCHEN FAVORITES
	APPLE CORER	• Comfortable grip with offset handle • Sharp teeth • Wide blade diameter	**CuisiPro Apple Corer** $9.95
	APPLE SLICER	• Sharp, serrated corer with 1-inch diameter • Ability to cut 8 or 16 slices • Comfortable handle	**Williams-Sonoma Dial-a-Slice Apple Divider** $19.95
	CORN STRIPPER	• Safer than using chef's knife • Attached cup to catch kernels • Comfortable grip and sharp blade	**OXO Good Grips Corn Stripper** $11.99
	TOMATO CORER	• Sharp teeth make easy, clean cuts • Lightweight, rounded-off plastic handle • Comfortable head-handle combination	**Norpro Tomato Core It** $2.99
	NUT CHOPPER	• Sharp, sturdy stainless steel chopping tines • Dishwasher-safe	**Progressive International Heavy Duty Nut Chopper** $8.89
	GRILL PAN	• Cast-iron pan with enamel coating for heat retention and easy cleanup • Tall ridges (4 to 5.5 mm high) to keep food above rendered fat • Generous cooking area	**Staub 12-Inch American Square Grill Pan and Press** $219.95 Best Buy: **Lodge Pre-Seasoned Square Grill Pan & Ribbed Panini Press** $18.97 (press sold separately for $14.58)

SPECIALTY PIECES	ITEM	WHAT TO LOOK FOR	TEST KITCHEN FAVORITES
	STOVETOP GRIDDLE	• Anodized aluminum for even heating • Nonstick coating • Lightweight (about 4 pounds) • Heat-resistant loop handles • At least 17 by 9 inches (large enough to span two burners) • Pour spout for draining grease	**Anolon Advanced Double Burner Griddle** $48.95
	OYSTER KNIFE	• Sturdy, flat blade with slightly curved tip for easy penetration • Slim, nonstick handle for secure, comfortable grip	**R. Murphy New Haven Oyster Knife** $16.65
	SEAFOOD SCISSORS	• Curved blade neatly snips off shells • Tidy removal of shrimp vein	**RSVP International Endurance Seafood Scissors** $14.99
	SILICONE MICROWAVE LID	• Thin, silicone round to cover splatter-prone food during microwave heating • Easy to clean • Doubles as jar opener	**Piggy Steamer** $18
	PIPING SET	• Contains all of the essentials: twelve 16-inch pastry bags; four plastic couplers; and the following Wilton tips: #4 round, #12 round, #70 leaf, #103 petal, #2D large closed star, #1M open star • All parts available at most crafts stores	**Test Kitchen Self-Assembled à La Carte Decorating Set** $12.20
	CHEESE WIRE	• Comfortable plastic handles • Narrow wire	**Fante's Handled Cheese Wire** $2.99
	PIZZA WHEEL	• Clear plastic wheel to prevent damage to pans • Comfortable, soft-grip handle	**OXO Good Grips 4-Inch Pizza Wheel** $12.99
	POTATO RICER	• Large hopper that can hold 1¼ cups sliced potatoes • Interchangeable fine and coarse disks • Sturdy, ergonomic handles	**RSVP International Potato Ricer** $13.95

SPECIALTY PIECES	ITEM	WHAT TO LOOK FOR	TEST KITCHEN FAVORITES
	TORTILLA WARMER	• Triple-layered sides with two layers of fabric around sheet of insulating plastic • 12-inch diameter to fit large wraps	**IMUSA 12-Inch Cloth Tortilla Warmer** $5.99
	INSULATED FOOD CARRIER	• Keeps food piping hot for over 3 hours • Fits two 13 by 9-inch baking dishes • Handy zippered pocket holds serving utensils	**Rachael Ray Expandable Lasagna Lugger** $26.95
	CUPCAKE AND CAKE CARRIER	• Fits both round and square cakes and cupcakes • Snap locks • Nonskid base • Collapses for easy storage	**Progressive Collapsible Cupcake and Cake Carrier** $29.95
	CAKE LIFTER	• Sturdy but small and slightly flexible • Rounded corners for visibility • Comfortable offset handle	**Fat Daddio's Cake Lifter** $11.88
	CAKE STAND	• Elevated rotating stand so you can hold the spatula steady for easy frosting • Solid, light construction	**Winco Revolving Cake Decorating Stand** $29.98
	CREAM WHIPPER	• Responsive lever better control and easy piping • Grips on handle and neck for easy refilling and cleanup	**iSi Gourmet Whip** $99.27
	SPICE/COFFEE GRINDER	• Electric, not manual, grinders • Deep bowl to hold ample amount of coffee beans • Good to have two, one each for coffee grinding and spice grinding	**Krups Fast-Touch Coffee Mill, Model 203** $19.99

SPECIALTY PIECES	ITEM	WHAT TO LOOK FOR	TEST KITCHEN FAVORITES
	INNOVATIVE TEAPOT	• Contained ultrafine-mesh strainer keeps tea leaf dregs separate • One-piece design for easy cleaning	**Adagio Teas IngenuiTEA** $14.95
	TRAVEL MUG	• Simple, leakproof lid design • Good heat retention • Easy-to-clean and dishwasher safe	**Timolino Icon 16-Ounces Signature Vacuum Travel Mug** $28
	WATER BOTTLE	• Clear plastic sides makes it easy to fill • Bi-level twist-on lid for easy sipping • Handy carrying loop	**Nathan LittleShot** $11.99
	WINE OPENER	• Durable design • Teflon-coated worm	**Pulltap's Classic Evolution Corkscrew by Pulltex** $39.95
	ELECTRIC WINE OPENER	• Sturdy, quiet corkscrew • Broad base that rests firmly on bottle	**Cuisinart Cordless Wine Opener with Vacuum Sealer** $39.95
	WINE AERATOR	• Long, tubelike design that exposes wine to air as it is being poured • Neat, hands-free aerating	**Nuance Wine Finer** $19.95

SPECIALTY PIECES	ITEM	WHAT TO LOOK FOR	TEST KITCHEN FAVORITES
	COCKTAIL SHAKER	• Holds at least 18 ounces to make one or two cocktails at once • Comfortable carafe-like shape • Wide mouth for easy filling, muddling, and cleaning	Cobbler Style: **Tovolo Stainless Steel 4-in-1 Cocktail Shaker** $29.99 Boston Style: **The Boston Shaker Professional Boston Shaker, Weighted** $14.50
	BEER SAVERS	• Fit both glass and plastic bottles • Preserves carbonation for up to 2 days	**Savebrands Beer Savers** $6.99 for six-pack
	COOLER	• Insulating layer of plastic lining • Lightweight, durable, sturdy, and easy to move, even when full • Easy to clean	**California Cooler Bags T-Rex Large Collapsible Rolling Cooler** $75
	SELTZER MAKER	• Easy to use and easy to control level of fizz • CO_2 canisters are long lasting and convenient to exchange at retail stores	**SodaStream Source Starter Kit** $99.95
	VACUUM SEALER	• Countertop, heat-sealed model • Works well with wide variety of bags, canisters, and rolls	**Weston Professional Advantage Vacuum Sealer** $189.99
	COMPOST BUCKET	• Plastic pail to collect food scraps for composter • Carbon filter prevents odors from escaping and allows oxygen to enter so decomposition can occur • Easy to open lid that latches securely in place • 2.4-gallon capacity	**Exaco Trading Kitchen Compost Waste Collector** $19.98

SPECIALTY PIECES	ITEM	WHAT TO LOOK FOR	TEST KITCHEN FAVORITES
MUST-HAVE ITEM	FIRE EXTINGUISHER	• Fast and effective • Intuitive to use and easy to lift • Powerful spray worked well on grease fire and burning fabric	**Kidde ABC Multipurpose Home Fire Extinguisher** $25.99

KITCHEN SUPPLIES	ITEM	WHAT TO LOOK FOR	TEST KITCHEN FAVORITES
MUST-HAVE ITEMS	PARCHMENT PAPER	• Sturdy paper for heavy doughs • Easy release of baked goods • At least 14 inches wide	**Little difference among various brands**
	PLASTIC WRAP	• Clings tightly and resticks well • Packaging with sharp teeth that aren't exposed (to avoid snags on clothing and skin) • Adhesive pad to hold cut end of wrap	**Glad Cling Wrap Clear Plastic** $1.20 per 100 square feet
	BUTTER SAVER	• Fits the end of standard-size stick of butter • Kept butter from picking up off-flavors for more than a week • Measures 1 tablespoon	**Savebrands Butter Saver** $4.99
	PAPER PLATES	• Roomy eating surface with steep lip • Thick paper holds up to 2 pounds of food	**Hefty Super Strong Paper Plates** $2.99 for 16 plates
	PLASTIC FOOD STORAGE CONTAINER	• Snap-style seal with ridge on underside to ensure tight seal • Low, flat rectangle for easy storage and more efficient heating and chilling • Made of plastic free of BPA (bisphenol-A)	**Snapware Airtight** $7.99 for 8-cup rectangle

KITCHEN SUPPLIES	ITEM	WHAT TO LOOK FOR	TEST KITCHEN FAVORITES
	DISH TOWEL	• Thin cotton for absorbency and flexibility • Dries glassware without streaks • Washes clean without shrinking	**Williams-Sonoma Striped Towels** $19.95 for set of four
	APRON	• Adjustable neck strap and long strings • Full coverage; chest area reinforced with extra layer of fabric • Stains wash out completely	**Bragard Travail Bib Apron** $27.95
	LIQUID DISH DETERGENT	• High concentration of surfactants to wash away oil • Clean scent	**Mrs. Meyer's Clean Day Liquid Dish Soap, Lavender** $3.99 for 16 fluid ounces
	DISH DRYING RACK	• Two roomy utensil holders • Seven-slot knife block • Ledge that can hang four wineglasses upside down for spot-free drying • Raised feet to hold it up off the counter	Innovative, Large: **Simple Human Steel Frame Dishrack** $63.57
		• Readily fits smaller items • Folds flat for easy storage • Best choice for small spaces or light loads	Innovative, Small: **Progressive Prepworks Collapsible Over-The-Sink Dish Drainer** $24.99
		• Fits dishes for a family of four • Angled mat tidily drains off water	Traditional/Best Buy: **Rubbermaid Antimicrobial Sink Drainer, Large, and Antimicrobial Drain Board, Large** $10.99 for basket, $7.38 for mat

STOCKING YOUR PANTRY

Using the best ingredients is one way to guarantee success in the kitchen. But how do you know what to buy? Shelves are filled with a dizzying array of choices—and price does not equal quality. Over the years, the test kitchen's blind tasting panels have evaluated thousands of ingredients, brand by brand, side by side, plain and in prepared applications, to determine which brands you can trust and which brands to avoid. In the chart that follows, we share the results, revealing our top-rated choices and the attributes that made them stand out among the competition. And because our test kitchen accepts no support from product manufacturers, you can trust our ratings. See AmericasTestKitchen.com for updates to these tastings.

	TEST KITCHEN FAVORITE	WHY WE LIKE IT	RUNNERS-UP
	ANCHOVIES **King Oscar Anchovies– Flat Fillets in Olive oil**	• Right amount of salt • Savory without being fishy • Firm, meaty texture • Minimal bones • Aged 4 to 6 months	Ortiz Anchovies in Olive Oil
	APPLESAUCE **Musselman's Lite**	• An unusual ingredient, sucralose, sweetens this applesauce without overpowering its fresh, bright apple flavor • Pinch of salt boosts flavor above weak, bland, and too-sweet competitors • Coarse, almost chunky texture, not slimy like applesauces sweetened with corn syrup	Musselman's Home Style
	BACON, SUPERMARKET **Farmland Thick Sliced Bacon and Plumrose Premium Thick Sliced**	• Good balance of saltiness and sweetness • Smoky and full flavored, not one-dimensional • Very meaty, not too fatty or insubstantial • Crisp yet hearty texture, not tough or dry	Boar's Head Brand Naturally Smoked Sliced and Hormel Black Label Original
	BARBECUE SAUCE **Bull's-Eye Original**	• Spicy, fresh tomato taste • Good balance of tanginess, smokiness, and sweetness • Robust flavor from molasses • Sweetened with sugar and molasses, not high-fructose corn syrup, which caramelizes and burns quickly	
	BEANS, CANNED BAKED **B&M Vegetarian**	• Firm and pleasant texture with some bite • Sweetened with molasses for complexity and depth	Bush's Best Original and Van Camp's Original

	TEST KITCHEN FAVORITE	WHY WE LIKE IT	RUNNERS-UP
	BEANS, CANNED BLACK **Bush's Best**	• Clean, mild, and slightly earthy flavor • Firm, almost al dente texture, not mushy or pasty • Good amount of salt	Goya and Progresso
	BEANS, CANNED CHICKPEAS **Pastene**	• Firm yet tender texture bests pasty and dry competitors • Clean chickpea flavor • Enough salt to enhance but not overwhelm the flavor	Goya
	BEANS, CANNED RED KIDNEY **Goya**	• Sweet with strong bean flavor • Beautiful red, plump beans • Smooth, creamy texture, not mushy, chalky, or too firm • Flavor boost from added sugar and salt	S&W
	BEANS, CANNED WHITE **Goya**	• Clean, earthy flavor • Smooth, creamy interior with tender skins • Not full of broken beans like some competitors	Bush's Best Cannellini Beans White Kidney Beans
	BREAD, MULTIGRAIN **Nature's Own Specialty 12 Grain**	• Substantial, chewy slices • Nutty, hearty seeds throughout and topped with rolled oats • Uses no white flour	Arnold 12 Grain and Pepperidge Farm 15 Grain
	BREAD, WHITE SANDWICH **Arnold Country Classics**	• Subtle sweetness, not tasteless or sour • Perfect structure, not too dry or too soft	Pepperidge Farm Farmhouse Hearty White
	BREAD, WHOLE-WHEAT SANDWICH **Arnold Whole Grains 100% Whole Wheat Bread**	• Mild nuttiness with clean wheat flavor and a touch of sweetness • Tender and chewy with crunchy flecks of bulgur on the crust	Pepperidge Farm Farmhouse 100% Whole Wheat Bread
	BREAD CRUMBS, PANKO **Ian's Panko Breadcrumbs, Original Style**	• Crisp, with a substantial crunch • Not too delicate, stale, sandy, or gritty • Oil-free and without seasonings or undesirable artificial flavors	

	TEST KITCHEN FAVORITE	WHY WE LIKE IT	RUNNERS-UP
	BROTH, BEEF **Better Than Bouillon** **Roasted Beef Base**	• Contains good amount of salt and multiple powerful flavor enhancers • Paste is economical, stores easily, and dissolves quickly in hot water	
	BROTH, CHICKEN **Swanson Chicken Stock**	• Strong chicken flavor, not watery, beefy, or vegetal • Hearty and pleasant aroma • Roasted notes, not sour, rancid, or salty like some competitors • Flavor-boosting ingredients include carrots, celery, and onions	Better Than Bouillon Chicken Base
	BROTH, VEGETARIAN **Orrington Farms Vegan** **Chicken Flavored Broth** **Base & Seasoning**	• Savory depth without off-tasting vegetable undertones • Easy to store • Yeast extract adds depth and richness	Swanson Certified Organic Vegetable Broth
	BROWNIE MIX **Ghirardelli Chocolate** **Supreme and Barefoot** **Contessa Outrageous** **Brownie Mix**	• Rich, balanced chocolate flavor from both natural and Dutch-processed cocoa powders • Moist, chewy, and fudgy with perfect texture	
	BUTTER, UNSALTED **Plugrá European-Style**	• Sweet and creamy • Complex tang and grassy flavor • Moderate amount of butterfat so that it's decadent and glossy but not so rich that baked goods are greasy	Land O'Lakes and Vermont Creamery European-Style
	BUTTER, SALTED **Lurpak Slightly Salted** **Butter**	• Made with cultured cream • Rich, creamy texture	Kate's Homemade, Plugrá European-Style, Land O'Lakes, Kerrygold Pure Irish, Challenge, and Organic Valley
	CHEESE, AMERICAN, **PRESLICED** **Boar's Head**	• Strong cheesy flavor, unlike some competitors • Higher content of cheese culture contributes to better flavor	Kraft Deli Deluxe
	CHEESE, ASIAGO **BelGioioso**	• Sharp, tangy, and complex flavor, not mild • Firm and not too dry • Melts, shreds, and grates well	

	TEST KITCHEN FAVORITE	WHY WE LIKE IT	RUNNERS-UP
	CHEESE, BLUE **Stella**	• Milder cheese is better for dressings • Crumbly texture • Nicely balanced flavor with mild sweetness	Danish Blue
	CHEESE, CHEDDAR, SHARP **Cabot Vermont Sharp Cheddar**	• Buttery, creamy texture • Nutty, complex sharpness	Tillamook, Cracker Barrel, Kraft Natural, Kerrygold Aged, and Sargento Tastings Aged Wisconsin
	CHEESE, CHEDDAR, EXTRA-SHARP **Cabot Private Stock**	• Balance of salty, creamy, and sweet flavors • Considerable but well-rounded sharpness, not overwhelming • Firm, crumbly texture, not moist, rubbery, or springy • Aged at least 12 months for complex flavor	Cabot Extra-Sharp Cheddar
	CHEESE, CHEDDAR, PRESLICED **Tillamook Presliced Sharp**	• Slightly crumbly, not rubbery or processed, texture characteristic of block cheddar • Strong, tangy, and salty flavor, not bland or too mild	Cabot All Natural Sharp and Cracker Barrel Natural Sharp
	CHEESE, CHEDDAR, ARTISINAL **Milton Creamery Prairie Breeze**	• Earthy complexity with nutty, buttery, and fruity flavors • Dry and crumbly with crystalline crunch, not rubbery or overly moist • Aged no more than 12 months to prevent overly sharp flavor	Cabot Cellars at Jasper Hill Clothbound Cheddar
	CHEESE, CHEDDAR, LOW-FAT **Cracker Barrel Reduced Fat Sharp**	• Ample creaminess • Strong cheesy flavor • Good for cooking	
	CHEESE, COTTAGE **Hood Country Style**	• Rich, well-seasoned, and buttery flavor • Velvety, creamy texture • Pillowy curds	Friendship 4% California Style and Breakstone's 4% Small Curd
	CHEESE, CREAM **Philadelphia Cream Cheese Brick Original**	• Rich, tangy, and milky flavor • Thick, creamy texture, not pasty, waxy, or chalky	Philadelphia Cream Cheese Spreads Original
	CHEESE, FETA **Mt. Vikos Traditional Feta**	• Strong tangy, salty flavor • Creamy, dense texture • Pleasing crumbly texture	Valbreso Feta

	TEST KITCHEN FAVORITE	WHY WE LIKE IT	RUNNERS-UP
	CHEESE, FONTINA For eating out of hand: **Fontina Val d'Aosta**	• Strong, earthy aroma • Somewhat elastic texture with small irregular holes • Grassy, nutty flavor—but can be overpowering in cooked dishes	
	For cooking: **Italian Fontina**	• Semisoft, super-creamy texture • Mildly tangy, nutty flavor • Melts well	
	CHEESE, GOAT **Laura Chenel's Chèvre**	• Rich-tasting, grassy, tangy flavor • Smooth and creamy both unheated and baked • High salt content	Vermont Creamery, Chevrion, and Cypress Grove
	CHEESE, GRUYÈRE **1655 Le Gruyère**	• Aged between 12 and 14 months • Crystalline structure with dense, fudgy texture • Deeply aged, caramelized, grassy flavors shine through even when cooked	Mifroma Le Gruyère Cavern Reserve
	CHEESE, MOZZARELLA **Polly-O Whole Milk Mozzarella Cheese**	• Creamy, rich flavor with a hint of salt reminiscent of fresh mozzarella • Elastic but not gooey when melted	Galbani Whole Milk Mozzarella
	CHEESE, PARMESAN, SUPERMARKET **Boar's Head Parmigiano-Reggiano**	• Rich and complex flavor balances tanginess and nuttiness • Dry, crumbly texture yet creamy with a crystalline crunch, not rubbery or dense • Aged a minimum of 12 months for better flavor and texture	Il Villagio Parmigiano-Reggiano 18 Month and Sarvecchio Parmesan
	CHEESE, PARMESAN PRESHREDDED **Sargento Artisan Blends Shredded Parmesan Cheese**	• Mix of small and large shreds • Blend of 10- and 18-month-aged Parmesan • Rich, nutty flavor	Kraft Natural
	CHEESE, PEPPERJACK **Boar's Head Monterey Jack Cheese with Jalapeño**	• Buttery, tangy cheese • Clean, balanced flavor with assertive spice	Tillamook Pepper Jack Cheese

	TEST KITCHEN FAVORITE	WHY WE LIKE IT	RUNNERS-UP
	CHEESE, PROVOLONE **Provolone Vernengo**	• Bold, nutty, and tangy flavor, not plasticky or bland • Firm, dry texture	
	CHEESE, RICOTTA **Belgioioso Ricotta Con Latte Whole Milk Ricotta Cheese**	• Rich, dense consistency • Slight sweetness thanks to sweet whey and small amount of milk	Galbani Whole Milk Ricotta Cheese and Calabro Whole Milk Ricotta Cheese
	CHEESE, SWISS For eating out of hand: **Edelweiss Creamery Emmenthaler**	• Subtle flavor with sweet, buttery, nutty, and fruity notes • Firm yet gently giving texture, not rubbery • Aged longer for better flavor, resulting in larger eyes • Mildly pungent yet balanced	Emmi Kaltbach
	For cooking: **Boar's Head Gold Label Switzerland Swiss Cheese**	• Mildly nutty flavor • Smooth texture when melted	
	For eating out of hand or cooking: **Emmi Emmenthaler Cheese AOC**	• Creamy texture • Salty mildness preferable for grilled cheese sandwiches	
	CHICKEN, WHOLE **Mary's Free Range Air-Chilled**	• Great, savory chicken flavor • Very tender • Air-chilled for minimum water retention and cleaner flavor	Bell & Evans Air-Chilled Premium Fresh
	CHICKEN, BREASTS, BONELESS SKINLESS **Bell & Evans Air-Chilled Boneless, Skinless**	• Juicy and tender with clean chicken flavor • Not salted or brined • Air-chilled • Aged on bone for at least six hours after slaughter for significantly more tender meat	Springer Mountain Farms and Eberly's Free Range Young Organic
	CHILI POWDER **Morton & Bassett**	• Bold, full-flavored heat • Multidimensional flavor from a blend of cayenne and other chiles • Spices that complement but don't overwhelm the chiles	Penzeys Spices

	TEST KITCHEN FAVORITE	WHY WE LIKE IT	RUNNERS-UP
	CHOCOLATE, DARK **Ghirardelli 60% Cacao Bittersweet Chocolate Premium Baking Bar**	• Creamy texture, not grainy or chalky • Complex flavor with notes of cherry and wine with slight smokiness • Balance of sweetness and bitterness	Callebaut Intense Dark L-60-40NV (60% Cacao)
	CHOCOLATE, MILK **Dove Silky Smooth**	• Intense, full, rich chocolate flavor • Super-creamy texture from abundant milk fat and cocoa butter • Not overwhelmingly sweet	Endangered Species All-Natural Smooth and Green & Black's Organic
	CHOCOLATE, DARK CHIPS **Ghirardelli 60% Cacao Bittersweet**	• Intense, complex flavor beats one-dimensional flavor of competitors • Low sugar content highlights chocolate flavor • High amount of cocoa butter ensures creamy, smooth texture, not gritty or grainy • Wider, flatter shape and high percentage of fat help chips melt better in cookie	Hershey's Special Dark Mildly Sweet
	CHOCOLATE, MILK CHIPS **Hershey's**	• Bold chocolate flavor outshines too-sweet, weak chocolate flavor of other chips • Complex with caramel and nutty notes • Higher fat content makes texture creamier than grainy, artificial competitors	
	CHOCOLATE, UNSWEETENED **Hershey's Unsweetened Baking Bar**	• Well-rounded, complex flavor • Assertive chocolate flavor and deep notes of cocoa	Valrhona Cacao Pate Extra 100% and Scharffen Berger Unsweetened Dark
	CHOCOLATE, WHITE CHIPS **Guittard Choc-Au-Lait**	• Creamy texture, not waxy or crunchy • Silky smooth meltability from high fat content • Complex flavor like high-quality real chocolate, no artificial or off-flavors	Ghirardelli Classic White
	CIDER, HARD **Angry Orchard Crisp Apple Hard Cider**	• Crisp and refreshing • Strong apple sweetness • Juicy complexity	Strongbow Gold Apple and Woodchuck Amber
	CINNAMON **Morton & Bassett Spices Ground Cinnamon**	• The perfect balance of sweet and spicy • Mellow in baked applications	Penzeys Vietnamese Cinnamon Ground and McCormick Ground Cinnamon

	TEST KITCHEN FAVORITE	WHY WE LIKE IT	RUNNERS-UP
	COCOA POWDER **Hershey's Natural Unsweetened**	• Full, strong chocolate flavor • Complex flavor with notes of coffee, cinnamon, orange, and spice	Droste
	COCONUT MILK **Aroy-D**	• Velvety, luxurious, and not overly thick texture • Balanced, clean coconut flavor	Goya Coconut Milk (Leche de Coco)
	COCONUT, SHREDDED **Now Real Food Organic Unsweetened Coconut, Shredded**	• Nutty, tropical flavor • Fluffy, crisp texture	Woodstock Foods Organic
	COFFEE, WHOLE BEAN, SUPERMARKET, Dark Roast: **Millstone Colombian Supremo**	• Deep, complex, and balanced flavor without metallic, overly acidic, or otherwise unpleasant notes • Smoky and chocolaty with a bitter, not burnt, finish	Starbucks Coffee House Blend
	Medium Roast: **Peet's Coffee Café Domingo**	• Extremely smooth but bold-tasting with a strong finish • Rich chocolate and toast flavors • Few defective beans, low acidity, and optimal moisture	Millstone Breakfast Blend
	COFFEE, DECAF **Maxwell House Decaf Original Roast**	• Smooth, mellow flavor without being acidic or harsh • Complex, with a slightly nutty aftertaste • Made with only flavorful Arabica beans	Peet's Decaf House Blend Ground and Starbucks Coffee Decaf House Blend
	CORNMEAL **Arrowhead Mills Organic Yellow**	• Clean, pure corn flavor comes from using whole-grain kernels • Ideal texture resembling slightly damp, fine sand, not too fine or too coarse	

	TEST KITCHEN FAVORITE	WHY WE LIKE IT	RUNNERS-UP
	CREOLE SEASONING **Tony Chachere's Original Creole Seasoning**	• Strong garlic and red pepper notes • Vibrant and zesty with a punch of heat	McCormick Perfect Pinch Cajun Seasoning
	CURRY POWDER **Penzeys Sweet**	• Balanced, neither too sweet nor too hot • Complex and vivid earthy flavor, not thin, bland, or one-dimensional NOTE: Available through mail order, 800-741-7787 or penzeys.com	
	DINNER ROLLS, FROZEN **Pepperidge Farm Stone Baked Artisan French Dinner Rolls**	• Tender on the inside with crispy crust • Has only seven ingredients • Tastes homemade, with a hint of salt	
	EGG WHITES, PROCESSED **Eggology 100% Egg Whites**	• Works well in egg white omelets • Pasteurized; safe for use in uncooked applications • Make satisfactory baked goods	
	FIVE-SPICE POWDER **Frontier Natural Products Co-op**	• Nice depth, not one-dimensional • Balanced heat and sweetness	Dynasty Chinese Five Spices, McCormick Gourmet Collection Chinese Five Spice, Dean & DeLuca Five Spice Blend, and Morton & Bassett Chinese Five Spice
	FLOUR, ALL-PURPOSE **King Arthur Unbleached Enriched**	• Fresh, toasty flavor • No metallic taste or other off-flavors • Consistent results across recipes • Made tender, flaky pie crust, hearty biscuits, crisp cookies, and chewy, sturdy bread	Gold Medal Enriched Bleached Presifted, Gold Medal Unbleached, and Heckers/Ceresota Unbleached Enriched Presifted
	Pillsbury Unbleached Enriched	• Clean, toasty, and hearty flavor • No metallic or other off-flavors • Consistent results across recipes • Made flaky pie crust, chewy cookies, and tender biscuits, muffins, and cakes	
	FLOUR, WHOLE-WHEAT **King Arthur Premium 100%**	• Finely ground for hearty but not overly coarse texture in bread and pancakes • Sweet, nutty flavor	Bob's Red Mill Organic

	TEST KITCHEN FAVORITE	WHY WE LIKE IT	RUNNERS-UP
	FRENCH FRIES, FROZEN **Alexia Organic Yukon Select Fries**	• Crispy exteriors with fluffy, creamy interiors • Earthy, potato-y flavor	Ore-Ida Golden Fries
	GIARDINIERA **Pastene**	• Sharp, vinegary tang • Crunchy mix of vegetables • Mellow heat that's potent but not overpowering	Scala Hot
	GNOCCHI **Gia Russa Gnocchi with Potato**	• Tender, pillowlike texture • Nice potato flavor • Slightly sour taste that disappears when paired with tomato sauce	De Cecco
	GRITS **Anson Mills**	• Full, ripe, fresh corn flavor • Nice chew while still thick and creamy	Arrowhead Mills and Bob's Red Mill
	HAM, BLACK FOREST DELI **Dietz & Watson**	• Good texture • Nice ham flavor	
	HAM, COUNTRY **Harper's Grand Champion Whole Country Ham**	• Aged 3 to 6 months • Porky and complex, with robust flavor and balanced salt levels • Available online or in some southern supermarkets	Burgers' Smokehouse Ready to Cook Country Ham and Edwards Virginia Traditions Uncooked Virginia Ham
	HAM, SPIRAL-SLICED, BONE-IN **Johnston County Spiral-Sliced Smoked Ham**	• Tender and moist • Nice smokiness and just enough sweetness	Burgers' Smokehouse Spiral-Sliced City Ham and Applewood Farms Spiral-Sliced Ham

TEST KITCHEN FAVORITE	WHY WE LIKE IT	RUNNERS-UP
HOISIN SAUCE Kikkoman	• Balances sweet, salty, pungent, and spicy flavors • Initial burn mellows into harmonious and aromatic blend without bitterness	
HONEY Nature Nate's 100% Pure Raw and Unfiltered Honey	• Bold notes of citrus, clover, and anise • Mild sweetness and slight acidity	Aunt Sue's Raw-Wild Honey and Sue Bee Clover Honey
HORSERADISH Boar's Head Pure Horseradish	• No preservatives, just horseradish, vinegar, and salt (found in refrigerated section) • Natural flavor and hot without being overpowering	Ba-Tampte Prepared Horseradish
HOT DOGS Nathan's Famous Skinless Beef Franks	• Meaty, robust, and hearty flavor, not sweet, sour, or too salty • Juicy but not greasy • Firm, craggy texture, not rubbery, mushy, or chewy	Kayem Skinless Beef Hot Dogs
HOT FUDGE SAUCE Hershey's Hot Fudge Topping	• True fudge flavor, not weak or overly sweet • Thick, smooth, and buttery texture	
HOT SAUCE Huy Fong Sriracha Hot Chili Sauce and Frank's RedHot Original	• Right combination of punchy heat, saltiness, sweetness, and garlic • Full, rich flavor • Mild heat that's not too hot	Original Louisiana and Tapatio Salsa Picante
ICE CREAM BARS Dove Bar Vanilla Ice Cream with Milk Chocolate	• Rich, prominent chocolate flavor • Thick, crunchy chocolate coating • Dense, creamy, ice cream with pure vanilla flavor • Milk chocolate, not coconut oil, listed first in coating ingredients	Häagen-Dazs Vanilla Milk Chocolate All Natural, Blue Bunny Big Alaska, and Good Humor Milk Chocolate
ICE CREAM CONES Joy Classic Waffle Cones	• Lightly sweet, with vanilla, toasty, and nutty flavors • Crunchy and crisp but not overly hard • Individual paper jackets keep things neat	Joy Sugar Cones, Keebler Waffle Cones, Keebler Sugar Cones, and Comet (Nabisco) Sugar Cones

	TEST KITCHEN FAVORITE	WHY WE LIKE IT	RUNNERS-UP
	ICE CREAM, CHOCOLATE **Friendly's Rich & Creamy Classic Chocolate**	• Ultra-creamy texture • Classic chocolate taste	Edy's Grand Rich & Creamy Chocolate
	ICE CREAM, VANILLA **Ben & Jerry's**	• Complex yet balanced vanilla flavor from real vanilla extract • Sweetness solely from sugar, rather than corn syrup • Creamy richness from both egg yolks and small amount of stabilizers	Häagen-Dazs Vanilla
	ICED TEA Loose leaf: **Tazo Iced Black Tea**	• Distinctive flavor with herbal notes • Balanced level of strength and astringency	Luzianne and Tetley Premium Blend
	Bottled, with lemon: **Lipton PureLeaf**	• Bright, balanced, and natural tea and lemon flavors • Uses concentrated tea leaves to extract flavor	Gold Peak
	JUICE, GRAPEFRUIT **Natalie's 100% Florida Grapefruit Juice**	• Balanced and bright flavor, not too sweet • Clean and refreshing crispness	Florida's Natural Ruby Red Grapefruit Juice
	JUICE, ORANGE **Natalie's 100% Florida Orange Juice**	• Blend of Hamlin, Pineapple, and Valencia oranges • Fresh, sweet, and fruity flavor without overly acidic, sour, or from-concentrate taste • Gentler pasteurization helps retain fresh-squeezed flavor • Pleasant amount of light pulp	Tropicana Pure Premium 100% Pure and Natural with Some Pulp
	JUICE, FROZEN ORANGE CONCENTRATE **Minute Maid Original Frozen Concentrated Orange Juice**	• Full-bodied orange flavor • Good texture, includes some pulp	Tropicana 100% Juice Frozen Concentrated Orange Juice
	KETCHUP **Heinz Organic**	• Clean, pure sweetness from sugar, not high-fructose corn syrup • Bold, harmonious punch of saltiness, sweetness, tang, and tomato flavor	Hunt's and Simply Heinz

	TEST KITCHEN FAVORITE	WHY WE LIKE IT	RUNNERS-UP
	LEMONADE **Natalie's Natural Lemonade**	• Natural-tasting lemon flavor from 20 percent real lemon juice, without artificial flavors or off-notes • Perfect balance of tartness and sweetness, unlike many overly sweet competitors	Simply Lemonade and Minute Maid Premium Frozen Concentrate
	MACARONI & CHEESE **Kraft Homestyle Macaroni & Cheese Classic Cheddar Cheese Sauce**	• Reinforces flavor with blue and cheddar cheeses • Uses creamy, clingy liquid cheese sauce • Dry noodles, rather than frozen, for substantial texture and bite • Crunchy, buttery breadcrumb topping	Kraft Velveeta Original
	MAPLE SYRUP **Uncle Luke's Pure Maple Syrup, Grade A Dark Amber**	• Inexpensive • Dark, molasses-y color • Rich caramel flavor that tastes pleasantly toasty in pie	Highland Sugarworks, Coombs Family Farms, Anderson's, Maple Grove Farms, Maple Gold, Spring Tree, and Camp Pure
	MAYONNAISE **Blue Plate Real Mayonnaise**	• Great balance of taste and texture • Tastes close to homemade NOTE: While it's one of the top-selling brands in the country, you'll have to mail-order it unless you live in the South or Southeast	Hellmann's Real Mayonnaise, Hellmann's Light Mayonnaise, Spectrum Organic Mayonnaise, and Duke's Mayonnaise
	MAYONNAISE, LIGHT **Hellmann's Light**	• Bright, balanced flavor close to full-fat counterpart, not overly sweet • Not as creamy as full-fat but passable texture NOTE: Hellmann's is known as Best Foods west of the Rocky Mountains	Hellmann's Canola Cholesterol Free
	MIRIN (JAPANESE RICE WINE) **Mitoku Organic Mikawa Mirin Sweet Rice Seasoning**	• Roasted flavor that is caramel-like and rich • Subtle salty-sweet and balanced flavor	Sushi Chef Mirin Sweetened Sake and Kikkoman Aji-Mirin Sweet Cooking Rice Seasoning

	TEST KITCHEN FAVORITE	WHY WE LIKE IT	RUNNERS-UP
	MOLASSES **Brer Rabbit All Natural Unsulphured Mild Flavor**	• Acidic yet balanced • Strong and straightforward raisin-y taste • Pleasantly bitter bite	Plantation Barbados Unsulphured and Grandma's Molasses Unsulphured Original
	MUSTARD, BROWN **Gulden's Spicy Brown Mustard**	• Complex flavor with both heat and gentle tang • Smooth, creamy texture that goes perfectly with hot dogs	French's Spicy Brown Mustard and Beaver Deli Mustard
	MUSTARD, COARSE-GRAIN **Grey Poupon Harvest Coarse Ground and Grey Poupon Country**	• Spicy, tangy burst of mustard flavor • High salt content amplifies flavor • Contains no superfluous ingredients that mask mustard flavor • Big, round seeds add pleasant crunch • Just enough vinegar, not too sour or thin	
	MUSTARD, DIJON **Trois Petits Cochons Moutarde de Dijon**	• Potent, bold, and very hot, not weak or mild • Good balance of sweetness, tanginess, and sharpness • Not overly acidic, sweet, or one-dimensional like competitors	Maille Dijon Originale Traditional and Roland Extra Strong
	MUSTARD, YELLOW **Annie's Naturals Organic**	• Lists mustard seeds second in the ingredients for rich mustard flavor • Good balance of heat and tang • Relatively low salt content	Gulden's, French's Classic, and Westbrae Natural
	OATS, ROLLED **Bob's Red Mill Old Fashioned Rolled Oats**	• Toasty flavor, even in cookies • Tender texture with just the right amount of chew • Hearty, tender texture and nutty flavor in oatmeal	Bob's Red Mill Extra Thick Rolled Oats
	OATS, STEEL-CUT **Bob's Red Mill Organic**	• Rich and complex oat flavor with buttery, earthy, nutty, and whole-grain notes • Creamy yet toothsome texture • Moist but not sticky NOTE: Not recommended for baking	Arrowhead Mills Organic Hot Cereal, Country Choice Organic, and Hodgson's Mill Premium

	TEST KITCHEN FAVORITE	WHY WE LIKE IT	RUNNERS-UP
	OLIVE OIL, SUPERMARKET **California Olive Ranch Everyday**	• Fruity, fragrant, and fresh with a complex finish • Flavor rivals winning high-end extra-virgin oil	Lucini Premium Select
	OLIVE OIL, EXTRA-VIRGIN, PREMIUM **Gaea Fresh Extra Virgin Olive Oil**	• Smooth, buttery, and balanced flavor • Sweet olive fruitiness with peppery aftertaste	Casa de Santo Amaro Selection Extra Virgin Olive Oil
	PANCAKE MIX **Hungry Jack Buttermilk Pancake and Waffle Mix**	• Flavorful balance of sweetness and tang well-seasoned with sugar and salt • Light, extra fluffy texture • Requires vegetable oil (along with milk and egg) to reconstitute the batter	Aunt Jemima Original
	PAPRIKA, SWEET **The Spice House Hungarian Sweet**	• Complex flavor with earthy, fruity notes • Bright and bold, not bland and boring • Rich, toasty aroma NOTE: Available only through mail order, 312-274-0378 or thespicehouse.com	Penzeys Hungary Sweet NOTE: Available through mail order, 800-741-7787 or penzeys.com
	PASTA, CHEESE RAVIOLI **Rosetto**	• Creamy, plush, and rich blend of ricotta, Romano, and Parmesan cheeses • Pasta with nice, springy bite • Perfect dough-to-filling ratio	Buitoni Four Cheese and Celentano
	PASTA, CHEESE TORTELLINI **Barilla Three Cheese**	• Robustly flavored filling from combination of ricotta, Emmentaler, and Grana Padano cheeses • Tender pasta that's sturdy enough to withstand boiling but not so thick that it becomes doughy	Seviroli and Buitoni Three Cheese
	PASTA, EGG NOODLES **Pennsylvania Dutch Wide Egg Noodles**	• Balanced, buttery flavor with no off-flavors • Light and fluffy texture, not gummy or starchy	De Cecco Egg Pappardelle and Light 'n Fluffy Egg Noodles, Wide

	TEST KITCHEN FAVORITE	WHY WE LIKE IT	RUNNERS-UP
	PASTA, ELBOW MACARONI **Barilla**	• Rich flavor from egg yolks • Firm, chewy bite • Wide corkscrew shape	Mueller's
	PASTA, FETTUCCINE **Garofalo Fettuccine**	• Wide, thick noodles that cook up plump and springy with mild, clean flavor • Retained perfect chew when tossed with sauce	De Cecco Fetuccine
	PASTA, FRESH **Contadina Buitoni Fettuccine**	• Firm but yielding, slightly chewy texture, not too delicate, gummy, or heavy • Faint but discernible egg flavor with no chemical, plasticky, or otherwise unpleasant flavors • Rough, porous surface absorbs sauce better than dried pasta	
	PASTA, LASAGNA NOODLES No-boil: **Barilla No-Boil**	• Taste and texture of fresh pasta • Delicate, flat noodles	Ronzoni and Pasta DeFino
	Whole-wheat: **Bionatura Organic 100% Whole Wheat**	• Complex nutly, rich wheat flavor • Substantial chewy texture without any grittiness	DeLallo 100% Organic
	PASTA, PENNE **Mueller's Penne Rigate**	• Hearty texture, not insubstantial or gummy • Wheaty, slightly sweet flavor, not bland	Benedetto Cavalieri Penne Rigate and De Cecco
	PASTA, SPAGHETTI **De Cecco Spaghetti No. 12**	• Rich, nutty, wheaty flavor • Firm, ropy strands with good chew, not mushy, gummy, or mealy	Rustichella D'Abruzzo Pasta Abruzzese di Semola di Grano Duro, Garofalo, and DeLallo Spaghetti No. 4
	PASTA, SPAGHETTI, GLUTEN-FREE **Jovial Organic Gluten-Free Brown Rice**	• High in fiber and protein with springy and clean taste • No gumminess or off-flavors as experienced with other brands	Andean Dream Gluten & Corn Free Quinoa Pasta

	TEST KITCHEN FAVORITE	WHY WE LIKE IT	RUNNERS-UP
	PASTA, SPAGHETTI, WHOLE-WHEAT Bionaturae Organic 100% Whole Wheat	• Chewy, firm, and toothsome, not mushy or rubbery • Full and nutty wheat flavor	Barilla PLUS Multigrain
	PASTA SAUCE Bertolli Tomato & Basil	• Fresh-cooked, balanced tomato flavor, not overly sweet • Pleasantly chunky, not too smooth or pasty • Not overseasoned with dry herbs like competitors	Francesco Rinaldi Traditional Marinara, Prego Marinara Italian, and Barilla Marinara
	PASTA SAUCE, PREMIUM Victoria Marinara Sauce	• Nice, bright acidity that speaks of real tomatoes • Robust flavor comparable to homemade	Classico Marinara with Plum Tomatoes and Olive Oil
	PEANUT BUTTER, CREAMY Skippy	• Smooth, creamy, and spreadable • Good balance of sweet and salty flavors	Jif Natural and Reese's
	PEPPERCORNS, BLACK Kalustyan's Indian Tellicherry	• Enticing and fragrant, not musty, aroma with flavor to back it up and moderate heat • Fresh, complex flavor at once sweet and spicy, earthy and smoky, fruity and floral NOTE: Available only by mail order, 800-352-3451 or kalustyans.com	Morton & Bassett Organic Whole
	PEPPERONI, SLICED Margherita Italian Style	• Nice balance of meatiness and spice • Tangy, fresh flavor with hints of fruity licorice and peppery fennel • Thin slices with the right amount of chew	Boar's Head
	PEPPERS, ROASTED RED Dunbars Sweet	• Balance of smokiness and sweetness • Mild, sweet, and earthy red pepper flavor • Firm texture, not slimy or mushy • Packed in simple yet strong brine of salt and water without distraction of other strongly flavored ingredients	Cento

	TEST KITCHEN FAVORITE	WHY WE LIKE IT	RUNNERS-UP
	PICKLES, BREAD-AND-BUTTER **Bubbies**	• Subtle, briny tang • All-natural solution that uses real sugar, not high-fructose corn syrup	
	PICKLES, WHOLE KOSHER DILL **Boar's Head**	• Authentic, garlicky flavor and firm, snappy crunch • Balanced salty, sour, and garlic flavors • Fresh and refrigerated, not processed and shelf-stable	Claussen
	PIE CRUST, READY-MADE **Wholly Wholesome 9" Certified Organic Traditional Bake at Home Rolled Pie Dough**	• Palm oil gives it a tender, flaky texture without artificial taste • Sold in sheets so you can use your own pie plate • Slightly sweet, rich flavor	
	PIZZA, PEPPERONI, FROZEN **Pizzeria! by DiGiorno Primo Pepperoni**	• Thick, crisp, and airy crust with a browned and charred bottom • Herby, zesty sauce • Very meaty pepperoni	Freschetta Brick Oven Crust Pepperoni and Italian Style Cheese and Red Baron Fire Baked Pepperoni Pizza
	POPCORN, BAGGED **Cape Cod Sea Salt Popcorn**	• Nutty, toasty corn flavor and well-calibrated salt • Hearty, puffy kernels that are crisp and crunchy on the outside with a tender interior	Smartfood Delight Sea Salt Popcorn
	PORK, PREMIUM **Snake River Farms American Kurobuta Berkshire Pork**	• Deep pink tint, which indicates higher pH level and more flavorful meat • Tender texture and juicy, intensely pork-y flavor	D'Artagnan Berkshire Pork Chops (Milanese-Style Cut)
	POTATO CHIPS **Lay's Kettle Cooked Original**	• Big potato flavor, no offensive off-flavors • Perfectly salted • Slightly thick chips that aren't too delicate or brittle • Not too greasy	Herr's Crisp 'N Tasty and Utz

	TEST KITCHEN FAVORITE	WHY WE LIKE IT	RUNNERS-UP
	POTATO CHIPS, REDUCED FAT **Cape Cod 40% Reduced Fat**	• Real potato flavor with excellent crunch and texture • Contains only potatoes, canola oil, and salt • With less sodium than many competitors, they have just the right balance of salt	Lay's Kettle Cooked Reduced Fat Extra Crunchy
	PRESERVES, PEACH **American Spoon Red Haven Peach Preserves**	• Bold, ripe peach taste and balanced sweetness • Loose and spreadable texture, similar to homemade preserves	Bonne Maman Peach Preserves and Smucker's Peach Preserves
	PRESERVES, RASPBERRY **Smucker's**	• Clean, strong raspberry flavor, not too tart or sweet • Not overly seedy • Ideal, spreadable texture, not too thick, artificial, or overprocessed	Trappist Red Raspberry Jam
	PRESERVES, STRAWBERRY **Welch's**	• Big, distinct strawberry flavor • Natural-tasting and not overwhelmingly sweet • Thick and spreadable texture, not runny, slimy, or too smooth	Smucker's and Smucker's Simply Fruit Spreadable Fruit
	RELISH, SWEET PICKLE **Cascadian Farm**	• Piquant, sweet flavor, lacks out-of-place flavors such as cinnamon and clove present in competitors • Fresh and natural taste, free of yellow dye #5 and high-fructose corn syrup • Good texture, not mushy like competitors	Heinz Premium
	RICE, ARBORIO **RiceSelect**	• Creamier than competitors • Smooth grains • Characteristic good bite of Arborio rice in risotto where al dente is ideal	Riso Baricella and Rienzi
	RICE, BASMATI **Tilda Pure**	• Very long grains expand greatly with cooking, a result of being aged for a minimum of one year, as required in India • Ideal, fluffy texture, not dry, gummy, or mushy • Nutty taste with no off-flavors • Sweet aroma	Kohinoor Super

	TEST KITCHEN FAVORITE	WHY WE LIKE IT	RUNNERS-UP
	RICE, BROWN **Lundberg Organic** **Long Grain Brown**	• Firm yet tender grains • Bold, toasty, nutty flavor • Works with a range of cooking methods • Includes the best instructions	Riceland Extra Long Grain Natural, Carolina Whole Grain, and Goya
	RICE, LONG-GRAIN WHITE **Lundberg Organic** **Long Grain White Rice**	• Nutty, buttery, and toasty flavor • Distinct, smooth grains that offer some chew without being overly chewy	Carolina Enriched Extra Long-Grain and Canilla Extra Long-Grain Enriched
	RICE, READY **Minute Ready to Serve** **White Rice**	• Parboiled long-grain white rice that is ready in less than 2 minutes • Toasted, buttery flavor • Firm grains with al dente bite	
	SALSA, JARRED GREEN **Frontera Tomatillo Salsa**	• Sweet and nuanced flavor with a roasted, smoky taste from charred tomatillo skins • A good amount of heat • Has no preservatives or stabilizers	Ortega Salsa Verde, Medium

	SALSA, HOT
	Pace Hot Chunky
		• Good balance of bright tomato, chile,
		  and vegetal flavors
		• Chunky, almost crunchy texture,
		  not mushy or thin
		• Spicy and fiery but not overpowering
			Newman's Own
			All Natural Chunky
			Hot and Herdez Hot
			Salsa Casera

	SALSA, MEDIUM **Chi-Chi's Medium Thick &** **Chunky Salsa**	• Fresh, balanced flavor; vegetables are firm and crunchy • Jalapeño chiles for medium-level heat	

	SALSA, MILD
	Chi-Chi's Mild Thick &
	Chunky Salsa
		• Hint of heat with good balance and sweet,
		  satisfying tomato flavor
		• Thick, smooth base fortified with concen-
		  trated crushed tomatoes and chunks
		  of vegetables	

	SALT **Maldon Sea Salt**	• Light and airy texture • Delicately crunchy flakes • Not so coarse as to be overly crunchy or gritty nor so fine as to disappear	Fleur de Sel de Camargue, Morton Coarse Kosher, and Diamond Crystal Kosher

	TEST KITCHEN FAVORITE	WHY WE LIKE IT	RUNNERS-UP
	SAUERKRAUT **Eden Organic Sauerkraut**	• Slight sweetness and subtle zing, bright tanginess • Small, soft shreds with just enough chew	Libby's Sauerkraut
	SAUSAGE, BREAKFAST **Jimmy Dean Fully Cooked Original Pork Sausage Links**	• Big pork flavor, not bland or overly spiced • Good balance of saltiness and sweetness with pleasantly lingering spiciness • Tender, super-juicy meat, not rubbery, spongy, or greasy	
	SOUP, CANNED CHICKEN NOODLE **Muir Glen Organic**	• Organic chicken and vegetables and plenty of seasonings give it a fresh taste and spicy kick • Firm, not mushy, vegetables and noodles • No off-flavors	Progresso Traditional
	SOUP, CANNED TOMATO **Progresso Vegetable Classics Hearty**	• Includes fresh, unprocessed tomatoes, not just tomato puree like some competitors • Tangy, slightly herbaceous flavor • Balanced seasoning and natural sweetness • Medium body and slightly chunky texture	Imagine Organic Vine Ripened
	SOY SAUCE **Kikkoman Soy Sauce**	• Good salty-sweet balance • Long fermentation (6 to 8 months) • Simple ingredient list (wheat, soybeans, water, and salt) with no added sugar or flavor enhancers	
	STEAK SAUCE **Heinz 57 Sauce**	• Mellow, restrained flavor that doesn't overpower the meat • Fruity, sweet, and tangy flavor with hints of heat and smoke • Smooth texture with enough body to cling to steak without being gluey	Lea & Perrins
	SWEETENED CONDENSED MILK **Borden Eagle Brand and Nestlé Carnation**	• Made with whole milk; creamier in desserts and balances more assertive notes from other ingredients	Nestlé Carnation
	TARTAR SAUCE **Legal Sea Foods**	• Creamy, nicely balanced sweet/tart base • Lots of vegetable chunks	McCormick Original

	TEST KITCHEN FAVORITE	WHY WE LIKE IT	RUNNERS-UP
	TEA, BLACK For plain tea: **Twinings English Breakfast**	• Bright, bold, and flavorful yet not too strong • Fruity, floral, and fragrant • Smooth, slightly astringent profile preferred for tea without milk	Lipton Black Tea
	With milk and sugar: **Tetley British Blend**	• Boasts caramel notes and full, deep, smoky flavors • Bold, fruity flavor	Celestial Seasonings English Breakfast Estate Tea
	TERIYAKI SAUCE **Annie Chun's All Natural**	• Distinct teriyaki flavor without offensive or dominant flavors, unlike competitors • Smooth, rich texture, not too watery or gluey	
	TOMATOES, CANNED CRUSHED **SMT Crushed Tomatoes**	• Bright, clear tomato flavor • Crushed tomatoes in liquid contribute thick, hearty texture	Red Pack Crushed Tomatoes in Puree
	TOMATOES, CANNED DICED **Hunt's**	• Bright, fresh tomato flavor that balances sweet and tart • Firm yet tender texture	Muir Glen Organic Diced Tomatoes
	TOMATOES, CANNED PUREED **Muir Glen Organic Tomato Puree**	• Full tomato flavor without any bitter, sour, or tinny notes • Pleasantly thick, even consistency, not watery or thin	Hunt's, Progresso, and Cento
	TOMATOES, CANNED WHOLE **Muir Glen Organic**	• Pleasing balance of bold acidity and fruity sweetness • Firm yet tender texture, even after hours of simmering	Hunt's
	TOMATO PASTE **Goya**	• Bright, robust tomato flavors • Balance of sweet and tart flavors	Pastene and Contadina

	TEST KITCHEN FAVORITE	WHY WE LIKE IT	RUNNERS-UP
	TORTILLA CHIPS **On the Border** **Café Style**	• Traditional, buttery sweetness and bright corn flavor • The perfect counterpart to salsa • Light, crisp exterior	Tostitos Original Restaurant Style and Santitas White Corn
	TORTILLAS, CORN **Maria and Ricardo's** **Handmade Style Soft** **Corn Tortillas, Yellow**	• Soft and pliable, don't crack when rolled up • Light, cornlike sweetness with a hint of nuttiness • Wheat gluten added to dough makes tortilla more cohesive and elastic	Mission White Corn Tortillas, Restaurant Style, Guerrero White Corn Tortillas, and La Banderita Corn Tortillas, White
	TORTILLAS, FLOUR **Old El Paso 6-Inch** **Flour Tortillas**	• Thin and flaky texture, not doughy or stale • Made with plenty of fat and salt	Mission
	TOSTADAS, CORN **Mission Tostadas** **Estilo Casero**	• Crisp, crunchy texture • Good corn flavor • Flavor and texture that are substantial enough to stand up to hearty toppings	Charras
	TUNA, CANNED **Wild Planet Wild** **Albacore**	• Rich, fresh-tasting, and flavorful, but not fishy • Hearty, substantial chunks of tuna	American Tuna Pole Caught Wild Albacore and Starkist Selects Solid White Albacore
	TUNA, CANNED PREMIUM **Nardin Bonito Del Norte** **Ventresca Fillets**	• Creamy, delicate meat and tender yet firm fillets • Full, rich tuna flavor	Tonnino Tuna Ventresca Yellowfin in Olive Oil
	TURKEY, WHOLE **Empire Kosher**	• Moist and dense texture without being watery, chewy, or squishy • Meaty, full turkey flavor • Buttery white meat • Koshering process renders brining unnecessary	Good Shepherd Ranch Heritage NOTE: Available through mail order, 785-227-5149 or reeseturkeys.net

	TEST KITCHEN FAVORITE	WHY WE LIKE IT	RUNNERS-UP
	VANILLA BEANS **McCormick** **Madagascar**	• Moist, seed-filled pods • Complex, robust flavor with caramel notes	Spice Islands Bourbon
	VANILLA EXTRACT **McCormick Pure**	• Strong, rich vanilla flavor where others are weak and sharp • Complex flavor with spicy, caramel notes and a sweet undertone	Rodelle Pure and Gold Medal Imitation by C.F. Sauer Co.
	VEGETABLE OIL, ALL-PURPOSE **Crisco Natural Blend Oil**	• Unobtrusive, mild flavor for stir-frying and sautéing and for use in baked goods and in uncooked applications such as mayonnaise and vinaigrette • Neutral taste and absence of fishy or metallic flavors when used for frying	Mazola Canola Oil
	VINEGAR, APPLE CIDER **Heinz Filtered Apple** **Cider Vinegar**	• Good balance of sweet and tart • Distinct apple flavor with a floral aroma and assertive, tangy qualities	
	VINEGAR, BALSAMIC **Bertolli Balsamic** **Vinegar of Modena**	• Tastes of dried fruit like figs, raisins, and prunes • Tastes pleasantly sweet once reduced or whisked into vinaigrette	Monari Federzoni of Modena, Colavita, Ortalli of Modena, Bellino, and Lucini Aged
	VINEGAR, RED WINE **Laurent du Clos**	• Crisp red wine flavor balanced by stronger than average acidity and subtle sweetness • Complex yet pleasing taste from multiple varieties of grapes	Pompeian Gourmet and Spectrum Naturals Organic

	TEST KITCHEN FAVORITE	WHY WE LIKE IT	RUNNERS-UP
	VINEGAR, WHITE WINE **Napa Valley Naturals** **Organic White Wine Vinegar**	• Balanced sweetness and acidity • Fruity and vibrant in vinaigrettes • Floral and aromatic notes with robust acidity in pickled vegetables	Star White Wine Vinegar
	WHIPPED TOPPING **Cool Whip Extra Creamy**	• Thick, silky, and luscious • Excellent, fresh cream flavor and just enough sweetness	Land O' Lakes Whipped Heavy Cream
	WORCESTERSHIRE SAUCE **Lea & Perrins Original** **Worcestershire Sauce**	• Balanced notes of vinegar, pepper, and tamarind • Distinctly punchy, bright tanginess in marinades	French's Worcestershire Sauce and Annie's Organic Vegan Worcestershire Sauce
	YOGURT, GREEK WHOLE MILK **Fage Total Classic**	• High in protein with no added stabilizers or thickeners • Rich, creamy, dense, faintly sweet flavor • Holds its own against garlicky sharpness of tzatziki sauce	Dannon Oikos Traditional and Wallaby Organic
	YOGURT, WHOLE-MILK **Brown Cow Cream** **Top Plain**	• Rich, well-rounded flavor, not sour or bland • Especially creamy, smooth texture, not thin or watery • Higher fat content contributes to flavor and texture	Stonyfield Farm Organic Plain

EPISODE DIRECTORY

2008
season one

2009
season two

2010
season three

2016
season nine

2017
season ten

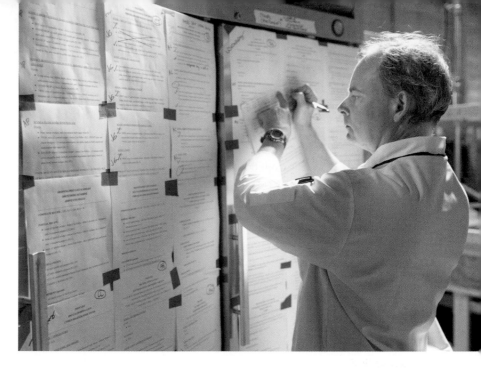

CONVERSIONS AND EQUIVALENTS

SOME SAY COOKING IS A SCIENCE AND AN ART. WE would say that geography has a hand in it, too. Flour milled in the United Kingdom and elsewhere will feel and taste different from flour milled in the United States. So we cannot promise that the loaf of bread you bake in Canada or England will taste the same as a loaf baked in the States, but we can offer guidelines for converting weights and measures. We also recommend that you rely on your instincts when making our recipes. Refer to the visual cues provided. If the bread dough hasn't "come together in a ball," as described, you may need to add more flour—even if the recipe doesn't tell you to. You be the judge.

The recipes in this book were developed using standard U.S. measures following U.S. government guidelines. The charts below offer equivalents for U.S., metric, and imperial (U.K.) measures. All conversions are approximate and have been rounded up or down to the nearest whole number.

EXAMPLE:

1 teaspoon	=	4.9292 milliliters, rounded up to 5 milliliters
1 ounce	=	28.3495 grams, rounded down to 28 grams

VOLUME CONVERSIONS

U.S.	METRIC
1 teaspoon	5 milliliters
2 teaspoons	10 milliliters
1 tablespoon	15 milliliters
2 tablespoons	30 milliliters
¼ cup	59 milliliters
⅓ cup	79 milliliters
½ cup	118 milliliters
¾ cup	177 milliliters
1 cup	237 milliliters
1¼ cups	296 milliliters
1½ cups	355 milliliters
2 cups (1 pint)	473 milliliters
2½ cups	591 milliliters
3 cups	710 milliliters
4 cups (1 quart)	0.946 liter
1.06 quarts	1 liter
4 quarts (1 gallon)	3.8 liters

WEIGHT CONVERSIONS

OUNCES	GRAMS
½	14
¾	21
1	28
1½	43
2	57
2½	71
3	85
3½	99
4	113
4½	128
5	142
6	170
7	198
8	227
9	255
10	283
12	340
16 (1 pound)	454

CONVERSIONS FOR INGREDIENTS COMMONLY USED IN BAKING

Baking is an exacting science. Because measuring by weight is far more accurate than measuring by volume, and thus more likely to achieve reliable results, in our recipes we provide ounce measures in addition to cup measures for many ingredients. Refer to the chart below to convert these measures into grams.

INGREDIENT	OUNCES	GRAMS
1 cup all-purpose flour*	5	142
1 cup whole-wheat flour	5½	156
1 cup granulated (white) sugar	7	198
1 cup packed brown sugar (light or dark)	7	198
1 cup confectioners' sugar	4	113
1 cup cocoa powder	3	85
4 tablespoons butter† (½ stick or ¼ cup)	2	57
8 tablespoons butter† (1 stick or ½ cup)	4	113
16 tablespoons butter† (2 sticks or 1 cup)	8	227

* U.S. all-purpose flour, the most frequently used flour in this book, does not contain leaveners, as some European flours do. These leavened flours are called self-rising or self-raising. If you are using self-rising flour, take this into consideration before adding leavening to a recipe.

† In the United States, butter is sold both salted and unsalted. We generally recommend unsalted butter. If you are using salted butter, take this into consideration before adding salt to a recipe.

OVEN TEMPERATURES

FAHRENHEIT	CELSIUS	GAS MARK (IMPERIAL)
225	105	¼
250	120	½
275	135	1
300	150	2
325	165	3
350	180	4
375	190	5
400	200	6
425	220	7
450	230	8
475	245	9

CONVERTING TEMPERATURES FROM AN INSTANT-READ THERMOMETER

We include doneness temperatures in many of the recipes in this book. We recommend an instant-read thermometer for the job. Refer to the above table to convert Fahrenheit degrees to Celsius. Or, for temperatures not represented in the chart, use this simple formula:

Subtract 32 degrees from the Fahrenheit reading, then divide the result by 1.8 to find the Celsius reading.

EXAMPLE:

"Roast chicken until thighs register 175 degrees."
To convert:

175°F − 32 = 143°
143° ÷ 1.8 = 79.44°C, rounded down to 79°C

index

Note: Page references in *italics* indicate photographs.

A

F

G

K

Kitchen supplies, ratings of, 624–25
Knives and more, ratings of, 596–98
Kolaches, 464, *465*

L

Lane Cake, *482*, 483
Lasagna
    Skillet, 294, *295*
    Skillet, with Sausage and Peppers, 294
    Spinach and Tomato, *296, 297*
Latin Fried Chicken, 244, *245*
Latin-Spiced Butter, 389
Lemon(s)
    -Caper Sauce, Grilled Salmon Steaks
        with, *382*, 383
    Chicken, Grilled Butterflied, 322, *323*
    Chicken, Roast, 166, *167*
    -Chocolate Truffles, 535
    and Herb Red Potato Salad, 418, *419*
    Icebox Cheesecake, 516, *517*
    juicing, 13
    Meringue Pie, Mile-High, *584,* 585
    Pie, Shaker, *564,* 565
    Pudding Cake, 514, *515*
    Salsa Verde, 195
    -Thyme Wood-Grilled Salmon, 378
Lettuce
    Chinese Chicken Salad, 78, *79*
    Grilled Caesar Salad, 398, *399*
Lexington Barbecue Sauce, 353

Lexington-Style Pulled Pork, *352, 353*
Lime
    -Coconut Cookies, 525
    -Ginger Glaze, 525
    Key, Pie, Icebox, 582, *583*
Loaded Baked Potato Omelet Filling, 423
Louisiana Seasoning, 131

M

Macaroni
    and Cheese, Best Potluck, 4, *5*
    and Cheese with Tomatoes, *2, 3*
Magic Chocolate Flan Cake, *492*, 493
Maine Blueberry Grunt, *546,* 547
Malted Milk Glaze, 525
Manchego and Chorizo Breakfast Pizza, 426
Manicotti, Baked, with Meat Sauce, *298, 299*
Marshmallow crème
    Chocolate Cream Cupcakes, *510,* 511
    Swiss Hazelnut Cake, 496, *497*
    Whoopie Pies, 532, *533*
Masa harina
    Puffy Tacos, *250, 251*
Mashed Potato Cakes, 152, *153*
    Blue Cheese and Bacon, 152
    Cheddar and Scallion, 152
Mashed Potato Casserole, *226, 227*
Measuring equipment, ratings of, 607–9
Meat
    scoring fat on, 377
    see also Beef; Pork
Meatballs and Marinara, 286, *287*

N

Nachos, Ultimate Spicy Beef, *234*, 235
Nashville Extra-Hot Fried Chicken, 60
Nashville Hot Fried Chicken, 60, *61*
Natchitoches Meat Pies, *104*, 105
New Orleans Barbecue Shrimp, 70, *71*
New Orleans Bourbon Bread Pudding, *554*, 555
New Orleans Muffulettas, *76*, 77
No-Cook Pizza Sauce, 303
No-Fear Single-Crust Pie Dough, 563
Noodles
  Chicken and Slicks, 178, *179*
  Chicken Chow Mein, *80*, 81
Nuts
  Brussels Sprout Salad, 218, *219*
  Brussels Sprout Salad with Cheddar, Hazelnuts, and Apple, 218
  Chocolate-Almond Truffles, 535
  Pine, and Capers, Stuffed Tomatoes with, 156
  Pine, and Pecorino, Roasted Green Beans with, 10
  Roasted Green Beans with Almonds and Mint, 10
  Roasted Green Beans with Goat Cheese and Hazelnuts, 10, *11*
  Stuffed Tomatoes with Currants and Pistachios, 156
  Swiss Hazelnut Cake, 496, *497*
  see also Pecan(s); Walnut(s)

O

Oklahoma Fried Onion Burgers, *86*, 87
Old-Fashioned Chocolate Frozen Custard, *558*, 559
Old-Fashioned Pecan Pie, 576, *577*
Old-Fashioned Roast Pork, *208*, 209
Old-Fashioned Roast Turkey with Gravy, 160, *161*
Old-Fashioned Vanilla Frozen Custard, *558*, 559
Olive Oil Potato Gratin, 150, *151*
Olives
  New Orleans Muffulettas, *76*, 77
  and Orange, Stuffed Tomatoes with, 156
One-Minute Salsa, 235
One-Pan Prime Rib and Roasted Vegetables, 198, *199*
One-Pan Roast Chicken with Fennel and Parsnips, 171
One-Pan Roast Chicken with Root Vegetables, *170*, 171
Onion(s)
  Caramelized, Herbed Mashed Sweet Potatoes with, 228
  chopping finely, 175
  Fried, Burgers, Oklahoma, *86*, 87
  Patty Melts, 84, *85*
  Pickled, *246*, 247
  Red, Pickled, *252*, 253
  Rings, Beer-Battered, 114, *115*
  Smothered Pork Chops, *38*, 39
  Soup, French, Slow-Cooker, *136*, 137
Orange(s)
  Chiffon Cake, 502
  Chinese Chicken Salad, 78, *79*
  and Olives, Stuffed Tomatoes with, 156
  –Poppy Seed Cookies, *524*, 525
  –Red Wine Sauce, 201
  Sour, Pie, *566*, 567

P

Q

R

Radish(es)

Hard-Cooked Eggs, and Capers, Tuna Salad
with, 14

and Sweet Potato, Chicken Baked in Foil
with, *176*, 177

Raisins

Classic Steak Sauce, 125

Lane Cake, *482*, 483

Morning Glory Muffins, *454*, 455

New Orleans Bourbon Bread Pudding, *554*, 555

Steak Sauce, 128

Ranch Fried Chicken, *62*, 63

Ranch Potato Salad, 410, *411*

Raspberry(ies)

Blitz Torte, *498*, 499

Chiffon Pie, 586, *587*

Summer Berry Pudding, 556, *557*

Recipe and culinary history

Basque cooking in California, 57

Bastien's Restaurant, 121

Big Bob Gibson's restaurant, 316

Bundt pans, 481

chicken Divan, 19

chicken Florentine, 16

chuck roast in foil, 203

cold-oven recipes, 508

Cornell chicken, 314

cowboy food lingo, 34

Delmonico potatoes, 141

Delmonico's restaurant, 141

Divan Parisien restaurant, 16, 19

Ebinger's Baking Company, 478

frozen fish sticks, 42

gelatin-based salads, 44

Recipe and culinary history *(cont.)*

grandma pizza, 300

Heinz ketchup, 22

Hidden Valley Ranch Dressing, 410

honeybees in America, 53

Horn and Hardart's automats, 3

"huli"-ed chicken, 313

Joe froggers, 528

Jucy Lucy burgers, 342

macaroni and cheese, 3

meatloaf, 22, 24

New Orleans Vietnamese community, 69

North Carolina barbecue, 353

Oberlin College dining plan, 490

Papa Kay Joe's, 359

Peach Park, 570

Pillsbury Bake-Off, 591

proper dining and tableware, 469

Salisbury steak, 33

sandwiches, 84

Shaker Lemon Pie, 565

smothered pork chops, 39

St. Louis–style pizza, 106

Sunbeam Mixmaster, 221

sweet-and-sour flavors, 409

sweetened condensed milk, 582

Syracuse salt potatoes, 224

whoopie pies, 532

Red Velvet Cake, 476, *477*

Red Wine–Orange Sauce, 201

Rhubarb-Strawberry Compote, 507

Rice

Arroz con Pollo, 242, *243*

Charleston Shrimp Perloo, *74*, 75

Easier Chicken Chimichangas, 254, *255*